PRACTICE MAKES PERFECT®

Complete German All-in-One

Ed Swick, Editor

Mc
Graw
Hill

New York Chicago San Francisco Lisbon London Madrid Mexico City
Milano New Delhi San Juan Seoul Singaporeo Sydney Toronto

1 2 3 4 5 6 7 8 9   LHS   24 23 22 21 20 19

ISBN   978-1-260-45514-4
MHID   1-260-45514-9

e-ISBN   978-1-260-45515-1
e-MHID   1-260-45515-7

Portions of this book are published under the following titles:

Practice Makes Perfect Complete German Grammar by Ed Swick
Practice Makes Perfect Intermediate German Grammar by Ed Swick
Practice Makes Perfect German Verb Tenses by Astrid Henschel
Practice Makes Perfect German Pronouns and Prepositions by Ed Swick
Practice Makes Perfect German Conversation by Ed Swick
Practice Makes Perfect German Sentence Builder by Ed Swick

McGraw-Hill Language Lab App
Audio recordings and flash cards are available to support your study of this book. Go to mhlanguagelab.com to access the online version of this application, or locate the mobile version of the app in the Apple App Store (for iPhone and iPad) and the Google Play Store (for Android devices).
Note: Internet access required for streaming audio.

McGraw-Hill books are available at special quantity discounts to use as premiums and sales promotions, or for use in corporate training programs. To contact a representative, please visit the Contact Us page at www.mhprofessional.com.

Contents

Preface

This book is a compilation of six German books, the subject matter of which includes all aspects of grammar and usage. The compilation book serves two purposes for acquiring the skills needed to be a confident user of German. Firstly, it is an excellent instrument for practicing the many intricacies of the grammar and structure of the language. Secondly, the book is a resource that contains the answers to questions most frequently on the minds of those learning German.

The book covers the major grammar topics that describe and explain how the various parts of speech function in a sentence, and, more importantly, it also provides abundant exercises for practice. In just this one book, the student has a comprehensive tool for learning and practicing his or her new language and a valuable resource that provides immediate answers to questions.

Technical terminology has been kept to a minimum but is introduced and explained when needed to describe an important concept. But the goal of the book is to hold such terminology to a minimum. For example, the term *elliptical clause* is a concept that must be memorized because at first glance those two words together have no precise meaning and merely *stand* for a special kind of clause. They describe a clause, in which something has been omitted. For example:

You are just as smart as Jim. = *You are just as smart as Jim* **is***.*

The verb (is) is left out of the final clause because it is understood. In this book, the term *elliptical clause* is avoided as much as possible, and the clause is more simply described as *omitting the verb* or *leaving out words that are understood.* Those replacement phrases provide simplicity and an instantaneous understanding of how the clause is structured and what meaning it provides. Avoiding technical terminology provides learners of German with a more immediate understanding of material being introduced or practiced.

The German Compilation book provides an all-encompassing look at German grammar and its application in both the written and spoken language. In addition, the large abundance of exercises provides a generous opportunity to practice what has been learned or a concept that learners may wish to master. Students of German are encouraged to use the extensive answer key to the exercises to check for accuracy and as an aid to assess the skill level that has been achieved.

One of the great advantages of using a compiled book like this is having access to a comprehensive collection of German language topics, thorough explanations of those topics, and a substantial amount of exercises with an answer key. It is to the user's advantage to review both small concepts and complete chapters until the German-learner's new skills can be used comfortably and confidently.

Pronunciation and gender

Pronunciation

Just like English and most other European languages, German uses the Latin alphabet as the basis for its writing. But the letters, in many cases, are pronounced slightly differently from English, and in four instances there are special letters for four sounds unique to German. Let's look at the German alphabet and its pronunciation.

LETTER	PHONETICS	EXAMPLE	
A a	ah	Maler	*painter*
B b	bay	Ball	*ball*
C c	tsay	Cent	*cent*
D d	day	dumm	*stupid*
E e	ay	weh	*sore*
F f	eff	finden	*find*
G g	gay	Garten	*garden*
H h	hah	Haus	*house*
I i	ee	ich	*I*
J j	yawt	ja	*yes*
K k	kah	Kind	*child*
L l	ell	Lampe	*lamp*
M m	emm	Mann	*man*
N n	enn	nein	*no*
O o	oh	Oma	*granny*
P p	pay	Park	*park*
Q q	koo	Quark	*curd cheese*
R r	air	rot	*red*
S s	ess	was	*what*
T t	tay	Tante	*aunt*
U u	oo	tut	*does*
V v	fow	Verbot	*ban*
W w	vay	wo	*where*
X x	ix	fixieren	*fix*
Y y	uepsilon	Gymnasium	*preparatory school*
Z z	tset	zehn	*ten*

German adds an umlaut to three vowels to change their pronunciation. These vowels are **ä**, **ö**, and **ü**. In addition, there is one special letter called ess-tset, which is the combination of an earlier form of an **s** and a **z**, and it looks like this: **ß**.

The vowel **ä** is pronounced very much like the German **e**. For example: **spät**, shpate, *late*. The vowel **ö** sounds something like the English sound *er* in the word *her*, but the *r* in that word is muted. For example: **können**, kernen, *can*. The sound of the vowel **ü** is made by pursing the lips to say *oo* but pronouncing *ee* in the mouth. For example: **Tür**, tuer, *door*. Note that the vowel **y** is pronounced in much the same way as **ü**. For example: **Gymnasium**, guem-nah-zee-oom, *preparatory school*.

The consonant sound of **ß** is identical to a double *s* in English. For example: **weiß**, vice, *white*.

Let's look at certain letter combinations that have their own unique sound.

LETTER	PHONETICS	EXAMPLE	
ch	*raspy* ch *as in Scottish* loch	nach	*after*
sch	sh	Schule	*school*
sp	shp	sparen	*save*
st	sht	Straße	*street*
au	ow	Frau	*woman*
äu	oy	läuft	*runs*
eu	oy	Freund	*friend*
ei	aye	mein	*my*
ie	ee	wie	*how*
th	t	Theater	*theater*
v	ff *but* v *in foreign words*	vor	*before*
		Vase	*vase*
tz	tz	Satz	*sentence*

Words that end in *voiced consonants* change to their *voiceless* counterparts.

IF A WORD ENDS IN . . .	PRONOUNCE IT AS . . .	EXAMPLE	
b	p	Leib	*body*
d	t	Bad	*bath*
g	k	Weg	*path*

The final syllable **-er** in a word is pronounced much like the final *-er* in a British English word, or something like *-uh*.

ÜBUNG
1·1

In the blank provided, write the letter of the pronunciation that matches the pronunciation of the German word.

_____ 1. Vater (*father*)   a. shern

_____ 2. Lampe (*lamp*)   b. shtate

_____ 3. Liebe (*love*)   c. foe-ghel

_____ 4. sagen (*say*)   d. shprach-eh

_____ 5. Bild (*picture*)   e. bilt

_____	6. machen (_make_)	f.	lee-beh
_____	7. warten (_wait_)	g.	fah-tuh
_____	8. Sprache (_language_)	h.	tsook
_____	9. Land (_country_)	i.	kahm
_____	10. Leute (_people_)	j.	loy-teh
_____	11. Vogel (_bird_)	k.	lunt
_____	12. kam (_came_)	l.	vahr-ten
_____	13. steht (_stands_)	m.	mahch-en
_____	14. Zug (_train_)	n.	zah-ghen
_____	15. schön (_pretty_)	o.	lahm-peh

Whenever in doubt about how a word is pronounced, refer to a good dictionary or speak to a German speaker. But be aware that just as with English, there are regional differences of pronunciation.

Gender

The gender of a noun can be masculine, feminine, or neuter. In English, the gender of masculine and feminine nouns is primarily determined by whether a living thing is male or female. Inanimate objects are called neuter. Look at these examples of English nouns that illustrate this:

MASCULINE/MALE	FEMININE/FEMALE	NEUTER/INANIMATE
boy	_girl_	_rock_
father	_mother_	_house_
actor	_actress_	_car_

There are some rare exceptions to this concept of gender. For example, ships are often referred to as feminine:

That's Old Ironsides. _She's a fine old ship._

Or a car might be considered feminine when there is a strong attachment to it:

My old Ford just won't run anymore. But she got me around for years.

The English speaker learning German has to put the English concept of gender aside and accept a different concept of gender—gender in the German language. For German gender is determined in more than one way. The easiest to understand is sexual gender. Most males are considered masculine, and most females are considered feminine. For example:

MASCULINE		FEMININE	
Mann	_man_	Frau	_woman_
Bruder	_brother_	Schwester	_sister_

Often, a suffix is attached to a masculine noun to make it feminine. You should be aware that this is a very common practice in German.

| Lehrer | (*male*) *teacher* | Lehrerin | (*female*) *teacher* |
| Schauspieler | *actor* | Schauspielerin | *actress* |

If a German noun is masculine, its definite article (*the*) is **der**. If it is feminine, its definite article is **die**. For example:

| der Mann | *the man* | die Frau | *the woman* |
| der Lehrer | *the teacher* | die Schauspielerin | *the actress* |

ÜBUNG
1·2

*In the blank provided, write the appropriate definite article for each noun—**der** or **die**.*

1. _____ Junge (*boy*)

2. _____ Lehrerin (*teacher*)

3. _____ Frau (*woman*)

4. _____ Diplomat (*diplomat*)

5. _____ Diplomatin (*diplomat*)

6. _____ Lehrer (*teacher*)

7. _____ Professor (*professor*)

8. _____ Professorin (*professor*)

9. _____ Schwester (*sister*)

10. _____ Bruder (*brother*)

German, like English, also has a neuter gender. But it does *not* necessarily refer to inanimate objects. The definite article (*the*) used with neuter nouns is **das**. Notice that neuter nouns can include persons as well as objects:

INANIMATE NEUTER NOUNS		ANIMATE NEUTER NOUNS	
das Haus	*the house*	das Kind	*the child*
das Auto	*the car*	das Mädchen	*the girl*

And masculine and feminine nouns can include objects as well as persons. For example:

MASCULINE		FEMININE	
der Garten	*the garden*	die Blume	*the flower*
der Stuhl	*the chair*	die Rose	*the rose*

Perhaps you are now wondering how you determine gender in German. Let's consider some signals to watch for. Masculine nouns:

- *Tend* to be those nouns that describe males

der Mann	*the man*

- Often end in -**er**, -**en**, or -**el**

der Pullover	*sweater*
der Brunnen	*well*
der Mantel	*coat*

Feminine nouns:

- *Tend* to be those that describe females

die Frau	*woman*

- End in -**in**

die Lehrerin	*teacher*

- End in -**ung**, -**heit**, -**keit**, -**ion**, -**schaft**, or -**tät**

die Übung	*exercise*
die Gesundheit	*health*
die Einsamkeit	*loneliness*
die Position	*position*
die Freundschaft	*friendship*
die Majorität	*majority*

- *Tend* to end in -**e**

die Lampe	*lamp*

Neuter nouns:

- End in -**chen** or -**lein** and are diminutives

das Mädchen	*girl*
das Röslein	*little rose*

- End in -**um**

das Gymnasium	*preparatory school*

- *Tend* to end in -**tum**

das Königtum	*kingdom*

These descriptions of gender are not rules; they are signals for determining the *likely* gender of a German noun. There are many exceptions, because often the choice of a noun's gender is based upon the traditional use of that noun. Sometimes the gender used in Germany is different from the gender used in Austria or Switzerland. The newcomer to German has to put up with this in the beginning stages of learning. But in time and with experience, using German gender correctly becomes a reality.

In the blank provided, write in the appropriate definite article (**der, die,** or **das**) for each of the following nouns.

1. _____ Kind (*child*)

2. _____ Schule (*school*)

3. _____ Tante (*aunt*)

4. _____ Onkel (*uncle*)

5. _____ Brüderlein (*little brother*)

6. _____ Studium (*studies*)

7. _____ Universität (*university*)

8. _____ Landschaft (*landscape*)

9. _____ Situation (*situation*)

10. _____ Wagen (*car*)

11. _____ Gärtner (*gardener*)

12. _____ Eigentum (*property*)

13. _____ Landkarte (*map*)

14. _____ Sportler (*athlete*)

15. _____ Boden (*floor*)

16. _____ Sängerin (*singer*)

17. _____ Sicherheit (*safety*)

18. _____ Mutter (*mother*)

19. _____ Katze (*cat*)

20. _____ Freiheit (*freedom*)

Definite and indefinite articles

Definite articles

Just as in English, the subject in a German sentence can be a noun or a pronoun. If the subject is a noun, it will illustrate its gender by being accompanied by either **der**, **die**, or **das**, the definite articles in German that all mean *the*. Naturally, to have a sentence, there has to be a verb and perhaps other elements in the sentence besides the subject. Let's look at some simple sentences that demonstrate masculine nouns, feminine nouns, and neuter nouns used as the subject of a sentence.

Masculine nouns

Der Mann ist hier.	*The man is here.*
Der Lehrer ist hier.	*The teacher is here.*
Der Stuhl ist hier.	*The chair is here.*
Der Wagen ist hier.	*The car is here.*
Der Schauspieler ist hier.	*The actor is here.*

Feminine nouns

Die Frau ist da.	*The woman is there.*
Die Lehrerin ist da.	*The teacher is there.*
Die Landkarte ist da.	*The map is there.*
Die Blume ist da.	*The flower is there.*
Die Schauspielerin ist da.	*The actress is there.*

Neuter nouns

Das Haus ist klein.	*The house is little.*
Das Auto ist klein.	*The car is little.*
Das Mädchen ist klein.	*The girl is little.*
Das Kind ist klein.	*The child is little.*
Das Gymnasium ist klein.	*The preparatory school is little.*

ÜBUNG

2·1

*Rewrite each sentence with the nouns provided in parentheses. Add the appropriate definite article—**der**, **die**, or **das**.*

FOR EXAMPLE: _____ ist hier.

(Mann) _____ *Der Mann ist hier.* _____

_____ ist da.

1. (Kind) _____
2. (Blume) _____
3. (Haus) _____
4. (Garten) _____
5. (Wagen) _____
6. (Stuhl) _____
7. (Auto) _____
8. (Bruder) _____
9. (Schwester) _____
10. (Sängerin) _____

_____ ist klein.

11. (Gymnasium) _____
12. (Katze) _____
13. (Sportler) _____
14. (Mädchen) _____
15. (Boden) _____
16. (Landkarte) _____
17. (Universität) _____
18. (Pullover) _____
19. (Schule) _____
20. (Kind) _____

_____ ist hier.

21. (Auto) _____
22. (Gärtnerin) _____
23. (Frau) _____

24. (Professorin) _____

25. (Junge) _____

The definite articles (**der, die, das**) are called **der**-words. Another word that can be used in place of a definite article is **dieser** (*this*), and it, too, is a **der**-word. Note how similar the ending of this word is to the ending of a definite article used with masculine, feminine, and neuter nouns.

Masculine

der Mann	dieser Mann	*this man*
der Lehrer	dieser Lehrer	*this teacher*
der Garten	dieser Garten	*this garden*

Feminine

die Schauspielerin	diese Schauspielerin	*this actress*
die Schule	diese Schule	*this school*
die Bluse	diese Bluse	*this blouse*

Neuter

das Kind	dieses Kind	*this child*
das Fenster	dieses Fenster	*this window*
das Bett	dieses Bett	*this bed*

ÜBUNG
2·2

*Rewrite each phrase by changing the definite article to the appropriate form of **dieser**.*

1. der Mann _____

2. die Frau _____

3. das Kind _____

4. die Blume _____

5. der Garten _____

6. die Gärtnerin _____

7. die Lehrerin _____

8. das Studium _____

9. das Bett _____

10. der Professor _____

11. der Diplomat _____

12. die Bluse _____

13. der Boden _____

14. das Fenster _____

15. die Schauspielerin _____

*Now supply the appropriate form of **dieser** for each of the following nouns.*

16. _____ Haus

17. _____ Universität

18. _____ Königtum

19. _____ Gärtner

20. _____ Lehrer

21. _____ Schule

22. _____ Mädchen

23. _____ Sänger

24. _____ Sängerin

25. _____ Landkarte

Indefinite articles

The German indefinite articles for the subject of a sentence are **ein** and **eine**, and both mean *a* or *an*. **Ein** is used with masculine and neuter nouns, and **eine** is used with feminine nouns. For example:

Masculine

ein Lehrer	*a teacher*
ein Arzt	*a doctor*
ein Fernsehapparat	*a television set*
ein Schauspieler	*an actor*

Feminine

eine Schule	*a school*
eine Mutter	*a mother*
eine Tochter	*a daughter*
eine Tante	*an aunt*

Neuter

ein Bett	*a bed*
ein Buch	*a book*
ein Restaurant	*a restaurant*
ein Bild	*a picture*

ÜBUNG

2·3

Rewrite each phrase by changing the definite article to the appropriate indefinite article.

1. die Lehrerin _____

2. der Junge _____

3. das Fenster _____

4. das Bett _____

5. die Universität _____

6. die Tante _____

7. das Mädchen _____

8. der Arzt _____

9. das Buch _____

10. der Fernsehapparat _____

11. die Tochter _____

12. das Restaurant _____

13. der Boden _____

14. die Mutter _____

15. das Bild _____

The indefinite articles are known as **ein**-words. Another such **ein**-word is **kein**, which means *not any* or *no*. Notice that its ending in the feminine is identical to the ending required with **eine**.

Masculine

kein Vater	*no father*
kein Bruder	*no brother*
kein Tisch	*no table*
kein Film	*no film, movie*

Feminine

keine Großmutter	*no grandmother*
keine Butter	*no butter*
keine Zeit	*no time*
keine Uhr	*no clock*

Neuter

kein Geld	*no money*
kein Fenster	*no window*
kein Rathaus	*no town hall*
kein Schlafzimmer	*no bedroom*

ÜBUNG
2·4

*Rewrite each phrase by changing the definite article to the appropriate form of **kein**.*

1. die Tochter _____

2. der Tisch _____

3. das Fenster _____

4. das Restaurant _____

5. der Gärtner _____

6. die Großmutter _____

7. der Arzt _____

8. die Ärztin _____

9. das Rathaus _____

10. die Butter _____

*In the blank provided, write the appropriate form of **kein** for each noun.*

11. _____ Junge

12. _____ Schlafzimmer

13. _____ Bild

14. _____ Schwester

15. _____ Tante

16. _____ Bruder

17. _____ Zeit

18. _____ Fernsehapparat

19. _____ Uhr

20. _____ Fenster

21. _____ Mantel

22. _____ Frau

23. _____ Geld

24. _____ Mutter

25. _____ Universität

*Rewrite each sentence twice, once by changing the definite article to the indefinite article and once by changing it to the appropriate form of **kein**.*

FOR EXAMPLE: Der Mann ist hier.

Ein Mann ist hier.

Kein Mann ist hier.

1. Die Frau ist da.

_____

_____

2. Das Restaurant ist klein.

_____

_____

3. Die Schule ist groß. (groß = *big*)

_____

_____

4. Die Mutter ist hier.

_____

_____

5. Der Film ist alt. (alt = *old*)

_____

_____

6. Das Bild ist klein.

_____

_____

7. Die Großmutter ist alt.

_____

_____

8. Der Tisch ist neu. (neu = *new*)

_____

_____

9. Das Restaurant ist groß.

_____

_____

10. Die Landkarte ist hier.

_____

_____

11. Die Tante ist alt.

_____

_____

12. Der Vater ist jung. (jung = *young*)

_____

_____

13. Das Rathaus ist neu.

_____

_____

14. Die Tochter ist jung.

_____

_____

15. Die Uhr ist da.

_____

_____

The subject of a sentence does not occur solely in statements. It is also used in questions. In a German question, the verb precedes the subject, and the rest of the sentence remains the same. For example:

STATEMENT	QUESTION	
Der Mann ist da.	Ist **der** Mann da?	_Is **the** man there?_
Diese Frau ist alt.	Ist **diese** Frau alt?	_Is **this** woman old?_
Eine Katze ist klein.	Ist **eine** Katze klein?	_Is **a** cat small?_
Kein Buch ist neu.	Ist **kein** Buch neu?	_Isn't **any** book new?_

ÜBUNG
2·6

Rewrite each statement as a question.

1. Der Film ist neu.

_____

2. Dieses Kind ist klein.

_____

3. Kein Lehrer ist da.

_____

4. Ein Restaurant ist da.

_____

5. Die Tochter ist jung.

_____

6. Dieser Arzt ist alt.

_____

7. Keine Schule ist neu.

_____

8. Kein Bild ist hier.

_____

9. Eine Uhr ist da.

_____

10. Die Großmutter ist alt.

_____

11. Dieser Professor ist jung.

_____

12. Ein Bett ist hier.

_____

13. Keine Butter ist da.

_____

14. Der Boden ist neu.

_____

15. Dieses Auto ist alt.

_____

ÜBUNG
2·7

In the blanks provided, write the appropriate forms of the definite article, indefinite article, **dieser,** *and* **kein.**

FOR EXAMPLE: _____ *der ein dieser kein* _____ Lehrer

DEF. ART.	INDEF. ART.	DIESER	KEIN	
1. _____	_____	_____	_____	Tochter
2. _____	_____	_____	_____	Ärztin
3. _____	_____	_____	_____	Bruder
4. _____	_____	_____	_____	Bild
5. _____	_____	_____	_____	Uhr

6. _____	_____	_____	_____	Fenster
7. _____	_____	_____	_____	Haus
8. _____	_____	_____	_____	Wagen
9. _____	_____	_____	_____	Gymnasium
10. _____	_____	_____	_____	Rathaus
11. _____	_____	_____	_____	Schlafzimmer
12. _____	_____	_____	_____	Tante
13. _____	_____	_____	_____	Großmutter
14. _____	_____	_____	_____	Mantel
15. _____	_____	_____	_____	Film
16. _____	_____	_____	_____	Schauspielerin
17. _____	_____	_____	_____	Diplomat
18. _____	_____	_____	_____	Restaurant
19. _____	_____	_____	_____	Schule
20. _____	_____	_____	_____	Bluse
21. _____	_____	_____	_____	Mutter
22. _____	_____	_____	_____	Vater
23. _____	_____	_____	_____	Buch
24. _____	_____	_____	_____	Kind
25. _____	_____	_____	_____	Garten
26. _____	_____	_____	_____	Gärtnerin
27. _____	_____	_____	_____	Arzt
28. _____	_____	_____	_____	Bett
29. _____	_____	_____	_____	Junge
30. _____	_____	_____	_____	Mädchen

Der-words

The definite and indefinite articles are called **der**-words and **ein**-words respectively. It is important to distinguish between **der**-words and **ein**-words in order to deal with adjective endings accurately.

A few words are categorized as *der-words*, because they follow the declensional patterns of the definite articles (**der, die**, and **das**). The **der**-words are usually introduced with a masculine ending even though different endings are used for the other genders. Only **jeder** does not have a form in the plural, and **solcher** tends to be used in the plural. The most commonly used **der**-words are:

SINGULAR	PLURAL
dieser (*this*)	diese (*these*)
jener (*that*)	jene (*those*)
jeder (*each, every*)	N/A
N/A	solche (*such, like that*)
welcher? (*which*)	welche? (*which*)

Notice that **welcher** is used to ask a question. If **welcher** replaces a definite article in a sentence that is not a question, the sentence must be changed to a question. For example:

Der Mann ist Soldat.	*The man is a soldier.*
Welcher Mann ist Soldat?	*Which man is a soldier?*

Remember that in questions the verb precedes the subject.

Just as the masculine form of **dieser, jener, jeder,** and **welcher** end in **-er** like **der**, the feminine form ends in **-e** like **die**, and the neuter form ends in **-s** like **das**:

FEMININE	NEUTER
diese	dieses
jene	jenes
jede	jedes
welche	welches

The **der**-words can replace the definite articles in sentences but must use the same gender ending as the **der**-word they replace. For example:

Der Lehrer wohnt in Hamburg.	*The teacher lives in Hamburg.*
Dieser Lehrer wohnt in Hamburg.	*This teacher lives in Hamburg.*
Die Ärztin ist krank.	*The doctor is sick.*
Jene Ärztin ist krank.	*That doctor is sick.*
Das Mädchen spricht Deutsch.	*The girl speaks German.*
Jedes Mädchen spricht Deutsch.	*Each girl speaks German.*
Die Männer arbeiten in einer Fabrik.	*The men work in a factory.*
Welche Männer arbeiten in einer Fabrik?	*Which men work in a factory?*

When the **der**-words are used in the accusative case, they still must conform to the ending of the article they replace. When it comes to masculine nouns, this means an ending different from the nominative: instead of **-er** as in the nominative, the accusative ending is **-en**. Look at the following sentences that illustrate **der**-words in the accusative case. Remember that feminine, neuter, and plural nouns make no change in the accusative case.

Kennen Sie **den** Lehrer?	*Do you know the teacher?*
Kennen Sie **jenen** Lehrer?	*Do you know that teacher?*
Sie arbeitet für **die** Frau.	*She works for the woman.*
Sie arbeitet für **diese** Frau.	*She works for this woman.*

Sie sieht **das** Kind.	*She sees the child.*
Sie sieht **jedes** Kind.	*She sees each child.*
Er liest **die** Zeitungen.	*He is reading the newspapers.*
Er liest **solche** Zeitungen.	*He is reading such newspapers (newspapers like that).*
Er bekommt **die** Bücher.	*He receives the books.*
Welche Bücher bekommt er?	*Which books does he receive?*

ÜBUNG
2·8

Reword each sentence by replacing the definite article with the **der**-words provided in parentheses.

1. Der Wagen ist sehr alt.

(dieser) _____

(welcher) _____

2. Die Kinder spielen Tennis.

(jener) _____

(welcher) _____

3. Sie kennt die Frau.

(jener) _____

(jeder) _____

4. Wir besuchen den Arzt.

(welcher) _____

(dieser) _____

5. Thomas hat die Zeitung (*newspaper*).

(jeder) _____

(jener) _____

6. Sie arbeiten für den Professor.

(dieser) _____

(jener) _____

7. Das Mädchen heißt (*is called*) Tina.

(dieser) _____

(welcher) _____

8. Herr Schneider verkauft den Wagen.

(dieser) _____

(jener) _____

9. Die Lehrerin kauft das Haus.

(dieser) _____

(welcher) _____

10. Die Männer helfen ihnen (*help them*).

(welcher) _____

(solcher) _____

Ein-words

Besides **ein** and **eine**, the possessive adjectives and **kein** (*no, not any*) are also **ein**-words. The possessive adjectives are:

PERSONAL PRONOUN	POSSESSIVE ADJECTIVE
ich	mein (*my*)
du	dein (*your*)
er	sein (*his/its*)
sie *s.*	ihr (*her/its*)
es	sein (*its/his/her*)
wir	unser (*our*)
ihr	euer (*your*)
Sie	Ihr (*your*)
sie *pl.*	ihr (*their*)
wer	wessen (*whose*)

Except for **wessen**, which does not show gender, all the possessive adjectives add an **-e** ending when they precede a feminine or plural noun in the nominative case. For example:

Mein Vater ist Lehrer.	*My father is a teacher.*
Meine Mutter ist Ärztin.	*My mother is a doctor.*
Sein Buch ist neu.	*His book is new.*
Seine Kinder sind zu Hause.	*His children are at home.*
Unser Wagen ist neu.	*Our car is new.*
Unsere Eltern sind in Italien.	*Our parents are in Italy.*
Kein Mann ist da.	*There isn't a man there.*
Keine Männer sind da.	*There aren't any men there.*
Wessen Haus ist das?	*Whose house is that?*
Wessen Kinder sind das?	*Whose children are those?*

Note that **wessen**, like **welcher**, introduces a question.

The possessive adjective **euer**, when used with a feminine or plural noun in the nominative case, changes its spelling slightly to **eure**.

Ist das **eure** Schwester?	*Is that your sister?*
Das sind **eure** Bücher.	*Those are your books.*

The accusative case with **ein**-words is similar to the accusative case with **der**-words. The feminine, neuter, and plural in the accusative case are identical to their use in the nominative case.

NOMINATIVE	ACCUSATIVE
eine Frau	eine Frau
mein Kind	mein Kind
eure Eltern	eure Eltern

Again, it is only the masculine that changes in the accusative case. And again, the change is to an -**en** ending.

NOMINATIVE	ACCUSATIVE
ein Freund	einen Freund
dein Bruder	deinen Bruder
kein Wagen	keinen Wagen

ÜBUNG
2·9

Reword each sentence with the possessive adjective in parentheses.

EXAMPLE _____ Vater ist alt.

(sein) *Sein Vater ist alt.*

_____ Schwester wohnt in Berlin.

1. (mein) _____

2. (ihr [*her*]) _____

3. (dein) _____

4. (euer) _____

5. (wessen) _____

Sind _____ Freunde (*friends*) in Heidelberg?

6. (Ihr) _____

7. (ihr [*their*]) _____

8. (unser) _____

9. (wessen) _____

10. (sein) _____

_____ Bruder ist Richter (*judge*).

11. (mein) _____

12. (euer) _____

13. (ihr [*her*]) _____

14. (sein) _____

15. (unser) _____

Ein/eine with questions

If **ein/eine** precedes a noun in a question, **ein/eine** does not change if the answer is in the positive.

Ist **ein** Mann hinter der Tür?	*Is a man behind the door?*
Ja, **ein** Mann ist hinter der Tür.	*Yes, a man is behind the door.*

If the answer is in the negative, **ein** changes to **kein**.

Ist **ein** Mann hinter der Tür?	*Is a man behind the door?*
Nein, **kein** Mann ist hinter der Tür.	*No, a man is not behind the door. (No, no man is behind the door.)*

Although nouns of nationality and professions are usually not accompanied by an article, it should be assumed that an *invisible* **ein** or **eine** precedes such nouns. When negated, they use **kein**.

Ist die Frau Lehrerin?	*Is the woman a teacher?*
Nein, die Frau ist **keine** Lehrerin.	*No, the woman is not a teacher.*

ÜBUNG
2·10

Answer each question in the positive and in the negative.

EXAMPLE   Ist ein Wagen in der Garage?

Ja, ein Wagen ist in der Garage.

Nein, kein Wagen ist in der Garage.

1. Wohnt ein Lehrer in diesem Haus?

_____

_____

2. Ist diese Dame Ärztin?

_____

_____

3. Ist eine Katze (*cat*) unter (*under*) dem Tisch?

_____

_____

4. Kommt ein Zug (*train*)?

_____

_____

5. Ist die Frau Richterin?

_____

_____

Pronouns, plurals, and the verb *sein*

·3·

In Chapters 1 and 2, you discovered just how great a role gender plays in German. Endings on **der**-words and **ein**-words signal the gender of a noun and follow a consistent pattern. That pattern continues when dealing with pronouns.

Just as in English, specific pronouns are used for certain kinds of nouns in German. Look at the following English nouns and the pronouns required to replace them:

MASCULINE NOUN	PRONOUN REPLACEMENT
the man	*he*
a boy	*he*
this doctor	*he*

FEMININE NOUN	PRONOUN REPLACEMENT
the girl	*she*
a mother	*she*
this lioness	*she*

NEUTER NOUN	PRONOUN REPLACEMENT
the tree	*it*
a book	*it*
this door	*it*

PLURAL NOUN	PRONOUN REPLACEMENT
the women	*they*
five houses	*they*
these workers	*they*

Note that all plurals in English—whether animate or inanimate—are replaced by the same pronoun: *they*. These pronouns, *he*, *she*, *it*, and *they*, are called third-person pronouns and replace nouns.

The German third-person pronouns also replace nouns and like English pronouns conform to the gender of the noun they replace. But remember that German gender is not always determined by the sex of an individual. Let's look at the German pronouns and how they replace nouns:

MASCULINE NOUN		PRONOUN REPLACEMENT	
der Mann	*the man*	er	*he*
ein Bruder	*a brother*	er	*he*
der Garten	*the garden*	er	*it*
dieser Tisch	*this table*	er	*it*

FEMININE NOUN		PRONOUN REPLACEMENT	
die Tochter	*the daughter*	sie	*she*
eine Ärztin	*a doctor*	sie	*she*
diese Landkarte	*this map*	sie	*it*
keine Bluse	*no blouse*	sie	*it*

NEUTER NOUN		PRONOUN REPLACEMENT	
das Mädchen	*girl*	es	*she*
ein Kind	*a child*	es	*he, she*
dieses Haus	*this house*	es	*it*
das Bild	*the picture*	es	*it*

ÜBUNG

3·1

In the blank provided, write the appropriate pronoun replacement for each noun.

1. das Restaurant _____

2. der Arzt _____

3. die Universität _____

4. der Gärtner _____

5. die Lehrerin _____

6. das Rathaus _____

7. das Bett _____

8. die Großmutter _____

9. der Boden _____

10. das Kind _____

11. ein Vater _____

12. eine Schule _____

13. ein Mädchen _____

14. ein Junge _____

15. ein Buch _____

16. kein Gymnasium _____

17. keine Tante _____

18. kein Tisch _____

19. keine Blume _____

20. kein Fenster _____

21. dieser Wagen _____

22. dieser Bruder _____

23. diese Tochter _____

24. dieses Haus _____

25. dieser Fernsehapparat _____

German plurals are formed in a variety of ways. A small number end in **-s**, and some examples are:

SINGULAR	PLURAL	
das Auto	die Autos	*cars*
die Kamera	die Kameras	*cameras*
das Sofa	die Sofas	*sofas*

All plural nouns use the definite article **die**, no matter what their gender is in the singular. Many masculine nouns form their plural by an **-e** ending or by an umlaut over **a**, **o**, or **u** plus an **-e** ending. For example:

SINGULAR	PLURAL	
der Tisch	die Tische	*tables*
der Schuh	die Schuhe	*shoes*
der Satz	die Sätze	*sentences*
der Stuhl	die Stühle	*chairs*

If a masculine noun ends in **-en**, **-er**, or **-el**, there is no additional ending, but sometimes an umlaut is added. For example:

SINGULAR	PLURAL	
der Boden	die Böden	*floors*
der Wagen	die Wagen	*cars*
der Sportler	die Sportler	*athletes*
der Lehrer	die Lehrer	*teachers*
der Mantel	die Mäntel	*coats*
der Onkel	die Onkel	*uncles*

But many other masculine nouns have their own plural formation and do not conform to simple patterns. For example:

SINGULAR	PLURAL	
der Mann	die Männer	*men*
der Junge	die Jungen	*boys*
der Soldat	die Soldaten	*soldiers*

Many feminine nouns form their plural by an **-n** or **-en** ending. For example:

SINGULAR	PLURAL	
die Blume	die Blumen	*flowers*
die Zeitung	die Zeitungen	*newspapers*
die Lampe	die Lampen	*lamps*
die Decke	die Decken	*blankets*

But many feminine nouns have a plural formation that is based upon what is commonly accepted or tradition. For example:

SINGULAR	PLURAL	
die Wand	die Wände	*walls*
die Mutter	die Mütter	*mothers*
die Tochter	die Töchter	*daughters*
die Wurst	die Würste	*sausages*

Many neuter nouns form their plural by an **-er** ending, often adding an umlaut to **a**, **o**, or **u**. But if the noun ends in **-chen** or **-lein**, no ending is required. For example:

SINGULAR	PLURAL	
das Haus	die Häuser	*houses*
das Land	die Länder	*countries*
das Kind	die Kinder	*children*
das Mädchen	die Mädchen	*girls*
das Röslein	die Röslein	*little roses*

It must be pointed out that there is no clear-cut way to always determine the plural of a noun; there are only *inconsistent patterns* and not always fixed rules. It is wise to check in a dictionary for the correct plural of a noun. Do not be frustrated by German plurals. Give yourself time and plenty of practice, and in due course the plurals will fall in line for you. Remember, practice makes perfect.

With this information about plurals, you are ready to look at the German third-person plural pronoun. And just like the English pronoun *they*, the German third-person plural pronoun is used for all plurals, no matter the gender of the singular noun. For example:

PLURAL NOUN		PRONOUN REPLACEMENT	
die Frauen	*women*	sie	*they*
die Männer	*men*	sie	*they*
die Sofas	*sofas*	sie	*they*
die Bücher	*books*	sie	*they*
die Brüder	*brothers*	sie	*they*
die Zeitungen	*newspapers*	sie	*they*

Let's look at some plurals used in complete sentences:

Die Männer sind hier.	*The men are here.*
Sie sind hier.	*They are here.*
Die Bücher sind alt.	*The books are old.*
Sie sind alt.	*They are old.*
Die Kinder sind jung.	*The children are young.*
Sie sind jung.	*They are young.*

Rewrite each sentence by changing the subject of the sentence to a pronoun.

1. Die Brüder sind jung.

_____

2. Die Frauen sind da.

_____

3. Die Mädchen sind klein.

_____

4. Die Jungen sind groß.

_____

5. Die Zeitungen sind neu.

_____

6. Die Töchter sind hier.

_____

7. Die Lehrer sind alt.

_____

8. Die Soldaten sind da.

_____

9. Die Tanten sind jung.

_____

10. Die Mäntel sind neu.

_____

*In the blank provided, write the pronoun that is the correct replacement for the nouns that follow. Note that these nouns are masculine, feminine, neuter, and plural. For feminine singular, write **sie** (sing.). For plural, write **sie** (pl.).*

1. das Haus _____

2. die Professorin _____

3. der Onkel _____

4. die Mütter _____

5. die Landkarten _____

6. das Mädchen _____

7. die Mädchen _____

8. die Länder _____

9. der Tisch _____

10. das Rathaus _____

11. ein Buch _____

12. keine Bücher _____

13. ein Bild _____

14. keine Großmutter _____

15. ein Soldat _____

16. kein Geld _____

17. diese Sofas _____

18. dieser Gärtner _____

19. diese Gärtner _____

20. diese Lampen _____

Do not let the similarity between the third-person singular pronoun **sie** and the third-person plural pronoun **sie** confuse you. Usage makes their distinction clear. It's like the English words *its* and *it's*. They sound exactly the same, but their usage avoids any confusion. In German, **sie** (*sing.*) is used with a singular verb, and **sie** (*pl.*) is used with a plural verb. For example:

sie ist	*she is*
sie sind	*they are*

ÜBUNG

3·4

Underline the noun that can be correctly substituted for the pronoun in each sentence.

FOR EXAMPLE: Es ist da.	eine Uhr	<u>das Haus</u>	kein Mann
1. Er ist klein.	der Mantel	ein Buch	kein Geld
2. Sie sind hier.	die Gärtnerin	die Landkarte	die Töchter
3. Es ist groß.	ein Wagen	ein Auto	keine Frauen
4. Sie sind alt.	die Onkel	keine Mutter	ein Junge

5. Sie ist neu.	keine Bücher	die Zeitungen	eine Kamera
6. Er ist da.	ein Arzt	kein Bild	diese Kinder
7. Sie sind klein.	ein Bruder	dieses Rathaus	die Würste
8. Sie sind alt.	die Schulen	diese Landkarte	keine Zeit
9. Es ist jung.	das Mädchen	kein Vater	ein Diplomat
10. Sie ist hier.	keine Mütter	diese Jungen	eine Lampe

There are also first-person and second-person pronouns in German. They are **ich** *I*, **du** *you*, **wir** *we*, **ihr** *you*, and **Sie** *you*. **Ich** and **wir** are first-person pronouns, and **du**, **ihr**, and **Sie** are second-person pronouns. Take a careful look at the following description of the second-person pronouns:

du	Singular and informal. Use with children, family, and friends.
ihr	Plural and informal. Use with children, family, and friends.
Sie	Singular or plural formal. Use with strangers and to show respect.

If you call someone by his or her first name (**Karl**, **Martin**, **Luise**), you should probably use **du**. Use **ihr** if you are speaking to more than one person. Use **Sie** when you address someone with a title (**Frau Braun**, **Herr Schmidt**, **Doktor Schneider**).

ÜBUNG
3·5

*In the blank provided, write the pronoun you should use to address the person identified in each line: **du**, **ihr**, or **Sie**.*

1. Herr Schäfer _____

2. Frau Bauer _____

3. Angela _____

4. Angela und Johann _____

5. Kinder _____

6. Tante Inge _____

7. Professor Braun _____

8. Onkel Karl _____

9. Frau Schneider und Doktor Benz _____

10. Stefan _____

You have encountered the verb **sein** (*to be*) only with third-person pronouns, but it is used with all pronouns. The changes the verb makes according to those pronouns are the *conjugation* of the verb **sein**.

ich bin	*I am*	wir sind	*we are*
du bist	*you are*	ihr seid	*you are*
er ist	*he is*	Sie sind	*you are*
sie ist	*she is*	sie sind	*they are*
es ist	*it is*		

ÜBUNG

3·6

*In the blank provided, write in the missing pronoun or form of the verb **sein**.*

1. es _____

2. ich _____

3. _____ seid

4. sie (*sing.*) _____

5. _____ bin

6. _____ bist

7. Sie _____

8. sie (*pl.*) _____

9. wir _____

10. es _____

11. du _____

12. ihr _____

No matter what pronoun or noun is the subject of a sentence, a question can be formed. And like the questions described in Chapter 2, they are formed by placing the verb before the subject:

Er ist klein.	*He is small.*
Ist **er** klein?	*Is **he** small?*

ÜBUNG

3·7

Rewrite each statement as a question.

1. Das Haus ist groß.

_____

2. Die Häuser sind klein.

_____

3. Er ist jung.

_____

4. Sie sind alt.

_____

5. Du bist klein.

_____

6. Wir sind Töchter.

_____

7. Die Kinder sind hier.

_____

8. Ihr seid Brüder.

_____

9. Sie ist Lehrerin.

_____

10. Die Stühle sind alt.

_____

11. Ich bin alt.

_____

12. Dieser Mann ist Professor.

_____

13. Sie ist neu.

_____

14. Es ist groß.

_____

15. Herr Braun! Sie sind Arzt.

_____

Pronouns in the nominative case

The English personal pronouns used as the subject of a sentence are equivalent to the German nominative case pronouns, which are used as the subject of a German sentence.

ENGLISH PRONOUNS	GERMAN PRONOUNS
I	ich
you	du, ihr, Sie
he	er
she	sie
it	es
we	wir
they	sie

The following examples show pronouns used as the subject of a sentence.

Ich wohne in Bonn.
I live in Bonn.

Sie ist meine Schwester.
She is my sister.

Wo sind **wir**?
Where are we?

The German pronouns are used in much the same way as the English pronouns, with the important exception of the pronouns that mean *you* (**du**, **ihr**, and **Sie**).
Use **du** when speaking to a small child, a family member, or a close friend.

Wie alt bist **du** jetzt, Franz? Sieben oder acht?
How old are you now, Franz? Seven or eight?

Use **ihr** when speaking to more than one child, family member, or close friend.

Erik! Gudrun! Kinder! Wo seid **ihr**?
Erik! Gudrun! Children! Where are you?

Use **Sie** when speaking to adults who are unfamiliar, as well as to people with whom you regularly deal on a formal basis (for example, your boss, your professor, your physician, and the local shopkeeper).

Können **Sie** mir sagen bitte, wo das Thaliatheater ist? (*to a stranger on the street*)
Can you please tell me where the Thalia Theater is?

Sind **Sie** heute beschäftigt, Herr Doktor?
Are you busy today, Doctor?

These differences can be generalized in the following chart.

du	a singular informal pronoun
ihr	a plural informal pronoun (the plural of du)
Sie	a singular or plural formal pronoun

The pronoun **sie** may sometimes seem confusing, because it can mean *she, they,* or (when capitalized—**Sie**) *you.* But Germans have no difficulty in distinguishing the meaning of this pronoun: The context of a conversation or of a written or printed text clearly indicates the intended meaning of **sie**.

„Kennst du diese Frau?" „Ja, **sie** ist meine Mutter."
"Do you know this woman?" "Yes, she's my mother."

„Kennst du diese Mädchen?" „Ja, **sie** sind meine Schwestern."
"Do you know these girls?" "Yes, they're my sisters."

„Sind **Sie** Deutscher?" „Nein, ich bin Schweizer."
"Are you German?" "No, I'm Swiss."

In addition, when sie means she, the verb is singular. When sie means they, the verb is plural.

Sie ist in Berlin.
She is in Berlin.

Sie sind in Berlin.
They are in Berlin.

German has two additional nominative case pronouns: wer and was. These are interrogative pronouns and ask the question *who* or *what*.

Wer ist das?
Who's that?

Was liegt auf dem Boden?
What's lying on the floor?

When changing a nominative case noun to a nominative case pronoun, the pronoun must have the same gender and number as the noun. Masculine nouns change to **er**, feminine nouns change to **sie**, and neuter nouns change to **es**. All plural nouns become **sie**.

Der Lehrer ist zu Hause.
The teacher is at home.
Er ist zu Hause.
He is at home.

Die Lehrerin ist zu Hause.
The teacher is at home.
Sie ist zu Hause.
She is at home.

Das Haus ist alt.
The house is old.
Es ist alt.
It's old.

Die Häuser sind alt.
The houses are old.
Sie sind alt.
They are old.

ÜBUNG

3·8

Rewrite each sentence, changing the word or phrase in boldface to the appropriate pronoun.

1. **Das Kind** hat lange geschlafen.

_____

2. Ist **die alte Frau** deine Großmutter?

_____

3. **Herr Keller** hat sich gestern das Bein gebrochen.

_____

4. **Viele Leute** kämpfen gegen das Schicksal.

   _____

5. Wo sind **die Stühle?**

   _____

6. **Sabine** wird den Ofen heizen.

   _____

7. **Die junge Ärztin** war mit dieser Arbeit zufrieden.

   _____

8. **Die Tiere und Pflanzen einer tropischen Insel** wachsen nicht hier.

   _____

9. Hat **Karl** meinen Pullover genommen?

   _____

10. **Das nette Mädchen** wohnt nicht weit von uns.

    _____

Each nominative case pronoun requires the use of a specific verb form. The following chart presents several verb types in the present tense and the form required for each pronoun.

	REGULAR VERB	IRREGULAR VERB	HABEN	SEIN	MODAL
ich	sage	lese	habe	bin	kann
du	sagst	liest	hast	bist	kannst
er	sagt	liest	hat	ist	kann
sie	sagt	liest	hat	ist	kann
es	sagt	liest	hat	ist	kann
wir	sagen	lesen	haben	sind	können
ihr	sagt	lest	habt	seid	könnt
sie	sagen	lesen	haben	sind	können
Sie	sagen	lesen	haben	sind	können

The forms for the past tense of these verbs follow.

	REGULAR VERB	IRREGULAR VERB	HABEN	SEIN	MODAL
ich	sagte	las	hatte	war	konnte
du	sagtest	lasest	hattest	warst	konntest
er	sagte	las	hatte	war	konnte
sie	sagte	las	hatte	war	konnte
es	sagte	las	hatte	war	konnte
wir	sagten	lasen	hatten	waren	konnten
ihr	sagtet	last	hattet	wart	konntet
sie	sagten	lasen	hatten	waren	konnten
Sie	sagten	lasen	hatten	waren	konnten

The interrogative pronouns **wer** and **was** use a third-person singular (**er**, **sie**, **es**) form of the verb.

The pronoun **es** is used in many *impersonal expressions*, which require a subject to make the sentence complete but which do not specify who or what is carrying out the action of the verb. The action is performed by an *impersonal it*. This kind of expression also occurs in English.

Es regnet.
It's raining. (What's raining? It!)

Es ist kalt.
It's cold.

Es wird schon dunkel.
It's already getting dark.

Titles, locations, and interrogatives

Titles

The three major titles for addressing a person are:

Herr	*Mr.*
Frau	*Mrs., Miss, Ms.*
Fräulein	*Miss*

The title **Fräulein** is generally not used anymore; it is considered somewhat sexist since it literally means *little woman*. Germans now use only **Frau** to refer to either a married or single woman.

The word **Herr** literally means *gentleman* and politely refers to an unfamiliar male. The word **Mann** means *man* or *husband* and is the more casual term used to refer to a man. Say **mein Herr** when you wish to convey the English meaning of *Sir*.

Mein Herr, ist das Ihr Buch?	*Sir, is that your book?*
Ist der Mann Sportler?	*Is the man an athlete?*
Mein Mann ist Richter.	*My husband is a judge.*

The word **Dame** means *lady* and politely refers to an unfamiliar female. The word **Frau** means *woman* or *wife* and is the more casual term used to refer to a woman.

Diese Dame ist Ärztin.	*This lady is a doctor.*
Diese Frau ist meine Schwester.	*This woman is my sister.*
Meine Frau heißt Angela.	*My wife's name is Angela.*

When addressing both men and women politely, you say **meine Damen und Herren** or **meine Herrschaften** (*ladies and gentlemen*).

If someone has a professional title, **Herr** and **Frau** precede those titles to be polite.

Herr Doktor/Frau Doktor	*doctor*
Herr Professor/Frau Professor	*professor*
Herr Minister/Frau Minister	*minister*
Herr Direktor/Frau Direktor	*principal, director*

When providing someone with your name, you usually say your last name first followed by your first name. An exchange with someone regarding your name would look like the following:

Guten Tag. Ich heiße Braun, Felix Braun.	*Hello. My name is Braun, Felix Braun.*
Guten Tag, **Herr** Braun.	*Hello, **Mr.** Braun.*

Using the name provided in parentheses, write a short dialogue like the one provided in the example that follows.

FOR EXAMPLE: (Tina Benz)

Guten Tag. Ich heiße Benz, Tina Benz.

Guten Tag, Frau Benz.

1. (Martin Schäfer)

_____

_____

2. (Boris Bauer)

_____

_____

3. (Angelika Schneider)

_____

_____

4. (Maria Schulze)

_____

_____

5. (Erik Neumann)

_____

_____

6. (Sonja Kraus)

_____

_____

7. (Heinrich Gasse)

_____

_____

8. (Marianne Becker)

_____

_____

9. (Thomas Schnell)

_____

_____

10. (Gabriele Kiefer)

_____

_____

Locations

Many geographical locations of the world have German names that are identical to their English names. And some are similar but still quite recognizable, and others are completely different in form. Let's look at some of these locations:

Kontinente (*Continents*)

Europa	*Europe*
Asien	*Asia*
Afrika	*Africa*
Nordamerika	*North America*
Südamerika	*South America*
Antarktis	*Antarctica*

Länder (*Countries*)

Deutschland	*Germany*
die USA	*the U.S.A.*
die Vereinigten Staaten von Amerika	*the United States of America*
England	*England*
Frankreich	*France*
Großbritannien	*Great Britain*
Italien	*Italy*
Norwegen	*Norway*
Polen	*Poland*
Russland	*Russia*
Spanien	*Spain*

Städte (*Cities*)

Berlin	*Berlin*
Hamburg	*Hamburg*
London	*London*
Madrid	*Madrid*
Moskau	*Moscow*
München	*Munich*
Paris	*Paris*
Rom	*Rome*
Warschau	*Warsaw*
Washington	*Washington*

When you wish to say that someone or something is in a certain location, use the German preposition **in** (*in*).

Paris ist **in Frankreich**.	*Paris is **in France**.*
Mein Vater wohnt **in Berlin**.	*My father lives **in Berlin**.*

Using the names and locations given, write brief sentences that tell where someone is and then where that person lives.

FOR EXAMPLE: Herr Braun/Deutschland

Herr Braun ist in Deutschland.

Herr Braun wohnt in Deutschland.

1. Frau Bauer/Italien

_____

_____

2. die Kinder/Russland

_____

_____

3. der Diplomat/Nordamerika

_____

_____

4. ein Richter/Rom

_____

_____

5. Frau Professor Schneider/München

_____

_____

6. der Direktor/Europa

_____

_____

7. meine Frau/Frankreich

_____

_____

8. mein Mann/Afrika

_____

_____

9. Ihr Bruder/Warschau

_____

_____

10. Ihre Töchter/Spanien

_____

_____

When the location is at a person's home, the phrase **zu Hause** (*at home*) should be used.

Die Dame ist **zu Hause**.	*The lady is **at home**.*
Der Herr ist **zu Hause**.	*The gentleman is **at home**.*

*Complete each sentence with the appropriate form of **sein** and the expression **zu Hause**.*

FOR EXAMPLE: Er _____ .

Er _____ *ist zu Hause* _____ .

1. Meine Tochter _____ .

2. Ich _____ .

3. Diese Frauen _____ .

4. Ihre Brüder _____ .

5. Du _____ .

6. Sie (*sing.*) _____ .

7. Wir _____ .

8. Mein Mann _____ .

9. Ihr _____ .

10. Sie (*pl.*) _____ .

The interrogative word **wo** (*where*) inquires into the location of someone or something. If the answer to such a question uses the German preposition **in** but the location is not a broad geographical name (i.e., continent, country, city), the definite article must accompany the preposition. With masculine and neuter nouns, the form used is **im** (*in the*, the contraction of **in dem**), and with feminine nouns, the form used is **in der** (*in the*).

Wo sind die Kinder?	*Where are the children?*
Sie sind im Park.	*They are in the park.*
Wo ist der Richter?	*Where is the judge?*
Er ist in der Bibliothek.	*He is in the library.*

Using the words given, write a question using the first word in parentheses that asks where someone or something is. Use the second word in parentheses to answer the question with the German preposition **in**.

FOR EXAMPLE: Frau Becker/die Schule

_____ *Wo ist Frau Becker?* _____

_____ *Frau Becker ist in der Schule.* _____

1. Ihre Mutter/der Keller (*basement, cellar*)

_____

_____

2. mein Bruder/die Garage (*garage*)

_____

_____

3. Martin und Angela/die Stadt (*city*)

_____

_____

4. ihr/die Kirche (*church*)

_____

_____

5. Thomas/das Café (*café*)

_____

_____

6. wir/das Wohnzimmer (*living room*)

_____

_____

7. ich/das Esszimmer (*dining room*)

_____

_____

8. Herr Doktor Bauer/das Hotel (*hotel*)

_____

_____

9. mein Onkel/der Garten

_____

_____

The interrogative word **wie** (*how*) can be used to ask what someone's name is. The word itself means *how*, and the German expression actually means *How is this person called?* For example:

Wie heißt der Mann?	*What is the man's name?*
Der Mann heißt Herr Braun.	*The man's name is Mr. Braun.*

ÜBUNG
4·5

*Using the name given in parentheses, ask what the person's name is (use **Mann** or **Frau** in each question), and then answer with the name provided.*

FOR EXAMPLE: (Maria)

Wie heißt die Frau?

Die Frau heißt Maria.

1. (Herr Schulze)

_____

_____

2. (Frau Schneider)

_____

_____

3. (Thomas)

_____

_____

4. (Anna Schäfer)

_____

_____

5. (Martin Neufeld)

_____

_____

6. (Erik Schmidt)

_____

_____

7. (Professor Benz)

_____

_____

8. (Doktor Tina Kiefer)

_____

_____

9. (Wilhelm Kassel)

_____

_____

10. (Angela)

_____

_____

The interrogatives **was** (_what_) and **wer** (_who_) ask what object something is or who someone is. For example:

Was ist das?	**What** _is that?_
Das ist ein Kino.	_That is a movie theater._
Was ist das?	**What** _is that?_
Das ist eine Bäckerei.	_That is a bakery._
Was ist das?	**What** _is that?_
Das ist ein Glas Bier.	_That is a glass of beer._
Wer ist das?	**Who** _is that?_
Das ist der Polizist.	_That is the police officer._
Wer ist das?	**Who** _is that?_
Das ist die Tänzerin.	_That is the dancer._
Wer ist das?	**Who** _is that?_
Das ist der Verkäufer.	_That is the salesman._

If the answer to these questions is a plural noun, the verb becomes the plural form **sind**.

Das sind meine Bücher.	_These are my books._
Das sind meine Kinder.	_These are my children._

*If the given word is an object, ask what the object is with **was**. Then answer the question. If the given word is a person, ask who the person is with **wer**. Then answer the question.*

FOR EXAMPLE: ein Haus

Was ist das?

Das ist ein Haus.

1. eine Kirche

_____

_____

2. ein Mantel

_____

_____

3. der Polizist

_____

_____

4. die Richterin

_____

_____

5. eine Bibliothek

_____

_____

6. Frau Schneider

_____

_____

7. die Zeitungen

_____

_____

8. Herr Bauer

_____

_____

9. Karl und Martin

_____

_____

10. die Garage

_____

_____

The interrogative word **wann** asks when something occurs.

Wann ist die Party?	**When** *is the party?*
Die Party ist heute.	*The party is today.*
Wann ist das Konzert?	**When** *is the concert?*
Das Konzert ist morgen.	*The concert is tomorrow.*
Wann ist das Examen?	**When** *is the exam?*
Das Examen ist am Freitag.	*The exam is on Friday.*
Wann ist Weihnachten?	**When** *is Christmas?*
Weihnachten ist im Dezember.	*Christmas is in December.*

The days of the week are:

Montag	*Monday*
Dienstag	*Tuesday*
Mittwoch	*Wednesday*
Donnerstag	*Thursday*
Freitag	*Friday*
Samstag *or* Sonnabend	*Saturday*
Sonntag	*Sunday*

Use the prepositional contraction **am (an dem)** to say *on* a certain day: **am Montag**.

The months of the year are:

Januar	*January*
Februar	*February*
März	*March*
April	*April*
Mai	*May*
Juni	*June*
Juli	*July*
August	*August*
September	*September*
Oktober	*October*
November	*November*
Dezember	*December*

Use the prepositional contraction **im (in dem)** to say *in* a certain month: **im Oktober**.

Answer each question with the cue words given.

FOR EXAMPLE: Freitag, September

Wann ist die Party?

Die Party ist am Freitag.

Die Party ist im September.

1. Montag, Januar

Wann ist das Konzert?

_____

_____

2. Dienstag, März

Wann ist das Examen?

_____

_____

3. Mittwoch, Mai

Wann ist die Reise (*trip*)?

_____

_____

4. Donnerstag, Juli

Wann ist die Oper (*opera*)?

_____

_____

5. Freitag, September

Wann ist Ihr Geburtstag (*birthday*)?

_____

_____

The verbs *haben* and *werden* and negation

The conjugations of the verbs **sein** (*to be*), **haben** (*to have*), and **werden** (*to become, get*) are important building blocks for understanding the tenses of the German language. Let's look at the present tense conjugation of these three verbs:

	sein	haben	werden
ich	bin	habe	werde
du	bist	hast	wirst
er	ist	hat	wird
sie (*sing.*)	ist	hat	wird
es	ist	hat	wird
wir	sind	haben	werden
ihr	seid	habt	werdet
Sie	sind	haben	werden
sie (*pl.*)	sind	haben	werden

Besides telling what someone or something *is*, **sein** is used to describe conditions or qualities. For example:

Das Buch **ist** lang.	*The book **is** long.*
Der Roman **ist** kurz.	*The novel **is** short.*
Der Artikel **ist** langweilig.	*The article **is** boring.*
Das Gedicht **ist** interessant.	*The poem **is** interesting.*
Das Wetter **ist** schlecht.	*The weather **is** bad.*
Die Geschichten **sind** gut.	*The stories **are** good.*
Die Prüfungen **sind** schwer.	*The tests **are** hard.*
Die Fragen **sind** leicht.	*The questions **are** easy.*
Es **ist** kalt.	*It **is** cold.*
Es **ist** heiß.	*It **is** hot.*
Es **ist** kühl.	*It **is** cool.*
Es **ist** warm.	*It **is** warm.*
Es **ist** regnerisch.	*It **is** rainy.*

Haben is used to show what someone possesses. For example:

Ich **habe** das Geld.	*I **have** the money.*
Du **hast** keine Zeit.	*You **have** no time.*
Er **hat** meine Schuhe.	*He **has** my shoes.*
Sie **hat** das Kleid.	*She **has** the dress.*
Wir **haben** viele Zeitungen.	*We **have** a lot of newspapers.*
Ihr **habt** wenig Geld.	*You **have** little money.*
Sie **haben** Ihre Fahrkarten.	*You **have** your tickets.*
Sie **haben** keine Prüfung.	*You do not **have** a test.*

It is also used in some special expressions.

Ich **habe** Sonja gern.	*I like Sonja.*
Er **hat** Durst.	*He is thirsty.*
Hast du Hunger?	*Are you hungry?*

Werden describes what a person becomes or how conditions are changing. For example:

Ich **werde** Zahnarzt.	*I **am becoming** a dentist.*
Du **wirst** krank.	*You **get** sick.*
Er **wird** gesund.	*He **gets** healthy.*
Sie **wird** Krankenschwester.	*She **becomes** a nurse.*
Wir **werden** Politiker.	*We **become** politicians.*
Ihr **werdet** böse.	*You **become** angry.*
Sie **werden** Rechtsanwalt.	*You **become** a lawyer.*
Es **wird** kalt.	*It **is getting** cold.*
Es **wird** dunkel.	*It **is getting** dark.*
Es **wird** hell.	*It **is getting** light.*

ÜBUNG
5·1

*In the blanks provided, write the appropriate conjugation of **sein**, **haben**, and **werden** for the subjects given.*

	1. sein	2. haben
ich	_____	_____
du	_____	_____
er	_____	_____
sie (*sing.*)	_____	_____
es	_____	_____
der Zahnarzt	_____	_____
wir	_____	_____
ihr	_____	_____
die Krankenschwester	_____	_____
Sie	_____	_____
sie (*pl.*)	_____	_____

	3. werden
ich	_____
du	_____
er	_____
sie (*sing.*)	_____
es	_____

wir	_____
ihr	_____
Sie	_____
sie (*pl.*)	_____
das Wetter	_____

As with other sentences formed as questions, the verb precedes the subject when posing a question with **sein**, **haben**, or **werden**.

Das Wetter **ist** schlecht.	*The weather **is** bad.*
Ist das Wetter schlecht?	***Is** the weather bad?*
Sie **hat** keine Zeit.	*She **has** no time.*
Hat sie keine Zeit?	*Doesn't she **have** any time?*
Es **wird** regnerisch.	*It **is getting** rainy.*
Wird es regnerisch?	*Will it **get** rainy?*

ÜBUNG
5·2

Rewrite each sentence as a question.

1. Ihr Bruder wird Zahnarzt.

   _____

2. Sie ist Tänzerin.

   _____

3. Ich habe Durst.

   _____

4. Dieser Artikel ist interessant.

   _____

5. Es ist heiß.

   _____

6. Frau Bauer wird Krankenschwester.

   _____

7. Die Kinder haben Hunger.

   _____

8. Es wird dunkel.

   _____

9. Sie haben keine Fahrkarten.

   _____

10. Erik hat Maria gern.

_____

11. Mein Onkel wird Rechtsanwalt.

_____

12. Sonja ist krank.

_____

13. Dieser Roman ist langweilig.

_____

14. Es wird am Montag kalt.

_____

15. Es ist kalt im Dezember.

_____

16. Das Gedicht ist kurz.

_____

17. Die Mädchen haben Karl gern.

_____

18. Wir sind zu Hause.

_____

19. Der Herr heißt Martin Schäfer.

_____

20. Frau Keller wird gesund.

_____

ÜBUNG
5·3

*Fill in the blank with the appropriate form of **sein, haben,** or **werden.***

1. Ich _____ Zeit.

2. _____ die Kinder zu Hause?

3. Es _____ heiß.

4. Thomas _____ Maria gern.

5. _____ du meine Fahrkarte?

6. Mein Geburtstag _____ im Juli.

7. Du _____ krank.

8. Meine Mutter _____ durst.

9. Es _____ regnerisch.

10. Meine Töchter _____ kein Geld.

11. _____ Sie die Zeitung?

12. Ihr _____ jung.

13. Diese Frau _____ Ärztin.

14. _____ diese Dame Ihre Tante?

15. _____ du die Bücher?

You have already discovered that the word **kein** (*no, not any*) is used to add a negative to a sentence. But be aware that **kein** is the negation of **ein**, as well as of any noun that is not preceded by a definite article.

Ich habe ein Buch	*I have a book.*
Ich habe **kein** Buch.	*I do **not** have a book.*
Er ist Zahnarzt.	*He is a dentist.*
Er ist **kein** Zahnarzt.	*He is **not** a dentist.*
Du hast Geld.	*You have money.*
Du hast **kein** Geld.	*You have **no** money.*
Das ist eine Landkarte.	*That is a map.*
Das ist **keine** Landkarte.	*That is **not** a map.*

You have probably noticed that when expressing one's profession or nationality, an article is not used. For example:

Ich bin Arzt.	*I am a physician.*
Er ist Deutscher.	*He is a German.*

Kein is used to negate such expressions.

Ich bin kein Arzt.	*I am not a physician.*
Er ist kein Deutscher.	*He is not a German.*

ÜBUNG

5·4

*Rewrite each sentence by adding the correct form of the negative **kein**.*

1. Er hat Schuhe.

_____

2. Du hast eine Zeitung.

_____

3. Frau Bauer ist Krankenschwester.

_____

4. Herr Schneider ist Politiker.

_____

5. Ich habe Zeit.

_____

6. Das ist ein Kleid.

_____

7. Er ist Polizist.

_____

8. Ein Tourist ist in Berlin.

_____

9. Wir haben am Mittwoch eine Prüfung.

_____

10. Hast du Geld?

_____

11. Das ist eine Bibliothek.

_____

12. Maria ist Tänzerin.

_____

13. Die Männer werden Politiker.

_____

14. Er hat ein Glas Bier.

_____

15. Das ist eine Kirche.

_____

When you answer a question with **nein** (*no*), it indicates that your response is negative. Besides using **kein** as a negative, adding the adverb **nicht** (*not*) is also a form of negation. **Nicht** is placed after a verb such as **sein**, before an adverb or adjective, or before a prepositional phrase.

Ist das Ihr Bruder?	*Is that your brother?*
Nein, das ist **nicht** mein Bruder.	*No, that is **not** my brother.*
Wird es kalt?	*Is it getting cold?*
Nein, es wird **nicht** kalt.	*No, it is **not** getting cold.*

Heißt sie Sonja Keller?	Is her name Sonja Keller?
Nein, sie heißt **nicht** Sonja Keller.	No, her name is **not** Sonja Keller.
Ist Martin zu Hause?	Is Martin at home?
Nein, Martin ist **nicht** zu Hause.	No, Martin is **not** at home.

Following the verb **haben**, place **nicht** after the object of the verb.

Wir haben die Fahrkarten **nicht**.	We do **not** have the tickets.
Haben Sie Ihr Buch **nicht**?	Don't you have your book?
Ich habe das Kleid **nicht**.	I do **not** have the dress.

ÜBUNG
5·5

Rewrite each sentence by using the negative **nicht**.

1. Die Touristen sind in Deutschland.

   _____

2. Mein Geburtstag ist im Oktober.

   _____

3. Das ist Herr Dorfmann.

   _____

4. Meine Schwester wohnt in der Stadt.

   _____

5. Wir haben am Freitag das Examen.

   _____

6. Ist Frau Benz zu Hause?

   _____

7. Es wird warm.

   _____

8. Das sind meine Bücher.

   _____

9. Sonja hat die Bluse.

   _____

10. Das ist der Lehrer.

    _____

11. Sie haben die Fahrkarten.

    _____

12. Ist das Herr Bauer?

    _____

13. Hast du die Zeitungen?

_____

14. Die Dame heißt Frau Becker.

_____

15. Sind das meine Schuhe?

_____

ÜBUNG

5·6

Fill in the blank with the missing negative word: **kein/keine** *or* **nicht**.

FOR EXAMPLE: Das ist _____ Herr Keller.

Das ist _____ *nicht* _____ Herr Keller.

1. Er heißt _____ Erik.

2. Wir wohnen _____ in Italien.

3. Ich habe _____ Geld.

4. Wir sind _____ Politiker.

5. Es wird am Sonntag _____ kalt.

6. Das ist _____ Gedicht.

7. Das ist _____ mein Gedicht.

8. Haben Sie Ihre Schuhe _____?

9. Mein Mann heißt _____ Heinrich.

10. Sind das _____ Ihre Bücher?

11. Das Examen ist _____ im Juni.

12. Ist Ihr Geburtstag _____ am Donnerstag?

13. Erik hat _____ Zeit.

14. Wird es _____ dunkel?

15. Meine Großmutter ist _____ krank.

16. Ich bin _____ zu Hause.

17. Er ist _____ der Verkäufer.

18. Ist die Landkarte _____ da?

19. Meine Tante wohnt _____ in München.

20. Habt ihr _____ Geld?

ÜBUNG

5·7

*Answer each question twice, once with **ja** and once with **nein**. Use **kein** and **nicht** appropriately.*

FOR EXAMPLE: Ist Herr Braun Ihr Vater?

Ja, Herr Braun ist mein Vater.

Nein, Herr Braun ist nicht mein Vater.

1. Hat sie Ihre Bücher?

_____

_____

2. Ist er Zahnarzt?

_____

_____

3. Wird es regnerisch?

_____

_____

4. Werden die Jungen Sportler?

_____

_____

5. Sind Sie Deutscher?

_____

_____

6. Seid ihr zu Hause?

_____

_____

7. Ist die Tänzerin in Paris?

_____

_____

8. Bin ich krank?

_____

_____

9. Hast du das Kleid?

_____

_____

The verbs *haben* and *werden* and negation   55

10. Wird es kühl?

_____

11. Habt ihr Zeit?

_____

_____

12. Wird Erik Student?

_____

_____

13. Ist der Onkel alt?

_____

_____

14. Sind wir in München?

_____

_____

15. Haben Sie Martin gern?

_____

_____

Negation

The German negative words are **nicht** and **kein**. They negate different elements of a sentence much like English.

English has two basic ways of using negation in a sentence. If the negative is adverbial, the adverb _not_ is used. The second kind of English negation is followed by _not a(n)_ or _no_. This form of negation is used to negate a noun (_This is **not a** problem_.). The determiner _no_ does not require the negative adverb _not_ (_I have **no** money_.).

Nicht

German is quite similar in its approach to negation. The adverb **nicht** is used to negate verbs. Let's look at a few examples.

Ich weiß **nicht**, wo Thomas ist.	_I do not know where Thomas is._
Ihr Mann schläft **nicht**.	_Her husband isn't sleeping._

In general, the adverb **nicht** is placed after the conjugated verb. But in a question or when something other than the subject begins the sentence, the verb precedes the subject, and the adverb **nicht** follows the subject. For example:

Kommst du **nicht** mit?	*Aren't you coming along?*
Heute arbeiten wir **nicht**.	*We're not working today.*
Nach dem Abendessen lese ich **nicht**.	*After supper I don't read.*

When sentences become more complicated, the position of **nicht** is not so simple. Let's look at some of the other positions that **nicht** can have in a sentence.

Nicht follows most adverbs.

Ich will heute **nicht** üben.	*I don't want to play today.*
Die Touristen sind noch **nicht** abgefahren.	*The tourists haven't departed yet.*

Nicht tends to follow direct objects.

Ich will diese Berge **nicht** fotografieren.	*I don't want to photograph these mountains.*
Erik hat seine Freundin **nicht** besucht.	*Erik didn't visit his girlfriend.*

Nicht precedes adverbs that identify manner (how).

Sie spielt die Geige **nicht** gut.	*She doesn't play the violin well.*
Warum kam er **nicht** schnell nach Hause?	*Why didn't he come home quickly?*

Nicht precedes most prepositional phrases.

Sie haben **nicht** auf uns gewartet.	*They didn't wait for us.*
Frauen arbeiten **nicht** in dieser Fabrik.	*Women do not work in this factory.*

If more than one of these elements is in a sentence [(1) adverb, (2) direct object, (3) adverb of manner, or (4) prepositional phrase], the rules suggested are still followed. For example:

Wir wollten (1) gestern **nicht** (3) ins Kino gehen.	*We didn't want to go to the movies yesterday.*
Der Vater hat (2) seine Kinder **nicht** (3) gut behandelt.	*The father didn't treat his children well.*
Ich bin (1) gestern **nicht** (4) in die Schweiz geflogen.	*I didn't fly to Switzerland yesterday.*

Just like English, German can put the negative **nicht** in other positions in order to emphasize a specific element in the sentence. When this occurs, a phrase introduced by **sondern** (*but rather*) usually follows.

Normal position of nicht

Sabine zeigt mir den neuen Wagen **nicht**.	*Sabine doesn't show me the new car.*
Ich komme morgen **nicht**.	*I'm not coming tomorrow.*

Nicht with a specific element

Sabine zeigt mir **nicht** den neuen Wagen, sondern den alten.	*Sabine doesn't show me the new car but rather the old one.*
Ich komme **nicht** morgen, sondern am Freitag.	*I'm not coming tomorrow but rather on Friday.*

*Reword each sentence by placing **nicht** in the appropriate position.*

EXAMPLE   Sie hat das Buch.

Sie hat das Buch nicht.

1. Sie können heute lange bleiben.

_____

2. Wohnen Sie in Darmstadt?

_____

3. Letzte Woche war sie noch krank.

_____

4. Mein Onkel singt schlecht.

_____

5. Unsere Gäste wollen heute Abend tanzen gehen.

_____

6. Warum beklagst (*complain*) du dich?

_____

7. Der Stuhl steht zwischen dem Schrank und dem Tisch.

_____

8. Soll die Lampe über dem Tisch hängen?

_____

9. Das alte Flugzeug fliegt schnell über die Wolken.

_____

10. Ich trage heute meinen Regenmantel (*raincoat*).

_____

11. Der Vogel sitzt auf dem hohen Dach (*high roof*).

_____

12. Gudrun hat ihren kleinen Bruder geschlagen.

_____

13. Er musste mich anrufen.

_____

14. Mozart war sehr musikalisch (*musical*).

_____

15. Warum hast du diesen Brief zerrissen (*torn up*)?

_____

16. Schreiben Sie den Brief an Ihre Tante?

_____

17. Diese Studenten haben fleißig gearbeitet.

_____

18. Sie ist gestern in der Nähe (*in the vicinity*) von Hannover gewesen.

_____

19. Hört der Regen (*rain*) auf?

_____

20. Die Jungen sind über die Brücke (*bridge*) gelaufen.

_____

21. Viele Studenten haben das Examen bestanden.

_____

22. Im Park sitzen die jungen Leute auf den Bänken (*benches*).

_____

23. In der Ferne (*distance*) erblickte der Wanderer die Räuber (*robbers*).

_____

24. Wir nehmen an dem Besuch der Oper teil (*participate in*).

_____

25. Mein Großvater kann sich an seine Jugend erinnern (*remember his youth*).

_____

ÜBUNG

5·9

*Reword each sentence by placing **nicht** in the position that emphasizes a specific element. Add an appropriate phrase introduced by **sondern**.*

EXAMPLE   Sie gibt mir das Buch nicht.

Sie gibt mir nicht das Buch, sondern die Zeitung.

1. Wir sind am Montag nicht abgefahren.

_____

2. Er will das kleine Haus nicht kaufen.

_____

3. Sie fahren heute nicht ins Restaurant.

_____

4. Er nennt den jungen Mann nicht einen Dieb (*calls the man a thief*).

_____

5. Die Studentin begegnete (*met*) dem Professor nicht.

_____

6. Das alte Lehrbuch (*textbook*) nützt (*be useful*) dem Studenten nicht.

_____

7. Ich hänge das Bild nicht über das Klavier.

_____

8. Der Junge will die neuen Wörter nicht vergessen.

_____

9. Die Kinder bitten die Mutter nicht um Süßigkeiten.

_____

10. Ich weiß die Hausnummer (*address*) nicht.

_____

Kein

The **ein**-word **kein** is a negative and modifies nouns. Unlike **nicht**, it is not used adverbially. It is, instead, the negative form of **ein** and means *not a*, *not any*, or *no*. Let's look at some examples in which **ein** is replaced by **kein**. Take note of the difference in the meaning of each pair of sentences.

Das ist **ein** Nilpferd.	*That is a hippopotamus.*
Das ist **kein** Nilpferd.	*That is not a hippopotamus.*
Haben Sie **einen** Pass?	*Do you have a passport?*
Haben Sie **keinen** Pass?	*Don't you have a passport?*
Ich brauche **ein** Hemd.	*I need a shirt.*
Ich brauche **kein** Hemd.	*I need no shirt./I don't need a shirt.*

Just like **ein**, **kein** can be used with all three genders and in all the cases. But remember that **kein** can also be used in the plural.

Singular

Wir warten auf einen Freund.	*We're waiting for a friend.*
Wir warten auf **keinen** Freund.	*We're not waiting for a friend.*

Ich habe einen Vogel gesehen.	*I saw a bird.*
Ich habe **keinen** Vogel gesehen.	*I didn't see a bird.*

Er hilft einem Ausländer damit.	*He helps a foreigner with it.*
Er hilft **keinem** Ausländer damit.	*He doesn't help any foreigner with it.*

Plural

Wir warten auf Freunde.	*We're waiting for friends.*
Wir warten auf **keine** Freunde.	*We're not waiting for any friends.*

Ich habe Vögel gesehen.	*I saw birds.*
Ich habe **keine** Vögel gesehen.	*I didn't see any birds.*

Er hilft Ausländern damit.	*He helps foreigners with it.*
Er hilft **keinen** Ausländern damit.	*He doesn't help any foreigners with it.*

ÜBUNG
5·10

*Reword each sentence by negating **ein** with **kein**.*

1. In diesem Haus wohnt ein Schauspieler (*actor*).

   _____

2. Hast du eine Prüfung bestanden?

   _____

3. Das Mädchen hat eine schöne Bluse verloren.

   _____

4. Gute Menschen helfen den Armen.

   _____

5. Der Uhrmacher zieht eine Uhr auf (*winds*).

   _____

6. Im Schatten verbergen sich Diebe (*hide in the shadows*).

   _____

7. Im März können Obstbäume (*fruit trees*) blühen (*bloom*).

   _____

8. Wachsen auf dieser tropischen Insel (*tropical island*) Tannen (*fir trees*)?

   _____

9. Dieser Fahrer hat ein Autorennen (*auto race*) gewonnen.

   _____

10. Die Schülerin lernt neue Wörter und ein Gedicht (*poem*).

   _____

11. An der Straßenecke stand ein Bettler (*beggar*).

_____

12. Auf dem Sportplatz (*athletic field*) rennen Kinder hin und her (*run around*).

_____

13. Warum reißt (*rip*) du ein Blatt (*page*) aus dem Buch?

_____

14. Unser Hund hat einen Fremden gebissen (*bit a stranger*).

_____

15. Unter dem Esstisch schlafen Katzen.

_____

16. Diese Sängerin (*singer*) hat wie eine Nachtigall (*nightingale*) gesungen.

_____

17. Der Erfinder (*inventor*) hat einen neuen Motor erfunden (*invented*).

_____

18. Ich schreibe Ansichtskarten und einen langen Brief.

_____

19. Er pfeift ein Lied (*whistles a song*).

_____

20. Sie können Kinder zu lernen zwingen.

_____

21. Das Mädchen hat einen Ball ins Wasser geworfen.

_____

22. Unfälle (*accidents*) geschehen täglich (*daily*).

_____

23. Hast du dem Kellner (*waiter*) ein Trinkgeld (*tip*) gegeben?

_____

24. Der Verkäufer (*salesman*) legte Waren (*goods*) auf den Tisch.

_____

25. In dieser Straße sind große Geschäfte (*stores*).

_____

Gar

The particle word **gar** emphasizes the negation of a word. It can be used with either **nicht** or **kein** and in both cases means *at all*. It is often added to an emphatic, negative response to a positive statement. For example:

Positive	Der Mann ist sehr krank.	*The man is very sick.*
Negative	Der Mann ist **gar** nicht krank.	*That man is not sick at all.*
Positive	Sie hat viel Geld.	*She has a lot of money.*
Negative	Sie hat **gar** kein Geld.	*She has no money at all.*

Let's look at more examples of the use of this participle word:

Er wird vorwärts kommen.	*He will get ahead.*
Er wird **gar** nicht vorwärts kommen.	*He will not get ahead at all.*
Es ist zu spät.	*It is too late.*
Es ist **gar** nicht zu spät.	*It is not too late at all.*
Sonja besitzt viele alte Bücher.	*Sonja owns many old books.*
Sonja besitzt **gar** keine alten Bücher.	*Sonja doesn't own any old books at all.*
Das Kind lernt neue Wörter.	*The child learns new words.*
Das Kind lernt **gar** keine neuen Wörter.	*The child doesn't learn any new words at all.*

The rules that govern the use of **nicht** and **kein** are not altered by the addition of the particle word **gar**.

Nie and nichts

The adverb **nie** (*never*) is sometimes stated as **niemals**. When added to a sentence, like other adverbs, it cannot be declined. Instead, it tells that the action of the verb in the sentence is *never carried out*. For example:

Er kommt **nie** pünktlich nach Hause.	*He never comes home on time.*
Ich bin **niemals** in Madrid gewesen.	*I have never been in Madrid.*
Warum sprichst du **nie** von deiner Frau?	*Why don't you ever speak of your wife?*
Ich will sie **niemals** besuchen.	*I never want to visit them.*

The negative indefinite pronoun **nichts** means *nothing*. It can be used like other pronouns; however, it never declines. It has only the one form. For example:

Nichts ist wichtiger als meine Familie.	*Nothing is more important than my family.*
Ich habe **nichts** zu sagen.	*I have nothing to say.*
Von mir bekam er **nichts** mehr.	*He got nothing more from me.*
Von **nichts** kommt **nichts**.	*You get nothing when you do nothing (don't show some effort).*

Choose the letter of the word or phrase that best completes each sentence.

1. In der Ferne sehe ich _____ .
   a. gar nicht   b. nichts   c. kein Mann   d. gar nicht

2. Wir haben die USA _____ besucht.
   a. niemals   b. gar   c. gar kein   d. keine

3. Mein Sohn braucht _____ .
   a. kein Wagen   b. nicht hier   c. keine neuen Schuhe   d. gar nicht

4. Wir sind _____ nicht in der Hauptstadt
   a. kein   b. gar kein   c. heute   d. gar nichts

5. Der König herrscht (*king rules*) _____ über das Land.
   a. gar kein   b. gar   c. nicht mehr   d. nichts

6. Ich muss heute Abend _____ schreiben.
   a. nicht Brief   b. ein Brief   c. diesen Briefen   d. keinen Brief

7. Ich will nicht dieses Buch lesen, _____ .
   a. und das andere   b. sondern das andere   c. sondern nicht ihn   d. aber das andere

8. Dieser alte Mann ist _____ .
   a. kranker   b. gar nicht gesund   c. nichts   d. gar kein

9. Ich kann das Examen _____ bestehen.
   a. noch nicht   b. gar keine   c. kein   d. kein mehr

10. Wir wollen unseren Urlaub _____ verbringen (*spend vacation*).
    a. gar nichts   b. keine Zeit   c. nicht in der Stadt   d. gar keine Reisen

The present tense and numbers

6

The present tense

You have already encountered the present tense of **haben**, **sein**, and **werden**. Other verbs in the present tense follow a similar pattern; that is, they conform to the same endings used following the personal pronouns. Compare **haben** with two other verbs in their present tense conjugation.

	haben	**lachen** (*laugh*)	**glauben** (*believe*)
ich	habe	lache	glaube
du	hast	lachst	glaubst
er/sie/es	hat	lacht	glaubt
wir	haben	lachen	glauben
ihr	habt	lacht	glaubt
Sie	haben	lachen	glauben
sie (*pl.*)	haben	lachen	glauben

The infinitive form of a verb is its basic form and usually ends in **-en**. English infinitives often appear with the particle *to*. Compare the German and English that follow:

    weinen *(to) cry*   **blühen** *(to) bloom*   **lachen** *(to) laugh*

The conjugational endings of the present tense are added to the verb after the infinitive ending has been dropped. Those endings are used with specific personal pronouns and are **-e**, **-st**, **-t**, and **-en**.

Many verbs follow this ending pattern in the present tense. Some are:

brauchen	*need*
decken	*cover/set (the table)*
denken	*think*
dienen	*serve*
fragen	*ask*
gehen	*go*
hoffen	*hope*
hören	*hear*
kaufen	*buy*
kommen	*come*
lächeln	*smile*
leben	*live*
lieben	*love*
machen	*make/do*
probieren	*try*
rauchen	*smoke*

sagen	*say*	
schicken	*send*	
schwimmen	*swim*	
setzen	*place/set*	
singen	*sing*	
sitzen	*sit*	
spielen	*play*	
stehen	*stand*	
stellen	*place/put*	
suchen	*look for/search*	
wohnen	*live/reside*	
zeigen	*show*	

Any of these verbs will add the conjugational endings in the present tense in the same way as illustrated previously. For example:

	brauchen	**stellen**	**wohnen**
ich	brauche	stelle	wohne
du	brauchst	stellst	wohnst
er/sie/es	braucht	stellt	wohnt
wir	brauchen	stellen	wohnen
ihr	braucht	stellt	wohnt
Sie	brauchen	stellen	wohnen
sie (*pl.*)	brauchen	stellen	wohnen

ÜBUNG
6·1

In the blanks provided, write the correct conjugations for the pronouns given.

1. | | machen | gehen | fragen |
|---|---|---|---|
| ich | _____ | _____ | _____ |
| du | _____ | _____ | _____ |
| er | _____ | _____ | _____ |

2. | | sagen | hören | zeigen |
|---|---|---|---|
| wir | _____ | _____ | _____ |
| ihr | _____ | _____ | _____ |
| Sie | _____ | _____ | _____ |

3. | | lachen | setzen | schwimmen |
|---|---|---|---|
| ich | _____ | _____ | _____ |
| sie (*sing.*) | _____ | _____ | _____ |
| sie (*pl.*) | _____ | _____ | _____ |

4. | | decken | probieren | schicken |
|---|---|---|---|
| du | _____ | _____ | _____ |

Sie	_____	_____	_____
ihr	_____	_____	_____

5.	denken	hoffen	lieben
ich	_____	_____	_____
du	_____	_____	_____
er	_____	_____	_____
wir	_____	_____	_____
ihr	_____	_____	_____
Sie	_____	_____	_____
sie (*pl.*)	_____	_____	_____

If the infinitive ending of a verb is preceded by the letter -**d** or -**t**, the second-person singular, and the second- and plural and the third-person singular endings become -**est** and -**et** respectively. For example:

	arbeiten (*work*)	**finden** (*find*)
ich	arbeite	finde
du	arbeitest	findest
er/sie/es	arbeitet	findet
wir	arbeiten	finden
ihr	arbeitet	findet
Sie	arbeiten	finden
sie (*pl.*)	arbeiten	finden

ÜBUNG
6·2

In the blanks provided, write the correct conjugation for each of the following verbs with the pronouns given.

	1. wetten (*bet*)	2. senden (*send*)
ich	_____	_____
du	_____	_____
er	_____	_____
wir	_____	_____
ihr	_____	_____
Sie	_____	_____
sie (*pl.*)	_____	_____

	3. meiden (*avoid*)	4. antworten (*answer*)
ich	_____	_____
du	_____	_____
er	_____	_____
wir	_____	_____
ihr	_____	_____
Sie	_____	_____
sie (*pl.*)	_____	_____

	5. husten (*cough*)
ich	_____
du	_____
er	_____
wir	_____
ihr	_____
Sie	_____
sie (*pl.*)	_____

If the infinitive ending is preceded by -**s**, -**ss**, -**ß**, -**z**, or -**tz**, the second-person singular ending becomes -**t**. For example:

	reißen (*tear*)
ich	reiße
du	reißt
er	reißt
wir	reißen
ihr	reißt
Sie	reißen
sie (*pl.*)	reißen

ÜBUNG

6·3

In the blank provided, write the correct conjugation for each of the following verbs with the pronouns given.

	1. setzen (*set*)	2. heißen (*be called*)
ich	_____	_____
du	_____	_____
er	_____	_____

wir   _____   _____

ihr   _____   _____

Sie   _____   _____

sie (*pl.*)   _____   _____

3. tanzen (*dance*)   **4. sitzen (*sit*)**

ich   _____   _____

du   _____   _____

er   _____   _____

wir   _____   _____

ihr   _____   _____

Sie   _____   _____

sie (*pl.*)   _____   _____

5. schmerzen (*hurt, pain*)   **6. reisen (*travel*)**

ich   _____   _____

du   _____   _____

er   _____   _____

wir   _____   _____

ihr   _____   _____

Sie   _____   _____

sie (*pl.*)   _____   _____

7. beißen (*bite*)   **8. niesen (*sneeze*)**

ich   _____   _____

du   _____   _____

er   _____   _____

wir   _____   _____

ihr   _____   _____

Sie   _____   _____

sie (*pl.*)   _____   _____

Some infinitives end in **-eln** and **-ern**. In such cases, only the final **-n** is dropped when the conjugational endings are added. And the **-en** conjugational ending becomes **-n**. For example:

	paddeln (*paddle/row*)
ich	paddele
du	paddelst
er	paddelt
wir	paddeln
ihr	paddelt
Sie	paddeln
sie (*pl.*)	paddeln

When using **wer** (*who*) or **man** (*one/you*) as the subject of a sentence, the third-person ending is required in the conjugation.

wer	hat	lacht	glaubt
man	hat	lacht	glaubt

In the blank provided, write the correct conjugation of the verb in bold with the pronoun given.

1. **sagen** ich _____

2. **machen** ihr _____

3. **schmeicheln** (*flatter*) wir _____

4. **hören** du _____

5. **schmelzen** (*melt*) es _____

6. **gehen** Sie _____

7. **fragen** sie (*sing.*) _____

8. **sein** ihr _____

9. **schließen** (*close*) du _____

10. **wohnen** sie (*pl.*) _____

11. **glauben** ich _____

12. **pflanzen** (*plant*) er _____

13. **bellen** (*bark*) sie (*sing.*) _____

14. **wandern** (*wander, hike*) ich _____

15. **werden** es _____

16. **rauchen** wer _____

17. **warten** (*wait*) sie (*sing.*) _____

18. **feiern** (*celebrate*) man _____

19. **baden** (*bathe*) du _____

20. **lächeln** ihr _____

21. **haben** er _____

22. **wünschen** (*wish*) du _____

23. **finden** wer _____

24. **kosten** es _____

25. **singen** ich _____

Numbers

There are many similarities between English numbers and German numbers. Look at the following list of German numbers, and consider how much they resemble their English counterparts.

0	null
1	eins
2	zwei
3	drei
4	vier
5	fünf
6	sechs
7	sieben
8	acht
9	neun
10	zehn
11	elf
12	zwölf
13	dreizehn
14	vierzehn
15	fünfzehn
16	sechzehn
17	siebzehn
18	achtzehn
19	neunzehn
20	zwanzig

The numbers 21 to 99 follow a pattern that once existed in English, but is now unique to German. Instead of *twenty-one*, German uses *one and twenty*.

21	einundzwanzig
22	zweiundzwanzig
30	dreißig
33	dreiunddreißig
40	vierzig
44	vierundvierzig
50	fünfzig
55	fünfundfünfzig
60	sechzig
66	sechsundsechzig
70	siebzig
77	siebenundsiebzig
80	achtzig

88	achtundachtzig
90	neunzig
99	neunundneunzig
100	hundert
200	zweihundert
500	fünfhundert
1 000	tausend
10 000	zehntausend
200 000	zweihunderttausend
1 000 000	eine Million
1 000 000 000	eine Milliarde
1 000 000 000 000	eine Billion

Notice that **Milliarde** is used where in English *billion* is said, and **Billion** in German means *trillion*.

The basic arithmetic structures in German look like this:

Addition

Zehn plus drei sind dreizehn.	*10 plus 3 is 13.*
or Zehn und drei sind dreizehn.	*10 and 3 is 13.*

Subtraction

Elf minus neun sind zwei.	*11 minus 9 is 2.*
or Elf weniger neun sind zwei.	*11 minus 9 is 2.*

Multiplication

Drei mal drei sind neun.	*3 times 3 is 9.*

Division

Zehn (geteilt) durch zwei sind fünf.	*10 divided by 2 is 5.*

In division, the word **geteilt** can be omitted.

ÜBUNG

6·5

Rewrite the following equations in German.

FOR EXAMPLE: 2 + 3 = 5 _____*zwei plus drei sind fünf*_____

1. 6 + 1 = 7 _____

2. 5 × 3 = 15 _____

3. 9 – 7 = 2 _____

4. 20 + 3 = 23 _____

5. 12 ÷ 3 = 4 _____

6. 100 – 50 = 50 _____

7. 88 + 2 = 90 _____

8. 200 ÷ 40 = 5 _____

9. 19 – 8 = 11 _____

10. 60 + 12 = 72 _____

Ordinals

Numbers have another form called *ordinals*. Ordinals function as adjectives and specify the *order* in which someone or something appears in a list. German ordinals from *first* to *nineteenth* end in **-te**. Ordinals from *twentieth* and higher end in **-ste**. Notice the few irregular forms in the following examples.

1	erste	*first*
2	zweite	*second*
3	dritte	*third*
4	vierte	*fourth*
5	fünfte	*fifth*
6	sechste	*sixth*
7	siebte	*seventh*
20	zwanzigste	*twentieth*
31	einunddreißigste	*thirty-first*
76	sechsundsiebzigste	*seventy-sixth*
100	hundertste	*hundreth*

In sentences the ordinals function like other adjectives:

Heute ist der **vierte** März.	*Today is the **fourth** of March.*
Ich habe sein **erstes** Gedicht gelesen.	*I read his **first** poem.*

ÜBUNG
6·6

Fill in the blank with the ordinal form of the number provided in parentheses. Add the necessary adjective endings. Use the ending **-e** after the definite article **der**. Use the ending **-en** after **am**.

FOR EXAMPLE: (4) Heute ist der _____*vierte*_____ Mai.

(4) Ihr Geburtstag ist am _____*vierten*_____ Juni.

1. (2) Heute ist der _____ Dezember.

2. (11) Mein Geburtstag ist am _____ Juni.

3. (3) Ist morgen der _____ Februar?

4. (1) Meine Frau ist am _____ gestorben.

5. (12) Dezember ist der _____ Monat.

6. (31) Mein Bruder kommt am _____ Oktober zu Besuch.

7. (21) War gestern der _____ April?

8. (10) Montag ist der _____ August.

9. (16) Der alte Mann ist am _____ Januar gestorben.

10. (7) Der Krieg endete am _____ Mai.

Usage of the Present Tense

In German the present tense is used when stating something that is taking place now, takes place often, or will take place in the near future. Therefore, **Wir essen Sauerkraut.** may mean:

> *We are eating sauerkraut now.*
> *We eat sauerkraut often or regularly.*
> *We are/will be eating sauerkraut soon.*
> (Let's hope there is some good pork with all this sauerkraut!)

The present tense is also used with seit and the dative to express actions, conditions, or states that are still continuing but began in the past. In English, the present perfect tense is used in this case:

> Er lernt seit drei Jahren Deutsch.   *He has been learning German
> for three years.*   (He is still learning it now.)

There are no progressive forms in German as there are in English (*am, are,* or *is* followed by the present participle ending in *-ing*) or emphatic forms (*do* or *does*). Thus:

> *he is coming* = **er kommt**
> *he does come* = **er kommt**
> *he comes* = **er kommt**

Personal Pronouns

A pronoun takes the place of a person or thing. *The book* is replaced by *it; the man* is replaced by *he.* The following is a chart of personal pronouns in German:

	Singular	Plural
First Person	ich (*I*)	wir (*we*)
Second Person	du (*you, familiar*)	ihr (*you, familiar*)
	Sie (*you, formal*)	Sie (*you, formal*)
Third Person	er, sie, es (*he, she, it*)	sie (*they*)

Du, ihr, and **Sie** all mean *you.* The familiar form **du** is used in speaking to a child under fifteen or sixteen years old, a relative, a close friend, or an animal. **Ihr** is used in speaking to several children under fifteen or sixteen years old, several relatives, several close friends, or several animals.

Sie (singular and plural) is used in speaking to one or several adults other than those listed above. Care has to be taken to use the formal and the familiar correctly. If you use the familiar du in speaking to an adult who is not a close friend, he or she may take offense.

Hans, was machst du?	*Hans, what are you doing?*
Vater, was machst du?	*Father, what are you doing?*
Hans und Peter, was macht ihr?	*Hans and Peter, what are you doing?*

| Herr Schmidt, was machen Sie? | *Mr. Schmidt, what are you doing?* |
| Herr Schmidt und Herr Braun, was machen Sie? | *Mr. Schmidt and Mr. Braun, what are you doing?* |

Note that the formal **Sie** is always capitalized. You never capitalize **ich** (unlike I in English)—it would portray arrogance.

Man is used very frequently in German speech. It is an indefinite pronoun and can be translated as *one, we, they, you, or people.*

| Man macht das nicht! | *One doesn't do that!* |
| Man kaut nicht mit offenem Mund! | *We don't chew with an open mouth!* |

Verb Position

In a *basic German sentence*, the conjugated verb is the second element. Usually the subject is the first element, followed by the verb.

| Wir **fahren** in die Stadt. | *We **drive** to town.* |
| Der Junge kommt morgen. | *The boy **comes** tomorrow.* |

When another element (not the subject) is in the first position, the subject stands behind the verb and the verb is again the second element.

| In die Stadt **fahren** wir. | *Into town we **drive**.* |
| Morgen **kommt** der Junge. | *Tomorrow the boy **comes**.* |

ÜBUNG
6·7

Change the following sentences so that they begin with the boldfaced word or words.

EXAMPLE: Luise lernt **Deutsch.**

Deutsch lernt Luise.

1. Heidi singt **schön.** _____

2. Müllers haben **viel Geld.** _____

3. Marie ist **nächste Woche** in Frankfurt. _____

4. Wir feiern **Weihnachten** mit den Großeltern. _____

5. Thomas ist **mein bester Freund.** _____

Verb Position with Question Words

When a *question word* such as **wann, wer, wie, wo, woher,** or **wohin** (*when, who, how, where, where from, or where to*) is used at the beginning of a question, the conjugated verb is also second.

| Wer **fährt** in die Stadt? | *Who **is driving** into town?* |
| Wann **kommt** der Junge? | *When **is** the boy **coming**?* |

ÜBUNG
6·8

Form questions using the question word given in parentheses.

EXAMPLE: Wir haben Hunger. (wer)
           Wer hat Hunger?

1. Die Kinder kommen morgen. (wer) _____

2. Sie machen einen Ausflug. (was) _____

3. Sie fahren an den See. (wohin) _____

4. Dort schwimmen sie. (wo) _____

5. Das machen sie oft. (warum) _____

Verb Position in General Questions

In a *general question*, when no question word is used, the order of the subject and the verb is reversed. The conjugated verb becomes the first element.

> **Fahren** wir in die Stadt?   *Are we driving into town?*
> **Kommt** der Junge?   *Is the boy coming?*

In a command the verb also comes first.

> **Geh** in die Schule.   *Go to school.*

This will be discussed further in Unit 8, Imperative Verbs.

ÜBUNG
6·9

Change the following sentences into general questions.

EXAMPLE: Er wohnt in Hamburg.
           Wohnt er in Hamburg?

1. Wir gehen jetzt schwimmen. _____

2. Jakob singt gut. _____

3. Paul singt besser. _____

4. Emma singt am besten. _____

5. Thomas ist oft in Leipzig. _____

6. Mutter geht oft einkaufen. _____

7. Müllers ziehen nach Ulm. _____

8. Der Bauer wohnt auf dem Land. _____

9. Der Lehrer liest viel. _____

10. Das Haus ist neu. _____

Note: *do, does, is,* and *are* are often used in English questions but not in German—only the verb and the noun or pronoun are used.

ÜBUNG
6·10

Translate the following questions into German.

EXAMPLE: What do you have?
Was hast du?

1. Are you working now? _____

2. Where do they live? _____

3. What are they selling here? _____

4. Are they buying a lot? _____

5. Does he sing loudly? _____

6. Are the children playing in the park? _____

7. Why is she always smiling? _____

8. Mr. Braun, are you going to the show? (**ins Kino?**) _____

9. Why don't I marry you? (**dich**) _____

10. Do we answer all the questions? (**beantworten**) _____

ÜBUNG
6·11

Change the following sentences into questions, using a question word where indicated.

EXAMPLE: Emma singt laut.
Singt Emma laut?

1. Peter tanzt gut. _____

2. Ulrich kommt heute. _____

3. Ulrich kommt heute. (wann) _____

4. Müllers wohnen jetzt in Berlin. _____

5. Müllers wohnen jetzt in Berlin. (wo) _____

6. Er hat viel Geld. _____

7. Er hat viel Geld. (warum) _____

8. Das ist mein Freund. (wer) _____

9. Du kommst bestimmt. _____

10. Er heißt Max. (wie) _____

Formation of the Present Tense

The Infinitive

The *infinitive form* of the verb is the basic verb form found in dictionaries. It has not been changed or conjugated. In addition, it does not agree with a subject and is not in a tense. In English, all infinitives include the word *to* (*to go, to come*). German infinitives stand alone and end in **-en** or **-n**.

komm**en**	to come
geh**en**	to go
lächel**n**	to smile

The use of infinitives will be discussed in Unit 18, Infinitives.

Present Tense Forms

The stem of the verb is formed by dropping the infinitive ending of **-en** or **-n**. The stem of **kommen** would therefore be **komm-**, of **gehen/geh-**, and of **lächeln/lächel-**. To form the present tense you add the following endings to the stem of the verb:

Singular

First Person	-e	ich komm**e**	*I come, I am coming, I do come*
Second Person (familiar)	-st	du komm**st**	*you come, you are coming, you do come*
Second Person (formal)	-en	Sie komm**en**	*you come, you are coming, you do come*
Third Person	-t	er komm**t**	*he comes, he is coming, he does come*
		sie komm**t**	*she comes, she is coming, she does come*
		es komm**t**	*it comes, it is coming, it does come*
		man komm**t**	*one comes, one is coming, one does come*

Plural

First Person	-en	wir komm**en**	*we come, we are coming, we do come*
Second Person (familiar)	-t	ihr komm**t**	*you come, you are coming, you do come*
Second Person (formal)	-en	Sie komm**en**	*you come, you are coming, you do come*
Third Person	-en	sie komm**en**	*they come, they are coming, they do come*

The following is a list of common verbs that follow this rule without exception:

beginnen	to begin	**decken**	to cover, to set (the table)
besuchen	to visit	**dienen**	to serve
bezahlen	to pay	**erklären**	to explain
blühen	to bloom	**erzählen**	to tell
brauchen	to need	**fragen**	to ask
danken	to thank	**gehen**	to go

lachen	to laugh	rauchen	to smoke
leben	to live	sagen	to say
lieben	to love	schauen	to look
machen	to make, to do	schicken	to send
probieren	to try	spielen	to play
prüfen	to test	suchen	to look for, to search
gehorchen	to obey	weinen	to cry
glauben	to believe	wiederholen	to repeat
hängen	to hang	wohnen	to live, reside
hoffen	to hope	zahlen	to pay
horchen	to listen	zählen	to count
hören	to hear	zeigen	to show, point
kommen	to come		

ÜBUNG

6·12

Write the present tense of the following verbs.

EXAMPLE: wohnen—ich

Ich wohne.

fragen

1. ich _____

2. du _____

3. Sie _____

4. er _____

5. wir _____

6. ihr _____

7. Emma _____

8. die Kinder _____

9. Herr Schmidt _____

kaufen

10. du _____

11. sie (*sing.*) _____

12. es _____

13. wir _____

14. Elisabeth und Emma _____

15. ich _____

machen

16. ihr _____

17. wir _____

18. du _____

19. Anna _____

20. Jakob und Michael _____

Translate the following sentences into German. Remember that there is no emphatic or progressive form (I do come, I am coming) *in German.*

EXAMPLE: He is learning German.

Er lernt Deutsch.

1. The class begins. _____

2. The children are visiting me. (**mich**) _____

3. Hans, what do you need? _____

4. Mrs. Schmidt, what do you need? _____

5. The teacher explains the assignment. (**die Aufgabe**) _____

6. What are they buying? _____

7. Is Emma coming? _____

8. Yes, Emma and Michael are coming. _____

9. What are you (*fam. pl.*) asking? _____

10. Where do the boys live? _____

11. I do thank you. (**dir**) _____

12. Do you love me? (**mich**) _____

13. I do not love you. (**dich**) _____

14. I love Peter. _____

15. The girl tries the sauerkraut. _____

16. The children are playing in the park. (**im Park**) _____

17. Mrs. Kugel repeats the lesson. _____

18. We don't cry. _____

19. We are laughing. _____

20. The parents are paying for this. (Note: *for* is understood in German) _____

Supply the correct form of the verb given in parentheses.

EXAMPLE: Was _____ (sagen) du?

   *Was **sagst** du?*

1. Wann _____ (beginnen) die Klasse?

2. Wir _____ (besuchen) Tante Gretel.

3. _____ (bezahlen) du immer alles?

4. Mutter _____ (decken) den Tisch.

5. Was _____ (fragen) du?

6. Ihr _____ (erzählen) immer so viel.

7. Der Lehrer _____ (erklären) alles gut.

8. Herr Frank, _____ (glauben) Sie das?

9. Goethe _____ (leben) nicht mehr.

10. Wir _____ (hoffen) alles Gute.

11. Fridolin _____ (lachen) immer blöd.

12. Ich _____ (rauchen) nicht mehr.

13. Das Kind _____ (weinen) laut.

14. _____ (hören) du die Musik?

15. Am Sonntag _____ (machen) wir nichts.

16. Die Kinder _____ (spielen) Schach.

17. Wie lange _____ (suchen) ihr die Straße?

18. Schmidts _____ (wohnen) in Görlitz.

19. _____ (lieben) du mich?

20. Die Bäume _____ (blühen) im Mai.

21. Frau Ross, _____ (brauchen) Sie Geld?

22. Das Mädchen _____ (zeigen) das Geschenk.

23. Warum _____ (schauen) du aus dem Fenster?

24. _____ (gehorchen) ihr euren Eltern?

25. Wir _____ (bewegen) uns nicht.

Verb Stems Ending in *-s*, *-ss*, *-ß*, *-z*, or *-tz*

When the stem of the verb ends in -s, -ss, -ß, -z, or -tz, the -s- of the second-person singular is dropped (**reisen—du reist; sitzen—du sitzt**). The following list of common verbs fall into this category:

beeinflussen	to influence	**reisen**	to travel
beißen	to bite	**reißen**	to tear
besitzen	to own	**schließen**	to close
beweisen	to prove	**sich setzen**	to sit down
genießen	to enjoy	**sitzen**	to sit
gießen	to pour	**tanzen**	to dance
heißen	to be called	**verletzen**	to injure
pflanzen	to plant	**verschmutzen**	to pollute
putzen	to clean		

ÜBUNG
6·15

*Insert the correct form of **heißen** in the following sentences:*

EXAMPLE: Wie _____ die Kinder?

Wie **heißen** die Kinder?

1. Wie _____ du?

2. Ich _____ Martin. Und er?

3. Er _____ Paul.

4. Wie _____ die Mädchen?

5. Sie _____ Elisabeth und Anna.

6. Der Mann _____ Bauer.

7. Wirklich? _____ Sie Bauer?

8. Ja, ich _____ Bauer.

9. Aber wie _____ ihr?

10. Wir _____ Jakob und Michael.

ÜBUNG
6·16

Complete the following sentences with the correct verb form.

EXAMPLE: Wohin _____ (reisen) du?

Wohin **reist** du?

1. Wir _____ (besitzen) ein großes Haus.

2. Was für ein Haus _____ (besitzen) du?

3. Wie _____ (heißen) du?

4. Der Hund _____ (beißen) die Katze.

5. _____ (genießen) du den Abend?

6. Die Bank _____ (schließen) um fünf Uhr.

7. Wo _____ (sitzen) du?

8. Warum _____ (tanzen) du nicht gern?

9. Im August _____ (reisen) Frau Müller nach Italien.

10. Inge und Jakob _____ (sich setzen) auf die Bank.

11. Du _____ (putzen) das Auto schon wieder?

12. Der Rauch _____ (verschmutzen) die Luft.

13. Du _____ (gießen) immer zu viel Wasser aus.

14. Der Vater _____ (beeinflussen) den Sohn.

15. _____ (pflanzen) du Blumen im Frühling?

Let's see if you have the rule down pat! Complete the following sentences.

EXAMPLE: Warum _____ (lachen) du immer?
            *Warum **lachst** du immer?*

1. Du _____ (heißen) jetzt Müller.

2. _____ (brauchen) du schon wieder Geld?

3. Du _____ (glauben) mir nicht?

4. _____ (tanzen) du jeden Samstagabend?

5. Du _____ (beißen) zu viel ab!

6. Wann _____ (reisen) du nach Berlin?

7. Du bringst mir nie Blumen. Wann _____ (überraschen) du mich?

8. Wie oft _____ (verletzen) du dich?

9. Du _____ (gehorchen) schon wieder nicht.

10. Wohin _____ (setzen) du dich jetzt?

11. Du _____ (pflanzen) schon wieder Rosen?

12. Was _____ (wünschen) du dir zum Geburtstag?

Verb Stems Ending in *-t*, *-d*, or *-n*

When the stem of the verb ends in -t, -d, or -n, an -e- is inserted between the stem and the ending of the verb in the second- and third-person singular and in the second-person plural, to aid in pronunciation.

	arbeiten (*to work*)	**zeichnen** (*to draw*)
du	arbeitest	zeichnest
er	arbeitet	zeichnet
ihr	arbeitet	zeichnet

The following common verbs fit this category:

antworten	to answer	**einladen**	to invite
arbeiten	to work	**erwarten**	to expect
baden	to bathe	**finden**	to find
beantworten	to answer a question/letter	**(sich) fürchten**	to be afraid, to fear
bedeuten	to mean	**heiraten**	to marry
beobachten	to notice, to watch	**kosten**	to cost
berichten	to report	**reden**	to talk
beten	to pray	**warten**	to wait
sich einbilden	to imagine	**zeichnen**	to draw

ÜBUNG
6·18

Supply the correct verb form in the following sentences.

EXAMPLE: Wie lange _____ (warten) du schon?

*Wie lange **wartest** du schon?*

1. Hans und Luise, wann _____ (heiraten) ihr?

2. Wir _____ (heiraten) im Sommer.

3. Sie (*pl.*) _____ (arbeiten) von morgens bis abends.

4. Wenn Hans nicht (arbeiten), _____ (beobachten) er die Mädchen

   die im Wasser _____ (baden).

5. Wenn die Sonne nicht _____ (scheinen), (baden) Elisabeth nicht.

6. Was _____ (bedeuten) dieses Wort?

7. Wann _____ (beantworten) ihr endlich diesen Brief?

8. _____ (fürchten) du dich wenn es dunkel ist?

9. Liesel _____ (fürchten) sich nicht wenn es dunkel ist.

10. Wie _____ (finden) du den Film?

11. Der Reporter _____ (berichten) alles.

12. Du _____ (arbeiten) wieder zu lange.

13. Was _____ (erwarten) du zum Geburtstag?

14. Kannst du bitte still sein? Du _____ (reden) und (reden).

15. Das Kind _____ (beten) jeden Abend.

16. Ihr _____ (finden) das schön.

17. Was _____ (kosten) dieses Buch?

Verb Stems Ending in *-el* or *-er*

When the stem of the verb ends in **-el** or **-er**, the infinitive ending is only **-n**. The **-e** in the first-person singular is often dropped, especially in speech.

        lächeln → **ich lächle**   *I smile*

Here are a few verbs belonging to this smaller group:

ändern	to change	**lächeln**	to smile
(sich) erinnern	to remember, to remind	**schütteln**	to shake
feiern	to celebrate	**steuern**	to steer
flüstern	to whisper	**verbessern**	to correct
klingeln	to ring (a bell)	**wandern**	to hike, wander

Complete these sentences with the verbs given.

EXAMPLE: Ich _____ (flüstern) nicht gern.
            *Ich **flüstere/flüstre** nicht gern.*

1. Deinen Geburtstag _____ (feiern) wir am Sonntag.

2. Ich _____ (schütteln) den Karton, denn ich weiß nicht was drin ist.

3. _____ (verbessern) du den Aufsatz?

4. Ja, ich _____ (verbessern) meine Aufsätze immer.

5. Der Wecker _____ (klingeln) immer zu früh.

6. Ich _____ (lächeln) immer wenn ich ihn sehe.

7. Ich _____ (erinnern) mich nicht an den Besuch.

8. Wir _____ (ändern) unsere Adresse wenn wir nach Berlin ziehen.

9. Ich _____ (steuern) das Rad durch die Menschenmenge.

10. Ich _____ (flüstern) nie in der Klasse.

Here are some exercises with the verbs used so far. Monika brings home her little friend Uwe. Her father is very controlling and interrogates him thoroughly. Form questions using the verbs in parentheses.

EXAMPLE: Was _____ (spielen) du am liebsten?

*Was **spielst** du am liebsten?*

1. Wie _____ (heißen) du?

2. Wo _____ (wohnen) du?

3. Woher _____ (kommen) deine Eltern?

4. Wo _____ (arbeiten) dein Vater?

5. _____ (arbeiten) deine grossen Geschwister?

6. Wie oft _____ (besuchen) ihr eure Großeltern?

7. _____ (rauchen) dein Bruder?

8. _____ (sitzen) du viel vor dem Fernseher?

9. _____ (besitzen) deine Eltern ihr eigenes Haus?

10. _____ (besitzen) du ein neues Rad?

11. _____ (putzen) du dein Zimmer oft?

12. _____ (benutzen) du manchmal den Bus?

13. _____ (kosten) dein Rad viel?

14. _____ (wandern) du gern?

15. _____ (gehorchen) du deinen Eltern?

16. _____ (finden) du Monika klug?

17. Was _____ (wünschen) du dir zum Geburtstag?

18. _____ (reden) du zu viel in der Schule?

19. _____ (zeichnen) du in deiner Freizeit?

20. _____ (reisen) du gern?

Here is another exercise using the verbs learned thus far. Complete the sentences with the verbs in parentheses.

EXAMPLE: Ich _____ (gehen) ins Bad.
            Ich **gehe** *ins Bad.*

1. Der Wecker _____ (klingeln).

2. Annemarie _____ (liegen) noch im Bett.

3. Die Mutter _____ (rufen) sie zweimal.

4. Annemarie _____ (gehen) ins Bad.

5. Sie (*sing.*) _____ (singen) laut.

6. In der Küche _____ (sitzen) sie am Tisch.

7. Die Mutter _____ (bringen) das Frühstück.

8. Sie (*sing.*) _____ (trinken) Kaffee.

9. _____ (trinken) du oft Kaffee?

10. Jemand _____ (klopfen) an die Tür.

11. Annemaries Freundin _____ (stehen) vor der Tür.

12. Sie (*sing., fam.*) _____ (besuchen) sie früh am Morgen.

13. _____ (besuchen) du Leute am frühen Morgen?

14. Die Freundin _____ (reden) leise mit Annemarie.

15. Die Mutter _____ (hören) nichts.

16. Die Mutter _____ (fragen) die Mädchen etwas.

17. Annemarie _____ (antworten) höflich.

18. Die Mädchen _____ (gehen) heute aufs Land.

19. Annemarie _____ (wandern) gern.

20. Die Freundin _____ (zeichnen) lieber.

21. Heute _____ (spielen) sie (*pl.*) aber Ball.

22. Jetzt _____ (kommen) drei Jungen.

23. Der Große _____ (heißen) Udo.

24. Er _____ (beobachten) Annemarie.

25. Annemarie _____ (grüßen) alle drei.

26. Alle _____ (lachen) zusammen.

27. Annemaries Freundin _____ (lächeln) viel.

28. Heute _____ (kommen) alle spät nach Hause.

29. Die Mutter _____ (warten) schon.

30. Annemarie _____ (finden) den Tag schön.

The Present Tense of *haben, sein,* and *werden*

Haben—*to have*, **sein**—*to be*, and **werden**—*to become* are irregular in the present tense. In the present tense, **haben** and **sein** are also used as helping verbs to form the present perfect and the future perfect tenses of other verbs. **Werden** is also used to form the future tense of other verbs. The following conjugations are for these three verbs:

	haben (*to have*)	**sein** (*to be*)	**werden** (*to become*)
ich	habe	bin	werde
du	hast	bist	wirst
er/sie/es	hat	ist	wird
wir	haben	sind	werden
ihr	habt	seid	werdet
sie/Sie	haben	sind	werden

ÜBUNG
6·22

*Supply the correct form of **haben**.*

EXAMPLE: Ich _____ kein Geld.

*Ich **habe** kein Geld.*

1. _____ du Hunger?

2. Ja, ich _____ großen Hunger. Und er?

3. Peter _____ immer Hunger.

4. _____ Herr Müller Hunger?

5. Herr Müller, _____ Sie Hunger?

6. Nein, ich _____ keinen Hunger.

7. Aber die Jungen _____ bestimmt Hunger.

8. Hans und Bjorn, _____ ihr Hunger?

9. Ja, wir _____ Hunger.

10. Ja, Kinder _____ immer Hunger.

*Supply the correct form of **sein**.*

EXAMPLE: Wo _____ du?

         *Wo **bist** du?*

1. Wie alt _____ du?

2. Ich _____ einundzwanzig Jahre alt.

3. Und Sie? Wie alt _____ Sie, Herr Braun?

4. Ich _____ fünfundvierzig Jahre alt.

5. Meine Frau _____ jünger.

6. Unsere Kinder _____ natürlich noch viel jünger.

7. Wie alt _____ ihr, Luise und Michael?

8. Wir _____ jünger.

9. Luise _____ zwölf.

10. Michael _____ acht.

*Supply the correct form of **werden**.*

EXAMPLE: _____ der Kaffee kalt?

         ***Wird** der Kaffee kalt?*

1. Im Winter _____ meine Mutter immer krank.

2. Wirklich? Ich _____ nie krank.

3. Und dein Vater, _____ er krank?

4. Nein. Nur meine Mutter. Aber manchmal _____ meine Großeltern auch krank.

5. Oma und Opa, _____ ihr im Winter oft krank?

6. Nein, wir _____ nicht oft krank.

7. Peter, _____ du oft krank?

8. Natürlich nicht. Ich _____ nie krank.

Answer the following questions with a complete sentence, using the cues given.

EXAMPLE: Wie heißt du? (Beate)
Ich heiße Beate.

1. Wie alt sind Sie? (zwanzig) _____

2. Haben Sie viel Geld? (ja) _____

3. Werden Sie oft nervös? (ja) _____

4. Jakob und Michael, wie alt seid ihr? (zwölf) _____

5. Habt ihr viel Geld? (ja) _____

6. Werdet ihr oft nervös? (ja) _____

7. Wie alt bin ich? (zwölf) _____

8. Was habe ich hier? (viel Geld) _____

9. Werde ich oft nervös? (ja) _____

10. Hast du Hunger? (ja) _____

Insert the correct form of the verb in the following sentences.

EXAMPLE: _____ (haben) du Hunger?
Hast du Hunger?

1. Wir _____ (haben) heute abend Besuch.

2. Wir _____ (feiern) den Geburtstag meines Bruders.

3. Er _____ (sein) zehn Jahre alt.

4. Ich _____ (sein) älter.

5. Ich _____ (freuen) mich auf die Feier.

6. Ich _____ (lächeln) viel.

7. Meine Mutter _____ (werden) etwas nervös wenn wir Besuch haben.

8. Aber es _____ (sein) ein Familienabend.

9. Meine Großeltern _____ (sein) schon hier.

10. Sie (*pl.*) _____ (wohnen) in Potsdam.

11. Meine Tante Emma _____ (sitzen) schon im Wohnzimmer.

12. Sie (*sing.*) _____ (haben) immer ein schönes Geschenk.

13. Wo _____ (sitzen) du?

14. Entschuldigung, das Telefon _____ (klingeln).

15. Es _____ (sein) mein Vetter.

16. Er _____ (haben) keine Zeit.

17. Er _____ (arbeiten) heute Abend.

18. Rolf und Gerd (haben) immer Zeit, wenn wir _____ (feiern).

19. Na, das _____ (sein) klar.

20. Wir _____ (haben) immer Zeit.

21. Wann _____ (beginnen) also die Feier?

22. _____ (warten) ihr noch auf jemand?

23. Ich _____ (haben) Hunger auf Kuchen.

24. Du _____ (haben) immer Hunger!

Direct objects and the accusative case

You have encountered nouns and pronouns that have been used primarily as the subject of a sentence. The form of a noun or pronoun used as the subject of a sentence is the *nominative case* of that noun or pronoun. For example, each subject that follows shown in bold is in the nominative case:

Der Mann wohnt in Berlin.	*The man lives in Berlin.*
Eine Lehrerin ist Amerikanerin.	*A teacher is an American.*
Dieses Haus ist alt.	*This house is old.*
Ich bin Rechtsanwalt.	*I am a lawyer.*
Du hast keine Fahrkarten.	*You don't have any tickets.*
Er hat Sonja gern.	*He likes Sonja.*
Sie kauft eine Bluse.	*She buys a blouse.*
Es wird kalt.	*It is getting cold.*
Wir sind zu Hause.	*We are at home.*
Ihr lernt Deutsch.	*You learn German.*
Sie heißen Karl Benz.	*Your name is Karl Benz.*
Sie sind Kinder.	*They are children.*
Wer ist das?	*Who is that?*
Was ist das?	*What is that?*

Another important case in German is the *accusative case*. In many instances, you will find that the accusative case is identical to the nominative case, especially in the case of nouns. If a masculine noun is in the accusative case, the **der**-word or **ein**-word that precedes it changes its form slightly. For example:

NOMINATIVE	ACCUSATIVE
der Arzt	den Arzt
ein Wagen	einen Wagen
dieser Bruder	diesen Bruder
kein Mantel	keinen Mantel
mein Tisch	meinen Tisch
Ihr Computer	Ihren Computer

It should be obvious that the masculine accusative noun is preceded by a determiner that ends in **-en**.

In the blank provided, rewrite each noun and its determiner in their accusative form.

1. der Lehrer _____

2. der Roman _____

3. ein Artikel _____

4. ein Zahnarzt _____

5. dieser Politiker _____

6. dieser Mann _____

7. mein Geburtstag _____

8. mein Onkel _____

9. Ihr Wagen _____

10. kein Sportler _____

It is only with masculine nouns that you have to be concerned about a new ending. Feminine, neuter, and plural nouns are identical in form in both the nominative and the accusative. For example:

	NOMINATIVE	ACCUSATIVE
FEMININE	die Dame	die Dame
	eine Tänzerin	eine Tänzerin
	diese Bluse	diese Bluse
NEUTER	das Buch	das Buch
	Ihr Auto	Ihr Auto
	mein Gedicht	mein Gedicht
PLURAL	die Bücher	die Bücher
	diese Kinder	diese Kinder
	keine Prüfungen	keine Prüfungen

In the blank provided, rewrite each noun and its determiner in their accusative form.

1. der Schauspieler _____

2. meine Schuhe _____

3. Ihre Tante _____

4. ein Stuhl _____

5. das Mädchen _____

6. ein Gymnasium _____

7. keine Schwester _____

8. dieses Wetter _____

9. keine Zeit _____

10. eine Landkarte _____

11. ein Mantel _____

12. ein Kind _____

13. Ihre Prüfung _____

14. das Examen _____

15. mein Garten _____

16. keine Universität _____

17. der Boden _____

18. die Schule _____

19. mein Pullover _____

20. Ihre Schwester _____

21. dieser Garten _____

22. meine Bücher _____

23. das Glas _____

24. dieses Fenster _____

25. eine Schauspielerin _____

The accusative case is used to identify the *direct object* in a sentence. To find the direct object in a sentence, first identify the subject of the sentence. Then find the verb and determine that it is conjugated correctly for the subject. Look at the other elements in the sentence. Then ask *what* or *whom* with the subject and verb of the sentence, and the answer to that question is the direct object. Let's look at some example sentences in English:

SENTENCE FOLLOWED BY QUESTION	ANSWER: THE DIRECT OBJECT
John borrows my car. *What does John borrow?*	*my car*
We help the woman in that house. *Whom do we help in that house?*	*the woman*
I need some extra cash. *What do I need?*	*some extra cash*
Mrs. Jones met Mary's teacher. *Whom did Mrs. Jones meet?*	*Mary's teacher*

The direct object in a German sentence is determined in the same way. Ask a question with **was** or **wen** (accusative form of **wer** = *whom*). For example:

Sentence followed by question and answer

Martin kauft **meinen Wagen**.	*Martin buys **my car**.*
Was kauft Martin?	***What** does Martin buy?*
meinen Wagen	***my car***
Tina kennt **diese Dame**.	*Tina knows **this lady**.*
Wen kennt Tina?	***Whom** does Tina know?*
diese Dame	***this lady***
Mein Bruder liebt **das Mädchen**.	*My brother loves **the girl**.*
Wen liebt mein Bruder?	***Whom** does my brother love?*
das Mädchen	***the girl***
Der Junge hat **keine Bücher**.	*The boy has **no books**.*
Was hat der Junge?	***What** does the boy have?*
keine Bücher	***no books***

ÜBUNG
7·3

Underline the direct object in each of the following sentences.

1. Ich habe keine Zeit.

2. Mein Vater kennt Frau Schneider.

3. Wir hören Radio.

4. Onkel Peter sucht die Kinder.

5. Sie kauft ein Kleid und einen Pullover.

6. Liebst du dieses Mädchen?

7. Werner hat Maria gern.

8. Meine Schwestern kaufen einen Wagen.

9. Wir lernen Deutsch.

10. Der Rechtsanwalt braucht Geld.

11. Sie hat keinen Mantel.

12. Findet ihr den Roman?

13. Wir haben ein Problem.

14. Lieben Sie meinen Bruder?

15. Kennen Sie diese Schauspielerin?

Just as pronouns can be used as the subject of a sentence, so too can they be used as direct objects. Note how the English personal pronouns are different as subjects and as direct objects.

SUBJECT	DIRECT OBJECT
I	*me*
you	*you*
he	*him*
she	*her*
it	*it*
we	*us*
you	*you*
they	*them*
who	*whom*
what	*what*

German does something very similar.

SUBJECT	DIRECT OBJECT
ich	mich
du	dich
er	ihn
sie (*sing.*)	sie (*sing.*)
es	es
wir	uns
ihr	euch
Sie	Sie
sie (*pl.*)	sie (*pl.*)
wer	wen
was	was

ÜBUNG
7·4

Rewrite each sentence with the correct accusative case form of the pronouns in parentheses.

FOR EXAMPLE: Er hat _____.

(es) _____*Er hat es*_____.

1. Kennst du _____?

   (ich) _____

   (er) _____

   (sie [*sing.*]) _____

   (wir) _____

2. Ja, ich habe _____.

   (er) _____

   (sie [*sing.*]) _____

   (es) _____

   (sie [*pl.*]) _____

3. Doktor Bauer hat _____ gern.

(du) _____

(er) _____

(wir) _____

(ihr) _____

4. Meine Großmutter liebt _____.

(ich) _____

(du) _____

(sie [*sing.*]) _____

(sie [*pl.*]) _____

5. Die Männer suchen _____.

(du) _____

(wir) _____

(ihr) _____

(Sie) _____

*Using the word in boldface as your cue, write a question with **was** or **wen**.*

FOR EXAMPLE: Martin hat **einen Mantel**.

Was hat Martin?

1. Die Frauen brauchen **Geld**.

_____

2. Meine Schwester kennt **diesen Herrn** nicht.

_____

3. Ich liebe **Rosen**.

_____

4. Wir suchen **Ihre Tochter**.

_____

5. Herr Benz kauft **ein Glas Bier**.

_____

6. Werner und Karl finden **einen Pullover**.

_____

7. Ihr habt **die Fahrkarten**.

_____

8. Mein Bruder braucht **Schuhe**.

_____

9. Martin sucht **einen Zahnarzt**.

_____

10. Sie hören **Ihren Vater**.

_____

11. Ich frage **meine Tante**.

_____

12. Die Kinder decken **den Tisch**.

_____

13. Erik liebt **die Amerikanerin**.

_____

14. Sabine hat **ein Problem**.

_____

15. Die Jungen kaufen **einen Computer**.

_____

In the blank provided, write the pronoun that correctly replaces the noun in boldface. Some answers will be in the nominative case, some in the accusative case.

FOR EXAMPLE: Werner hat **das Geld**. _____ _es_ _____

1. **Der Junge** ist zu Hause. _____

2. Wir kaufen **einen Wagen**. _____

3. Erik und Tina suchen **ein Restaurant**. _____

4. Wer hat **die Landkarte**? _____

5. Der Zahnarzt liebt **Frau Bauer**. _____

6. Hat **Sonja** eine Blume? _____

7. Kaufen **die Männer** das Haus? _____

8. Meine Schwester hat **Werner Schmidt** gern. _____

9. Ich liebe **diesen Roman**. _____

10. Thomas zeigt **das Fenster**. _____

11. Wer kennt **diesen Mann**? _____

12. Was hat **Herr Schneider**? _____

13. Der Student findet **das Examen**. _____

14. Wir suchen **das Gymnasium**. _____

15. Liebst du **das Kind**? _____

Accusative case

The accusative case is needed to identify *direct objects* or *objects that follow accusative prepositions*. Determining which word in a sentence is the direct object is rather simple: ask *whom* or *what* of the verb. The answer is the direct object. For example in English:

> *John likes Mary.*
> *Whom does John like?* (*Mary* is the direct object.)
>
> *She bought a car.*
> *What did she buy?* (*Car* is the direct object.)

The same questions can be asked to determine the direct object in a German sentence. For example:

> Erik hat Tina gern. *Erik likes Tina.*
> Wen hat Erik gern? *Whom does Erik like?* (**Tina** is the direct object.)
>
> Sie kauft ein Kleid. *She buys a dress.*
> Was kauft sie? *What does she buy?* (**Kleid** is the direct object.)

The interrogative pronoun **wer** (*who*) is used as the subject of a sentence: **Wer ist das?** (*Who is that?*) Its accusative case form is **wen** (*whom*) and is used to ask about a direct object: **Wen besuchen Sie?** (*Whom are you visiting?*) The interrogative pronoun **was** (*what*) is the same in the nominative and accusative cases: **Was ist das? Was sehen Sie?** (*What is that? What do you see?*)

Direct objects that are feminine, neuter, or plural nouns use the same definite and indefinite articles as in the nominative case. There are no declensional changes that take place.

Feminine

NOMINATIVE	**Die Lehrerin** spricht Deutsch.	*The teacher speaks German.*
ACCUSATIVE	Kennen Sie **die Lehrerin**?	*Do you know the teacher?*

Neuter

NOMINATIVE	**Das Kind** spielt im Garten.	*The child is playing in the garden.*
ACCUSATIVE	Wir sehen **ein Kind**.	*We see a child.*

Plural

NOMINATIVE	**Die Bücher** sind alt.	*The books are old.*
ACCUSATIVE	Warum kaufst du **die Bücher**?	*Why are you buying the books?*

The masculine definite and indefinite articles change in the accusative case to **den** and **einen**. Therefore, when a masculine noun is used as a direct object, it must use the accusative form of the articles. For example:

NOMINATIVE	**Ein Arzt** wohnt in dieser Straße.	*A doctor lives on this street.*
ACCUSATIVE	Ich besuche **einen Arzt**.	*I am visiting a doctor.*
NOMINATIVE	**Der Tisch** is neu.	*The table is new.*
ACCUSATIVE	Er verkauft **den Tisch**.	*He sells the table.*

ÜBUNG
7·7

Based on the word given in bold in each sentence, ask a question that begins with **wen** *or* **was**.

EXAMPLE   Thomas hat **Gudrun** gern.

   Wen hat Thomas gern?

1. Die Männer bauen (*build*) **ein Haus**.

   _____

2. Herr Schneider hat **das Geld**.

   _____

3. Wir besuchen **den Lehrer**.

   _____

4. Der Tourist kennt **die Amerikanerin**.

   _____

5. Martin braucht (*needs*) **eine Zeitung**.

   _____

6. Niemand (*no one*) versteht **das Problem**.

   _____

7. Ich sehe **die Kinder**.

   _____

8. Karin hat **Erik** gern.

   _____

9. Er verkauft **das Haus**.

_____

10. Wir sehen **die Lehrerinnen**.

_____

_____

ÜBUNG
7·8

Reword the sentence with the nouns provided in parentheses.

EXAMPLE   Wir sehen _____.

(der Mann) _Wir sehen den Mann._

Haben Sie _____?

1. (ein Heft [_notebook_]) _____

2. (die Briefe [_letters_]) _____

3. (der Stuhl [_chair_]) _____

4. (eine Bluse [_blouse_]) _____

5. (das Geld [_money_]) _____

Ich kaufe ein _____.

6. (Wagen [_car_]) _____

7. (Zeitung [_newspaper_]) _____

8. (Bücher) _____

9. (Lampe) _____

10. (Handy [_cell phone_]) _____

Accusative case form of personal pronouns

Pronouns are not only used as the subject of a sentence but also as the direct object of a sentence. Each of the personal pronouns has an accusative case form. They are:

NOMINATIVE	ACCUSATIVE
ich	mich
du	dich
er	ihn

sie *s.*	sie *s.*
es	es
wir	uns
ihr	euch
Sie	Sie
sie *pl.*	sie *pl.*
wer	wen
was	was

As direct objects, they look like this:

Ein Freund besucht **mich**.	*A friend is visiting me.*
Ich kenne **ihn** nicht.	*I don't know him.*
Die Kinder haben **sie** gern.	*The children like them.*

ÜBUNG
7·9

Reword each sentence with the pronouns provided in parentheses.

EXAMPLE   Er besucht _____.

(wir) *Er besucht uns.*

Die Frauen sehen _____.

1. (ich) _____

2. (du) _____

3. (sie *s.*) _____

4. (es) _____

5. (ihr) _____

Niemand versteht _____.

6. (er) _____

7. (wir) _____

8. (Sie) _____

9. (sie *pl.*) _____

10. (ich) _____

Accusative prepositions

Nouns and pronouns that follow the accusative prepositions must also be in the accusative case. The accusative prepositions are:

bis	*until*
durch	*through*
für	*for*
gegen	*against*
ohne	*without*
wider	*against*
um	*around*

The translations for the previous accusative prepositions are the basic translations. When some of these prepositions are used with certain verbs, their English translation is altered. For example:

sich interesssieren **für**	*be interested in*
bitten **um**	*ask for*

In sentences, the accusative prepositions are used like this:

Der Zug fährt **durch** einen Tunnel.	*The train is going through a tunnel.*
Das ist ein Geschenk **für** die Kinder.	*This is a gift for the children.*
Warum kommt sie **ohne** ihn?	*Why does she come without him?*
Er schlägt **gegen** die Tür.	*He beats against the door.*

If the object of the accusative preposition is a pronoun that has replaced an inanimate noun, a *prepositional adverb* is formed. A prepositional adverb is a combination of **da(r)**- plus the preposition. For example: **dadurch** (*through it*) and **darum** (*around it*). The prefix **dar**- is used with prepositions that begin with a vowel.

ÜBUNG
7·10

Reword each sentence with the nouns and pronouns provided in parentheses.

EXAMPLE   Das ist ein Geschenk für _____.

(der Lehrer) *Das ist ein Geschenk für den Lehrer.*

Die Kinder gehen durch _____.

1. (die Straße [*street*]) _____

2. (ein Tunnel) _____

3. (der Park) _____

4. (ein Garten) _____

Ich habe etwas (*something*) für _____.

5. (sie [*she*]) _____

6. (er [*he*]) _____

7. (ihr) _____

8. (die Männer) _____

Warum ist er gegen _____?

9. (wir) _____

10. (es [*it*]) _____

11. (sie [*it*]) _____

12. (der Krieg [*war*]) _____

13. (ich) _____

14. (du) _____

15. (Sie) _____

Pronouns in the accusative case

When an English noun is made the direct object in a sentence, it does not change—it looks like it does when it is the subject of a sentence. Most English pronouns, however, change when used as a direct object.

SUBJECT	DIRECT OBJECT
The **boy** is ten years old.	Do you know the **boy?**
He is ten years old.	Do you know **him?**
The **woman** is quite young.	Do you know the **woman?**
She is quite young.	Do you know **her?**

The following chart gives the subject and direct object forms of the personal pronoun in English.

SUBJECT PRONOUNS	DIRECT OBJECT PRONOUNS
I	*me*
you	*you*
he	*him*
she	*her*
it	*it*
we	*us*
they	*them*

German treats nouns somewhat differently. Masculine singular nouns require a new form of the article when used as a direct object. Feminine, neuter, and plural nouns do not change their article when used as direct objects. German direct objects are expressed in the accusative case.

NOMINATIVE NOUNS	ACCUSATIVE NOUNS	
der Laden	den Laden	*the store*
die Kreide	die Kreide	*the chalk*
das Flugzeug	das Flugzeug	*the airplane*
die Leute	die Leute	*the people*

Most German pronouns have a different form when used as direct objects in the accusative case. The only exceptions are **sie** (*sing.*), **es**, **sie** (*pl.*), and **was**.

NOMINATIVE PRONOUNS	ACCUSATIVE PRONOUNS
ich	mich
du	dich
er	ihn
sie (*sing.*)	sie
es	es
wir	uns
ihr	euch
sie (*pl.*)	sie
Sie	Sie
wer	wen
was	was

To use the accusative pronouns correctly, you must know how to identify a direct object. In English, you ask whom or what of the verb; the answer is the direct object.

| *John kissed Mary.* | *Whom did he kiss?* | ***Mary*** = *direct object* |
| *I bought a new car.* | *What did I buy?* | ***a new car*** = *direct object* |

The same test can be used in German. You ask wen or was of the verb; the answer is the direct object.

| Hans küsste Maria. | Wen küsste Hans? | **Maria** = direct object (accusative case) |
| Ich kaufte einen neuen Wagen. | Was kaufte ich? | **einen neuen Wagen** = direct object (accusative case) |

Pronouns substituted for direct object nouns must be accusative case pronouns.

„Hans küsste Maria." „Wirklich? Hans küsste **sie**?"
"Hans kissed Maria." *"Really? Hans kissed her?"*
„Ich kaufte einen neuen Wagen." „Wirklich? Du kauftest **ihn**?"
"I bought a new car." *"Really? You bought it?"*

Notice that the pronouns substituted in these examples are the same gender and number as the nouns they replace and are, of course, in the accusative case: **Maria → sie** and **einen neuen Wagen → ihn**.

The following examples show each of the accusative case pronouns in German used as a direct object in complete sentences.

ich	Der Tiger hat **mich** angegriffen.	*The tiger attacked me.*
du	Sie kennen **dich** nicht.	*They don't know you.*
er	Sie hat **ihn** nie geliebt.	*She never loved him.*
sie	Jede Woche besuche ich **sie**.	*I visit her every week.*
es	Er versteht **es** nicht.	*He doesn't understand it.*
wir	Karin hat **uns** eingeladen.	*Karin invited us.*

ihr	Er wird **euch** nie vergessen.	*He will never forget you.*
sie	Ich kann **sie** nicht sehen.	*I can't see them.*
Sie	Ich werde **Sie** vorstellen.	*I'll introduce you.*
wer	**Wen** hast du besucht?	*Whom did you visit?*
was	**Was** haben Sie gekauft?	*What did you buy?*

ÜBUNG
7·11

Rewrite each sentence, changing the word or phrase in boldface to the appropriate pronoun.

1. Im Sommer werden wir **unsere Verwandten in New York** besuchen.

   _____

2. Ich kenne **das Mädchen** nicht.

   _____

3. Gudrun hat **die Fragen** zu langsam beantwortet.

   _____

4. Kannst du **ihre Handschrift** lesen?

   _____

5. Wir haben **den Zug** verpasst!

   _____

6. Wer kann **dieses Problem** lösen?

   _____

7. Mutter hat **meinen Regenmantel** im Keller gefunden.

   _____

8. Der Blitz hat **zwei Pferde** getötet.

   _____

9. Martin wird **eine weiße Nelke** kaufen.

   _____

10. Ich liebe **das schöne Wetter**.

    _____

In rare instances, there can be two accusative objects in the same sentence.

Frau Schuhmann hat **die Kinder** (1) **die neue Rechtschreibung** (2) gelehrt.
Mrs. Schuhmann taught the children the new orthography.

Sie nannte **den Dieb** (1) **einen Lügner** (2).
She called the thief a liar.

If pronouns replace accusative nouns, they must, of course, be accusative case pronouns.

Frau Schuhmann hat **sie** die neue Rechtschreibung gelehrt.
Mrs. Schuhmann taught them the new orthography.

Sie nannte **ihn** einen Lügner.
She called him a liar.

Sentences with two accusative objects tend to occur with only a few verbs: **heißen**, **kosten**, **lehren**, **nennen**, **rufen**, **schelten**, **schimpfen**, and **taufen**.

When substituting a pronoun for an accusative noun, you must be aware of not only the proper case for the pronoun but also its gender. The English inanimate pronoun is always *it*, but German inanimate nouns can be masculine, feminine, or neuter. Therefore, the accusative form of the pronoun must be the same gender as the noun in the accusative case.

„Verstehst du **diesen Satz**?"   „Nein, ich verstehe **ihn** nicht."
"Do you understand this sentence?"   "No, I don't understand it."

„Verstehst du **diese Oper**?"   „Nein, ich verstehe **sie** nicht."
"Do you understand this opera?"   "No, I don't understand it."

„Verstehst du **dieses Problem**?"   „Nein, ich verstehe **es** nicht."
"Do you understand this problem?"   "No, I don't understand it."

„Verstehst du **diese Sätze**?"   „Nein, ich verstehe **sie** nicht."
"Do you understand these sentences?"   "No, I don't understand them."

It is only with animate nouns that German and English replace nouns with pronouns in a similar way.

„Kennst du **diesen Mann**?"   „Nein, ich kenne **ihn** nicht."
"Do you know this man?"   "No, I don't know him."

„Kennst du **diese Dame**?"   „Nein, ich kenne **sie** nicht."
"Do you know this lady?"   "No, I don't know her."

„Kennst du **dieses Kind**?"   „Nein, ich kenne **es** nicht."
"Do you know this child?"   "No, I don't know him/her."

„Kennst du **diese Leute**?"   „Nein, ich kenne **sie** nicht."
"Do you know these people?"   "No, I don't know them."

ÜBUNG
7·12

Rewrite each sentence, changing the accusative case pronoun to any appropriate noun.

1. Ich habe ihn in Kanada kennen gelernt.

_____

2. Wo hast du es gefunden?

_____

3. Er hat sie auf dem Tisch stehen gelassen.

_____

4. Onkel Karl hat ihn versteckt.

_____

5. Wirst du uns besuchen?

_____

6. Man baut sie am Rande des Waldes.

_____

7. Tante Luise hat es auf das Bett gelegt.

_____

Note: When changing a noun phrase that includes **ich** to a pronoun, you must use a form of **wir**.

> **Karl und ich** warten noch.
> _Karl and I are still waiting._
> **Wir** warten noch.
> _We're still waiting._
>
> Sie kennen **Karl und mich**.
> _They know Karl and me._
> Sie kennen **uns**.
> _They know us._

As shown in these examples, this substitution can be used for a nominative subject (**Karl und ich** = **wir**) and for an accusative direct object (**Karl und mich** = **uns**).

ÜBUNG
7·13

Rewrite each sentence as a question, replacing the noun or pronoun in boldface with either wer or was.

EXAMPLE   Er hat es gefunden.

_____Was hat er gefunden?_____

1. Ich werde meinen Urlaub in Innsbruck verleben.

_____

2. Mein Vetter kennt ihn nicht.

_____

3. Martin kaufte das Geschenk für seine Schwester.

_____

4. Sie hat seit ihrer Jugend Sport getrieben.

   _____

5. Der Arbeitslose verdient nichts.

   _____

6. Wir treffen sie am Hauptbahnhof.

   _____

7. Meine Tante hat den Pförtner gefragt.

   _____

8. Ich liebe meine Heimat am meisten.

   _____

9. Seine Eltern haben Sie im Kaufhaus gesehen.

   _____

10. Solche Umstände ärgern mich.

    _____

Circle the pronoun that best completes each sentence.

1. Ich habe _____ einfach vergessen.   mich | es | du

2. Sie sieht _____ auf dem Dach.   ihn | wir | ihr

3. Wir müssen _____ fragen.   sie | ihr | ich

4. Morgen kaufen wir _____.   uns | Sie | ihn

5. Die Kinder dürfen _____ nicht tun.   du | dich | es

6. Wo sind meine Schuhe? Hast du _____?   sie | es | ihn

7. Ich höre _____ singen.   er | euch | wir

8. Wir besuchen _____ im Krankenhaus.   ihr | ich | sie

9. Mögen Sie _____ nicht?   er | ich | ihn

10. Wir haben _____ verpasst!   ihn | mich | ihr

Pronouns

Pronouns are words that stand in place of a noun. In German, third person pronouns must be true to the gender, number, and case of the nouns they replace:

der Mann → *masculine singular nominative* → er
die Frau → *feminine singular dative* → ihr
das Kind → *neuter singular accusative* → es
die Kinder → *plural nominative* → sie

First, let's look at all the personal pronouns in the three cases and as possessive adjectives:

NOM.	ACC.	DAT.	POSS.	
ich	mich	mir	mein	*I, me, my*
du	dich	dir	dein	*you, your (informal singular)*
er	ihn	ihm	sein	*he/it, his/its*
sie	sie	ihr	ihr	*she/it, her/its*
es	es	ihm	sein	*it, its*
wir	uns	uns	unser	*we, us, our*
ihr	euch	euch	euer	*you, your (informal plural)*
Sie	Sie	Ihnen	Ihr	*you, your (formal singular or plural)*
sie	sie	ihnen	ihr	*they, them, their*

Most German personal pronouns are used like their English counterparts. But the third person pronouns (**er, sie, es**) reflect the gender of the word they replace: masculine, feminine, or neuter—whether animate or inanimate. The English meaning of the noun should not be considered, because sexual gender does not determine the gender of a German pronoun. For example:

MASCULINE		PRONOUN	
der Lehrer	*teacher*	er	*he*
der Garten	*garden*	er	*it*

FEMININE		PRONOUN	
die Richterin	*judge*	sie	*she*
die Blume	*flower*	sie	*it*

NEUTER		PRONOUN	
das Kind	*child*	es	*he, she*
das Dorf	*village*	es	*it*

In the plural, the German and English third person pronouns are used identically: gender is not considered, and all nouns are replaced by a single pronoun, **sie** (*they*):

PLURAL		PRONOUN	
die Leute	*people*	sie	*they*
die Zeitungen	*newspapers*	sie	*they*

In the blank provided, write the pronoun that can replace each noun: **er**, **sie**, **es**, *or* **sie** *plural*.

1. Vater _____

2. Hochschule _____

3. Universität _____

4. Katze _____

5. Schülerinnen _____

6. Rathaus _____

7. Fragen _____

8. Kaffee _____

9. Satz _____

10. Papier _____

Man

The third person pronoun **man** is generally translated as *one*. But in reality it has other English translations: *you, they, someone, people,* and certain phrases expressed in the passive voice. For example, the most common use of **man** is in sentences such as these:

Man soll nicht fluchen.	***One** should not curse.*
Man kann nie wissen.	***You** can never tell.*
Man hat ihn dafür verprügelt.	***They** beat him up for it.*

But other translations can also be used for this pronoun:

Man wartet vor dem Eingang.	*Someone is waiting in front of the entrance.*
Damals glaubte man, dass die Erde flach war.	*Back then people believed the earth was flat.*
Man hat herausgefunden, dass sie das Geld gestohlen hat.	*It was discovered that she stole the money.*

The pronoun **man** is not a substitute for a specific noun. It is used to express what people do in general or to point out that the person or persons carrying out an action are unknown. **Man** is used only as a replacement for people and is only used in the nominative case. If another case is required, a form of **einer** is used:

Man ist froh, wenn **einem** ein kleines Geschenk gegeben wird.	*One is happy when one is given a little gift.*

When forming German sentences, it is wise to consider carefully whether the English relates to people in general or specific people. This will help to determine whether **man** is the appropriate pronoun for a sentence. For example:

Man liebte den alten König.	*People loved the old king. (general)*
Das Volk des Dorfes liebte den alten König.	*The people of the village loved the old king. (specific)*

*Rewrite each sentence, changing the underlined words and phrases to **man** or **einer**, as appropriate. Make any other necessary changes.*

EXAMPLE: <u>Die Jungen</u> sollen nicht fluchen.

<u>Man</u> soll nicht fluchen.

1. <u>Die Politiker</u> erwarten von den Bürgern Respekt.

_____

2. Oft tut <u>der Mann</u>, was <u>er</u> nicht tun soll.

_____

3. Die Firma soll <u>ihnen</u> mehr Lohn geben.

_____

4. <u>Den Kindern</u> soll so viel wie möglich geholfen werden.

_____

5. <u>Es</u> wird oft gesagt, dass sie miteinander nie auskommen werden.

_____

6. <u>Die Frauen</u> müssen ihn lange kennen, bis <u>sie</u> ihn verstehen.

_____

7. <u>Ein Fremder</u> stand am Fenster und klopfte.

_____

Irregular verbs in the present tense

8

You have already encountered the present tense conjugation of verbs that follow a regular pattern. For example:

	LERNEN	SPIELEN
ich	lerne	spiele
du	lernst	spielst
er/sie/es	lernt	spielt
wir	lernen	spielen
ihr	lernt	spielt
Sie	lernen	spielen
sie (*pl.*)	lernen	spielen

You have also been introduced to three irregular verbs that break that pattern:

	HABEN	SEIN	WERDEN
ich	habe	bin	werde
du	hast	bist	wirst
er/sie/es	hat	ist	wird
wir	haben	sind	werden
ihr	habt	seid	werdet
Sie	haben	sind	werden
sie (*pl.*)	haben	sind	werden

Several other verbs break that pattern, and they tend to fall into one of two major groups: verbs that add an umlaut in the second-person and third-person singular, and verbs that make a vowel change in the second-person and third-person singular.

The addition of an umlaut

Only the vowels **a**, **o**, and **u** can have an umlaut, and the addition of that diacritical mark changes the pronunciation of the vowel. This can occur in an irregular present tense conjugation, but only in the second-person and third-person singular (**du**, **er**, **sie** [*sing.*], **es**), primarily with the vowel **a,** and in one instance with the vowel **o**. Let's look at the form that this irregular conjugation takes:

	fahren (drive)	laufen (run)	stoßen (kick)
ich	fahre	laufe	stoße
du	fährst	läufst	stößt
er/sie/es	fährt	läuft	stößt
wir	fahren	laufen	stoßen
ihr	fahrt	lauft	stoßt
Sie	fahren	laufen	stoßen
sie (*pl.*)	fahren	laufen	stoßen

Other verbs that follow this irregular present tense conjugational pattern are:

backen, bäckst, bäckt	*bake*
braten, brätst, brät	*fry, roast*
fallen, fällst, fällt	*fall*
fangen, fängst, fängt	*catch*
halten, hältst, hält	*hold*
lassen, lässt, lässt	*let*
raten, rätst, rät	*advise*
schlafen, schläfst, schläft	*sleep*
schlagen, schlägst, schlägt	*beat*
tragen, trägst, trägt	*carry, wear*
wachsen, wächst, wächst	*grow*
waschen, wäschst, wäscht	*wash*

ÜBUNG
8·1

In the blank, rewrite each verb in parentheses with the subject provided.

1. (fahren) du _____

2. (haben) er _____

3. (fallen) wir _____

4. (raten) sie (*sing.*) _____

5. (raten) ihr _____

6. (backen) ich _____

7. (braten) du _____

8. (halten) es _____

9. (lassen) er _____

10. (fangen) sie (*pl.*) _____

11. (waschen) du _____

12. (stoßen) sie (*sing.*) _____

13. (sein) ihr _____

14. (wachsen) er _____

15. (schlafen) Sie _____

16. (tragen) du _____

17. (schlagen) der Mann _____

18. (fangen) die Lehrerin _____

19. (fallen) mein Bruder _____

20. (raten) du _____

21. (schlafen) das Kind _____

22. (werden) ihr _____

23. (halten) du _____

24. (waschen) ich _____

25. (tragen) die Dame _____

Write the full conjugation of each verb with the subjects provided.

	1. wachsen	2. tragen
ich	_____	_____
du	_____	_____
er	_____	_____
wir	_____	_____
ihr	_____	_____
Sie	_____	_____
man	_____	_____

	3. fallen	4. schlagen
ich	_____	_____
du	_____	_____
er	_____	_____
wir	_____	_____
ihr	_____	_____
Sie	_____	_____
man	_____	_____

	5. braten	6. stoßen
ich	_____	_____
du	_____	_____
er	_____	_____
wir	_____	_____
ihr	_____	_____
Sie	_____	_____
man	_____	_____

	7. lassen	8. schlafen
ich	_____	_____
du	_____	_____
er	_____	_____
wir	_____	_____
ihr	_____	_____
Sie	_____	_____
man	_____	_____

Vowel change e to i

When a verb has a vowel change in an irregular present tense conjugation, that vowel change occurs primarily with the vowel **e**. An exception is the vowel **ö** in the verb **erlöschen** (*go out, die out*), which forms **erlischst** and **erlischt** in the second-person and third-person singular respectively. Let's look at the form that this irregular conjugation takes:

	brechen (*break*)	**essen** (*eat*)	**nehmen** (*take*)
ich	breche	esse	nehme
du	brichst	isst	nimmst
er/sie/es	bricht	isst	nimmt
wir	brechen	essen	nehmen
ihr	brecht	esst	nehmt
Sie	brechen	essen	nehmen
sie (*pl.*)	brechen	essen	nehmen

Other verbs that follow this irregular present tense conjugational pattern are:

bergen, birgst, birgt	*rescue*
erschrecken, erschrickst, erschrickt	*be startled*
fressen, frisst, frisst	*eat* (*for animals*)
geben, gibst, gibt	*give*
gelten, giltst, gilt	*be valid*
helfen, hilfst, hilft	*help*
melken, milkst, milkt	*milk*

messen, misst, misst	*measure*
schmelzen, schmilzt, schmilzt	*melt*
sprechen, sprichst, spricht	*speak*
stechen, stichst, sticht	*stick, prick*
sterben, stirbst, stirbt	*die*
treffen, triffst, trifft	*meet*
treten, trittst, tritt	*step, kick*
verderben, verdirbst, verdirbt	*spoil*
vergessen, vergisst, vergisst	*forget*
werfen, wirfst, wirft	*throw*

In the blank, rewrite each verb in parentheses with the subject provided.

1. (brechen) du _____

2. (vergessen) sie (*sing.*) _____

3. (sprechen) ihr _____

4. (treten) er _____

5. (stechen) ich _____

6. (messen) wir _____

7. (schmelzen) es _____

8. (werfen) du _____

9. (erschrecken) Sie _____

10. (geben) er _____

11. (helfen) sie (*sing.*) _____

12. (sterben) sie (*pl.*) _____

13. (essen) wir _____

14. (fressen) der Hund (*dog*) _____

15. (nehmen) er _____

16. (treffen) du _____

17. (bergen) die Männer _____

18. (gelten) es _____

19. (melken) ich _____

20. (treten) du _____

21. (essen) mein Freund (*friend*) _____

22. (werfen) ihr _____

23. (geben) Ihre Töchter _____

24. (sterben) er _____

25. (brechen) meine Kinder _____

Write the full conjugation of each verb with the subjects provided.

	1. essen	2. helfen
ich	_____	_____
du	_____	_____
er	_____	_____
wir	_____	_____
ihr	_____	_____
Sie	_____	_____
man	_____	_____

	3. verderben	4. nehmen
ich	_____	_____
du	_____	_____
er	_____	_____
wir	_____	_____
ihr	_____	_____
Sie	_____	_____
man	_____	_____

	5. sprechen	6. sterben
ich	_____	_____
du	_____	_____
er	_____	_____
wir	_____	_____
ihr	_____	_____
Sie	_____	_____
man	_____	_____

	7. geben	8. treffen
ich	_____	_____
du	_____	_____
er	_____	_____
wir	_____	_____
ihr	_____	_____
Sie	_____	_____
man	_____	_____

Vowel change **e** to **ie**

Other verbs that have the vowel **e** in their stem change that vowel to an **ie** in the second-person and third-person singular. For example:

	lesen (*read*)	**geschehen** (*happen*)	**empfehlen** (*recommend*)
ich	lese	N/A	empfehle
du	liest	N/A	empfiehlst
er/sie/es	liest	geschieht	empfiehlt
wir	lesen	N/A	empfehlen
ihr	lest	N/A	empfehlt
Sie	lesen	N/A	empfehlen
sie (*pl.*)	lesen	geschehen	empfehlen

Other verbs that follow this irregular present tense conjugational pattern are:

sehen, siehst, sieht	*see*
stehlen, stiehlst, stiehlt	*steal*

ÜBUNG
8·5

Write the full conjugation of each verb with the subjects provided.

	1. sehen	2. stehlen
ich	_____	_____
du	_____	_____
er	_____	_____
wir	_____	_____
ihr	_____	_____
Sie	_____	_____
man	_____	_____

	3. empfehlen	4. lesen
ich	_____	_____
du	_____	_____
er	_____	_____
wir	_____	_____
ihr	_____	_____
Sie	_____	_____
man	_____	_____

The verb **wissen**

The verb **wissen** (*know*) has an irregular present tense conjugation, but its irregularities occur not only with the second-person and third-person singular but also with the first-person singular. Let's look at this conjugation:

	wissen
ich	weiß
du	weißt
er/sie/es	weiß
wir	wissen
ihr	wisst
Sie	wissen
sie (*pl.*)	wissen

ÜBUNG
8·6

In the blank, rewrite each verb in parentheses with the subject provided.

1. (brechen) er _____

2. (fahren) wir _____

3. (sein) ihr _____

4. (stehlen) sie (*sing.*) _____

5. (fallen) du _____

6. (fangen) man _____

7. (sehen) ich _____

8. (geschehen) es _____

9. (nehmen) er _____

10. (lassen) Sie _____

11. (stoßen) du _____

12. (werden) es _____

13. (wissen) sie (*sing.*) _____

14. (helfen) sie (*sing.*) _____

15. (empfehlen) wir _____

16. (lesen) du _____

17. (schlafen) er _____

18. (wissen) wer _____

19. (messen) ihr _____

20. (laufen) es _____

21. (stehlen) Sie _____

22. (treten) du _____

23. (raten) ihr _____

24. (wissen) ich _____

25. (sprechen) man _____

26. (raten) sie (*sing.*) _____

27. (geschehen) was _____

28. (lassen) es _____

29. (haben) du _____

30. (wissen) wir _____

ÜBUNG

8·7

Using the word in parentheses as the new subject, rewrite the sentence as a question.

FOR EXAMPLE: (er) Wir lernen Deutsch.

Lernt er Deutsch?

1. (man) Wir sprechen Englisch.

_____

2. (du) Sie läuft nach Hause (*home, homeward*).

_____

3. (er) Ich nehme die Fahrkarten.

_____

4. (ihr) Sie gibt kein Geld.

_____

5. (er) Sie fahren nach Hause.

_____

6. (wer) Wir sehen die Bibliothek.

_____

7. (sie [*pl.*]) Sie isst kein Brot (*bread*).

_____

8. (ich) Ihr empfehlt den Roman.

_____

9. (du) Ich fange den Ball (*ball*).

_____

10. (er) Wir wissen nichts (*nothing*).

_____

11. (Sie) Sie tritt mir auf den Fuß (*steps on my foot*).

_____

12. (Thomas) Ich helfe Sonja und Sabine.

_____

13. (du) Wir lesen die Zeitung.

_____

14. (sie [*sing.*]) Er bricht sich den Arm (*breaks his arm*).

_____

15. (meine Schwester) Ich trage einen Pullover.

_____

See Appendix A for a complete list of verbs with present tense irregularities.

Verbs with stem-vowel changes from *a* to *ä* and *au* to *äu*

Many verbs with a stem vowel of **a** change in the second-person singular (**du**) and third-person singular (**er, sie, es**) from **a** to **ä**. Verbs with **au** change to **äu**. There is no change in the endings of these verbs in the present tense.

	fallen (*to fall*)	**laufen** (*to run*)
ich	falle	laufe
du	fällst	läufst
er, sie, es	fällt	läuft
wir	fallen	laufen
ihr	fallt	lauft
sie/Sie	fallen	laufen

Common verbs with a vowel change from **a** to **ä** or **au** to **äu** are:

backen	to bake	**lassen**	to let
blasen	to blow	**laufen**	to run
braten	to roast	**raten**	to guess, to advise
einladen	to invite	**wachsen**	to grow
empfangen	to receive	**saufen**	to drink (*said of animals*)
fahren	to go (*by vehicle*)	**schlafen**	to sleep
fangen	to catch	**schlagen**	to hit
gefallen	to please	**verlassen**	to leave
halten	to hold, to stop	**waschen**	to wash

Your friends are discussing how long various people would like to sleep after a late night out. Make sentences out of the cues given.

EXAMPLE: ich—11 Uhr
Ich schlafe bis elf Uhr.

1. der Peter—12 Uhr _____

2. die Eltern—7 Uhr _____

3. Steffi und Ulla—2 Uhr nachmittags _____

4. du—10 Uhr _____

5. Luise—9 Uhr _____

*You and your friends are at a marathon and are discussing how everyone is running. Make sentences out of the cues given, using a form of **laufen**.*

EXAMPLE: ich—schnell
Ich laufe schnell.

1. die Liesel—langsam _____

2. die Kinder—nicht _____

3. du—schnell _____

4. der Lehrer—schneller _____

5. ihr—am schnellsten _____

Peter has a day off. See what happens to him. Complete the sentences with the correct verb form.

EXAMPLE: Peter _____ (gehen) zum Auto.
          Peter geht zum Auto.

1. Peter _____ (haben) einen freien Tag.

2. Er _____ (empfangen) eine Einladung von seinen Freunden.

3. Er _____ (fahren) mit ihnen aufs Land.

4. Es _____ (sein) ein schöner Tag.

5. Die Sonne _____ (scheinen) und der Wind (blasen) nicht.

6. Dort _____ (wachsen) viele wilde Blumen, hier (wachsen) ein großer Baum.

7. Das Auto _____ (halten) unter einem Baum.

8. Sie (*pl.*) _____ (verlassen) das Auto.

9. Sie (*pl.*) _____ (spielen) Ball.

10. Peter _____ (fangen) den Ball.

11. Hans _____ (laufen) schnell hin und her.

12. Manchmal _____ (lassen) er den Ball fallen.

13. Jetzt _____ (haben) Peter, Hans, und Max Hunger.

14. Hans _____ (braten) Würstchen.

15. Eine Wurst_____ (fallen) auf das Gras.

16. Das _____ (machen) nichts.

17. Die Jungen _____ (waschen) sich die Hände und essen.

18. _____ (waschen) du dir die Hände bevor du isst?

19. Alles _____ (schmecken) gut.

20. Max _____ (schlafen) jetzt.

21. Die anderen _____ (lesen) ein Buch.

22. Der Tag _____ (gefallen) ihnen sehr gut.

23. Abends _____ (fahren) sie (*pl.*) nach Hause.

Verbs with a stem-vowel change from *e* to *i* or to *ie*

Some verbs have a vowel change from **e** to **i** or to **ie** in the second- and third-person singular. Again there is no change in the endings of these verbs in the present tense.

	geben (*to give*)	**sehen** (*to see*)
ich	gebe	sehe
du	gibst	siehst
er/sie/es	gibt	sieht
wir	geben	sehen
ihr	gebt	seht
sie/Sie	geben	sehen

Common verbs with a vowel change from **e** to **i**:

brechen	to break	**sterben**	to die
essen	to eat	**treffen**	to meet
geben	to give	**treten**	to step
helfen	to help	**vergessen**	to forget
nehmen	to take	**werfen**	to throw
sprechen	to speak		

Note: the following are other spelling changes that take place in the second- and third-person singular:

- **nehmen** drops the **h** and doubles the **m: du nimmst, er/sie/es nimmt**

- **treten** adds a **t: du trittst, er tritt**

ÜBUNG
8·11

Was essen wir? *Let's decide what everyone will eat. Make sentences using the cues given.*

EXAMPLE: Lotte—Kekse
Lotte isst Kekse.

1. ich—Kuchen _____

2. Max—Brötchen _____

3. die Großeltern—Schinken _____

4. der Chef—Speck _____

5. die Familie—Tomaten _____

6. du—Eis _____

7. wir—Brot _____

8. ihr—Sauerkraut _____

9. Herr Schmidt, Sie—Erdbeertorte _____

10. Frau Braun—Hähnchen _____

Common verbs with a vowel change from **e** to **ie**:

befehlen	to command, order
empfehlen	to recommend
geschehen	to happen
lesen	to read
sehen	to see
stehlen	to steal

ÜBUNG
8·12

Was lesen wir? What is everyone reading? Make sentences using the cues given.

EXAMPLE: Lotte—den Brief
Lotte liest den Brief.

1. ich—die Zeitung _____

2. er—den Roman _____

3. wir—die Nachrichten _____

4. du—den Brief _____

5. die Geschwister—die Postkarte _____

6. Herr Wagner—den Bericht _____

7. ihr—die Bücher _____

8. Frau Schmidt, Sie—das Buch _____

9. Peter und ich—die Geschichte _____

10. Fräulein Brunn und Frau Mahl, Sie—das Gedicht _____

ÜBUNG
8·13

*You have become close friends with a colleague. Though you used to say **Sie** to each other,
you now use **du** (**Ihr duzt euch jetzt**.), and therefore the questions he used to ask you using
the **Sie** form need to be rephrased using **du**.*

EXAMPLE: Wie lange helfen Sie dem Kind?
Wie lange hilfst du dem Kind?

1. Wie lange fahren Sie Auto? _____

2. Wie lange arbeiten Sie hier? _____

3. Wie lange lernen Sie Deutsch? _____

4. Wie lange sammeln Sie Briefmarken? _____

5. Wie lange braten Sie den Schinken? _____

6. Wie lange schlafen Sie am Wochenende? _____

7. Wie lange lesen Sie abends? _____

8. Wie lange laufen Sie jeden Morgen? _____

9. Wie oft empfangen Sie Gäste? _____

10. Wie lange lächeln Sie schon? _____

11. Wie lange backen Sie den Kuchen? _____

12. Wie lange reden Sie über Politik? _____

13. Wie lange beobachten Sie die Kinder? _____

14. Wie lange fürchten Sie sich vor dem Krieg? (dich) _____

15. Wie lange beten Sie abends? _____

ÜBUNG

8·14

Answer the following questions using nicht oft.

EXAMPLE: Wie oft sprichst du Deutsch?
Ich spreche nicht oft Deutsch.

1. Wie oft klingelst du schon? _____

2. Wie oft schüttelst du den Apfelbaum? _____

3. Wie oft änderst du die Haare? _____

4. Wie oft verbesserst du das Kind? _____

5. Wie oft flüsterst du mit dem Freund? _____

6. Wie oft fährst du Auto? _____

7. Wie oft feierst du Geburtstag? _____

8. Wie oft redest du mit Marie? _____

9. Wie oft badest du den Hund? _____

10. Wie oft erinnerst du ihn an den Geburtstag? _____

You receive a letter from your best friend. Of course, you are anxious to read it. However, as you walk back from the mailbox it is raining and some of the letters get smeared. Correct the letter before you put it away.

EXAMPLE: L_____be Inge!
Liebe Inge!

Jetzt b _____ ich schon zwei Wochen in der Schweiz. Wir wohn _____am

See. Die Berge s_____ groß und schön. Ich klett _____oft in den Bergen.

Beate _____ (helfen) mir dabei. Sie mach _____es viel besser. Pauline

klett _____ nicht mit uns. Sie läuf _____ jeden Morgen. Dann

trink _____ Pauline viel Wasser und _____ss _____ viel Obst. Sie

g _____ b _____ mir auch Obst zum Essen. Ich nehm _____ es

natürlich gern. N _____ du Obst wenn man es dir g _____ b _____ ?

Später treff _____ wir uns mit Freunden. Max verg _____ ss _____ oft

zu kommen. Das _____ t schade. Luise tr _____ fft uns immer. Nachmittags

lesen wir oft. Pauline l _____ einen französischen Roman. Sie läch _____ oft

beim Lesen. Montags komm _____ immer eine Frau und wasch _____ die

Wäsche für uns. Sie spr _____ nicht mit uns. Sie i _____ immer still und

arbeit _____ schnell. Das si _____ unsere Ferien. Hoffentlich

g _____ b _____ es gutes Wetter bis wir nach Hause komm _____ .

Ich habe es nicht gern wenn der Wind bl _____ st. Tr _____ ff _____

du mich im Café wenn ich wieder zu Hause bin?

Deine Emma

Imperatives

Imperatives are commands given, for the most part, to the second-person pronoun *you*. In English, the infinitive of a verb without the particle word *to* is used to give a casual command and the same form with the addition of the word *please* is used to give a more formal or polite command:

Sit down.   *Sit down, please.*   *Sign here.*   *Sign here, please.*

German is similar but not identical. For one thing, German has three forms for the pronoun *you*: **du**, **ihr**, and **Sie**. Therefore, there are three imperative forms that correspond to the usual uses of those three pronouns: informal singular, informal plural, and formal singular or plural, respectively:

du imperative + predicate → command
ihr imperative + predicate → command
Sie imperative + predicate → command

With many German verbs, the stem of the verb becomes the stem of the imperative form. The stem of a verb is the infinitive minus the -(e)n ending (**machen** – **mach**). The **du**-form adds an -**e** to the stem, the **ihr**-form adds a -**t**, and the **Sie**-form adds an -**en** and is paired with the pronoun **Sie**. Look at the following examples:

	DU	IHR	SIE	
lachen	lache!	lacht!	lachen Sie!	*laugh*
kaufen	kaufe!	kauft!	kaufen Sie!	*buy*
warten	warte!	wartet!	warten Sie!	*wait*

The -**e** ending of the **du**-form is optional for most verbs. However, if the stem of the verb ends in -**d** or -**t** the ending is not optional and must be retained:

stellen	stell(e)!	stellt!	stellen Sie!	*put*
senden	sende!	sendet!	senden Sie!	*broadcast*
streiten	streite!	streitet!	streiten Sie!	*quarrel*

If a verb requires an umlaut in the second- and third-persons singular in the present tense conjugations, for example, **tragen—trägst**, **trägt** (*to carry*), the imperative forms follow the pattern above and the umlaut is not used:

- ♦ **Du** imperative:

    verb stem(e) + !
    Schlag(e) + !
    Hit!

- ♦ **Ihr** imperative:

    verb stem + -t + !
    Schlagt + !
    Hit!

- ♦ **Sie** imperative:

    verb stem + -en + Sie + !
    Schlagen + Sie + !
    Hit!

But if a verb forms its singular second- and third-persons present tense conjugations with a vowel shift to -**i**- or -**ie**-, the **du**-form of the imperative is formed from the second-person present tense conjugation (**du**) minus the -**st** ending and never adds an -**e** ending. The other two forms follow the previous pattern. For example:

geben	gib!	gebt!	geben Sie!	*give*
helfen	hilf!	helft!	helfen Sie!	*help*
sehen	sieh!	seht!	sehen Sie!	*see*

A notable exception to this rule is **werden**:

werden	werde!	werdet!	werden Sie!	*become*

The only verb that has its own imperative pattern is **sein**. It forms the imperative from the infinitive:

sein	sei!	seid!	seien Sie!	*be*

Inseparable and separable prefixes act the same way in an imperative sentence as they do in any other sentence:

besuchen	besuche!	besucht!	besuchen Sie!	*visit*
zuhören	hör zu!	hört zu!	hören Sie zu!	*listen*

Note that imperatives are punctuated with an exclamation point in German.

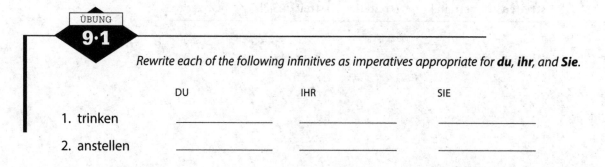

ÜBUNG
9·1

*Rewrite each of the following infinitives as imperatives appropriate for **du**, **ihr**, and **Sie**.*

	DU	IHR	SIE
1. trinken	_____	_____	_____
2. anstellen	_____	_____	_____

3. tun   _____   _____   _____

4. brechen   _____   _____   _____

5. empfehlen   _____   _____   _____

6. abfahren   _____   _____   _____

7. sein   _____   _____   _____

8. nehmen   _____   _____   _____

9. essen   _____   _____   _____

10. stehlen   _____   _____   _____

*Using the word or phrase in parentheses as your cue, write an appropriate **du-**, **ihr-**, or **Sie-**form command with the infinitive provided.*

EXAMPLE: (Kind) gehen   <u>Geh zur Schule!</u>

1. (Mutter und Vater) helfen _____

2. (Doktor Schmidt) essen _____

3. (Richter) schreiben _____

4. (Arzt und Pflegerin) besuchen _____

5. (Bruder) sein _____

6. (Hund) fressen _____

7. (Freund) einladen _____

8. (Tochter) werden _____

9. (Kinder) antworten _____

10. (Touristen) aussteigen _____

Addressing groups

There is another form of imperative that is used when a command is not directed at any particular individual and is meant to give information to people at large instead. These imperatives can be heard over loudspeakers or read on signs in public places. Their formation is quite simple: The infinitive is used as the imperative form and is usually found at the end of the phrase. For example:

Den Rasen nicht betreten!	*Keep off the grass.*
Nicht rauchen!	*No smoking.*
Gepäck aufmachen!	*Open (your) baggage.*

Change the following infinitives to imperatives that address people in general. The information in parentheses tells where the action takes place. Add any necessary words.

EXAMPLE: aufmachen (*at the border*)
            <u>Gepäck aufmachen!</u>

1. zurückbleiben (*on the platform as a train arrives*)

   _____

2. anfassen (*a sign on a museum exhibit*)

   _____

3. anstellen (*an announcement about where to line up*)

   _____

4. aussteigen (*an announcement to get off the streetcar*)

   _____

5. sitzen bleiben (*a sign indicating that one should remain seated in this area*)

   _____

Imperatives with **wir**

Most commands are given to the second person pronoun *you*. But in both English and German it is possible to include yourself in the command and thereby make it seem a bit more polite. In fact, it sounds more like a suggestion than an imperative. In English, this is done by beginning a verb phrase with *let's*:

Let's get something to eat.	*Let's leave soon.*

The German version of this type of command is equally simple. The present tense conjugation of a verb in the first person plural (**wir**) with the verb preceding the pronoun is all that is required:

Essen wir im italienischen Restaurant!	*Let's eat at an Italian restaurant.*
Kaufen wir einen neuen Wagen!	*Let's buy a new car.*
Fahren wir jetzt ab!	*Let's leave now.*

verb 1 wir 1 complement 1 !
Gehen + wir + nach Hause + !
Let's go home.

A similar expression is formed by using the verb **lassen** (*to let*). It can include the speaker or not, as we shall see below, but must conform, regardless, to the second-person pronoun required by the circumstances: informal or formal, singular or plural. Therefore, a distinction is made among the **du**-, **ihr**-, and **Sie**-forms. First, let us look at the basic imperative, meaning *let*, not *let's* (i.e., not including the speaker). For example:

Lass ihn ausreden! (du)	*Let him finish speaking.*
Lasst die Kinder spielen! (ihr)	*Let the children play.*
Lassen Sie sie warten! (Sie)	*Let them wait.*

lass/lasst/lassen Sie 1 object 1 infinitive 1 !
Lassen Sie + ihn + mitkommen + !
Let him come along.

If you add the accusative pronoun **uns** (*us*) to the equation, you have once again a form that means *let's*. For example:

Lass uns nicht mehr streiten! (du)   *Let's not quarrel anymore.*
Lasst uns bald gehen! (ihr)   *Let's go soon.*
Lassen Sie uns darüber sprechen! (Sie)   *Let's talk about it.*

lass uns/lasst uns/lassen Sie uns 1 complement 1 !
Lass uns + jetzt gehen + !
Let's go now.

ÜBUNG
9·4

Rewrite the following sentences as imperatives with **wir**. *Careful: The sentences provided are in a variety of tenses.*

EXAMPLE: Er ging schnell nach Hause.

                         Gehen wir schnell nach Hause!

1. Die Freunde segelten in den Hafen.

   _____

2. Die Frau ist am Marktplatz eingestiegen.

   _____

3. Sie aßen im Schnellimbiss.

   _____

4. Sie liest die amerikanischen Zeitungen.

   _____

5. Ihr seid nicht um die Ecke gefahren.

   _____

6. Er legte die Kinder aufs Bett.

   _____

7. Ich muss einen Polizisten fragen, wo die Bank ist.

   _____

*Rewrite each sentence with **lassen** to form an imperative that begins with the meaning* let. *Conjugate **lassen** for the pronoun **du**. Then rewrite the imperative changing the direct object to **uns** and thereby the meaning of the verb to* let's.

EXAMPLE: Martin spricht darüber.

  <u>Lass Martin darüber sprechen!</u>

  <u>Lass uns darüber sprechen!</u>

1. Sie schlafen morgen aus.

  a. _____

  b. _____

2. Er ißt den letzten Apfel.

  a. _____

  b. _____

3. Er schwimmt nicht im kalten Fluss.

  a. _____

  b. _____

*Follow the same directions, but conjugate **lassen** for **ihr** instead of **du**.*

4. Die Mädchen spielen mit den Kindern.

  a. _____

  b. _____

5. Er besucht die neue Kunsthalle.

  a. _____

  b. _____

*Follow the same directions, but conjugate **lassen** for **Sie** instead of **du**.*

6. Sie fängt um achtzehn Uhr an.

  a. _____

  b. _____

7. Herr Bauer kehrt in die Heimat zurück.

  a. _____

  b. _____

Imperatives

The imperative form is the command form of a verb. In English there is only one imperative form, and it is the base form, or infinitive, of a verb. For example:

> *Sit.*
> *Stand up.*
> *Go away.*
> *Be as quiet as possible.*

Imperatives are directed at the second person (*you*), and since there are three forms of *you* in German, there are three imperative forms, one for each of these pronouns: **du**, informal singular; **ihr**, informal plural; and **Sie**, formal singular or plural.

The **du**-form is derived from the infinitive with the -**en** ending omitted. Sometimes, an optional **e** is added to this imperative form.

Lach! (Lache!)	*Laugh!*	Komm! (Komme!)	*Come!*	Sing! (Singe!)	*Sing!*
Spiel!	*Play!*	Such!	*Search!*	Trink!	*Drink!*
Lern!	*Learn!*	Wein!	*Cry!*	Schreib!	*Write!*

If an infinitive ends in -**eln**, -**ern**, -**igen**, or -**men**, the -**e** ending is not optional and must be included in the **du** imperative.

Öffne! (öffnen)	*Open!*	Entschuldige! (entschuldigen)	*Excuse!*
Atme! (atmen)	*Breathe!*	Lächele! (lächeln)	*Smile!*
Wandere! (wandern)	*Hike!*	Behandele! (behandeln)	*Treat!*

If the present tense of a verb is irregular and has an umlaut in the second-person and third-person singular, that umlaut does not occur in the imperative. However, if the irregularity is a change from **e** to **i** or **ie**, that form of irregularity appears in the **du** imperative. For example:

Fahr! (*Drive!*)	fahren, du fährst, er fährt
Lauf! (*Run!*)	laufen, du läufst, er läuft
Gib! (*Give!*)	geben, du gibst, er gibt
Sieh! (*See!*)	sehen, du siehst, er sieht

The **ihr** imperative is in most cases identical to the present tense conjugation for **ihr**. The same is true of the **Sie** imperative, except that the pronoun **Sie** accompanies the imperative form. For example:

INFINITIVE	**IHR** IMPERATIVE	**SIE** IMPERATIVE	
lachen	Lacht!	Lachen Sie!	*Laugh!*
arbeiten	Arbeitet!	Arbeiten Sie!	*Work!*
geben	Gebt!	Geben Sie!	*Give!*
helfen	Helft!	Helfen Sie!	*Help!*

*In the blanks provided, write the **du**, **ihr**, and **Sie** imperative forms for each infinitive.*

INFINITIVE	DU	IHR	SIE
1. trinken			
2. kaufen			
3. nehmen			
4. paddeln			
5. schlafen			
6. gehen			
7. sprechen			
8. hören			
9. stehlen			
10. schwimmen			

The separable prefixes separate from the verb in the imperative, but the inseparable prefixes remain affixed to the verb. For example:

ausgeben (*spend*)	Gib aus!	Gebt aus!	Geben Sie aus!
verkaufen (*sell*)	Verkauf!	Verkauft!	Verkaufen Sie!

*In the blanks provided, write the **du**, **ihr**, and **Sie** imperative forms for each infinitive.*

INFINITIVE	DU	IHR	SIE
1. abfahren			
2. gewinnen			
3. bekommen			
4. mitbringen			
5. zumachen			
6. versuchen			
7. erschlagen			
8. ansehen			
9. aufhören			
10. ankommen			

The verbs **haben**, **sein**, and **werden** always play a special role, and their imperatives are no exception.

haben	Hab!	Habt!	Haben Sie!
sein	Sei!	Seid!	Seien Sie!
werden	Werde!	Werdet!	Werden Sie!

ÜBUNG
9·8

*Rewrite each sentence as an imperative. But take care to use the correct form for **du**, **ihr**, or **Sie**. The words in parentheses are your signal to tell you to whom the imperative is addressed, and you need to provide the form that is appropriate for an informal singular or plural imperative or the form that is appropriate for a formal singular or plural imperative.*

FOR EXAMPLE: Die Kinder spielen Tennis. *The children play tennis.*

(Herr Braun) _____*Spielen Sie Tennis!*_____ (Herr Braun is addressed formally.)

1. Meine Mutter ist gesund. *My mother is well.*

   (das Kind) _____

2. Der Mann steht auf. *The man stands up.*

   (Professor Schmidt) _____

3. Sie machen die Fenster auf. *They open the windows.*

   (Hans und Sabine) _____

4. Die Männer essen in der Küche. *The men eat in the kitchen.*

   (Karl) _____

5. Meine Eltern besuchen Onkel Heinz. *My parents visit Uncle Heinz.*

   (Tina, Max und Erik) _____

6. Ich verkaufe den alten Wagen. *I sell the old car.*

   (Frau Schneider) _____

7. Wir warten an der Tür. *We wait at the door.*

   (mein Bruder) _____

8. Die Touristen sprechen nur Deutsch. *The tourists only speak German.*

   (Thomas) _____

9. Die Gäste kommen um sieben Uhr. *The guests come at seven o'clock.*

   (Herr Benz und Frau Keller) _____

10. Sie helfen mir damit. *They help me with that.*

    (mein Freund) _____

The present perfect tense

Usage of the present perfect tense

In oral conversation, when speaking about something that has happened in the past, German uses the *present perfect tense*:

Ich habe gegessen.	*I have eaten.*
Ich habe gekauft.	*I have bought.*

In English there are different ways of saying the same thing: *I have eaten, I have been eating, I did eat*, and most often, *I ate*; or *I have bought, I have been buying, I did buy*, and again most often, *I bought*. In German, since the present perfect tense is the tense most often used in speech, it is often called the *conversational past*. The present perfect tense is also used in all kinds of informal writing.

Formation of the present perfect tense

In German, as in English, the present perfect tense is a compound tense. It is formed by using the present tense of **haben** or **sein** and the past participle (**gekauft**—*bought*, **gesagt**—*said*). The helping verb **haben** or **sein** is conjugated and must agree with the subject. The past participle is placed in the final position, except in a dependent clause.

Ich **habe** das Buch **gekauft**.	*I **have bought** the book.*
Du **hast** das Buch **gekauft**.	*You **have bought** the book.*
Er/sie/es **hat** das Buch **gekauft**.	*He/she/it **has bought** the book.*
Wir **haben** das Buch **gekauft**.	*We **have bought** the book.*
Ihr **habt** das Buch **gekauft**.	*You (pl.) **have bought** the book.*
Sie/Sie **haben** das Buch **gekauft**.	*They/You (form.) **have bought** the book.*

Ich **bin** in die Schule **gegangen**.	*I **have gone** to school.*
Du **bist** in die Schule **gegangen**.	*You **have gone** to school.*
Er/sie/es **ist** in die Schule **gegangen**.	*He/she/it **has gone** to school.*
Wir **sind** in die Schule **gegangen**.	*We **have gone** to school.*
Ihr **seid** in die Schule **gegangen**.	*You (pl.) **have gone** to school.*
Sie/Sie **sind** in die Schule **gegangen**.	*They/You (form.) **have gone** to school.*

German verbs may be broken up into two major groups: weak and strong. The way in which the past tense of the verb is formed determines whether a verb is weak or strong. A weak verb does not change its stem in the past tense forms. A strong verb changes its stem vowel and sometimes the consonants in the past tense forms, as can be seen in the verb shown above—**gehen/ gegangen**.

Present perfect tense of weak verbs

The present perfect tense is a compound tense, so you need a helping verb. Weak verbs take the helping verb **haben**. **Haben** must be conjugated to agree with the subject.

Weak verbs do not change their stems in the past tense forms (**er hat gespielt, er spielte**—*he has played, he played* / **ich habe getanzt, ich tanzte**—*I have danced, I danced*).

Regular weak verbs form their past participles by adding the prefix **ge-** to the third-person singular. Therefore, the past participle of **sagen**, as an example, is formed like this:

> third-person singular of **sagen** is **sagt**
> no stem change
> add the prefix **ge-**:
> = **gesagt**

Here is a conjugation of all persons:

Ich **habe** nichts **gesagt**.	*I **have said** nothing.*
Du **hast** nichts **gesagt**.	*You **have said** nothing.*
Er/sie/es **hat** nichts **gesagt**.	*He/she/it **has said** nothing.*
Wir **haben** nichts **gesagt**.	*We **have said** nothing.*
Ihr **habt** nichts **gesagt**.	*You (pl.) **have said** nothing.*
Sie/Sie **haben** nichts **gesagt**.	*They/You (form.) **have said** nothing.*

-d, -t, -et; -m, -n

If the stem of the verb ends in **-d** or **-t**, you add an **-e-** between the stem and the **-t** suffix, as in the present tense: **arbeiten, gearbeitet; baden, gebadet**. To aid pronunciation an **-e-** is also added between the stem and the **-t** suffix in some verbs whose stems end in **-m** or **-n**: **öffnen, geöffnet; atmen, geatmet**; but **lernen, gelernt; wohnen, gewohnt**.

ÜBUNG
10·1

Your father wants you to mow the lawn. Tell your father that it has already been done.

EXAMPLE: Luise. _____
Luise hat es schon gemacht.

1. Opa _____.

2. Ich _____.

3. Herr Lange _____.

4. Wir _____.

5. Jakob und Michael _____.

6. Herr Müller und Frau Müller _____.

7. Emma _____.

Mother wants you to do a number of things before you go away for the weekend. Tell her you have already done these.

EXAMPLE: Deck den Tisch.

Ich habe den Tisch schon gedeckt.

1. Kauf Brot. _____

2. Spiel mit Ännchen. _____

3. Öffne die Fenster. _____

4. Bade den Hund. _____

5. Pack den Koffer. _____

6. Putz das Zimmer. _____

7. Arbeite im Garten. _____

8. Besuch die Nachbarn. _____

9. Lern Spanisch. _____

10. Antworte dem Vater. _____

Tante Gretel comes for a visit and tells all the news about her family and the rest of the relatives. Change the following sentences to the present perfect tense.

EXAMPLE: Benita lernt Polnisch.

Benita hat Polnisch gelernt.

1. Onkel Dieter und Tante Edith bauen ein neues Haus. _____

2. Es kostet viel Geld. _____

3. Sie borgen Geld auf der Bank. _____

4. Sie arbeiten viel im Haus. _____

5. Tante Edith putzt die Fenster oft. _____

6. Sie kauft neue Möbel. _____

7. Sie wünscht sich einen schönen Garten. _____

8. Sie sucht Blumen für den Garten. _____

9. Sie braucht viel Geld. _____

10. Sie zeigt das Haus den Freunden. _____

11. Das Haus macht ihr Freude. _____

12. Opa und Oma atmen oft laut. _____

13. Sie wohnen nicht mehr alleine. _____

14. Oma weint oft. _____

15. Sie sagt nicht viel. _____

16. Die Zwillinge spielen Ball. _____

17. Sie baden oft. _____

18. Sie lachen laut. _____

19. Sabine tanzt mit dem neuen Freund. _____

20. Sie wartet oft auf Post von ihm. _____

haben or *sein* as the Auxiliary Verb in Perfect Tenses

Although **haben** is used as the helping verb by most verbs in the present perfect tense, **sein** is used by some instead of **haben**. When the main verb shows a change of position (such as running, but not dancing [since you can dance in one place]) or a change of condition (such as dying), **sein** is used. These sentences show a change of position:

Er ist nach Hause gegangen.   *He has gone home.*
Die Kinder sind in den Park gelaufen.   *The children have run to the park.*

sein with a Change of Position

The following are common verbs that show a change of position and therefore take sein as a helping verb:

fahren	**ist gefahren**	to go (by vehicle)
fallen	**ist gefallen**	to fall
fliegen	**ist geflogen**	to fly
folgen	**ist gefolgt**	to follow
gehen	**ist gegangen**	to go
kommen	**ist gekommen**	to come
kriechen	**ist gekrochen**	to creep, to crawl
laufen	**ist gelaufen**	to run
reisen	**ist gereist**	to travel
reiten	**ist geritten**	to ride (on horseback)

rennen	ist gerannt	to run
schwimmen	ist geschwommen	to swim
sinken	ist gesunken	to sink
springen	ist gesprungen	to jump

ÜBUNG
10·4

Axel and his friends spend an afternoon in the park. Insert the correct helping verb, either haben or sein, in the space provided.

EXAMPLE: Axel _____ in den Park gekommen.

*Axel **ist** in den Park gekommen.*

1. Die Kinder _____ in den Park gegangen.

2. Dort _____ sie (*pl.*) Ball gespielt.

3. Axel _____ an den See gelaufen.

4. Er _____ den Ball ins Wasser geworfen.

5. Der Ball _____ tief gesunken.

6. Axel _____ ins Wasser gesprungen.

7. Er _____ den Ball geholt.

8. Er _____ ans Ufer geschwommen.

9. Dann _____ er auf das Gras gekrochen.

10. Die anderen Kinder _____ da auf ihn gewartet.

sein with a Change of Condition

You will see a change of condition in these sentences:

Das Kind **ist** schnell eingeschlafen.   *The child **has** fallen asleep quickly.*
Wir **sind** nicht krank geworden.   *We **did** not become ill.*

The following verbs show a change of condition and therefore take **sein** as a helping verb:

aufwachen	ist aufgewacht	to wake up
einschlafen	ist eingeschlafen	to fall asleep
ertrinken	ist ertrunken	to drown
gebären	hat geboren	to give birth
	ist geboren	to be born
geschehen	ist geschehen	to happen
passieren	ist passiert	to happen
sterben	ist gestorben	to die
wachsen	ist gewachsen	to grow
werden	ist geworden	to become

Heiko's teacher asks the class what they know about Johann Wolfgang von Goethe. Supply the correct missing helping verb in the students' answers.

EXAMPLE: Silke: Goethe _____ *Faust geschrieben.*
Silke: Goethe **hat** *Faust geschrieben.*

1. Thomas: Goethe _____ in Frankfurt geboren.

2. Heide: Dort _____ er aufgewachsen.

3. Erika: Er _____ in Straßburg studiert.

4. Ute: Er _____ da eine Pastorstochter geliebt.

5. Sebastian: Er _____ viele Gedichte geschrieben.

6. Fritz: In 1786 _____ er nach Italien gereist.

7. Heike: Er _____ in Mittenwald übernachtet.

8. Michael: _____ er da gleich eingeschlafen?

9. Annchen: In Goethes Leben _____ wirklich viel passiert.

10. Franz: 1832 _____ Goethe gestorben.

sein with Verbs of Rest

Sein is also used with two verbs of rest: **sein**—*to be*; **bleiben**—*to remain.*

Er ist im Geschäft gewesen.   *He has been in the store. (He was in the store.)*
Ich bin im Bett geblieben.   *I have stayed in bed. (I stayed in bed.)*

Where is Werner? Fill in the correct helping verb in the space provided.

EXAMPLE: Werner _____ in der Schule geblieben.
Werner **ist** *in der Schule geblieben.*

1. Werner _____ nicht hier gewesen.

2. Er _____ zu Hause geblieben.

3. Er _____ krank geworden.

4. Dann _____ er viel Saft getrunken.

5. Seine Großeltern _____ bei ihm geblieben.

haben with Some Verbs of Motion

Some verbs of motion can take a direct object. When this is done, the verb takes haben as a helping verb.

Ich habe das neue Auto gefahren.	*I have driven the new car.*
Der Pilot hat die Passagiere nach München geflogen.	*The pilot has flown the passengers to Munich.*

Haben is also used when the verb indicates motion within a place rather than motion toward a place.

Der Junge hat im See geschwommen.	*The boy swam in the lake.*
Das Kind hat auf dem Teppich gekrochen.	*The child crawled on the carpet.*

ÜBUNG
10·7

Jörg has a rushed morning. In the following sentences he tells about it. Supply the correct form of the helping verb (haben or sein).

EXAMPLE: Er _____ ins Wasser gefallen.
Er ist ins Wasser gefallen.

1. Ich _____ früh aufgestanden.

2. Ich _____ nicht lange im Bett gelegen.

3. Ich _____ ins Bad gegangen.

4. Ich _____ mir die Zähne geputzt.

5. In der Küche _____ ich Orangensaft getrunken.

6. Ich _____ auch Toast gegessen.

7. Leider _____ ein Stück Toast auf den Fußboden gefallen.

8. Es _____ mir schon einmal passiert.

9. Es _____ da nicht liegen geblieben.

10. Ich _____ es in den Müll geworfen.

11. Es _____ spät geworden.

12. Ich _____ an die Bushaltestelle gelaufen.

13. Ich _____ auf den Bus gewartet.

14. Der Bus _____ gleich gekommen.

15. Ich _____ eingestiegen.

16. Im Bus _____ ich nach hinten gegangen.

17. Ich _____ mich hingesetzt.

18. Ich _____ etwas die Zeitung gelesen.

19. Ich _____ so müde gewesen.

20. Dann _____ ich eingeschlafen.

21. Der Busfahrer _____ mich aufgeweckt.

22. Ich _____ schwer aufgewacht.

23. Ich _____ alle meine Sachen genommen.

24. Ich _____ an die Bustür gegangen.

25. Dann _____ ich ausgestiegen.

26. Es _____ ein kalter Morgen gewesen.

27. Ich _____ nicht zu spät gekommen. Ich mag meine Arbeit nicht. Ich möchte lieber Busfahrer werden.

28. Ich _____ aber noch nie einen Bus gefahren.

29. Na ja, wenn ich reich geworden _____, brauche ich nicht arbeiten.

30. Bis jetzt _____ das aber noch nicht geschehen!

Present perfect tense of strong verbs

A strong verb changes its stem and sometimes its consonants when forming the past or perfect tenses. The past participle of strong verbs is formed by adding **ge-** to the beginning and **-(e)n** to the end of the stem (**getan** is an exception).

laufen	**ge**lauf**en**
sehen	**ge**seh**en**

Besides that, many strong verbs change the stem vowel in the past participle from **i** to **u**, **e** to **a**, **e** to **o**, etc.:

gehen	geg**a**ngen
sprechen	gespr**o**chen

Common verbs with a change from **e** to **o**:

befehlen	**befohlen**	to order, command
brechen	**gebrochen**	to break
empfehlen	**empfohlen**	to recommend
heben	**gehoben**	to lift
nehmen	**genommen**	to take
sprechen	**gesprochen**	to speak
stehlen	**gestohlen**	to steal
sterben	**gestorben**	to die
treffen	**getroffen**	to meet
werfen	**geworfen**	to throw

Common verbs with a change from **e** to **a**:

gehen	**gegangen**	to go
stehen	**gestanden**	to stand

Common verbs with a change from **i**, **ie**, or **ü** to **o**:

fliegen	**geflogen**	to fly
frieren	**gefroren**	to freeze
lügen	**gelogen**	to lie
riechen	**gerochen**	to smell
schieben	**geschoben**	to push
schließen	**geschlossen**	to close
schwimmen	**geschwommen**	to swim
verlieren	**verloren**	to lose
ziehen	**gezogen**	to pull, to move (change residence)

Common verbs with a change from **ei** to **i** or **ie**:

beißen	**gebissen**	to bite
greifen	**gegriffen**	to grab
leihen	**geliehen**	to lend
pfeifen	**gepfiffen**	to whistle
reiten	**geritten**	to ride (on horseback)
schreiben	**geschrieben**	to write
schweigen	**geschwiegen**	to keep quiet
steigen	**gestiegen**	to climb
streiten	**gestritten**	to quarrel

Common verbs with a change from **i** to **u**:

binden	**gebunden**	to tie
finden	**gefunden**	to find
singen	**gesungen**	to sing
sinken	**gesunken**	to sink
springen	**gesprungen**	to jump
trinken	**getrunken**	to drink

Common verbs with a change from **i** or **ie** to **e**:

bitten	**gebeten**	to ask
liegen	**gelegen**	to lie (down)
sitzen	**gesessen**	to sit

Other common verbs:

essen	**gegessen**	to eat
haben	**gehabt**	to have
sein	**gewesen**	to be
tun	**getan**	to do
werden	**geworden**	to become, to get

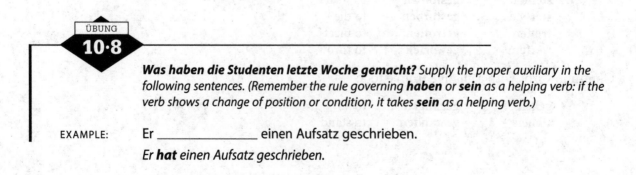

ÜBUNG
10·8

Was haben die Studenten letzte Woche gemacht? *Supply the proper auxiliary in the following sentences. (Remember the rule governing **haben** or **sein** as a helping verb: if the verb shows a change of position or condition, it takes **sein** as a helping verb.)*

EXAMPLE: Er _____ einen Aufsatz geschrieben.

*Er **hat** einen Aufsatz geschrieben.*

1. Sie (*pl.*) _____ früh in die Uni gefahren.

2. Dort _____ sie (*pl.*) andere Freunde getroffen.

3. Sie (*pl.*) _____ sich gegenseitig die Hand gegeben.

4. Das neue Mädchen _____ viel zu sagen gehabt.

5. Das viele Sprechen _____ Martin zu viel geworden.

6. Sie (*pl.*) _____ zusammen in den Saal gegangen.

7. Dort _____ Martin keinen freien Platz gefunden.

8. Eine schöne Blonde _____ ihm aber geholfen.

9. Der Professor _____ sehr laut gesprochen.

10. Ich _____ nicht geschlafen.

11. Wir _____ ins Heft geschrieben.

12. Ein Buch _____ auf den Boden gefallen.

13. Die Freunde _____ dann in die Mensa gegangen.

14. Dort _____ sie (*pl.*) Kaffee getrunken.

15. Das neue Mädchen _____ Brötchen gegessen.

ÜBUNG

10·9

Supply the helping verb (for the third-person singular) and the past participle of the following verbs.

EXAMPLES: schlafen   *hat geschlafen*
           fallen   *ist gefallen*

1. essen _____

2. trinken _____

3. nehmen _____

4. sitzen _____

5. liegen _____

6. springen _____

7. kommen _____

8. laufen _____

9. gehen _____

10. schwimmen _____

11. reiten _____

12. schreiben _____

13. lesen _____

14. geben _____

15. helfen _____

16. treffen _____

17. singen _____

18. sprechen _____

19. sterben _____

20. fahren _____

21. fliegen _____

22. werden _____

23. sein _____

24. haben _____

25. tun _____

ÜBUNG
10·10

The teacher wants to know what the students know about Otto von Bismarck. Supply the correct past participle in the students' answers.

EXAMPLE: Emma: (wohnen) Er hat in Berlin _____.
*Emma: Er hat in Berlin **gewohnt**.*

1. Peter: (lernen) Er hat viel in der Schule _____.

2. Luise: (werden) Er ist Rechtsanwalt _____.

3. Angela: (sprechen) Er hat im Parlament _____.

4. Birgit: (fahren) Er ist nach Russland _____.

5. Christoph: (reisen) Nach Frankreich ist er auch _____.

6. Sabine: (sein) Er ist ein großer Diplomat _____.

7. Hans: (reiten) Er ist viel in der Armee _____.

8. Ulrich: (helfen) Er hat den Kranken _____.

9. Holger: (unterschreiben) Er hat einen Vertrag mit Russland _____.

10. Erich: (schweigen) Er hat nicht gern _____.

11. Elsa: (haben) Er hat viel Land in Magdeburg _____.

12. Leo: (essen) Er hat gern Hering _____.

13. Beate: (trinken) Er hat viel Tee mit dem Kaiser _____.

14. Uwe: (ziehen) Am Ende seines Lebens ist er auf sein Gut _____.

15. Anke: (sterben) 1898 ist er _____.

ÜBUNG
10·11

Magda is talking to her friend on the phone and tells her what she and her family did all day. Change the following sentences to the present perfect tense.

EXAMPLE:　　Ich sehe einen Film.
Ich habe einen Film gesehen.

1. Wir essen ein gutes Frühstück. _____

2. Ich trinke viel Kaffee. _____

3. Die Kinder gehen in die Schule. _____

4. Sie fahren mit dem Bus. _____

5. Sie spielen auf dem Schulplatz. _____

6. Sie lernen in der Klasse. _____

7. Ich putze die Küche. _____

8. Harold arbeitet im Garten. _____

9. Er pflanzt Tomaten. _____

10. Ich kaufe sie beim Gärtner. _____

11. Sie kosten nicht viel. _____

12. Habt ihr dieses Jahr auch Tomaten? _____

13. Es wird heute Abend kalt. _____

14. Es friert schon lange nicht. _____

15. Moment, ruft der Nachbar? _____

ÜBUNG
10·12

Wo warst du gestern? *You came home late last night and your mother wants to know everything that happened. Change the following conversation to the present perfect tense.*

EXAMPLE:　　Du: Wir kaufen ein Eis.
Wir haben ein Eis gekauft.

1. Du: Ich fahre mit Michael in die Stadt.

_____

2. Mutter: Was macht ihr da?

_____

3. Du: Wir gehen in die Geschäfte.

_____

4. Mutter: Kauft ihr etwas?

_____

5. Du: Ja, ich kaufe eine neue Bluse. Sie kostet nicht viel.

_____

6. Mutter: Und dann?

Du: Wir sehen einen Film. Ich finde ihn sehr interessant.

_____

7. Mutter: Was macht ihr dann?

_____

8. Du: Wir holen etwas zum Essen.

_____

9. Mutter: Was isst du?

_____

10. Du: Ich esse ein Stück Torte und trinke Kaffee.

_____

11. Mutter: Wie lange bleibt ihr im Restaurant?

_____

12. Du: Wir sitzen da vielleicht zwei Stunden. Wir sprechen viel zusammen. Michael gibt mir ein neues Foto. Ich nehme es natürlich. Sonst tun wir nichts. Wir steigen ins Auto und fahren nach Hause.

_____

_____

_____

Present perfect tense of mixed verbs

Mixed verbs have a vowel change in the past participle, just as strong verbs do. However, the past participle of mixed verbs ends in **-t**, which is a characteristic of weak verbs. This group of verbs is rather small. The following is a list of these verbs.

Past participles of mixed verbs:

brennen	**gebrannt**	to burn
bringen	**gebracht**	to bring
denken	**gedacht**	to think

kennen	gekannt	to know
nennen	genannt	to name
rennen	gerannt	to run
senden	gesandt	to send
wenden	gewandt	to turn
wissen	gewusst	to know

ÜBUNG
10·13

The following letter is from a jilted lover. Rewrite the following sentences in the present perfect tense.

EXAMPLE: Kennst du mich nicht mehr?
Hast du mich nicht mehr gekannt?

1. Ich denke oft an dich. _____

2. Ich denke wir sind (waren) gute Freunde. _____

3. Du bringst mir Geschenke. _____

4. Du sendest mir Liebesbriefe. _____

5. Du nennst mich »Liebling«. _____

6. Jetzt wendest du dich von mir. _____

7. Ich weiss nicht was falsch war. _____

8. Mein Herz brennt noch nie so vor Schmerz. _____

9. Liebst du mich nie? _____

ÜBUNG
10·14

A visit to a friend. Change the following sentences to the present perfect tense.

EXAMPLE: Wir trinken Tee.
Wir haben Tee getrunken.

1. Ich kenne dich gut.

_____

2. Wir wissen alle wo du wohnst.

_____

3. Sonst weiß es niemand.

_____

4. Wir kommen zu dir.

_____

5. Zuerst schreiben wir einen Brief.

   _____

6. Du sitzt auf der Couch.

   _____

7. Wir gehen ins Haus.

   _____

8. Du machst Tee.

   _____

9. Wir essen Kuchen.

   _____

10. Das Feuer brennt im Ofen.

    _____

11. Der Hund rennt im Garten herum.

    _____

12. Es regnet.

    _____

13. Das Dienstmädchen bringt uns einen Regenschirm.

    _____

14. Wir nehmen den Regenschirm.

    _____

15. Wir sagen, »Auf Wiedersehen«.

    _____

Present perfect tense with separable prefixes

If the verb has a separable prefix (such as **ab-**, **ein-**, **mit-**, **vor-**, **zu-**, etc.), the **ge-** of the participle is placed between the separable prefix and the verb.

	INFINITIVE	PAST PARTICIPLE
Weak Verb	aufpassen	aufgepasst
Strong Verb	weggehen	weggegangen

Sie hat immer aufgepasst.   She always paid attention.
Wann seid ihr weggegangen?   When did you leave?

Complete the following sentences with the correct past participle.

EXAMPLE: Gestern sind alle (fortfahren).
             *Gestern sind alle **fortgefahren**.*

1. Wann hast du Luise _____ (abholen)?

2. Sie ist gestern _____ (ankommen).

3. Was hat sie _____ (anziehen)?

4. Die Kinder sind alle _____ (hereinkommen).

5. Vater hat sie alle _____ (hereinlassen).

6. Was haben sie _____ (mitbringen)?

7. Sie haben sich viel _____ (umsehen).

8. Warum hast du die Tür _____ (zumachen)?

9. Darüber habe ich noch nicht _____ (nachdenken).

10. Herr Wende, haben Sie alles Geld _____ (zurückgeben)?

Change the following conversations to the present perfect tense.

EXAMPLE: Wann rufst du an?   *Wann **hast** du **angerufen**?*
             Ich rufe nachmittags an.   *Ich **habe** nachmittags **angerufen**.*

1. Wann stehst du auf? _____

   Ich mache das immer um sieben Uhr. _____

2. Was brennt dort nieder? _____

   Das ist bestimmt das alte Haus. _____

3. Werft ihr den Müll heraus? _____

   Natürlich nicht. Das passiert nie. _____

4. Stellst du das schöne Mädchen vor? _____

   Nein. Ich kenne sie nicht. _____

5. Wann kommt der Bus an? _____

   Das geschieht um zwei Uhr. _____

6. Fällt der Ball schon wieder ins Wasser hinein? _____

   Ja. Klaus passt wieder nicht auf. _____

7. Reißt der Gärtner alle Blumen heraus? _____

   Ja. Er pflanzt sie nicht um. _____

8. Wann kommt ihr mit den Freunden zusammen? _____

   Das weiß ich nicht. _____

9. Nimmst du die Äpfel mit? _____

   Nein. Ich lasse sie hier. _____

10. Wir hören mit dem Singen auf. _____

    Gut. Das hört sich wirklich nicht gut an. _____

Present perfect tense with inseparable prefixes

The inseparable prefixes—so called because they are never separated from the verb—are **be-**, **emp-**, **ent-**, **er-**, **ge-**, **miss-**, **ver-**, and **zer-**. Verbs with inseparable prefixes do not take the usual **ge-** prefix to form the past participle.

	INFINITIVE	PAST PARTICIPLE
Weak Verb	besuchen	besucht
Strong Verb	beginnen	begonnen

Common verbs with inseparable prefixes are listed in Unit 4.

ÜBUNG
10·17

*Change the following conversation to the present perfect tense or the simple past, as appropriate. (Some of the sentences will use the simple past, since the present perfect is seldom used with **sein**, **werden**, and **haben**.)*

EXAMPLE: Was kaufst du ein?   *Was hast du eingekauft?*
          Ich kaufe nichts ein.   *Ich habe nichts eingekauft.*

Wo wart ihr letzten Sommer?

1. Wir fahren in die Alpen.

   _____

2. Bernd kommt mit.

   _____

3. Wir haben viel Spaß.

   _____

4. Was macht ihr alles?

   _____

5. Wir reiten in den Wald hinein.

   _____

6. Wir klettern in den Bergen.

   _____

7. Luise klettert immer schnell hinunter.

   _____

8. Sie passt aber gut auf.

   _____

9. Sie tut sich nicht weh.

   _____

10. Nachmittags schwimmen wir viel.

    _____

11. Die Jungen werfen die Mädchen gern ins Wasser hinein.

    _____

12. Wir bringen immer etwas zum Essen und Trinken mit.

    _____

13. Die Jungen spielen Ball.

    _____

14. Bernd gibt immer den Ball zurück.

    _____

15. Er macht das nicht gern.

    _____

16. Was habt ihr abends vor?

    _____

17. Wir gehen in die Stadt hinein.

    _____

18. Wir schauen uns einen Film an.

    _____

19. Wir gehen zum Essen aus.

    _____

20. Zu früh kehren wir nach Hause zurück.

    _____

Our car is gone! Change the following sentences to the present perfect tense.

EXAMPLE: Die Polizei mißtraut uns nicht.
Die Polizei hat uns nicht mißtraut.

1. Wir rufen die Polizei an. _____

2. Unser neues Auto verschwindet. _____

3. Wir begreifen nicht warum. _____

4. Wir besitzen es noch nicht lange. _____

5. Unser Nachbar verkauft es uns. _____

6. Es gefällt mir sehr gut. _____

7. Die Polizei verlangt Beweis. _____

8. Ich beweise dass es mir gehört. _____

9. Ich beschreibe es genau. _____

10. Ich weiss genau wie das Auto aussieht. _____

Wer war Albert Einstein? Now the teacher wants to know what the students know about Albert Einstein. Change the students' responses to the present perfect tense.

EXAMPLE: Axel: 1940 nimmt er die amerikanische Staatsbürgerschaft an.
Axel: 1940 hat er die amerikanische Staatsbürgerschaft angenommen.

1. Peter: 1879 kommt er zur Welt.

_____

2. Beate: Er wächst in Deutschland auf.

_____

3. Friedel: Er besucht die Schule in München und in der Schweiz.

_____

4. Emma: Er spielt Violine.

_____

5. Jörg: Er erfindet die Relativitätstheorie.

_____

6. Dieter: 1921 bekommt er den Nobelpreis in Physik.

_____

7. Jürgen: Er verheiratet sich mit seiner Kusine Elsa.

   _____

8. Brigitte: Er entscheidet sich nach Amerika auszuwandern.

   _____

9. Anna: Er verlässt Deutschland.

   _____

10. Ruth: 1933 wandert er nach Amerika aus.

    _____

11. Hilde: Er unterrichtet an der Universität in Princeton.

    _____

12. Ulrike: Da zieht er in ein einfaches Haus.

    _____

13. Anke: Er bespricht vieles mit seiner Frau.

    _____

14. Inge: Der Präsident Roosevelt empfängt einen Brief von ihm.

    _____

15. Fritz: Im Brief beschreibt er die Entwicklung einer Atombombe in Deutschland.

    _____

16. Achim: Er unterstützt den Zionismus.

    _____

17. Marie: Er hilft vielen Menschen.

    _____

18. Michael: Er vergisst die Armen nicht.

    _____

19. Luise: In seinem Leben geschieht wirklich viel.

    _____

20. Thomas: 1955 stirbt er in Princeton.

    _____

Present perfect tense with verbs ending in -ieren

Verbs ending in **-ieren** also do not take the usual ge- prefix to form the past participle. The past participle of these verbs is the same as the third-person singular in the present tense.

Infinitive	Past Participle
musizieren—er **musiziert**	**musiziert**
reparieren—er **repariert**	**repariert**

Sie haben im Park **musiziert**.	*They **made music** in the park.*
Er hat das Auto **repariert**.	*He has **repaired** the car.*

The following is a list of some of the more common verbs ending in **-ieren**:

sich amüsieren	to amuse oneself
dekorieren	to decorate
demonstrieren	to demonstrate
existieren	to exist
fotografieren	to photograph
funktionieren	to function
informieren	to inform
sich interessieren für	to be interested in
sich konzentrieren	to concentrate
korrigieren	to correct
musizieren	to make music
operieren	to operate
passieren	to happen
probieren	to try
sich rasieren	to shave
regieren	to rule, govern
reparieren	to repair
servieren	to serve
studieren	to study
telefonieren	to telephone

ÜBUNG
10·20

*Change the following sentences to the present perfect tense. Remember that the present perfect tense is usually not used with **haben** and **sein**. The simple past is used instead.*

EXAMPLE: Hier existieren keine tropischen Vögel.
Hier haben keine tropischen Vögel existiert.

1. Was passiert am Wochenende?

   _____

2. Wir korrigieren zuerst unsere Hausaufgaben.

   _____

3. Wir konzentrieren uns dabei und es geht schnell.

   _____

4. Dann amüsieren wir uns.

   _____

5. Sabine telefoniert mit uns.

   _____

6. Sie informiert uns dass sie Karten für ein Konzert hat.

_____

7. »Die Blonden Herren« musizieren schön.

_____

8. Wir besuchen alle das Konzert.

_____

9. Dann fahren wir in ein schönes Restaurant.

_____

10. Wir bestellen Kaffee und Kuchen.

_____

11. Heiko probiert die Sachertorte.

_____

12. Die Kellnerin serviert große Stücke.

_____

13. Alles schmeckt gut.

_____

14. Sie fotografiert uns auch.

_____

15. Das macht alles Spaß.

_____

16. Wir verlassen fröhlich das Restaurant.

_____

17. Schreck! Das Auto funktioniert nicht!

_____

18. Peter repariert es aber schnell.

_____

19. Der Motor springt an.

_____

20. Das ist unser Wochenende!

_____

Present perfect tense of modal auxiliaries and of *sein* and *haben*

The present perfect tense forms **gedurft**, **gekonnt**, **gemocht**, **gemusst**, **gesollt**, and **gewollt** are used only when the modal is the only verb:

Er hat das gemocht.	*He has liked it.*
Sie hat das nicht gewollt.	*She did not want this.*

When another verb is combined with a modal, the present perfect tense uses a double infinitive. **Sie hat die Aufgabe machen müssen**. This is addressed in more detail in Chapter 24. In most cases the simple past is preferred: **Sie wollte zu Hause bleiben**.

    Sein and **haben** are used more often in the simple past tense (**war**, **hatten**) than in the present perfect tense. However, sometimes you will come across phrases like:

Ich habe die Grippe gehabt.	*I have had the flu.*
Er ist hier gewesen.	*He has been here.*

Subordinate clauses and the present perfect tense

When using a subordinate clause, the finite verb (the verb that is conjugated to agree with the subject) is placed in the last position.

Er war krank, weil er zu viel grüne Äpfel gegessen **hat**.	*He was ill because he ate too many green apples.*
Ich weiß, dass ich zu schnell gelaufen **bin**.	*I know that I ran too fast.*

Past perfect and future tense

Past perfect tense

The past perfect tense is identical in structure to the present perfect tense. The difference is that the auxiliary (**haben** or **sein**) is conjugated in the past tense rather than in the present tense. Compare the following verbs conjugated in the present perfect and the past perfect tenses.

	Present perfect	**Past perfect**
ich	habe gesprochen	hatte verstanden
du	hast gesprochen	hattest verstanden
er/sie/es	hat gesprochen	hatte verstanden
wir	haben gesprochen	hatten verstanden
ihr	habt gesprochen	hattet verstanden
Sie	haben gesprochen	hatten verstanden
sie (*pl.*)	haben gesprochen	hatten verstanden

	Present perfect	**Past perfect**
ich	bin gegangen	war gefahren
du	bist gegangen	warst gefahren
er/sie/es	ist gegangen	war gefahren
wir	sind gegangen	waren gefahren
ihr	seid gegangen	wart gefahren
Sie	sind gegangen	waren gefahren
sie (*pl.*)	sind gegangen	waren gefahren

Use the present perfect tense to describe an action that began in the past but has ended in the present or is ongoing in the present. Use the past perfect tense to describe an action that began and ended in the past.

ÜBUNG

11·1

In the blank provided, write the past perfect conjugation for the verb in parentheses with the accompanying subject.

1. (ziehen) wir _____

2. (bleiben) ich _____

3. (singen) du _____

4. (reisen) sie (*sing.*) _____

5. (zumachen) meine Schwester _____

6. (sterben) der Mann _____

7. (fliegen) wir _____

8. (essen) Sie _____

9. (erwarten) ihr _____

10. (spielen) ich _____

11. (anziehen) er _____

12. (passieren) es _____

13. (besuchen) du _____

14. (lachen) ihr _____

15. (schlagen) sie (*pl.*) _____

16. (gefallen) es _____

17. (fallen) er _____

18. (einschlafen) das Baby _____

19. (rennen) wir _____

20. (wissen) niemand _____

21. (kommen) Sonja _____

22. (bekommen) ihr _____

23. (zerstören) sie (*pl.*) _____

24. (vergessen [*forget*]) ich _____

25. (geschehen) es _____

The past perfect tense

The past perfect is formed in the same manner as the present perfect—auxiliary verb plus past participle. However, the past perfect uses the *past* tense of the auxiliary **haben** or **sein**. It is, again, the past participle that determines whether to use **haben** or **sein**, and the past participle is again placed at the end of a clause or sentence. The past perfect is used to show events that happened before other past events.

Bevor er die Prüfung bestand,   *Before he passed the test, he*
hatte er viel studiert.   *had studied a lot.*

The following is the conjugation of the past perfect with verbs that take **haben** or **sein**:

Ich **hatte** lange geschlafen.   *I **had** slept long.*
Du **hattest** lange geschlafen.   *You **had** slept long.*
Er/sie/es **hatte** lange geschlafen.   *He/she/it **had** slept long.*

Wir **hatten** lange geschlafen.	*We **had** slept long.*
Ihr **hattet** lange geschlafen.	*You (pl.) **had** slept long.*
Sie/Sie **hatten** lange geschlafen.	*They/You (form.) **had** slept long.*
Ich **war** nach Hause gegangen.	*I **had** gone home.*
Du **warst** nach Hause gegangen.	*You **had** gone home.*
Er/sie/es **war** nach Hause gegangen.	*He/she/it **had** gone home.*
Wir waren nach Hause gegangen.	*We **had** gone home.*
Ihr wart nach Hause gegangen.	*You (pl.) **had** gone home.*
Sie/Sie waren nach Hause gegangen.	*They/You (form.) **had** gone home.*

ÜBUNG

11·2

Supply the correct auxiliary verb to form the past perfect tense.

EXAMPLE: Er _____ den Brief geschrieben.

*Er **hatte** den Brief geschrieben.*

1. Ich _____ in die Schule gegangen.

2. Der Lehrer _____ schon gewartet.

3. Die anderen Schüler _____ auch gekommen.

4. Sie (*pl.*) _____ mit dem Bus gefahren.

5. Beate _____ für alle ein Geschenk mitgebracht.

6. Wir _____ uns alle gefreut.

7. Das Lernen _____ heute viel Spaß gemacht.

8. Bernd _____ nicht eingeschlafen.

9. Er _____ gut aufgepasst.

10. Wann _____ eure Schule begonnen?

ÜBUNG

11·3

*Complete the sentences in the past perfect tense, beginning with **Bevor wir in die Schweiz flogen.***

EXAMPLE: wir telefonieren mit Onkel Alois
Bevor wir in die Schweiz flogen, hatten wir mit Onkel Alois telefoniert.

1. wir fahren an die Nordsee

_____

2. wir besuchen das Reisebüro

_____

3. wir machen Pläne

_____

4. wir kaufen die Flugkarten

_____

5. wir packen die Koffer

_____

ÜBUNG
11·4

*Complete these sentences in the past perfect tense, beginning with **Ich ging nach Hause, denn**.*

EXAMPLE: das Restaurant macht zu
             Ich ging nach Hause, denn das Restaurant hatte zugemacht.

1. ich sehe den Film schon

_____

2. ich besuche die Großmutter schon

_____

3. ich gehe schon in den Park

_____

4. ich kaufe alles ein

_____

5. ich besichtige das Museum

_____

ÜBUNG
11·5

*Complete the sentences in the past perfect tense, beginning with **Als Weihnachten kam**.*

EXAMPLE: wir putzen schon das Haus
             Als Weihnachten kam, hatten wir schon das Haus geputzt.

1. wir kaufen schon für jeden ein Geschenk

_____

2. wir packen schon die Geschenke schön ein

_____

3. die Eltern schmücken schon den Weihnachtsbaum

_____

4. Hans backt Plätzchen

_____

5. wir sind noch nicht in der Kirche

_____

6. der Adventskranz liegt auf dem Tisch

_____

7. wir singen oft Weihnachtslieder

_____

8. Hans lädt Tante Gretel und ihre Familie ein

_____

9. die Kinder haben schon vier Tage Ferien

_____

10. es schneit noch nicht

_____

Future tense

Consider how English can *imply* a future tense meaning with a present tense conjugation. For example:

> On Monday we fly to Rome.
> Next month we're buying a cottage on Slocum Lake.

This present tense verb usage to suggest a future tense meaning is also quite common in German. But remember that German does not have a progressive present tense (*we're buying, they're helping, I am studying*). Let's look at some German examples of the present tense verb used to mean the future tense:

> Morgen fährt Onkel Heinrich nach Prag.   *Tomorrow Uncle Heinrich is driving to Prague.*
> Nächste Woche muss ich viel mehr arbeiten.   *Next week I have to work a lot more.*
> Der Zug kommt um vierzehn Uhr.   *The train arrives at two P.M.*

Naturally, to be perfectly clear, one can translate the previous example sentences as:

> *Tomorrow Uncle Heinrich will drive to Prague.*
> *Next week I shall have to work a lot more.*
> *The train will arrive at two P.M.*

*Reword each present tense sentence twice: once with the future tense inferred and once with the future auxiliary **werden**. Begin each sentence with **nächste Woche**.*

EXAMPLE   Er reist in die Stadt.

Nächste Woche reist er in die Stadt.

Nächste Woche wird er in die Stadt reisen.

1. Die Jungen helfen uns im Garten.

_____

_____

2. Die Lehrerin erklärt (*explains*) das Problem.

_____

_____

3. Sie kaufen ein Haus im Vorort (*suburb*).

_____

_____

4. Die Reiter (*riders*) reiten in den Wald (*woods*).

_____

_____

5. Er geht täglich spazieren.

_____

_____

*Follow the same directions, but begin each sentence with **nächstes Jahr**.*

6. Die Stadt baut hier einen Wolkenkratzer (*skyscraper*).

_____

_____

7. Der Schriftsteller (*writer*) schreibt einen neuen Roman.

_____

_____

8. Wir ziehen (*move*) nach München (*Munich*).

_____

_____

9. Erik besucht ein Gymnasium (*preparatory school*).

_____

_____

10. Er wird wieder gesund.

_____

_____

Modal auxiliaries in the future tense

When writing the modal auxiliaries in the future tense, **werden** is conjugated and the modal auxiliary stands at the end of the sentence accompanied by an infinitive. This structure is identical to the double infinitive structure described in Chapter 24. The difference is the use of **werden** in place of **haben**. For example:

PRESENT	Rolf **kann** gut schwimmen.	*Rolf can swim well.*
FUTURE	Rolf **wird** gut schwimmen **können**.	*Rolf will be able to swim well.*
PRESENT	Ich **muss** mehr arbeiten.	*I have to work (study) more.*
FUTURE	Ich **werde** mehr arbeiten **müssen**.	*I will have to work (study) more.*
PRESENT	Du **darfst** ihnen helfen.	*You may help them.*
FUTURE	Du **wirst** ihnen helfen **dürfen**.	*You will be allowed to help them.*
PRESENT	Meine Schwester **will** in Freiburg studieren.	*My sister wants to study in Freiburg.*
FUTURE	Meine Schwester **wird** in Freiburg studieren **wollen**.	*My sister will want to study in Freiburg.*

There are four other verbs that require the use of a double infinitive structure in the future tense: **helfen**, **hören**, **lassen**, and **sehen**. Just as a double infinitive is formed with these verbs in the perfect tenses, they also form a double infinitive in the future tense. For example:

PRESENT	Wir **helfen** ihm arbeiten.	*We help him work.*
FUTURE	Wir **werden** ihm arbeiten **helfen**.	*We will help him work.*
PRESENT	Ich **höre** den Mann pfeifen.	*I hear the man whistling.*
FUTURE	Ich **werde** den Mann pfeifen **hören**.	*I will hear the man whistling.*
PRESENT	Thomas **lässt** sein Fahrrad reparieren.	*Thomas gets his bicycle repaired.*
FUTURE	Thomas **wird** sein Fahrrad reparieren **lassen**.	*Thomas will get his bicycle repaired.*
PRESENT	Ihr **seht** die Jungen Fußball spielen.	*You see the boys play soccer.*
FUTURE	Ihr **werdet** die Jungen Fußball spielen **sehen**.	*You will see the boys play soccer.*

Reword each present tense sentence in the past tense, present perfect tense, and future tense.

1. Tina kann schnell tippen (*type*).

   PAST _____

   PRESENT PERFECT _____

   FUTURE _____

2. Wann kommst du wieder nach Hause?

   PAST _____

   PRESENT PERFECT _____

   FUTURE _____

3. Peter muss einen Kuchen backen.

   PAST _____

   PRESENT PERFECT _____

   FUTURE _____

4. Ich gebe ihr ein paar Rosen.

   PAST _____

   PRESENT PERFECT _____

   FUTURE _____

5. Felix will mit Sonja tanzen.

   PAST _____

   PRESENT PERFECT _____

   FUTURE _____

6. Wieder hören wir den Mann schreien.

   PAST _____

   PRESENT PERFECT _____

   FUTURE _____

7. Der Boxer gewinnt den Kampf (*wins the match*).

   PAST _____

   PRESENT PERFECT _____

   FUTURE _____

8. Niemand sieht ihn das Buch stehlen.

PAST _____

PRESENT PERFECT _____

FUTURE _____

9. Viele Unfälle (*accidents*) geschehen hier.

PAST _____

PRESENT PERFECT _____

FUTURE _____

10. Wir helfen ihr die Briefe schreiben.

PAST _____

PRESENT PERFECT _____

FUTURE _____

11. Wir dürfen nicht im Wald wandern.

PAST _____

PRESENT PERFECT _____

FUTURE _____

12. Man muss vorsichtig (*careful*) sein.

PAST _____

PRESENT PERFECT _____

FUTURE _____

13. Bist du wieder in Heidelberg?

PAST _____

PRESENT PERFECT _____

FUTURE _____

14. Ich habe leider keine Zeit.

PAST _____

PRESENT PERFECT _____

FUTURE _____

15. Wo lassen Sie Ihre Uhr reparieren?

PAST _____

PRESENT PERFECT _____

FUTURE _____

The future tense

The future tense is composed of the conjugated present tense of **werden** and an infinitive. The infinitive is always placed at the end of the clause.

Ich **werde** Deutsch lernen.	*I will learn German.*
Du **wirst** Deutsch lernen.	*You will learn German.*
Er/sie/es **wird** Deutsch lernen.	*He/she/it will learn German.*
Wir **werden** Deutsch lernen.	*We will learn German.*
Ihr **werdet** Deutsch lernen.	*You (pl.) will learn German.*
Sie/Sie **werden** Deutsch lernen.	*They/you (form.) will learn German.*

Adverbs of time

When an adverb of time, such as **bald**, **morgen**, or **nächste Woche**, is included in a clause, the present tense is used instead of the future tense. The adverb already expresses the future.

Wir fahren **morgen** in die Stadt.	*Tomorrow we will drive to town.*
Er kommt **bald**.	*He will come soon.*

ÜBUNG
11·8

Rewrite the following sentences using the future tense.

EXAMPLE: Marlies isst ein Eis.
Marlies wird ein Eis essen.

1. Ich habe viel Geld. _____

2. Wir schwimmen im See. _____

3. Peter kauft ein Auto. _____

4. Wohnst du in Bonn? _____

5. Müllers bauen ein großes Haus. _____

6. Seid ihr vorsichtig? _____

7. Frau Wendt, haben Sie Durst? _____

8. Die Mädchen spielen Ball. _____

9. Tante Friede besucht uns. _____

10. In dem Kleid siehst du gut aus! _____

Rewrite the following sentences using the future tense, if needed.

EXAMPLE: Er kommt nach Hause.
Er wird nach Hause kommen.

1. Ich kaufe mir ein Eis.

   _____

2. Nächstes Jahr verkaufen Müllers ihr Haus.

   _____

3. Hast du Hunger?

   _____

4. Ab morgen mache ich Diät.

   _____

5. Wir besuchen morgen Onkel Alex.

   _____

6. Tante Luise kommt mit.

   _____

7. Alle gehen ins Restaurant.

   _____

8. Der Kellner findet einen guten Platz am Fenster.

   _____

9. Alles schmeckt gut.

   _____

10. Nächstes Mal besuchen wir wieder das gleiche Restaurant.

    _____

Position and form of modals

Modals are in the infinitive form when the clause expresses the *future tense*. The modal is in the last position and follows the dependent infinitive.

Du **wirst** in die Schule **gehen müssen**.	*You will have to go to school.*
In Deutschland **wird** Emma viel **sehen wollen**.	*Emma will want to see a lot in Germany.*

Again, change the following sentences to the future tense.

EXAMPLE: Ich will in die Schule gehen.
            Ich werde in die Schule gehen wollen.

1. Müllers wollen an die Nordsee fahren.

   _____

2. Herr Wendt will aber in den Bergen Ferien machen.

   _____

3. Das Pferd müssen sie zu Hause lassen.

   _____

4. Man darf Pferde nicht ins Ferienhaus mitbringen.

   _____

5. Ihren Hund dürfen sie mitnehmen.

   _____

The Wendts are planning a vacation in the mountains. What will they all do? Change the following sentences to the future tense, unless there is a reason not to.

EXAMPLE: Peter fällt ins Wasser.
            Peter wird ins Wasser fallen.

1. Vater fährt das Auto.

   _____

2. Wir kommen müde an.

   _____

3. Am ersten Morgen schlafen wir lange.

   _____

4. Vater kocht ein gutes Frühstück.

   _____

5. Die Kinder wollen Ball spielen.

   _____

6. Peter und Hans gehen wandern.

   _____

7. Marie schwimmt.

_____

8. Alle haben Hunger.

_____

9. Sie sind sehr müde.

_____

10. Abends spielen sie Karten.

_____

11. Morgen wollen sie früh aufstehen.

_____

12. Mutter geht ins Dorf und will ein gutes Bauernbrot kaufen.

_____

13. Das schmeckt sehr gut.

_____

14. Der Urlaub gefällt ihnen gut.

_____

15. Nächstes Jahr reisen sie wieder in die Berge.

_____

Expressing probability

Probability in the present tense can also be expressed by using the future tense with adverbs such as **bestimmt**, **schon**, **sicher**, and **wohl**.

Er wird wohl in der Schule sein.
Sie werden bestimmt viel Geld haben.

He is probably at school.
They probably have a lot of money.

ÜBUNG
11·12

The Müllers went to the North Sea on their vacation. Make sentences telling what they are probably doing, using **sicher** or **wohl**.

EXAMPLE: Wo schwimmt Angela? (See)
Sie wird wohl im See schwimmen.

1. Wo spielen die Kinder Ball? (am Strand)

_____

2. Wohin gehen die großen Jungen? (in den Wald)

_____

3. Was will Herr Müller essen? (Fisch)

_____

4. Wie ist das Wetter? (gut)

_____

5. Was machen sie wenn sie müde sind? (lesen)

_____

6. Wie lange schlafen sie? (bis zehn)

_____

7. Was trägt Angela? (Shorts)

_____

8. Was müssen die Kinder trinken? (Milch)

_____

9. Was bauen die Kinder im Sand? (Schlösser)

_____

10. Was gibt es zum Essen? (Fisch)

_____

ÜBUNG
11·13

What will happen when the two families get home? Make sentences using the future tense, where necessary.

EXAMPLE: Müllers / haben / eine gute Heimfahrt
Müllers werden eine gute Heimfahrt haben.

1. Morgen / sein / Müllers und Wendts / zu Hause.

_____

2. Sie / auspacken / das Auto.

_____

3. Sie / tragen / die Koffer / ins Haus.

_____

4. Mutter / machen / das Abendessen.

_____

5. Alle / essen wollen / viel.

_____

6. Es / schmecken / alles gut.

_____

7. Sie / trinken / Limonade.

_____

8. Marie / anrufen / ihre Freundin.

_____

9. Peter / mähen müssen / den Rasen / morgen.

_____

10. Herr Müller / gehen / zur Arbeit / übermorgen.

_____

11. Die Kinder / haben / wohl / noch keine Schule.

_____

12. Sie / bleiben / zu Hause.

_____

13. Die Mutter / waschen / die Wäsche.

_____

14. Angela / helfen müssen / der Mutter.

_____

15. Sie / sprechen / bestimmt / über den Urlaub.

_____

Separable and inseparable prefixes and imperatives

Prefixes

The meaning and use of German verbs are changed by the addition of prefixes. This occurs in English, but not as frequently as in German. Look at a few English verbs and how their meaning is altered by prefixes.

| *have* | *trust* | *believe* | *report* |
| *behave* | *entrust* | *relieve* | *transport* |

German has three types of prefixes: inseparable prefixes, separable prefixes, and those prefixes that are sometimes inseparable and sometimes separable. The inseparable prefixes are **be-**, **emp-**, **ent-**, **er-**, **ge-**, **ver-**, and **zer-**. They are called inseparable because they remain affixed to the verb in a conjugation. Compare verbs with no prefix and verbs with an inseparable prefix.

	warten	**erwarten** (*expect*)	**hören**	**gehören** (*belong to*)
ich	warte	erwarte	höre	gehöre
du	wartest	erwartest	hörst	gehörst
er/sie/es	wartet	erwartet	hört	gehört
wir	warten	erwarten	hören	gehören
ihr	wartet	erwartet	hört	gehört
Sie	warten	erwarten	hören	gehören
sie (*pl.*)	warten	ewarten	hören	gehören

When a prefix is added to a verb, it is not the conjugation that changes, but the meaning of the verb and, therefore, the use of the verb. If a verb has an irregular present tense conjugation, those irregularities remain intact when an inseparable prefix is added. For example:

	lassen	**entlassen** (*release*)	**halten**	**behalten** (*keep*)
ich	lasse	entlasse	halte	behalte
du	lässt	entlässt	hältst	behältst
er/sie/es	lässt	entlässt	hält	behält
wir	lassen	entlassen	halten	behalten
ihr	lasst	entlasst	haltet	behaltet
Sie	lassen	entlassen	halten	behalten
sie (*pl.*)	lassen	entlassen	halten	behalten

A list of commonly used verbs with inseparable prefixes follows:

bekommen	*receive, get*	besuchen	*visit*	begrüßen	*greet*
empfangen	*receive*	empfehlen	*recommend*	empfinden	*feel*
entdecken	*discover*	entfernen	*remove*	entlaufen	*run away*
ersetzen	*replace*	erstaunen	*amaze*	ertragen	*bear*
gebrauchen	*use*	gefallen	*please, like*	gewinnen	*win, gain*
verstehen	*understand*	verkaufen	*sell*	versprechen	*promise*
zerstören	*destroy*	zerreißen	*tear up*	zerschmettern	*smash*

ÜBUNG
12·1

In the blank, rewrite each verb in parentheses with the subject provided.

1. (erfahren [*experience*]) du _____

2. (entlassen) sie (*sing.*) _____

3. (empfangen) die Dame _____

4. (bekommen) ich _____

5. (empfehlen) ihr _____

6. (verkaufen) Sie _____

7. (besuchen) du _____

8. (gefallen) es _____

9. (erstaunen) er _____

10. (gebrauchen) die Jungen _____

11. (verstehen) wir _____

12. (gelingen [*succeed*]) es _____

13. (zerstören) sie (*pl.*) _____

14. (begrüßen) ich _____

15. (erschlagen [*kill*]) er _____

16. (entlaufen) das Mädchen _____

17. (beschreiben [*describe*]) man _____

18. (empfinden) Sie _____

19. (bekommen) er _____

20. (gefallen) sie (*pl.*) _____

21. (ertragen) der Herr _____

22. (versuchen [*try*]) ich _____

23. (gewinnen) du _____

24. (enlassen) sie (*pl.*) _____

25. (behalten) du _____

Write the full conjugation of each verb phrase with the subjects provided.

Bekommen einen Brief (*Receive a letter*)

1. ich _____

2. du _____

3. er _____

4. wir _____

5. ihr _____

6. Sie _____

7. man _____

Empfangen sie mit Blumen (*Receive, greet her with flowers*)

8. ich _____

9. du _____

10. er _____

11. wir _____

12. ihr _____

13. Sie _____

14. niemand (*no one*) _____

Entdecken eine kleine Insel (*Discover a little island*)

15. ich _____

16. du _____

17. er _____

18. wir _____

19. ihr _____

20. Sie _____

21. der Professor _____

Verstehen kein Wort (*Not understand a word*)

22. ich _____

23. du _____

24. er _____

25. wir _____

26. ihr _____

27. Sie _____

28. die Touristen (*tourists*) _____

Zerreißen die Zeitschriften (*Tear up the magazines*)

29. ich _____

30. du _____

31. er _____

32. wir _____

33. ihr _____

34. Sie _____

35. man _____

The separable prefixes are prepositions and adverbs and form a very large group. They are called separable, because in the conjugation of a verb, the prefix separates from the verb and becomes the final element in a sentence. For example, using the prefixes **mit-**, **fort-**, and **vor-**:

Einen Freund mitbringen (*Bring along a friend*)
Ich bringe einen Freund mit.
Du bringst einen Freund mit.
Er bringt einen Freund mit.
Wir bringen einen Freund mit.
Ihr bringt einen Freund mit.
Sie bringen einen Freund mit.
Meine Eltern bringen einen Freund mit. (*My parents*)

Den Weg zu Fuß fortsetzen (*Continue the journey on foot*)
Ich setze den Weg zu Fuß fort.
Du setzt den Weg zu Fuß fort.
Sie (*sing.*) setzt den Weg zu Fuß fort.
Wir setzen den Weg zu Fuß fort.
Ihr setzt den Weg zu Fuß fort.
Sie setzen den Weg zu Fuß fort.
Sie (*pl.*) setzen den Weg zu Fuß fort.

Die Gäste vorstellen (*Introduce the guests*)
Ich stelle die Gäste vor.
Du stellst die Gäste vor.
Er stellt die Gäste vor.
Wir stellen die Gäste vor.

Ihr stellt die Gäste vor.
Sie stellen die Gäste vor.
Mein Mann stellt die Gäste vor.

If the conjugated verb is irregular in the present tense, the addition of a separable prefix does not alter the conjugation. For example:

Das neue Gemälde ansehen (*Look at the new painting*)
Ich sehe das neue Gemälde an.
Du siehst das neue Gemälde an.
Er sieht das neue Gemälde an.
Wir sehen das neue Gemälde an.
Ihr seht das neue Gemälde an.
Sie sehen das neue Gemälde an.
Man sieht das neue Gemälde an.

A list of verbs with some commonly used separable prefixes follows:

abfahren	*depart*	abspülen	*rinse off*	abreißen	*tear down*
ankommen	*arrive*	anbieten	*offer*	anfangen	*begin*
aufräumen	*tidy up*	aufmachen	*open*	aufstehen	*stand up*
ausgeben	*spend*	aussehen	*look like*	aussteigen	*get off, alight*
beibringen	*teach*	beistehen	*stand by*	beitragen	*contribute*
fortfahren	*continue*	fortbleiben	*stay away*	forteilen	*hurry away*
mitgehen	*go along*	mitnehmen	*take along*	mitsingen	*sing along*
nachdenken	*think about*	nachfolgen	*follow*	nachkommen	*come later*
vorbereiten	*prepare*	vorlesen	*read aloud*	vortragen	*perform*
umbringen	*kill*	umkommen	*die*	umziehen	*change clothes*
weglaufen	*run away*	weggehen	*go away*	wegnehmen	*take away*
zurückgehen	*go back*	zurückbleiben	*stay behind*	zurücknehmen	*take back*
zumachen	*close*	zunehmen	*increase*	zuhören	*listen to*

ÜBUNG
12·3

In the blank, rewrite each verb in parentheses with the subject provided.

1. (ankommen) ihr _____

2. (umbringen) sie (*pl.*) _____

3. (mitnehmen) er _____

4. (zurückgehen) wir _____

5. (vorbereiten) mein Vater _____

6. (umziehen) ich _____

7. (anfangen) sie (*sing.*) _____

8. (weglaufen) ihr _____

9. (zumachen) die Touristen _____

10. (umkommen) sie (*pl.*) _____

11. (wegnehmen) er _____

12. (beibringen) ich _____

13. (aufhören) Sie _____

14. (vorstellen) meine Gäste _____

15. (aufmachen) die Ärztin _____

16. (weglaufen) der Hund _____

17. (mitbringen) wir _____

18. (fortsetzen) Tina und Werner _____

19. (anbieten) du _____

20. (aufräumen) sie (*sing.*) _____

Write the full conjugation of each verb phrase with the subjects provided.

Abfahren um neun Uhr (*Depart at nine o'clock*)

1. ich _____

2. du _____

3. er _____

4. wir _____

5. ihr _____

6. Sie _____

7. man _____

Zumachen die Fenster und die Türen (*Close the windows and the doors*)

8. ich _____

9. du _____

10. er _____

11. wir _____

12. ihr _____

13. Sie _____

14. niemand _____

Beibringen ihnen Deutsch (*Teach them German*)

15. ich _____

16. du _____

17. er _____

18. wir _____

19. ihr _____

20. Sie _____

21. man _____

Aufhören damit (*Stop that*)

22. ich _____

23. du _____

24. er _____

25. wir _____

26. ihr _____

27. Sie _____

28. Martin _____

Ausgeben zwanzig Euro (*Spend twenty euros*)

29. ich _____

30. du _____

31. er _____

32. wir _____

33. ihr _____

34. Sie _____

35. wer _____

A relatively small group of prefixes can be either separable or inseparable. If they are separable, the accented syllable is the prefix itself. If they are inseparable, the accented syllable is the stem of the verb. Let's look at a few examples of these prefixes.

SEPARABLE		INSEPARABLE	
dúrchfallen	*fail*	durchzíehen	*pass through*
überwerfen	*throw over*	übertréiben	*exaggerate*
úmkommen	*die*	umármen	*embrace*
únterkommen	*find housing*	untersúchen	*investigate*
vólltanken	*fill the gas tank*	vollzíehen	*carry out, complete*
wíderrufen	*retract*	widerspréchen	*contradict*
wíederkommen	*come back*	wiederhólen	*repeat*

In the following, compare how the same prefix is used as a separable prefix and then as an inseparable prefix.

Ich komme morgen **wieder**.   *I'll come back tomorrow.*
Ich **wieder**hole den Satz.   *I repeat the sentence.*

Write the full conjugation of each verb phrase with the subjects provided.

Umkommen vor Langeweile (*Die of boredom*)

1. ich _____

2. du _____

3. er _____

4. wir _____

5. ihr _____

6. Sie _____

7. man _____

Unterbrechen die Rede (*Interrupt the speech*)

8. ich _____

9. du _____

10. er _____

11. wir _____

12. ihr _____

13. Sie _____

14. niemand _____

Prefixes

In European languages, prefixes play a significant role in changing the meaning of a verb. Consider the following English verbs and how prefixes alter them.

NON-PREFIX VERB	PREFIX ADDED
do	*undo*
go	*forego*
have	*behave*

English words that are derived from Latin have even more variations when prefixes are added. For example:

press	*port*
compress	*deport*
depress	*export*
express	*import*
impress	*transport*

German uses prefixes in the same way. It is important to remember that the base verb does not always give a clue to the meaning of that verb with a prefix added. For example:

VERB	ENGLISH
kommen	*come*
bekommen	*receive*
entkommen	*escape*
verkommen	*go bad, go to the dogs*

Inseparable prefixes

There are three types of German prefixes: inseparable prefixes, separable prefixes, and prefixes that can be either inseparable or separable.

The inseparable prefixes are **be-**, **emp-**, **ent-**, **er-**, **ge-**, **ver-**, and **zer-**. These prefixes are called *inseparable*, because they do not separate from the stem of the verb when the verb is conjugated. When these prefixes are added to a verb, their present tense conjugations are not altered. This occurs with both regular and irregular verbs. For example:

	Regular verb **benutzen** *use*	Irregular verb **erwarten** *expect*
ich	benutze	erwarte
du	benutzt	erwartest
er	benutzt	erwartet
wir	benutzen	erwarten
ihr	benutzt	erwartet
Sie	benutzen	erwarten
sie *pl.*	benutzen	erwarten
man	benutzt	erwartet

	vergeben *forgive*	**entlassen** *release*
ich	vergebe	entlasse
du	vergibst	entlässt
er	vergibt	entlässt
wir	vergeben	entlassen
ihr	vergebt	entlasst
Sie	vergeben	entlassen
sie *pl.*	vergeben	entlassen
man	vergibt	entlässt

Remember that if a verb stem ends in -t or -d, the second-person singular and plural and the third-person singular change the endings -st and -t to -est and -et, respectively. Verb stems that end in -s, -ss, -ß, -z, and -tz do not add the ending -st in the second-person singular. They just add -t. For example: **du reist** *drive*, **du hasst** *hate*, **du musst** *must*, **du weißt** *know*, **du heizt** *heat*, **du sitzt** *sit*.

ÜBUNG
12·6

Reword each sentence with the subjects provided.

Ich bekomme ein paar Briefe.

1. Du _____ .

2. Sie *s.* _____ .

3. Wir _____ .

4. Ihr _____ .

Es gehört (*belongs to*) einem Soldaten (*soldier*).

5. Das Buch _____ .

6. Sie *pl.* _____ .

7. Sie *s.* _____ .

8. Diese Stiefel (*boots*) _____ .

Meine Eltern erfahren etwas Wichtiges (*learn something important*).

9. Ich _____ .

10. Du _____ .

11. Er _____ .

12. Ihr _____ .

Empfehlen (*recommend*) Sie dieses Restaurant?

13. _____ du _____ ?

14. _____ ihr _____ ?

15. _____ Herr Benz _____ ?

16. _____ sie *s.* _____ ?

Warum zerstören (*destroy*) sie die alte Kirche?

17. _____ die Soldaten _____ ?

18.	_____ er	_____ ?
19.	_____ die Männer	_____ ?
20.	_____ wir	_____ ?

Separable prefixes

There are numerous separable prefixes, and most of them are derived from prepositions and adverbs. They are called *separable* because they separate from the stem of the infinitive and are placed at the end of the sentence when conjugated in the present tense. Some commonly used separable prefixes are: **ab-**, **auf-**, **bei-**, **her-**, **hin-**, **klar-**, **mit-**, **nach-**, **weiter-**, and **zu-**. This is by far not the end of the list of inseparable prefixes.

Knowing which prefix is separable is possible by remembering which prefixes are inseparable. If the prefix in question is not in the list of inseparable prefixes (**be-**, **emp-**, **ent-**, **er-**, **ge-**, **ver-**, and **zer**), it is separable. Let's look at some example sentences. Note the position of the prefix when the verb is conjugated.

abfahren *depart*
Wir fahren um acht Uhr **ab**.   *We depart at eight o'clock.*

ankommen *arrive*
Wann kommt der nächste Zug **an**?   *When does the next train arrive?*

klarmachen *make clear*
Er macht mir seine Idee nicht **klar**.   *He does not make his idea clear to me.*

mitkommen *come along*
Kommst du **mit**?   *Are you coming along?*

zuhören *listen to*
Wir hörten dem Professor **zu**.   *We listened to the professor.*

ÜBUNG
12·7

Reword each sentence with the subjects provided.

Ich mache das Fenster zu (*close*).

1. Du _____.

2. Sie *s.* _____.

3. Wir _____.

4. Ihr _____.

Er bringt einen Freund mit (*bring along*).

5. Sie *pl.* _____.

6. Wir _____.

7. Der Arzt _____ .

8. Die Ärzte _____ .

Sie sieht sehr hübsch aus (*looks beautiful*).

9. Seine Töchter _____

10. Diese junge Dame _____ .

11. Ihr _____ .

12. Du _____ .

Er fahre morgen zurück (*drive back*).

13. Ich _____ .

14. Du _____ .

15. Sie *pl.* _____ .

16. Niemand _____ .

Die Hunde laufen weg (*run away*).

17. Er _____ .

18. Die Katze _____ .

19. Der Dieb (*thief*) _____ .

20. Die Soldaten _____ .

Using the string of words provided, create a present tense sentence.

EXAMPLE   wir / ankommen / morgen
           Wir kommen morgen an.

1. die Kinder / aufstehen (*get up*) / um sieben Uhr

_____

2. warum / aufmachen (*open*) / du / die Fenster

_____

3. die Schüler / zuhören / aufmerksam (*attentively*)

_____

4. meine kleine Schwester / einschlafen (*fall asleep*) / früh

_____

5. die Touristen / aussteigen (*get off, out*) / am Marktplatz (*market square*)

   _____

6. niemand / zumachen (*close*) / die Tür

   _____

7. Herr Schiller / anziehen (*put on*) / ein neuer Anzug (*suit*)

   _____

8. seine Freundin / anrufen (*call, telephone*) / er / jeden Tag

   _____

9. die Sportler (*athletes*) / zurückkommen / langsam und müde (*slowly and tired*)

   _____

10. der Bus / abfahren / pünktlich (*punctually*)

    _____

11. viele Reisende (*travelers*) / umsteigen (*transfer*) / am Hauptbahnhof (*main railway station*)

    _____

12. Erik / sich ausziehen / im Umkleideraum

    _____

13. er / sich hinsetzen (*sit down*) / daneben

    _____

14. du / weiterschicken (*send on*) / das Paket

    _____

15. nachkommen (*come later*) / deine Familie / ?

    _____

Verbs that combine with both separable and inseparable prefixes

There are numerous verbs that are combined with either separable or inseparable prefixes. These prefixes do not determine the conjugation. They change the meaning of the verb and determine the position of the prefix. For example:

	Inseparable prefix **verstehen** *understand*	Separable prefix **aufstehen** *get up, stand up*
ich	verstehe	stehe . . . auf
du	verstehst	stehst . . . auf
er	versteht	steht . . . auf
wir	verstehen	stehen . . . auf

ihr	versteht	steht . . . auf
Sie	verstehen	stehen . . . auf
sie *pl.*	verstehen	steht . . . auf
man	versteht	steht . . . auf

Conjugate each verb in the present tense with the pronouns provided.

1. beschreiben *describe*

   ich _____

   du _____

   er _____

   wir _____

   ihr _____

   Sie _____

   sie *pl.* _____

   man _____

2. anschreiben *write up*

   _____

   _____

   _____

   _____

   _____

   _____

   _____

   _____

3. sich ergeben *resign oneself*

   ich _____

   du _____

   er _____

   wir _____

   ihr _____

   Sie _____

   sie *pl.* _____

   man _____

4. ausgeben *spend*

   _____

   _____

   _____

   _____

   _____

   _____

   _____

   _____

5. erschlagen *strike dead*

   ich _____

   du _____

   er _____

   wir _____

   ihr _____

6. vorschlagen *suggest*

   _____

   _____

   _____

   _____

   _____

Sie	_____	_____
sie *pl.*	_____	_____
man	_____	_____

Using the string of words provided, form a present tense sentence.

EXAMPLE   wir / aussteigen / hier
Wir steigen hier aus.

Notice that the verbs have either a separable or inseparable prefix.

1. mein Bruder / aufstehen / um sechs Uhr

   _____

2. das Rathaus / sich befinden / in dieser Straße

   _____

3. wir / aufwachen (*wake up*) / sehr früh

   _____

4. ich / empfangen / sie / mit gelben Rosen

   _____

5. die Studenten / erlernen (*learn*) / zwei Sprachen (*languages*)

   _____

6. meine Tante / besuchen / ich / in der Stadt

   _____

7. die Mädchen / sich umziehen (*change clothes*) / schnell

   _____

8. die Ausländer / besichtigen / die Altstadt (*old city*)

   _____

9. der Studienrat (*teacher*) / anrufen / meine Eltern

   _____

10. der Lehrer / benutzen / die Tafel (*blackboard*)

    _____

11. alt / Mauern / zerfallen (*crumble*) / zu Staub (*into dust*)

    _____

12. klein / Schülerinnen / erröten / vor Scham (*embarrassed, in shame*)

    _____

13. niemand / einladen (*invite*) / neu / Studentin

_____

14. warum / zusammenbrechen (*collapse*) / neu / Brücke / ?

_____

15. wir / einkaufen (*shop*) / beim Bäcker (*at the baker's*)

_____

Prefixes that are inseparable and separable

A few prefixes are used both as inseparable prefixes and separable prefixes. When they are used as inseparable prefixes, the stress is *on the stem of the verb*. When they are used as separable prefixes, the stress is *on the prefix*. The preposition **um** can be used as such a prefix. Note where the stress is in the infinitive and in the conjugation of the verb.

	umármen *embrace*	**úmkommen** *die*
ich	umárme	komme um
du	umármst	kommst um
er	umármt	kommt um
wir	umármen	kommen um
ihr	umármt	kommt um
Sie	umármen	kommen um
sie *pl.*	umármen	kommen um
man	umármt	kommt um

Other prepositions that can act as either an inseparable or separable prefix are **durch**, **über**, **unter**, **voll**, **wider**, and **wieder**.

ÜBUNG
12·11

*Conjugate each verb with **ich**, **er**, and **wir** in the present tense. Note where the stress is and position the prefix accordingly.*

1. übertréiben *exaggerate*   2. wíedergeben *give back*

   ich _____   _____

   er _____   _____

   wir _____   _____

3. durchdríngen *penetrate*

ich _____

er _____

wir _____

4. wíderrufen *retract*

_____

_____

_____

5. vólltanken *fill up the gas tank*

ich _____

er _____

wir _____

6. únterkommen *find lodging*

_____

_____

_____

7. wiederhólen *repeat*

ich _____

er _____

wir _____

8. dúrchfallen *fail*

_____

_____

_____

Imperative verbs

The imperative forms are used to express commands or to give instructions. In German, as in English, the verb is in the first position in the command. An exclamation point is not always used after a written command in German; it is used only after strong emphatic commands. There are three main imperative forms. All of them use the present tense.

Formal commands

When addressing one or several people formally, the formal command is used. In the formal command the verb has the **-en** ending of the **Sie** form. The pronoun **Sie** is always added.

Kommen Sie her.	*Come here.*
Trinken Sie Wasser.	*Drink water.*

ÜBUNG
12·12

Frau Müller has landed a job in an office. Many instructions are given to her on the first day. Make commands with the following cues.

EXAMPLE: die Rechnungen bezahlen
Bezahlen Sie die Rechnungen.

1. die Post reinbringen _____

2. die Briefe sortieren _____

3. einen Brief tippen _____

4. Das Telefon bedienen _____

5. Briefmarken kaufen _____

6. den Computer einschalten _____

7. mehr Papier bestellen _____

8. den Schreibtisch aufräumen _____

9. die Formulare ausfüllen _____

10. zur Bank gehen _____

Familiar commands

Singular

When you are on a **du** basis with a person, the familiar command, singular, is used. In order to form the familiar command, singular, the **du** form of the present tense without the -**(e)st** ending is used and an -**e** is added or left off.

- If the stem ends in -**eln**, -**ern**, -**ig**, -**n**, or -**m**, an -**e** must be added.

sammeln	du sammelst	samm(e)le
verbessern	du verbesserst	verbess(e)re
sich rechtfertigen	du rechtfertigst dich	rechtfertige dich
rechnen	du rechnest	rechne
atmen	du atmest	atme

- However, if the consonant preceding -**m** or -**n** is -**l**-, -**m**-, -**n**-, -**r**-, or -**h**-, the final -**e** may be dropped.

    komm(e)
    lern(e)

- If the stem ends in -**t** or -**d**, an -**e** is added, but sometimes this is optional with the -**d** ending.

sich fürchten	du fürchtest dich	fürchte dich nicht
warten	du wartest	warte
einladen	du lädst ein	ladt(e) ein

- If the stem ends in a vowel, the -**e** is usually kept.

schreien	schreie
säen	säe

- If there is a vowel change from **e** to **i** or **ie** in the stem, an -**e** is not added.

essen	du isst	iss
lesen	du liest	lies

- For all other instances, the addition of an -**e** in the familiar command, singular, is optional.

    leg(e)
    steh(e)
    lieb(e)

- If the second-person singular has an umlaut, the umlaut is not used in the **du** command.

fahren	du fährst	fahr(e)
waschen	du wäschst	wasch(e)

When Frau Müller comes home she has to take care of her daughter. She gives her the following directions. Make commands with the following cues.

EXAMPLE: Deutsch lernen
Lerne Deutsch.

1. in deinem Zimmer spielen _____

2. dir die Hände waschen _____

3. ruhig am Tisch sitzen _____

4. die Milch trinken _____

5. das Gemüse essen _____

6. nicht laut schreien _____

7. den Tisch abräumen _____

8. ein Buch lesen _____

9. den Schlafanzug anziehen _____

10. ins Bett gehen _____

11. süß schlafen _____

12. morgen früh aufstehen _____

13. die Hausaufgaben nicht vergessen _____

14. in der Schule viel lernen _____

15. nicht zu spät nach Hause kommen _____

Plural

When addressing several people with whom you are on a **du** basis, the familiar command, plural, is used. This command form has the same form as the second-person plural. The personal pronoun **ihr** is dropped.

Lernt.	*Learn.*
Esst.	*Eat.*
Wartet.	*Wait.*
Schaut.	*Look.*

Frau Müller's daughter, Sabine, hears the following instructions that are given to her and her classmates. Make commands with the following cues.

EXAMPLE: reinkommen
             Kommt rein.

1. ruhig sitzen _____

2. die Hand heben _____

3. still sein _____

4. nicht laut werden _____

5. die Bücher nehmen _____

6. die Geschichte lesen _____

7. einen Aufsatz schreiben _____

8. keine Fehler machen _____

9. nicht mit den Nachbarn sprechen _____

10. den Aufsatz noch einmal abschreiben _____

11. den Film ansehen _____

12. die Hausaufgaben für morgen haben _____

13. das Pausenbrot essen _____

14. auf dem Schulplatz spielen _____

15. jetzt nach Hause gehen _____

Exhortations (mild commands, inclusive commands)

When expressing *let us* (*Let's go.* / *Let's eat.*), the first-person plural is used, with inverted word order.

Essen wir jetzt.	*Let's eat now.*
Spielen wir heute Schach.	*Let's play chess today.*

Sabine and her friends are trying to decide what to do on the weekend. Make inclusive commands with the clues given.

EXAMPLE: einen Film sehen
             Sehen wir einen Film.

1. schwimmen gehen _____

2. in den Park fahren _____

3. Ball spielen _____

4. ein Buch lesen _____

5. Hausaufgaben machen _____

6. ein Eis essen _____

7. eine Limonade trinken _____

8. einen Turm bauen _____

9. malen _____

10. Karl besuchen _____

The command forms of sein and werden

The command forms of these two verbs are somewhat irregular:

Seien Sie.	Sei.	Seid.	Seien wir.
Werden Sie.	Werde.	Werdet.	Werden wir.

ÜBUNG
12·16

Make commands by following the given directions.

EXAMPLES: Sage Peter und Michael, dass sie still sein sollen.
Seid still.
Sage Herrn Müller, dass er still sein soll.
Seien Sie still.

1. Sage Michael und Jakob, dass sie still sein sollen. _____

2. Sage Herrn Peters, dass er gesund werden soll. _____

3. Sage Annchen, dass sie lieb sein soll. _____

4. Sage Herrn Wurster und Herrn Riske, dass sie geduldig sein sollen. _____

5. Sage Anke, dass sie nicht krank werden soll. _____

6. Sage dem Nachbarn, dass er nicht böse sein soll. _____

7. Sage den Kindern, dass sie nicht nervös werden sollen. _____

8. Sage den Eltern, dass sie geduldig sein sollen. _____

9. Sage dem Hans, dass er Glück haben soll. _____

10. Sage den Geschwistern, dass sie groß werden sollen. _____

Give the four imperative forms of the following verbs.

EXAMPLE: schlafen

Schlafen Sie, Schlaf(e), Schlaft, Schlafen wir

1. fahren _____

2. helfen _____

3. essen _____

4. nehmen _____

5. mitkommen _____

6. schreien _____

7. sehen _____

8. werden _____

9. sein _____

10. haben _____

Make commands by following the given directions.

EXAMPLE: Sagen Sie Peter, dass er ein neues Buch kaufen soll.

Kauf ein neues Buch.

1. Sagen Sie Frau Braun, dass sie ins Café gehen soll.

_____

2. Sagen Sie Peter, dass er still sein soll.

_____

3. Sagen Sie Luise und Hannah, dass sie draußen spielen sollen.

_____

4. Sagen Sie Marianne, dass sie leise sprechen soll.

_____

5. Sagen Sie Ute, dass sie ein neues Kleid kaufen soll.

_____

6. Sagen Sie den Kindern, dass sie nicht krank werden sollen.

_____

7. Sagen Sie Max, dass er den Rasen mähen soll.

_____

8. Sagen Sie den Mädchen, dass sie ihr Zimmer aufräumen sollen.

_____

9. Sagen Sie Emma, dass sie sich die Hände waschen soll.

_____

10. Sagen Sie den Damen, dass sie hier sitzen sollen.

_____

11. Sagen Sie dem Jungen, dass er keine Angst haben soll.

_____

12. Sagen Sie Max und Hans, dass sie vorsichtig sein sollen.

_____

13. Sagen Sie dem Onkel Fritz, dass er die Tür zumachen soll.

_____

14. Sagen Sie dem Nachbarn, dass er den Hund einschließen soll.

_____

15. Sagen Sie dem Kind, dass es die Geschichte vorlesen soll.

_____

16. Sagen Sie den Herren, dass sie langsam fahren sollen.

_____

17. Sagen Sie Jakob und Michael, dass sie ins Wasser laufen sollen.

_____

Accusative prepositions and interrogatives

The German accusative case is used to identify direct objects. In the following sentence, the bolded word is the direct object.

> Martin kauft **meinen Wagen**.   *Martin buys **my car**.*

It answers the question *What does Martin buy?* If the direct object is a person, it answers the question *Whom does Martin see?*

> Martin sieht **meinen Bruder**.   *Martin sees **my brother**.*

Remember that only masculine nouns have a declensional change in the accusative case.

	MASCULINE	FEMININE	NEUTER	PLURAL
nom	der Mann	die Frau	das Kind	die Kinder
acc	den Mann	die Frau	das Kind	die Kinder

Another function of the accusative case is to identify the object of an accusative preposition. The accusative prepositions are:

bis	*until, 'til*
durch	*through*
entlang	*along(side), down*
für	*for*
gegen	*against*
ohne	*without*
wider	*against, contrary to (poetical)*
um	*around, at (a time of the clock)*

Nouns that follow one of these prepositions will appear in the accusative case. For example:

Er bleibt **bis** nächsten Montag.	*He is staying **until** next Monday.*
Sie laufen **durch** das Haus.	*They run **through** the house.*
Sie gehen die Straße **entlang**.	*They go **down** the street.*
Das ist ein Geschenk **für** Ihren Mann.	*That is a gift **for** your husband.*
Er schlägt **gegen** die Tür.	*He bangs **on** the door.*
Er kommt **ohne** Frau Benz.	*He comes **without** Ms. Benz.*
Es ist **wider** alle Vernunft.	*It is **against** all reason.*
Sie fahren schnell **um** die Ecke.	*They drive quickly **around** the corner.*

Note that **entlang** follows the accusative object: **die Straße entlang**.

ÜBUNG

13·1

Complete each sentence with the given phrases.

FOR EXAMPLE: Ich bleibe bis _____.

(sechs Uhr) _____ *Ich bleibe bis sechs Uhr.* _____

(Montag) _____ *Ich bleibe bis Montag.* _____

Ein Vogel fliegt durch _____. *A bird flies through . . . .*

1. das Fenster _____

2. die Tür _____

3. der Garten _____

4. der Wald (*woods*) _____

Ich habe diese Blumen für _____. *I have these flowers for . . . .*

5. Ihre Mutter _____

6. Ihr Vater _____

7. mein Onkel _____

8. meine Schwestern _____

Ist er gegen _____? *Is he against . . . .*

9. dieser Rechtsanwalt _____

10. meine Idee (*idea*) _____

11. Ihre Freundin _____

12. mein Bruder _____

Kommen Sie ohne _____? *Are you coming without . . . .*

13. ein Geschenk _____

14. Ihr Großvater (*grandfather*) _____

15. ein Regenschirm (*umbrella*) _____

16. Ihre Bücher _____

Sie sorgt sich um _____. *She worries about . . . .*

17. mein Sohn (*son*) _____

18. dieses Problem _____

19. meine Eltern _____

20. der Zahnarzt _____

Pronouns also have a new form in the accusative case. Compare the nominative case and accusative case pronouns that follow.

NOMINATIVE	ACCUSATIVE
ich	mich
du	dich
er	ihn
sie (*sing.*)	sie (*sing.*)
es	es
wir	uns
ihr	euch
Sie	Sie
sie (*pl.*)	sie (*pl.*)
wer	wen
was	was

The accusative case pronouns are used when the pronoun is a direct object. For example:

Meine Schwester besucht **mich**.	*My sister visits **me**.*
Kennst du **ihn**?	*Do you know **him**?*
Die Kinder lieben **euch**.	*The children love **you**.*

ÜBUNG

13·2

In the blank provided, write the correct accusative case form of the pronoun provided in parentheses.

FOR EXAMPLE: (ich) Die Kinder lieben _____*mich.*_____

1. (Sie) Meine Familie begrüßt _____.

2. (du) Ich kenne _____ nicht.

3. (es) Die Jungen essen _____.

4. (sie [*pl.*]) Wir haben _____.

5. (er) Die Schüler legen _____ auf den Tisch. (*The students lay it on the table.*)

6. (wir) Die Touristen fotografieren _____. (*The tourists photograph us.*)

7. (ihr) Er liebt _____ nicht.

8. (ich) Meine Eltern besuchen _____ in Hamburg.

9. (wer) _____ siehst du?

10. (was) _____ schreibt der Mann?

11. (sie [*sing.*]) Die Mädchen suchen _____.

12. (er) Niemand liest _____.

13. (du) Meine Mutter ruft _____ an. (*My mother phones you.*)

14. (wir) Die Frauen begrüßen _____.

15. (es) Wer bekommt _____?

If a pronoun follows an accusative preposition, the pronoun must be in the accusative case. For example:

Ich habe ein Geschenk für **dich**.   *I have a gift for **you**.*
Sie schickt die Nachricht durch **ihn**.   *She sends the news through **him**.*

ÜBUNG
13·3

Complete each sentence with the pronouns provided in parentheses. Note that some sentences will require a nominative case pronoun and others an accusative case pronoun. If the pronoun is in the nominative case, it is the subject of the sentence, which can affect the conjugation of the verb.

FOR EXAMPLE: _____ hat kein Geld.

(ich) _____ *Ich habe kein Geld.* _____

(er) _____ *Er hat kein Geld.* _____

_____ wohnt in Heidelberg.

1. (du) _____

2. (wir) _____

3. (ihr) _____

4. (Sie) _____

5. (sie [*sing.*]) _____

Erik spielt gegen _____. *Erik plays against . . . .*

6. (ich) _____

7. (er) _____

8. (wir) _____

9. (ihr) _____

10. (sie [*pl.*]) _____

Meine Eltern sorgen sich um _____.

11. (du) _____

12. (sie [*sing.*]) _____

13. (ihr) _____

14. (Sie) _____

15. (sie [*pl.*]) _____

_____ entdeckt eine kleine Insel.

16. (ich) _____

17. (er) _____

18. (wir) _____

19. (Sie) _____

20. (wer) _____

Sie gehen ohne _____ wandern. *They go hiking without . . . .*

21. (du) _____

22. (er) _____

23. (sie [*sing.*]) _____

24. (wir) _____

25. (ihr) _____

The third-person pronouns (**er**, **sie** [*sing.*], **es**, and **sie** [*pl.*]) are the replacements for nouns. If those nouns refer to persons or other animates, a prepositional phrase as previously illustrated is used. For example:

Ich komme **ohne** meine Eltern.	*I come **without** my parents.*
Ich komme **ohne** sie.	*I come **without** them.*

But if the noun refers to an inanimate object, a different type of prepositional phrase is formed. It is called a *prepositional adverb*. A prepositional adverb is the combination of the prefix **da-** and the preposition. For example:

dadurch	*through it*
dafür	*for it*
dagegen	*against it*
darum	*around it*

Because the preposition **um** begins with a vowel, the prefix becomes **dar-**.

In the blank provided, write the prepositional phrase with the pronoun replacement for the noun in the original prepositional phrase.

FOR EXAMPLE: für den Mann _____ *für ihn* _____

1. durch das Fenster _____

2. um die Kinder _____

3. für meine Eltern _____

4. für diesen Artikel _____

5. gegen die Tänzerin _____

6. um die Ecke _____

7. durch meinen Bruder _____

8. für meinen Freund und mich _____

9. gegen diese Idee _____

10. ohne Frau Keller _____

11. wider den Rechtsanwalt _____

12. um meine Freundin _____

13. durch den Wald _____

14. ohne meinen Sohn _____

15. um die Stadt _____

You have encountered the interrogatives **wer**, **wen**, **was**, **wo**, **wie**, and **wann**. Two more important interrogative words are **warum** (*why*) and **wessen** (*whose*).

Warum asks for a reason for an action. The most common response is with the conjunction **denn** (*because*).

Warum ist Tina zu Hause?	*Why is Tina at home?*
Sie ist zu Hause, **denn** sie ist krank.	*She is at home, because she is sick.*

Wessen asks about ownership. And the response often requires the use of a possessive pronoun. They are:

PRONOUN	POSSESSIVE
ich	mein
du	dein
er	sein
sie (*sing.*)	ihr
es	sein
wir	unser
ihr	euer
Sie	Ihr
sie (*pl.*)	ihr
wer	wessen

The possessive pronouns are **ein**-words and show gender and case like the other **ein**-words.

MASCULINE	FEMININE	NEUTER	PLURAL
dein Bruder	deine Schwester	dein Kind	deine Kinder
unser Freund	unsere Freundin	unser Haus	unsere Bücher

Let's look at some example questions with **wessen** and possible answers to those questions:

Wessen Buch ist das?	*Whose book is that?*
Das ist dein Buch.	*That is your book.*
Wessen Eltern wohnen da?	*Whose parents live there?*
Seine Eltern wohnen da.	*His parents live there.*
Wessen Vater spricht Deutsch?	*Whose father speaks German?*
Euer Vater spricht Deutsch.	*Your father speaks German.*

ÜBUNG
13·5

*Using the provided phrases, answer the questions that ask **warum**.*

FOR EXAMPLE: Warum ist er nicht hier?

Er hat keine Zeit. _____*Er ist nicht hier, denn er hat keine Zeit.*_____

1. Warum ist Sabine in Berlin?

   Sie besucht ihren Onkel. _____

   Sie arbeitet in der Hauptstadt. _____

   Sie sucht einen Freund. _____

2. Warum bleibt er in Kanada?

   Er lernt Englisch. _____

   Seine Eltern wohnen da. _____

   Seine Freundin arbeitet in Toronto. _____

3. Warum kaufst du einen VW?

   Ich brauche ein Auto. _____

   Ein BMW ist teuer. (*expensive*) _____

   Ein VW ist billig. (*cheap*) _____

ÜBUNG
13·6

*Using the pronoun provided in parentheses as your cue, answer the questions that ask **wessen**. Use the appropriate possessive pronoun form.*

FOR EXAMPLE: Wessen Haus ist das?

(ich) _____*Das ist mein Haus.*_____

Wessen Hut ist das?

1. (er) _____

2. (sie [*sing.*]) _____

3. (wir) _____

4. (ihr) _____

5. (Sie) _____

Wessen Freund sieht er?

6. (ich) _____

7. (du) _____

8. (ihr) _____

Accusative prepositions and interrogatives   205

9. (Sie) _____

10. (sie [*pl.*]) _____

Wessen Fahrrad (*bicycle*) kaufen sie?

11. (du) _____

12. (er) _____

13. (sie [*sing.*]) _____

14. (wir) _____

15. (ihr) _____

Wessen Eltern wohnen in der Hauptstadt?

16. (ich) _____

17. (du) _____

18. (er) _____

19. (wir) _____

20. (sie [*pl.*]) _____

The interrogative **wie** is often combined with other words to form new interrogatives. For example:

wie alt	*how old*
wie hoch	*how high*
wie klein	*how small*
wie lange	*how long*
wie oft	*how often*
wie schnell	*how fast*
wie spät	*how late*
wie viel	*how much*

The following questions demonstrate such interrogatives:

Wie alt ist er?	*How old is he?*
Wie hoch ist das Rathaus?	*How high is city hall?*
Wie oft gehst du in die Bibiliothek?	*How often do you go to the library?*
Wie viel kostet das Hemd?	*How much does the shirt cost?*

ÜBUNG
13·7

Write the question with **wie** *that would be asked to elicit each of the answers provided.*

FOR EXAMPLE: Er ist vier Jahre alt. (*He is four years old.*)

Wie alt ist er?

1. Sie fährt jeden Tag in die Stadt. (*She drives into the city every day.*)

_____

2. Sie bleiben nur vier Tage hier. (*They are staying here for only four days.*)

_____

3. Das Buch kostet elf Euro. (*The book costs eleven euros.*)

_____

4. Sie kommt zwei Stunden zu spät. (*She is coming two hours too late.*)

_____

5. Der alte Herr hat viel Geld. (*The old gentleman has a lot of money.*)

_____

An interrogative can be formed by the combination of an accusative preposition and **wen**. It asks *whom* with the meaning of the preposition. For example:

für wen	*for whom*
gegen wen	*against whom*
ohne wen	*without whom*

If the object of the preposition is not a person but an inanimate object, a prepositional adverb is formed with the prefix **wo(r)-**. **Wor-** is used with prepositions that begin with a vowel. For example:

wofür	*for what*
wogegen	*against what*
worum	*around what*

ÜBUNG
13·8

In the blank provided, write the question that asks about the underlined prepositional phrase. In the second blank, write the correct prepositional phrase with a pronoun that can replace the underlined prepositional phrase in each sentence.

FOR EXAMPLE: Er hat ein Buch für seine Schwester.

Für wen hat er ein Buch?

für sie

Er sorgt sich um das Problem.

Worum sorgt er sich?

darum

1. Thomas war gegen seine Familie. (*Thomas was against his family.*)

_____

_____

2. Frau Braun fährt ohne ihre Kinder ab. (*Ms. Braun departs without her children.*)

_____

_____

3. Ich schreibe den Brief <u>für den Schüler</u>. (*I write the letter for the pupil.*)

_____

_____

4. Der Sportler schwimmt <u>durch den Fluss</u>. (*The athlete swims through the river.*)

_____

_____

5. Die Zwillinge danken uns <u>für die Geschenke zum Geburtstag</u>. (*The children thank us for the gifts for their birthday.*)

_____

_____

6. Die Jungen laufen <u>durch den Friedhof</u>. (*The boys run through the cemetery.*)

_____

_____

7. Der alte Mann bittet <u>um Hilfe</u>. (*The old man asks for help.*)

_____

_____

8. Ich kenne ein gutes Mittel <u>gegen die Krankheit</u>. (*I know a good remedy for the disease.*)

_____

_____

9. Erik kommt nach Hause <u>ohne seine Freundin</u>. (*Erik comes home without his girlfriend.*)

_____

_____

10. Wir schicken das Paket <u>durch die Post</u>. (*We send the package through the mail.*)

_____

_____

Accusative prepositions

English nouns do not decline when they are used as direct objects or in prepositional phrases. In German, however, direct objects and objects of accusative prepositions are functions of the accusative case, and masculine nouns make declensional changes in this case.

	NOMINATIVE CASE	ACCUSATIVE CASE
Masculine	der Vater	den Vater
Feminine	die Frau	die Frau
Neuter	das Kind	das Kind
Plural	die Lampen	die Lampen

The following are the most common accusative prepositions, and masculine nouns in phrases with these prepositions must appear in the accusative case. Remember: Feminine, neuter, and plural nouns do not decline in the accusative case.

bis	*until, up to*	gegen	*against*
durch	*through*	ohne	*without*
entlang	*along, down*	um	*around, about*
für	*for*	wider	*against, contrary to*

In the following examples, notice how nouns appear in accusative prepositional phrases and how the masculine definite article changes.

> Ich habe etwas für **den Mann.**
> *I have something for the man.*

> Er bittet um **die Adresse.**
> *He asks for the address.*

> Sie laufen durch **das Haus.**
> *They run through the house.*

> Er kommt ohne **die Kinder.**
> *He comes without the children.*

Unlike the other accusative prepositions, the preposition **entlang** follows its noun object.

> Der Weg führte den Fluss **entlang.**
> *The path went along the river.*

When accusative prepositions are used with pronouns that refer to animate nouns, the prepositional phrase consists of preposition + accusative pronoun.

> Es ist ein Geschenk **für dich.**
> *It's a gift for you.*

> Kommst du **ohne ihn?**
> *Are you coming without him?*

> Ich denke er ist **gegen mich.**
> *I think he's against me.*

If you ask the question *whom* with an accusative preposition, the nominative **wer** changes to the accusative **wen.**

> Das ist ein Geschenk für meinen Bruder.
> **Für wen** ist das Geschenk?
> *Whom is the gift for?*

> Er hat gegen den Dieb gesprochen.
> **Gegen wen** hat er gesprochen?
> *Whom did he speak against?*

> Die Touristen stehen um den Reiseleiter.
> **Um wen** stehen die Touristen?
> *Whom are the tourists standing around?*

Rewrite each sentence, using the appropriate form of the word or phrase in parentheses to fill in the blank.

1. Eine Fledermaus ist durch _____ geflogen.

   a. (das Haus) _____

   b. (die Scheune) _____

   c. (der große Lesesaal) _____

   d. (unsere Schule) _____

2. Warum ist er gegen ?_____

   a. (seine Kinder) _____

   b. (sein Sohn) _____

   c. (ihr älterer Bruder) _____

   d. (seine Tante) _____

3. Der neue Manager handelte ohne _____.

   a. (jede Rücksicht auf uns)_____

   b. (Vernunft) _____

   c. (Überlegung) _____

4. Ich möchte bis _____ bleiben.

   a. (Freitag) _____

   b. (nächster Samstag) _____

   c. (morgen) _____

5. Welcher Weg führt _____ entlang?

   a. (der schöne Bach) _____

   b. (dieser Wald) _____

   c. (jener Zaun) _____

   d. (kein Fluss) _____

*Fill in each blank with the appropriate preposition. Choose from **für**, **bis**, and **um**.*

1. Ich habe mich immer _____ meine Familie bemüht.

2. Morgen fahren wir _____ Freiburg.

3. Darf ich _____ Ihren Vornamen bitten?

4. Erich hat _____ 40 Euro zwei alte Pullover verkauft.

5. Ich habe Onkel Heinz _____ das nette Geschenk gedankt.

6. Diese Arbeit ist typisch _____ einen achtjährigen.

7. Ich war oft _____ meine Eltern besorgt.

8. Ich werde mit dir _____ an das Ende der Straße gehen.

9. Kommen Sie _____ dreizehn Uhr?

10. Der Stadtgraben ging _____ die ganze Stadt.

Multiple usages

The meaning of the accusative prepositions shown in the lists and examples above is their *basic meaning*. Accusative prepositions, however, have more than one use and therefore have to be translated into English appropriately to achieve the intended meaning.

Bis

Bis is generally used to show movement toward a goal, and that goal can be a location, an amount, or a point in time. When used with locations, it often means *as far as* or *up to*.

bis Berlin	*as far as Berlin*
bis hier	*up to here*

With amounts, it means *up to* or *as much as*.

bis 100 Euro	*as much as 100 euros*
bis 10 Liter	*up to ten liters*

Notice that no article is used in the expressions above. However, when an article is used, a second preposition tends to accompany **bis**.

Wir gingen bis **zum** Irrgarten.
We went as far as the maze.

Sie fliegen bis **über** die Wolken.
They're flying up over the clouds.

Er bleibt hier bis **nach** den Ferien.
He's staying here until after vacation.

In these examples, the translation of **bis** varies, although the general idea of *up to, until,* or *as far as* is still expressed in some form to show movement toward a goal.

Durch

Durch means *through* or *across* and identifies movement through a certain space.

Wir laufen durch den Wald.
We run through the woods.

Ich schwimme durch den Fluss.
I swim across the river.

But when **durch** is used to express movement across time, the meaning changes slightly.

Wir lebten den Herbst durch in Wien.
We lived through the fall in Vienna.

Es geschieht durch die Geschichte.
It occurs throughout history.

Notice that the preposition **durch** in the expression **den Herbst durch** follows its object. In the passive voice, **durch** is used to indicate the cause of an action.

Der Mann ist durch einen Unfall getötet worden.
The man was killed due to an accident.

Durch also describes the *means* by which an action is carried out.

Wir werden die Geschenke durch die Post schicken.
We'll send the gifts by mail.

Für

Für means *for* and signifies that something is being done for the benefit of someone or something. In this meaning, it is the opposite of **gegen** (*against*).

Luise arbeitet für ihre Familie.
Luise works for her family.

Ich kämpfe für ein besseres Leben.
I struggle for a better life.

Für can also signify a replacement for someone or something else.

Der Freund schreibt die Briefe für seinen kranken Kameraden.
The friend writes the letters for his sick pal.

Für is also used to express an amount of money or a price.

Ich arbeite nur für Geld.
I'm just working for the money.

Sie kauft für 5 Euro einen Schlips.
She buys a tie for 5 euros.

Gegen

Gegen has the basic meaning *against*. It is the opposite of **für**.

Warum kämpfen sie immer gegeneinander?
Why are they always fighting against one another?

Die Jungen sind gegen den Strom geschwommen.
The boys swam against the current.

Gegen also means *approximately* or *toward* in expressions of time or amount.

Sie sind gegen 23 Uhr angekommen.
They arrived toward 11 P.M.

Mein Urgroßvater ist jetzt gegen 90 Jahre alt.
My great-grandfather is almost 90 years old now.

Ohne

Ohne indicates that someone or something is not present. Its general meaning is *without*.

Der arme Mann ist jetzt ohne Wohnung.
The poor man is now without an apartment.

Das junge Ehepaar ist noch ohne Kinder.
The young couple is still without children.

Um

Um is used to express the time as shown on a clock.

Es ist um Mitternacht geschehen.
It happened at midnight.

Ich komme um 10 Uhr nach Hause.
I'll come home at 10 o'clock.

This preposition is also frequently used to mean *around* and implies a circular motion around a person or object.

Die Planeten bewegen sich endlos um die Sonne.
The planets move endlessly around the sun.

Um is also used with certain verbs to achieve a specific meaning, and in such instances **um** can have a variety of translations.

er bemüht sich um	*he acts on behalf of*
ich bitte um	*I ask for*
wir weinen um	*we cry about*
sie kümmert sich um	*she cares about/for*

Wider

Wider, like **gegen**, is the opposite of **für**. It means *against* or *contrary to*, but is used less often than **gegen** and is found most frequently in poetic language.

Der Chef handelte wider alle Vernunft.
The boss acted against all reason.

Der-words

Der-words are demonstratives that replace definite articles. They identify the gender of a noun like definite articles and decline in the same way. The **der**-words are **dieser** (*this*), **jener** (*that*), **jeder** (*each*), **solcher** (*such*), and **welcher** (*which*). Gender is shown in the nominative case of **der**-words and singular adjectives that follow end in -**e**.

	DIESER	JENER	JEDER
Masculine	dieser gute Mann	jener gute Mann	jeder gute Mann
Feminine	diese nette Frau	jene nette Frau	jede nette Frau
Neuter	dieses alte Haus	jenes alte Haus	jedes alte Haus
Plural	diese guten Kinder	jene guten Kinder	—

Notice that **jeder** (*each*) is used only in the singular.

Following an accusative preposition, a masculine **der**-word declines like the definite article, and the ending of an adjective that follows becomes **-en**.

für dies**en** neu**en** Lehrer	*for this new teacher*
bis jen**en** froh**en** Tag	*until that happy day*
um jed**en** schön**en** Garten	*around each beautiful garden*
durch welch**en** alt**en** Bahnhof	*through which old railway station*

Ein-words

Ein-words are demonstratives that replace indefinite articles. They are the possessive pronouns (**mein, dein, sein, ihr, unser, euer, ihr, Ihr**) and **kein** (*no, not any*). With **ein**-words, gender is shown in the adjective.

MASCULINE	FEMININE	NEUTER	PLURAL
mein alt**er** Mantel	deine neu**e** Mappe	mein rot**es** Buch	deine guten Kinder
sein alt**er** Wagen	ihre neu**e** Lampe	sein rot**es** Auto	ihre guten Kinder
unser alt**er** Onkel	eure neu**e** Schule	Ihr rot**es** Hemd	unsere guten Kinder
kein alt**er** Mann	keine neu**e** Tasse	kein rot**es** Dach	keine guten Kinder

Following an accusative preposition, a masculine **ein**-word declines like the indefinite article, and the ending of an adjective that follows becomes **-en**.

um mein**en** rot**en** Mantel	*around my red coat*
für dein**en** nett**en** Bruder	*for your nice brother*
durch Ihr**en** schön**en** Garten	*through your beautiful garden*
ohne unser**en** neu**en** Freund	*without our new friend*

ÜBUNG
13·11

Fill in each blank with any appropriate phrase.

1. Diese Leute haben viel für _____ getan.

2. Der blinde Mann stieß gegen _____.

3. Gegen _____ sind wir endlich nach Hause gekommen.

4. Die Party fängt um _____ an.

5. Die Wanderer müssen durch _____ schwimmen.

6. Morgen reisen wir nur bis _____.

7. Wir gingen bis zu _____.

8. Mein Vater geht niemals ohne _____ aus dem Haus.

9. Ich habe es für _____ gekauft.

10. Die Mädchen gingen _____ entlang.

11. Der Polizist hat um _____ gebeten.

12. Die alte Scheune wurde durch _____ zerstört.

13. Wie kannst du das ohne _____ tun?

14. Warum ist Helmut gegen _____?

15. Sie hat sich selten um _____ gekümmert.

Regular verbs in the past tense and word order

Regular past tense

A large group of German verbs form the past tense by following the same conjugational pattern. This past tense form is called the *regular past tense*. The basic suffix for the regular past tense is **-te**. Look at the following verbs for the full conjugation.

	glauben (*believe*)	**folgen** (*follow*)	**tanzen** (*dance*)
ich	glaubte	folgte	tanzte
du	glaubtest	folgtest	tanztest
er/sie/es	glaubte	folgte	tanzte
wir	glaubten	folgten	tanzten
ihr	glaubtet	folgtet	tanztet
Sie	glaubten	folgten	tanzten
sie (*pl.*)	glaubten	folgten	tanzten

ÜBUNG
14·1

In the blank provided, write the past tense conjugation of the given verb for the subject provided.

1. ich _____ spielen

2. du _____ hören

3. wir _____ sagen

4. Sie _____ fragen

5. der Diplomat _____ reisen (*travel*)

6. sie (*sing.*) _____ machen

7. ihr _____ stellen

8. sie (*pl.*) _____ setzen

9. er _____ dienen

10. ich _____ sorgen

11. seine Eltern _____ holen (*get, fetch*)

12. du _____ suchen

216

13. wir _____ kaufen

14. ihr _____ pflanzen (*plant*)

15. Erik _____ flüstern (*whisper*)

Write the full conjugation of each verb with the subjects provided.

1. lernen   2. lächeln

ich   _____   _____

du   _____   _____

er   _____   _____

wir   _____   _____

ihr   _____   _____

Sie   _____   _____

man   _____   _____

3. feiern (*celebrate*)   4. leben

ich   _____   _____

du   _____   _____

er   _____   _____

wir   _____   _____

ihr   _____   _____

Sie   _____   _____

wer   _____   _____

5. lieben   6. wohnen

ich   _____   _____

du   _____   _____

er   _____   _____

wir   _____   _____

ihr   _____   _____

Sie   _____   _____

Tina   _____   _____

If a verb stem ends in **-t** or **-d**, the basic regular past tense ending will be **-ete**. For example:

	arbeiten (*work*)	**baden** (*bathe*)
ich	arbeitete	badete
du	arbeitetest	badetest
er/sie/es	arbeitete	badete
wir	arbeiteten	badeten
ihr	arbeitetet	badetet
Sie	arbeiteten	badeten
sie (*pl.*)	arbeiteten	badeten

Write the full conjugation of each verb with the subjects provided.

1. enden (*end*)   **2. fürchten** (*fear*)

ich _____   _____

du   _____   _____

er   _____   _____

wir _____   _____

ihr _____   _____

Sie _____   _____

man _____   _____

3. reden (*talk*)   **4. antworten** (*answer*)

ich _____   _____

du   _____   _____

er   _____   _____

wir _____   _____

ihr _____   _____

Sie _____   _____

wer _____   _____

The separable and inseparable prefixes function in the same way in the regular past tense as they do in the present tense. For example:

	zumachen (*close*)	**erzählen** (*tell*)
ich	machte zu	erzählte
du	machtest zu	erzähltest
er/sie/es	machte zu	erzählte
wir	machten zu	erzählten
ihr	machtet zu	erzähltet
Sie	machten zu	erzählten
sie (*pl.*)	machten zu	erzählten

In the blank provided, write the past tense conjugation of the given verb for the subject provided.

1. ich _____ warten

2. du _____ besuchen

3. er _____ erwarten (*expect*)

4. wir _____ abholen (*pick up, fetch*)

5. ihr _____ vorbereiten (*prepare*)

6. Sie _____ nachfragen (*inquire*)

7. sie (*sing.*) _____ verkaufen

8. seine Eltern _____ zuhören (*listen*)

9. man _____ aufhören (*stop, cease*)

10. ein Lehrer _____ verlangen (*demand*)

11. ich _____ umpflanzen (*transplant*)

12. sie (*pl.*) _____ zurückkehren (*turn back, return*)

13. wir _____ sagen

14. du _____ einkaufen (*shop*)

15. ihr _____ ersetzen (*replace*)

The past tense

Usage of the past tense

The past tense is usually used to tell a story or a sequence of past events.

Er öffnete die Tür des Cafés und schaute sich um. Als er sie sah, lächelte er vor Freude und eilte auf sie zu.	*He opened the door of the café and looked around. When he saw her, he smiled happily and hurried toward her.*

The past tense is also used to express customary or repeated actions.

An heißen Tagen kaufte sie ein Erdbeereis.	*On hot days she always bought a strawberry ice cream.*

Whereas the present perfect tense is generally preferred in conversation, when using the verbs **haben**, **sein**, and **werden** and the modal auxiliaries **dürfen**, **können**, **mögen**, **müssen**, **sollen**, and **wollen**, the past tense is preferred.

Er **hatte** viel Geld.	*He had lots of money.*
Wir **mussten** um sechs Uhr aufstehen.	*We had to get up at six o'clock.*

When a clause is introduced by **als** (*when*), the past tense is always used.

Als er sie **sah, lächelte** er.   *When he saw her, he smiled.*

In all other cases involving back-and-forth conversation, the present perfect is used.

Weak verbs

German verbs may be broken up into two major groups: weak and strong. The way the past tense of the verb is formed determines whether a verb is weak or strong. Weak verbs do not have a vowel change in the stem in the past tenses. The past tense of weak verbs is formed by adding **-t** to the stem and then adding the following endings:

spielen (*to play*)

ich spiel**te**	wir spiel**ten**
du spiel**test**	ihr spiel**tet**
er/sie/es spiel**te**	sie/Sie spiel**ten**

Note that the first- and third-person singular are the same. Verbs whose stem ends in **-t** or **-d** add an extra **-e-** between the stem and the **-te** suffix: **arbeiten—arbeitete, warten—wartete**. This is done to aid pronunciation.

baden (*to bathe or swim*)

ich bad**ete**	wir bad**eten**
du bad**etest**	ihr bad**etet**
er/sie/es bad**ete**	sie/Sie bad**eten**

An **-e-** is also added to some verbs whose stem ends in **-m** or **-n**: **atmen—atmete, öffnen— öffnete**; but **lernen—lernte, wohnen—wohnte**.

Verbs with separable prefixes are separated in the past tense in the same manner as in the present tense.

Er macht die Tür zu.	*He closes the door.*
Er machte die Tür zu.	*He closed the door.*

ÜBUNG
14·5

Change the following verb phrases to the past tense.

EXAMPLE: Er tanzt.
        *Er **tanzte**.*

1. Ich wohne. _____

2. Er atmet. _____

3. Das Baby weint. _____

4. Hörst du nichts? _____

5. Herr Müller raucht. _____

6. Wir suchen etwas _____

7. Lernt ihr viel? _____

8. Die Mädchen öffnen es. _____

9. Wartest du? _____

10. Schmidts kaufen es. _____

11. Sie arbeiten. _____

12. Was sagst du? _____

13. Was spielt ihr? _____

14. Sie lächelt. _____

15. Er wohnt in Berlin. _____

Your sister talks about the childhood you shared. Insert the proper past tense verbs in the following sentences.

EXAMPLE: Oft _____ (reden) wir abends.
　　　　　Oft **redeten** wir abends.

1. Unsere Familie _____ (machen) immer viel.

2. Vater _____ (arbeiten) jeden Tag.

3. Die Kinder _____ (lernen) in der Schule.

4. Mutter _____ (kochen) jeden Tag mehrere Mal.

5. Sie (*sing., fam.*) _____ (kaufen) immer viel Obst und Gemüse.

6. Das Essen _____ (schmecken) immer gut.

7. Sie (*sing., fam.*) _____ (ernähren) uns gut.

8. Oma _____ (pflanzen) oft neue Blumen, oder sie _____ (putzen) das Haus.

9. Mein großer Bruder _____ (mähen) den Rasen.

10. Abends _____ (erholen) sich alle beim Kartenspiel, oder wir _____ (beschäftigen) uns mit Musik.

11. Die Kinder _____ (spielen) alle ein Instrument.

12. Wir _____ (üben) viel und _____ (verbessern) uns.

13. Vater _____ (achten) darauf dass wir jeden Tag _____ (üben).

14. Der Musikunterricht _____ (kosten) viel.

15. Aber die Eltern _____ (meinen) es _____ (lohnen) sich.

Word order

In a German sentence where the subject begins the sentence, the verb follows the subject.

Mein Vater **spricht** kein Englisch.　　　*My father **speaks** no English.*
Das Haus **ist** sehr klein.　　　　　　　*The house **is** very small.*

　　But if something other than the subject begins the sentence, the verb will precede the subject. For example:

Wir **fahren** nach Hause.　　　　　　　*We **are driving** home.*
Heute **fahren** wir nach Hause.　　　　　*Today we **are driving** home.*

Mein Bruder **arbeitet** in der Stadt.　　　*My brother **works** in the city.*
Im Winter **arbeitet** mein Bruder in der Stadt.　*In winter my brother **works** in the city.*

ÜBUNG
14·7

Rewrite the following sentences with the phrase in parentheses as the first element of the sentence.

FOR EXAMPLE:　(heute) Ich gehe zum Park. (*I am going to the park.*)
　　　　　　　　　Heute gehe ich zum Park.

1. (im Sommer) Die Kinder schwimmen gern. (*The children like to swim.*)

　　_____

2. (in Deutschland) Das Wetter ist oft sehr schön. (*The weather is often very nice.*)

　　_____

3. (gestern [*yesterday*]) Unsere Eltern kauften einen neuen Wagen.

　　_____

4. (heute) Meine Töchter spielen Schach. (*My daughters are playing chess.*)

　　_____

5. (um sieben Uhr [*at seven o'clock*]) Ich stehe auf. (*I get up.*)

　　_____

6. (morgen [*tomorrow*]) Meine Familie reist nach Paris. (*My family is traveling to Paris.*)

　　_____

7. (gestern) Wir wohnten noch in München. (*We still lived in Munich.*)

　　_____

8. (im Mai) Sie feierten meinen Geburtstag. (*They celebrated my birthday.*)

　　_____

9. (im Frühling [*in the spring*]) Ich besuchte meine Tante in Amerika.

   _____

10. (morgen) Du verkaufst dein Fahrrad. (*You sell your bicycle.*)

   _____

Word order is not affected when using the four conjunctions **und**, **aber**, **oder**, and **denn**. For example:

Ich lerne Spanisch, **und** Maria lernt Deutsch.	*I learn Spanish, **and** Maria learns German.*
Das Haus ist alt, **aber** es ist sehr groß.	*The house is old, **but** it is very big.*
Hat er einen Bruder, **oder** hat er eine Schwester?	*Does he have a brother, **or** does he have a sister?*
Sie bleibt zu Hause, **denn** sie ist krank.	*She stays home **because** she is sick.*

ÜBUNG

14·8

*Combine each pair of sentences with the conjunction **und**.*

1. Ich spiele das Klavier. Sonja singt. (*I play the piano. Sonja sings.*)

   _____

2. Martin wohnt in der Hauptstadt. Ich wohne in Bremen. (*Martin lives in the capital. I live in Bremen.*)

   _____

3. Der Hund ist krank. Die Katze ist alt. (*The dog is sick. The cat is old.*)

   _____

*Combine each pair of sentences with the conjunction **aber**.*

4. Ich lese den Roman. Ich verstehe nichts. (*I read the novel. I understand nothing.*)

   _____

5. Mein Bruder ist stark. Er ist faul. (*My brother is strong. He is lazy.*)

   _____

6. Das Wetter ist schön. Wir bleiben zu Hause. (*The weather is good. We stay at home.*)

   _____

*Combine each pair of sentences with the conjunction **oder**.*

7. Sind sie reich? Sind sie arm? (*Are they rich? Are they poor?*)

   _____

8. Kaufte sie ein Kleid? Kaufte sie eine Bluse? (*Did she buy a dress? Did she buy a blouse?*)

_____

Combine each pair of sentences with the conjunction **denn**.

9. Der Mann arbeitet nicht. Er ist müde. (*The man is not working. He is tired.*)

_____

10. Die Touristen verstehen nichts. Sie sprechen kein Deutsch. (*The tourists do not understand anything. They do not speak German.*)

_____

Some conjunctions require a significant change in word order. Two such conjunctions are **dass** and **weil**. In a phrase that follows these conjunctions, the verb becomes the last element in the sentence. Notice how the position of the verb changes when the example sentence is placed after one of these conjunctions.

Er wohnt in der Schweiz.	*He lives in Switzerland.*
Ich weiß, **dass** er in der Schweiz **wohnt**.	*I know **that** he lives in Switzerland.*
Die alte Frau hat kein Geld.	*The old woman has no money.*
Karl sagt, **dass** die alte Frau kein Geld **hat**.	*Karl says **that** the old woman has no money.*
Sie ist müde.	*She is tired.*
Sie legt sich hin, **weil** sie müde **ist**.	*She lies down, **because** she is tired.*
Er hat eine gute Stimme.	*He has a good voice.*
Er singt gern, **weil** er eine gute Stimme **hat**.	*He likes to sing, **because** he has a good voice.*

ÜBUNG
14·9

Complete each sentence with the given phrase.

FOR EXAMPLE: Ich weiß, dass _____.

Er ist krank.

Ich weiß, dass er krank ist.
_____

Ich weiß, dass _____.

1. Du kauftest einen neuen VW.

_____

2. Meine Eltern wohnten viele Jahre im Ausland. (*My parents lived abroad for many years.*)

_____

3. Frau Keller besuchte deinen Bruder.

_____

4. Ihr Sohn schwimmt sehr gut.

_____

5. Er spielt sehr schlecht Klavier. (*He plays the piano very badly.*)

   _____

   Meine Tante wohnt in Berlin, weil _____.

6. Ihre Tochter wohnt da. (*Her daughter lives there.*)

   _____

7. Ihr Mann arbeitet in der Hauptstadt. (*Her husband works in the capital.*)

   _____

8. Sie hat da eine große Wohnung. (*She has a large apartment there.*)

   _____

9. Wohnungen in Berlin sind billig. (*Apartments in Berlin are cheap.*)

   _____

10. Sie geht gern ins Theater. (*She likes going to the theater.*)

   _____

ÜBUNG
14·10

Circle the letter of the word or phrase that best completes each sentence.

1. Mein Onkel _____ das Klavier.
   a. lebte
   b. kaufen
   c. spielte
   d. verkauftet

2. _____ machte die Fenster zu.
   a. Die Männer
   b. Niemand
   c. Seine Töchter
   d. Du

3. Mein Sohn wohnt in Bonn, _____ meine Tochter wohnt in Heidelberg.
   a. und
   b. wer
   c. dass
   d. wen

4. _____ fahren wir in die Schweiz.
   a. Weil
   b. Sie
   c. Heute
   d. Was

5. Im _____ schwimmen wir gern.
   a. Hauptstadt
   b. Thomas und ich
   c. Straße
   d. Sommer

6. Wir wissen, _____ Herr Schmidt Frau Benz gern hat.
   a. denn
   b. oder
   c. dass
   d. wessen

7. Was _____ der Mann?
   a. erzählte
   b. verstehst
   c. bekommen
   d. zumachen

8. Sie bleibt zu Hause, _____ sie ist sehr krank.
   a. weil
   b. dass
   c. wann
   d. denn

9. _____ feierten wir meinen Geburtstag.
   a. Gestern
   b. Aber
   c. Morgen
   d. Meine Eltern

10. Was _____ ihr?
    a. antwortetet
    b. verkauftest
    c. lernte
    d. besuchten

Indirect objects and the dative case

You have already discovered that direct objects in German take the accusative case. Indirect objects, however, take the dative case. An indirect object is usually a person or other living thing and is the object in a sentence *to whom* or *for whom* something is done. Let's look at some examples in English:

> *John gives Mary a book. (To whom does John give a book?)*
> → **Mary** *is the indirect object.*

> *We buy the children some ice cream. (For whom do we buy some ice cream?)*
> → **The children** *are the indirect object.*

It works the same way in German:

> Johann gibt **seiner Frau** ein Buch.   *Johann gives **his wife** a book.*
> **Wem** gibt er ein Buch?   ***To whom** does he give a book?*
> → **seiner Frau** *is the indirect object.*

> Ich kaufe **den Kindern** neue Schuhe.   *I buy **the children** new shoes.*
> **Wem** kaufe ich neue Schuhe?   ***For whom** do I buy new shoes?*
> → **den Kindern** *is the indirect object.*

Indirect objects in German are in the dative case. The dative case declension requires the following endings:

MASCULINE	FEMININE	NEUTER	PLURAL
dem Mann	der Frau	dem Kind	den Kindern
einem Lehrer	einer Lehrerin	einem Mädchen	keinen Lehrern
diesem Arzt	dieser Ärztin	diesem Kind	diesen Frauen

Notice that the dative plural noun has an **-n** ending.

ÜBUNG
15·1

Rewrite each of the following phrases in the dative case.

1. der Rechtsanwalt _____

2. die Dame _____

3. das Kind _____

4. die Leute (*people*) _____

5. keine Krankenschwester _____

6. diese Mädchen _____

7. ein Schüler _____

8. meine Brüder _____

9. unsere Freundin _____

10. eure Eltern _____

ÜBUNG
15·2

Rewrite each sentence with the phrase provided. Note each phrase will be the indirect object of the sentence.

Ich schicke _____ einen Brief.

1. mein Vater _____

2. diese Dame _____

3. unser Professor _____

4. ihre Freunde _____

5. deine Mutter _____

Wir schenkten _____ einen Computer. (*We gave . . . a computer.*)

6. unsere Töchter _____

7. seine Tante _____

8. das Mädchen _____

9. der Zahnarzt _____

10. ihr Onkel _____

Was geben Sie _____?

11. Ihre Frau _____

12. seine Kinder _____

13. diese Sportler _____

14. die Tänzerin _____

15. die Schauspieler _____

Some masculine nouns require an additional **-n** or **-en** ending in the accusative and dative cases. They are certain old German words and foreign words with the accent on the final syllable. In addition, masculine words that end in **-e** also have this ending.

nom	der Herr	der Mensch	der Diplomat	der Junge
acc	den Herrn	den Menschen	den Diplomaten	den Jungen
dat	dem Herrn	dem Menschen	dem Diplomaten	dem Jungen

Just as pronouns have an accusative form, they also have a dative declension.

NOMINATIVE	ACCUSATIVE	DATIVE
ich	mich	mir
du	dich	dir
er	ihn	ihm
sie (*sing.*)	sie (*sing.*)	ihr
es	es	ihm
wir	uns	uns
ihr	euch	euch
Sie	Sie	Ihnen
sie (*pl.*)	sie (*pl.*)	ihnen
wer	wen	wem

ÜBUNG
15·3

Rewrite each sentence with the pronoun or noun provided. Note that each pronoun or noun will be the indirect object of the sentence.

Ich gebe es _____.

1. du _____

2. er _____

3. sie (*sing.*) _____

4. der Löwe (*lion*) _____

5. mein Student _____

Niemand sendet _____ ein Geschenk. (*No one sends . . . a gift.*)

6. ich _____

7. wir _____

8. ihr _____

9. dieser Herr _____

10. der Soldat (*soldier*) _____

Diese Frau kaufte _____ eine Zeitschrift. (*This woman bought . . . a magazine.*)

11. Sie _____

12. sie (*pl.*) _____

13. dieser Schauspieler _____

14. diese Schauspielerin _____

15. ich _____

The same dative declension is required in prepositional phrases that are introduced by a dative preposition. The dative prepositions are as follows:

aus	*out, from*
außer	*except for, apart from*
bei	*by, near, at (the home)*
gegenüber	*opposite, across from*
mit	*with*
nach	*after, to a region*
seit	*since*
von	*from, of*
zu	*to, to (someone's home)*

Let's look at the dative prepositions as they are used in phrases.

aus der Flasche	*out of the bottle*
außer mir	*except for me*
bei meinen Eltern	*at my parents' house*
dem Rathaus gegenüber	*opposite the town hall*
mit Ihnen	*with you*
nach dem Konzert	*after the concert*
seit dem Krieg	*since the war*
von meinem Freund	*from my friend*
zu uns	*to our house*

If a pronoun refers to an inanimate object, it cannot be used as the object of a dative preposition. Instead, a prepositional adverb with **da-** or **dar-** is formed. **Dar-** precedes the prepositions that start with a vowel. To use prepositional adverbs in questions, use the prefixes **wo-** and **wor-**. For example:

von der Schule	davon	*from it*	wovon?
mit dem Auto	damit	*with it*	womit?
aus dem Fenster	daraus	*out of it*	woraus?

However, **gegenüber** does not form a prepositional adverb and follows pronouns. It can either precede or follow nouns. For example:

ihm gegenüber	*opposite him*
gegenüber dem Park	*opposite the park*
dem Park gegenüber	*opposite the park*

Rewrite each sentence with the pronoun or noun provided.

Wir sprechen mit _____.

1. der Polizist _____

2. ein Gärtner (*gardener*) _____

3. sie (*pl.*) _____

Doktor Schneider ist heute bei _____.

4. sie (*sing.*) _____

5. wir _____

6. sein Sohn _____

Das ist ein Geschenk von _____.

7. er _____

8. ich _____

9. ein Matrose (*sailor*) _____

Kommst du nach _____ zu mir?

10. das Konzert _____

11. die Oper (*opera*) _____

12. ihre Vorlesungen (*lectures*) _____

Die Kinder laufen zu _____.

13. der Stadtpark (*city park*) _____

14. die Schule _____

15. du _____

ÜBUNG

15·5

Rewrite each prepositional phrase after changing the noun object to a pronoun.

1. von einem Freund _____

2. mit diesem Buch _____

3. bei deiner Freundin _____

4. gegenüber einem Soldaten _____

5. aus der Schule _____

6. nach der Oper _____

7. zu der Tür _____

8. zu den Gästen _____

9. außer diesem Studenten _____

10. mit Herrn Keller _____

There is a group of verbs called *dative verbs*. The object of such verbs must be in the dative case. The English translation of sentences with dative verbs makes the object of these verbs appear to be direct objects. But in German they are not in the accusative case. Here is a list of some commonly used dative verbs:

begegnen	*meet, encounter*
danken	*thank*
dienen	*serve*
drohen	*threaten*
folgen	*follow*
gefallen	*like, please*
gehören	*belong to*
glauben	*believe*
helfen	*help*
imponieren	*impress*
raten	*advise*
schaden	*harm*
vertrauen	*trust*

In sentences they look like this.

Ich **glaube** dir nicht.	*I do not **believe** you.*
Wir **danken** den Gästen.	*We **thank** the guests.*
Das **imponierte** uns.	*That **impressed** us.*

ÜBUNG
15·6

Rewrite each sentence with the pronoun or noun provided.

Die Jungen helfen _____ damit.

1. die Frauen _____

2. ich _____

3. wir _____

4. ihre Freunde _____

5. sie (*pl.*) _____

Ich danke _____ dafür.

6. du _____

7. er _____

8. Sie _____

9. meine Freundin _____

10. der Matrose _____

Wo begegneten Sie _____?

11. die Diplomaten _____

12. sie (*sing.*) _____

13. mein Freund _____

14. sie (*pl.*) _____

15. seine Großmutter _____

ÜBUNG
15·7

Circle the letter of the word or phrase that best completes each sentence.

1. Ich _____ ihm nicht.
   a. sehe
   b. versuche
   c. vertraue
   d. erwarte

2. Thomas gibt _____ eine Blume.
   a. ihr
   b. dich
   c. ihn
   d. Sie

3. Die Kinder spielen _____.
   a. damit
   b. Ihnen
   c. außer
   d. seit

4. Die Kirche ist dem Rathaus _____.
   a. gegenüber
   b. bei
   c. davon
   d. womit

5. Er _____ uns ein neues Fahrrad.
   a. besucht
   b. imponiert
   c. erzählte
   d. kaufte

6. Mein Onkel schickte _____ einen Brief.
   a. ihn
   b. sie
   c. euer
   d. mir

7. Die Jungen laufen aus _____ Schule.
   a. diese
   b. einem
   c. der
   d. ihren

8. Warum _____ du mir nicht?
   a. findest
   b. machst
   c. sendest
   d. glaubst

9. Nach _____ Konzert fahren wir nach Hause.
   a. der
   b. diesen
   c. diese
   d. dem

10. Meine Schwester tanzt mit _____.
    a. einem Soldaten
    b. es
    c. dieser Kirche
    d. der Löwe

Dative case

The dative case has three primary functions: (1) It identifies the indirect object of a sentence. (2) It is used with the object of a dative preposition. (3) It is used with the object of a dative verb.

Indirect objects

Let's identify what an indirect object is in English. An indirect object tells *to whom* something is given and *for whom* something is made available. The *something* in sentences that have an indirect object is the direct object.

> *Thomas gives his wife a gift.* (**To whom** *does Thomas give a gift?*)
> → **His wife** *is the indirect object, and* **a gift** *is the direct object.*

> *We bought him new gloves.* (**For whom** *did we buy new gloves?*)
> → *The pronoun* **him** *is the indirect object, and* **new** *gloves is the direct object.*

German works in the same way. One difference is that a single word is used in German to ask *to whom* or *for whom*: **wem**. **Wem** is the dative form of **wer**. The following example sentences are the German translation of the previous English examples.

> Thomas gibt seiner Frau ein Geschenk.
> **Wem** gibt Thomas ein Geschenk?

→ **Seiner Frau** *is the indirect object, and* **ein Geschenk** *is the direct object.*

> Wir kauften ihm neue Handschuhe.
> **Wem** kauften wir neue Handschuhe?

→ *The pronoun* **ihm** *is the indirect object, and* **neue Handschuhe** *is the direct object.*

Nouns used as indirect objects

In Chapter 2 the difference between **der**-words and **ein**-words was described. That difference is where the gender of a noun is shown: in the **der**-word or in the adjective following an **ein**-word. This difference does not occur in the dative case. All endings for **der**-words, **ein**-words, and adjectives follow the same patterns.

	DER-WORDS WITH DATIVE ENDINGS	**EIN**-WORDS WITH DATIVE ENDINGS
MASCULINE	dem, diesem, welchem	einem, keinem, unserem
FEMININE	der, jener, jeder	einer, meiner, ihrer
NEUTER	dem, diesem, jedem	einem, deinem, eurem
PLURAL	den, jenen, solchen	N/A, seinen, Ihren

When a noun is used as an indirect object, the appropriate dative ending must be used with **der**-words and **ein**-words. For example:

Ich gebe **dem Lehrer** fünf Euro.	*I give the teacher five euros.*
Er schickt **seiner Schwester** die Bücher.	*He sends his sister the books.*
Sie zeigt **diesen Touristen** das Museum.	*She shows these tourists the museum.*

Be aware that the translation of the German indirect object can be stated as a prepositional phrase in English. For example, with the previous German sentences:

> *I give five euros **to the teacher**.*
> *He sends the books **to his sister**.*
> *She shows the museum **to the tourists**.*

In the dative plural, the plural noun adds the ending **-n** if the noun does not already end in **-n**.

> den Lehrer**n**
> meinen Freunde**n**
> keinen Kinder**n**

When adjectives modify nouns in the dative case, the dative case ending must be added to the adjectives. Following **der**-words or **ein**-words, the dative case adjective ending is always **-en**: **diesem jungen Mann**, **der alten Frau**, **meinen kleinen Kindern**.

Give each noun phrase as it would appear in the blank of the sentence provided.

EXAMPLE   Er gibt _____ ein Geschenk.

(die Frau) *der Frau*

Erik schenkte _____ einen Ring.

1. (seine Freundin) _____

2. (der Arzt) _____

3. (dieses Mädchen) _____

4. (seine Brüder) _____

5. (meine Schwester) _____

Was zeigen Sie _____?

6. (diese Leute) _____

7. (jener Mann) _____

8. (Ihre Tochter) _____

9. (meine Kinder) _____

10. (der Gast [*guest*]) _____

Morgen bringt er _____ ein paar Blumen (*a couple flowers*)?

11. (jene Dame) _____

12. (seine Lehrerinnen) _____

13. (unser Onkel) _____

14. (die Mädchen) _____

15. (deine Mutter) _____

Give each noun phrase with the accompanying adjective as it would appear in the blank of the sentence provided.

EXAMPLE   Er gibt _____ ein Geschenk.

(alt / die Frau) *der alten Frau*

Ich schickte _____ einen Brief (*letter*).

1. (deutsch / meine Verwandten) _____

2. (jünger / sein Bruder) _____

3. (nett / eure Eltern) _____

4. (hübsch [*pretty*] / seine Schwester) _____

5. (amerikanisch / unsere Gäste) _____

Was gebt ihr _____?

6. (klein / jene Kinder) _____

7. (älter / diese Jungen) _____

8. (neu / eure Freunde) _____

9. (jung / die Dame) _____

10. (komisch [*funny*] / der Mann) _____

Pronouns used as indirect objects

Pronouns can be used as indirect objects. When this occurs, the pronouns must be in their dative case form. The dative case forms of the personal pronouns are:

NOMINATIVE	DATIVE
ich	mir (*me*)
du	dir (*you*)
er	ihm (*him, it*)
sie *s.*	ihr (*she, it*)
es	ihm (*it*)
wir	uns (*us*)
ihr	euch (*you*)
sie *pl.*	ihnen (*them*)
Sie	Ihnen (*you*)
wer	wem (*whom*)

Let's look at how personal pronouns appear as indirect objects in a few sample sentences.

Sie geben **mir** die Zeitung.	*They give me the newspaper.*
Was schenken Sie **uns**?	*What are you giving (presenting to) us?*
Seine Tante zeigt **ihm** das Bild.	*His aunt shows him the picture.*

When the direct object in a sentence is a noun, it follows the indirect object. This occurs whether the indirect object is a noun or a pronoun.

Ich schicke meinem Freund **ein Buch**.	*I send my friend a book.*
Ich schicke ihm **ein Buch**.	*I send him a book.*

But if the direct object is a pronoun, it will precede the indirect object. This, too, occurs whether the indirect object is a noun or a pronoun.

Noun as direct object	Sie schickt dem Mann **neue Handschuhe**.	*She sends the man new gloves.*
Pronoun as direct object	Sie schickt **sie** dem Mann.	*She sends them to the man.*
Noun as direct object	Wir geben ihr **einen Hut**.	*We give her a hat.*
Pronoun as direct object	Wir geben **ihn** ihr.	*We give it to her.*

You will notice that when the noun direct object is changed to a pronoun direct object, the pronoun conforms to the number, case, and gender of the noun: **neue Handschuhe = sie, einen Hut = ihn**.

ÜBUNG
15·10

Reword each sentence with the pronoun provided.

EXAMPLE   (ich) Sie gibt _____ das Buch.

Sie gibt mir das Buch.

1. (du) Schenkte sie _____ die Handschuhe?

   _____

2. (wir) Die Kinder bringen _____ ein paar Blumen.

   _____

3. (ihr) Die Touristen schickten _____ Ansichtskarten (*picture postcards*).

   _____

4. (sie *pl.*) Ich zeigte _____ die alten Bilder.

   _____

5. (Sie) Er gibt _____ die Briefe.

   _____

ÜBUNG
15·11

Reword each sentence by changing the noun phrase in bold to the appropriate pronoun.

EXAMPLE   Sie gibt **dem Mann** das Buch.

Sie gibt ihm das Buch.

1. Zeigen Sie **den Gästen** die alten Landkarten (*maps*)?

   _____

2. Was gibt sie **den kleinen Kindern**?

_____

3. Erik schenkt **seiner neuen Freundin** einen Ring.

_____

4. Seine Verwandten schickten **dem Jungen** ein Geschenk.

_____

5. Sie geben **Erik und mir** ein paar Euro.

_____

Reword each sentence twice. First, change the indirect object to a pronoun. Then change the direct object to a pronoun.

EXAMPLE   Er gibt dem Mann einen Hut.

Er gibt ihm einen Hut.

Er gibt ihn ihm.

Sie zeigten den Gästen den neuen Wagen.

1. _____

2. _____

Gibst du der Lehrerin eine Blume?

3. _____

4. _____

Die Kinder bringen ihrer Tante ein Geschenk.

5. _____

6. _____

Tina kaufte meinem Bruder und mir neue Handschuhe.

7. _____

8. _____

Wir schicken dem Arzt eine Ansichtskarte.

9. _____

10. _____

Dative prepositions

The nine dative prepositions are:

aus	*out, out of*
außer	*except*
bei	*by, with, at*
gegenüber	*opposite, across from*
mit	*with*
nach	*after*
seit	*since*
von	*from, of*
zu	*to*

Nouns and pronouns that follow the dative prepositions must be in the dative case. For example:

Er wohnt **bei** seiner Tante.	*He lives at his aunt's house.*
Kommst du **mit** uns?	*Are you coming with us?*
Nach dem Konzert geht er nach Hause.	*After the concert, he goes home.*
Das ist ein Brief **von** ihr.	*That's a letter from her.*

ÜBUNG
15·13

*Complete each sentence with the noun provided in parentheses. Add any **der**-word or **ein**-word plus an adjective.*

EXAMPLE   Sie kommt mit _____.

(Frau) *Sie kommt mit der alten Frau.*

Martin wohnt bei _____.

1. (Onkel) _____

2. (Freunde) _____

Sprechen Sie mit _____?

3. (Töchter) _____

4. (Richter) _____

Erik wohnt gegenüber _____.

5. (Bahnhof [*railroad station*]) _____

6. (Schule) _____

Niemand (*no one*) sieht mich außer _____.

7. (Bruder) _____

8. (Freundin) _____

Wohin geht ihr nach _____?

9. (Konzert) _____

10. (Oper [*opera*]) _____

Reword each sentence with the pronouns provided in parentheses.

Warum sprecht ihr mit _____?

1. (wir) _____

2. (er) _____

3. (ich) _____

4. (sie *s.*) _____

5. (sie *pl.*) _____

Erik wohnt nicht weit von _____.

6. (sie *s.*) _____

7. (sie *pl.*) _____

8. (du) _____

9. (ihr) _____

10. (wir) _____

The preposition **gegenüber** has two positions when accompanied by its object. If the object is a pronoun, **gegenüber** will *follow* the object pronoun.

Er sitzt uns **gegenüber**.   *He is sitting across from us.*

If the object of **gegenüber** is a noun, it usually precedes the noun object.

Sonja wohnte **gegenüber** der Bibliothek.   *Sonja lived across from the library.*

But if that noun refers to a person, **gegenüber** tends to follow the noun.

Warum steht er dem Lehrer **gegenüber**?   *Why is he standing opposite the teacher?*

ÜBUNG
15·15

*Complete the sentence with each of the words provided in parentheses. Place **gegenüber** in the correct position.*

Wer wohnt _____?

1. (ihr) _____

2. (Frau Schneider) _____

3. (der Bahnhof) _____

4. (die neue Schule) _____

5. (Sie) _____

Martin und Tina sitzen _____.

6. (die Lehrerin) _____

7. (unsere Gäste) _____

8. (sie *pl.*) _____

9. (der Stadtpark [*city park*]) _____

10. (ich) _____

Prepositional adverbs

When a prepositional phrase introduces a pronoun that is a replacement for an inanimate noun, the typical prepositional phrase is not formed. Instead, a *prepositional adverb* is used. A prepositional adverb is a combination of the prefix **da(r)-** and a preposition. For example: **davon** (*from it*), **daraus** (*out of it*), **danach** (*after it*). Compare the difference in the formation of a prepositional phrase with a pronoun that replaces an animate noun and one that replaces an inanimate noun.

Animate

Er fährt mit einem Freund.   *He's driving with a friend.*
Er fährt **mit ihm**.   *He's driving with him.*

Inanimate

Er fährt mit dem Bus.   *He's going by bus.*
Er fährt **damit**.   *He's going by it.*

To ask a question with a preposition and a pronoun that replaces an inanimate noun, combine the prefix **wo(r)-** with the preposition: **wovon** (*from where*), **womit** (*with what*), **wobei** (*by what*).

The prefixes **dar-** and **wor-** add the consonant **r** to the base prefix **da-** and **wo-**. These prefixes are used with prepositions that begin with a vowel. In addition, be aware that prepositional adverbs are also formed with accusative prepositions (see Chapter 2), and the same rules apply as with dative prepositions. For example:

| Dative prepositions | dazu, danach, daraus / wozu, wonach, woraus |
| Accusative prepositions | dadurch, dafür, darum / wodurch, wofür, woraus |

ÜBUNG
15·16

Reword each prepositional phrase by changing the object of the preposition to a pronoun. If the object is inanimate, form a prepositional adverb. Note that some accusative prepositions are included.

1. mit dem Mann _____

2. mit dem Auto _____

3. von meinem Vater _____

4. durch einen Tunnel _____

5. nach dem Konzert _____

6. für seine Kinder _____

7. für klassische Musik (*classical music*) _____

8. bei seinem Onkel _____

9. bei einem Glas Wein (*glass of wine*) _____

10. aus Gold (*made of gold*) _____

Dative verbs

German has a category of verbs that does not exist in English. The translation of sentences that contain such verbs often suggests that the object of the verbs is a direct object. But that is not correct. This category of verbs requires the nouns and pronouns that follow them to be in the dative case. Such verbs are:

antworten	*answer*
begegnen	*meet, encounter*
danken	*thank*
dienen	*serve*
drohen	*threaten*
folgen	*follow*
gehören	*belong to*
gratulieren	*congratulate*
helfen	*help*
imponieren	*impress*
passen	*fit, suit*
passieren	*happen to*
vertrauen	*trust*
widersprechen	*contradict*

Let's look at some example sentences with dative verbs. Note that the object of these verbs is in the dative case, but the English translation of the sentences uses the objects of these verbs as direct objects.

Im Stadtpark **begegnete** ich **einem Freund**.	*I met a friend in the city park.*
Warum **folgst** du **mir**?	*Why are you following me?*
Die Kinder **helfen ihrem Vater**.	*The children help their father.*
Wie kannst du **ihm vertrauen**?	*How can you trust him?*

Two verbs that have an irregular present tense conjugation are among the dative verbs. In the second- and third-person singular, the vowel **e** changes to an **i**.

	helfen *to help*	**widersprechen** *to contradict*
ich	helfe	widerspreche
du	hilfst	widersprichst
er/sie/es	hilft	widerspricht
wir	helfen	widersprechen
ihr	helft	widerspricht
sie *pl.*	helfen	widersprechen
Sie	helfen	widersprechen

Reword each sentence with the noun phrases and pronouns provided in parentheses.

Kannst du _____ helfen?

1. (wir) _____

2. (er) _____

3. (dieser alte Mann) _____

4. (meine Eltern) _____

5. (jeder neue Schüler) _____

Warum widerspricht er _____?

6. (ich) _____

7. (jene Dame) _____

8. (sein eigener Vater [*his own father*]) _____

9. (ihr) _____

10. (sie *s.*) _____

Sein Tanzen (*dancing*) imponiert _____ nicht.

11. (sie *pl.*) _____

12. (du) _____

13. (unsere Gäste) _____

14. (sein jüngerer Bruder) _____

15. (die hübsche Ärztin) _____

Irregular verbs in the past tense

Verbs that follow a consistent pattern in forming the past tense use the regular past tense ending -**te**. But many verbs do not conform to this pattern. They form their past tense in irregular ways. This also occurs in English. For example:

REGULAR PAST TENSE	IRREGULAR PAST TENSE
talk → talked	come → came
like → liked	see → saw
miss → missed	go → went

German is similar to English in that it usually forms the irregular past tense by a vowel change rather than with a past tense suffix. The vowels **e**, **o**, **u**, **i**, and **ie** in the verb stem often change to the vowel **a** to form the past tense. For example:

INFINITIVE	PRESENT TENSE	PAST TENSE
beginnen	er beginnt	begann
bitten	er bittet	bat
essen	er isst	aß
finden	er findet	fand
geben	er gibt	gab
helfen	er hilft	half
kommen	er kommt	kam
lesen	er liest	las
liegen	er liegt	lag
nehmen	er nimmt	nahm
schwimmen	er schwimmt	schwamm
sehen	er sieht	sah
singen	er singt	sang
sitzen	er sitzt	saß
sprechen	er spricht	sprach
stehen	er steht	stand
treffen	er trifft	traf
trinken	er trinkt	trank
tun	er tut	tat

Other vowel changes can also occur in the irregular past tense.

INFINITIVE	PRESENT TENSE	PAST TENSE
beißen	er beißt	biss
bleiben	er bleibt	blieb
einladen	er lädt ein	lud ein
fahren	er fährt	fuhr

fallen	er fällt	fiel
fangen	er fängt	fing

INFINITIVE	PRESENT TENSE	PAST TENSE
fliegen	er fliegt	flog
frieren	er friert	fror
gehen	er geht	ging
greifen	er greift	griff
halten	er hält	hielt
heißen	er heißt	hieß
lassen	er lässt	ließ
laufen	er läuft	lief
leihen	er leiht	lieh
lügen	er lügt	log
rufen	er ruft	rief
scheinen	er scheint	schien
schießen	er schießt	schoss
schlafen	er schläft	schlief
schlagen	er schlägt	schlug
schließen	er schließt	schloss
schreiben	er schreibt	schrieb
steigen	er steigt	stieg
tragen	er trägt	trug
wachsen	er wächst	wuchs
waschen	er wäscht	wusch
verlieren	er verliert	verlor
ziehen	er zieht	zog

Now let's look at the complete conjugation of the irregular past tense.

	geben (*give*)	schreiben (*write*)	verlieren (*lose*)
ich	gab	schrieb	verlor
du	gabst	schriebst	verlorst
er/sie/es	gab	schrieb	verlor
wir	gaben	schrieben	verloren
ihr	gabt	schriebt	verlort
Sie	gaben	schrieben	verloren
sie (*pl.*)	gaben	schrieben	verloren

Prefixes function with irregular verbs in the same way as they function with regular verbs in the present or past tense.

	abfahren (*depart*)	beschreiben (*describe*)
ich	fuhr ab	beschrieb
du	fuhrst ab	beschriebst
er/sie/es	fuhr ab	beschrieb
wir	fuhren ab	beschrieben
ihr	fuhrt ab	beschriebt
Sie	fuhren ab	beschrieben
sie (*pl.*)	fuhren ab	beschrieben

In the blank provided, write the past tense of the given verb with the subject provided.

1. laufen (*run*) er _____

2. kommen (*come*) du _____

3. gehen (*go*) wir _____

4. sprechen (*speak*) ich _____

5. versprechen (*promise*) sie (*sing.*) _____

6. trinken der Matrose _____

7. essen ihr _____

8. ziehen (*pull*) sie (*pl.*) _____

9. heißen die Tänzerin _____

10. singen Sie _____

11. waschen du _____

12. treffen er _____

13. lassen ich _____

14. bekommen sie (*sing.*) _____

15. annehmen (*accept*) wir _____

16. anrufen (*call, phone*) Sie _____

17. verstehen (*understand*) sein Bruder _____

18. tun (*do*) wir _____

19. helfen du _____

20. schlafen er _____

21. aussteigen (*get off, alight*) ich _____

22. anfangen (*start*) sie (*pl.*) _____

23. scheinen (*seem*) es _____

24. erfinden (*invent*) ihr _____

25. sitzen niemand _____

Write the full conjugation of each verb with the subjects provided.

1. halten   2. fallen

ich   _____   _____

du   _____   _____

er   _____   _____

wir   _____   _____

ihr   _____   _____

Sie   _____   _____

man   _____   _____

3. schließen (*close*)   4. begreifen (*understand, grasp*)

ich   _____   _____

du   _____   _____

er   _____   _____

wir   _____   _____

ihr   _____   _____

Sie   _____   _____

wer   _____   _____

5. ausgeben (*spend*)   6. fliegen (*fly*)

ich   _____   _____

du   _____   _____

er   _____   _____

wir   _____   _____

ihr   _____   _____

Sie   _____   _____

Tina   _____   _____

Three important verbs that are irregular in the present tense are also irregular in the past tense. Let's look at their conjugations:

	haben	sein	werden
ich	hatte	war	wurde
du	hattest	warst	wurdest
er/sie/es	hatte	war	wurde
wir	hatten	waren	wurden
ihr	hattet	wart	wurdet
Sie	hatten	waren	wurden
sie (*pl.*)	hatten	waren	wurden

You have probably noticed that the first-person and second-person singular past tense endings are always identical. This is true of both regular and irregular verbs.

ich lachte	ich suchte	ich sprach	ich lief
er lachte	er suchte	er sprach	er lief

Write the full conjugation of each verb with the subjects provided.

1. haben   **2. sein**

ich   _____   _____

du   _____   _____

er   _____   _____

wir   _____   _____

ihr   _____   _____

Sie   _____   _____

man   _____   _____

3. werden

ich   _____

du   _____

er   _____

wir   _____

ihr   _____

Sie   _____

wer   _____

A small group of verbs have a vowel change in the past tense. But they also have a **-te** past tense suffix. Such verbs are called *mixed*. These verbs are:

INFINITIVE	PAST TENSE	
brennen	er brannte	*burn*
bringen	er brachte	*bring*
denken	er dachte	*think*
kennen	er kannte	*know, be acquainted*
nennen	er nannte	*name*
rennen	er rannte	*run*
senden	er sandte	*send*
wenden	er wandte	*turn*
wissen	er wusste	*know, have knowledge*

The same past tense endings that are used in the regular past tense are used with this group of verbs. For example:

ich	brannte
du	branntest
er/sie/es	brannte
wir	brannten
ihr	branntet
Sie	brannten
sie (*pl.*)	brannten

ÜBUNG

16·4

In the blank provided, write the past tense of the verb in parentheses with the subject provided.

1. (kennen) er _____

2. (denken) du _____

3. (wissen) ich _____

4. (bringen) sie (*pl.*) _____

5. (nennen) Sie _____

6. (rennen) sie (*sing.*) _____

7. (wenden) wir _____

8. (senden) ihr _____

9. (brennen) du _____

10. (wissen) Sie _____

Write the full conjugation of each verb with the subjects provided.

	1. kennen	2. denken
ich	_____	_____
du	_____	_____
er	_____	_____
wir	_____	_____
ihr	_____	_____
Sie	_____	_____
man	_____	_____

	3. wissen	4. bringen
ich	_____	_____
du	_____	_____
er	_____	_____
wir	_____	_____
ihr	_____	_____
Sie	_____	_____
wer	_____	_____

In the blank provided, write in the correct past tense conjugation of the verb in parentheses.

FOR EXAMPLE: Er _____*sprach*_____ mit seinem Bruder. (sprechen)

1. Wir _____ ihn nicht. (kennen)

2. Er _____, dass sie krank war. (wissen)

3. _____ Sie keine Zeit? (haben)

4. Herr Walthers _____ reich. (sein)

5. Es _____ sehr kalt. (werden)

6. Sie _____ ihre Tochter Tina. (nennen)

7. Ich _____, dass Erik in Berlin war. (denken)

8. Sonja _____ ein Problem. (haben)

9. Mein Onkel _____ gesund. (werden)

10. _____ du zu Hause? (sein)

Rewrite each sentence in the past tense.

FOR EXAMPLE: Er ist in Berlin.

_____ *Er war in Berlin.* _____

1. Es wird um sieben Uhr dunkel.

_____

2. Er kommt ohne seine Frau.

_____

3. Die Kinder haben Durst.

_____

4. Was bringen Sie uns?

_____

5. Meine Eltern fahren zu alten Freunden.

_____

6. Ich weiß es nicht.

_____

7. Siehst du die Berge (*mountains*)?

_____

8. Das Wetter wird schlecht.

_____

9. Ich sende ihm eine Ansichtskarte (*postcard*).

_____

10. Der Junge steht um sechs Uhr auf.

_____

11. Kennt ihr diesen Herrn?

_____

12. Nennt sie ihren Namen (*name*)?

   _____

13. Wo bist du?

   _____

14. Ich rufe meine Freundin an.

   _____

15. Lesen Sie eine Zeitschrift?

   _____

Strong verbs

All strong verbs have a stem vowel change in the past tense. The first-person singular (**ich**) and third-person singular (**er/sie/es**) are the same and have no endings. The other persons (**du, wir, ihr, sie/Sie**) have the same endings as in the present tense. However, when the stem ends in **-s** or **-ß**, the second-person singular (**du**) adds an **-e-** before the ending for ease of pronunciation: **du aßest**, **du bewiesest**.

singen (*to sing*)

ich sang	wir sang**en**
du sang**st**	ihr sang**t**
er/sie/es sang	sie/Sie sang**en**

Following is a list of strong verbs in the past tense (note the vowel changes):

i or *ie* to *a*

beginnen	**begann**	*to begin*
binden	**band**	*to tie*
bitten	**bat**	*to ask*
ertrinken	**ertrank**	*to drown*
finden	**fand**	*to find*
gewinnen	**gewann**	*to win*
liegen	**lag**	*to lie (down)*
schwimmen	**schwamm**	*to swim*
singen	**sang**	*to sing*
sitzen	**saß**	*to sit*
springen	**sprang**	*to jump*
trinken	**trank**	*to drink*

e, *ie*, or *ü* to *o*

anbieten	**bot an**	*to offer*
fliegen	**flog**	*to fly*
frieren	**fror**	*to freeze*
heben	**hob**	*to lift*
lügen	**log**	*to lie*
schieben	**schob**	*to push*
schießen	**schoss**	*to shoot*
schließen	**schloss**	*to close*

verbieten	verbot	to forbid
verlieren	verlor	to lose
ziehen	zog	to pull, to move (change residence)

ei to i or ie

begreifen	begriff	to comprehend
beißen	biss	to bite
beschreiben	beschrieb	to describe
bleiben	blieb	to stay, remain
greifen	griff	to reach, to grab
heißen	hieß	to be named, to command
leihen	lieh	to lend
pfeifen	pfiff	to whistle
reiten	ritt	to ride (on horseback)
scheinen	schien	to shine, seem
schreiben	schrieb	to write
schreien	schrie	to shout
steigen	stieg	to climb
vergleichen	verglich	to compare

e to a

essen	aß	to eat
geben	gab	to give
geschehen	geschah	to happen
helfen	half	to help
lesen	las	to read
nehmen	nahm	to take
sehen	sah	to see
sprechen	sprach	to speak
stehen	stand	to stand
stehlen	stahl	to steal
sterben	starb	to die
treffen	traf	to meet
treten	trat	to step
vergessen	vergaß	to forget
werfen	warf	to throw

a to u

einladen	lud ein	to invite
fahren	fuhr	to go (by vehicle)
schlagen	schlug	to beat, hit
tragen	trug	to carry, to wear
wachsen	wuchs	to grow
waschen	wusch	to wash

a, ä, au, u, or e to ie or i

blasen	blies	to blow
fallen	fiel	to fall
fangen	fing	to catch
gehen	ging	to go
halten	hielt	to hold
hängen	hing	to hang

lassen	ließ	to let, to leave
laufen	lief	to run
rufen	rief	to call
schlafen	schlief	to sleep
verlassen	verließ	to leave

o or u to a

bekommen	bekam	to receive
kommen	kam	to come
tun	tat	to do

Give the past tense of the following verbs in the first- or third-person singular.

EXAMPLE: fliegen
            flog

1. finden _____

2. gewinnen _____

3. gehen _____

4. trinken _____

5. sitzen _____

6. singen _____

7. helfen _____

8. lesen _____

9. stehen _____

10. heißen _____

11. verlieren _____

12. lügen _____

13. sprechen _____

14. essen _____

15. geben _____

16. schreiben _____

17. tun _____

18. vergessen _____

19. laufen _____

20. kommen _____

21. nehmen _____

22. finden _____

23. bleiben _____

24. schwimmen _____

25. einladen _____

Conjugate the following verbs in the past tense.

EXAMPLE: trinken—ich
           ich trank

gehen

1. ich _____

2. du _____

3. wir _____

4. Jakob _____

5. ihr _____

6. Jakob und Michael _____

trinken

7. ich _____

8. wir _____

9. Elisabeth _____

10. ihr _____

11. Frau Wendt _____

tun

12. ich _____

13. Sie _____

14. alle _____

15. er _____

essen

16. du _____

17. ich _____

18. Herr Müller und Herr Schulz _____

19. ihr _____

20. Herr Müller _____

Write the verb in parentheses in the past tense.

EXAMPLE: (kommen) ich
ich kam

1. (helfen) die Mutter _____

2. (schlafen) die Kinder _____

3. (treffen) wir _____

4. (nehmen) du _____

5. (geben) Oma _____

6. (gehen) ich _____

7. (schwimmen) die Jungen _____

8. (werfen) ihr _____

9. (singen) der Lehrer _____

10. (finden) du _____

11. (beginnen) die Klasse _____

12. (geschehen) es _____

13. (fahren) das Auto _____

14. (vergessen) ich _____

15. (sprechen) Frau Wendt _____

Marlies and her friends spend a few days in Hamburg. Change the following sentences to the past tense.

EXAMPLE: Sie spricht immer laut.
Sie sprach immer laut.

1. Marlies und ihre Freunde fahren nach Hamburg.

_____

2. Ute steuert das neue Auto.

_____

3. Sie übernachten in einer kleinen Pension.

_____

4. Das Auto parken sie hinter der Pension.

_____

5. Sie stehen früh auf.

_____

6. Sie essen ein gutes Frühstück.

_____

7. Ute trinkt drei Tassen Kaffee.

_____

8. Dann ziehen sie sich die Jacken an und gehen zur U-Bahn.

_____

9. In der Innenstadt besichtigen sie das alte Rathaus und das Museum.

_____

10. Nachmittags machen sie eine Hafenrundfahrt.

_____

11. Der Kapitän sieht sehr gut aus.

_____

12. Viele Leute sitzen im Boot.

_____

13. Sie sehen aber alles gut.

_____

14. Nach der Rundfahrt steigen sie schnell aus.

_____

15. Sie nehmen ein Taxi zu einem berühmten Restaurant.

_____

16. Im Restaurant finden sie noch einen freien Tisch.

_____

17. Sie bestellen gebratenen Fisch.

_____

18. Die Kellnerin bedient sie gut.

_____

19. Alles schmeckt wunderbar.

_____

20. Sie geben der Kellnerin ein großes Trinkgeld.

_____

21. Müde verlassen sie das Restaurant.

_____

22. Sie legen sich müde ins Bett.

_____

23. Der Tag gefällt ihnen sehr gut.

_____

24. Sie vergessen ihn nie.

_____

Mixed verbs

Mixed verbs also have a vowel change in the past tense. However, they have the **-te** suffix, which is a characteristic of weak verbs.

The following is a list of mixed verbs:

brennen	**brannte**	_to burn_
bringen	**brachte**	_to bring_
denken	**dachte**	_to think_
kennen	**kannte**	_to know_
nennen	**nannte**	_to name_
rennen	**rannte**	_to run_
senden	**sandte**	_to send_
wenden	**wandte**	_to turn_
wissen	**wusste**	_to know_

Change the following sentences to the past tense.

EXAMPLE: Das Kind rennt schnell.
           Das Kind **rannte** schnell.

1. Das Licht brennt schon im Haus. _____

2. Es klopft an der Tür. _____

3. Ich gehe hin und mache die Tür auf. _____

4. Ein fremder Mann steht da. _____

5. Er nennt seinen Namen. _____

6. Ich kenne ihn nicht. _____

7. Er weiß aber, wer ich bin. _____

8. Ich denke mir, »Etwas stimmt nicht!« _____

9. Was machen wir? _____

10. Wende ich mich um und schließe die Tür? _____

11. Sende ich den Mann weg? _____

12. Bringe ich ihn ins Haus? _____

13. Ich denke nach. _____

14. Auf einmal erkenne ich ihn! _____

ÜBUNG
16·13

Change the following sentences to the past tense.

EXAMPLE: Ich sende dich weg.
            Ich **sandte** dich weg.

1. Wir fahren zu alten Freunden.

   _____

2. Wir kennen sie schon viele Jahre.

   _____

3. Meine Frau nennt sie unsere besten Freunde.

   _____

4. Sie wissen viel über uns.

   _____

5. Manchmal denke ich sie wissen zu viel.

   _____

6. Wir bringen frische Tomaten aus unserem Garten mit.

   _____

7. Die Fahrt dauert lange.

   _____

8. Ihre Kinder rennen uns entgegen.

   _____

9. Alle freuen sich sehr.

_____

10. Wir bleiben den ganzen Nachmittag da.

_____

haben, sein, and werden

The past tense of the auxiliary verbs **haben**, **sein**, and **werden** is irregular. Whereas all other verbs (except modals) are used in the present perfect tense in conversation, these auxiliary verbs are usually used in the simple past tense.

Present Perfect:	Ich **bin** in der Stadt **gewesen**.
Preferred Past:	Ich **war** in der Stadt.

Following is the conjugation of the three auxiliary verbs in the past tense:

haben (*to have*)		sein (*to be*)		werden (*to become*)	
ich hatte	wir hatten	ich war	wir waren	ich wurde	wir wurden
du hattest	ihr hattet	du warst	ihr wart	du wurdest	ihr wurdet
er/sie/es hatte	sie/Sie hatten	er/sie/es war	sie/Sie waren	er/sie/es wurde	sie/Sie wurden

Insert the correct form of haben in the past tense.

EXAMPLE: Ich _____ Hunger.

*Ich **hatte** Hunger.*

1. Wir _____ viel Geld.

2. _____ ihr auch viel Geld?

3. Ich _____ viel Geld.

4. Er _____ aber nicht viel Geld.

5. Müllers _____ viel Geld.

6. Herr Müller, _____ Sie viel Geld?

7. Luise, _____ du viel Geld?

Insert the correct form of sein in the past tense.

EXAMPLE: Ich _____ einmal schön.

Ich **war** einmal schön.

1. Ich _____ reich.

2. _____ du reich?

3. Paulinchen und ich _____ immer reich.

4. _____ Meiers reich?

5. Walter Meier _____ reich.

6. Stimmt das, Herr Meier, _____ Sie reich?

7. Max und Georg, _____ ihr reich?

Insert the correct form of werden in the past tense.

EXAMPLE: Ich _____ krank.

Ich **wurde** krank.

1. Wann _____ wir reich?

2. Ich _____ 1990 reich.

3. Wendts _____ nie reich.

4. Peter _____ vor dreißig Jahren reich.

5. Wann _____ ihr reich?

6. Meine Familie _____ noch nicht reich.

7. Herr Wendt, _____ Sie nicht reich?

Change the following conversational exchanges to the past tense.

EXAMPLE: Wo bist du? Ich bin im Garten.
Wo **warst** du? Ich **war** im Garten.

1. Wo ist Anna? Sie ist in der Schule.

2. Wirst du oft krank? Ich werde nie krank.

_____

3. Haben die Kinder Hunger? Nein, Peter hat aber Durst.

_____

4. Wann wird es dunkel? Es wird um acht dunkel.

_____

5. Wo seid ihr? Wir sind im Auto.

_____

6. Hast du Durst? Ja, ich habe Durst.

_____

7. Habt ihr am Wochenende Besuch? Ja, die Großeltern sind da.

_____

8. Bist du fremd hier? Ja, ich bin fremd.

_____

9. Frau Schrank, sind Sie oft im Theater? Ich bin selten im Theater.

_____

10. Wir werden nervös wenn er da ist. Wieso denn? Er ist harmlos.

_____

Regular past tense conjugations

The German regular past tense is a relatively simple structure. The suffix **-te** is added to the stem of a verb accompanied by the appropriate conjugational ending: **-e**, **-st**, **-en**, or **-t**. For example:

	besuchen *visit*	**fragen** *ask*
ich	besuchte *visited*	fragte *asked*
du	besuchtest	fragtest
er	besuchte	fragte
wir	besuchten	fragten
ihr	besuchtet	fragtet
Sie	besuchten	fragten
sie *pl.*	besuchten	fragten
man	besuchte	fragte

If the stem of a verb ends in -**d** or -**t**, an -**e** will precede the past tense ending.

	enden *end*	**antworten** *answer*
ich	endete *ended*	antwortete *answered*
du	endetest	antwortetest
er	endete	antwortete
wir	endeten	antworteten
ihr	endetet	antwortetet
Sie	endeten	antworteten
sie *pl.*	endeten	antworteten
man	endete	antwortete

Irregular past tense

The irregular past tense in German is formed in much the same way as the irregular past tense in English: the stem of the verb changes its vowel sound or sometimes changes the whole stem without the regular past tense suffix (-**te**). Let's look at a few English verbs that have an irregular past tense.

PRESENT	PAST
be	*was/were*
build	*built*
go	*went*
have	*had*
see	*saw*

Note how German forms an irregular past tense in the same way.

INFINITIVE	PRESENT TENSE FIRST/THIRD PERSON	PAST TENSE FIRST/THIRD PERSON
fahren	fahre/fährt	fuhr
gehen	gehe/geht	ging
kommen	komme/kommt	kam
sehen	sehe/sieht	sah
singen	singe/singt	sang

After the irregular past tense stem has been formed, the appropriate conjugational endings are added: -**st**, -**en**, or -**t**.

	tragen/trug *carry/wear*	**sprechen/sprach** *speak*
ich	trug *carried/wore*	sprach *spoke*
du	trugst	sprachst
er	trug	sprach
wir	trugen	sprachen
ihr	trugt	spracht
Sie	trugen	sprachen
sie *pl.*	trugen	sprachen
man	trug	sprach

Note that the first- and third-person singular require no ending.

ÜBUNG
16·18

Conjugate each verb in the past tense with the pronouns provided.

1. beschreiben/beschrieb *described*

ich _____

du _____

er _____

wir _____

ihr _____

Sie _____

sie *pl.* _____

man _____

2. tun/tat *did*

_____

_____

_____

_____

_____

_____

_____

_____

3. fliegen/flog *flew*

ich _____

du _____

er _____

wir _____

ihr _____

Sie _____

sie *pl.* _____

man _____

4. verstehen/verstand *understood*

_____

_____

_____

_____

_____

_____

_____

_____

The verbs haben, sein, and werden

The verbs **haben**, **sein**, and **werden** play an important role in the conjugations of verbs. They help form the various tenses. But they also can stand alone and have their own meaning. Each of them is irregular and looks like this in the past tense:

	haben/hatte *had*	**sein/war** *was/were*	**werden/wurde** *became*
ich	hatte	war	wurde
du	hattest	warst	wurdest
er	hatte	war	wurde
wir	hatten	waren	wurden

ihr	hattet	wart	wurdet
Sie	hatten	waren	wurden
sie *pl.*	hatten	waren	wurden
man	hatte	war	wurde

ÜBUNG
16·19

Reword each sentence with the subjects provided.

Ich hatte ihre Tasche (*purse*).

1. Du _____ .

2. Sie *s.* _____ .

3. Wir _____ .

4. Ihr _____ .

Mein Freund war in der Schweiz.

5. Wir _____ .

6. Sie *s.* _____ .

7. Die Ausländer _____ .

8. Seine Verwandten _____ .

Wurde er Lehrer?

9. _____ du _____ .

10. _____ sie *pl.* _____ .

11. _____ Sie _____ .

12. _____ dein Sohn _____ .

Wir hatten genug (*enough*) Geld.

13. Niemand _____ .

Ich war den ganzen Tag in der Stadt.

14. Ihr _____ .

Seine Großmutter wurde sehr krank.

15. Du _____ .

Prefixes

The inseparable and separable prefixes function the same way in the past tense as in the present tense with both regular and irregular verbs. For example:

REGULAR PAST TENSE		IRREGULAR PAST TENSE	
er suchte	*sought/looked for*	er fuhr	*drove*
er besuchte	*visited*	er erfuhr	*experienced*
er suchte aus	*chose/picked out*	er fuhr ab	*departed*

REGULAR PAST TENSE		IRREGULAR PAST TENSE	
er kaufte	*bought*	er stand	*stood*
er verkaufte	*sold*	er verstand	*understood*
er kaufte ein	*shopped*	er stand auf	*stood up*

Let's look at a few more commonly used verbs that have an irregular past tense. Be aware that many verbs that have an irregular past tense form do not have an irregular present tense form.

INFINITIVE		PRESENT TENSE THIRD-PERSON SINGULAR	PAST TENSE THIRD-PERSON SINGULAR
beginnen	*begin*	beginnt	begann
bitten	*ask, request*	bittet	bat
bleiben	*stay*	bleibt	blieb
brechen	*break*	bricht	brach
essen	*eat*	isst	aß
fallen	*fall*	fällt	fiel
finden	*find*	findet	fand
fliegen	*fly*	fliegt	flog
geschehen	*happen*	geschieht	geschah
halten	*hold*	hält	hielt
laufen	*run*	läuft	lief
riechen	*smell*	riecht	roch
scheinen	*shine, seem*	scheint	schien
schlagen	*hit*	schlägt	schlug
schließen	*close*	schließt	schloss
schwimmen	*swim*	schwimmt	schwamm
sitzen	*sit*	sitzt	saß
steigen	*climb*	steigt	stieg
trinken	*drink*	trinkt	trank
waschen	*wash*	wäscht	wusch
werfen	*throw*	wirft	warf
ziehen	*pull*	zieht	zog

This is only a partial list of irregular past tense verbs. See the Appendix at the end of this book for the complete list. Refer to the Appendix to form the irregular past tense with accuracy.

Reword each present tense sentence in the past tense. Note that some verbs have a regular
past tense and some have an irregular past tense.

1. Martin trinkt keine Milch.

_____

2. Das Kind sieht sehr süß (*sweet*) aus.

_____

3. Lauft ihr zum Stadtpark?

_____

4. Ich bin sehr müde.

_____

5. Er verkauft sein Fahrrad.

_____

6. Sabine bekommt ein paar Nelken (*carnations*) von Erik.

_____

7. Der junge Mann steigt am Marktplatz aus.

_____

8. Er befindet sich in einer Großstadt.

_____

9. Essen Sie gern Rotkohl (*red cabbage*)?

_____

10. Der Ausländer spricht sehr langsam.

_____

11. Meine Kinder lernen Deutsch.

_____

12. Wir wohnen bei unseren Großeltern.

_____

13. Professor Benz ruft meinen Sohn an.

_____

14. Wir bleiben eine Woche in Berlin.

_____

15. Warum schlägst du das arme Pferd?

   _____

16. Felix wäscht sich die Hände.

   _____

17. Es wird wieder kalt.

   _____

18. Gehen die Soldaten nach Hause?

   _____

19. Brauchen Sie ein Hemd?

   _____

20. Der Sportler bricht sich den Finger.

   _____

21. Erik wirft mir den Ball zu.

   _____

22. Ich rieche die schönen Rosen.

   _____

23. Sie schließt nur ein Fenster.

   _____

24. Warum sitzen deine Eltern in der Küche?

   _____

25. Mein Wörterbuch (*dictionary*) fällt in den Schmutz (*dirt*).

   _____

26. Habt ihr keine Zeit?

   _____

27. Es geschieht ihm nichts.

   _____

28. Stefan bittet um den nächsten Tanz (*next dance*).

   _____

29. Viele Touristen fliegen nach Europa.

   _____

30. Erik nimmt das Buch unter den Arm.

   _____

Modal auxiliaries in the present and past tenses

The modal auxiliaries are a group of verbs that can act alone or together with other verbs. The modals are the auxiliary verbs, and the accompanying verbs are in infinitive form. Let's look at some examples of how modals function in English and change the meaning of a sentence.

Modal **can**	You **can** ride the bike.
Modal **may**	You **may** ride the bike.
Modal **must**	You **must** ride the bike.

The German modal auxiliaries function in the same way. They are:

dürfen	*may, be allowed to*
können	*can, be able to*
mögen	*may, might, like*
müssen	*must, have to*
sollen	*should, be supposed to*
wollen	*want*

These verbs follow a unique pattern in the present tense.

	dürfen	**können**	**mögen**
ich	darf	kann	mag
du	darfst	kannst	magst
er	darf	kann	mag
wir	dürfen	können	mögen
ihr	dürft	könnt	mögt
Sie	dürfen	können	mögen
sie (*pl.*)	dürfen	können	mögen

	müssen	**sollen**	**wollen**
ich	muss	soll	will
du	musst	sollst	willst
er	muss	soll	will
wir	müssen	sollen	wollen
ihr	müsst	sollt	wollt
Sie	müssen	sollen	wollen
sie (*pl.*)	müssen	sollen	wollen

On the lines provided, rewrite the sentence with the correct conjugation of the modal auxiliary for the subjects given.

Wir <u>wollen</u> zu Hause bleiben. (*We want to stay home.*)

1. Ich _____.

2. Du _____.

3. Er _____.

4. Sie _____.

Thomas <u>soll</u> ihr helfen. (*Thomas should help her.*)

5. Sie (*sing.*) _____.

6. Sie (*pl.*) _____.

7. Wir _____.

8. Ihr _____.

Ich <u>kann</u> den Brief nicht lesen. (*I cannot read the letter.*)

9. Du _____.

10. Wer _____?

11. Sie _____.

12. Ihr _____.

Sie <u>dürfen</u> die Bibliothek benutzen. (*You are allowed to use the library.*)

13. Ich _____.

14. Sie (*sing.*) _____.

15. Wir _____.

16. Die Studenten _____.

Er <u>muss</u> heute abend arbeiten. (*He has to work this evening.*)

17. Du _____.

18. Sie _____.

19. Ihr _____.

20. Niemand _____.

The modal auxiliary **mögen** has some special uses. It can be used alone to mean that someone likes to do something. For example:

Sie **mag** gern Eis.   *She likes ice cream.*

When used with an infinitive, **mögen** can mean *must*, but not in the sense of what someone is obliged to do but rather *what is the likely possibility*. It is most commonly used with the verb **sein**. For example:

Die Frau **mag** vierzig sein.   *The woman must be forty.*

With other verbs, its meaning is *may* or *be allowed to*.

Du **magst** gehen, wohin du willst.   *You may go wherever you want.*

ÜBUNG
17·2

On the lines provided, rewrite the sentence with the correct conjugation of the modal auxiliary **mögen** *for the subjects given.*

mögen gern Bier (*to like beer*)

1. Ich _____.

2. Du _____.

3. Er _____.

4. Wir _____.

5. Ihr _____.

6. Sie _____.

7. Sie (*pl.*) _____.

8. Die Männer _____.

mögen jünger sein (*must be younger*)

9. Ich _____.

10. Du _____.

11. Sie (*sing.*) _____.

12. Wir _____.

13. Ihr _____.

14. Sie _____.

15. Sie (*pl.*) _____.

16. Frau Keller _____.

The past tense of the modal auxiliaries resembles the regular past tense. However, if a modal has an umlaut in the infinitive, that umlaut is omitted in the past tense. For example:

	dürfen	können	mögen
ich	durfte	konnte	mochte
du	durftest	konntest	mochtest
er	durfte	konnte	mochte
wir	durften	konnten	mochten
ihr	durftet	konntet	mochtet
Sie	durften	konnten	mochten
sie (*pl.*)	durften	konnten	mochten

	müssen	sollen	wollen
ich	musste	sollte	wollte
du	musstest	solltest	wolltest
er	musste	sollte	wollte
wir	mussten	sollten	wollten
ihr	musstet	solltet	wolltet
Sie	mussten	sollten	wollten
sie (*pl.*)	mussten	sollten	wollten

ÜBUNG
17·3

Rewrite the present tense sentences in the past tense.

1. Du sollst fleißig (*diligently*) arbeiten.

   _____

2. Wir müssen ihnen helfen.

   _____

3. Ich will eine Reise durch Italien machen. (*I want to take a trip through Italy.*)

   _____

4. Der Mann mag viel älter sein. (*The man must be much older.*)

   _____

5. Der Ausländer (*foreigner*) kann es nicht verstehen.

   _____

6. Sie dürfen nicht länger bleiben. (*You may not stay any longer.*)

   _____

7. Wir sollen mehr Geld sparen. (*We should save more money.*)

   _____

8. Du musst an deine Mutter schreiben. (*You have to write to your mother.*)

   _____

9. Wollt ihr bei uns übernachten? (*Do you want to spend the night at our house?*)

_____

10. Können die Jungen kochen? (*Can the boys cook?*)

_____

The verb **mögen** has a special and very high-frequency usage in its subjunctive form. (The subjunctive is described in detail in Chapters 26 and 27.) It is the polite form used in place of *want*.

Ich **will** ein Glas Bier.	I *want* a glass of beer.
Ich **möchte** ein Glas Bier.	I *would like* a glass of beer.
Er **will** wissen, wo du wohnst.	He *wants* to know where you live.
Er **möchte** wissen, wo du wohnst.	He *would like* to know where you live.

This form of **mögen** can also be used with an accompanying infinitive. For example:

Möchten Sie eine Fahrkarte kaufen?	*Would* you *like* to buy a ticket?
Sie **möchte** etwas essen.	She *would like* something to eat.

ÜBUNG

17·4

*Rewrite each sentence by adding the correct form of **möchte**.*

FOR EXAMPLE: Er steht spät auf.

Er möchte spät aufstehen.

1. Ich besuche das Theater.

_____

2. Gehen Sie nach Hause?

_____

3. Er kauft neue Handschuhe.

_____

4. Frau Benz fragt den Polizisten.

_____

5. Niemand schreibt die Briefe.

_____

6. Trinkst du etwas?

_____

7. Wir frühstücken um neun Uhr. (*We have breakfast at nine o'clock.*)

_____

8. Fahrt ihr mit uns?

_____

9. Sie liest die neue Zeitung.

_____

10. Ich steige hier aus.

_____

Six other verbs—**lassen**, **sehen**, **hören**, **helfen**, **lernen**, **gehen**—function in a similar way to modal auxiliaries. They have a basic meaning and can stand alone in a sentence. But they can also be used with an accompanying infinitive. For example:

Er **lässt** seinen Wagen waschen.	He **gets** his car washed.
Wir **sahen** die Kinder spielen.	We **saw** the children playing.
Hörst du die Mädchen singen?	Do you **hear** the girls singing?
Ich **half** ihr den Koffer tragen.	I **helped** her carry the suitcase.
Er **lernte** seine Mutter verstehen.	He **learned** to understand his mother.
Sie **gehen** heute schwimmen.	They **go** swimming today.

Just like the modals, these verbs can be used in either the present tense or past tense as just illustrated.

ÜBUNG
17·5

If the sentence is in the present tense, rewrite it in the past tense. If it is in the past, rewrite it in the present.

1. Sie lässt ein neues Kleid machen. (_She has a new dress made._)

_____

2. Er half seinem Vater kochen.

_____

3. Der Hund hört zwei Männer kommen.

_____

4. Gehst du um elf Uhr spazieren? (_Are you going for a walk at eleven?_)

_____

5. Ich sah sie im Garten arbeiten.

_____

6. Die Schüler lernen lesen und schreiben.

_____

7. Sie gingen am Montag radfahren. (*They went biking on Monday.*)

_____

8. Wir ließen das alte Fahrrad reparieren. (*We had the old bike repaired.*)

_____

9. Niemand hilft uns die Sätze übersetzen. (*No one helped us translate the sentences.*)

_____

10. Hörtet ihr ihn pfeifen? (*Did you hear him whistling?*)

_____

ÜBUNG
17·6

Add the provided subject and verb to the sentence, and make any necessary changes. Retain the tense of the original verb.

FOR EXAMPLE: Die Kinder schlafen.   er, sehen

Er sieht die Kinder schlafen.

1. Seine Freunde flüstern vor der Tür.   Erik, hören

_____

2. Erik bereitete das Frühstück vor. (*Erik prepared breakfast.*)   wir, helfen

_____

3. Thomas trägt große Pakete. (*Thomas is carrying large packages.*)   ihr, sehen.

_____

4. Sie sprachen Deutsch.   ich, hören

_____

5. Frau Bauer macht die Küche sauber. (*Ms. Bauer cleans up the kitchen.*)   er, helfen

_____

Circle the letter of the word or phrase that best completes each sentence.

1. Niemand _____ uns damit helfen.
   a. lässt
   b. wollten
   c. kann
   d. durftet

2. Wolltest _____ in der Hauptstadt arbeiten?
   a. mein Freund
   b. meine Freunde
   c. ihr
   d. du

3. Ich _____ die kleine Uhr reparieren.
   a. ließ
   b. wollten
   c. könnt
   d. sollt

4. Wir hörten die Kinder _____.
   a. kamen
   b. müssen
   c. arbeiteten
   d. singen

5. Der alte Hund _____ einen jungen Mann kommen.
   a. lässt
   b. will
   c. sieht
   d. konnte

6. Gestern _____ ich meinen Sohn vom Rathaus abholen.
   a. kann
   b. soll
   c. helfe
   d. musste

7. Was _____ Sie gern trinken?
   a. mögen
   b. sehen
   c. wollte
   d. hören

8. Wo _____ er das Hemd machen?
   a. ließ
   b. könnt
   c. möchten
   d. lerntet

9. Möchte _____ mich morgen besuchen?
    a. ihr
    b. ihn
    c. wir
    d. sie

10. Ich will im Juni ins Ausland _____.
    a. lassen
    b. reisen
    c. bekommen
    d. lernen

Modal auxiliaries

Both English and German have a group of helping verbs called modal auxiliaries. They are **dürfen**—*to be allowed to*, **können**—*to be able to*, **mögen** (and **möchten**)—*to like*, **müssen**—*to have to*, **sollen**—*to be supposed to*, and **wollen**—*to want to*.

Conjugation of the modal auxiliaries

These verbs are irregular in the present tense singular. The **ich** and **er/sie/es** forms have no endings and are identical. There is a vowel change in the singular in all verbs except **sollen** and **möchten**. In the plural the verbs are regular.

	dürfen (*may, to be allowed to*)	**können** (*to be able to*)	**mögen** (*to like*)	**möchten** (*would like to*) (*actually the past subjunctive of* **mögen**)
ich	darf	kann	mag	möchte
du	darfst	kannst	magst	möchtest
er/sie/es	darf	kann	mag	möchte
wir	dürfen	können	mögen	möchten
ihr	dürft	könnt	mögt	möchtet
sie/Sie	dürfen	können	mögen	möchten

	müssen (*to have to*)	**sollen** (*to be supposed to*)	**wollen** (*to want to*)
ich	muss	soll	will
du	musst	sollst	willst
er/sie/es	muss	soll	will
wir	müssen	sollen	wollen
ihr	müsst	sollt	wollt
sie/Sie	müssen	sollen	wollen

Modals used with infinitives

A modal is usually used in combination with another verb that is in the infinitive form. The conjugated modal is in the second position while the infinitive is placed at the end of the sentence or clause.

Ich **muss** die Hausaufgaben **machen**.	*I have to do the homework.*
Er **will** das Auto **haben**.	*He wants to have the car.*

ÜBUNG
17·8

*Make sentences with the cues given and the correct form of **dürfen** or **können**.*

EXAMPLE: Wir können hier sitzen. (Ich)
Ich kann hier sitzen.

1. Das Kind darf zu Hause bleiben. (ich) _____

2. Wir dürfen in den Park gehen. (ihr) _____

3. Man darf nicht rauchen. (Kinder) _____

4. Inge kann Auto fahren. (ich) _____

5. Leo kann Deutsch lernen. (wir) _____

6. Sie können viel erzählen. (die Kellnerin) _____

7. Wir können die Speisekarte lesen. (die Freunde) _____

8. Ich kann den heißen Kaffee trinken. (ihr) _____

9. Elisabeth darf ins Kino gehen. (du) _____

10. Jakob und Anna dürfen den Film sehen. (wir) _____

11. Ich darf den Kuchen nicht essen. (Frau Kranz) _____

12. Die Feier darf jetzt beginnen. (die Ferien) _____

13. Können wir das Auto kaufen? (Herr Bohl, Sie) _____

14. Könnt ihr tanzen? (du) _____

15. Wir können den Brief schreiben. (die Sekretärin) _____

ÜBUNG
17·9

*Answer the questions with the correct form of **müssen**.*

EXAMPLE: Warum sitzt du hier?
Ich muss hier sitzen.

1. Warum lernst du Deutsch? _____

2. Warum sprecht ihr so leise? _____

3. Warum laufen die Kinder so schnell? _____

4. Warum arbeitet der Vater so spät? _____

5. Warum gehen wir zu den Nachbarn? _____

6. Herr Schmidt, warum wohnen Sie in Berlin? _____

7. Herr Bohl und Herr Winkel, warum verkaufen Sie Ihre Autos? _____

8. Muss ich zu den Nachbarn gehen? Ja, _____

ÜBUNG

17·10

*Supply the correct form of **möchten** or **sollen**.*

EXAMPLE: Ich _____ (möchten) Kuchen essen.
*Ich möchte **Kuchen** essen.*

1. Inge und Leo _____ (möchten) ins Kino gehen.

2. Inge _____ (möchten) einen Liebesfilm sehen, aber Leo _____ (möchten) einen Krimi sehen.

3. Was _____ (sollen) sie (*pl.*) tun?

4. Ich meine, Inge _____ (sollen) einen Liebesfilm sehen, und Leo _____ (sollen) einen Krimi sehen.

5. Sie (pl.) _____ (möchten) aber zusammen sein. _____ (möchten) du alleine ins Kino gehen? Ich _____ (möchten) das nicht.

6. Du _____ (möchten) nie allein sein!

7. Peter und du, ihr _____ (möchten) immer unter vielen Leuten sein!

ÜBUNG

17·11

*Supply the correct form of mögen in the following sentences. **Mögen** (to like) often stands alone, without another verb.*

EXAMPLE: Ich _____Schokolade.
*Ich **mag** Schokolade.*

1. _____ du Vanilleeis?

2. Ja, ich _____ es.

3. Peter _____ auch Vanilleeis.

4. Hans und Jakob _____ aber Schokoladeneis lieber.

5. Liesel und Gretel, _____ ihr Vanilleeis?

6. Nein, wir _____ es nicht.

7. Und Herr Braun, _____ Sie Vanilleeis? Na, klar! Ich esse alles!

*Supply the correct form of **wollen**.*

EXAMPLE: Was _____ Sie essen, Frau Kuhl?
*Was **wollen** Sie essen, Frau Kuhl?*

1. Beate, was _____ du tun?

2. Ich _____ schwimmen gehen.

3. Luise _____ auch schwimmen gehen.

4. Peter und Franz, _____ ihr schwimmen gehen?

5. Nein, wir _____ nicht.

6. Wir _____ Rad fahren.

Modal position in a subordinate clause

In a *subordinate clause*, the conjugated modal is put after the infinitive at the end of the clause and is therefore the last element in the sentence (whenever the subordinate clause is the last clause).

Ich weiß nicht, warum ich das lernen **muss**.   *I don't know why I **have to** learn that.*
Er muss Geld haben, wenn er das Auto haben **will**.   *He has to have money if he **wants to** have the car.*

Form sentences using the given cues.

EXAMPLE: (aufstehen, müssen, gehen) Wir / früh, weil wir in die Schule.
Wir stehen früh auf, weil wir in die Schule gehen müssen.

1. (essen, möchten, abnehmen) Ich / nicht viel, weil / ich.

_____

2. (Sport treiben, wollen, sein) Er / da er fit.

_____

3. (ziehen, können, schwimmen) Sie (*pl.*) / an den Bodensee, weil sie da immer.

_____

4. (müssen, lernen, wollen, bestehen) Lotte / viel, wenn sie die Prüfung.

_____

5. (verkaufen, können, haben) Wir / unser Haus, damit wir viel Geld.

_____

6. (wissen, sollen, sein) Die Kinder / nicht, warum sie / still.

   _____

7. (müssen, sein, können, schlafen) Es / still, damit das Kind.

   _____

8. (verstehen, dürfen, gehen) Die Mädchen / nicht, warum sie nicht ins Kino.

   _____

9. (lernen, wollen, bleiben) Anton / viel, weil er nicht dumm.

   _____

10. (besuchen, möchten, sprechen) Wir / Tante Margarete, da wir mit ihr.

    _____

Omission of the infinitive

When the meaning of the infinitive is clear, the infinitive is often omitted.

Kannst du Klavier spielen?	*Can you play piano?*
Nein, ich **kann nicht**.	*No, I can't.*
Ich **darf das nicht**.	*I may not (do) that.*

ÜBUNG
17·14

Translate these expressions into German.

EXAMPLE: He has to.
           Er muss.

1. Mr. Volker, would you like more coffee? _____

2. Leo, do you know German? _____

3. I have to. _____

4. We want it. _____

5. What does he want here? _____

6. I want it. _____

7. Must you? (**ihr**) _____

8. He can't. _____

9. You may. (**du**) _____

10. Would you like it? (**Sie**) _____

Make sentences out of the given phrases.

EXAMPLE: (möchten, schlafen) Die Kinder / lange.
Die Kinder möchten lange schlafen.

1. (bekommen) Wir / Besuch.

_____

2. (wollen, besuchen) Alte Freunde / uns.

_____

3. (sollen, ankommen) Sie (*pl.*) / heute Nachmittag.

_____

4. (hoffen, wollen, bleiben) Ich / dass sie (*pl.*) / ein paar Tage.

_____

5. (haben, sein) Wir / immer viel Spaß / wenn sie (*pl.*) hier.

_____

6. (geben) Es / viel zu tun.

_____

7. (müssen, sein) Das Haus / sauber.

_____

8. (müssen, vorbereiten) Mutter / das Essen.

_____

9. (wollen, arbeiten) Vater / noch im Garten.

_____

10. (wollen, mähen) Er und Peter / den Rasen.

_____

11. (sollen, gießen) Peter / auch die Blumen.

_____

12. (sagen, sollen, bringen) Mutter / dass ich / frische Blumen ins Haus.

_____

13. (mögen) Ich / die gelben Tulpen.

_____

14. (möchten, stellen) Ich / einen großen Strauß / auf den Tisch.

_____

15. (wollen, backen) Mutter / noch schnell / einen Kuchen.

_____

16. (dürfen, bleiben) Er / nicht zu lange / im Ofen.

_____

17. (können, riechen) Ich / ihn schon.

_____

18. (sein) Endlich / alles fertig.

_____

19. (müssen, warten, kommen) Wir / noch etwas / bis der Besuch.

_____

20. (stehen, warten) Peter / am Fenster und.

_____

21. (können, sehen) Jetzt / er das Auto.

_____

22. (wollen, begrüßen) Wir / sie alle.

_____

23. (sollen, sich setzen) Die Gäste.

_____

24. (möchten, gehen) Sie (*pl.*) / aber in den Garten.

_____

25. (wollen, essen) Wir / da.

_____

26. (sollen, sein) Das Wetter / schön.

_____

27. (möchten, trinken) Frau Marx / etwas.

_____

28. (wollen, erzählen) Herr Marx / viel.

_____

29. (müssen, lachen) Wir / viel.

_____

30. (dürfen, aufbleiben) Die Kinder / lange.

_____

Modal auxiliaries and double infinitives

The modal auxiliaries are verbs that combine with an infinitive and shade the meaning of that infinitive to suggest *desire*, *obligation*, *ability*, or *permission*. Consider the following English sentences that include a modal auxiliary.

Desire	*I **want to** visit my uncle.*
Obligation	*I **have to** visit my uncle.*
Ability	*I **can** visit my uncle.*
Permission	*I **may** visit my uncle.*

The German modal auxiliaries function in a very similar way. Let's look at the present tense conjugation of each of them.

dürfen *may, allowed to*		**können** *can, be able to*	
ich darf	wir dürfen	ich kann	wir können
du darfst	ihr dürft	du kannst	ihr könnt
er darf	sie (*pl.*) dürfen	er kann	sie (*pl.*) können

mögen *like*		**müssen** *must, have to*	
ich mag	wir mögen	ich muss	wir müssen
du magst	ihr mögt	du musst	ihr müsst
er mag	sie (*pl.*) mögen	er muss	sie (*pl.*) müssen

sollen *should*		**wollen** *want to*	
ich soll	wir sollen	ich will	wir wollen
du sollst	ihr sollt	du willst	ihr wollt
er soll	sie (*pl.*) sollen	er will	sie (*pl.*) wollen

Notice that the conjugation with the singular pronouns (**ich**, **du**, **er**) is different from the conjugation with the plural pronouns (**wir**, **ihr**, **sie** *pl.*).

The modal auxiliaries can combine with infinitives. When this occurs, the infinitive is the last element in the sentence. For example:

Das **darfst** du nicht **sagen**.	*You're not allowed to say that.*
Wir **können** euch **helfen**.	*We can help you.*
Wie lange **muss** ich **warten**?	*How long do I have to wait?*
Ihr **sollt** sofort damit **aufhören**!	*You should stop that immediately!*
Er **will** in die Stadt **fahren**.	*He wants to drive to the city.*

The modal auxiliary **mögen** has some unique usages. When it stands alone in a sentence, it means *like*. For example:

> Der Mann **mag** mich nicht. *The man doesn't like me.*

But combined with an infinitive, the meaning is more like *may* or *might*. For example:

> Wie viel Wasser **mag** das sein? *How much water might that be?*

A very high-frequency function of **mögen** occurs when it is conjugated in the past subjunctive. (The subjunctive is taken up in Chapters 26 and 27.) In that form, the verb can stand alone or be combined with an infinitive and means *would like*.

Möchten Sie ein Glas Bier?   *Would you like a glass of beer?*
Ich **möchte** gerne wissen,   *I would really like to know what that*
was das bedeutet.   *means.*

ÜBUNG
17·16

Reword each sentence by conjugating the modal auxiliary provided in parentheses in the present tense with the subject of the sentence. Make any other necessary changes.

EXAMPLE   Er geht nach Hause.

(wollen) *Er will nach Hause gehen.*

Sie spricht Deutsch und Italienisch.

1. (können) _____

2. (wollen) _____

Ich bleibe den ganzen Tag (*whole day*) zu Hause.

3. (müssen) _____

4. (sollen) _____

Meine Schwester kommt nicht mit.

5. (dürfen) _____

6. (wollen) _____

Schreibst du ihm einen Brief?

7. (können) _____

8. (müssen) _____

Was isst sie zu ihrem Essen?

9. (mögen) _____

10. (wollen) _____

Modal auxiliaries in the past tense and with past participles

When the modals are conjugated in the past tense, they resemble regular verbs. The past tense suffix (**-te**) is used with all the modal auxiliaries, but, if there is an umlaut in the infinitive, the umlaut is omitted in the past tense. For example:

dürfen	ich durfte, du durftest, er durfte, wir durften, ihr durftet
können	ich konnte, du konntest, er konnte, wir konnten, ihr konntet
mögen	ich mochte, du mochtest, er mochte, wir mochten, ihr mochtet
müssen	ich musste, du musstest, er musste, wir mussten, ihr musstet
sollen	ich sollte, du solltest, er sollte, wir sollten, ihr solltet
wollen	ich wollte, du wolltest, er wollte, wir wollten, ihr wolltet

If a modal auxiliary is not accompanied by an infinitive, the past participle that is formed resembles the past participle of a regular verb. If the infinitive has an umlaut, the umlaut is omitted in the past participle. The present perfect tense auxiliary and the past perfect tense auxiliary are **haben** and **hatten**, respectively. For example:

dürfen	er hat/hatte gedurft
können	er hat/hatte gekonnt
mögen	er hat/hatte gemocht
müssen	er hat/hatte gemusst
sollen	er hat/hatte gesollt
wollen	er hat/hatte gewollt

ÜBUNG
17·17

Conjugate each modal auxiliary in the present, past, and present perfect tenses with the subject provided.

1. (wollen)

PRESENT er _____

PAST er _____

PRESENT PERFECT er _____

2. (müssen)

PRESENT wir _____

PAST wir _____

PRESENT PERFECT wir _____

3. (sollen)

PRESENT ihr _____

PAST ihr _____

PRESENT PERFECT ihr _____

4. (können)

PRESENT er _____

PAST sie *pl.* _____

PRESENT PERFECT ich _____

5. (mögen)

PRESENT sie *s.*_____

PAST du _____

PRESENT PERFECT wir _____

6. (dürfen)

PRESENT er _____

PAST ich _____

PRESENT PERFECT du _____

Wissen and kennen

Conjugation of wissen

Wissen is an irregular verb in the singular forms of the present tense. Like the modals, it has the same conjugation in the first- and third-person singular.

wissen

ich weiß	wir wissen
du weißt	ihr wisst
er/sie/es weiß	sie/Sie wissen

ÜBUNG
18·1

Insert the correct form of wissen in the following sentences.

EXAMPLE: du wie er heißt?
           Weißt du wie er heißt?

1. _____ du wo der Park ist?

2. Ja, ich _____ es.

3. _____ der Peter wo der Park ist?

4. Ja, Peter und Michael _____ wo er ist.

5. Luise und Anna, _____ ihr wo er ist?

6. Ja, wir _____ wo er ist.

7. Aber, Frau Kunkel, _____ Sie wo der Park ist?

8. Ja, natürlich. Alle _____ wo der Park ist.

Meanings of wissen and kennen

The English meaning of both **wissen** and **kennen** is *to know*.
   Wissen means to know something as a fact.

Ich weiß wie alt er ist.	*I know how old he is.*
Er weiß wo das Rathaus ist.	*He knows where the city hall is.*

Kennen means to be acquainted or familiar with a person, place, or thing.

Er kennt das hübsche Mädchen. *He knows the pretty girl.*
Wir kennen Dresden sehr gut. *We know Dresden very well.*

ÜBUNG
18·2

*Complete the following sentences with a form of **kennen** or **wissen**.*

EXAMPLE: Maria _____, wer ich bin.
Maria weiß, wer ich bin.

1. Müllers _____ die Schweiz gut.

2. Ich _____, wo Zürich ist.

3. _____ du das Museum?

4. Sie _____ (sing., fam.) nicht was sie will.

5. Herr Müller denkt, er _____ alles.

6. _____ sie (*pl.*), wo Schulzes wohnen?

7. Du _____ den Roman nicht?

8. Frau Blau, _____ Sie wie das Mädchen heißt?

9. _____ ihr, wann der Besuch kommt?

10. Ihr _____ euch doch, oder nicht?

ÜBUNG
18·3

Translate the following statements and questions into German.

EXAMPLE: She knows where the book is.
Sie weiß wo das Buch ist.

1. Paul, what do you know? _____

2. I know nothing. _____

3. Mr. Brach knows Köln well. _____

4. She knows the girl. _____

5. Miss Schmalz, do you know Hamburg? _____

6. Lotte and Beate, do you know how much that costs? _____

7. We don't know that. _____

8. I know Mrs. Broch. _____

9. Girls, do you know where the book is? _____

10. We know the area (**die Gegend**) well. _____

Imperatives

The formation of an imperative or *command* in German is not quite as simple as it is in English. Commands are given to the second person (*you*), and so German has three forms of imperative because German has three words for *you*: **du**, **ihr**, and **Sie**.

Imperatives come from the infinitive of a verb, but the second-person singular conjugation in the present tense must be taken into consideration. If a verb is regular in the present tense, its imperative is quite easy. The **ihr**-form is like the present tense conjugation (**stellt**, **macht**, **hört**). The **Sie**-form is also the present tense conjugation of the pronoun **Sie** with the pronoun following the verb (**stellen Sie**, **machen Sie**, **hören Sie**).

The **du**-form of imperative requires a bit more thought. It is formed from the stem of an infinitive. In many cases, an optional **-e** is added: (**stell[e]**, **mach[e]**, **hör[e]**). Let's look at a variety of verbs with these three forms of imperative. It is very common to conclude an imperative statement with an exclamation point.

INFINITIVE	DU-FORM	IHR-FORM	SIE-FORM	ENGLISH
fragen	Frage(e)!	Fragt!	Fragen Sie!	*ask*
leben	Leb(e) !	Lebt!	Leben Sie!	*live*
pfeifen	Pfeif(e)!	Pfeift!	Pfeifen Sie!	*whistle*
spielen	Spiel(e)!	Spielt!	Spielen Sie!	*play*
suchen	Such(e)!	Sucht!	Suchen Sie!	*search, look for*

If a verb ends in **-eln**, **-ern**, **-nen**, **-igen**, or **-men**, the **-e** in the **du**-form is not an option. It must be used.

INFINITIVE	DU-FORM	IHR-FORM	SIE-FORM	ENGLISH
lächeln	Lächele!	Lächelt!	Lächeln Sie!	*smile*
hämmern	Hämmere!	Hämmert!	Hämmern Sie!	*hammer*
öffnen	Öffne!	Öffnet!	Öffnen Sie!	*open*
entschuldigen	Entschuldige!	Entschuldigt!	Entschuldigen Sie!	*excuse*
atmen	Atme!	Atmet!	Atmen Sie!	*breathe*

If a verb has an irregularity in the present tense that is in the form of a vowel change from **e** to **i** or **ie**, that irregularity occurs in the **du**-form of the imperative. For example:

INFINITIVE	DU-FORM	IHR-FORM	SIE-FORM	ENGLISH
geben	Gib!	Gebt!	Geben Sie!	*give*
sehen	Sieh!	Seht!	Sehen Sie!	*see*

Three verbs that must always be given special attention are **haben**, **sein**, and **werden**.

INFINITIVE	DU-FORM	IHR-FORM	SIE-FORM	ENGLISH
haben	Hab(e)!	Habt!	Haben Sie!	*have*
sein	Sei!	Seid!	Seien Sie!	*be*
werden	Werde!	Werdet!	Werden Sie!	*become, get*

Separable and inseparable prefixes function in the imperative as they do in the present or past tense: only separable prefixes change their position and are located at the end of an utterance. For example:

INFINITIVE	DU-FORM	IHR-FORM	SIE-FORM	ENGLISH
aufhören	Hör(e) auf!	Hört auf!	Hören Sie auf!	*stop, cease*
mitkommen	Komm(e) mit!	Kommt mit!	Kommen Sie mit!	*come along*
besuchen	Besuch(e)!	Besucht!	Besuchen Sie!	*visit*
erwarten	Erwarte!	Erwartet!	Erwarten Sie!	*expect, await*

ÜBUNG
18·4

*Reword each sentence as an imperative in the **du**-form, **ihr**-form, and **Sie**-form.*

EXAMPLE   Thomas fragt den Lehrer.

Frag den Lehrer!

Fragt den Lehrer!

Fragen Sie den Lehrer!

1. Wir sagen es auf Deutsch.

_____

_____

2. Ich empfehle ein Restaurant.

_____

_____

3. Wir bleiben in der Hauptstadt.

_____

_____

4. Er probiert den Kuchen.

_____

_____

_____

5. Er probiert den Mantel an.

_____

_____

_____

6. Wir fahren nach Hause.

_____

_____

_____

7. Sie jagt den Hund weg.

_____

_____

_____

8. Die Kinder singen lauter.

_____

_____

_____

9. Ich zerreiße den Brief.

_____

_____

_____

10. Er ist artig (*behaved*).

_____

_____

_____

The accusative-dative prepositions

19

You have already had experience with the accusative prepositions (**bis, durch, für, gegen, ohne, wider, um**) and the dative prepositions (**aus, außer, bei, gegenüber, mit, nach, seit, von, zu**). Another category of prepositions can require either the accusative case or the dative case. These prepositions are:

an	*at*
auf	*on, onto*
hinter	*behind*
in	*in, into*
neben	*next to*
über	*over*
unter	*under, among*
vor	*before, in front of*
zwischen	*between*

Choosing the correct case is quite simple. If the preposition indicates a motion to a place, use the accusative. If the preposition indicates a location, use the dative. For example:

Er läuft **an** die Tür. (*acc.*)	*He runs **to** the door.*
Er steht **an** der Tür. (*dat.*)	*He stands **at** the door.*
Ich gehe **in** die Bibliothek. (*acc.*)	*I go **into** the library.*
Ich lese **in** der Bibliothek. (*dat.*)	*I read **in** the library.*
Er setzt sich **zwischen** die Kinder.	*He sits down **between** the children.*
Er sitzt **zwischen** den Kindern.	*He sits **between** the children.*

The signal to use the accusative case is most often a *verb of motion*. This kind of verb indicates that someone or something is moving from one place to another. Typical verbs of motion are:

fahren	*drive, travel*
fliegen	*fly*
gehen	*go*
kommen	*come*
laufen	*run*
legen	*lay*
reisen	*travel*
rennen	*run*
setzen	*set*
stellen	*place*

The signal to use the dative case with these prepositions is a verb that indicates a stationary position or a locale where the action is being carried out. Such verbs include:

arbeiten	*work*
bleiben	*remain, stay*
kaufen	*buy*
liegen	*lie*
schlafen	*sleep*
sitzen	*sit*
stehen	*stand*
verkaufen	*sell*
warten	*wait*

In the blank provided, complete each sentence with the correct form of words in parentheses.

FOR EXAMPLE: (die Bank) Er wartet vor _____ *der Bank.* _____

Er stellte sein Fahrrad hinter _____.

1. (das Haus) _____

2. (die Tür) _____

3. (die Bäume [*trees*]) _____

4. (die Garage [*garage*]) _____

5. (der Laden [*shop*]) _____

Der Matrose will neben _____ sitzen.

6. (dieses Mädchen) _____

7. (unsere Eltern) _____

8. (seine Freundin) _____

9. (ein Schulkamerad [*school friend*]) _____

10. (der Fernsehapparat [*television set*]) _____

Geht ihr in _____?

11. (der Keller [*cellar*]) _____

12. (die Kirche) _____

13. (das Restaurant) _____

14. (die Garage) _____

15. (dieser Laden) _____

Der alte Hund wollte auf _____ schlafen.

16. (unser Bett) _____

17. (das Sofa) _____

18. (eine Decke [*blanket*]) _____

19. (diese Kissen [*pillows*]) _____

20. (der Boden [*floor*]) _____

Wir hängen sein Bild über _____. *We hang his picture over . . .*

21. (das Klavier) _____

22. (der Tisch) _____

23. (der Schrank [*cabinet*]) _____

24. (die Stühle [*chairs*]) _____

25. (das Sofa) _____

Some verbs are not clear signals as to whether *motion* or *location* is indicated. Study the following two lists, which contain verbs that are followed by accusative-dative prepositions, but use only one of those cases.

Accusative

sich beklagen über	*complain about*
denken an	*think about*
sich erinnern an	*remember*
sich freuen auf	*look forward to*
sich freuen über	*be glad about*
glauben an	*believe in*
reden über	*talk about*
schreiben an	*write to*
schreiben über	*write about*
sprechen über	*speak about*
sich verlieben in	*fall in love with*
warten auf	*wait for*

Dative

erkennen an	*recognize by*
leiden an	*suffer from*
schützen vor	*protect from*
sterben an	*die from*
teilnehmen an	*take part in*
warnen vor	*warn against*

Some prepositions tend to form a contraction with the definite article that follows. For example:

an das	→	ans
an dem	→	am
auf das	→	aufs
bei dem	→	beim
für das	→	fürs
in das	→	ins
in dem	→	im
um das	→	ums

von dem	→	vom
zu dem	→	zum
zu der	→	zur

Although the preposition followed by a definite article is a correct form, it is more common to hear it used in its contracted form.

CORRECT		MORE COMMON
an dem Tor	*at the gate*	am Tor
in dem Garten	*in the garden*	im Garten

ÜBUNG
19·2

Rewrite the following prepositional phrases in their contracted form wherever possible.

1. auf dem Sofa _____

2. in der Schule _____

3. an dem Theater _____

4. in dem Wasser (*water*) _____

5. vor der Tür _____

6. an dem Fluss (*river*) _____

7. auf das Bett _____

8. in das Rathaus _____

9. an dem Bahnhof (*train station*) _____

10. auf den Stühlen _____

Dative-accusative prepositions

A special category of prepositions can use either the dative case or the accusative case. Therefore, they are called the *dative-accusative prepositions*. They are:

an	*at*
auf	*on*
hinter	*behind*
in	*in*
neben	*next to*
über	*over*
unter	*under*
vor	*before, in front of*
zwischen	*between*

Dative case

The dative case is used with these prepositions when a *location* is being described: *at the door, in the house, between two books,* and so on. For example, in German:

an der Tür	*at the door*
auf dem Tisch	*on the table*
hinter einem Baum	*behind a tree*
im (in dem) Klassenzimmer	*in the classroom*
neben seinem Freund	*next to his friend*
über dem Haus	*over the house*
unter dieser Decke	*under this blanket*
vor dem Rathaus	*in front of city hall*
zwischen meinen Eltern	*between my parents*

It is common to form a contraction with a preposition and the definite article. Some of the most common contractions are:

im = in dem	am = an dem
ins = in das	ans = an das
zum = zu dem	beim = bei dem
zur = zur	vom = von dem

As with other functions of the dative case, the adjective ending used with these prepositions in the dative case with both **der**-words and **ein**-words is always **-en**.

hinter dieser alt**en** Schule	*behind this old school*
in einem klein**en** Haus	*in a little house*
vor der neu**en** Kirche	*in front of the new church*

ÜBUNG
19·3

Complete each sentence with the phrase provided in parentheses.

Die Katzen schlafen unter _____.

1. (dieser Tisch) _____

2. (eine alte Decke) _____

3. (der warme Ofen) _____

Warum warten die Kinder an _____?

4. (die Tür) _____

5. (die kleinen Fenster [*windows*]) _____

6. (unser Tor [*gate*]) _____

Spielen die Jungen Schach (*chess*) in _____?

7. (der kalten Keller [*basement*]) _____

8. (meine Garage) _____

9. (ein anderes Zimmer [*other room*]) _____

Wir steigen vor _____ um (*transfer transportation*).

10. (eine Bäckerei [*bakery*]) _____

11. (die neue Bank) _____

12. (das Einkaufszentrum [*shopping mall*]) _____

Was seht ihr über _____?

13. (jener Fernsehturm [*TV tower*]) _____

14. (diese großen Bäume [*trees*]) _____

15. (die Berge [*mountains*]) _____

Using noun phrases, reword each sentence twice.

1. Warum willst du auf _____ schlafen?

_____

_____

2. Hinter _____ wohnt eine alte Frau.

_____

_____

3. Eine Schauspielerin (*actress*) steht zwischen _____.

_____

_____

4. Sabine bleibt an _____ stehen (*remains standing*).

_____

_____

5. Erik will neben _____ sitzen.

_____

_____

6. Unsere Eltern kauften ein Haus in _____

_____

_____

7. Ein großes Bild hängt (*hangs*) über _____.

_____

_____

8. Der kleine Hund liegt (*is lying*) unter _____.

_____

_____

9. Warum steht der Polizist (*police officer*) vor _____?

_____

_____

10. Eine neue Stehlampe (*floor lamp*) steht neben _____.

_____

_____

Pronouns and the dative-accusative prepositions

A pronoun can be used in the dative case as an indirect object, as the object of a dative verb, or following the dative prepositions. This is also true following the dative-accusative prepositions. For example:

Indirect object	Ich gebe **ihm** ein paar Euro.	*I give him a couple euros.*
Dative verb	Martin hilft **ihnen** im Garten.	*Martin is helping them in the garden.*
Dative preposition	Der Lehrer spricht mit **uns**.	*The teacher speaks with us.*
Dative-accusative preposition	Hinter **mir** sitzt ein Hund.	*A dog is sitting behind me.*

However, if the pronoun is a replacement for an inanimate noun, remember that a prepositional adverb should be used in place of a prepositional phrase. For example:

ANIMATE NOUN	INANIMATE NOUN
neben dem Mann = neben **ihm**	an der Tür = daran
zwischen den Frauen? = zwischen **ihnen**?	vor dem Rathaus? = wovor?

Reword each sentence, changing the noun in the prepositional phrase to a pronoun. If the noun is inanimate, use a prepositional adverb.

EXAMPLE   Wir wohnen neben Herrn Benz.

Wir wohnen neben ihm.

1. Er geht zwei Schritte (*steps*) vor seinem Vater.

    _____

2. Der Hund erkennt (*recognizes*) die Frau an ihrer Stimme (*voice*).

    _____

3. Hier sind wir endlich wieder unter (*among*) Freunden.

    _____

4. Warum stehst du vor dem Fenster?

    _____

5. Die Kinder fürchten sich vor den Gefahren (*dangers*).

    _____

6. Sie irren sich in Ihren Freunden (*wrong about your friends*).

    _____

7. Jemand (*someone*) steht hinter jenem Tor.

    _____

8. Man soll sich vor einer Erkältung schützen (*protect against a cold*).

    _____

9. Die Jungen warten neben der Lehrerin.

    _____

10. Er schläft zwischen zwei großen Bäumen.

    _____

Follow the same directions, but make each new sentence a question.

EXAMPLE   Wir wohnen neben Herrn Benz.

Neben wem wohnen wir?

11. Die Kinder spielen unter dem Tisch.

    _____

12. Der Mann ist sehr eifersüchtig (*jealous*) auf seine Frau.

    _____

13. Die Touristen steigen vor dem Bahnhof aus *(get off in front of the train station)*.

_____

14. Ein großes Bild hängt über dem Klavier *(piano)*.

_____

15. Die Katze verbirgt sich *(hides)* in einer Schublade *(drawer)*.

_____

Accusative case

The accusative case is used with the dative-accusative prepositions when the prepositional phrase indicates *movement or motion to a place*. This is different from the use of the dative case with these prepositions that indicates *location*. This distinction is also made in English with a couple of prepositions that have two varieties. For example:

LOCATION	MOVEMENT
in the house	*into the house*
on the roof	*onto the roof*

German achieves this difference of meaning by the use of two cases: dative and accusative.

Verbs of motion combined with the dative-accusative prepositions most often require the accusative case, because movement to a place is involved. Some commonly used verbs of motion are **fahren**, **fliegen**, **gehen**, **hängen**, **laufen**, **legen**, **setzen**, **stecken**, and **stellen**. In sentences, they are used like this:

Morgen **fahren** wir **in** die Schweiz.	*Tomorrow we're driving to Switzerland.*
Das Flugzeug **fliegt über** den See.	*The airplane flies over the lake.*
Die Mädchen **gehen hinter** das Haus.	*The girls go behind the house.*
Er **hängt** ein Bild **neben** die Lampe.	*He hangs a picture next to the lamp.*
Die Hunde **laufen an** die Tür.	*The dogs run to the door.*
Er **legt** Zeitungspapier **auf** den Boden.	*He puts newspaper on the floor.*
Frau Kohl **setzt** sich **zwischen** ihre Kinder.	*Ms. Kohl sits down between her children.*
Ich **stecke** das Geld **in** meine Tasche.	*I put (stick) the money in my pocket.*
Sie **stellte** die Vase **auf** den Tisch.	*She put the vase on the table.*

ÜBUNG
19·6

Reword each sentence with the phrases provided in parentheses.

EXAMPLE   Sie setzt sich neben _____.

(der Mann) *Sie setzt sich neben den Mann.*

Jetzt fahren wir in _____.

1. (die Berge [*mountains*]) _____

2. (ein langer Tunnel) _____

3. (die neue Garage) _____

Sie hängt einen Spiegel (*mirror*) über _____.

4. (der Esstisch [*dining room table*]) _____

5. (mein Bett) _____

6. (der Bücherschrank [*bookcase*]) _____

Was stecktest du in _____?

7. (deine Tasche) _____

8. (ihre Handschuhe [*gloves*]) _____

9. (dein Mund [*mouth*]) _____

Der Bus fährt bis vor _____.

10. (der neue Bahnhof) _____

11. (das Einkaufszentrum [*shopping mall*]) _____

12. (unsere Schule) _____

Herr Keller stellte den Korb (*basket*) hinter _____.

13. (die Tür) _____

14. (der alte Esstisch) _____

15. (der große Bücherschrank) _____

Complete each sentence with any logical noun phrase.

1. Warum laufen die Jungen an _____?

2. Erik legt das Buch auf _____.

3. Mein Vater fährt den Wagen hinter _____.

4. Ich stellte die Bücher in _____.

5. Die neue Studentin setzt sich neben _____.

6. Tina hängt einen Spiegel über _____.

7. Der Hund kriecht (*crawls*) unter _____.

8. Eine Straßenbahn (*streetcar*) fährt bis vor _____.

9. Sie stellt eine Stehlampe zwischen _____ .

10. Der Junge steckte einen Bleistift in _____ .

Pronouns and prepositional adverbs

When a pronoun replaces a noun that follows a dative-accusative preposition, there are some other differences to consider between animate and inanimate nouns. If the noun is animate, the procedure already described is still followed: the pronoun replaces the noun in the prepositional phrase in the same case that the noun was in. For example:

Er ist eifersüchtig auf seine Frau.
Er ist eifersüchtig **auf sie**.   *He is jealous about his wife.*

Sie geht zwei Schritte vor ihrem Vater.
Sie geht zwei Schritte **vor ihm**.   *She walks two steps ahead of him.*

When inanimate nouns are replaced by pronouns, a prepositional adverb is formed.

Ein Bild hängt über dem Klavier.
Ein Bild hängt **darüber**.   *A picture hangs above it.*

Eine Straßenbahn fährt vor das Rathaus.
Eine Straßenbahn fährt **davor**.   *A streetcar drives up in front of it.*

So far, the patterns of changing from noun to pronoun conform to what was presented earlier. However, when questions are formed, differences do occur when the noun that is replaced by a pronoun is inanimate. When the noun is inanimate, a question can begin with a prepositional adverb introduced by **wo(r)-** or often by the interrogative words **wo** and **wohin**. **Wo** is used to ask about a dative case location, and **wohin** is used to ask about a motion to a place in the accusative case. For example:

Dative case
Der Hund schläft unter dem Tisch.   *The dog is sleeping under the table.*
Worunter schläft der Hund?   *What is the dog sleeping under?*
Wo schläft der Hund?   *Where is the dog sleeping?*

Die Schlüssel liegen in der Schublade.   *The keys are in the drawer.*
Worin liegen die Schlüssel?   *What are the keys in?*
Wo liegen die Schlüssel?   *Where are the keys?*

Accusative case
Das Flugzeug fliegt über den See.   *The airplane flies over the lake.*
Worüber fliegt das Flugzeug?   *What is the airplane flying over?*
Wohin fliegt das Flugzeug?   *Where is the airplane flying?*

Er setzt sich an den Tisch.   *He seats himself at the table.*
Woran setzt er sich?   *What does he seat himself at?*
Wohin setzt er sich?   *Where does he seat himself?*

The main difference between a question that is introduced by a prepositional adverb and a question introduced by the interrogatives **wo** and **wohin** is *specificity*. The prepositional adverb gives precise meaning as to location or movement. The interrogatives are more general.

*Create one question for the prepositional phrase in each sentence by changing the noun in the prepositional phrase to a pronoun. If the object of the preposition is an animate noun, create one question. If the object is an inanimate noun, create two questions, one with a prepositional adverb and the other with the interrogative **wo** or **wohin**.*

EXAMPLE   Ein Buch liegt auf dem Tisch.

Worauf liegt ein Buch?

Wo liegt ein Buch?

1. Eine Katze schläft im Korb.

_____

_____

2. Der Junge steht vor seinem bösen (*angry*) Vater.

_____

_____

3. Das Kind will zwischen seinen älteren Schwestern sitzen.

_____

_____

4. Eine Maus (*mouse*) kriecht unter das Klavier.

_____

_____

5. Sie stellt die Milch (*milk*) in den Kühlschrank (*refrigerator*).

_____

_____

6. Ein Poster hängt über meinem Schreibtisch.

_____

_____

7. Sie schreibt einen Brief an ihre Tante.

_____

_____

8. Sein Moped (*motor scooter*) steht an der Mauer (*wall*).

_____

_____

9. Sie fahren ihre Fahrräder (*bicycles*) hinter das Haus.

_____

_____

10. Alle essen in diesem Zimmer.

_____

_____

Prepositions and verbs

The dative-accusative prepositions are used with certain verbs to form a meaning that is not always directly translatable into English. A common example is **warten auf**. The words mean *wait on* or *wait upon*, but the translation is *wait for*. Other high-frequency combinations of prepositions and verbs are:

angst haben vor (D)	*be afraid of*
denken an (A)	*think about*
eifersüchtig sein auf (D)	*be jealous of*
schreiben an (A)	*write to*
schreiben über (A)	*write about*
sich freuen auf (A)	*look forward to*
sich freuen über (A)	*be glad about*
sich fürchten vor (D)	*be afraid of*
sich gewöhnen an (A)	*get accustomed to/used to*
sich irren an (D)	*be wrong about*
sich schützen vor (D)	*protect oneself against/from*
sich stoßen an (D)	*bump (oneself) on/against*
sich verlieben in (A)	*fall in love with*

In the previous list, the letters D and A indicate that the preposition requires either the use of the dative case (D) or the accusative case (A). Let's look at a few example sentences.

Wir warten auf unsere Verwandten.	*We wait for our relatives.*
Ich denke oft an mein Leben in Bonn.	*I often think of my life in Bonn.*
Erik schreibt über den Unfall.	*Erik is writing about the accident.*
Ich freue mich auf euren Besuch.	*I'm looking forward to your visit.*
Ich kann mich nicht an dieses Haus gewöhnen.	*I can't get used to this house.*
Martin verliebt sich in meine Schwester.	*Martin falls in love with my sister.*

Verbs shown with the reflexive pronoun **sich** change that pronoun depending upon the subject of the sentence. For example:

Ich freue **mich** darüber.	*I'm glad about it.*
Du freust **dich** darüber.	*You're glad about it.*
Er freut **sich** darüber.	*He's glad about it.*
Sie freut **sich** darüber.	*She's glad about it.*
Wir freuen **uns** darüber.	*We're glad about it.*
Ihr freut **euch** darüber.	*You're glad about it.*
Sie freuen **sich** darüber.	*You/They are glad about it.*

In many cases, when a German verb requires a reflexive pronoun, the English translation has no reflexive pronoun as illustrated above. In other cases, the English verb may be accompanied by a reflexive pronoun as well. For example:

Wir schützen uns vor dem Hund.	*We protect ourselves from the dog.*
Ich schütze mich vor dem Hund.	*I protect myself from the dog.*

Reflexive pronouns will be taken up in detail in Chapter 23.

ÜBUNG
19·9

Choose the letter of the word or phrase that best completes each sentence.

1. Monika verliebte sich _____ meinen Cousin.
   a. vor   b. in   c. am   d. im

2. _____ hängen die Bilder?
   a. Wohin   b. Woher   c. Wo   d. An das

3. Ich _____ oft an meine Familie in Deutschland.
   a. warte   b. sage   c. fürchte   d. denke

4. Die Kinder freuen sich schon _____ deine Geburtstagsparty (*birthday party*).
   a. an   b. auf   c. vor   d. in

5. Ich schreibe jeden Tag an _____.
   a. meinen Freund   b. meinen Kindern   c. meiner neuen   d. mein alter Onkel
      in Wien   Freundin   in der Schweiz

6. _____ fliegen diese Flugzeuge?
   a. Wo   b. An wem   c. Worüber   d. Auf sich

7. Gewöhnst du dich _____?
   a. auf das große   b. an die neue   c. in eine junge   d. vor dem
      Haus   Wohnung   Dame   schlechten Wetter

8. Warum bist du immer so _____ auf mich?
   a. freut   b. eifersüchtig   c. verliebt   d. fürchtest

9. Meine Mutter _____ einen Spiegel über mein Bett.
   a. schreibt   b. freuen   c. setze   d. hängt

10. Wir müssen lange auf _____ warten.
    a. den nächsten Zug   b. einer Straßenbahn   c. unseren Freunden   d. unseren
                                                                                Freundinnen

11. Das Kind steht _____ seinem Onkel und seiner Tante.
    a. in   b. im   c. zwischen   d. auf

12. Am Freitag muss ich in die Schweiz _____.
    a. besuchen   b. fahren   c. gehe   d. fliege

13. Die Schüler bleiben _____ Klassenzimmer.
    a. auf das   b. in   c. auf dem   d. im

14. Niemand fürchtete sich _____.
    a. wovor   b. davor   c. woran   d. daran

15. Sabine verliebte sich _____.
    a. in ihren Lehrer   b. mit diesem Herrn   c. auf ihrem Freund   d. darüber

Genitive case, the comparative, and the superlative

Genitive case

The genitive case is the fourth and last case in the German language. One of its functions is to provide the vehicle for showing possession. In English, possession is shown in two ways: with an apostrophe *s* or by the preposition *of*.

> *the woman's new dress*
> *the color of the sky*

The German genitive case functions in place of those two types of English possession.

das neue Kleid der Frau	*the woman's new dress*
die Farbe des Himmels	*the color of the sky*

The genitive case endings for **der**-words and **ein**-words follow:

MASCULINE	FEMININE	NEUTER	PLURAL
des Mannes	der Frau	des Kindes	der Kinder
dieses Jungen	dieser Dame	dieses Hauses	dieser Leute
eines Wagens	einer Schule	eines Buches	deiner Brüder
keines Gartens	keiner Zeitung	keines Gymnasiums	keiner Schüler

The typical genitive noun ending for masculine and neuter nouns is -s. But many nouns that are monosyllabic or end in a sibilant sound (**s, ss, ß, sch**) use the ending -**es**. Also, masculine nouns that are certain old German words or foreign words with the accent on the final syllable add an -**n** or -**en** in the genitive case.

> des Stuhles
> des Einflusses (*influence*)
> des Herrn
> des Diplomaten

ÜBUNG
20·1

*In the blank provided, write the genitive case form for each noun given. Use the correct form of the **der**-word or **ein**-word.*

1. die Tasse (*cup*) _____

2. dieses Glas _____

3. meine Eltern _____

4. seine Tochter _____

5. eine Prüfung _____

6. Ihr Bleistift (*pencil*) _____

7. das Geld _____

8. ihre Gesundheit (*health*) _____

9. unser Garten _____

10. das Flugzeug (*airplane*) _____

11. dieser Zug _____

12. die Blume _____

13. diese Nacht (*night*) _____

14. dein Geburtstag _____

15. unsere Freundinnen (*girlfriends*) _____

16. der Hund _____

17. ihre Katze _____

18. das Jahr _____

19. diese Pferde (*horses*) _____

20. ein Apfel (*apple*) _____

21. kein Dichter (*poet*) _____

22. die Gäste _____

23. der Student _____

24. ein Löwe _____

25. das Schiff (*ship*) _____

In the blank provided, complete each sentence by writing the noun in parentheses in the genitive case.

FOR EXAMPLE: (mein Bruder) Die Frau ___*meines Bruders*___ ist sehr krank. (*My brother's wife is very sick.*)

1. (seine Schwester) Die Kinder _____ müssen zu Hause bleiben.

2. (die Lehrer) Viele (*many*) _____ helfen ihnen.

3. (dieser Herr) Die Jacke (*jacket*) _____ ist alt.

4. (meine Töchter) Das Schlafzimmer (*bedroom*) _____ ist sehr schön.

5. (unser Gast) Der Mantel _____ liegt auf dem Boden.

6. (der Chef [*boss*]) Hast du die Rede _____ gehört?

7. (ihr Freund) Das Haus _____ ist weit von hier.

8. (dieses Problem) Die Lösung (*solution*) _____ ist sehr einfach (*simple*).

9. (deine Tante) Das Auto _____ ist kaputt (*broken*).

10. (Ihre Freundin) Wurde die Tochter _____ Ärztin?

In the spoken language, it is common to substitute a prepositional phrase introduced by **von** for the genitive case.

WRITTEN OR FORMAL LANGUAGE	SPOKEN LANGUAGE	
das Haus meines Bruders	das Haus von meinem Bruder	*my brother's house*
viele der Kinder	viele von den Kindern	*many of the children*

Just as certain prepositions require the accusative or dative case, certain prepositions require the genitive case, as well.

anstatt *or* statt	*instead of*
angesichts	*in the face of*
außerhalb	*outside of*
diesseits	*this side of*
jenseits	*that side of*
trotz	*despite/in spite of*
unterhalb	*below*
während	*during*
wegen	*because of*

Nouns that follow these prepositions will be in the genitive case. For example:

anstatt meines Bruders	*instead of my brother*
diesseits der Grenze	*this side of the border*
trotz des Wetters	*in spite of the weather*
während des Krieges	*during the war*
wegen eines Sturmes	*because of a storm*

ÜBUNG
20·3

Rewrite each sentence with the words provided.

Wegen _____ bleiben alle zu Hause. (*Because of . . . everyone stays home.*)

1. der Regen (*rain*) _____

2. das Gewitter (*storm*) _____

3. seine Erkältung (*his cold*) _____

4. das Wetter _____

5. die Prüfungen _____

Wir waren während _____ in Kanada. (*We were in Canada during . . .*)

6. mein Geburtstag _____

7. der Krieg _____

8. der Angriff (*attack*) _____

9. die Konferenz _____

10. die Verhandlungen (*negotiations*) _____

Anstatt _____ musste ich ihr helfen. (*Instead of . . . I had to help her.*)

11. mein Onkel _____

12. die Jungen _____

13. ein Matrose _____

14. die Familie _____

15. unsere Eltern _____

Trotz _____ wollte sie nicht Tennis spielen. (*In spite of . . . she did not want to play tennis.*)

16. unsere Freundschaft (*friendship*) _____

17. das Wetter _____

18. der Sonnenschein (*sunshine*) _____

19. mein Alter (*my age*) _____

20. meine Bitte (*request*) _____

Wir wohnten diesseits _____. (*We lived on this side of . . .*)

21. der Fluss (*river*) _____

22. die Grenze (*border*) _____

23. die Brücke (*bridge*) _____

24. die Berge (*mountains*) _____

25. die Alpen (*Alps*) _____

Possession

In English, possession is shown by an apostrophe *s*, *s* apostrophe, or with the preposition *of* and answers the question *whose*. For example: *the man's car, the woman's dress, the boys' boat, the girls' DVDs, the color of money.* German, too, can use an **s** to show possession, but that form tends to occur only with names. An apostrophe is not used. For example:

Mozarts Opern	*Mozart's operas*
Eriks Eltern	*Erik's parents*
Frau Schneiders Sohn	*Ms. Schneider's son*

With other types of nouns, the genitive endings are applied to form a possessive, and in German it answers the question **wessen**. For example:

Wessen Buch ist das?	*Whose book is that?*
Das ist das Buch **des Lehrers**.	*That's the teacher's book.*
Wessen Brief liest du?	*Whose letter are you reading?*
Ich lese den Brief **meiner Schwester**.	*I'm reading my sister's letter.*
Wessen Auto kaufen Sie?	*Whose car are you buying?*
Ich kaufe das Auto **dieses Mannes**.	*I'm buying this man's car.*

ÜBUNG
20·4

Using the string of words provided, create a sentence that says that he wants to buy the object belonging to the person in the string of words.

EXAMPLE   die Lampe / diese Frau

Er will die Lampe dieser Frau kaufen.

1. der Wagen / ein Freund _____

2. das Fahrrad / diese Kinder _____

3. der Hut / ein General _____

4. die Bücher / jene Lehrerin _____

5. der Regenschirm (*umbrella*) / mein Onkel _____

6. die Blumen / dieses Mädchen _____

7. die Katze / diese Mädchen _____

8. der Ring / seine Freundin _____

9. die Schuhe (*shoes*) / ein Tänzer (*dancer*) _____

10. der Spiegel (*mirror*) / ihr Großvater _____

Adjectives

Just like in the dative case, the adjective ending used in the genitive case with both **der**-words and **ein**-words is -en: **eines kleinen Hauses** (*of a little house*), **dieser netten Tänzerin** (*of this nice dancer*), **solcher roten Rosen** (*of such red roses*).

Complete the sentence with the adjective provided in parentheses. Add the genitive adjective ending.

1. (alt) Die Temperatur in dem _____ Ofen (*oven*) ist zu hoch (*high*).

2. (jünger) Die Noten (*grades*) seiner _____ Tochter sind schlecht.

3. (neu) Wir hören die Rede (*speech*) des _____ Kanzlers (*chancellor*).

4. (deutsch) Die Wohnung (*apartment*) meiner _____ Verwandten ist groß.

5. (groß) Die Ausstellung des _____ Museums ist interessant.

6. (älter) Das Schlafzimmer (*bedroom*) eurer _____ Kinder ist klein.

7. (jung) Die Gesundheit (*health*) seiner _____ Frau ist besser.

8. (amerikanisch) Erik ist ein Freund dieser _____ Touristen.

9. (russisch) Die Musik jenes _____ Balletts (*ballet*) ist sehr schön.

10. (erst [*first*]) Was ist der Titel ihres _____ Gedichts (*poem*)?

Using the string of words provided, create a question that asks where the object of the person is.

EXAMPLE   Hemd / dies / jung / Mann

Wo ist das Hemd dieses jungen Mannes?

1. Spielzeug (*toy*) / die / jünger / Kinder

_____

2. Bücher / der / neu / Schüler

_____

3. Hotel / mein / ausländisch (*foreign*) / Gäste

_____

4. Rathaus / dies / klein / Dorf (*village*)

_____

5. Schuhe / die / hübsch (*beautiful*) / Tänzerin

_____

Using the string of words, write a sentence that says that the person's relatives are driving to the specified place.

EXAMPLE   Verwandten / der / jungen / Mann / Berlin

Die Verwandten des jungen Mannes fahren nach Berlin.

6. Schwestern / mein / neu / Frau / Frankreich (*France*)

_____

7. Chef (*boss*) / Ihr / jünger / Bruder / Brüssel (*Brussels*)

_____

8. Wirtin (*landlady*) / dein / krank / Mutter / München (*Munich*)

_____

9. Sohn / die / jung / Ärztin / Heidelberg

_____

10. Freund / das / hübsch / Mädchen / Österreich (*Austria*)

_____

Using the string of words, write a sentence that asks whether you see the object or relative of the person.

EXAMPLE   Wagen / der / alt / Mann

Sehen Sie den Wagen des alten Mannes?

11. Freund / mein / älter / Bruder

_____

12. Haus / der / reich (*rich*) / Richter

_____

13. Tante / ihr / ausländisch / Verwandten

_____

14. Fahrrad / unser / jünger / Tochter

_____

15. Kleider (*dresses*) / dies / hübsch / Tänzerinnen

_____

Genitive prepositions

There are four high-frequency genitive prepositions. They are:

(an)statt	*instead of*
trotz	*in spite of*

| während | *during* |
| wegen | *because of* |

Nouns that follow these genitive prepositions must have the appropriate genitive case endings. For example:

Anstatt/Statt meines Bruder kommt
meine Schwester mit.
*Instead of my brother, my sister
   comes along.*

Trotz des kalten Regens gehen wir
schwimmen.
In spite of the cold rain, we go swimming.

Während des letzten Krieges wohnten
sie in der Schweiz.
During the last war, they lived in Switzerland.

Wegen einer langen Krankheit bleibt
sie zu Hause.
Because of a long illness, she stays at home.

ÜBUNG
20·7

*Complete each sentence with any phrase that includes a **der**-word or **ein**-word, an
adjective, and a noun.*

EXAMPLE   Anstatt *meines guten Freundes* hilft mir mein Bruder.

1. Wir waren während _____ in Hamburg.

2. Wegen _____ werden die Kinder sehr krank.

3. Trotz _____ geht sie mit Martin tanzen.

4. Anstatt _____ schickt sie uns einen Brief.

5. Ich kann wegen _____ nicht kommen.

6. Während _____ bleiben meine Eltern in
Bonn.

7. Trotz _____ beginnt das Autorennen
(*car race*) um elf Uhr.

8. Statt _____ schreibt unsere Tante die
Postkarten.

9. Während _____ besuchen wir viele Museen.

10. Wegen _____ ist das Geschäft geschlossen
(*store is closed*).

11. Trotz _____ ist der Mann noch nicht fünfzig
Jahre alt (*years old*).

12. Anstatt _____ kauft er einen goldenen Ring.

13. Wegen _____ ist die Autobahn nicht
befahrbar (*impassable*).

14. Während _____ wohnte seine Familie im
Norden (*north*).

15. Trotz _____ gehen sie heute wandern
(*hiking*).

Comparative and superlative

The comparative is a comparison between two persons or things. The superlative describes the person or thing that has no equal. In English these two forms look like the following:

COMPARATIVE: *He is **taller** than James.*
SUPERLATIVE: *She is the **tallest** in her family.*

Just like English, German adds **-er** to many adjectives or adverbs to form the comparative. For example:

kleiner	*smaller*
netter	*nicer*
schöner	*prettier, nicer*
kühler	*cooler*
heißer	*hotter*
weiter	*farther*

Often an umlaut is added in the comparative. For example:

alt	→ älter	*older*
kalt	→ kälter	*colder*
jung	→ jünger	*younger*

Unlike English, there is no difference between the adjective and adverb forms of the comparative and superlative.

ADJECTIVE: **Er ist schnell/schneller/am schnellsten.**
ADVERB: **Sie läuft schnell/schneller/am schnellsten.**

ÜBUNG
20·8

In the blank provided, write the comparative form of each adjective or adverb.

1. schnell (*fast*) _____

2. langsam (*slow*) _____

3. grün (*green*) _____

4. weiß (*white*) _____

5. dick (*thick, fat*) _____

6. neu _____

7. lang (*long*) _____

8. schwer (*heavy, difficult*) _____

9. leicht (*light, easy*) _____

10. kurz (*short*) _____

11. nah (*near*) _____

12. hell (*bright*) _____

13. alt _____

14. fleißig (*diligent*) _____

15. breit (*wide, broad*) _____

The superlative is often formed as a prepositional phrase introduced by **am** (**an dem**). It uses the ending **-sten**. For example:

am kleinsten	*the smallest*
am schnellsten	*the fastest*
am schwersten	*the hardest*

If the adjective or adverb ends in **-d**, **-t**, **-s**, **-ss**, **-ß**, **-sch**, or **-z**, the superlative ending becomes **-esten**.

am ältesten	*the oldest*
am blödesten	*the most stupid*
am hübschesten	*the most beautiful*

And a slight spelling shift takes place in the comparative with adjectives and adverbs that end in **-el**, **-er**, and **-en**.

POSITIVE	COMPARATIVE	SUPERLATIVE
dunkel (*dark*)	dunkler	am dunkelsten
teuer (*expensive*)	teurer	am teuersten
trocken (*dry*)	trockner	am trockensten

English uses another form of comparative and superlative with long words—particularly foreign words.

more interesting	*most interesting*
more talkative	*most talkative*

German does not follow this pattern. The same approach to comparative and superlative used with shorter words is also used with longer words.

POSITIVE	COMPARATIVE	SUPERLATIVE	
interessant	interessanter	am interessantesten	*more/most interesting*
wichtig	wichtiger	am wichtigsten	*more/most important*
glücklich	glücklicher	am glücklichsten	*more/most fortunate*

Just like English, German has a few comparative and superlative forms that are irregular.

POSITIVE		COMPARATIVE	SUPERLATIVE
bald	*soon*	eher	am ehesten
groß	*big*	größer	am größten
gut	*good*	besser	am besten
hoch	*high*	höher	am höchsten
nah	*near*	näher	am nächsten
viel	*much*	mehr	am meisten

Comparisons are made by using the word **als** (*than*). The superlative requires no such word.

Mein Freund ist älter **als** mein Bruder. *My friend is older **than** my brother.*
Mein Freund ist am ältesten. *My friend is the oldest.*

Read the original sentence with the positive form of the adjective or adverb. Then using the first signal in parentheses, make a comparison with the noun in the original sentence. Using the second signal in parentheses, write the sentence in the superlative.

FOR EXAMPLE: Mein Vater ist alt.

(mein Onkel, mein Großvater)
Mein Vater ist älter als mein Onkel.
Mein Großvater ist am ältesten.

1. Seine Tochter war jung.

(seine Schwester, Tante Angela)

_____

_____

2. Die Kinder laufen langsam.

(Thomas, mein Sohn)

_____

_____

3. Das Gymnasium ist groß.

(die Grundschule *primary school*, die Universität *university*)

_____

_____

4. Erik spricht gut.

(seine Kusine *cousin*, der Professor)

_____

_____

5. Der Doppeldecker (*biplane*) fliegt hoch.

(der Zeppelin, diese Flugzeuge)

_____

_____

6. Unsere Gäste kamen spät (*late*).

(ich, du)

_____

_____

7. Diese Geschichte (*story*) war langweilig (*boring*).

   (ihr Roman, sein Gedicht)

   _____

   _____

8. Diese Straßen sind breit.

   (unsere Straße, die Autobahn [*superhighway*])

   _____

   _____

9. Diese Prüfung ist schwer.

   (die Hausaufgabe [*assignment*], das Examen)

   _____

   _____

10. Frau Bauer kam früh (*early*).

    (ihr Mann, ihr)

   _____

   _____

The future perfect, negation, and imperatives

As in English, the future perfect tense is rarely used in German. When it is used, it usually expresses past probability.

Er **wird** nach Hamburg **gefahren sein**.	He **has probably driven** to Hamburg.
Sie **werden** ein neues Auto **gekauft haben**.	They **probably bought** a new car.

The future perfect tense is also used to express an action or event that will have been completed in the future.

Wenn er heiratet, **wird** er sechs Jahre **studiert haben**.	When he gets married, he **will have studied** six years.

As you can see in the examples, the future perfect is formed with the past participle and the future tense of the auxiliary verb (**er *wird haben*, er *wird sein***). Note the position of the conjugated auxiliary verb. It stays right next to the subject. Whether to use **haben** or sein is decided by the past participle.

Ich werde geschlafen haben.	*I will have slept./I have probably slept.*
Du wirst geschlafen haben.	*You will have slept./You have probably slept.*
Er/sie/es wird geschlafen haben.	*He/she/it will have slept./ He/she/it has probably slept.*
Wir werden geschlafen haben.	*We will have slept./We have probably slept.*
Ihr werdet geschlafen haben.	*You (pl.) will have slept./You (pl.) have probably slept.*
Sie/sie werden geschlafen haben.	*You (form.)/They will have slept./You (form.)/They have probably slept.*

We are still talking about what probably happened on the Wendts' and the Müllers' vacations. Insert the future perfect auxiliary verb in the following sentences.

EXAMPLE: Sie (pl.) _____ lange gefahren _____.

Sie **werden** lange gefahren **sein**.

1. Sie (*pl.*) _____ müde angekommen _____.

2. Am ersten Morgen _____ sie (*pl.*) lange geschlafen _____.

3. Mutter _____ ein gutes Frühstück gekocht _____.

4. Die Kinder _____ Ball gespielt _____.

5. Peter und Hans _____ wandern gegangen _____.

6. Marie _____ ein Bauernbrot gekauft _____.

7. Das _____ gut geschmeckt _____.

8. Abends _____ sie Karten gespielt _____.

9. Du _____ Hunger gehabt _____.

10. Der Urlaub _____ ihnen gut gefallen _____.

Marie Wendt is now seventeen. Let's predict what will have happened to her ten years from now. Make sentences using the future perfect with the cues given.

EXAMPLE: wohl nach Italien fahren

Sie wird wohl nach Italien gefahren sein.

1. das Gymnasium beenden

_____

2. die Universität besuchen

_____

3. einen Beruf lernen

_____

4. ein Auto kaufen

_____

5. eine Ferienreise in die Alpen machen

_____

6. in die eigene Wohnung ziehen

_____

7. wenig Geld haben

_____

8. die Bekanntschaft eines jungen Mannes machen

_____

9. sich verlieben

_____

10. heiraten

_____

ÜBUNG
21·3

The Wendts talk about what they suppose will have happened on Marie's honeymoon. What will the couple probably have done? Make sentences using the future perfect with the cues given.

EXAMPLE: im Wald spazieren gehen

Sie werden im Wald spazieren gegangen sein.

1. in die Berge fahren _____

2. gut ankommen _____

3. im See schwimmen _____

4. ins Dorf gehen _____

5. Souvenirs kaufen _____

6. in einem guten Restaurant essen _____

7. eine Spazierfahrt machen _____

8. einen Film sehen _____

9. sich küssen _____

10. viel miteinander sprechen _____

Marie and her new husband wonder what her family at home has been doing. Make sentences using the future perfect with the cues given.

EXAMPLE: die Familie—sich die Fotos ansehen

Die Familie wird sich die Fotos angesehen haben.

1. die Eltern—sich bei den Gästen bedanken

_____

2. die Eltern—sich von den Gästen verabschieden

_____

3. Vater—die Hochzeitsrechnung bezahlen

_____

4. Vater—zur Arbeit gehen

_____

5. Mutter—sich ausruhen

_____

6. Mutter—im Garten arbeiten

_____

7. die Großeltern—nach Hause fahren

_____

8. die Geschwister—den Kuchenrest aufessen

_____

9. Tante Erika—mit Mutter telefonieren

_____

10. alle—uns vermissen

_____

The future perfect tense is composed of the conjugation of **werden** accompanied by a past participle and its appropriate auxiliary (**haben** or **sein**). The structure can be illustrated in the following way:

   werden + past participle + **haben**
or
   werden + past participle + **sein**

Like English, German does not use this tense with regularity. When it is used, it usually infers a *probability* or an *action that will be completed some time in the future*. Let's look at some sentences in the future perfect tense:

Sie **wird** nach Hause **gefahren sein**.	She **probably has driven** home.
Er **wird** das alte Fahrrad **verkauft haben**.	He **probably has sold** the old bike.
Wenn sie zurückkommen, **werden** sie vier Jahre im Ausland **gewohnt haben**.	When they come back, they **will have lived** overseas for four years.
Wenn ich ein Haus kaufe, **werde** ich mehr als zehn Monate **gearbeitet haben**.	When I buy a house, I **will have worked** for more than ten months.

Rewrite each sentence in the future perfect tense.

FOR EXAMPLE: Er lernt Englisch.

Er wird Englisch gelernt haben.

1. Wir fahren sechs Stunden lang (*for six hours*).

2. Die Touristen reisen wohl (*probably*) nach Polen.

3. Die Jungen spielen Fußball (*soccer*).

4. Die Wanderer (*hikers*) haben Durst.

5. Der Schüler kauft ein Würstchen (*sausage*).

6. Du isst den ganzen Kuchen (*the whole cake*).

7. Karl lernt wohl einen Beruf (*profession*).

8. Die Party gefällt allen (*everyone*).

9. Wir schlafen mehr als neun Stunden.

10. Die Reisenden (*travelers*) kommen zu spät an.

Rewrite each present tense sentence in the past tense, present perfect tense, past perfect tense, future tense, and the future perfect tense.

FOR EXAMPLE: Er lernt Englisch.

Er lernte Englisch.

Er hat Englisch gelernt.

Er hatte Englisch gelernt.

Er wird Englisch lernen.

Er wird Englisch gelernt haben.

1. Mein Onkel bezahlt die Rechnung (*pay the bill*).

2. Die Mädchen schwimmen im Fluss.

3. Wir sprechen oft mit unseren Nachbarn (*neighbors*).

4. Meine Verwandten (*relatives*) reisen nach Amerika.

5. Ich arbeite für Herrn Dorf.

6. Mein Sohn besucht (*attends*) die Universität.

7. Sie zieht sich eine schöne Bluse an.

8. Viele Jugendliche (*young people*) wandern im Wald.

9. Er macht alle Fenster auf.

10. Die Gäste essen mehr als dreimal (*three times*) mexikanisch (*Mexican food*).

_____

_____

_____

_____

_____

_____

Relative pronouns

When a noun in one sentence is identical to a noun in a second sentence, one of the nouns can be replaced by a *relative pronoun*. That pronoun connects the two sentences and functions like a conjunction. Look at this English example:

> *My brother likes cars. My brother bought a red sports car.*
> *My brother, **who** likes cars, bought a red sports car.*

German relative pronouns function in the same way, but German has to consider gender and case. Therefore, the pattern for German relative pronouns, which are for the most part definite articles, largely follows the declension pattern of definite articles.

	MASCULINE	FEMININE	NEUTER	PLURAL
nom	der	die	das	die
acc	den	die	das	die
dat	dem	der	dem	denen
gen	dessen	deren	dessen	deren

The German relative pronouns can be translated as *who*, *that*, or *which*. The gender and case of the noun that is replaced by a relative pronoun must be the gender and case used with the relative pronoun. For example:

Mein Bruder wohnt in Leipzig.	*My brother lives in Leipzig.*
Erik will **meinen Bruder** besuchen.	*Erik wants to visit my brother.*
Mein Bruder, **den** Erik besuchen will, wohnt in Leipzig.	*My brother, whom Erik wants to visit, lives in Leipzig.*

The first use of **mein Bruder** is the *antecedent*, and the second becomes the *relative pronoun*. Notice that the word order of the verbs in the relative clause has the conjugated verb as the last element in the relative clause (**... den Erik besuchen will.**).
The genitive relative pronoun is a substitute for a possessive pronoun.

Meine Tante ist sehr alt.	*My aunt is very old.*
Ihr Sohn kommt selten vorbei.	*Her son seldom comes by.*

The word **ihr** refers to **Tante**, and since **Tante** is feminine and **ihr** is a possessive, the feminine genitive form of the relative pronoun is used here. The fact that **Sohn** is masculine does not affect the relative pronoun; therefore, the relative pronoun used in this sentences is **deren**:

Meine Tante, **deren** Sohn selten vorbeikommt, ist sehr alt.	*My aunt, **whose** son seldom comes by, is very old.*

If a preposition is used to determine the case of the relative pronoun, that preposition must precede the relative pronoun. For example:

> der Mann, **mit dem** ich gesprochen habe
> die Schule, **zu der** die Kinder laufen

In the blank provided, write the relative pronoun that can be substituted for the given phrase. If a preposition is used, use the preposition with the relative pronoun.

FOR EXAMPLE: für den Mann _____ *für den* _____

1. das Mädchen _____

2. mit den Kindern _____

3. sein Buch _____

4. den Gästen _____

5. den Bahnhof _____

6. in der Oper _____

7. nach dem Konzert _____

8. ihre Eltern _____

9. von den Ausländern _____

10. seine Bücher _____

11. dem Fluss _____

12. in das Haus _____

13. ihr Vater _____

14. die Uhr _____

15. durch diesen Mann _____

Rewrite each numbered sentence as a relative clause for the provided sample sentence.

FOR EXAMPLE: Der Lehrer, _____, wurde wieder krank.

Mein Vater wollte mit dem Lehrer sprechen.

_____ *mit dem mein Vater sprechen wollte* _____

Das Flugzeug, _____, landete um vier Uhr. (*landed at four o'clock*)

1. Das Flugzeug ist ein Düsenjäger (*jet fighter*).

_____

2. Ein kleiner Vogel sitzt auf dem Flugzeug.

   _____

3. Niemand konnte das Flugzeug reparieren.

   _____

4. Die Fluggäste steigen in das Flugzeug ein.

   _____

Herr Bauer tanzt mit der Frau, _____.

5. Die Frau ist Amerikanerin.

   _____

6. Ihre Kinder besuchen eine Schule in der Stadt.

   _____

7. Viele Männer wollen mit der Frau tanzen.

   _____

8. Ich habe gestern auf die Frau gewartet.

   _____

Wir helfen den alten Leuten, _____.

9. Die alten Leute haben alles verloren.

   _____

10. Ihre Töchter können ihnen nicht helfen.

    _____

11. Wir haben einmal (*once*) für die alten Leute gearbeitet.

    _____

12. Alle Nachbarn lieben die alten Leute.

    _____

Er schläft auf einem Bett, _____.

13. Das Bett ist viel zu groß.

    _____

14. Der Hund schläft auch auf dem Bett.

    _____

15. Sein Großvater hatte das Bett vierzig Jahre vorher (*forty years earlier*) gekauft.

    _____

The **der**-word **welcher** can replace the definite article as a relative pronoun. This can occur in all cases except the genitive.

	MASCULINE	FEMININE	NEUTER	PLURAL
nom	welcher	welche	welches	welche
acc	welchen	welche	welches	welche
dat	welchem	welcher	welchem	welchen
gen	dessen	deren	dessen	deren

This form of relative pronoun functions in the same way as the definite article. For example:

Das ist das Haus, **welches** mein Freund gekauft hat.

*That is the house **that** my friend bought.*

Ich besuche meine Verwandten, **mit welchen** mein Bruder jetzt wohnt.

*I am visiting my relatives, **with whom** my brother now lives.*

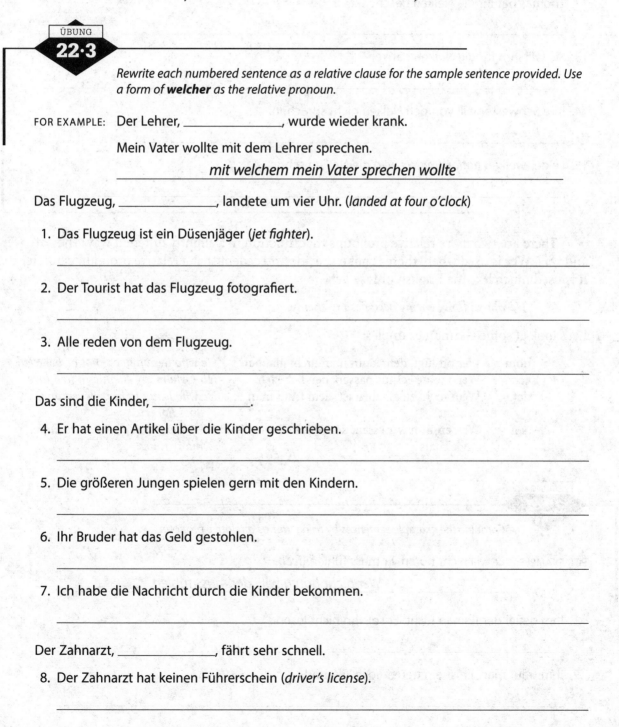

ÜBUNG
22·3

*Rewrite each numbered sentence as a relative clause for the sample sentence provided. Use a form of **welcher** as the relative pronoun.*

FOR EXAMPLE: Der Lehrer, _____, wurde wieder krank.

Mein Vater wollte mit dem Lehrer sprechen.

_____*mit welchem mein Vater sprechen wollte*_____

Das Flugzeug, _____, landete um vier Uhr. (*landed at four o'clock*)

1. Das Flugzeug ist ein Düsenjäger (*jet fighter*).

_____

2. Der Tourist hat das Flugzeug fotografiert.

_____

3. Alle reden von dem Flugzeug.

_____

Das sind die Kinder, _____.

4. Er hat einen Artikel über die Kinder geschrieben.

_____

5. Die größeren Jungen spielen gern mit den Kindern.

_____

6. Ihr Bruder hat das Geld gestohlen.

_____

7. Ich habe die Nachricht durch die Kinder bekommen.

_____

Der Zahnarzt, _____, fährt sehr schnell.

8. Der Zahnarzt hat keinen Führerschein (*driver's license*).

_____

9. Frau Keller hat den Zahnarzt gern.

_____

10. Diese Fußgänger wollen mit dem Zahnarzt sprechen.

_____

11. Der Polizist gab dem Zahnarzt einen Strafzettel (*ticket*).

_____

Seine Freundin liebt die Nelken (*carnations*), _____.

12. Thomas hat ihr die Nelken geschenkt.

_____

13. Sie will ihm für die Nelken danken.

_____

14. Ihre Schwester will von den Nelken nicht sprechen.

_____

15. Leider welken (*unfortunately wilt*) die Nelken schon.

_____

There are two more relative pronouns that function in a slightly different way. They are **wer** and **was**. **Wer** is used where there is not a specific antecedent that a relative pronoun can refer to. It is used much like the English phrase *he who*.

> *He who aids my enemy becomes my enemy.*

Let's look at some German examples:

nom	**Wer** oft lügt, dem kann man nicht glauben.	*He **who** lies often cannot be believed.*
acc	**Wen** meine Feinde hassen, den liebe ich.	*Him **whom** my enemies hate I love.*
dat	**Wem** nicht zu glauben ist, dem traut man nicht.	*He **who** is not to be believed one does not trust.*
gen	**Wessen** Brot wir essen, dem danken wir vielmals.	*Him **whose** bread we eat we thank many times.*

ÜBUNG
22·4

*Combine the example sentences by using **wer** as a relative pronoun.*

FOR EXAMPLE: Er will nicht hören. Er muss fühlen (*feel*).

Wer nicht hören will, der muss fühlen.

1. Ihm gefiel der Roman nicht. Er soll ihn nicht lesen.

_____

2. Ihm traut man. Er ist ein treuer (*loyal*) Freund.

_____

3. Er ist nicht für uns. Er ist gegen uns.

_____

4. Wir laden ihn ein. Wir geben ihm den teuersten Sekt (*champagne*).

_____

5. Ich trinke seinen Wein. Ich bleibe ihm treu.

_____

6. Der Freund liebt ihn. Der Feind hasst ihn.

_____

7. Man kennt ihn nicht. Man bleibt ihm fern.

_____

8. Ich habe ihn gesehen. Ich werde ihn nie vergessen.

_____

9. Der Politiker spricht mit ihm. Er wird der neue Kandidat (*candidate*).

_____

10. Ich habe seine Freundschaft (*friendship*). Ich bleibe ihm ein guter Freund.

_____

Was acts similarly but uses certain words that signal that this form of relative pronoun is required. Such words include **alles, nichts, manches, vieles,** and **etwas.** It is also used after **das** when it is used as a demonstrative pronoun. The meaning of **was** in this structure is *that which*.

Ich kaufe **alles, was** billig ist.	*I buy **everything that** is cheap.*
Sie haben **etwas, was** Sie verkaufen können.	*You have **something that** you can sell.*
Er sagte **das, was** nicht zu glauben war.	*He said **(that which) what** was not to be believed.*

Use **was** also when the antecedent of the relative clause is an entire sentence. For example:

Martin ist Lehrer geworden, **was** seinen Vater sehr erstaunte.	*Martin became a teacher, **which** really astounded his father.*
Er isst ungekochtes Fleisch, **was** uns entsetzt.	*He eats uncooked meat, **which** horrifies us.*

If a preposition needs to accompany the relative pronoun **was**, a prepositional adverb is formed.

Der Professor spricht über das Internet, **wofür** ich mich sehr interessiere.	*The professor is speaking about the Internet, **in which** I am very interested. (not **für das**)*

If a neuter adjective is used as a noun and is the antecedent of a relative pronoun, **was** is used.

Die reiche Dame kaufte **das Beste, was** der Verkäufer hatte.	*The rich lady bought **the best (thing) that** the salesman had.*
Was war **das Erste, was** das Kind gesagt hat?	*What was **the first (thing) that** the child said?*

*Combine the example sentences by using **was** as a relative pronoun.*

FOR EXAMPLE: Ich habe etwas. Etwas wird dir gefallen.

Ich habe etwas, was dir gefallen wird.

1. Der Mann sagte alles. Alles war voller Unsinn (*nonsense*).

   _____

2. Das ist das Schrecklichste (*most terrible thing*). Ich habe das Schrecklichste gesehen.

   _____

3. Es gibt (*there is*) vieles. Vieles ist sehr gefährlich (*dangerous*).

   _____

4. Sie hat das Teuerste. Das Teuerste ist nicht immer das Beste.

   _____

5. Singe etwas! Wir haben etwas noch nicht gehört.

   _____

6. Thomas hat ein Auto gestohlen. Seine Eltern haben nichts davon gewusst.

   _____

7. Unsere Tante muss heute abreisen. Wir bedauern (*regret*) das sehr.

   _____

8. Sie hat nichts verstanden. Ich habe das gesagt.

   _____

9. Wir vergessen alles. Der Politiker hat alles versprochen.

   _____

10. Unsere Nachbarn machen Krach (*noise*). Der Krach stört uns.

    _____

German has two forms of relative pronouns: one is derived from the definite articles (**der, die, das**) and the other is a declined form of **welcher**. Both types are translated as *that, who,* or *which*. The case ending and number of the relative pronoun is determined by how it is used: singular or plural subject, object, or possessive.

Definite article form of relative pronouns

Let's look at the declension of the definite article form of relative pronouns:

CASE	MASCULINE	FEMININE	NEUTER	PLURAL
NOMINATIVE	der	die	das	die
ACCUSATIVE	den	die	das	die
DATIVE	dem	der	dem	denen
POSSESSIVE	dessen	deren	dessen	deren

As you can see, the pattern of the declension of the relative pronouns is identical to the declension of the definite articles, except for the dative plural and the possessive. The relative pronouns form a possessive adjective in place of the genitive case just like other pronouns.

A relative pronoun can be used to combine two sentences that have the same element in them. One of those elements is omitted, and a relative pronoun replaces it. The conjugated verb takes up the final position in the relative clause. For example:

Kennen Sie den Mann? Der Mann **steht** an der Ecke.	*Do you know the man? The man is standing on the corner.*
Kennen Sie den Mann, **der** an der Ecke **steht**?	*Do you know the man who is standing on the corner?*

The element **Der Mann** is the masculine subject of the second sentence. It is replaced by the masculine singular relative pronoun **der**. That relative pronoun *relates* to the phrase **den Mann** (its antecedent) in the first sentence. It is the same number and gender as **den Mann** but is in the nominative case, because the relative pronoun is used as the subject of the relative clause. Just as in other aspects of German, number, gender, and case must be taken into consideration with relative pronouns.

Let's look at some example sentences. Take note of how the relative pronoun changes as the number and gender change.

Ich sehe den Jungen, **der** Tennis spielt.	*I see the boy who is playing tennis.*
Ich sehe die Frau, **die** Tennis spielt.	*I see the woman who is playing tennis.*
Ich sehe das Mädchen, **das** Tennis spielt.	*I see the girl who is playing tennis.*
Ich sehe die Männer, **die** Tennis spielen.	*I see the men who are playing tennis.*

Note that relative clauses are generally set off by commas.

ÜBUNG
22·6

Combine each pair of sentences, making the second sentence a relative clause.

EXAMPLE Wo ist der Gast? Der Gast kommt aus Berlin?

Wo ist der Gast, der aus Berlin kommt?

1. Das ist die Lehrerin. Die Lehrerin wird mir helfen.

   _____

2. Das Land ist meine Heimat. Ich liebe das Land.

   _____

3. Es war einmal eine Königin. Die Königin hatte eine hübsche Tochter.

   _____

4. Wo ist der Hund? Der Hund bellt so laut.

_____

5. Seht ihr die Vögel? Die Vögel singen so schön.

_____

6. Sie haben die Weingläser verloren (*lost wine glasses*). Die Weingläser waren sehr teuer.

_____

7. Warum kaufst du das Pferd? Das Pferd ist alt und krank.

_____

8. Wir besuchten unsere Verwandten. Unsere Verwandten wohnten in Leipzig.

_____

9. Erik hat einen Fernsehapparat. Der Fernsehapparat hat einen großen Bildschirm (*screen*).

_____

10. Ihr Sohn hat morgen Geburtstag. Ihr Sohn wird neun Jahre alt.

_____

Relative pronouns that replace nouns in the accusative, dative, and genitive cases

Relative pronouns also replace nouns that are in the accusative, dative, and genitive cases. First let's look at examples of the use of these cases with a masculine noun and its relative pronoun.

Accusative direct object
Wo ist der Lehrer, **den** sie anrufen wollen?

Where is the teacher whom they want to call?

Accusative preposition
Wo ist der Lehrer, **für den** Erik gearbeitet hat?

Where is the teacher for whom Erik worked?

Dative indirect object
Wo ist der Lehrer, **dem** wir die Bücher geben wollen?

Where is the teacher to whom we want to give the books?

Dative preposition
Wo ist der Lehrer, **mit dem** sein Vater reden will?

Where is the teacher with whom his father wants to speak?

Dative verb
Wo ist der Lehrer, **dem** ich im Park begegnete?

Where is the teacher whom I met in the park?

Genitive possessive
Wo ist der Lehrer, **dessen** Schüler so gut Englisch sprechen?

Where is the teacher whose students speak English so well?

Now let's change the gender of these sentences to feminine. Note how the declension of the relative pronoun changes to reflect the new gender.

Wo ist die Lehrerin, **die** sie anrufen wollen?	*Where is the teacher whom they want to call?*
Wo ist die Lehrerin, **für die** Erik gearbeitet hat?	*Where is the teacher for whom Erik worked?*
Wo ist die Lehrerin, **der** wir die Bücher geben wollen?	*Where is the teacher to whom we want to give the books?*
Wo ist die Lehrerin, **mit der** sein Vater reden will?	*Where is the teacher with whom his father wants to speak?*
Wo ist die Lehrerin, **der** ich im Park begegnete?	*Where is the teacher whom I met in the park?*
Wo ist die Lehrerin, **deren** Schüler so gut Englisch sprechen?	*Where is the teacher whose students speak English so well?*

If the antecedent of the relative pronoun is changed to neuter or plural, the appropriate declensional changes occur to reflect the new gender or number.

ÜBUNG
22·7

Change the antecedent in each sentence to the ones provided in parentheses. Make the necessary declensional changes to the relative pronoun to reflect the new gender or number of the antecedent.

EXAMPLE   Er spricht mit **dem Mann**, der ihm helfen wird.

(die Frau) *Er spricht mit der Frau, die ihm helfen wird.*

1. Sie findet **die Bluse**, die sie gestern gekauft hat.

(das Kleid) _____

(die Briefmarken [*stamps*]) _____

(der Hut) _____

2. Kennen Sie **die Leute**, die in Darmstadt wohnen?

(der Ausländer) _____

(die Studenten) _____

(die Studentin) _____

3. Ich begegnete **einem Nachbarn**, dessen Vater gestorben ist.

(eine Dame) _____

(die Brüder) _____

(ein Kind) _____

4. Das ist **die Richterin**, von der ich das Geschenk bekommen habe.

(die Leute) _____

(der Richter) _____

(unsere Gäste) _____

5. **Die Frau**, für die wir gearbeitet haben, ist nach Bonn gezogen (*moved*).

(die Männer) _____

(der Engländer) _____

(das Mädchen) _____

_____

ÜBUNG
22·8

Use the phrases provided as relative clauses to complete each sentence.

EXAMPLE   Er spricht mit dem Mann, _____.

(Der Mann wohnt in der Nähe.) *Er spricht mit dem Mann, der in der Nähe wohnt.*

Ich habe den Roman, _____.

1. (Karl will den Roman übersetzen [*translate*].) _____

2. (Viele Leute sind vom Roman begeistert [*taken with*].) _____

3. (Der Schriftsteller [*writer*] des Romans war Hesse.) _____

Sabine spielte mit den Kindern, _____.

4. (Der Reporter hat über die Kinder geschrieben.) _____

5. (Die Eltern der Kinder waren krank.) _____

6. (Der Lehrer fragte nach den Kindern.) _____

Die Witwe (*widow*), _____, wohnt jetzt in Bayern (*Bavaria*).

7. (Der Mann der Witwe ist vor zwei Monaten gestorben.) _____

8. (Niemand wollte der Witwe helfen.) _____

9. (Ihre Kinder können für die Witwe nicht sorgen [*care*].) _____

Sie erzählte (*told*) von einem König, _____.

10. (Der König hatte vier starke Söhne.) _____

11. (Das Volk liebte den König sehr.) _____

12. (Die Tochter des Königs hatte goldene Haare.) _____

Stefan fotografiert die Soldaten, _____.

13. (Der Bürgermeister des Dorfes hasst die Soldaten.) _____

14. (Niemand will von den Soldaten sprechen.) _____

15. (Die Soldaten waren tapfer [*brave*] im Kampf.) _____

Using **welcher** as a relative pronoun

For the most part, the use of **welcher** as a relative pronoun is identical to the use of the definite articles. The only exception is the possessive form, which is not composed from a declension of **welcher** but rather from the declension of the definite articles. Let's look at the declension of **welcher** as a relative pronoun:

CASE	MASCULINE	FEMININE	NEUTER	PLURAL
NOMINATIVE	welcher	welche	welches	welche
ACCUSATIVE	welchen	welche	welches	welche
DATIVE	welchem	welcher	welchem	welchen
POSSESSIVE	dessen	deren	dessen	deren

Note in the following example sentences how **welcher** is employed as a relative pronoun in exactly the same way as the definite articles. Its translation is *that*, *who*, or *which* just like the definite articles.

Wo ist der Lehrer, **welchen** sie anrufen wollen?	*Where is the teacher whom they want to call?*
Wo ist die Lehrerin, für die Erik gearbeitet hat?	*Where is the teacher, for whom Erik worked?*
Wo ist das Kind, **welchem** wir die Bücher geben wollen?	*Where is the child to whom we want to give the books?*
Wo sind die Kinder, mit denen ihr Vater reden will?	*Where is the child with whom their father wants to speak?*
Wo ist der Gast, **dessen** Frau Krankenschwester ist?	*Where is the guest whose wife is a nurse?*

It is important to pay strict attention to the German formation of relative clauses that have a preposition introducing the relative pronoun. In German, the preposition always precedes the relative pronoun and stands at the beginning of the relative clause. English is more flexible. Consider how the following German clause can be translated more than one way in English.

> Das ist der Mann, mit dem Erik gesprochen hat.
> *That is the man with whom Erik spoke.*
> *That is the man whom Erik spoke with.*
> *That is the man that Erik spoke with.*
> *That is the man Erik spoke with.*

German never omits the relative pronoun as in the fourth English translation.

Change the antecedent in each sentence to the ones provided in parentheses. Make the necessary declensional changes to the relative pronoun to reflect the new gender or number of the antecedent. Use a form of **welcher** as the relative pronoun.

EXAMPLE   Er spricht mit **dem Mann**, welcher ihm helfen wird.

(die Frau) *Er spricht mit der Frau, welche ihm helfen wird.*

1. Sie findet **die Bluse,** welche sie gestern gekauft hat.

   (das Kleid) _____

   (die Briefmarken [*stamps*]) _____

   (der Hut) _____

2. Kennen Sie **die Leute**, welche in Darmstadt wohnen?

   (der Ausländer) _____

   (die Studenten) _____

   (die Studentin) _____

3. Ich begegnete **einem Nachbarn**, dessen Vater gestorben ist.

   (eine Dame) _____

   (die Brüder) _____

   (ein Kind) _____

4. Das ist **die Richterin**, von welcher ich das Geschenk bekommen habe.

   (die Leute) _____

   (der Richter) _____

   (unsere Gäste) _____

5. **Die Frau**, für welche wir gearbeitet haben, ist nach Bonn gezogen (*moved*).

   (die Männer) _____

   (der Engländer) _____

   (das Mädchen) _____

Using a form of the definite article as the relative pronoun, complete each sentence with any appropriate relative clause.

1. Er besuchte seinen Onkel, _____.

2. Der Kaufmann, _____, reist sehr weit.

3. Erik verkaufte die Bücher, _____.

4. Kennen Sie die Amerikanerin, _____?

5. Die Künstlerin (*artist*), _____, ist gestorben.

6. Heidelberg ist eine Stadt, _____.

7. Die Herren, _____, sind Ausländer.

8. Die Leute, _____, sind umgezogen (*moved away*).

9. Frau Benz ist jetzt eine Witwe, _____.

*Follow the same directions. Use a form of **welcher** as the relative pronoun.*

10. Der Aufsatz (*essay*), _____, ist schwer.

11. Die Polizei fand die Wanderer, _____.

12. Der Wagen, _____, ist ein BMW.

13. Wir wohnen in einem Land, _____.

14. Viele helfen dem Jungen, _____.

15. Ist das das Pferd, _____.

16. Ich sehe das Fenster, _____.

17. Mein Nachbar, _____, ist krank geworden.

18. Er sitzt auf einem Stuhl, _____.

19. Wir begegneten der Richterin, _____.

A relative pronoun is a word that reflects back to an antecedent in one sentence and connects that sentence with another sentence, combining the two sentences into one. The English relative pronouns are *that*, *who*, and *which*.

> *The story is true. I'm going to tell you the story.*
> *The story **that** I'm going to tell you is true.*

> *The mayor is quite popular. The mayor happens to be in Spain.*
> *The mayor, **who** happens to be in Spain, is quite popular.*

*The medicine is strong. The medicine is now available over the
counter.*
*The medicine, **which** is now available over the counter, is strong.*

But English also has an elliptical relative construction, which omits the pronoun from the relative clause.

With the pronoun	*The boy **that** I saw had red hair.*
Without the pronoun	*The boy **I** saw had red hair.*

Der/die/das

German generally replaces each of these types of English relative pronouns with a definite article that serves as a relative pronoun. The declension of the definite article used as a relative pronoun is identical to the declension of the definite article alone, with the exception of the genitive case and the dative plural.

	Masculine	Feminine	Neuter	Plural
Nominative	der	die	das	die
Accusative	den	die	das	die
Dative	dem	der	dem	**denen**
Genitive	**dessen**	**deren**	**dessen**	**deren**

Although the German relative pronoun looks like a definite article, its meaning is *that, who,* or *which.* In its use as a relative pronoun, the definite article retains the gender, number, and case of the noun replaced in the relative clause.

When two German sentences share the same noun, one of the nouns can be changed to a relative pronoun and the two sentences can be combined into one.

Erich besuchte **eine Tante. Eine Tante** wohnt in Heidelberg.
Erich besuchte **eine Tante, die** in Heidelberg wohnt.
Erich visited an aunt who lives in Heidelberg.

Notice that the relative pronoun die has the same gender, number, and case as the noun, **eine Tante**, that it replaces. In the relative clause, the conjugated verb **wohnt** is the last element in the clause. This occurs in all relative clauses, which are subordinate clauses and require the conjugated verb at the end.

As the gender, number, and case of a noun replaced by a relative pronoun changes, so, too, must the relative pronoun change.

Nominative masculine singular

Heinz will einen Wagen, **der** neuer ist.
Heinz wants a car that is newer.

Accusative feminine singular

Wir treffen die Dame, **die** meine Mutter kennt.
We meet the lady that my mother knows.

Dative neuter singular

Er sucht das Mädchen, **mit dem** er getanzt hat.
He's looking for the girl he danced with.

Ich helfe den Touristen, **deren** Verwandte hier in der Stadt wohnen.
I help the tourists whose relatives live here in the city.

In the example for the dative neuter singular, notice that the German preposition mit stands directly in front of the relative pronoun dem. Although English is more flexible about the position of a preposition in a relative clause, the German preposition always stands in front of the relative pronoun.

> . . . *the girl with whom he danced.*
> . . . *the girl that he danced with.* } ... das Mädchen, mit dem er getanzt hat.
> . . . *the girl he danced with.*

Whatever the position of the English preposition, the German preposition has only one place in the relative clause.

> Hier ist der Kleiderschrank, **in dem** meine Anzüge aufbewahrt sind.
> *Here's the wardrobe that my suits are kept in.*

> In der Ferne ist der Tunnel, **durch den** der Zug fahren wird.
> *In the distance is the tunnel that the train will travel through.*

> Das ist ein Bild von meinen Söhnen, **von denen** ich heute diese Blumen
> bekommen habe.
> *This is a picture of my sons, from whom I received these flowers today.*

The genitive of the relative pronoun replaces a possessive modifier or the genitive case of a noun.

> Kennst du den Mann? Seine Frau ist gestern gestorben.
> Kennst du den Mann, **dessen** Frau gestern gestorben ist?
> *Do you know the man whose wife died yesterday?*

> Werner besuchte die Schauspielerin. Ihr Talent ist weltberühmt.
> Werner besuchte die Schauspielerin, **deren** Talent weltberühmt ist.
> *Werner visited the actress whose talent is world famous.*

> Sie helfen den Touristen. Ihre Pässe sind ungültig.
> Sie helfen den Touristen, **deren** Pässe ungültig sind.
> *They help the tourists whose passports are invalid.*

In sentences where a possessive relative pronoun is used, the modified noun remains in the sentence (in the sentences above, **dessen** *Frau*, **deren** *Talent*, **deren** *Pässe*). Because the possessive relative pronoun reflects back to the antecedent in the first sentence, it must have the gender and number of that antecedent. The noun that is modified does not affect the form of the possessive relative pronoun.

> Kennst du den Mann, **dessen** Frau gestern gestorben ist?
> (**dessen** replaces **seine**, which refers to **Mann**)

In the sentence above, the word **Frau** could be replaced by other nouns of different genders and number and the sentence would remain structured in the same way.

> Kennst du den Mann, **dessen** Vater gestern gestorben ist?
> *Do you know the man whose father died yesterday?*

> Kennst du den Mann, **dessen** Kind gestern gestorben ist?
> *Do you know the man whose child died yesterday?*

Kennst du den Mann, **dessen** Schwester gestern gestorben ist?
Do you know the man whose sister died yesterday?

Kennst du den Mann, **dessen** Freunde gestern gestorben sind?
Do you know the man whose friends died yesterday?

The noun that **dessen** modifies does not determine the gender or number of the relative pronoun—the antecedent **Mann** does. If the antecedent changes, the possessive relative pronoun may also change.

Kennst du **die Frau, deren** Vater gestern gestorben ist?
Do you know the woman whose father died yesterday?

Kennst du **das Kind, dessen** Vater gestern gestorben ist?
Do you know the child whose father died yesterday?

Kennst du **den Arzt, dessen** Vater gestern gestorben ist?
Do you know the physician whose father died yesterday?

Kennst du **die Kinder, deren** Vater gestern gestorben ist?
Do you know the children whose father died yesterday?

The genitive relative pronoun may also be used to replace a genitive noun.

Kennst du den Mann? Die Frau **des Mannes** ist gestern gestorben.
Kennst du den Mann, **dessen** Frau gestern gestorben ist?
Do you know the man whose wife died yesterday?

Wo sind die Blumen? Der Geruch **der Blumen** ist so schön.
Wo sind die Blumen, **deren** Geruch so schön ist?
Where are the flowers whose scent (the scent of which) is so pretty?

Ich suche den Rechtsanwalt. Ich habe die Mappe **des Rechtsanwalts** gefunden.
Ich suche den Rechtsanwalt, **dessen** Mappe ich gefunden habe.
I'm looking for the lawyer whose briefcase I found.

Sie kann der Lehrerin nicht antworten. Die Fragen **der Lehrerin** sind sehr schwierig.
Sie kann der Lehrerin, **deren** Fragen sehr schwierig sind, nicht antworten.
She can't answer the teacher whose questions are very hard.

Thus, both a possessive modifier and a genitive noun can be replaced in the very same way by a genitive relative pronoun.

ÜBUNG
22·11

Rewrite the relative clause in each sentence, taking into account each new antecedent.

1. Er findet ein Buch, das seinem Freund gehört.

   a. Er findet einen Handschuh, _____.

   b. Er findet eine Mappe, _____.

   c. Er findet die Anzüge, _____.

2. Ich sprach mit einem Freund, den Liese neulich kennen gelernt hat.

   a. Ich sprach mit einer Freundin, _____.

b. Ich sprach mit dem Mädchen, _____.

c. Ich sprach mit den Ausländern, _____.

3. Klaus kennt die Frau, von der die anderen gesprochen haben.

   a. Klaus kennt den Herrn, _____.

   b. Klaus kennt die Leute, _____.

   c. Klaus kennt das Kind, _____.

4. Sie besuchte die Dame, deren Nachbar aus England kommt.

   a. Sie besuchte ihre Verwandten, _____.

   b. Sie besuchte den Professor, _____.

   c. Sie besuchte die Krankenschwester, _____.

Welcher

Frequently, relative pronouns formed from definite articles are replaced by **welcher**. The endings for this form of the relative pronoun are the same as the ones used with **welcher** when it is a modifier, with the exception of the genitive case.

	Masculine	Feminine	Neuter	Plural
Nominative	welcher	welche	welches	welche
Accusative	welchen	welche	welches	welche
Dative	welchem	welcher	welchem	welchen
Genitive	**dessen**	**deren**	**dessen**	**deren**

Example phrases follow.

der Hund, der stundenlang bellt OR der Hund, welcher stundenlang bellt
the dog that barks for hours

das Haus, das weiß ist OR das Haus, welches weiß ist
the house that's white

die Bücher, die er liest OR die Bücher, welche er liest
the books that he reads

Like **der/die/das** used as a relative pronoun, **welcher** retains the gender, number, and case of the noun it replaces in a relative clause. When **welcher** is the relative pronoun in a clause, the conjugated verb is still the last element in the clause.

Der Schüler, welcher nichts **lernt**, ist faul.
The pupil who isn't learning anything is lazy.

In German, relative clauses are separated from the rest of the sentence by commas; this is not necessarily so in English, where the presence or absence of commas typically impacts the meaning of the sentence.

Rewrite each sentence, changing the definite article used as a relative pronoun to the appropriate form of **welcher.**

1. Der Tourist, mit dem er gesprochen hat, war Ausländer.

   _____

2. Der Schriftsteller, dessen Romane viel bewundert werden, ist jetzt achtzig Jahre alt.

   _____

3. Sie haben Beethoven ein Denkmal gesetzt, das ein junger Bildhauer geschaffen hat.

   _____

4. Sie kauft neue Gläser, aus denen man nur Wein trinken wird.

   _____

5. Der Zug, der langsam fährt, ist kein Eilzug.

   _____

Was

In certain cases, **was** is used as a relative pronoun. This occurs when the antecedent of the relative pronoun is **alles, etwas, nichts,** or **viel(es).**

> Ich verstehe **alles, was** Sie sagen.
> *I understand everything you're saying.*

> Sie kaufte **etwas, was** wirklich zu teuer war.
> *She bought something that was really too expensive.*

> Hans lernt **nichts, was** gelehrt wird.
> *Hans isn't learning anything that is being taught.*

> Es gibt **viel(es), was** dem Körper schaden kann.
> *There's a lot that can harm the body.*

In addition, when **das** is used as a demonstrative pronoun, **was** is used as the relative pronoun.

> Ich lese ein bisschen von **dem, wa**s er geschrieben hat.
> *I read a little of what he wrote.*

When an adjective is used as a neuter noun, **was** is used as the relative pronoun.

> Ich brauche **das Beste, was** Sie haben.
> *I need the best that you have.*

Was is also used as a relative pronoun when the antecedent of the relative clause is an entire clause.

> **Sie fing an zu weinen, was** ihn sehr überrascht hat.
> *She started to cry, which really surprised him.*

When **was** is the subject (as, for instance, in **... was dem Körper schaden kann** above) or direct object (as in **... was er geschrieben hat** above) of a relative clause, it does not make a declensional change. When **was** is the object of a preposition, a form like a prepositional adverb is used: **wo(r)-** + preposition.

> In zwei Tagen fängt Fasching an, **worauf** ich mich sehr freue.
> *Fasching starts in two days, which I'm really looking forward to.*

> Sie verkaufte alles, **womit** sie nach Berlin gezogen war.
> *She sold everything she moved to Berlin with.*

Prepositional adverbs are discussed in Chapter 23.

The interrogatives **wer** and **was** are used as special relative pronouns, where in English *whoever/whosoever* or *whatever/whatsoever* is used. In some instances, these two pronouns can be translated simply as *who* or *what*. **Wer** or **was** begins the first clause, and **der** or **das** is used in the second clause, although **der** and **das** can sometimes be omitted.

> **Wer** nicht lernen will, **dem** wird nichts gelingen.
> *Whoever does not want to learn will succeed at nothing.*

> **Was** du findest, **das** gehört jetzt dir.
> *What you find now belongs to you.*

Wer in this usage can be declined in all cases.

Nominative	**wer**
Accusative	**wen**
Dative	**wem**
Genitive	**wessen** (**Wessen** is sometimes pronounced as **wes**.)

Example sentences follow.

> Wer ihn trifft, (der) vergisst ihn nie.
> *Whoever meets him never forgets him.*

> Wen man befreit, den befreundet man.
> *Whomever you free you make your friend.*

> Wem man nicht traut, dem bleibt man fern.
> *Stay away from whomever you don't trust.*

> Wessen Brot wird gegessen, dessen Lied wird gesungen.
> *Whoever's bread is eaten, his song will be sung.*

ÜBUNG

22·13

Fill in each blank with the appropriate relative pronoun.

1. Die Zeitung, von _____ der Held gelobt wurde, war das Abendblatt.

2. Die Uhr, _____ an der Wand hängt, war ein Geschenk von meiner Mutter.

3. Mein Mann gibt mir alles, _____ ich verlange.

4. _____ nicht mein Freund ist, der ist mein Feind.

5. Ich kaufte einen schweren Mantel, _____ ich im Winter tragen werde.

6. Das große Haus, _____ an der Ecke gebaut wird, ist furchtbar teuer.

7. Ich brauche einen Schrank, in _____ ich mein Geld aufbewahren kann.

8. Sie sucht ein Thermometer, mit _____ sie das Fieber ihres Sohnes messen kann.

9. Das ist der Lehrer, _____ Schüler durchgefallen sind.

10. Siehst du den Wagen, _____ ich gestern gekauft habe?

ÜBUNG
22·14

Complete each sentence with any appropriate relative clause.

1. Am Himmel sehe ich die Sterne, _____ .

2. Er gab mir etwas, _____ .

3. Das sind die Soldaten, von denen _____ .

4. Er kaufte sich einen Schlips, _____ .

5. Ich lese nichts, wofür _____ .

Relative pronouns are commonly used to combine two sentences that have the same noun or pronoun in both. One of them is changed to a relative pronoun, and the sentences are then combined:

> **identical noun + identical noun**
> *Do you know **the man**? + **The man** is a thief.*
> *Do you know the man, <u>who</u> is a thief?*

Two types of relative pronouns

In German, there are two basic types of relative pronouns. One is formed from the definite article, and the other is formed from the **der**-word **welcher**. Naturally, in German you have to consider the gender, number, and case when using relative pronouns. Let's look at their declension:

	MASCULINE	FEMININE	NEUTER	PLURAL
Definite article				
Nominative:	der	die	das	die
Accusative:	den	die	das	die
Dative:	dem	der	dem	denen
Possessive:	dessen	deren	dessen	deren
Welcher				
Nominative:	welcher	welche	welches	welche
Accusative:	welchen	welche	welches	welche
Dative:	welchem	welcher	welchem	welchen
Possessive:	dessen	deren	dessen	deren

Notice that both the definite article form and the **welcher** form have the identical possessive adjective where the genitive case would normally occur.

Just like English relative pronouns, German relative pronouns combine two sentences that have the same noun or pronoun in both. But in German, gender, number, and case must be considered. If the noun replaced by a relative pronoun is nominative, the relative pronoun must be nominative. For example:

Der Junge ist Amerikaner. Der Junge lernt Deutsch.	*The boy is an American. The boy is learning German.*
Der Junge, der Deutsch lernt, ist Amerikaner.	*The boy, who is learning German, is an American.*
Der Junge, welcher Deutsch lernt, ist Amerikaner.	⟶
Wo sind die Kinder? Die Kinder spielen Schach.	*Where are the children? The children are playing chess.*
Wo sind die Kinder, die Schach spielen?	*Where are the children who are playing chess?*
Wo sind die Kinder, welche Schach spielen?	⟶

main clause + der/die/das + relative clause with verb in final position
Das ist der Mann, + der + unser Haus kaufte.
That's the man who bought our house.

main clause + welcher + relative clause with verb in final position
Das ist der Mann, + welcher + unser Haus kaufte.
That's the man who bought our house.

If the noun replaced by a relative pronoun is accusative, the relative pronoun must be accusative. For example:

Sie ist die Frau. Thomas liebt die Frau.	*She is the woman. Thomas loves the woman.*
Sie ist die Frau, die Thomas liebt.	*She is the woman that Thomas loves.*
Sie ist die Frau, welche Thomas liebt.	
Er sprach mit dem Herrn. Niemand kennt den Herrn.	*He spoke with the gentleman. No one knows the gentleman.*
Er sprach mit dem Herrn, den niemand kennt.	*He spoke with the gentleman whom no one knows.*
Er sprach mit dem Herrn, welchen niemand kennt.	

If the noun replaced by a relative pronoun is dative, the relative pronoun must be dative. For example:

Kennst du die Leute? Er spricht mit den Leuten.	*Do you know the people? He is talking to the people.*
Kennst du die Leute, mit denen er spricht?	*Do you know the people that he is talking to?*
Kennst du die Leute, mit welchen er spricht?	
Die Dame ist eine Verwandte. Er hilft der Dame.	*The lady is a relative. He helps the lady.*
Die Dame, der er hilft, ist eine Verwandte.	*The lady that he helps is a relative.*
Die Dame, welcher er hilft, ist eine Verwandte.	

If the noun replaced by a relative pronoun is in the genitive case or is a possessive adjective, the relative pronoun must be in the possessive adjective form. For example:

Er sieht den Lehrer. Die Schüler des Lehrers singen ein Lied.   *He sees the teacher. The teacher's students are singing a song.*

Er sieht den Lehrer, dessen Schüler ein Lied singen.   *He sees the teacher whose students are singing a song.*

Das ist die Richterin. Ihr Sohn wurde verhaftet.   *That's the judge. Her son was arrested.*

Das ist die Richterin, deren Sohn verhaftet wurde.   *That's the judge whose son was arrested.*

In the last example, the possessive adjective **ihr** refers to the noun **Richterin** and therefore is replaced by the corresponding feminine, singular relative pronoun.

It is probably wise to remind you that English has three types of relative pronouns: (1) *who* and *which*, which introduce a *non-restrictive* relative clause that gives parenthetical information; (2) *that*, which introduces a *restrictive* relative clause that helps to define the antecedent; and (3) an elliptical relative pronoun, which is understood but not spoken or written. All three types of English relative pronouns can be translated into German by the German definite article or **welcher**. For example:

Der Mann, den ich sah, ist ein Freund.   *The man, whom I saw, is a friend.*
     The man that I saw is a friend.
     The man I saw is a friend.

When the case of a German relative pronoun is determined by its accompanying preposition, the preposition precedes the relative pronoun. The position of a preposition in an English relative clause is more flexible. For example:

Das ist der Mann, für den er arbeitet.   *That's the man for whom he works.*
     That's the man that he works for.
     That's the man he works for.

Wo ist die Dame, mit der ich sprach?   *Where's the lady with whom I spoke?*
     Where's the lady that I spoke with?
     Where's the lady I spoke with?

ÜBUNG
22·15

Combine the following pairs of sentences by changing one of the identical nouns (or its corresponding possessive adjective) to the appropriate relative pronoun in its definite article form. Remember to take gender, number, and case into account.

EXAMPLE: Peter hat einen Wagen. Sie will den Wagen kaufen.

     Peter hat einen Wagen, den sie kaufen will.

1. Die Frau wollte die Suppe nicht probieren. Ihre Tochter ist Köchin.

_____

2. Er hilft seinen Verwandten. Seine Verwandten wohnen in den Bergen.

_____

3. Sie segelten zu einer Insel. Die Insel wurde von keinen Menschen bewohnt.

_____

4. Es ist ein deutsches Flugzeug. Das Flugzeug ist eben gelandet.

_____

5. Der alte Herr musste bei seinem Bruder wohnen. Sein Vermögen ging verloren.

_____

6. Er trifft einen Freund auf der Straße. Das Gesicht seines Freundes ist ganz blass.

_____

7. Sie sieht die Soldaten. Das kleine Dorf wurde von den Soldaten besetzt.

_____

8. Die Universität ist weltbekannt. In den Räumen der Universität findet eine Konferenz statt.

_____

9. Der Mann ist neulich gestorben. Tina hat für den Mann gearbeitet.

_____

10. Der Stuhl ist alt und wackelig. Oma sitzt auf dem Stuhl.

_____

ÜBUNG

22·16

Complete each of the following sentences twice, using the relative pronoun in each of the cases specified.

EXAMPLE: Thomas kauft den Hut.

(nom.) <u>Thomas kauft den Hut, der zu groß ist.</u>

(dat.) <u>Thomas kauft den Hut, von dem Luise gesprochen hat.</u>

1. Er lud seine Freunde ein.

   a. (nom.) _____

   b. (acc.) _____

2. Wer hat die Uhr gekauft?

   a. (acc.) _____

   b. (dat.) _____

3. Andreas spielte mit dem Hund.

   a. (dat.) _____

   b. (poss.) _____

4. Alle respektieren die Richterin.

    a. (acc.) _____

    b. (dat.) _____

5. Sie fotografierte die jungen Soldaten.

    a. (nom.) _____

    b. (acc.) _____

Wer and der

There is another aspect to relative pronouns. When no specific person is referred to in a sentence, the pronoun **wer** is used as a relative pronoun. It is usually paired with **der**, and the English meaning of this concept is *he, who,* or *who(so)ever*. For example:

> *He who lies about me is no friend of mine.*
> *Whoever threw that snowball is in a lot of trouble.*

Since German declines words like **wer** and **der**, this kind of relative pronoun usage can appear in all the cases:

Wer oft lügt, den respektiert niemand.	*He who often lies is respected by no one.*
Wen die Polizei verhaftet, dem kann man nicht helfen.	*No one can help the one, whom the police arrest.*
Wem das imponiert, der ist wohl naiv.	*Whomever that impresses is probably naive.*
Wessen Brot man isst, dessen Lied man singt.	*If you eat his bread, you must dance to his tune.* (A saying)

You will notice that the declension of **wer** and **der** is dependent upon the use of each in its own clause.

Was

Something similar occurs with **was**. Use **was** if it refers to no specific object and can be translated as *that, which,* or *what(ever)*. For example:

Was billig ist, ist nicht immer gut.	*That which is cheap is not always good.*
Was sie sagte war Unsinn.	*What(ever) she said was nonsense.*

Was is also used as a relative pronoun after the demonstrative pronoun **das**. For example:

Sie verstand nichts von dem, was ich sagte.	*She didn't understand anything I said.*
Hast du das, was ich brauche?	*Do you have what I need?*

Was also becomes a relative pronoun after the following words: **alles, etwas, nichts, manches,** and **vieles**. For example:

Ist das alles, was Sie sagen wollen?	*Is that everything you want to say?*
Ich habe etwas, was dich freuen wird.	*I have something that will make you happy.*

Manches, was sie sagt, ist Unsinn.	*Some of what she says is nonsense.*
Rede nichts, was nicht alle hören dürfen.	*Say nothing that not everyone is allowed to hear.*
Es gibt vieles, was ich vergessen will.	*There's a lot that I want to forget.*

If an adjective is used as a noun, **was** acts as its relative pronoun:

| Das ist das Schönste, was ich jemals gesehen habe. | *That's the most beautiful thing I've ever seen.* |
| Das war das Erste, was er sah. | *That was the first thing he saw.* |

In addition, the relative pronoun **was** is used to introduce a relative clause when the antecedent is an entire clause. For example:

| Onkel Karl reist heute ab, was ich sehr bedaure. | *Uncle Karl is leaving today, which I regret very much.* |
| Sie hat die Prüfung bestanden, was uns sehr erstaunte. | *She passed the test, which really surprised us.* |

When a preposition is required with the relative pronoun **was**, the compound form **wo(r)** plus preposition is used. For example:

| Hier gibt es nichts, wofür er sich interessiert. | *There's nothing here that interests him.* |
| Peter geht an die Universität, worauf sein Vater sehr stolz ist. | *Peter is going to college, which makes his father very proud.* |

ÜBUNG 22·17

*Complete each sentence with an appropriate phrase that includes **wer** as the relative pronoun. Be careful to use the correct case of **wer**.*

EXAMPLE: <u>Wer mir in Not hilft</u>, der ist ein guter Freund.

1. _____, den kann sie nicht lieben.

2. _____, dem glaube ich nicht.

3. _____, der soll es nicht lesen.

4. _____, dem bleibt man fern.

5. _____, der ist gegen mich.

*Now complete each sentence with an appropriate conclusion beginning with a form of **der**.*

6. Wem es nicht gefällt, _____.

7. Wer nicht gehorcht, _____.

Complete the following sentences with an appropriate antecedent for a **was** relative pronoun or an appropriate relative clause that is introduced by **was**.

EXAMPLE: Das ist alles, <u>was ich zu sagen habe.</u>

1. Ist das das Beste, was _____?

2. Der Kranke hat etwas gegessen, was _____.

3. Sie haben eine gute Prüfung abgelegt, was _____.

4. _____, was billiger ist?

5. _____, worum sich niemand kümmert.

6. _____, was unvergesslich war.

7. Der Reisende erzählte vieles, was _____.

8. _____, worüber ich mich gar nicht freute.

9. Das war das Dümmste, was _____.

This exercise contains a variety of relative pronoun types. Complete each sentence with an appropriate relative clause.

1. Er tanzt mit der Ausländerin, _____.

2. Sie möchte alles wissen, _____.

3. Der alte Hund ist gestorben, _____.

4. Tue nichts, _____!

5. Die Leute, _____, fingen an zu schreien.

6. Hamburg ist eine Handelsstadt, _____.

7. _____, mit dem will ich nichts zu tun haben.

8. Mein Onkel hat etwas gefunden _____.

Write an original sentence that contains a relative clause. Use the word or phrase in parentheses as the relative pronoun.

1. (was)

_____

2. (mit denen)

_____

3. (dessen)

_____

4. (worüber)

_____

5. (welcher)

_____

Modifiers, adverbs, reflexive pronouns, and conjunctions

Modifiers

We can group German modifiers into three groups: the **der-** and **ein-**words, adjectives, and intensifiers. The **der-** and **ein-**words are already familiar to you, but here we shall add a few more to their list as well as some special *determiners*.

DER-WORDS		EIN-WORDS	
der/die/das	*the*	ein/eine	*a*
dieser	*this*	kein	*no/not any*
jener	*that*	mein	*my*
jeder	*each, every*	dein	*your*
welcher	*which*	sein	*his, its*
mancher	*some, many a*	ihr	*her, their*
solcher	*such*	unser	*our*
		euer	*your*
		Ihr	*your*

You have already seen in Chapter 2 how adjective endings are affected by **der-**words and **ein-**words. But **solcher** requires some further explanation.

Solcher is used primarily with plural nouns. Notice that the adjective endings are identical to those for other **der-**words.

	PLURAL NOUN	PLURAL NOUN
nom	solche jungen Frauen	solche netten Leute
acc	solche jungen Frauen	solche netten Leute
dat	solchen jungen Frauen	solchen netten Leuten
gen	solcher jungen Frauen	solcher netten Leute

When used with singular nouns, **solcher** functions more like a declined adjective than a **der-**word and follows **ein**. For example:

Ein solcher Roman ist unvergesslich.	*Such a novel is unforgettable.*
Sie kaufte **eine solche** Bluse.	*She bought such a blouse.*
Ein solches Buch kann ich nicht lesen.	*I cannot read such a book.*

It can also be used in its undeclined form as a replacement for **so** (*such*).

so ein Haus	→ solch ein Haus	*such a house*
so eine Blume	→ solch eine Blume	*such a flower*

In the blanks provided, write in the missing adjective endings in each phrase.

1. mit ein_____ alt_____ Herrn

2. für dies_____ hübsch_____ Dame

3. solch_____ interessant_____ Gedichte

4. dein_____ erst_____ Geschichte

5. unser_____ best_____ Freunde

6. von jed_____ gut_____ Bürger (*citizen*)

7. ohne sein_____ neu_____ Freundin

8. zu ein_____ klein_____ Kirche

9. bei jen_____ groß_____ Restaurant

10. ein_____ solch_____ Flugzeug

11. solch_____ laut (*loud*) _____ Flugzeuge

12. durch welch_____ jung_____ Mann?

13. aus kein_____ klein_____ Fenster

14. Ihr_____ schön_____ Garten

15. nach ein_____ lang_____ Oper

There are two more **der**-words to consider. They are **alle** (*all*) and **beide** (*both*) and are used only with plural nouns.

	ALLE	BEIDE
nom	alle jungen Frauen	beide netten Leute
acc	alle jungen Frauen	beide netten Leute
dat	allen jungen Frauen	beiden netten Leuten
gen	aller jungen Frauen	beider netten Leute

There are also five other determiners, which are used only with plural nouns. They are:

einige	*some*	viele	*many*
mehrere	*several*	wenige	*few*
sämtliche	*all, all the*		

The declension with these determiners is different from those used with **der**-words and **ein**-words. For example:

	EINIGE	VIELE
nom	einige junge Frauen	viele nette Leute
acc	einige junge Frauen	viele nette Leute
dat	einigen jungen Frauen	vielen netten Leuten
gen	einiger junger Frauen	vieler netter Leute

Remember that comparative and superlative adjectives can be fully declined like other adjectives. In Chapter 20 you used them primarily in the dative case with the preposition **an: am schnellsten**, **am besten**, and so on. Let's look at their full declension.

	HIS BEST FRIEND (MASC.)	*HER NICEST DRESS* (NEUT.)
nom	sein bester Freund	ihr schönstes Kleid
acc	seinen besten Freund	ihr schönstes Kleid
dat	seinem besten Freund	ihrem schönsten Kleid
gen	seines besten Freundes	ihres schönsten Kleides

There are cases when no **der**-word, **ein**-word, or other determiner is used with an adjective and noun. Such cases have their own special declension. For example:

	COLD WATER (NEUT.)	*HOT COFFEE* (MASC.)	*FRESH MILK* (FEM.)	*NICE PEOPLE* (PL.)
nom	kaltes Wasser	heißer Kaffee	frische Milch	nette Leute
acc	kaltes Wasser	heißen Kaffee	frische Milch	nette Leute
dat	kaltem Wasser	heißem Kaffee	frischer Milch	netten Leuten
gen	kalten Wassers	heißen Kaffees	frischer Milch	netter Leute

ÜBUNG

23·2

Write the full declension for the words provided in parentheses.

1. (solch/nett/Kinder)

nom _____

acc _____

dat _____

gen _____

2. (wenig/deutsch/Männer)

_____

_____

_____

_____

3. (jeder/alt/Herr)

nom _____

acc _____

dat _____

gen _____

4. (ein/solch/Flugzeug)

_____

_____

_____

_____

5. (dein/best/Prüfung)

nom _____

acc _____

dat _____

gen _____

6. (gut/Wetter)

_____

_____

_____

_____

Adverbs

Certain modifiers merely intensify the meaning of the adjective they modify. Intensifiers are adverbs and do not decline. The most commonly used intensifiers are:

ganz	*quite*	völlig	*completely, totally*
sehr	*very*	ziemlich	*rather, pretty*
total	*totally, completely*		

And two others are used mostly in the negative:

gar	*at all*	überhaupt	*at all*

Let's look at these adverbs in sentences. Note that they can modify both adjectives and adverbs.

Das Wetter ist wieder **ganz** schlecht.	*The weather is **quite** bad again.*
Dieses Mädchen läuft **sehr** schnell.	*This girl runs **very** fast.*
Ich bin **total/völlig** erschöpft.	*I am **totally** exhausted.*
Wir haben **ziemlich** viele Gäste eingeladen.	*We invited **pretty** many guests.*
Das ist **gar** nicht wahr.	*That is not true **at all**.*
Ich habe **gar** kein Geld.	*I have no money **at all**.*
Er versteht **überhaupt** nichts.	*He does not understand anything **at all**.*
Wir hatten **überhaupt** keine Zeit.	*We had no time **at all**.*

ÜBUNG
23·3

Rewrite each sentence with the modifiers provided.

FOR EXAMPLE: Er ist krank.

sehr _____ *Er ist sehr krank.* _____

Die Kinder waren müde.

1. ganz _____

2. sehr _____

3. ziemlich _____

4. gar nicht _____

5. total _____

Sein Gedicht ist gut.

6. ziemlich _____

7. überhaupt nicht _____

8. ganz _____

9. sehr _____

10. gar nicht _____

Reflexive pronouns

The German reflexive pronouns are:

SUBJECT PRONOUN	ACCUSATIVE REFLEXIVE	DATIVE REFLEXIVE	
ich	mich	mir	*myself*
du	dich	dir	*yourself*
er	sich	sich	*himself*
sie (*sing.*)	sich	sich	*herself*
es	sich	sich	*itself*
wir	uns	uns	*ourselves*
ihr	euch	euch	*yourselves*
Sie	sich	sich	*yourself, yourselves*
sie (*pl.*)	sich	sich	*themselves*
wer	sich	sich	*himself, herself*

Reflexive pronouns are used when the direct object or indirect object of a sentence is the same person or object as the subject. Compare the following pairs of sentences:

Er fragt uns, wo sie ist.	*He asks us where she is.*
Er fragt **sich**, wo sie ist.	*He asks **himself** where she is.*

Ich kaufe euch ein Fahrrad.	*I buy you a bicycle.*
Ich kaufe **mir** ein Fahrrad.	*I buy **myself** a bicycle.*

The accusative and dative reflexive pronouns can also be used with accusative or dative prepositions and as the object of dative verbs.

Er denkt nur an **sich**.	*He only thinks about **himself**.*
Warum widersprichst du **dir**?	*Why do you contradict **yourself**?*

ÜBUNG
23·4

Rewrite each sentence by changing the underlined word to an appropriate reflexive pronoun.

FOR EXAMPLE: Wir kaufen dem Mann ein Glas Bier.

Wir kaufen uns ein Glas Bier.

1. Martin kaufte etwas für seine Freundin.

_____

2. Ihr habt nur an euren Bruder gedacht.

_____

3. Wir helfen der Frau, so oft wir können.

_____

4. Ich verberge (*hide*) das Geschenk hinter der Tür.

_____

5. Er setzte das Paket auf den kleinen Stuhl.

   _____

6. Wer wollte ihm ein Würstchen bestellen?

   _____

7. Sie konnte uns nicht helfen.

   _____

8. Wäschst du die Kinder im Badezimmer (*bathroom*)?

   _____

9. Ich frage ihn, warum er weint.

   _____

10. Warum widersprecht ihr dem alten Herrn?

    _____

11. Mutter wird Frau Dorf ein paar (*a couple of*) Nelken kaufen.

    _____

12. Sie finden gar keine Plätze (*seats*) für sie.

    _____

13. Karl hat mich an die große Prüfung erinnert.

    _____

14. Wo kann er den Hund waschen?

    _____

15. Wir ärgern (*annoy*) euch nicht darüber.

    _____

Reflexive pronouns

English reflexive pronouns, which end in *-self* (singular) and *-selves* (plural), are the reflexive counterparts of subject pronouns.

Personal pronoun	Reflexive pronoun
I	*myself*
you	*yourself*
he	*himself*
she	*herself*
it	*itself*
we	*ourselves*
you	*yourselves*
they	*themselves*

German does not use a suffix to form reflexive pronouns. Instead, the accusative or dative form of the personal pronoun—except for the third-person singular and plural forms—is used as the reflexive form. Just as in English, German reflexive pronouns are the counterparts of subject pronouns.

Nominative	Accusative reflexive	Dative reflexive
ich	mich	mir
du	dich	dir
er	**sich**	**sich**
sie	**sich**	**sich**
es	**sich**	**sich**
wir	uns	uns
ihr	euch	euch
sie	**sich**	**sich**
Sie	**sich**	**sich**
man	**sich**	**sich**
wer	**sich**	**sich**
was	**sich**	**sich**

Since singular and plural nouns are in the third person, their reflexive pronoun form is always **sich**.

The accusative reflexive pronoun is used to replace the accusative object of a verb. When the object of the verb is *not* the same person or thing as the subject of the sentence, a reflexive pronoun is not used.

Karl ärgert **seinen Vater**.
Karl annoys his father.

Was fragst du **ihn**?
What are you asking him?

Helga schützt **sie** davor.
Helga protects her from it.

But when the object of the verb is the same person or thing as the subject, the reflexive counterpart of the subject is used.

Karl ärgert **sich**.
Karl annoys himself. / Karl is annoyed.

Was fragst du **dich**?
What are you asking yourself?

Helga schützt **sich** davor.
Helga protects herself from it.

Rewrite each sentence, changing the direct object in boldface to the appropriate reflexive pronoun.

1. Ich möchte **meine Freundin** vorstellen.

   _____

2. Wir haben **den Professor** wieder geärgert.

   _____

3. Du musst **die Kinder** vor einer Erkältung schützen.

   _____

4. Habt ihr **die Kinder** angekleidet?

   _____

5. Wie können sie **die Lage** ändern?

   _____

6. Meine Mutter fragt **meinen Vater**, was geschehen ist.

   _____

7. Frau Schneider hat **die Katze** auf einen Stuhl gesetzt.

   _____

8. Du hast **mich** schon überzeugt.

   _____

9. Der wahnsinnige Mann hat **sie** getötet.

   _____

10. Ich wasche **ihn**.

    _____

When the object of a verb is not the same person or thing as the subject of the sentence, a reflexive pronoun is not used.

> Wir trauen **dir** diese Arbeit zu.
> _We entrust you with this job._
>
> Ich kaufe **dem Kind** eine Blume.
> _I buy the child a flower._
>
> Er bestellt **ihr** eine Tasse Tee.
> _He orders her a cup of tea._

But when the dative object of the verb is the same person or thing as the subject, the dative reflexive counterpart of the subject is used.

> Wir trauen **uns** diese Arbeit zu.
> *We entrust ourselves with this job.*

> Ich kaufe **mir** eine Blume.
> *I buy myself a flower.*

> Er bestellt **sich** eine Tasse Tee.
> *He orders himself a cup of tea.*

The accusative case is used for direct objects and after prepositions that take the accusative case. An accusative reflexive pronoun is used in these two instances just as a noun or a personal pronoun is.

> Ich freue mich auf die Ferien.
> *I'm looking forward to vacation.*

> Er hat es nur für sich getan.
> *He has only done it for himself.*

The dative case is used for indirect objects, with dative verbs, and after dative prepositions. A dative reflexive pronoun is used in these three instances just as a noun or a personal pronoun is.

> Er findet sich einen neuen Schlips.
> *He finds a new tie for himself.*

> Sie helfen sich, so gut sie können.
> *They help themselves as well as they can.*

> Ich habe kein Geld bei mir.
> *I don't have any money on me.*

ÜBUNG
23·6

Rewrite each sentence, changing the dative object in boldface to the appropriate reflexive pronoun.

1. Die Mutter putzt **dem kleinsten Kind** die Zähne.

   _____

2. Gudrun hilft **den anderen**, so gut sie kann.

   _____

3. Martin und Erich wollen **uns** ein Spiel kaufen.

   _____

4. Warum musst du **dem Lehrer** widersprechen?

   _____

5. Ich kämme **ihm** die Haare.

   _____

6. Darf ich **meinem Freund** ein Stück Kuchen nehmen?

   _____

7. Meine Schwester hat **mir** ein interessantes Buch gefunden.

   _____

8. Er kaufte **seinem besten Freund** eine Armbanduhr.

   _____

9. Das wird sie **Ihnen** nie verzeihen.

   _____

10. Habt ihr **den Kindern** die Mäntel ausgezogen?

    _____

ÜBUNG
23·7

Rewrite each sentence, changing the accusative or dative object in boldface to the appropriate reflexive pronoun.

1. Was hat **es** bewegt?

   _____

2. Ich kann **diesen armen Leuten** nicht helfen.

   _____

3. Haben Sie **Ihrem Mann** nicht widersprochen?

   _____

4. Wir haben **den jungen Kandidaten** vorgestellt.

   _____

5. Wer hat **sie** gewaschen?

   _____

6. Sie hat **ihren Mann** an die Italienreise erinnert.

   _____

7. Man soll **den Manager** nicht ärgern.

   _____

8. Herr Finkler hat **seinem einzigen Sohn** einen neuen Wagen gekauft.

   _____

9. Sie haben **uns** ein paar Pralinen genommen.

_____

10. Du musst **sie** ändern.

_____

In order to achieve a specific meaning, some verbs require a reflexive pronoun to act as part of the verb. If the reflexive pronoun is omitted, the meaning is changed. These are called reflexive verbs and are identified as such in dictionaries, because the addition of a reflexive pronoun is important to the meaning of the verb. Examples of the range of meaning and use of the verb **vorstellen** follow.

> Ich kann ihn vorstellen.
> _I can introduce him._

In this example, **vorstellen** is not a reflexive verb; it is a transitive verb with a direct object (**ihn**).

> Ich kann mich vorstellen.
> _I can introduce myself._

In this example, **vorstellen** is also not a reflexive verb; it is a transitive verb with a reflexive direct object (**mich**). It is not a reflexive verb, because the meaning remains the same whether the direct object is a reflexive pronoun or some other word.

> Ich kann mir das vorstellen.
> _I can imagine that._

In this example, the verb **sich vorstellen** is a dative reflexive verb that means to _imagine_. This meaning is achieved only if the reflexive pronoun remains part of the verb. If the subject changes, the reflexive pronoun must change accordingly.

> Du kannst dir das vorstellen.
> _You can imagine that._

> Er kann sich das vorstellen.
> _He can imagine that._

> Sie kann sich das vorstellen.
> _She can imagine that._

> Wir können uns das vorstellen.
> _We can imagine that._

Following is a list of other reflexive verbs that require a reflexive pronoun to act together with the verb to achieve a desired meaning.

sich einbilden (_dative reflexive_)	_to imagine something_
sich erkälten (_accusative reflexive_)	_to catch cold_
sich irren (_accusative reflexive_)	_to be wrong_
sich vornehmen (_dative reflexive_)	_to intend to do something_

German has numerous other reflexive verbs. To be certain that a reflexive pronoun is required to achieve a particular meaning, check the dictionary entry for the verb. For example, the entry for the verb **benehmen** may appear as follows.

> **benehmen** 1. *ir.v.a.* take away. 2. *v.r.* behave, demean oneself.

Definition 1 identifies **benehmen** as an **ir**regular **v**erb and transitive (that is, **a**ctive), meaning *take away*. Definition 2 identifies it as a **v**erb that is **r**eflexive, meaning *to behave* or *demean oneself*. This two-letter abbreviation (**v.r.**) tells you that this verb is reflexive and achieves its meaning by acting together with a reflexive pronoun in its conjugation.

ich benehme mich	*I behave myself*
du benimmst dich	*you behave yourself*
er benahm sich	*he behaved himself*
sie hat sich benommen	*she has behaved herself*
wir hatten uns benommen	*we had behaved ourselves*
sie werden sich benehmen	*they will behave themselves*

Verbs that have to do with getting dressed require special consideration. Three high-frequency verbs are derived from the infinitive **ziehen** and combined with prefixes that change the basic meaning of the verb.

anziehen	*to put on (clothes)*
ausziehen	*to take off (clothes)*
umziehen	*to change (clothes)*

These three verbs can be used with a direct object. The meaning is that someone is putting on, taking off, or changing certain clothing.

> Ich möchte den neuen Regenmantel anziehen.
> *I'd like to put on the new raincoat.*

> Die nassen Kinder zogen ihre Hemden aus.
> *The wet children took off their shirts.*

> Der schwitzende Läufer zieht die Schuhe um.
> *The sweating runner changes shoes.*

The same verbs can be used with an accusative reflexive pronoun to refer to dressing in general, with no particular article of clothing specified.

> Nach einer langen Dusche habe ich mich angezogen.
> *After a long shower I got dressed.*

> Der schüchterne Junge will sich nicht ausziehen.
> *The shy boy doesn't want to undress.*

> Kannst du dich nicht schneller umziehen?
> *Can't you change faster?*

Finally, these verbs can be used with an indirect object in the form of a dative reflexive pronoun. In addition, the sentence also contains a direct object (an article of clothing).

> Sie möchte sich ein blaues Kleid anziehen.
> *She'd like to put on a blue dress.*

Willst du dir den schweren Mantel ausziehen?
Do you want to take off the heavy coat?

Er hat sich die Stiefel umziehen wollen.
He wanted to change his boots.

ÜBUNG
23·8

Rewrite each sentence, using the subjects in parentheses and changing the accusative or dative object in boldface to the appropriate reflexive pronoun. Be sure to make any necessary changes to the verb.

1. Seine Freundin denkt nur an **ihn**.

   a. (ich) _____

   b. (du) _____

   c. (die Kinder) _____

   d. (Sie) _____

2. Gerda kaufte **mir** neue Handschuhe.

   a. (ich) _____

   b. (er) _____

   c. (wir) _____

   d. (du) _____

3. Wir brauchen Hustentropfen für **unsere Tochter**.

   a. (der alte Mann) _____

   b. (sie [*sing.*]) _____

   c. (ihr) _____

   d. (Erich) _____

ÜBUNG
23·9

Rewrite each sentence, changing the reflexive pronoun to any appropriate noun or noun phrase.

1. Wir werden uns diese Arbeit zutrauen.

   _____

2. Braucht ihr das Geld für euch?

   _____

3. Ich kann mich nicht davon überzeugen.

_____

4. Sie dürfen sich auf diese Bank setzen.

_____

5. Marianne stellte sich neben ihren Vater.

_____

6. Meine Eltern haben sich einen bunten Teppich gekauft.

_____

7. Er fragt sich, ob das eine Dummheit ist.

_____

8. Du sollst dich sofort vorstellen.

_____

9. Karl hat sich einen guten Platz gesucht.

_____

10. Ich ziehe mir das Hemd an.

_____

Circle the pronoun that best completes each sentence.

1. Ich habe das Geld für _____ gebraucht.   ihm | sich | mich

2. Wie hast du _____ wieder erkältet?   dich | ihr | dir

3. Karl möchte _____ ein neues Fahrrad kaufen.   sich | ihn | es

4. Das werden Sie _____ nie verzeihen.   mich | euch | sich

5. Darf ich _____ vorstellen?   euch | sich | du

6. Bitte setzen Sie _____!   uns | sich | ihm

7. Martin will _____ den Pullover ausziehen.   mich | dich | sich

8. Wo kann ich _____ die Hände waschen?   sich | uns | mir

9. Hast du _____ wieder umgezogen?   dir | dich | Ihnen

10. Er hat _____ diese Arbeit zugetraut.   mir | Sie | ihn

Conjunctions

In previous chapters you encountered a variety of conjunctions, among them those that require the conjugated verb to be the last element in a sentence. For example:

> Ich weiß, **dass** Herr Braun krank ist.
> Sie bleibt zu Hause, **weil** das Wetter schlecht ist.

Like **dass** and **weil**, when interrogative words combine two sentences, they function as conjunctions and place the conjugated verb at the end of a sentence.

Let's look at interrogative words that ask a question and compare them to their use as conjunctions.

Wo ist Herr Schneider?	*Where is Mr. Schneider?*
Wissen Sie, **wo** Herr Schneider ist?	*Do you know where Mr. Schneider is?*
Wie alt ist ihre Schwester?	*How old is her sister?*
Niemand fragte, **wie alt** ihre Schwester ist.	*No one asked how old her sister is.*
Wen werden seine Eltern besuchen?	*Whom will his parents visit?*
Er liest in dem Brief, **wen** seine Eltern besuchen werden.	*He reads in the letter whom his parents will visit.*

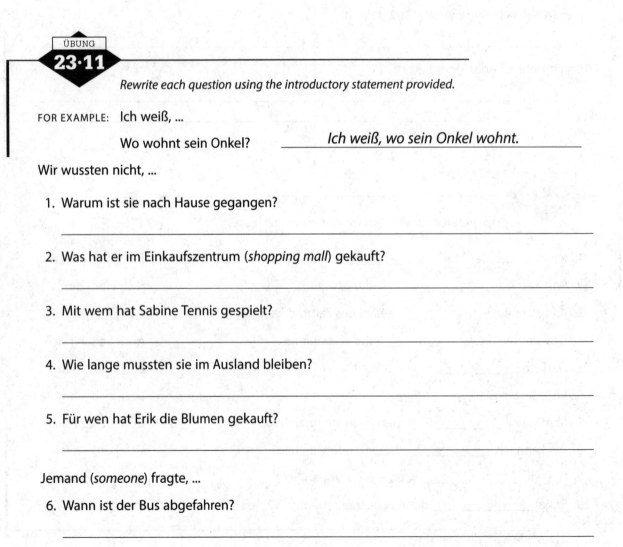

ÜBUNG
23·11

Rewrite each question using the introductory statement provided.

FOR EXAMPLE:　Ich weiß, …

Wo wohnt sein Onkel?　　　*Ich weiß, wo sein Onkel wohnt.*

Wir wussten nicht, …

1. Warum ist sie nach Hause gegangen?

   _____

2. Was hat er im Einkaufszentrum (*shopping mall*) gekauft?

   _____

3. Mit wem hat Sabine Tennis gespielt?

   _____

4. Wie lange mussten sie im Ausland bleiben?

   _____

5. Für wen hat Erik die Blumen gekauft?

   _____

Jemand (*someone*) fragte, …

6. Wann ist der Bus abgefahren?

   _____

7. Wessen Mercedes hat der Mann gestohlen?

_____

8. Wohin sind die Jungen gelaufen?

_____

9. Wofür hat sich der Wissenschaftler (*scientist*) interessiert?

_____

10. Warum widersprichst du dir immer?

_____

Können Sie mir sagen, ...?

11. Um wie viel Uhr kommt der Zug?

_____

12. Wem soll ich damit helfen?

_____

13. Was ist geschehen?

_____

14. Wie viel kosten diese Hemden?

_____

15. Wonach hat der Polizist gefragt?

_____

Conjunctions that combine words, phrases, and sentences

Conjunctions are used to combine two words, phrases, or sentences. For example, with the conjunction **und**:

Combined words	Vater **und** Mutter	*father and mother*
Combined phrases	die Bevölkerung Deutschlands **und** die Bevölkerung Frankreichs	*Germany's population and France's population*
Combined sentences	Erik arbeitet in der Stadt, **und** Sabine arbeitet zu Hause.	*Erik works in the city, and Sabine works at home.*

There are five conjunctions with which no change in word order is required when combining sentences: **aber** (*but*), **denn** (*because*), **oder** (*or*), **sondern** (*but rather*), and **und** (*and*). For example:

Die Katze schläft auf dem Sofa, **aber** der Hund schläft unter dem Tisch.	*The cat sleeps on the sofa, but the dog sleeps under the table.*

Sie bleibt zu Hause, **denn** sie ist wieder krank.	*She stays home because she is sick again.*
Willst du in die Oper gehen, **oder** willst du ins Theater gehen?	*Do you want to go to the opera, or do you want to go to the theater?*
Ich arbeite nicht bei der Bank, **sondern** ich arbeite bei der Post.	*I don't work at the bank, but rather I work for the post office.*
Klaudia ist Lehrerin, **und** ihr Bruder ist Schuldirektor.	*Klaudia is a teacher, and her brother is a principal.*

The conjunction **sondern** introduces a clause that follows one that is negated by **nicht** or **kein** (Ich arbeite **nicht** bei der Bank, **sondern** ich arbeite bei der Post.). It is common to omit redundant information in the **sondern**-clause. For example:

Ich arbeite nicht bei der Bank, **sondern** bei der Post.

This omission of repeated information is also possible with the other conjunctions.

ÜBUNG

23·12

Complete each sentence with any appropriate clause.

1. Ich habe ein neues Fahrrad, aber _____.

2. Meine Cousine wohnt in Bayern (*Bavaria*), aber _____.

3. Peter mag kaltes Wetter, denn _____.

4. Wir werden bis morgen warten, denn _____.

5. Sollen wir ins Theater gehen, oder _____?

6. Du kannst dich im Keller waschen, oder _____.

7. Ich höre nicht gern Radio (*do not like*), sondern _____.

8. Er möchte keinen Kuchen essen, sondern _____.

9. Tina deckt (*sets*) den Tisch, und _____.

10. Im Juni fliegen wir nach New York, und _____.

Conjunctions that introduce a subordinate clause

Other German conjunctions introduce a subordinate clause. Subordinate clauses require the conjugated verb to be the last element in the sentence. Such clauses can be the first clause in a sentence or the second clause. Some commonly used subordinating conjunctions are:

als ob	*as if*
als	*when, as*
da	*since (the reason), as*
dass	*that*

ehe	*before*
nachdem	*after*
ob	*whether (if)*
obwohl	*although*
seitdem	*since (the time)*
während	*while*
weil	*because*
wenn	*whenever, if*

Let's look at some example sentences. Notice that the underlined conjugated verb is the last element in the clause.

Als ich in Hamburg <u>wohnte</u>, ging ich oft in die Oper.	*When I lived in Hamburg, I often went to the opera.*
Sie kann den Artikel nicht lesen, **weil** sie kein Deutsch <u>kann</u>.	*She can't read the article, because she doesn't know any German.*
Nachdem wir gegessen <u>haben</u>, fahren wir mit dem Bus ins Kino.	*After we've eaten, we'll take the bus to the movies.*
Ich weiß nicht, **ob** ich das Examen bestanden <u>habe</u>.	*I don't know if I passed the exam.*
Wenn ich meinen Nachbarn <u>helfe</u>, geben sie mir ein paar Euro.	*Whenever I help my neighbors, they give me a couple of euros.*

ÜBUNG
23·13

Complete each clause with any appropriate phrase.

1. Während _____, musste ich eine kleine Volksschule besuchen.

2. Da _____, konnte er nicht aufstehen.

3. Ehe _____, möchte ich die Speisekarte (*menu*) lesen.

4. Obwohl _____, konnten wir den Tisch nicht aufheben (*lift*).

5. Als _____, lernte ich einen berühmten Dichter (*famous poet*) kennen.

6. Wissen Sie, ob _____?

7. Der Schuldirektor sagt, dass _____.

8. Er hat viel Englisch gelernt, seitdem _____.

9. Wir können nicht schwimmen gehen, weil _____.

10. Herr Bauer macht die Küche sauber (*cleans*), nachdem _____.

Double infinitive structures

Double infinitives are not used in English, but this unique structure of German verbs is very simple to understand and use. The double infinitive occurs in the perfect tenses and in the future.

As variously discussed in Chapters 10, 11, and 21, in the perfect tenses there is an auxiliary (**haben** or **sein**) and a past participle.

Der Mann **hat** es **gekauft**.	Die Frau **ist** nach Hause **gegangen**.

And in the future tense, the auxiliary **werden** is accompanied by an infinitive.

Es **wird** heute **regnen**.	Die Kinder **werden** damit **spielen**.

When a modal auxiliary is combined with an infinitive in the present or past tense, the modal is conjugated, and the infinitive is the last element in the sentence.

Ich **will** es verkaufen.	*I **want** to sell it.*
Die Frau **kann** uns helfen.	*The woman **can** help us.*
Er **musste** zu Hause bleiben.	*He **had** to stay home.*
Sie **durfte** die Bibliothek benutzen.	*She was **allowed** to use the library.*

But in the perfect tenses of modal auxiliaries, the auxiliary **haben** is combined with a double infinitive—an infinitive followed by a modal in the infinitive form. For example:

Ich habe es **vekaufen wollen**.	*I have **wanted to sell** it.*
Die Frau hatte uns **helfen können**.	*The woman had **been able to help** us.*
Er hat zu Hause **bleiben müssen**.	*He has **had to stay** home.*
Sie hat die Bibliothek **benutzen dürfen**.	*She was **allowed to use** the library.*

The same thing occurs in the future tense. **Werden** is followed by a double infinitive.

Ich werde es **vekaufen wollen**.	*I will **want to sell** it.*
Die Frau wird uns **helfen können**.	*The woman will **be able to help** us.*
Er wird zu Hause **bleiben müssen**.	*He will **have to stay** home.*
Sie wird die Bibliothek **benutzen dürfen**.	*She will **be allowed to use** the library.*

Rewrite each sentence in the present perfect tense.

1. Du sollst deine Pflicht (*duty*) tun.

   _____

2. Der Mann kann nicht schwimmen.

   _____

3. Man muss sehr vorsichtig (*careful*) sein.

   _____

4. Dürfen sie mit der Katze spielen?

   _____

5. Niemand will mit mir tanzen.

   _____

6. Können Sie die Berge (*mountains*) sehen?

   _____

Rewrite each sentence in the past perfect tense.

7. Er will ins Ausland reisen.

   _____

8. Was soll er tun?

   _____

9. Die Jungen können für Sie arbeiten.

   _____

10. Ihr müsst den Hund waschen.

    _____

11. Hier darf man nicht rauchen (*smoke*).

    _____

Rewrite each sentence in the future tense.

12. Erik will ins Restaurant gehen.

    _____

13. Kannst du ihm helfen?

    _____

14. Ich soll in die Stadt fahren.

_____

15. Wir müssen ihn vom Flughafen abholen (*pick up*).

_____

The double infinitive structure occurs with several other verbs:

helfen	*help*
hören	*hear*
lassen	*get, have (something done)*
sehen	*see*

The double infinitive structure with these verbs can be used in the perfect and future tenses. For example:

Er hat mir in der Küche **arbeiten helfen**.	He **helped** me **work** in the kitchen.
Ich hatte die Kinder **singen hören**.	I **heard** the children **singing**.
Sie wird das Auto **reparieren lassen**.	She will **have** the car **repaired**.

ÜBUNG
24·2

Rewrite each sentence in the present perfect and future tenses.

1. Er lässt das neue Auto waschen.

_____

_____

2. Er hört seine Eltern im Keller flüstern (*whisper*).

_____

_____

3. Wir sehen den Düsenjäger über dem Wald fliegen.

_____

_____

4. Herr Dorf lässt einen neuen Anzug (*suit*) machen.

_____

_____

5. Der Junge hilft mir das alte Radio reparieren.

_____

_____

Write each phrase in the present, past, present perfect, and future tenses with the subject provided in parentheses.

FOR EXAMPLE: wollen es verkaufen (ich)

Ich will es verkaufen.

Ich wollte es verkaufen.

Ich habe es verkaufen wollen.

Ich werde es verkaufen wollen.

1. können seine Rede nicht verstehen (sie [*sing.*])

_____

_____

_____

_____

2. hören den Mann Gitarre (*guitar*) spielen (wir)

_____

_____

_____

_____

3. müssen ins Ausland reisen (du)

_____

_____

_____

_____

4. sehen die Mädchen im Fluss schwimmen (wer?)

_____

_____

_____

_____

5. dürfen nicht nach Hause gehen (der kranke Mann)

_____

_____

_____

_____

6. sollen eine neue Schule besuchen (ich)

_____

_____

_____

_____

7. können schwimmen (viele Leute)

_____

_____

_____

8. wollen die Suppe probieren (*taste the soup*) (er)

_____

_____

_____

_____

9. lassen die Software installieren (*install the software*) (der Wissenschaftler)

_____

_____

_____

_____

10. helfen ihnen die Tulpen pflanzen (*plant the tulips*) (die Soldaten)

_____

_____

_____

_____

ÜBUNG

24·4

Circle the letter of the word or phrase that best completes each sentence.

1. Die Ballerina wird in Berlin tanzen _____.
   a. muss
   b. haben können
   c. wollen
   d. gemocht

2. Niemand _____ sie im Wald wandern sehen.
   a. hat
   b. wurde
   c. ist
   d. geworden

3. Sie werden heute zu Hause _____ müssen.
   a. blieben
   b. bleiben
   c. geblieben
   d. bleibt

4. Karl _____ mit Herrn Keller sprechen.
   a. mögen
   b. sollt
   c. können
   d. wollte

5. _____ du Ski laufen (*skiing*)?
   a. Müssen
   b. Hast
   c. Kannst
   d. Bist

6. Der Matrose _____ an die Nordsee (*North Sea*) fahren wollen.
   a. wird
   b. haben
   c. konnte
   d. sollen

7. Ihr _____ keinen Wein trinken.
   a. will
   b. müssen
   c. dürft
   d. habt

8. Niemand hat ihn vom Bahnhof abholen _____.
   a. gewollt
   b. können
   c. möchte
   d. musste

9. Frau Bauer _____ ein neues Kleid machen.
   a. ließ
   b. konnten
   c. wollen
   d. hörte

10. Das darf _____ nicht sagen.
    a. du
    b. alle
    c. man
    d. viele Leute

11. Was _____ du zu deinem Essen (*with your food*) trinken?
    a. magst
    b. siehst
    c. lernte
    d. wollen

12. Thomas _____ sich die Haare schneiden (*get a haircut*).
    a. können
    b. half
    c. sollt
    d. lässt

13. Warum _____ die arme Frau sterben müssen?
    a. ist
    b. hat
    c. war
    d. haben

14. Meine Verwandten _____ in die Berge fahren.
    a. sehen
    b. soll
    c. wollten
    d. hören

15. Der Professor konnte das Examen _____.
    a. kommen hören
    b. schreiben können
    c. nicht finden
    d. nicht gelesen

16. Ich werde meine Freundin in Berlin _____.
    a. besuchen wollen
    b. nicht gesehen
    c. angerufen
    d. ankommen müssen

17. Sie hat ihm den Fernsehapparat _____.
    a. gekauft haben
    b. reparieren helfen
    c. abgefahren sein
    d. lassen

18. Wir haben die Sportler Fußball _____.
    a. machen lassen
    b. wollten lernen
    c. gespielt
    d. spielen sehen

19. Habt ihr das Baby _____?
    a. gehalten haben
    b. nicht helfen
    c. fahren dürfen
    d. weinen hören

20. Ich muss noch ein paar Wochen _____.
    a. warten
    b. schon gemacht
    c. gereist sein
    d. können

Infinitive clauses

A German infinitive clause is composed of the word **zu** and an infinitive. A variety of other elements can accompany **zu** and the infinitive to form a phrase. For example:

zu sprechen	*to speak*
mit ihnen zu sprechen	*to speak with them*
ein bisschen lauter zu sprechen	*to speak a little louder*

Note that **zu** and the infinitive are the final elements of the clause.

ÜBUNG
24·5

Change each present tense sentence into an infinitive clause.

FOR EXAMPLE: Er hilft uns.

uns zu helfen

1. Wir lernen eine Sprache.

_____

2. Ich gebe ihr sechs Euro.

_____

3. Sie bringt ihm ein Glas Wasser.

_____

4. Du wartest an der Ecke.

_____

5. Sie haben mehr Zeit (*more time*).

_____

6. Alle fragen nach meiner Tochter.

_____

7. Ich arbeite in einer Fabrik (*factory*).

_____

8. Erik sieht ihn nicht.

_____

9. Es wird schlechter.

_____

10. Ich bin heute in der Hauptstadt.

_____

Prefixes must be taken into account when working with infinitive clauses. Inseparable prefixes on infinitives are simply preceded by the word **zu.**

NO PREFIX	INSEPARABLE PREFIX
zu kommen	zu bekommen
zu stehen	zu verstehen
zu warten	zu erwarten

The word **zu** is placed between the infinitive and a separable prefix, and the verb is written as one word.

NO PREFIX	INSEPARABLE PREFIX
zu fangen	anzufangen
zu bringen	beizubringen
zu fahren	abzufahren

ÜBUNG

24·6

Change each present tense sentence into an infinitive clause.

FOR EXAMPLE: Er versteht Deutsch.

_____ *Deutsch zu verstehen* _____

1. Wir besuchen eine Schule in Bremen.

   _____

2. Er vergisst die Fahrkarten.

   _____

3. Sabine kommt um acht Uhr an.

   _____

4. Sie ziehen sich um (*change clothes*).

   _____

5. Ihr kehrt bald (*soon*) zurück.

   _____

6. Ich empfehle es.

   _____

7. Sie bringt einen Freund mit.

   _____

8. Er verkauft einen alten Koffer (*suitcase*).

   _____

9. Ich stelle die Gäste vor.

_____

10. Sie steigen in der Schillerstraße aus.

_____

If an auxiliary accompanies a verb, it functions as the infinitive in the infinitive clause. For example:

AUXILIARY **SEIN**	INFINITIVE CLAUSE	
Er ist abgefahren.	abgefahren zu sein	_to have departed_
Sie ist hier geblieben.	hier geblieben zu sein	_to have stayed here_

AUXILIARY **HABEN**	INFINITIVE CLAUSE	
Ich habe nichts gefunden.	nichts gefunden zu haben	_to have found nothing_
Sie haben das Geld gestohlen.	das Geld gestohlen zu haben	_to have stolen the money_

MODAL AUXILIARY	INFINITIVE CLAUSE	
Sie kann es verstehen.	es verstehen zu können	_to be able to understand it_
Du musst ihm helfen.	ihm helfen zu müssen	_to have to help him_
Ich will länger schlafen.	länger schlafen zu wollen	_to want to sleep longer_

ÜBUNG
24·7

Change each sentence into an infinitive clause.

FOR EXAMPLE: Er hat Deutsch gelernt.

_____ _Deutsch gelernt zu haben_ _____

1. Wir sind zum Einkaufszentrum gefahren.

_____

2. Man soll ihnen danken.

_____

3. Es ist sehr kalt geworden.

_____

4. Du hast die Polizei angerufen.

_____

5. Ihr könnt nicht schneller laufen.

_____

6. Frau Keller hat eine Tasse Tee (_a cup of tea_) bestellt.

_____

7. Ich muss in die Schweiz reisen.

_____

8. Er hat einen Regenschirm (*umbrella*) mitgenommen.

_____

9. Sie ist langsam hereingekommen.

_____

10. Erik darf nicht alleine fahren.

_____

Infinitive clauses are most commonly used as replacements for nouns or noun phrases. For example:

Russisch ist schwierig.	*Russian is difficult.*
Russisch zu erlernen ist schwierig.	*To learn Russian is difficult.*
Er ging nach Hause ohne Tina.	*He went home without Tina.*
Er ging nach Hause, ohne seinen Regenschirm mitzunehmen.	*He went home without taking along his umbrella.*

Often sentences are introduced by **es** when that pronoun is *standing in* for an infinitive clause that ends the sentence. For example:

Es ist sehr wichtig einen Führerschein zu haben.	*It is very important to have a driver's license.*
Fiel **es** dir nicht ein deine Eltern anzurufen?	*Did it not occur to you to phone your parents?*

ÜBUNG
24·8

Change each numbered sentence into an infinitive clause that completes the main sentence.

FOR EXAMPLE: Es ist wichtig _____.

Man lernt eine zweite Sprache.

_____*Es ist wichtig eine zweite Sprache zu lernen.*_____

Es ist schwierig _____.

1. Ich verstehe den kranken Mann. _____

2. Wir lesen in dem dunklen Wohnzimmer. _____

3. Er rennt so schnell wie ein Pferd (*horse*). _____

4. Sie wohnen in einer kleinen Wohnung. _____

5. Sie arbeitet ohne einen Computer. _____

Ist es leicht (*easy*) _____?

6. Ich bekomme einen neuen Ausweis (*identity card*). _____

7. Sie erziehen (*raise*) elf Kinder. _____

8. Wir schicken einige Pakete nach Afghanistan. _____

9. Du trägst die schweren Koffer zum Bahnhof. _____

10. Er ist Politiker. _____

Four prepositions are frequently used with infinitive clauses: **anstatt zu, außer zu, ohne zu**, and **um zu**. The meaning of the prepositions is retained when used with infinitive phrases, except for **um**, which in English is translated as *in order to*. Let's look at some example sentences:

Sie ging nach Hause, **anstatt** uns damit **zu** helfen.	She went home **instead of** helping us with it.
Ich konnte nichts tun, **außer** mit ihm darüber **zu** streiten.	I could not do anything **except** argue with him about it.
Die Kinder verließen die Schule, **ohne** Abschied von der Lehrerin **zu** nehmen.	The children left the school **without** saying good-bye to the teacher.
Der Mann stiehlt das Geld, **um** Geschenke für seine Freundin **zu** kaufen.	The man steals the money **in order** to buy his girlfriend presents.

The phrase **um zu** can also be used following adjectives, in which case the meaning of *in order to* no longer applies. It can be simply translated as *to*.

Der Mann war zu schwach, **um** den schweren Koffer **zu** tragen.	The man was too weak to carry the heavy suitcase.

ÜBUNG
24·9

Change each numbered sentence into an infinitive clause with the provided preposition to complete the main sentence.

FOR EXAMPLE: Sie geht nach Hause, ohne _____.

Sie bezahlt dafür.   *Sie geht nach Hause, ohne dafür zu bezahlen.*

Sie trägt keinen Mantel. *Sie geht nach Hause, ohne einen Mantel zu tragen.*

Erik sass einfach da, anstatt _____.

1. Er arbeitet im Garten. _____

2. Er schreibt den wichtigen Brief. _____

3. Er bereitet die Suppe vor. _____

Was konnten sie tun, außer _____?

4. Sie heben den armen Mann auf (*lift up*). _____

5. Sie bestellen noch eine Flasche Wein. _____

6. Sie strafen den unartigen (*naughty*) Jungen. _____

Sie fuhr mit dem Bus ab, ohne _____.

7. Sie hat eine Fahrkarte gekauft. _____

8. Sie nimmt von uns Abschied. _____

9. Sie weint. _____

Du bist jetzt alt genug, um _____.

10. Du wählst deine Kleider (clothing) aus (choose). _____

11. Du dienst beim Militär (in the military). _____

12. Du arbeitest in der Fabrik. _____

Sie sind nach Weimar gezogen, um _____.

13. Sie können mehr Geld verdienen (earn). _____

14. Sie suchen einen guten Job. _____

15. Sie untersuchen (research) Goethes Leben (life). _____

Infinitive clauses

German infinitives end in -en or -n. They are most often paired with modal auxiliaries or certain other verbs that are used as auxiliaries, for example: **helfen**, **hören**, **lassen**, and **sehen**. In sentences, the infinitives used together with these auxiliaries become the last element in a sentence or clause.

Modal auxiliaries

Er **muss** sofort nach Hause **gehen**.	He has to go home immediately.
Kannst du das **erklären?**	Can you explain that?
Wir **wollten** um acht **frühstücken**.	We wanted to have breakfast at eight.

Other auxiliaries

Martin **hört** die Frau **weinen**.	Martin hears the woman crying.
Sehen Sie die Vögel darüber **fliegen?**	Do you see the birds flying above it?
Er **ließ** seinen Wagen **waschen**.	He had his car washed.

Formation of infinitive clauses

Infinitives can also be used in so-called *infinitive clauses*, which require the use of the word **zu** with the infinitives. Infinitive clauses can be used in sentences that begin with **es**, an impersonal subject. That sentence is most often a statement that is explained by the infinitive clause. For example:

Es ist wichtig, ehrlich **zu sein**.	It is important to be honest.
(Statement: "Es ist wichtig." Explanation: "ehrlich zu sein.")	

Es war unmöglich, den Mann **zu retten**.	It was impossible to rescue the man.
(Statement: "Es war unmöglich." Explanation: "den Mann zu retten.")	

If the infinitive in an infinitive clause has an inseparable prefix, **zu** merely precedes the infinitive. But if the infinitive has a separable prefix, **zu** stands between the prefix and the verb and all the elements are written as one word. For example:

versprechen (*promise*) = **zu versprechen**
aussprechen (*pronounce*) = **auszusprechen**

When an infinitive or participle is accompanied by an auxiliary and they are used in an infinitive clause, the auxiliary is used as an infinitive and is preceded by **zu** and follows the accompanying infinitive or participle. For example:

Ich muss arbeiten. = **arbeiten zu müssen**	*to have to work*
Wir lassen den Wagen reparieren. = **den Wagen reparieren** **zu lassen**	*to have the car repaired*
Er hat es gesagt. = **es gesagt zu haben**	*to have said it*
Es wird von ihr zerbrochen. = **von ihr zerbrochen zu werden**	*to be broken by her*

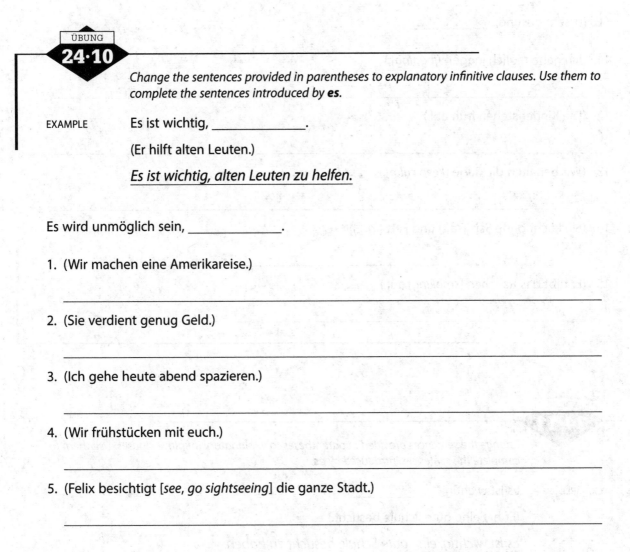

ÜBUNG
24·10

Change the sentences provided in parentheses to explanatory infinitive clauses. Use them to complete the sentences introduced by **es**.

EXAMPLE   Es ist wichtig, _____.

(Er hilft alten Leuten.)

Es ist wichtig, alten Leuten zu helfen.

Es wird unmöglich sein, _____.

1. (Wir machen eine Amerikareise.)

_____

2. (Sie verdient genug Geld.)

_____

3. (Ich gehe heute abend spazieren.)

_____

4. (Wir frühstücken mit euch.)

_____

5. (Felix besichtigt [*see, go sightseeing*] die ganze Stadt.)

_____

Es ist notwendig (*necessary*), _____.

6. (Wir schreiben einen anderen Brief.)

   _____

7. (Sie erlernt zwei fremde Sprachen.)

   _____

8. (Wir erziehen die Kinder richtig.)

   _____

9. (Der Bürgermeister verwaltet [*manages*] die Stadt besser.)

   _____

10. (Man wiederholt das lange Gedicht jeden Tag.)

    _____

Es ist sehr gesund, _____.

11. (Ich gehe täglich joggen [*jogging*].)

    _____

12. (Die Kinder stehen früh auf.)

    _____

13. (Wir behalten die Ruhe [*keep calm*].)

    _____

14. (Sie kocht ohne Salz [*salt*] und Fett [*fat*].)

    _____

15. (Er gibt das Rauchen [*smoking*] auf.)

    _____

ÜBUNG

24·11

*Change the sentences provided in parentheses to explanatory infinitive clauses. Use them to complete the sentences introduced by **es**.*

EXAMPLE   Es ist wichtig, _____.

(Er hat eine gute Schule besucht.)

Es ist wichtig, eine gute Schule besucht zu haben.

Es war Schade (*pity*), _____.

1. (Wir haben das Spiel verloren.)

   _____

2. (Sie haben den Mann entlassen.)

   _____

3. (Sie muss nach Schweden ziehen [*move*].)

   _____

4. (Seine Frau hat zu viel Geld ausgegeben [*spent*].)

   _____

5. (Wir sind vergebens [*for nothing, in vain*] so weit gefahren.)

   _____

Es war eine gute Idee, _____.

6. (Sie will an eine Universität gehen.)

   _____

7. (Ich finde einen guten Job.)

   _____

8. (Wir bleiben gesund und froh.)

   _____

9. (Erik kann zwei musikalische Instrumente spielen.)

   _____

10. (Sie lässt ein neues Kleid machen.)

   _____

Verbs that introduce infinitive clauses

There is a list of verbs that often introduce infinitive clauses. The most common of these verbs are:

anfangen	*begin, start*
aufhören	*cease, stop*
beabsichtigen	*intend*
beginnen	*begin, start*
brauchen	*need*
hoffen	*hope*
vergessen	*forget*
versuchen	*attempt, try*
wünschen	*wish*

Let's look at some example sentences with some of these verbs:

Er **fängt an**, ziemlich gut zu singen.   *He starts to sing rather well.*
Wir **beabsichtigen**, ein neues Haus in   *We intend to build a new house in*
     Mannheim zu bauen.   *Mannheim.*
Du **brauchst** nicht davor Angst zu haben.   *You need not fear that.*
Ich **vergaß**, meinen Regenschirm mitzubringen.   *I forgot to bring my umbrella along.*
Wir **wünschen**, dieses Konzert bald wieder   *We wish to listen to this concert again soon.*
     zu hören.

ÜBUNG
24·12

Combine the two clauses provided by changing the second one to an infinitive clause.

EXAMPLE   Er beginnt. Er singt sehr laut.

     Er beginnt, sehr laut zu singen.

1. Ich vergesse. Ich erzähle von meiner Europareise.

2. Wir haben versucht. Wir sprechen mit dem Bürgermeister.

3. Meine Eltern hoffen. Sie können jeden Abend spazieren gehen.

4. Du musst aufhören. Du spielst mit den kleinen Welpen.

5. Sie fangen an. Sie arbeiten früh am Morgen.

6. Ich hoffe. Ich kann in den Ferien (*vacation*) länger schlafen.

7. Niemand versucht. Niemand folgt dem entlaufenden (*fleeing*) Taschendieb.

8. Sabine will nicht aufhören. Sabine tanzt mit ihrem neuen Freund.

9. Die Großeltern wünschen sehr. Sie besuchen ihre Kinder und Enkel in Bremen.

10. Tina hat vergessen. Tina bringt ein Geschenk mit.

Infinitive clauses as nouns

Infinitive clauses can function in place of a noun or noun phrase used as the subject of the sentence. This occurs in English as well as in German. For example:

> **To help with the dishes** *is a chore that Mike hated.*
> **To get good grades** *has always been my goal.*
> **To win at chess** *was her greatest wish.*

In German, the infinitive accompanied by **zu** occurs at the end of the clause and is followed by the rest of the sentence. For example:

Ihm damit zu helfen war völlig unmöglich.	*To help him with that was quite impossible.*
Schnell zu tippen ist sehr schwer.	*To type quickly is very hard.*
Reich zu sein wird nur ein Wunsch bleiben.	*To be rich will remain only a wish.*

Because the infinitive clause replaces a noun or noun phrase, it can also function as the object of a verb or preposition. Consider the following examples when the infinitive clause is used as the direct object:

Ich verspreche dir **früh nach Hause zu kommen**.	*I promise you to come home early.*
Er hat uns empfohlen **die Kunsthalle zu besuchen**.	*He recommended to us to visit the art museum.*

When the infinitive clause follows a preposition, the preposition is formed as a prepositional adverb, which is then followed by the infinitive clause.

Wir freuen uns **darüber von den Gästen gratuliert zu werden**.	*We are happy to be congratulated by the guests.*
Die Jungen interessieren sich **dafür ein Baumhaus zu bauen**.	*The boys are interested in building a tree house.*

ÜBUNG

24·13

Complete each phrase with two appropriate infinitive clauses.

1. _____ ist notwendig.

   _____ ist notwendig.

2. _____ war nicht leicht.

   _____ war nicht leicht.

3. Erik hat mir versprochen _____.

   Erik hat mir versprochen _____.

4. Kleine Sabine träumt (*dreams*) davon _____.

   Kleine Sabine träumt davon _____.

5. Freuen Sie sich darauf (*look forward to*) _____?

   Freuen Sie sich darauf _____?

Prepositions commonly used with infinitive clauses

Infinitive clauses are frequently used with certain prepositions. The most commonly used of these prepositions are **anstatt** *instead of*, **ohne** *without*, and **um** *around*. In the case of **um**, the meaning of the preposition is lost, and a new meaning is derived from the preposition being used in combination with the infinitive clause. In all cases, the preposition will introduce the clause, and the infinitive will be the last element of the clause. Let's look at some examples.

Anstatt zu

Karl spielte mit Thomas, **anstatt** mit seiner Schwester **zu spielen**.	*Karl played with Thomas instead of playing with his sister.*
Wir lernen Französisch, **anstatt** Englisch **zu lernen**.	*We learn French instead of learning English.*
Die Jungen stehen am Ufer, **anstatt** dem Mann **zu helfen**.	*The boys stand on shore instead of helping the man.*

Ohne zu

Sie tauchte ins Wasser, **ohne** an ihre Sicherheit **zu denken**.	*She dove into the water without thinking of her safety.*
Lars benutzt die neue Säge, **ohne** Erlaubnis von seinem Vater **zu bekommen**.	*Lars uses the new saw without asking his father for permission.*
Tina antwortete, **ohne** von der Lehrerin **gefragt zu werden**.	*Tina answered without being asked by the teacher.*

Um zu

Die Frau lief in die Mitte der Straße, **um** die Katze **zu retten**.	*The woman ran into the middle of the street in order to rescue the cat.*
Sie arbeiten viel, **um** vorwärts **zu kommen**.	*They work a lot in order to get ahead.*
Der Gelehrte blieb zu Hause, **um** ein Buch **zu übersetzen**.	*The scholar remained at home in order to translate a book.*

ÜBUNG
24·14

Reword each incomplete sentence with any appropriate infinitive clauses.

Er sieht den ganzen Abend fern, anstatt _____.

1. _____

2. _____

3. _____

4. _____

5. _____

Die Touristen sind nach Hause gefahren, ohne _____.

6. _____

7. _____

8. _____

9. _____

10. _____

Tina und Felix müssen viel arbeiten, um _____.

11. _____

12. _____

13. _____

14. _____

15. _____

Stefan wird nicht vergessen, _____.

16. _____

17. _____

18. _____

19. _____

20. _____

Meine Mutter träumt davon _____.

21. _____

22. _____

23. _____

24. _____

25. _____

The passive voice

The sentences that you have been working with in this book so far have been in the *active voice*. The active voice is composed of a subject and a verb and a variety of other accompanying elements.

Er ist ein netter Mann	*He is a nice man.*
Ich kaufte einen Mantel.	*I bought a coat.*
Wir gehen zum Stadtpark.	*We go to the city park.*

The passive voice is composed of the same elements that are in an active-voice sentence that has a *transitive verb*. The transitive verb is essential, because only such verbs can have a direct object. For example, **küssen** is a transitive verb.

Martin küsste das Mädchen.	*Martin kissed the girl.*

In the example sentence, **das Mädchen** is the direct object. Let's look at the way English forms a passive-voice sentence from this example sentence. The subject becomes the object of the preposition *by*: *by Martin*. The direct object becomes the subject of the passive sentence: *the girl*. The verb *to be* is conjugated in the same tense as the original verb for the subject *the girl*: *the girl was*. The verb becomes a past participle: *kissed*. Put together, these elements create a passive sentence.

The girl was kissed by Martin.

It is a passive-voice sentence because the subject of the active sentence is now in a passive position in the new sentence and no longer functions as the subject.

Forming the German passive-voice sentence is similar. The subject of the active-voice sentence becomes the object of the preposition **von**: **von Martin**. The direct object becomes the subject of the passive sentence: **das Mädchen**. The verb **werden** is conjugated in the same tense as the original verb for the subject **das Mädchen**: **das Mädchen wurde**. The verb becomes a past participle: **geküsst**. When these elements are put together, a passive sentence is created.

Das Mädchen **wurde** von Martin **geküsst**.	*The girl was kissed by Martin.*

This sentence as well as all other passive sentences can occur in other tenses. For example:

PRESENT	Das Mädchen wird von Martin geküsst.	*The girl is kissed by Martin.*
PAST	Das Mädchen wurde von Martin geküsst.	*The girl was kissed by Martin.*
PRES PERF	Das Mädchen ist von Martin geküsst worden.	*The girl has been kissed by Martin.*
FUTURE	Das Mädchen wird von Martin geküsst werden.	*The girl will be kissed by Martin.*

396

Notice that the past participle for **werden** in the passive voice is **worden**. Use **geworden** only when the verb means *to become* or *to get*:

Es ist kalt geworden.   *It has become cold.*

Let's look at another example of how an active-voice sentence is changed to a passive-voice sentence.

ACTIVE	Er bestellt ein Glas Bier.	*He orders a glass of beer.*
PASSIVE	Ein Glas Bier **wird** von ihm **bestellt**.	*A glass of beer is ordered by him.*

It is necessary for the verb **werden** to be in the same tense as the original verb in the active sentence. Since **bestellt** is in the present tense, **wird** is used in the present-tense passive sentence. Let's look at this sentence in the other tenses:

PRESENT	Ein Glas Bier wird von ihm bestellt.
PAST	Ein Glas Bier wurde von ihm bestellt.
PRES PERF	Ein Glas Bier ist von ihm bestellt worden.
FUTURE	Ein Glas Bier wird von ihm bestellt werden.

ÜBUNG
25·1

Rewrite each passive sentence in the missing tenses.

1. Present Die Maus wird von der Eule gefressen. (*The mouse is eaten by the owl.*)

   Past _____

   Pres perf _____

   Future _____

2. Present _____

   Past   Der Kranke wurde von der Ärztin geheilt. (*The sick man was healed by the doctor.*)

   Pres perf _____

   Future _____

3. Present _____

   Past _____

   Pres perf Der Artikel ist von ihm gelesen worden. (*The article has been read by him.*)

   Future _____

4. Present _____

   Past _____

   Pres perf _____

   Future Die Briefe werden von mir geschrieben werden. (*The letters will be written by me.*)

5. Present _____

Past <u>Die Schüler wurden vom Lehrer unterrichtet.</u> (*The pupils were taught by the teacher.*)

Pres perf _____

Future _____

6. Present _____

Past _____

Pres perf _____

Future <u>Die Anzüge werden vom Schneider genäht werden.</u> (*The suits will be sewn by the tailor.*)

7. Present <u>Das Brot wird von Herrn Benz gekauft.</u> (*The bread is bought by Mr. Benz.*)

Past _____

Pres perf _____

Future _____

8. Present _____

Past _____

Pres perf <u>Eine Tasse Kaffee ist von der Kellnerin gebracht worden.</u> (*A cup of tea is brought by the waitress.*)

Future _____

The prepositional phrase that is formed with **von** does not always appear in a passive sentence. In such a case, the *doer* of the action in the active-voice sentence remains anonymous. For example:

Das Rathaus wurde im Stadtzentrum gebaut.
The city hall was built in the center of the city.

The builder of the city hall is not provided in the example sentence and remains anonymous.

Also, **von** can be replaced by **durch** when the object of that preposition is the *means* by which the action of the verb was carried out or is the *cause* of that action. For example:

Der Mann wurde **durch** einen Unfall getötet.   *The man was killed **due to** an accident.*
Der Brief wird **durch** die Post befördert.   *The letter is sent **in** the mail.*

Rewrite the following active-voice sentences in the passive voice. Retain the tense of the original.

1. Der Feind (*enemy*) hat das Dorf (*village*) zerstört.

   _____

2. Ein Waldbrand bedroht (*forest fire threatens*) den Bauernhof (*farm*).

   _____

3. Ein Schuss (*shot*) tötete den alten Hund.

   _____

4. Der Bauer (*farmer*) wird viele Schweine aufziehen (*raise pigs*).

   _____

5. Der Lehrer hat die Aufsätze verbessert (*corrected the themes*).

   _____

If the object of the verb in an active sentence is in the dative case, the dative case will also be used in the passive sentence. For example:

Sie halfen meiner Mutter.	*They helped my mother.*
Meiner Mutter wurde von ihnen geholfen.	*My mother was helped by them.*
Niemand hat ihm geglaubt.	*No one believed him.*
Ihm ist von niemandem geglaubt worden.	*He was believed by no one.*

Rewrite the active-voice sentences in the passive voice. Retain the tense of the original verb. Note that some of the sentences have dative verbs in them.

1. Sein Gedicht imponierte dem Professor.

   _____

2. Ich habe der alten Frau geholfen.

   _____

3. Du hast dem König (*king*) gut gedient.

   _____

4. Alle werden das Lied (*song*) singen.

   _____

5. Der Dieb droht uns mit einer Pistole (*pistol*).

_____

6. Ich habe den Mann in Berlin gesehen.

_____

7. Der Soldat dankte mir für das Geschenk.

_____

8. Die Kinder werden das Eis essen.

_____

9. Das Rauchen (*smoking*) schadet der Gesundheit (*health*).

_____

10. Ein guter Freund hat ihm geraten.

_____

There can be both accusative and dative objects in an active-voice sentence. In such cases, the accusative object always becomes the subject of the passive-voice sentence. For example:

Er gab der Frau eine Zeitung.	*He gave the woman a newspaper.*
Eine Zeitung wurde der Frau von ihm gegeben.	*A newspaper was given to the woman by him.*

It is possible, however, to begin the passive-voice sentence with the dative object while still using the accusative object as the subject of the passive-voice sentence.

Der Frau wurde **eine Zeitung** von ihm gegeben.

German has another form of passive that uses **sein** as its auxiliary in place of **werden**. When **sein** is used, the meaning of the sentence is changed. With **werden**, the meaning is that an action is taking place:

Das Haus **wird** gebaut.	*The house is being built.*

With **sein**, the meaning is that the action is completed and the participle tells what the condition of the subject is. That is, the participle acts more like an adjective than a verb:

Das Haus **ist** gebaut.	*The house is (already) built.*

Let's look at a few more examples:

Das Theater **wurde** zerstört.	*The theater was being destroyed.*
Das Theater **war** zerstört.	*The theater was (already) destroyed.*
Ihr Finger **wird** verletzt.	*Her finger is (getting) injured.*
Ihr Finger **ist** verletzt.	*Her finger is (already) injured.*

Modal auxiliaries can be used in passive-voice sentences. But in such cases, the verb **werden** is used as an infinitive and follows the past participle in the sentence. For example:

Dem alten Mann **muss** geholfen werden.	*The old man **must** be helped.*
Kann das Radio nicht repariert werden?	***Can** the radio not be repaired?*
Erik **soll** nicht eingeladen werden.	*Erik **should** not be invited.*
Dieser Aufsatz **durfte** nicht geschrieben werden.	*This theme was not **allowed** to be written.*
Er wird fotografiert werden **wollen**.	*He **will** want to be photographed.*

ÜBUNG
25·4

Rewrite each sentence with the modal auxiliaries provided.

FOR EXAMPLE   Das Buch wird nicht gelesen.

müssen _____ *Das Buch muss nicht gelesen werden.* _____

Ein Haus wird hier gebaut.

1. müssen _____

2. können _____

3. sollen _____

Ihm wurde damit geholfen.

4. wollen _____

5. sollen _____

6. können _____

Das Problem wird auch von ihr verstanden.

7. können _____

8. müssen _____

Das Auto wird nicht repariert werden.

9. können _____

10. müssen _____

A special phrase is often used in place of a passive voice conjugation: **es/das lässt sich**. It is a replacement for the modal **können** in a passive structure and is used with an infinitive rather than a past participle. For example:

Das **lässt sich** nicht sagen.	*That **cannot be** said.*
Es **lässt sich** leicht tun.	*It **can** easily **be** done.*

This structure can be used in all the tenses.

PRESENT	Das **lässt sich** nicht tun.	*That **cannot be** done.*
PAST	Das **ließ sich** nicht tun.	*That **could not be** done.*
PRES PERF	Das hat **sich** nicht tun **lassen**.	*That **could** not **be** done.*
FUTURE	Das wird **sich** nicht tun **lassen**.	*That will not **be able to be** done.*

ÜBUNG
25·5

Rewrite each passive sentence in the missing tenses.

1. Present Das lässt sich nicht leicht ändern (change easily).

Past _____

Pres perf _____

Future _____

2. Present _____

Past Das Geld konnte nicht gefunden werden.

Pres perf _____

Future _____

3. Present _____

Past _____

Pres perf _____

Future Diese Probleme werden sich schnell lösen lassen.

4. Present _____

Past _____

Pres perf Ihnen ist dafür gedankt worden.

Future _____

5. Present Der Hund ist gewaschen.

Past _____

Pres perf _____

Future _____

The passive voice

Active voice versus passive voice

Verbs can be either in the active or in the passive voice. This is true in English and in German. In the active voice, the subject is *active*. It performs the action of the verb.

Der Junge isst den Kuchen.   *The boy eats the cake.*

In the above sentence, the subject is the boy and he is performing the action and most likely enjoying it! Therefore, this is an active sentence.

When the subject of the verb is the thing or person the action is being done to, the sentence is passive.

Der Kuchen wird von dem   *The cake is being eaten by the boy.*
   Jungen gegessen.

The cake, **der Kuchen**, is the subject in the above sentence. The cake is not doing any action—the action is being done to it. It is, therefore, a passive sentence.

The passive voice is formed with the auxiliary verb **werden** and the past participle of the main verb. The past participle is used in all tenses, even the present.

Active Voice

Present:	Brauns bauen das große Haus.
	The Brauns are building the large house.
Present Perfect:	Brauns haben das große Haus gebaut.
	The Brauns have built the large house.
Past:	Brauns bauten das große Haus.
	The Brauns built the large house.
Past Perfect:	Brauns hatten das große Haus gebaut.
	The Brauns had built the large house.
Future:	Brauns werden das große Haus bauen.
	The Brauns will build the large house.
Future Perfect:	Brauns werden das große Haus gebaut haben.
	The Brauns will have built the large house.

Passive Voice

Present:	Das große Haus wird von Brauns gebaut.
	The large house is being built by the Brauns.
Present Perfect:	Das große Haus ist von Brauns gebaut worden.
	The large house has been built by the Brauns.
Past:	Das große Haus wurde von Brauns gebaut.
	The large house was built by the Brauns.
Past Perfect:	Das große Haus war von Brauns gebaut worden.
	The large house had been built by the Brauns.
Future:	Das große Haus wird von Brauns gebaut werden.
	The large house will be built by the Brauns.
Future Perfect:	Das große Haus wird von Brauns gebaut worden sein.
	The large house will have been built by the Brauns.

Note that in the passive, the past participle is the last element in the sentence or clause in the present or past tense. In the perfect tenses of the passive (present perfect, past perfect, and future perfect), **worden** is used instead of **geworden**, with **sein** as the auxiliary. **Worden** is placed after the past participle.

ÜBUNG
25·6

Change the following sentences into the given passive tense.

EXAMPLE: Das Lied wird von Anke gesungen.
             Present Perfect: *Das Lied ist von Anke gesungen worden.*

Der Brief wird von der Mutter geschrieben.

1. Present Perfect: _____

2. Past Perfect: _____

3. Future: _____

4. Future Perfect: _____

5. Past: _____

von or durch

When the passive voice tells you who performed the action (who the agent is), **von** is used, followed by the dative case.

    Das Haus wird **von** dem Mann gebaut.   *The house is being built by the man.*

When the passive voice tells you the means by which something is brought about or done, **durch** is used, followed by the accusative case.

    Das Haus wurde **durch** den Sturm zerstört.   *The house was destroyed by the storm.*

ÜBUNG
25·7

Answer the following questions with the cues given, using von.

EXAMPLE: Wer empfiehlt das Restaurant? (der Nachbar)
             Das Restaurant wird von dem Nachbarn empfohlen.

1. Wer besucht das gute Restaurant? (die Freunde)

_____

2. Wer bestellt den gebratenen Fisch? (der junge Mann)

_____

3. Wer isst die Sachertorte? (das Mädchen)

_____

4. Wer bringt das Essen zum Tisch? (der Kellner)

_____

5. Wer bezahlt die Rechnung? (das Paar)

_____

ÜBUNG
25·8

Answer the following questions with the cues given, using durch.

EXAMPLE: Wie wurde der Baum zerstört? (der Frost)
Der Baum wurde durch den Frost zerstört.

1. Wie wurde Deutsch gelernt? (viel Mühe)

_____

2. Wie wurde das Kind geweckt? (laute Musik)

_____

3. Wie wurde die Kirche zerstört? (der Sturm)

_____

4. Wie wurdest du geheilt? (Medizin)

_____

5. Wie wurde die Ratte getötet? (Gift)

_____

Impersonal passive constructions

A passive construction without a subject or an agent is called an *impersonal passive construction*.

The sentence **Das Haus wird von dem Mann gebaut** tells you who the agent is (**Mann**). However, there are often passive sentences where the agent is omitted, as if the corresponding active sentence has no subject.

Das Haus wurde gebaut.	*The house was being built.*
Das Haus wurde zerstört.	*The house was destroyed.*

Who or what did the previously mentioned things to the house? The sentences don't tell us. The agent is not named.

The pronoun **es** can also begin an impersonal passive construction when no other words precede the verb. The English equivalent would be *there is* or *there are*.

Es wird viel gelernt.	*There is a lot being learned.*
Es wurde viel Geld ausgegeben.	*A lot of money was spent.*
Es werden viel Äpfel gegessen.	*There are a lot of apples being eaten.*

What activities are being done by the Müllers on the weekend? Supply the form of werden and the past participle of the given verb. Notice the sentences don't tell us who does what.

EXAMPLE: Der Rasen _____ nachmittags _____ (mähen).
               *Der Rasen **wird** nachmittags **gemäht**.*

1. Das Geschirr _____ mit heissem Wasser _____ (spülen).

2. Die Betten _____ morgens _____ (machen).

3. Das Auto _____ gut _____ (waschen).

4. Die Blumen _____ _____ (giessen).

5. Das Kino _____ abends _____ (besuchen).

Restate the following sentences, beginning with Es.

EXAMPLES: Hier wird viel gearbeitet.
                Es wird hier viel gearbeitet.

                Im Sommer wurde viel geschwommen.
                Es wurde im Sommer viel geschwommen.

1. Abends wird musiziert. _____

2. Dem Lehrer wurde nicht geantwortet. _____

3. Dem Kind wird nichts geglaubt. _____

4. Am Wochenende wurde viel gegessen. _____

5. In den Ferien wurde viel gewandert. _____

sein and the Passive Voice

When using the passive with **sein**, the resulting state of the action is emphasized, rather than the process of the action (which is emphasized when using **werden**). It is formed in the same way as the **werden** passive but with **sein** taking the place of **werden**.

| **werden** | Das Bett wird gemacht. | *The bed is being made.* |
| **sein** | Das Bett ist gemacht. | *The bed is made.* (the job has been completed) |

The **sein** passive is usually used only in the present and the past tenses.

ÜBUNG
25·11

Inge has passed her exams with flying colors. Leo is throwing her a party and is making sure everything is in order. Make sentences using the cues given.

EXAMPLE: der Tisch—decken
             Der Tisch ist gedeckt.

1. die Getränke—kühlen _____

2. die Würstchen—braten _____

3. der Kuchen—servieren _____

4. die Küche—aufräumen _____

5. die Wohnung—schmücken _____

Then Leo makes sure he looks good.

6. die Haare—kämmen _____

7. das Gesicht—waschen _____

8. die Zähne—putzen _____

9. der Bart—rasieren _____

10. die Krawatte—binden _____

ÜBUNG
25·12

Translate the following sentences into German, showing what was completed before it was time to leave for school. Use the past tense.

EXAMPLE: The homework was done.
             Die Hausaufgabe war gemacht.

1. The book was read. _____

2. The essay (**der Aufsatz**) was written. _____

3. The bag (**die Tasche**) was packed. _____

4. The breakfast was eaten. _____

5. The teeth were brushed. _____

6. The coat was put on. _____

7. The bag was taken. _____

8. The door was closed. _____

Substitutes for the passive voice

Where English uses the passive, German frequently substitutes one of a number of active constructions for the passive voice.

man

Man (meaning *one*, *they*, *you*, *we*, or *people*) is frequently used whenever the agent is indefinite.

Man macht das nicht!	*One doesn't do that! (That isn't done.)*
Das lernt man leicht.	*That is easy to learn.*

ÜBUNG
25·13

Restate the following passive sentences, using man.

EXAMPLE: Wie wird das auf Deutsch gesagt?
Wie sagt man das auf Deutsch?

1. Wie wird das Wort geschrieben? _____

2. Das Lied wird laut gesungen. _____

3. Der Kuchen wird mit der kleinen Gabel gegessen. _____

4. Die Suppe wird langsam gekocht. _____

5. Viel Geld wurde für diese Bilder bezahlt. _____

6. Das Kind wird ins Bett gebracht. _____

7. Die Tür wurde zugemacht. _____

8. Das Licht wird ausgemacht. _____

When changing a sentence that uses **man** into a true passive sentence, **man** is dropped.

Man singt das Lied leise.	*They sing the song quietly.*
Das Lied wird leise gesungen.	*The song is being sung quietly.*

ÜBUNG 25·14

*Was wird alles in der Klasse gemacht? Change the following sentences into passive sentences, beginning with **Es wird**.*

EXAMPLE: Man macht die Rechenaufgabe.
Es wird die Rechenaufgabe gemacht.

1. Man sitzt ruhig. _____

2. Man hebt die Hand. _____

3. Man schreibt ins Heft. _____

4. Man spricht nicht mit den Nachbarn. _____

5. Man passt gut auf. _____

sein...zu + Infinitive

A form of **sein** plus an adjective, followed by **zu** and an infinitive, is also often used instead of the passive voice.

Er ist schwer zu verstehen.   *He is hard to understand.*
Das Gedicht ist leicht zu lernen.   *The poem is easy to learn.*

ÜBUNG 25·15

*Answer the following questions in the affirmative with a **sein...zu** + infinitive construction.*

EXAMPLE: Kann man das Dorf leicht finden?
Ja, es ist leicht zu finden.

1. Kann man den Wein billig herstellen? _____

2. Kann man die Tür leicht leise öffnen? _____

3. Kann man die Sprache leicht lernen? _____

4. Kann man das Auto schwer verkaufen? _____

5. Kannst du das Kind gut verstehen? _____

sich lassen + Infinitive

A form of **sich lassen** + an infinitive can also be substituted for the passive voice. The phrase suggests that the action is possible.

Das Stroh lässt sich zu Gold spinnen.   *It is possible to spin straw into gold.*
Das Männlein lässt sich leicht erkennen.   *It is possible to recognize the little man easily.*

Rewrite the following sentences using a **sich lassen** + infinitive construction. Some of the items are in the past and need to take the past tense of **lassen**.

EXAMPLES: Man kann Deutsch leicht lernen.
Deutsch lässt sich leicht lernen.

Konnte man den Fisch leicht braten?
Ließ sich der Fisch leicht braten?

1. Den Stuhl kann man reparieren. _____

2. Den Patient kann man retten. _____

3. Kann man das Lied leicht singen? _____

4. Kann man die Straße gleich finden? _____

5. Das wird mit Schwierigkeit gemacht. _____

6. Das wurde schnell erklärt. _____

7. Die Frage konnte man schwer beantworten. _____

8. Das Geld wurde schnell ausgegeben. _____

9. Das Mädchen kann man sehen. _____

10. Das Geld kann man leicht verlieren. _____

What are the eating habits of Germans? Change the following sentences from the active to the passive. Remember, when changing a sentence from the active to the passive, the direct object of the active sentence becomes the subject of the passive.

EXAMPLES: Die meisten Familien trinken abends Tee.
Tee wird von den meisten Familien abends getrunken.

Man isst viel Obst.
Viel Obst wird gegessen.

1. Die Leute essen viel Spätzle im Süden.

_____

2. Man legt die linke Hand nicht in den Schoß.

_____

3. Man trinkt Getränke ohne Eis.

_____

4. Man isst die Hauptmahlzeit meistens mittags.

   _____

5. Zum Frühstück essen die Leute oft frische Brötchen.

   _____

6. Abends isst man viel Kartoffelsalat und Würstchen.

   _____

7. Die Kinder bringen ein Pausenbrot in die Schule mit.

   _____

8. Sonntagnachmittags serviert man Kaffee und Kuchen.

   _____

9. Man lädt oft Besuch zum Kaffee ein.

   _____

10. Obstkuchen isst man oft mit Schlagsahne.

    _____

11. Die Kinder trinken Kakao.

    _____

12. Der Besuch bringt Blumen.

    _____

ÜBUNG

25·18

How was life when Oma was young? Change the following sentences to the passive using the past tense.

EXAMPLE: Die Mutter pflanzte viel Gemüse.
           Viel Gemüse wurde von der Mutter gepflanzt.

1. Frauen machten die Arbeit im Haus.

   _____

2. Die Frau versorgte die Kinder.

   _____

3. Der Mann brachte das Geld ins Haus.

   _____

4. Junge Männer lernten einen Beruf.

   _____

5. Junge Mädchen lernten die Arbeit im Haus.

   _____

6. Man backte das Brot zu Hause.

   _____

7. Man aß selten Kuchen.

   _____

8. Die Leute schrieben viele Briefe.

   _____

9. Die Waschfrau wusch die Wäsche mit der Hand.

   _____

10. Man fuhr viel mit dem Rad oder ging zu Fuß.

    _____

ÜBUNG
25·19

Remember Rumpelstilzchen? Indicate whether each of the following sentences is in the active voice, passive voice, or passive voice with sein or is using a substitute for the passive voice.

EXAMPLES: Die Tochter wurde vom Vater zum König gebracht. (*passive voice*)
             Der Vater brachte die Tochter zum König. (*active voice*)
             Man brachte die Tochter zum König. (*substitute for passive voice*)

1. Der König führte die Müllerstochter in die Kammer. _____

2. Die Tür ist geschlossen. _____

3. Das Stroh wurde in die Kammer gebracht. _____

4. Das lässt sich nicht machen. _____

5. Es ist nicht leicht Stroh zu Gold zu spinnen. _____

6. Das Stroh wurde vom Männlein zu Gold gesponnen. _____

7. Bis zum Morgen wurde gearbeitet. _____

8. Dann wurde das Halsband weggegeben. _____

9. Das Gold wurde dem König gezeigt. _____

10. Er wollte noch mehr Gold haben. _____

11. Es ist leicht nie genug zu haben. _____

12. Man konnte den Namen nicht raten. _____

13. Der Name wurde vom Männlein gesungen. _____

14. Das Singen wurde vom Boten gehört. _____

15. Man freute sich den Namen zu wissen. _____

16. Das Kind wurde von der Königin geliebt. _____

17. Das schöne Kind ließ sich leicht lieben. _____

18. Der Fuß wurde vom Männlein rausgerissen. _____

19. Das Männlein war wütend und starb. _____

20. Der Name Rumpelstilzchen wird selten einem Kind gegeben. _____

Passive voice

The passive voice in English is composed of a conjugated form of *be* (*am, is, are, was, were, have been, will be*) and a past participle.

> It **is being fixed.**
> The man **was fired** by his boss.
> You **will be rewarded** by the new mayor.

Formation of the passive voice

The German passive voice is composed of a conjugated form of **werden** and a past participle.

First, let's review this important verb **werden**. The verb **werden** has three specific functions. When it accompanies an infinitive, it is used as the auxiliary of the future tense. For example:

> Ich **werde** in die Schweiz reisen.   *I will travel to Switzerland.*

When it stands alone it means *become* or *get*. Let's look at this verb in the various tenses.

> Es **wird** sehr kalt.   *It's getting very cold.*
> Es **wurde** sehr kalt.   *It got very cold.*
> Es **ist** sehr kalt **geworden.**   *It got/has gotten very cold.*
> Es **wird** sehr kalt **werden.**   *It will get very cold.*

The third function of **werden** is its use as the auxiliary of a transitive past participle. This is the *passive voice*, and in the passive voice, **werden** is translated as a conjugated form of *be* (*am, is, are, was, were, have been, will be*). It is important to remember that intransitive verbs or verbs of motion are not used in the passive voice.

The major difference between the active voice and the passive voice is how the subject and direct object of an active voice sentence change in a passive voice sentence: the subject becomes the *object of a preposition*, and the direct object becomes the *subject*. Let's look at an example in English:

ACTIVE VOICE	PASSIVE VOICE
The boy kissed her.	*She was kissed by the boy.*

The direct object *her* has become the subject *she* of the passive voice sentence. The subject of the active voice sentence (*the boy*) is now in a passive position in the passive voice sentence and is introduced by the preposition *by* (*by the boy*).

Let's look at some German examples of active voice sentences and how they are changed to the passive voice. When making the change to the passive voice, the passive voice sentence must be in the same tense as the active voice sentence from which it is derived.

PRESENT TENSE ACTIVE VOICE	PRESENT TENSE PASSIVE VOICE
Der Mann verkauft den Wagen.	Der Wagen wird von dem Mann verkauft.
The man sells the car.	*The car is sold by the man.*

PAST TENSE ACTIVE VOICE	PAST TENSE PASSIVE VOICE
Ich zerbrach die Vase.	Die Vase wurde von mir zerbrochen.
I smashed the vase.	*The vase was smashed by me.*

PRESENT PERFECT ACTIVE SENTENCE	PRESENT PERFECT PASSIVE SENTENCE
Wir haben die Blumen gekauft.	Die Blumen sind von uns gekauft worden.
We (have) bought the flowers.	*The flowers were/have been bought by us.*

FUTURE ACTIVE SENTENCE	FUTURE PASSIVE SENTENCE
Diese Frau wird die Kinder finden.	Die Kinder werden von dieser Frau gefunden werden.
This woman will find the children.	*The children will be found by this woman.*

The participle **geworden** is only used when the meaning of **werden** is *become* or *get*. The participle **worden** is only used when it means *been* in a passive voice sentence. Both, however, use **sein** as their auxiliary.

Sie **ist** krank **geworden**.   *She became/has become ill.*
Sie **ist** von Erik geküsst **worden**.   *She was/has been kissed by Erik.*

Note that the preposition **von** is used to mean *by* in passive voice sentences. The object of **von** is always in the dative case.

Es wurde **von ihm** zerbrochen.   *It was smashed by him.*
Es wurde **von einem Freund** zerbrochen. *It was smashed by a friend.*
Es wurde **von der Schülerin** zerbrochen. *It was smashed by the schoolgirl.*

ÜBUNG
25.20

Reword each passive voice sentence in the missing tenses.

1. PRESENT Der Anzug wird von dem Schneider genäht (*tailor, sewn*).

PAST _____

PRESENT PERFECT _____

FUTURE _____

2. PRESENT _____

   PAST Von wem wurde das Haus gebaut?

   PRESENT PERFECT _____

   FUTURE _____

3. PRESENT _____

   PAST _____

   PRESENT PERFECT Die Schüler sind von dem Lehrer unterrichtet (*instructed*) worden.

   FUTURE _____

4. PRESENT _____

   PAST _____

   PRESENT PERFECT _____

   FUTURE Die neue Übung wird von ihr gelesen werden.

5. PRESENT Ein Glas Wein wird von dem Kellner (*waiter*) gebracht.

   PAST _____

   PRESENT PERFECT _____

   FUTURE _____

6. PRESENT _____

   PAST Kleider und Blusen wurden von ihr verkauft.

   PRESENT PERFECT _____

   FUTURE _____

7. PRESENT _____

   PAST _____

   PRESENT PERFECT Die alte Kirche ist von den Touristen besucht worden.

   FUTURE _____

8. PRESENT _____

   PAST _____

   PRESENT PERFECT _____

   FUTURE Die Wörter werden von der Schülerin gelernt werden.

9. PRESENT Die Fenster werden von meiner Tante aufgemacht.

   PAST _____

   PRESENT PERFECT _____

   FUTURE _____

10. PRESENT _____

   PAST <u>Wer wurde von ihnen verhaftet (*arrested*)?</u>

   PRESENT PERFECT _____

   FUTURE _____

Maintaining the tense of the active voice sentence, reword each active voice sentence in the passive voice.

EXAMPLE   Sie kaufte den roten Hut.

   Der rote Hut wurde von ihr gekauft.

1. Der Student braucht neue Schuhe.

   _____

2. Die Malerin (*painter*) aß ein belegtes Brot (*sandwich*).

   _____

3. Diese Männer dressierten (*trained*) die Pferde.

   _____

4. Eine neue Dichterin (*poet*) hat diese Gedichte geschrieben.

   _____

5. Die Kinder werden die Lehrbücher (*textbooks*) lesen.

   _____

6. Meine Eltern haben die Ausländer eingeladen (*invited*).

   _____

7. Sie werden eine neue Werkstatt (*workshop*) bauen.

   _____

8. Die Arbeiter beendeten (*ended*) die Arbeit.

   _____

9. Meine Großmutter bäckt (*bakes*) einen Kuchen.

   _____

10. Herr Keller hat die Kinder gerufen.

   _____

11. Der Fleischer (*butcher*) wird die Tiere schlachten (*slaughter*).

    _____

12. Der Bauer zieht die Schweine auf (*raises*).

    _____

13. Der Gast hat drei Flaschen Wein bestellt.

    _____

14. Ein Gelehrter (*scholar*) erlernt viele Sprachen.

    _____

15. Die Mechaniker werden den alten Wagen reparieren.

    _____

16. Meine Frau fütterte das Baby.

    _____

17. Der Tischler hat einen Hammer und eine Säge (*saw*) benutzt.

    _____

18. Frau Schäfer entlässt (*fires*) einige Angestellte (*employees*).

    _____

19. Die Studentinnen werden das große Zimmer mieten (*rent*).

    _____

20. Felix hat die Fahrkarten wieder vergessen.

    _____

The preposition durch

The preposition **durch** can be translated as *by* in a passive sentence just like **von**. But there is a difference. Use **von** when the object of that preposition is the actual *doer* of the action of the verb. This is most often a person. For example:

> Sie ist **von ihrem Vater** geküsst worden.   *She was kissed by her father.*

Use **durch** to suggest that *something caused* the action of the verb to be carried out or that the action of the verb is *due to* the object of the preposition **durch**. This is most often a thing. For example:

> Das Haus ist **durch ein Erdbeben**   *The house was destroyed by (due to)*
> zerstört worden.   *an earthquake.*

In some cases, **von** can be used with a thing when that thing is the actual doer of the action. Compare the following two sentences:

Das Gebäude wurde **durch** einen
   Bombenangriff zerstört.
Das Gebäude wurde **von** einer
   Bombe zerstört.

The building was destroyed by (due to)
   a bombing attack.
The building was destroyed
   by a bomb.

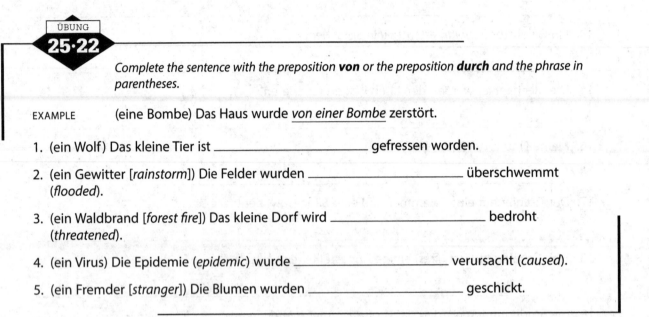

ÜBUNG
25·22

Complete the sentence with the preposition **von** or the preposition **durch** and the phrase in parentheses.

EXAMPLE   (eine Bombe) Das Haus wurde *von einer Bombe* zerstört.

1. (ein Wolf) Das kleine Tier ist _____ gefressen worden.

2. (ein Gewitter [*rainstorm*]) Die Felder wurden _____ überschwemmt
   (*flooded*).

3. (ein Waldbrand [*forest fire*]) Das kleine Dorf wird _____ bedroht
   (*threatened*).

4. (ein Virus) Die Epidemie (*epidemic*) wurde _____ verursacht (*caused*).

5. (ein Fremder [*stranger*]) Die Blumen wurden _____ geschickt.

Passive and the dative case

Many transitive verbs in German are used with a dative object. These are the dative verbs, and although the object of the verbs is a direct object in the English translation, the object of the German verbs is in the dative case. For example:

Wir **helfen** dem Mann.   *We help the man.*
Ich **glaube** der Frau nicht.   *I don't believe the woman.*

The dative verbs can be used to form a passive voice sentence. But unlike direct objects in the accusative case, which become the nominative subject in the passive voice sentence, *dative case objects remain in the dative case*. The subject of such a passive voice sentence is **es**, and therefore the verb **werden** is conjugated for the third-person singular. It is very common to omit **es**. For example:

ACTIVE VOICE SENTENCE	PASSIVE VOICE SENTENCE
Wir helfen dem Mann.	Dem Mann wird von uns geholfen.
We help the man.	*The man is helped by us.*
Ich glaube der Frau nicht.	Der Frau wird von mir nicht geglaubt.
I don't believe the woman.	*The woman is not believed by me.*

	Die Gäste haben ihr gedankt.	Ihr ist von den Gästen gedankt worden.
	The guests (have) thanked her.	*She was/has been thanked by the guests.*
	Das wird dem Arzt imponieren.	Dem Arzt wird davon imponiert werden.
	That will impress the doctor.	*The doctor will be impressed by that.*

Just like other sentences that are changed from the active voice to the passive voice, the tense is identical in both types of sentences.

ÜBUNG
25·23

Reword each of the following passive voice sentences in the missing tenses.

1. PRESENT Ihr wird von niemandem geglaubt.

   PAST _____

   PRESENT PERFECT _____

   FUTURE _____

2. PRESENT _____

   PAST Dem Herrn wurde für seine Hilfe von uns gedankt.

   PRESENT PERFECT _____

   FUTURE _____

3. PRESENT _____

   PAST _____

   PRESENT PERFECT Den Schülern ist von dem Lehrer gratuliert worden.

   FUTURE _____

4. PRESENT _____

   PAST _____

   PRESENT PERFECT _____

   FUTURE Der Gesundheit wird durch Rauchen geschadet werden.

5. PRESENT Den Touristen wird von dem Dieb gedroht.

   PAST _____

   PRESENT PERFECT _____

   FUTURE _____

6. PRESENT _____

PAST Dem Professor wurde nicht von den Studenten widersprochen.

PRESENT PERFECT _____

FUTURE _____

7. PRESENT _____

PAST _____

PRESENT PERFECT Der alten Dame ist von ihm geschmeichelt worden.

FUTURE _____

8. PRESENT _____

PAST _____

PRESENT PERFECT _____

FUTURE Uns wird immer von ihnen vertraut werden.

9. PRESENT Den verlorenen Kindern wird von dem Polizisten geholfen.

PAST _____

PRESENT PERFECT _____

FUTURE _____

10. PRESENT Dem König wird von einem jungen Mädchen gedient.

PAST _____

PRESENT PERFECT _____

FUTURE _____

Expressing an indirect object with the dative case

The dative case is also used to express an indirect object. This function of the dative can also appear in a passive voice sentence. But if there is an indirect object in a sentence, then there must also be a direct object. And the direct object in an active voice sentence becomes the subject of a passive voice sentence. Be aware that this is different from the use of dative verbs in the passive. Another difference is the position of the dative object in the passive sentence. It can begin the sentence, or the subject can begin the sentence. Let's look at some examples:

ACTIVE VOICE SENTENCE	PASSIVE VOICE SENTENCE
Erik gibt der Frau die Geschenke. _Erik gives the woman the gifts._	Der Frau werden die Geschenke von Erik gegeben. _The woman is given the gifts by Erik._
	or Die Geschenke werden der Frau von Erik gegeben. _The gifts are given to the woman by Erik._

Sie kaufte ihrem Bruder einen Schlips.	Ihrem Bruder wurde ein Schlips von ihr gekauft.
She bought her brother a tie.	*Her brother was bought a tie by her.*
	or Ein Schlips wurde ihrem Bruder von ihr gekauft.
	A tie was bought for her brother by her.
Er hat es ihnen gezeigt.	Ihnen ist es von ihm gezeigt worden.
He showed it to them.	*They were shown it by him.*
	or Es ist ihnen von ihm gezeigt worden.
	It was shown to them by him.

Remember that the subject of passive voice sentences as illustrated can be any number or person. Therefore, the verb **werden** can have a variety of endings, unlike dative verbs in the passive voice, which are always conjugated for **es**.

ÜBUNG
25·24

Reword each active voice sentence in the passive voice twice: once with the indirect object beginning the sentence and once with the direct object beginning the sentence. If there is no direct object in the sentence, restate it once. Retain the tense of the original sentence.

1. Sie brachte mir Blumen.

    _____

    _____

2. Thomas hat der Amerikanerin einen Teller (*plate, bowl*) Suppe bestellt.

    _____

    _____

3. Die Touristen werden das Museum fotografieren.

    _____

    _____

4. Viele schicken der armen Frau Geld.

    _____

    _____

5. Ich gab ihr eine kleine Überraschung (*surprise*).

    _____

    _____

6. Die Lehrerin hat ihnen die Bücher ausgeteilt (*distributed*).

    _____

    _____

7. Unser Sohn wird uns einen Fernsehapparat (TV) schenken.

_____

8. Seine Cousine sendet ihm viele E-Mails.

_____

9. Er wird seiner Tochter einen Wagen kaufen.

_____

10. Die Malerin zeigte uns die Gemälde.

_____

_____

Choose the letter of the word or phrase that best completes each sentence.

1. Ich _____ von den Eltern geliebt.
   a. habe   b. werde   c. wurden   d. kann

2. Pferde wurden _____ aufgezogen.
   a. von den Bauern   b. worden   c. geworden   d. ins Dorf

3. Ein neues Gedicht ist von ihm _____.
   a. gelernt worden   b. einem Schüler   c. schreiben   d. von dem Jungen

4. Die Schule ist _____ ein Erdbeben zerstört worden.
   a. durch   b. davon   c. wurde   d. von

5. _____ wurde nicht damit geholfen.
   a. Ihm   b. Das Mädchen   c. Von den Kindern   d. Sie

6. Das Brot _____ vom Bäcker gebacken werden.
   a. ist   b. sind   c. wurde   d. wird

7. Es ist wieder kalt _____.
   a. gebaut worden   b. geworden   c. wurden   d. von uns

8. Die Kinder wurden _____ unterrichtet.
   a. durch ein Gewitter   b. es   c. morgen   d. von einer neuen Lehrerin

9. _____ wurdet von einem alten Freund eingeladen.
   a. Wir   b. Uns   c. Er   d. Ihr

10. Wir werden dem alten Mann _____.
    a. geholfen worden   b. helfen   c. geglaubt   d. glauben werden

11. Mir ist für meine Hilfe _____.
    a. gedankt worden   b. dienen   c. gratulieren   d. gesehen worden
                                                                  werden

12. Uns _____ die Briefe von einer Cousine geschickt.
    a. wird   b. wurde   c. ist worden   d. wurden

13. _____ du von der neuen Ärztin behandelt worden?
    a. War   b. Hast   c. Ist   d. Bist

14. _____ sind von den Kindern gesammelt worden.
    a. Der Gast   b. Die Malerin   c. Viele Bücher   d. Dieses Gemälde

15. Die Garage ist _____ zerstört worden.
    a. von einer Bombe   b. es regnete   c. durch die Felder   d. ein schreckliches
                                                                                Gewitter

The subjunctive

Forming the subjunctive

The subjunctive conjugations have endings that are readily recognized, because they resemble so closely the endings of the German past tense. The subjunctive falls into two categories: the present subjunctive, or subjunctive I, and the past subjunctive, or subjunctive II. In this book, they will be called subjunctive I and II.

The subjunctive I conjugation is formed from the stem of a verb and the following endings: **-e, -est, -e, -en, -et, -en**. There are no differences between regular and irregular verbs or modal auxiliaries. For example:

	stellen	**besuchen**	**können**	**abfahren**
ich	stelle	besuche	könne	fahre ab
du	stellest	besuchest	könnest	fahrest ab
er	stelle	besuche	könne	fahre ab
wir	stellen	besuchen	können	fahren ab
ihr	stellet	besuchet	könnet	fahret ab
Sie	stellen	besuchen	können	fahren ab

Let's look at the three special verbs of the German language in subjunctive I.

	haben	**sein**	**werden**
ich	habe	sei	werde
du	habest	seiest	werdest
er	habe	sei	werde
wir	haben	seien	werden
ihr	habet	seiet	werdet
Sie	haben	seien	werden

ÜBUNG
26·1

Write the full subjunctive I conjugation for each of the following verbs.

1.	müssen	tragen	versuchen
ich	_____	_____	_____
du	_____	_____	_____
er	_____	_____	_____
wir	_____	_____	_____

ihr	_____	_____	_____
Sie	_____	_____	_____

2.

	ansehen	laufen	interessieren
ich	_____	_____	_____
du	_____	_____	_____
er	_____	_____	_____
wir	_____	_____	_____
ihr	_____	_____	_____
Sie	_____	_____	_____

3.

	wissen	wollen	ausgeben (*spend*)
ich	_____	_____	_____
du	_____	_____	_____
er	_____	_____	_____
wir	_____	_____	_____
ihr	_____	_____	_____
Sie	_____	_____	_____

The subjunctive II conjugation is derived from the past tense of a verb. In the subjunctive II conjugation, there is an important difference in how regular and irregular verbs are formed. Regular verbs are identical to the regular past tense. For example:

	machen	vorstellen	verkaufen
ich	machte	stellte vor	verkaufte
du	machtest	stelltest vor	verkauftest
er	machte	stellte vor	verkaufte
wir	machten	stellten vor	verkauften
ihr	machtet	stelltet vor	verkauftet
Sie	machten	stellten vor	verkauften

The subjunctive II conjugation of irregular verbs is formed from the irregular past tense of the verb. If the past tense has an umlaut vowel (**a, o, u**), an umlaut is added in the subjunctive II conjugation. The endings used in this conjugation are **-e, -est, -e, -en, -et, -en**. Let's look at some example verbs:

	sehen	bleiben	versprechen	abfahren
ich	sähe	bliebe	verspräche	führe ab
du	sähest	bliebest	versprächest	führest ab
er	sähe	bliebe	verspräche	führe ab
wir	sähen	blieben	versprächen	führen ab
ihr	sähet	bliebet	versprächet	führet ab
Sie	sähen	blieben	versprächen	führen ab

Modal auxiliaries form their past tense with a **-te** suffix, and if there is an umlaut in the infinitive, it is omitted in the past tense. However, in the subjunctive II conjugation, the umlaut is added.

	sollen	**müssen**	**können**	**mögen**
ich	sollte	müsste	könnte	möchte
du	solltest	müsstest	könntest	möchtest
er	sollte	müsste	könnte	möchte
wir	sollten	müssten	könnten	möchten
ihr	solltet	müsstet	könntet	möchtet
Sie	sollten	müssten	könnten	möchten

A small list of irregular verbs forms a new stem for the subjunctive II conjugation. They are:

INFINITIVE	SUBJUNCTIVE II	
empfehlen	empföhle	*recommend*
gelten	gölte/gälte	*be valid*
helfen	hülfe	*help*
schwimmen	schwömme	*swim*
schwören	schwüre	*swear*
stehen	stünde/stände	*stand*
sterben	stürbe	*die*
verderben	verdürbe	*spoil*
verstehen	verstünde/verstände	*understand*
werben	würbe	*recruit*
werfen	würfe	*throw*

ÜBUNG

26·2

Write the full subjunctive II conjugation for each of the following verbs.

1. schlafen   essen   wollen

ich _____   _____   _____

du   _____   _____   _____

er   _____   _____   _____

wir _____   _____   _____

ihr _____   _____   _____

Sie _____   _____   _____

2. einladen   trinken   mitgehen

ich _____   _____   _____

du   _____   _____   _____

er   _____   _____   _____

	wir		
	ihr		
	Sie		

3.

	dürfen	verstehen	anrufen
ich			
du			
er			
wir			
ihr			
Sie			

The verbs **haben**, **sein**, and **werden** are conjugated in the following ways in subjunctive II:

	haben	sein	werden
ich	hätte	wäre	würde
du	hättest	wärest	würdest
er	hätte	wäre	würde
wir	hätten	wären	würden
ihr	hättet	wäret	würdet
Sie	hätten	wären	würden

The mixed verbs have a unique form that does not conform to regular or irregular verb patterns in the subjunctive.

	wissen	denken	brennen
ich	wüsste	dächte	brennte
du	wüsstest	dächtest	brenntest
er	wüsste	dächte	brennte
wir	wüssten	dächten	brennten
ihr	wüsstet	dächtet	brenntet
Sie	wüssten	dächten	brennten

Write the full subjunctive II conjugation for each of the following verbs.

1.

	nennen	erkennen	sein
ich			
du			
er			
wir			

ihr	_____	_____	_____
Sie	_____	_____	_____

2.	haben	bringen	werden
ich	_____	_____	_____
du	_____	_____	_____
er	_____	_____	_____
wir	_____	_____	_____
ihr	_____	_____	_____
Sie	_____	_____	_____

Using the subjunctive

The subjunctive I conjugation is used most frequently in *indirect discourse*. When reporting what someone else has said, the verb in the reported statement will be in subjunctive I. For example:

Thomas sagte, dass seine Freundin krank **sei**.	*Thomas said that his girlfriend **is** sick.*
Sie berichtete, dass der Richter nach Paris fahren **werde**.	*She reported that the judge **will** travel to Paris.*
Er fragte, ob Tina es verkauft **habe**.	*He asked whether (if) Tina bought it.*
Wir fragten, ob Karl ihnen helfen **könne**.	*We asked whether Karl **can** help them.*

If the subjunctive I form is identical to the indicative, the subjunctive II conjugation is used.

Er sagte, dass sie in Frankreich **wohnten**.	*He said that they **live** in France.*
Erik fragte, ob die Kinder es verstehen **könnten**.	*Erik asked whether the children **can** understand it.*

ÜBUNG
26·4

Rewrite the incomplete sentence as indirect discourse using the given phrase.

FOR EXAMPLE: Er sagte, dass _____.

Sie wohnt in Hamburg.   *Er sagte, dass sie in Hamburg wohne.*

Der Reporter berichtete, dass _____.

1. Der Kanzler (*chancellor*) wird bald gesund.

_____

2. Niemand versteht die Rede.

_____

3. Die Touristen reisen nach Italien.

_____

4. Die alte Frau ist gestorben.

_____

5. Herr Dorf wird in Polen wohnen.

Sie haben ihn gefragt, ob _____.

6. Ist seine Frau wieder in der Schweiz?

_____

7. Können die Kinder Fußball spielen?

_____

8. Hat er genug Geld?

_____

9. Wissen sie, wo sie ist?

_____

10. Muss der Junge bestraft werden?

_____

If a sentence is in the past, present perfect, or past perfect tense, it is structured like the present perfect tense in subjunctive I. For example:

Er sang gut.	Sie sagte, dass er gut **gesungen habe**.
Er hat gut gesungen.	Sie sagte, dass er gut **gesungen habe**.
Er hatte gut gesungen.	Sie sagte, dass er gut **gesungen habe**.
Er ging mit.	Sie fragte, ob er **mitgegangen sei**.
Er ist mitgegangen.	Sie fragte, ob er **mitgegangen sei**.
Er war mitgegangen.	Sie fragte, ob er **mitgegangen sei**.

If a modal auxiliary is in the past tense, the present perfect structure is not used and the modal is conjugated in subjunctive II.

Er konnte gut singen.	Sie sagte, dass er gut singen **könnte**.	_She said that he could sing well._

It is possible to omit **dass** in indirect discourse, which changes the word order. For example:

Er sagte, er **habe** gut gesungen.	_He said he sang well._
Sie berichtete, der Mann **verstehe** das Problem nicht.	_She reported the man does not understand the problem._

Rewrite the incomplete sentence as indirect discourse using the given phrase.

Der Richter hat gesagt, dass _____.

1. Der Junge spielte mit dem Hund.

   _____

2. Wir haben die Uhr verloren.

   _____

3. Sie waren mit dem Bus gefahren.

   _____

4. Erik stahl das Auto.

   _____

5. Der Dieb war zwei Stunden im Keller.

   _____

Sonja berichtete, dass _____.

6. Sie hatten eine neue Speise (*food*) gekocht.

   _____

7. Karl kam zu spät.

   _____

8. Ihre Tochter hat gut getanzt.

   _____

9. Mein Vater gab ihr zehn Euro.

   _____

10. Martin dachte oft an uns.

   _____

In conversational German it is common to use a subjunctive II conjugation in indirect discourse.

FORMAL	CONVERSATIONAL
Sie sagte, er **habe** keine Zeit.	Sie sagte, er **hätte** keine Zeit.

The subjunctive II conjugation is also used when stating a *wish* that is introduced by **wenn** (*if*). For example:

Wenn mein Vater nur hier **wäre**!	*If only my father **were** here.*
Wenn wir doch bei unseren Eltern **wären**!	*If we **were** only with our parents.*
Wenn sie nur mehr Zeit **hätte**!	*If only she **had** more time.*

Wenn can be omitted; then the sentence would begin with the verb:

Wäre mein Vater nur hier!	*If only my father **were** here.*
Könntest du doch ihnen helfen!	*If you **could** only help them.*
Hätte er doch seine Frau nie verlassen!	*If only he **had** not left his wife.*

ÜBUNG
26·6

Rewrite each sentence as a wish *statement with* **wenn** *in subjunctive II.*

FOR EXAMPLE: Er hat mehr Geld.

Wenn er mehr Geld hätte!

1. Ich bin in meiner Heimat (*home/homeland*).

_____

2. Er hat mehr Mut (*courage*).

_____

3. Wir haben mehr Glück (*luck*) gehabt.

_____

4. Er ist nicht in die Stadt gefahren.

_____

5. Du hast besser gearbeitet.

_____

The subjunctive II conjugation is used in clauses that are introduced by **als ob** or **als wenn** (*as if*). For example:

Er sprach, **als ob** er alles verstehen **könnte**.	*He spoke **as if** he could understand everything.*
Sie tat so, **als wenn** sie viel schöner **wäre**.	*She acted **as if** she were much prettier.*

Complete each sentence with the phrases provided.

Der Mann schrie (*screamed*), als ob _____.

1. Er ist verletzt.

   _____

2. Er hasst (*hates*) uns.

   _____

3. Wir sind taub (*deaf*).

   _____

Ihr Gesicht sah aus (*her face looked*), als ob _____.

4. Sie ist sehr krank gewesen.

   _____

5. Sie kann ihm überhaupt nicht glauben.

   _____

6. Sie hat ein Ungeheuer (*monster*) gesehen.

   _____

Die Frau tat so, als ob _____.

7. Sie liebt ihn.

   _____

8. Sie hat den Mann nie kennen gelernt (*never became acquainted with*).

   _____

9. Ich bin ihr Diener (*servant*).

   _____

10. Sie kann perfekt Deutsch sprechen.

    _____

The conjunction **wenn** is used in another form that requires a subjunctive II conjugation. This occurs in a *conditional* sentence. Conditional sentences set a condition with a proposed result. In English, they look as follows:

CONDITION	RESULT
If John were here,	he would surely help me.
If I were rich,	I would buy a new sports car.

German structures conditional sentences in the same way. Where the English word *would* is used in the *result* clause, German uses the subjunctive II verb **würde**. For example:

Wenn er hier wäre, **würde** er mir helfen.	*If he were here, he **would** help me.*
Wenn ich reich wäre, **würde** ich ein großes Haus kaufen.	*If I were rich, I **would** buy a big house.*
Wenn sie mehr Zeit hätte, **würde** sie eine Suppe vorbereiten.	*If she had more time, she **would** prepare a soup.*

It is possible to place the conditional clause at the end of the sentence.

Er **würde** mir helfen, wenn er hier wäre.

To indicate conditions and results in the past, the present perfect structure is used. In such cases, the verb **würde** can be omitted.

Wenn er hier gewesen wäre, hätte er mir geholfen.	*If he had been here, he would have helped me.*
Wenn sie mehr Zeit gehabt hätte, hätte sie eine Suppe vorbereitet.	*If she had had more time, she would have prepared a soup.*

The verb **würde** can also be omitted if there is a modal auxiliary in the sentence.

Wenn ich sie sähe, könnte ich sie begrüßen.	*If I saw them, I could say hello to them.*
Wenn er eine Fahrkarte hätte, müsste er nach Bonn reisen.	*If he had a ticket, he would have to travel to Bonn.*

To indicate conditions and results in the past, the present perfect structure is used in these sentences.

Wenn er eine Fahrkarte gehabt hätte, hätte er nach Bonn reisen müssen.	*If he had had a ticket, he would have had to travel to Bonn.*

ÜBUNG
26·8

*Combine each pair of sentences by introducing the first sentence as a **wenn**-clause and making the second clause the result.*

FOR EXAMPLE: Er hat mehr Zeit. Er besucht seinen Onkel.
Wenn er mehr Zeit hätte, würde er seinen Onkel besuchen.

1. Tina gewinnt im Lotto. Sie kauft sich einen Pelzmantel (*fur coat*).

    _____

2. Der Mann schläft lange. Er kann nicht arbeiten.

    _____

3. Sie fand das verlorene Geld. Sie musste es dem Polizisten geben.

    _____

4. Das Wetter ist schlecht gewesen. Ich bin nicht auf das Land gefahren.

_____

5. Der Student war nicht aufmerksam (*attentive*). Er machte einen großen Fehler (*mistake*).

_____

6. Es ist nicht so weit. Ich gehe dorthin zu Fuß.

_____

7. Das Mädchen hat ein Gymnasium besucht. Sie konnte an einer Universität studieren.

_____

8. Die Frau arbeitet besser. Sie verdient (*earns*) mehr.

_____

9. Sie hat uns angerufen. Ich habe sie vom Bahnhof abgeholt.

_____

10. Du bist wieder gesund. Du musst wieder einen Job finden.

_____

Subjunctive I

Mood: Indicative and Subjunctive

The verb tenses you have studied so far have been in the indicative mood. The indicative mood expresses fact or reality.

> Ich gehe in die Schule.　　　*I am going to school.*

The subjunctive mood, on the other hand, indicates a subjective attitude on the part of the speaker and shows uncertainty, possibility, doubt, wish, or desire.

> Er sagt, er gehe in die Schule.　　*He says he is going to school.*

He *says* he is going, though he may not go. When using the subjunctive in indirect discourse, the speaker indicates that he or she doesn't take responsibility for the accuracy of what is being said.

There are two ways of forming the subjunctive in German. Usually they are referred to as subjunctive I, or special subjunctive, and subjunctive II, or general (more common) subjunctive. Here we will use the terms *subjunctive I* and *subjunctive II*. Both subjunctives have a present and past form. But they only have one past form each—no present perfect, simple past, or past perfect, as in the indicative. Probable happenings in the future are expressed by using the present form. The terms *present-time* and *past-time subjunctive* are used quite often when referring to the two tenses of the subjunctive. We will use these terms here.

Use and Formation of the Subjunctive I

The use of the subjunctive I is fading away, now being found mostly in formal, literary German. In spoken German it is generally only used with the **er/sie/es** form, because this form is clearly different from the indicative.

Indicative	Subjunctive I
er/sie/es hat	er/sie/es habe
er/sie/es macht	er/sie/es mache
er/sie/es isst	er/sie/es esse

Subjunctive I is mainly used in indirect discourse—the speaker telling what someone else says or said.

Er sagt immer, er habe kein Geld.   *He always says he has no money. (though maybe he does)*

Sie meint, sie singe am besten.   *She thinks she is the best singer.*

Present-Time Subjunctive I

The *present-time* subjunctive I is made up of the infinitive stem and the subjunctive I endings.

kommen	
ich komme	wir kommen
du kommest	ihr kommet
er/sie/es komme	sie/Sie kommen

Verbs that have a vowel change in the indicative in the second- and third-person singular do not have this change in the subjunctive I. Therefore, **er isst** would be **er esse**; **er schläft** would be **er schlafe**; and **er hat** would be **er habe**.

Sein is the only verb used somewhat frequently with all persons in the subjunctive I.

sein	
ich sei	wir seien
du seiest *or* seist	ihr seiet
er/sie/es sei	sie/Sie seien

ÜBUNG
26·9

*Andrea is in love and can't stop talking about her friend. Following are things Uwe, her new friend, supposedly says to her. Begin the sentences with **Er sagt**.*

EXAMPLE: Ich liebe dich.
    Er sagt, er liebe mich.

1. Ich finde dich sehr schön. _____

2. Du hast schöne Augen. _____

3. Ich bin so gern mit dir zusammen. _____

4. Ich kaufe dir ein schönes Geschenk. _____

5. Ich will mit dir ins Theater gehen. _____

6. Im Sommer gehe ich gern mit dir spazieren. _____

7. Dein Gang ist so anmutig. _____

8. Ich singe gern mit dir. _____

9. Ich denke oft an dich. _____

10. Es ist recht langweilig ohne dich. _____

Past-Time Subjunctive I

To form the *past-time subjunctive I*, use the subjunctive I of **haben** or **sein** and the past participle of the main verb.

Volker hat gesagt, er **habe** den Kuchen nicht **gegessen**.   *Volker said he did not eat the cake.*
Uschi sagte, sie **sei** gestern in Berlin **gewesen**.   *Uschi said she was in Berlin yesterday.*

ÜBUNG
26·10

*The new neighbor likes to brag about her life before moving here. Mother tells the family later what she said. Change the following sentences using the past-time subjunctive I. Start the sentence with **Sie sagte**.*

EXAMPLE: Ich habe ein schönes Kleid gekauft.
Sie sagte, sie habe ein schönes Kleid gekauft.

1. Ich habe zehn Pfund abgenommen.

   _____

2. Meine Frisur ist sehr modern.

   _____

3. Ich mache viermal in der Woche Gymnastik.

   _____

4. Ich koche jede Woche eine neue Speise.

   _____

5. Ich backe immer den besten Kuchen.

   _____

6. Unser Wohnzimmer hat einen neuen Teppich.

   _____

7. Anton, mein Sohn, bekommt immer gute Noten.

   _____

8. Gabriela, meine Tochter, ist die schönste in der Klasse.

   _____

9. Mein Mann hat die zweite Lohnerhöhung bekommen.

   _____

10. Mein Vater gibt mir oft Geld.

   _____

Indirect Questions

The subjunctive I is also used in indirect questions. The sentence could be started with **Er fragte**, or with **Er wollte wissen**. The verb is at the end of the main clause.

Er fragte, wieviel das Kind **wisse**. *He asked how much the child knew.*

ÜBUNG
26·11

*Holger has a new girlfriend. His mother wants to know all about her. He is upset about all her questioning and tells his friend about it. Rewrite the following questions using the present-time subjunctive I. Begin the paragraph with **Sie wollte wissen**.*

EXAMPLE: Wie alt ist sie?
Sie wollte wissen, wie alt sie sei.

1. Wie heißt sie? _____

2. Wie sieht sie aus? _____

3. Ist sie intelligent? (ob) _____

4. Wo wohnt sie? _____

5. Wer sind ihre Eltern? _____

6. Was für eine Arbeit hat der Vater? _____

7. Hat die Familie Geld? (ob) _____

8. Was macht sie in ihrer Freizeit? _____

9. Spricht sie gutes Deutsch? (ob) _____

10. Kann sie gut kochen? (ob) _____

sollen in Commands

When reporting a *command*, **sollen** is usually used.

Mach das Bett.   *Make the bed.*
Mutter sagte, ich solle das Bett machen.   *Mother said I should make the bed.*

ÜBUNG
26·12

Michael comes home and tells what his music teacher told him to do. Rewrite the commands, reporting what he was told to do.

EXAMPLE: Spiel nicht so laut.
             Er sagte, ich solle nicht so laut spielen.

1. Übe jeden Tag. _____

2. Sitz gerade. _____

3. Schau nicht auf die Finger. _____

4. Spiel am Ende des Stückes leiser. _____

5. Kauf ein neues Musikheft. _____

Expressing a Wish

When *expressing a wish*, the third person of subjunctive I is used. Some of these wishes are idiomatic in nature and occur mostly in literature or have a religious origin, and they are taken from there to use in speech.

Lang lebe der König!	*Long live the king!*
Gott segne euch!	*God bless you!*

ÜBUNG
26·13

Give the English meaning of the following wishes.

EXAMPLE: Gott segne dich!
             God bless you!

1. Gott sei Dank! _____

2. Dein Wille geschehe! _____

3. Gott behüte dich! _____

4. Dein Reich komme! _____

5. Es lebe die Freiheit! _____

The Brauers receive a letter from Emma telling about her experiences in Germany. Mother is the first to read it and then talks about it. Rewrite the following sentences in the subjunctive I, telling what Mother said. Begin the sentences with **Sie schreibt**. Be careful: some of the sentences should be in the present-time and some in the past-time subjunctive I.

EXAMPLE: Ich bin gut in Frankfurt gelandet.
            Sie schreibt, sie sei gut in Frankfurt gelandet.

1. Ich habe im Flugzeug geschlafen.

   _____

2. Frankfurt ist eine schöne Stadt.

   _____

3. Ich habe die Altstadt besichtigt.

   _____

4. Ich habe das Goethehaus interessant gefunden.

   _____

5. Ich bin nach München gefahren.

   _____

6. Ich war einen ganzen Nachmittag im Englischen Garten.

   _____

7. In den Alpen bin ich zweimal geklettert.

   _____

8. Ich habe viele Souvenirs gekauft.

   _____

9. Ich habe oft Wiener Schnitzel gegessen.

   _____

10. Ich habe Luthers Wartburg in Thüringen interessant gefunden.

    _____

11. Ich habe genug Geld mitgebracht.

    _____

12. Ich habe auch eine Schifffahrt auf dem Rhein gemacht.

    _____

13. Andreas hat auch viel Spaß.

    _____

14. Er hat ein schönes Mädchen kennen gelernt.

_____

15. Sie wohnt in Bonn.

_____

Use and Formation of the Subjunctive II

The more common subjunctive II, or general subjunctive, is used to express conditions, hypotheses, and wishes.

Er hätte genug Geld das Auto zu kaufen.	*He would have enough money to buy the car.*
Die alte Stadt wäre interessanter.	*The old city would be more interesting.*

The Present-Time Subjunctive II

The *present-time subjunctive II* of weak verbs is identical to the past forms of the indicative (active voice). Remember that the present-time subjunctive is also used to express the future, since there is no separate future form.

	lernen	warten
ich	lernte	wartete
du	lerntest	wartetest
er/sie/es	lernte	wartete
wir	lernten	warteten
ihr	lerntet	wartetet
sie/Sie	lernten	warteten

Er meinte immer, er lernte am besten in der Klasse.	*He always thought he was the best student in the class.*
Sie behauptet, wir warteten nicht lange genug.	*She claims we don't wait long enough.*

The present-time subjunctive II forms of mixed verbs are also the same as the past forms of the indicative, except that an umlaut is added when possible.

ich dachte	ich dächte
du wusstest	du wüsstest
es brannte	es brännte

Kannte (**kennen**) does not take an ä but stays kennte.

Wüsstest du wie er heißt?	*Would you know what his name is?*
Kennte er die Frau?	*Would he know the woman?*

The present-time subjunctive II of strong verbs is formed by adding the subjunctive endings **-e**, **-est**, **-e**, **-en**, **-et**, and **-en** to the indicative past tense stem of the verb. If the stem has a vowel of **a**, **o**, or **u**, an umlaut is added.

	bleiben	geben
ich	bliebe	gäbe
du	bliebest	gäbest
er/sie/es	bliebe	gäbe

wir	blieben	gäben
ihr	bliebet	gäbet
sie/Sie	blieben	gäben

	haben	**sein**
ich	hätte	wäre
du	hättest	wärest
er/sie/es	hätte	wäre
wir	hätten	wären
ihr	hättet	wäret
sie/Sie	hätten	wären

The subjunctive verb endings -**est** and -**et** are often contracted to -**st** and -**t**, especially in speech.

du blieb**est**—du blieb**st**   ihr blieb**et**—ihr blieb**t**
du gäb**est**—du gäb**st**   ihr gäb**et**—ihr gäb**t**

Bliebst du länger in Italien,   *Would you stay longer in Italy, if you had*
    wenn du Geld hättest?   *money?*

When a modal verb has an umlaut in the infinitive of the indicative, it also has an umlaut in the present-time subjunctive II.

können   Könntest du morgen kommen?
dürfen   Dürfte er draußen spielen?
sollen   Solltest du nicht ins Bett gehen?

ÜBUNG
26·15

Magda would like to go to the park. Make phrases saying that the following people would like to go to the park as well.

Magda ginge gern.

EXAMPLE: Wir _____ auch gern.
              Wir gingen auch gern.

1. Frau Kohl _____ auch gern.

2. Wir _____ auch gern.

3. Die Mädchen _____ auch gern.

4. Du _____ auch gern.

5. Ihr _____ auch gern.

6. Ich _____ auch gern.

7. Er _____ auch gern.

8. Herr und Frau Bohl _____ auch gern.

Change the following active sentences to the present-time subjunctive II.

EXAMPLE: Ich kann das machen.
Ich könnte das machen.

1. Wir kaufen es gern. _____

2. Wir haben aber kein Geld. _____

3. Mutter muss es uns geben. _____

4. Gibt sie es gern? _____

5. Das weiß ich nicht. _____

6. Die Kinder sagen immer, Vater verdient viel. _____

7. Bringt ihr das Geld dann? _____

8. Wir denken nicht daran. _____

9. Kennt er die neuen Nachbarn? _____

10. Bist du am Wochenende hier? _____

11. Ich soll jetzt gehen. _____

12. Kommst du morgen wieder? _____

13. Wenn du es willst. _____

14. Wir gehen jetzt nach Hause. _____

15. Schreibt ihr uns einen Brief? _____

16. Arbeitest du lange? _____

17. Nein, ich bin zu müde. _____

18. Nennt sie das Kind Rumpelstilzchen? _____

19. Das will ich nicht. _____

20. Er hat es aber gern. _____

Modal Verbs in the Subjunctive II

Subjunctive II modal verbs are often used to form polite questions, requests, or statements.

Könntest du, bitte, die Tür zumachen?	*Could you, please, close the door?*
Dürfte ich, bitte, telefonieren?	*May I telephone, please?*

26·17

Little Jens is sick in bed and has many requests. Make sentences with the cues given in parentheses.

EXAMPLE: (können, haben) ich ein Glas Wasser?
Könnte ich ein Glas Wasser haben?

1. (dürfen, essen) ich ein Stück Schokolade? _____

2. (können, ausmachen) du das Licht? _____

3. (dürfen, fernsehen) ich? _____

4. (können, lesen) der Vater ein Buch? _____

5. (dürfen, spielen) Paul mit mir? _____

26·18

The subjunctive II is also used to express wishes. Lars tells his grandmother what everyone would like for Christmas. Make sentences with the cues given.

EXAMPLE: ich—neues Fahrrad
Ich hätte gern ein neues Fahrrad.

1. Inge—neue Puppe _____

2. die Zwillinge—elektrischen Zug _____

3. der Vater—neuen Pullover _____

4. ich—Fußball _____

5. Peter und ich—viel Schokolade _____

26·19

Luise and her friends stop at a restaurant for refreshments. She orders for everyone. Make sentences with the cues given.

EXAMPLE: Peter—ein Vanilleeis
Peter hätte gern ein Vanilleeis.

1. ich—ein Stück Torte _____

2. Marie—eine Limo _____

3. Hans und Lars—eine Pizza _____

4. Frank, was du? _____

5. Beate und ich—ein Erdbeereis _____

The Past-Time Subjunctive II

The *past-time subjunctive II* is formed by using the subjunctive II form of **sein** (**wäre**) or **haben** (**hätte**) and the past participle of the main verb.

ich hätte gespielt (*I would have played*) ich wäre gegangen (*I would have gone*)
du hättest gespielt   du wär(e)st gegangen
er/sie/es hätte gespielt   er/sie/es wäre gegangen
wir hätten gespielt   wir wären gegangen
ihr hättet gespielt   ihr wäret gegangen
sie/Sie hätten gespielt   sie/Sie wären gegangen

Er hätte gern den Kuchen gegessen.   *He would have liked to eat the cake.*
Sie wären gern in den Park gegangen.   *They would have liked to go to the park.*

ÜBUNG
26·20

Change the following sentences to the past-time subjunctive II.

EXAMPLE: Das ist eine gute Idee.
             Das wäre eine gute Idee gewesen.

1. Er kommt heute nicht. _____

2. Sie nimmt wieder nichts mit. _____

3. Das ist nett. _____

4. Wir haben viel Geld. _____

5. Die Kinder lernen viel. _____

6. Er geht schnell nach Hause. _____

7. Kennt sie die Stadt? _____

8. Ich weiß nichts davon. _____

9. Wir besuchen die Oma oft. _____

10. Er macht die Reise. _____

11. Axel kauft einen neuen Anzug. _____

12. Peter macht nie seine Hausaufgaben. _____

13. Er findet das langweilig. _____

14. Das ärgert den Lehrer. _____

15. Peter spielt aber lieber. _____

Modal Verbs in the Past-Time Subjunctive II

When *modal verbs* are conjugated in the past-time subjunctive II, the modal verb stays in its infinitive form and serves as the past participle. The modal past participle is always in the last position. It follows the infinitive of the main verb.

Er hätte den Kuchen essen **wollen**. *He would have liked to eat the cake.*
Sie hätten in den Park gehen **sollen**. *They should have gone to the park.*

Change the following sentences to the past-time subjunctive II.

EXAMPLE: Sie müsste mehr lernen.
Sie hätte mehr lernen müssen.

1. Emma müsste mehr Geld mitnehmen.

   _____

2. Sie wollte alles sehen.

   _____

3. Andreas wollte mehr Zeit in Deutschland haben.

   _____

4. Sie sollten länger in Deutschland bleiben.

   _____

5. Sie könnten dann mehr sehen.

   _____

6. Ich wollte auch mitfahren.

   _____

7. Ich müsste nicht immer zu Hause bleiben.

   _____

8. Die Reise sollte länger sein.

   _____

9. Sie müssten nicht so früh zurückkommen.

   _____

10. Wolltest du auch eine Reise machen?

    _____

The *würde* Construction

Würden (the subjunctive II form of **werden**) plus an infinitive is often used instead of the subjunctive II form. This is especially true for the present-time subjunctive. The meaning does not change when using the **würde** construction. This construction is especially used when:

1. The subjunctive form of the verb could be interpreted as the indicative past:

   Wenn Anna mehr spielte, lernte sie nicht genug.

A clearer sentence would be:
Wenn Anna mehr spielte, würde sie nicht genug lernen.

2. Use of the subjunctive II verb would be considered awkward:

Wenn das Kind allein stünde, käme die Mutter.
Wenn das Kind allein stehen würde, käme die Mutter.

Very seldom would you use the **würde** construction to replace **hätte**, **wäre**, or the subjunctive II of the modals (**dürfte**, **könnte**, **müsste**, **möchte**, **sollte**, or **wollte**).

ÜBUNG
26·22

*Supply the correct form of **würden** in the following sentences.*

EXAMPLE: Peter _____ mehr Deutsch lernen.
*Peter **würde** mehr Deutsch lernen.*

1. Ilse _____ mehr Deutsch lernen.

2. Ich _____ mehr Deutsch lernen.

3. Du _____ mehr Deutsch lernen.

4. Wir _____ mehr Deutsch lernen.

5. Peter und ich _____ mehr Deutsch lernen.

6. Ihr _____ mehr Deutsch lernen.

7. Herr Lutz, Sie _____ mehr Deutsch lernen.

ÜBUNG
26·23

Andreas and Emma's father had advice for them before they left for Germany.
A. Complete the following sentences using the present-time subjunctive II construction.

EXAMPLE: Es wäre schön, wenn ihr an den Bodensee _____ (fahren).
*Es wäre schön, wenn ihr an den Bodensee **führet**.*

1. Es wäre schön, wenn ihr mehr Zeit _____ (haben).

2. Es wäre besser, wenn ihr nur zwei Koffer _____ (nehmen).

3. Es wäre besser, wenn ihr mehr Deutsch _____ (lernen).

4. Es wäre besser, wenn Emma nicht allein _____ (ausgehen).

5. Es wäre schön, wenn ihr meinen Freund in Duisburg _____ (besuchen).

6. Es wäre besser, wenn Andreas das Geld hier _____ (umtauschen).

7. Es wäre besser, wenn ihr ein Hotelzimmer _____ (reservieren).

8. Es wäre besser, wenn ihr nur Deutsch _____ (sprechen).

9. Es wäre besser, wenn Andreas die Koffer _____ (nehmen).

10. Es wäre sicherer, wenn Emma nie allein _____ (sein).

B. Rewrite the above sentences using the würde construction, if appropriate. Remember that the würde construction is not used to replace hätte, wäre, or the subjunctive II of the modals.

EXAMPLE: Es wäre schön, wenn ihr an den Bodensee führet.
             Es wäre schön, wenn ihr an den Bodensee fahren würdet.

1. _____

2. _____

3. _____

4. _____

5. _____

6. _____

7. _____

8. _____

9. _____

10. _____

ÜBUNG
26·24

*Emma and Andreas's sister is unhappy she could not go to Germany, so she proceeds to say what she would do differently in their place. Use the **würde** construction in the following sentences.*

EXAMPLE: Ich nehme mehr Geld mit.
             Ich würde mehr Geld mitnehmen.

1. Ich packe nur einen Koffer.

   _____

2. Ich fahre auf die Insel Sylt.

   _____

3. Ich kaufe mir neue Kleider.

   _____

4. Ich fahre mit dem Taxi zum Flugplatz.

   _____

5. Ich esse oft Schwarzwälder Torte.

_____

6. Ich reise nach Thüringen.

_____

7. Der Vater schickt mir bestimmt mehr Geld.

_____

8. Meine Freundin und ich gehen jeden Tag spazieren.

_____

9. Meine Reise kostet nicht so viel.

_____

10. Ich übernachte in einer Jugendherberge.

_____

Conditional Sentences

Conditional sentences have two clauses: the **wenn** clause (*if* clause), or condition, and the conclusion. The conditions under which an event mentioned in the conclusion may or may not take place are found in the **wenn** clause.

Wenn er Geld hat, kauft er das Haus.	*If he has money, he buys (will buy) the house.*
Wenn er Geld hätte, würde er das Haus kaufen.	*If he had money, he would buy the house.*

There are three types of conditional sentences: conditions of fact, unreal conditions, and speculation about the past.

Conditions of Fact

These sentences have conditions that can be fulfilled. Use the indicative verb forms in these sentences.

Present

Wenn ich viel lerne, weiß ich viel.	*If I study a lot, I will know a lot.*
Wenn sie genug Geld haben, kaufen sie das Haus.	*If they have enough money, they will buy the house.*

When using the past tense in a conditional sentence of fact, regular or repeated action in the past is implied.

Present

Wenn die Arbeiter Durst hatten, tranken sie Wasser.	*When/whenever the workers were thirsty, they drank water.*
Wenn es heiß war, kaufte sie sich ein Erdbeereis.	*When/whenever it was hot, she bought herself strawberry ice cream.*

ÜBUNG
26·25

Combine the groups of two sentences, making a real condition. Notice the position of the verbs.

EXAMPLE: Es ist kalt. Sie zieht sich warm an.
*Wenn es kalt **ist**, **zieht** sie sich warm an.*

1. Klaus hat Hunger. Er isst sein Pausenbrot.

   _____

2. Ich habe Geld. Ich fahre nach Freudenstadt.

   _____

3. Die Sonne scheint. Die Kinder gehen schwimmen.

   _____

4. Es regnet. Sie gehen nach Hause.

   _____

5. Sie sind müde. Sie gehen ins Bett.

   _____

Unreal Conditions

If the conditions are unreal—meaning that it is possible they could be fulfilled, although there is no guarantee of this happening—the present-time subjunctive II is used. This form is often used to express wishes.

Wenn er nur bald kommen würde!	*If he only came soon!*
Wenn ich viel Geld hätte, könnte ich nach Egypten fahren.	*If I had a lot of money, I could go to Egypt. (It is questionable whether I will ever have enough extra money for this, but it could happen.)*

If two present-time subjunctive II verbs (aside from **haben**, **sein**, and the modals) are used in a conditional sentence, the **würde** construction should be used for clarity. Remember that the subjunctive II of weak verbs is the same as the indicative past form and that using this form could confuse the meaning.

Not: Wenn sie mit mir telefonierte, sagte ich ihr alles.	
But: Wenn sie mit mir telefonierte, würde ich ihr alles sagen.	*If she telephoned me, I would tell her everything.*

Emma's mother gets frustrated with her sometimes. Here she expresses her wishes to her husband. Make sentences using the **würde** construction (except with **haben** or **sein**) with the given cues.

EXAMPLE: nur ihr Zimmer aufräumen
Wenn sie nur ihr Zimmer aufräumen würde.

1. nur nicht so lange am Telefon sprechen

   _____

2. nur mehr zu Hause helfen

   _____

3. nur bessere Noten bekommen

   _____

4. nur nicht so oft in die Disko gehen

   _____

5. nur nicht so viel Geld ausgeben

   _____

6. nur bessere Freunde haben

   _____

7. nur nicht so lange schlafen

   _____

8. sich nur nicht mit der Schwester streiten

   _____

9. nur die Kleider aufhängen

   _____

10. nur die Oma besuchen

   _____

*Emma tells what she would do if certain conditions were fulfilled. Note that the subjunctive II is used in the condition and a **würde** construction is used in the conclusion.*

EXAMPLE: Wenn ich Zeit habe, gehe ich zur Oma.
Wenn ich Zeit hätte, würde ich zur Oma gehen.

1. Wenn ich Geld habe, kaufe ich mir etwas schönes.

   _____

2. Wenn ich Lust habe, gehe ich ins Kino.

   _____

3. Wenn ich ein gutes Buch habe, lese ich.

   _____

4. Wenn das Wetter schön ist, machen meine Freunde und ich einen Ausflug.

   _____

5. Wenn es warm ist, gehen wir schwimmen.

   _____

Speculation About the Past

To speculate how conditions might have been in the past, use the past-time subjunctive II. Remember, the event happened in the past, so the condition can no longer be fulfilled.

Wenn er Geld gehabt hätte, hätte er das Auto gekauft.	*If he had had money, he would have bought the car.* (He didn't have money, so he didn't buy it. End of story.)
Wenn sie hier gewesen wäre, hätte ich mit ihr gesprochen.	*If she had been here, I would have spoken to her.*

Starting with the Conclusion

In all three types of conditions you can start the sentence with the conclusion, followed by the **wenn** clause.

Ich weiß viel, wenn ich viel lerne.
Sie würde telefonieren, wenn sie Zeit hätte.
Ich hätte mit ihr gesprochen, wenn sie hier gewesen wäre.

Omitting *wenn*

Especially in written German, the **wenn** can be omitted. If this is done, the verb comes first in what would have been the **wenn** clause. Usually this is only possible if that clause (the condition, which is the subordinate clause) comes first.

Hätte sie Zeit, telefonierte sie.
Wäre sie hier gewesen, hätte ich mit ihr gesprochen.

*Emma's Oma is not always the happiest person; she likes to talk about how things could have been different. Begin each sentence with **Wenn ich klug gewesen wäre...***

EXAMPLE: ich lerne mehr in der Schule
Wenn ich klug gewesen wäre, hätte ich mehr in der Schule gelernt.

1. ich spare weniger Geld

   _____

2. ich mache mehr Reisen

   _____

3. ich habe weniger Kinder

   _____

4. ich heirate einen reicheren Mann

   _____

5. ich streite mich nicht so viel mit meiner Schwester

   _____

6. ich mache mehr Sport

   _____

7. ich kaufe mir schönere Sachen

   _____

8. ich wohne auf dem Land

   _____

9. ich lerne Auto fahren

   _____

10. ich nehme mir ein Dienstmädchen

   _____

ÜBUNG
26·29

Was würde Emma tun, wenn sie nicht nach Deutschland fahren könnte? *Complete the following sentences with the given cues.*

EXAMPLE: Freunde besuchen
Wenn Emma nicht nach Deutschland fahren könnte, würde sie Freunde besuchen.

1. weinen _____

_____

2. böse sein _____

_____

3. nach Chicago fahren _____

_____

4. in ihrem Zimmer sitzen _____

_____

5. ihre Freundin anrufen _____

_____

ÜBUNG
26·30

Was würden Müllers tun, wenn sie eine Million Euro hätten? *Complete the following sentences with the given cues.*

EXAMPLE: nicht mehr arbeiten
Wenn Müllers eine Million Euro hätten, würden sie nicht mehr arbeiten.

1. ein neues Haus bauen _____

_____

2. nach Australien fliegen _____

_____

3. ein Haus an der Nordsee kaufen _____

_____

4. zwei neue Mercedes kaufen _____

_____

5. keine Geldsorgen haben _____

_____

More on the subjunctive mood

The German subjunctive mood is expressed in two conjugational forms: the *present subjunctive*, which is also called *subjunctive I*, and the *past subjunctive*, which is also called *subjunctive II*. Here the two forms will be referred to by the latter names. Both subjunctive I and II use the same conjugational endings. For the first, second, and third persons singular, they are **-e**, **-est**, and **-e**. For the first, second, and third persons plural, they are **-en**, **-et**, and **-en**. The verb **sein** is the only exception in subjunctive I.

Subjunctive I

In the subjunctive I conjugation, irregularities do not occur. All verbs use their verb stem [infinitive minus **-(e)n**] and add the subjunctive I conjugational endings. For example:

	finden	**können**	**haben**	**werden**	**sein**
ich	finde	könne	habe	werde	sei
du	findest	könnest	habest	werdest	seiest
er	finde	könne	habe	werde	sei
wir	finden	können	haben	werden	seien
ihr	findet	könnet	habet	werdet	seiet
sie	finden	können	haben	werden	seien

Note that a modal auxiliary (**können**) does not deviate from the subjunctive I pattern.

When prefixes are added to verbs, the verbs still conform to this conjugational pattern.

	bekommen	**mitnehmen**
ich	bekomme	nehme mit
du	bekommest	nehmest mit
er	bekomme	nehme mit
wir	bekommen	nehmen mit
ihr	bekommet	nehmet mit
sie	bekommen	nehmen mit

The primary use of the subjunctive I conjugation is with verbs used in *indirect discourse*. Direct discourse is a statement that someone makes and usually is enclosed by quotation marks in writing.

> Mary: "Erik has a test tomorrow."

Indirect discourse is the retelling of what someone has said.

> Mary said that Erik has a test tomorrow.

In the German translation of these sentences, the verb in Mary's statement (*has*) is conjugated in subjunctive I in the indirect discourse sentence.

> Maria: „Erik hat morgen eine Prüfung."
> Maria sagte, dass Erik morgen eine Prüfung **habe**.

Let's look at a couple more examples:

> Erik: „Meine Freundin ist Krankenschwester."   *"My girlfriend is a nurse."*
> Erik sagte, dass seine Freundin Krankenschwester **sei**.

> Der Lehrer: „Kann das Kind Deutsch verstehen?"   *"Can the child understand German?"*
> Der Lehrer fragte, ob das Kind Deutsch verstehen **könne**.

If the clause in indirect discourse is introduced with a present tense verb, the subjunctive I conjugation is not used. For example:

> Erik **sagt**, dass seine Freundin Krankenschwester **ist**.
> Der Lehrer **fragt**, ob das Kind Deutsch **versteht**.

The conjunction **dass** is sometimes omitted in indirect discourse. This means a change in word order.

> Erik sagte, seine Freundin **sei** Krankenschwester.

However, the use of **dass** is more common.

When a yes-no question is asked in direct discourse, the clause with the indirect discourse is introduced by **ob** (*whether, if*). If the question begins with an interrogative word, the clause is introduced by that interrogative word used as a conjunction. For example:

> Sabine: „Lernt sie Mathematik?"   *"Is she learning mathematics?"*
> Sabine fragte, **ob** sie Mathematik lerne.

> Thomas: „**Wo** wohnt der alte Herr?"   *"Where does the old gentleman live?"*
> Thomas fragte, **wo** der alte Herr wohne.

When a statement is made in the past tense or a perfect tense, its structure in indirect discourse is in the form of a present perfect tense verb. For example:

> „Er lernte Deutsch." = Sie sagte, dass er Deutsch **gelernt habe**.
> „Er hat Deutsch gelernt." = Sie sagte, dass er Deutsch **gelernt habe**.
> „Er hatte Deutsch gelernt." = Sie sagte, dass er Deutsch **gelernt habe**.

Complete each sentence with the direct discourse statements provided. Do not change the subject of the sentence in direct discourse.

Der Reporter berichtete (*reported*), dass _____.

1. „Die Kanzlerin macht eine Reise nach Russland."

   _____

2. „Die Touristen sind in der Hauptstadt gewesen."

   _____

3. „Der Dieb ist gestern Abend verhaftet (*arrested*) worden."

   _____

4. „Die deutsche Wirtschaft (*economy*) wird immer stärker."

   _____

Die Dame hat gefragt, ob _____.

5. „Hat er das Problem verstanden?"

   _____

6. „Will Ihr Sohn auch spielen?"

   _____

7. „Sind die Gäste noch im Wohnzimmer?"

   _____

8. „Musst du so laut singen?"

   _____

Jemand fragte, _____.

9. „Wo arbeitet Frau Keller jetzt?"

   _____

10. „Warum hat Felix so viele Schulden (*debts*)?"

    _____

11. „Wohin fährt dein Bruder?"

    _____

12. „Wie viel Geld gibt der reiche Herr aus?"

    _____

Sie sagte, dass _____.

13. „Lars ist wieder sehr krank geworden."

_____

14. „Die laute Musik stört (*disturbs*) sie."

_____

15. „Ihr Mann wird seinen Pass vergessen."

_____

16. „Das Unwetter (*storm*) soll bald aufhören."

_____

Der Reiseführer hat uns erzählt, dass _____.

17. „Die alte Burg ist vor hundert Jahren zerstört worden."

_____

18. „Der letzte König hat in der Burg gewohnt."

_____

19. „Ein neues Theater wird neben dem Rathaus gebaut."

_____

20. „Man kann im Garten spazieren."

_____

ÜBUNG
27·2

Complete each sentence with the direct discourse statements provided. Do not change the subject of the sentence in direct discourse.

Frau Schneider teilte mit (*informed*), dass _____.

1. „Mein Bruder war vor einem Jahr in Afrika."

_____

2. „Der neue Professor kam aus Amerika."

_____

3. „Der Gast hat noch nicht gefrühstückt."

_____

4. „Die Ausländer sind zu lange im Museum geblieben."

_____

5. „Das Mädchen hatte zu wenig Geld."

_____

Der Richter hat geschrieben, dass _____.

6. „Niemand durfte dieses Gebiet betreten (*enter this area*)."

_____

7. „Der Fluss überschwemmte viel Land."

_____

8. „Meine Frau gewöhnte sich (*became accustomed*) nicht an die Seeluft."

_____

9. „Der Verbrecher (*criminal*) hat seine Rechte (*rights*) verloren."

_____

10. „Es gab nichts Schöneres als den Anblick der Berge (*view of the mountains*)."

_____

Subjunctive II

The subjunctive II conjugation is derived from the past tense of a verb. Regular verbs in subjunctive II resemble their regular past tense form. If the past tense form of the verb is irregular and has an umlaut vowel, an umlaut is added in subjunctive II. Let's look at some examples.

	Regular verb	Irregular verbs			
	sagen	gehen	kommen	haben	sein
ich	sagte	ginge	käme	hätte	wäre
du	sagtest	gingest	kämest	hättest	wärest
er	sagte	ginge	käme	hätte	wäre
wir	sagten	gingen	kämen	hätten	wären
ihr	sagtet	ginget	kämet	hättet	wäret
sie	sagten	gingen	kämen	hätten	wären

Modal auxiliaries that have an umlaut in the infinitive will also have an umlaut in the subjunctive II conjugation. Those without an umlaut do not have one in subjunctive II. For example:

	können	müssen	wollen	sollen
ich	könnte	müsste	wollte	sollte
du	könntest	müsstest	wolltest	solltest
er	könnte	müsste	wollte	sollte
wir	könnten	müssten	wollten	sollten
ihr	könntet	müsstet	wolltet	solltet
sie	könnten	müssten	wollten	sollten

Verbs that have a mixed conjugation are unique in that some of them break the subjunctive II pattern.

	brennen	kennen	rennen	senden	bringen	denken
ich	brennte	kennte	rennte	sandte	brächte	dächte
du	brenntest	kenntest	renntest	sandtest	brächtest	dächtest
er	brennte	kennte	rennte	sandte	brächte	dächte
wir	brennte	kennten	rennten	sandten	brächten	dächten
ihr	brennte	kenntet	renntet	sandtet	brächtet	dächtet
sie	brennten	kennten	rennten	sandten	brächten	dächten

ÜBUNG
27·3

Give the subjunctive I and subjunctive II conjugations of each verb.

1. schlafen

	subjunctive I	subjunctive II
ich	_____	_____
du	_____	_____
er	_____	_____
wir	_____	_____
ihr	_____	_____
sie	_____	_____

2. reisen

	subjunctive I	subjunctive II
ich	_____	_____
du	_____	_____
er	_____	_____
wir	_____	_____
ihr	_____	_____
sie	_____	_____

3. austrinken (*finish drinking*)

ich	_____	_____
du	_____	_____
er	_____	_____
wir	_____	_____
ihr	_____	_____
sie	_____	_____

4. vergessen

_____	_____
_____	_____
_____	_____
_____	_____
_____	_____
_____	_____

5. wissen

ich   _____   _____

du   _____   _____

er   _____   _____

wir   _____   _____

ihr   _____   _____

sie   _____   _____

6. aufmachen

_____   _____

_____   _____

_____   _____

_____   _____

_____   _____

_____   _____

7. denken

ich   _____   _____

du   _____   _____

er   _____   _____

wir   _____   _____

ihr   _____   _____

sie   _____   _____

8. abfahren

_____   _____

_____   _____

_____   _____

_____   _____

_____   _____

_____   _____

9. erwarten (*expect, await*)

ich   _____   _____

du   _____   _____

er   _____   _____

wir   _____   _____

ihr   _____   _____

sie   _____   _____

10. dürfen

_____   _____

_____   _____

_____   _____

_____   _____

_____   _____

_____   _____

The subjunctive II conjugation replaces the subjunctive I conjugation in indirect discourse *when the subjunctive I verb is identical to the indicative.* For example:

> Er sagte, dass seine Kinder zu Hause **bleiben**   *He said that his children are staying home.*
> (identical to indicative **bleiben**).

> Er sagte, dass seine Kinder zu Hause **blieben** (subjunctive II replaces subjunctive I).

This occurs most often in the first-person singular and the first- and third-person plural.

> Er sagte, dass ich zu schnell **führe** (replaces **fahre**).   *He said that I drive too fast.*
> Er sagte, dass wir gut **tanzten** (replaces **tanzen**).   *He said that we dance well.*
> Er sagte, dass sie keine Zeit **hätten** (replaces **haben**).   *He said that they have no time.*

ÜBUNG

27·4

Complete each sentence with the direct discourse statements provided. Do not change the subject of the sentence in direct discourse.

Der Arzt fragte, ob _____ .

1. „Haben sie ein Rezept (*prescription*) dafür?"

   _____

2. „Habe ich einen Preis gewonnen?"

   _____

3. „Werden wir unsere Verwandten besuchen?"

   _____

4. „Sind die Sportler (*athletes*) schon auf dem Sportplatz?"

   _____

5. „Spreche ich nur Deutsch?"

   _____

Herr Benz antwortete, dass _____ .

6. „Die Männer machen Überstunden (*overtime*)."

   _____

7. „Diese Bücher gehören (*belong to*) ihm."

   _____

8. „Die älteren Schüler wandern im Wald."

   _____

9. „Sonne und Meer (*sea*) machen jeden Menschen (*person*) gesund."

   _____

10. „Wir werden um vier Uhr abreisen."

    _____

Subjunctive II in spoken language

The subjunctive I conjugation is used most often in indirect discourse in formal language, particularly in writing. It is more common to use subjunctive II conjugations in the spoken language. For example:

WRITTEN LANGUAGE	SPOKEN LANGUAGE
Sie sagte, dass ihr Mann krank **sei**. *She said that her husband is sick.*	Sie sagte, dass ihr Mann krank **wäre**.

ÜBUNG
27·5

Complete each sentence with the direct discourse statements provided as they would be said in the spoken language. Do not change the subject of the sentence in direct discourse.

Der neue Student hat gefragt, _____.

1. „Woher wissen wir darüber?"

   _____

2. „Warum hat sie die Vorträge (*lectures*) nicht besucht?"

   _____

3. „Was kann man mit 200 Euro kaufen?"

   _____

4. „Wie lange hat das Theaterstück (*play*) gedauert (*lasted*)?"

   _____

5. „Wem willst du diesen alten Laptop schenken?"

   _____

Doktor Frank erzählte, dass _____.

6. „Seine Geschichte war total richtig."

   _____

7. „Die Studentin aus Frankreich ist leider durchgefallen (*failed*)."

   _____

8. „Viele Einwohner des Dorfes (*residents of the village*) werden dadurch krank werden."

   _____

9. „Er glaubte dem Diplomaten aus Asien nicht."

_____

10. „Sein Sohn kam mit dem Präsidenten ins Gespräch (*conversation*)."

_____

Subjunctive II with **wenn**-clauses

Another important use of subjunctive II is in a so-called **wenn**-clause (*if-clause*). This kind of clause expresses a *wish* or a *desired outcome*. For example, in English:

> *If only my brother were home from Afghanistan.*
> *If you could have seen how she looked in that dress.*

English frequently adds *only* to *if*-clauses. German does not have to include **nur**.
Verbs in German **wenn**-clauses are conjugated in subjunctive II. For example:

Wenn Onkel Heinz nicht so krank **wäre**!	*If Uncle Heinz were not so sick.*
Wenn es wärmer gewesen **wäre**!	*If only it had been warmer.*

The conjunction **wenn** is often omitted from the sentence, but the meaning remains the same. Modern English tends not to omit *if*.

Hätte ich nur mehr Zeit zu Hause!	*If I only had more time at home.*
Wäre meine Frau noch am Leben!	*If my wife were only still alive.*

Wenn is also used to introduce a clause that expresses an *unreal or desired condition*, followed by a clause that indicates what the *result* would be if that condition were achieved. Let's look at a couple of English examples first because English has a similar structure:

UNREAL OR DESIRED CONDITION	RESULT
If she would marry me,	*I would be the happiest of men.*
If the rain would stop,	*the children could go out and play.*

It is possible to place the *if-clause* in the second position. For example:

RESULT	UNREAL OR DESIRED CONDITION
He would buy her a necklace	*if he had a bit more money.*

Now let's look at some German examples. Note that the verbs in both clauses are conjugated in subjunctive II. In the result clause, the auxiliary **würde** accompanies an infinitive and most often means *would*. However, if there already is another auxiliary (**haben**, **sein**, **werden**, or modal auxiliary) in the clause, **würde** can be omitted.

Wenn sie mich wirklich **liebte, würde** ich sehr froh sein.	*If she really loved me, I would be very happy.*
Wenn Thomas nach Hause **käme, würde** sie sich sehr freuen.	*If Thomas came home, she would be so glad.*
Wenn ich ein bisschen älter gewesen **wäre, hätte** ich ein Auto kaufen können.	*If I had been a little older, I would have been able to buy a car.*

Wenn das Unwetter gefährlich (*dangerous*)   *If the thunderstorm became dangerous,*
   wäre, **müssten** die Kinder zu Hause   *the children would have to remain home.*
   bleiben.

The word **so** often introduces the result clause.

Wenn sie mich wirklich liebte, **so** würde ich mich sehr freuen.

*Using the phrases provided, create original **wenn**-clauses.*

EXAMPLE   (intelligenter sein) *Wenn er nur intelligenter wäre!*

1. (schneller arbeiten) _____

2. (reich sein) _____

3. (einen guten Job haben) _____

4. (Eltern besuchen können) _____

5. (mich lieben) _____

*Combine the pairs of sentences, making the first sentence a **wenn**-clause.*

EXAMPLE   Sie kommt nach Hause. Ich freue mich darüber.

   Wenn sie nach Hause käme, würde ich mich darüber freuen.

1. Martin spricht Deutsch. Er kann mit seinem Urgroßvater (*great-grandfather*) sprechen.

   _____

2. Sie ist damals (*then, back then*) gesund gewesen. Sie hat den Arzt nicht gebraucht.

   _____

3. Lars hat es gewusst. Er hat nicht gefragt.

   _____

4. Wir gewinnen im Lotto (*lottery*). Wir kaufen ein neues Haus in der Stadt.

   _____

5. Er kann ihr helfen. Sie ist sehr dankbar (*grateful*).

   _____

6. Du hast Flügel (*wings*). Du kannst wie ein Vogel (*bird*) fliegen.

   _____

7. Erik hat den Bürgermeister getroffen. Er hat mit ihm darüber gesprochen.

   _____

8. Sie arbeiten mehr. Sie verdienen mehr Geld.

   _____

9. Das Wetter ist schlecht gewesen. Ich bin nicht aufs Land gefahren.

   _____

10. Die Studentin ist aufmerksam (*attentive, careful*). Sie macht keine Fehler (*mistakes*).

    _____

There are a few verbs that make an irregular change in subjunctive II. They are:

INFINITIVE	SUBJUNCTIVE II
empfehlen (*recommend*)	empföhle (*also* empfähle)
helfen (*help*)	hülfe (*also* hälfe)
stehen (*stand*)	stünde (*also* stände)
sterben (*die*)	stürbe
verstehen (*understand*)	verstünde
werfen (*throw*)	würfe

Subjunctive II with **als ob**

Another conjunction that requires the use of subjunctive II is **als ob** (*as if*). **Als ob** can also be said as **als wenn**. Let's look at a couple examples in English, which uses this conjunction in the same way as German:

> *She acts as if she were the brightest in the class.*
> *He hobbled as if he had injured his foot.*

Notice that the subjunctive form of the verb is also used in the English examples.

In German, the verb in the **als ob**–clause is conjugated in subjunctive II and stands at the end of the clause. For example:

Sie tut so, **als ob** sie am schnellsten laufen **könnte**.	*She acts as if she could run the fastest.*
Der Mann redete, **als ob** er alles **wüsste**.	*The man talked as if he knew everything.*
Der Junge sagte nichts, **als ob** er stumm geworden **wäre**.	*The boy said nothing as if he had become mute.*

Complete each sentence with the sentences in parentheses.

EXAMPLE   Sie tut so, als ob _____.

(Sie kennt mich nicht.) *Sie tut so, als ob sie mich nicht kennte.*

Der Gast machte ein Gesicht, als ob _____.

1. (Die Suppe schmeckt [*tastes*] nicht gut.)

   _____

2. (Er ist sehr traurig [*sad*]).

   _____

3. (Er versteht sie falsch.)

   _____

4. (Der Gastgeber [*host*] ist unhöflich gewesen.)

   _____

5. (Das Essen ist zu scharf [*spicy*].)

   _____

Mein Bruder führt ein Leben [*conducts his life*], als wenn _____.

6. (Er ist reich geworden.)

   _____

7. (Unser Vater ist Millionär.)

   _____

8. (Man kann von Wein und Bier leben.)

   _____

9. (Seine Gesundheit [*health*] kann nie ein Ende haben.)

   _____

10. (Er hat keine Freunde mehr.)

   _____

The subjunctive mood

The subjunctive mood is often avoided in modern English by many English speakers. The subjunctive mood is still an important part of the language and needs to be carefully considered in order to write good German sentences.

Subjunctive conjugations

There are two basic conjugations in the German subjunctive: One is called *subjunctive I* or *the present subjunctive* and the other is called *subjunctive II* or *the past subjunctive*. The terms *subjunctive I* and *subjunctive II* will be used here.

The following conjugational endings are basic to both forms of the subjunctive:

ich	-e	wir	-en
du	-est	ihr	-et
er/sie/es	-e	Sie/sie	-en

But subjunctive I applies them to the stem of the infinitive, and subjunctive II applies them to a past tense form. Let's look at some examples:

Suchen (*to look for*) is a regular verb. The subjunctive I conjugation has only a slight difference from the indicative present tense conjugation. And subjunctive II is identical to the indicative past tense conjugation:

	SUBJUNCTIVE I	SUBJUNCTIVE II
ich	suche	suchte
du	suchest	suchtest
er	suche	suchte
wir	suchen	suchten
ihr	suchet	suchtet
sie	suchen	suchten

Laufen (*to run*) is an irregular verb. Both subjunctive I and II are different in some degree from the indicative conjugation:

	SUBJUNCTIVE I	SUBJUNCTIVE II
ich	laufe	liefe
du	laufest	liefest
er	laufe	liefe
wir	laufen	liefen
ihr	laufet	liefet
sie	laufen	liefen

Kommen (*to come*) is also an irregular verb. But its irregular past tense form (**kam**) has an umlaut vowel (**a, o, u**). When an irregular verb has an umlaut vowel, its subjunctive II forms will require an umlaut:

	SUBJUNCTIVE I	SUBJUNCTIVE II
ich	komme	käme
du	kommest	kämest
er	komme	käme
wir	kommen	kämen
ihr	kommet	kämet
sie	kommen	kämen

Kennen (*to know*) is an irregular verb that has a vowel change in the past tense and also has the past tense suffix **-te** (**kannte**). When this verb is conjugated in subjunctive II, the vowel change is avoided. This also occurs with other verbs in this category, such as **nennen** (*to name*) and **brennen** (*to burn*):

	SUBJUNCTIVE I	SUBJUNCTIVE II
ich	kenne	kennte
du	kennest	kenntest
er	kenne	kennte
wir	kennen	kennten
ihr	kennet	kenntet
sie	kennen	kennten

Denken (*to think*) is another irregular verb that has a vowel change in the past tense and also has the past tense suffix **-te** (**dachte**). When this verb is conjugated in subjunctive II, the vowel change is maintained and an umlaut is added. This also occurs with other verbs in this category, such as **bringen** (*to bring*) and **wissen** (*to know*):

	SUBJUNCTIVE I	SUBJUNCTIVE II
ich	denke	dächte
du	denkest	dächtest
er	denke	dächte
wir	denken	dächten
ihr	denket	dächtet
sie	denken	dächten

Modals and the umlaut

Müssen (*to have to*) and other modal auxiliaries that have an umlaut in the infinitive keep the umlaut in subjunctive II. Modals that do not have an umlaut in the infinitive, e.g., **wollen** (*to want*), do not have one in subjunctive II:

	MÜSSEN	WOLLEN
ich	müsse/müsste	wolle/wollte
du	müssest/müsstest	wollest/wolltest
er	müsse/müsste	wolle/wollte
wir	müssen/müssten	wollen/wollten
ihr	müsset/müsstet	wollet/wolltet
sie	müssen/müssten	wollen/wollten

The auxiliaries **sein** (*to be*), **haben** (*to have*), and **werden** (*shall, will*) play an important role in tense formation. Let's look at their subjunctive I and II conjugations:

	SEIN	HABEN	WERDEN
ich	sei/wäre	habe/hätte	werde/würde
du	seiest/wärest	habest/hättest	werdest/würdest
er	sei/wäre	habe/hätte	werde/würde
wir	seien/wären	haben/hätten	werden/würden
ihr	seiet/wäret	habet/hättet	werdet/würdet
sie	seien/wären	haben/hätten	werden/würden

Indirect discourse

Indirect discourse is the retelling of what someone else has said or asked. In *spoken* German, there is a tendency to use a subjunctive II conjugation in indirect discourse:

Er sagte, dass Frau Schmidt krank wäre.   *He said that Ms. Schmidt was sick.*

But in *written* German, sentences in indirect discourse more frequently conjugate verbs in subjunctive I:

Er sagte, dass Frau Schmidt krank sei.   *He said that Ms. Schmidt was sick.*

This use of the subjunctive I and subjunctive II conjugations occurs with both *indirect discourse* and *indirect questions*. For example:

Der Redner sagte, dass der globale Klimawandel noch ein Problem sei.   *The speaker said that global warming was still a problem.*

Die Zeitung berichtete, dass der Präsident nach Berlin fliegen werde.   *The newspaper reported that the president would fly to Berlin.*

Herr Benz fragte, ob ihre Mannschaft gewonnen habe.   *Mr. Benz asked whether their team had won.*

sagen + dass + subjunctive I verb → indirect discourse

fragen + ob + subjunctive I verb → indirect question

When the subjunctive I conjugation is identical to the indicative present tense (for the verb **haben**, for instance, where the subjunctive I, **wir haben**, is identical to the indicative, **wir haben**), use the subjunctive II conjugation (**wir hätten**) in place of the subjunctive I conjugation. For example:

Karl erzählte, dass die Kinder im Garten (spielen) spielten.   *Karl said that the children were playing in the garden.*

Sie fragte, ob sie genug Geld (haben) hätten.   *She asked whether they had enough money.*

Use **ob** (*whether, if*) to introduce indirect discourse questions that can be answered with **ja** or **nein**:

Kann er verstehen? (Ja, er kann verstehen.)   *Can he understand? (Yes, he can understand.)*

Erik fragte, ob er verstehen könne.   *Erik asked whether he could understand.*

If a question is posed using an interrogative word, that interrogative word becomes the conjunction in indirect discourse and a subjunctive I conjugation is required. For example:

Wo wohnt er jetzt?
Er fragte, wo er jetzt wohne.   *He asked where he was living now.*
Warum ist sie wieder krank geworden?
Er fragte, warum sie wieder krank geworden sei.   *He asked why she had gotten sick again.*
Wie viel Geld brauchen sie?
Er fragte, wie viel Geld sie brauchten.   *He asked how much money they needed.*

It is important to consider the tense of a verb in direct discourse. The past tense form of the subjunctive I conjugation in indirect discourse is not identical to the indicative past tense form. For example:

Present tense:	„Er singt sehr gut."	
Indirect discourse:	Sabine sagte, dass er sehr gut singe.	*Sabine said that he sings very well.*
Past tense:	„Er sang sehr gut."	

or

Present perfect tense:	„Er hat sehr gut gesungen."	
Indirect discourse:	Sabine sagte, dass er sehr gut gesungen habe.	*Sabine said that he had sung very well.*
Future tense:	„Er wird sehr gut singen."	
Indirect discourse:	Sabine sagte, dass er sehr gut singen werde.	*Sabine said that he would sing very well.*

Direct discourse verbs in the past or perfect tenses are formed like present perfect conjugations when they are reported in indirect discourse:

er sang	→	er habe gesungen
er hat gesungen	→	er habe gesungen
er reiste	→	er sei gereist
er ist gereist	→	er sei gereist

ÜBUNG
27·9

*Fill in the blanks with the subjunctive I and subjunctive II third person singular (**er**) conjugation of the verbs and verb phrases provided.*

EXAMPLE: tun   <u>tue</u>   <u>täte</u>

1. helfen   _____   _____

2. bleiben   _____   _____

3. besuchen   _____   _____

4. mitbringen   _____   _____

5. sein gekommen   _____   _____

6. werden sprechen   _____   _____

7. müssen lachen   _____   _____

8. essen   _____   _____

9. nennen   _____   _____

10. werden gefunden werden   _____   _____

Complete each line of indirect discourse with four original phrases, using the verbal signals given.

EXAMPLE: Er sagte, dass _____.

kaufen Er sagte, dass er einen neuen Wagen gekauft habe.

1. Der Reporter berichtete, dass _____.

    a. küssen _____

    b. stehlen _____

    c. regieren _____

    d. bleiben _____

2. Professor Benz fragte, ob _____.

    a. schreiben _____

    b. finden _____

    c. sich benehmen _____

    d. zerstören _____

3. Sie teilte mit, dass _____.

    a. werden bestraft _____

    b. müssen verteidigen _____

    c. können bauen _____

    d. haben gesehen _____

4. Frau Kamps erzählte, dass _____.

    a. imponieren _____

    b. ausgeben _____

    c. verbessern _____

    d. angreifen _____

Als ob, als wenn

The subjunctive II conjugation has another function besides being the preferred conjugation in German conversational indirect discourse. It is also used after the conjunctions **als ob** and **als wenn** (*as if*) and is an important element of writing good sentences:

Martin tut so, als ob er alles wüsste.	*Martin acts as if he knew everything.*
Sie spricht, als wenn ich ein dummes Kind wäre.	*She speaks as if I were a stupid child.*

With the conjunctions **als ob** and **als wenn**, just as with other subordinating conjunctions such as **dass** and **ob**, the conjugated verb in the subordinating clause is the final element.

ÜBUNG
27·11

*Complete each sentence three times, each time introducing a subordinating clause with **als ob**.*

EXAMPLE:
a. Der Torwart spielte, <u>als ob er krank wäre.</u>

b. Der Torwart spielte, <u>als ob er nicht laufen könnte.</u>

c. Der Torwart spielte, <u>als ob das Tor schon verteidigt wäre.</u>

1. a. Meine Schwester tut so, _____.

   b. _____

   c. _____

2. a. Der alte Mann lacht, _____.

   b. _____

   c. _____

3. a. Die Kinder singen, _____.

   b. _____

   c. _____

4. a. Meine Mutter weinte, _____.

   b. _____

   c. _____

5. a. Herr Keller spricht, _____.

   b. _____

   c. _____

Wenn

The subordinating conjunction **wenn** (*if*) also requires a verb with a subjunctive II conjugation in the clause that follows it. Again, since **wenn** is a subordinating conjunction, the verb in the subordinate clause will be the last element in the sentence.

Clauses that are introduced by **wenn** suggest a *wish* and can often stand alone without a main clause. The conjunction can be omitted from the sentence and presumed to be understood. In that case, the conjugated verb begins the sentence. For example:

Wenn wir nur mehr Geld hätten!   *If only we had more money!*
Hätten wir nur mehr Geld!
Wenn er nicht so jung gestorben wäre!   *If he hadn't died so young!*
Wäre er nicht so jung gestorben!
Wenn ich sie doch nicht verlassen hätte! *If only I hadn't left her!*
Hätte ich sie doch nicht verlassen!

Notice that the words **doch** and **nur** are often added to these sentences for emphasis.

*Use the information in the sentence provided to form a wish statement with **wenn**. Then rewrite the sentence, omitting **wenn**.*

EXAMPLE: Er ist nicht gesund.

     a. <u>Wenn er doch gesund wäre!</u>

     b. <u>Wäre er doch gesund!</u>

1. Ihr seid nicht bei mir.

    a. _____

    b. _____

2. Das Kind ist nicht fleißig.

    a. _____

    b. _____

3. Der arme Mann ist so unglücklich.

    a. _____

    b. _____

4. Ich kann ihnen nicht helfen.

    a. _____

    b. _____

5. Du hast so wenig Glück gehabt.

    a. _____

    b. _____

Subordinating clauses

Of course, you can also use a subordinate **wenn**-clause together with a main clause. In such cases, the **wenn**-clause sets a *condition* for the achievement of the action in the main clause: *If this condition existed, then this would occur.* In sentences of this type, a subjunctive II conjugation is used in both the **wenn**-clause and the main clause. When there is only one verb in the main clause, there is a tendency to use **würde** and an infinitive. For example, consider the following sentences with a condition set in the present:

Wenn es nicht so weit wäre, ginge ich   *If it weren't so far, I'd go there on foot.*
   zu Fuß dorthin.
Wenn es nicht so weit wäre, würde ich
   zu Fuß dorthin gehen.

Wenn wir genug Geld hätten, dann kauften wir ein neues Auto.	*If we had enough money, we'd buy a new car.*
Wenn wir genug Geld hätten, dann würden wir ein neues Auto kaufen.	

wenn-clause with subjunctive II verb + main clause with subjunctive II verb
Wenn es nicht so weit wäre, + führen wir dorthin.
If it weren't so far, we'd drive there.

or

wenn-clause with subjunctive II verb + main clause with würde + infinitive
Wenn es nicht so weit wäre, + würden wir dorthin + fahren.
If it weren't so far, we'd drive there.

If the main clause has more than one verb form in it, such as a modal and an infinitive, **würde** is not used:

Wenn sie hier wäre, könnte sie uns helfen.	*If she were here, she could help us.*
Wenn er älter wäre, müsste er nicht zur Schule gehen.	*If he were older, he wouldn't have to go to school.*

The emphasis of sentences such as these can be shifted by changing the positions of the **wenn**-clause and the main clause:

Wenn sie uns nicht um Hilfe bäte, könnten wir ihr nicht helfen.	*If she wouldn't ask us for help, we couldn't help her.*
Wir könnten ihr nicht helfen, wenn sie uns nicht um Hilfe bäte.	*We couldn't help her if she wouldn't ask us for help.*

ÜBUNG
27·13

Complete each sentence by setting a condition in the present.

EXAMPLE: Wenn ich mehr Zeit hätte, würde ich meiner Mutter helfen.

1. _____, würden wir in die Stadt fahren.

2. _____, könnten die Jungen im Garten spielen.

3. _____, würde ich in Hamburg übernachten.

4. _____, würde sie aufhören zu weinen.

Now complete each sentence by providing the main clause of the sentence.

5. Wenn Erik reicher wäre, _____.

6. Wenn Onkel Hans das Klavier spielen könnte, _____.

7. Wenn Frau Benz ihn kennte, _____.

8. Wenn sie auf dem Balkon stünden, _____.

It is possible to form sentences such as these with the condition set in the past. This requires a verb structure consisting of **haben** or **sein** plus a past participle. Since there is more than one verb form in the structure, **würde** is not used:

Wenn es nicht so weit gewesen wäre, wären wir zu Fuß dorthin gegangen.	*If it hadn't been so far, we would have gone there on foot.*
Wenn wir genug Geld gehabt hätten, dann hätten wir ein neues Auto gekauft.	*If we had had enough money, we would have bought a new car.*

ÜBUNG
27·14

Complete each sentence by setting a condition in the past.

EXAMPLE: <u>Wenn ich mehr Zeit gehabt hätte,</u> hätte ich meiner Mutter geholfen.

1. _____, wären wir nach München gefahren.

2. _____, hätte er länger bleiben können.

3. _____, wäre das Kind schneller gesund geworden.

4. _____, hätte ich ihre Rede verstanden.

Now complete each sentence by providing the main clause of the sentence.

5. Wenn Sonja nicht krank gewesen wäre, _____.

6. Wenn das Wetter besser geworden wäre, _____.

7. Wenn ich einen neuen Laptop gekauft hätte, _____.

8. Wenn das Baby hätte schlafen können, _____.

ÜBUNG
27·15

Using the verb cues provided, write original sentences in the conditional. If the verb cues are infinitives, form the condition in the present. If the verb cues are provided with an auxiliary and participle, form the condition in the past.

EXAMPLE: tanzen / sich freuen

<u>Wenn Andrea mit mir tanzte, würde ich mich sehr freuen.</u>

haben getanzt / haben sich gefreut

<u>Wenn Andrea mit mir getanzt hätte, hätte ich mich sehr gefreut.</u>

1. kommen / sein

_____

2. sein gekommen / sein gewesen

_____

3. haben geholfen / sein gewesen

   _____

4. haben gewusst / haben gefragt

   _____

5. sein / machen

   _____

6. sein / sein

   _____

7. haben / haben

   _____

8. sein gefahren / haben bleiben müssen

   _____

9. sein gewesen / sein gegangen

   _____

10. sein / schwimmen gehen

   _____

Building sentences

Declarative sentences and word order

Declarative sentences in both English and German consist of a subject and a predicate. In German, the subject is in the nominative case, and the verb in the predicate is conjugated appropriately for the subject and in a specific tense:

> subject + verb + predicate
> Karl + singt + gut.
> *Karl sings well.*

In the example above, the subject is **Karl** and the verb **singt** is conjugated in the present tense for the third person singular subject. This basic structure is used in great abundance in the language and can be modified in a variety of ways. Nonetheless, its simple formula is *subject plus predicate*. If one of those elements is missing, you don't have a sentence.

> Niemand kann ihn verstehen.　　*No one can understand him.*

And still others can be written in the passive voice:

> Deutsch wird hier gesprochen.　　*German is spoken here.*

In other words, a declarative sentence can take many forms.

Let's look at a series of sentences composed in this way. Take note of the subjects, the variety of verb types in the predicate, and the various tenses that can be used in declarative sentences. Many sentences are composed of a present perfect tense verb and the auxiliary **haben**:

> Karin hat in Leipzig gewohnt.　　*Karin lived in Leipzig.*

Remember that the present perfect tense is the more common form to use to describe an action in the past. The German simple past tense is used more often in a narrative. But both forms can be translated into English in the same way.

> Er hat an der Ecke gewartet.　　*He waited on the corner.*
> Er wartete an der Ecke.　　*He waited on the corner.*

Many are composed of a present perfect tense verb and the auxiliary **sein**:

> Sie sind nach Kanada　　*They emigrated to Canada.*
> 　ausgewandert.

The future tense usually requires the auxiliary **werden**:

> Die Kinder werden im Garten spielen.　*The children will play in the garden.*

Others can be a combination of a modal auxiliary and an infinitive.

Rewrite the following declarative sentences in the missing tenses.

1. Present   Martin spricht kein Englisch.

    Past   a. _____

    Present perfect   b. _____

    Future   c. _____

2. Present   a. _____

    Past   b. _____

    Present perfect   c. _____

    Future   Ich werde es machen können.

3. Present   a. _____

    Past   b. _____

    Present perfect   Eine Schlange hat den Frosch gefressen.

    Future   c. _____

4. Present   a. _____

    Past   Über dem Wald flogen viele Vögel.

    Present perfect   b. _____

    Future   c. _____

Negation

Declarative sentences do not always make positive statements. They can be made negative by adding a negative word to the sentence or by changing a positive subject to a negative subject.

The most common way to negate a sentence is by the addition of the adverb **nicht** (*not*):

Karl singt gut.	*Karl sings well.*
Karl singt nicht gut.	*Karl doesn't sing well.*

German usually places **nicht** in front of the element that is negated. However, if that element is the verb itself, **nicht** follows the conjugated form or stands between the auxiliary and the corresponding infinitive or participle. **Nicht** also follows an adverb or adverbial phrase that describes *time* or *place* or an object that is in the *accusative case*:

Es geht nicht.	*That won't work.*
Sie sind nicht zu Hause gewesen.	*They weren't at home.*
Er konnte gestern Nacht nicht schlafen.	*He couldn't sleep last night.*
Sie kennt den Mann nicht.	*She doesn't know the man.*

Nicht precedes a prepositional phrase or an adverbial that describes the *manner* in which something was done:

> **subject + verb + nicht + prepositional phrase**
> Sie + fahren + nicht + nach Hause.
> *They're not driving home.*

English often requires the auxiliary *do/does* when negating. This does not occur in German:

Sie warten nicht auf Katrin.	*They **don't** wait for Katrin.*
Er versteht nicht.	*He **doesn't** understand.*
Onkel Fritz kommt nicht.	*Uncle Fritz isn't coming.*

When the English verb *to be* is the negated verb, a form *do/does* is not used. When negating a noun, **kein** (*no, not any*) is used:

> **kein + noun**
> keine + Bücher
> *no/not any books*

Ich habe kein Geld.	*I don't have any money.*
Jack kennt keine Deutschen.	*Jack doesn't know any Germans.*
Es dauert keine fünf Minuten.	*It won't last more than five minutes.*

ÜBUNG
28·2

*Rewrite each sentence, negating the underlined element with **nicht**.*

EXAMPLE: Sie laufen in den Garten.
            Sie laufen nicht in den Garten.

1. Das ist das beste Buch.

   _____

2. Sie ist am Nachmittag angekommen.

   _____

3. Ihr Mann ist bei einem Unglück umgekommen.

   _____

4. Er hat helfen wollen.

   _____

5. Frau Schneider hat sich wohl gefühlt.

   _____

6. Die Studenten sitzen im Lesesaal.

   _____

7. Seine Frau hat ihn betrogen.

   _____

*Rewrite each sentence, negating the underlined element with the correct form of **kein**.*

EXAMPLE: Luise hat <u>eine Zeitung</u>.
Luise hat <u>keine Zeitung</u>.

1. Meine Großmutter trinkt <u>Kaffee</u>.

_____

2. Boris hat <u>interessante Bücher</u> gefunden.

_____

3. Ich habe <u>eine Tante</u> in London.

_____

4. Der Dieb hat <u>ein Wort</u> gesagt.

_____

5. In diesem Wald gibt es <u>Bären</u>.

_____

6. Ich werde das unter <u>diesen Umständen</u> tun.

_____

7. Ich habe heute Abend <u>viel Zeit</u>.

_____

*Rewrite each sentence, negating the underlined element with the correct form of **kein** or with **nicht**, whichever is appropriate.*

1. Ihr Sohn hat <u>mitgehen wollen</u>.

_____

2. Die Leute gehen <u>in seinen Laden</u>.

_____

3. Ich klebte die Marke <u>auf den Brief</u>.

_____

4. Der Bodensee ist <u>der größte</u> See.

_____

5. <u>Ein Mann</u> spricht mit ihm.

_____

6. Die Lehrerin brauchte <u>einen Kugelschreiber</u>.

_____

7. Der betrunkene Mann fährt <u>schnell</u>.

_____

Niemand, nichts, and niemals

The negative pronouns **niemand** (_no one, nobody_) and **nichts** (_nothing_) are high-frequency words and are commonly used to negate a sentence. The same is true of the adverb **nie** or **niemals** (_never_). **Niemand** and **nichts** can act as subjects or objects. Compare their use in the following examples:

Niemand besucht sie.	_No one is visiting them._
Sie versteht niemanden.	_She doesn't understand anybody._
Nichts interessiert ihn.	_Nothing interests him._
Ich habe nichts für die Kinder.	_I have nothing for the children._

Nie / niemals is used adverbially:

Er geht nie (niemals) ins Kino.	_He never goes to the movies._

Just like **jemand**, **niemand** can have a declensional ending in the accusative and dative cases. That ending, however, is optional:

Nominative	jemand	niemand
Accusative	jemand _or_ jemanden	niemand _or_ niemanden
Dative	jemand _or_ jemandem	niemand _or_ niemandem

ÜBUNG
28·5

Change the underlined word(s) in each sentence to the appropriate negative word: **niemand**, **nichts**, _or_ **nie** (**niemals**). _Take care to change the respective verb if necessary._

EXAMPLE: Thomas hat <u>zehn Euro</u>.
Thomas hat nichts.

1. <u>Die Mädchen</u> wollen Schlittschuh laufen.

_____

2. Der Polizist wird <u>den Dieb</u> verhaften.

_____

3. Manfred geht <u>alle paar Tage</u> in die Stadt.

_____

4. Meine Verwandten waren <u>gestern</u> in Berlin.

   _____

5. Sonja wird <u>ihre kranke Tante</u> in Hamburg besuchen.

   _____

6. Er will <u>etwas</u> zu essen haben.

   _____

7. Sonja hat <u>ein Heft und zwei Bleistifte</u> gekauft.

   _____

Word order

The sentences you have encountered so far all began with the subject. But German sentences can begin with other elements as well. When this occurs, the verb in the sentence precedes the subject. Consider the following sentences. Notice that the English sentences cannot always follow the German word order, particularly when the German sentence begins with a direct object:

ADVERB	**Gestern** war er in der Stadt.	*Yesterday he was in the city.*
DIRECT OBJECT	**Das** verstehe ich nicht.	*I don't understand that.*
CLAUSE	**Als ich in Berlin war**, besuchte ich meinen Onkel.	*When I was in Berlin, I visited my uncle.*

In the previous examples, the German sentences began with an adverb (**Gestern**), a direct object (**Das**), and a clause (**Als ich in Berlin war**). And in each case the subject was preceded by the verb:

non-subject element + verb + subject → inverted subject and verb

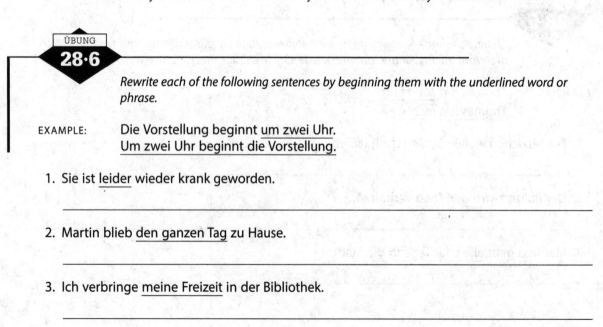

ÜBUNG
28·6

Rewrite each of the following sentences by beginning them with the underlined word or phrase.

EXAMPLE: Die Vorstellung beginnt <u>um zwei Uhr</u>.
<u>Um zwei Uhr beginnt die Vorstellung.</u>

1. Sie ist <u>leider</u> wieder krank geworden.

   _____

2. Martin blieb <u>den ganzen Tag</u> zu Hause.

   _____

3. Ich verbringe <u>meine Freizeit</u> in der Bibliothek.

   _____

4. Ich begegnete meinen Nachbarn, <u>als ich um die Ecke kam</u>.

_____

5. Ich möchte <u>im Herbst</u> nach Italien reisen.

_____

6. Sie geht oft ins Theater, <u>wenn sie in London ist</u>.

_____

7. Meine Tante wohnte <u>letzten Sommer</u> bei ihrem Sohn.

_____

It is important to remember that German sentences that begin with some element other than the subject cannot always be translated word for word into English. For example:

Den Mann beißt der Hund.

Those words translate as _the man bites the dog_, but the German sentence begins with the direct object and must, therefore, be translated into English as _the dog bites the man_.

ÜBUNG
28·7

Rewrite each of the following sentences by placing the direct object at the beginning of the sentence.

EXAMPLE: Der Hund beißt den Mann.
<u>Den Mann beißt der Hund.</u>

1. Er hat den Wecker reparieren lassen.

_____

2. Sie wissen das nicht.

_____

3. Die Jungen spielen Schach.

_____

4. Man muss das nicht.

_____

5. Die Frau kaufte einen Mantel im Kaufhaus.

_____

Rewrite the following sentences by beginning each one first with an adverb, then with a prepositional phrase, and finally with a clause of your choosing.

1. Meine Familie isst italienisch.

    a. Adverb _____

    b. Prepositional phrase _____

    c. Clause _____

2. Sonja spielte Tennis.

    a. Adverb _____

    b. Prepositional phrase _____

    c. Clause _____

3. Seine Freundin wird einen neuen Wagen kaufen.

    a. Adverb _____

    b. Prepositional phrase _____

    c. Clause _____

4. Beethoven komponierte diese Sinfonie.

    a. Adverb _____

    b. Prepositional phrase _____

    c. Clause _____

Compose sentences using the words provided in each list. Add the grammatically necessary words that are missing.

EXAMPLE: morgen / kommen / er / mit / Freund / nach Hause
          Morgen kommt er mit einem Freund nach Hause.

1. in / Woche / werden / wir / wieder / Wien / sein

    _____

2. Mutter / müssen / um / sechs / aufstehen / und / Stadt / fahren

    _____

3. als / ich / in / Hauptstadt / sein / gehen / ich / oft / Museum

    _____

Write original sentences. Begin each one with the cue words provided.

EXAMPLE: (heute)
             <u>Heute werde ich meine Tante in Berlin besuchen.</u>

1. (jemand)

   _____

2. (vor einer Woche)

   _____

3. (um zehn Uhr)

   _____

Interrogative sentences

In both English and German, there is a variety of ways to form questions. In German questions that concern the action of a verb and in some English questions, the verb precedes the subject:

> **verb + subject**
> Ist + Martin zu Hause?
> *Is Martin at home?*

But if the question concerns the action of a verb, English most often uses the auxiliary *to do* to form the question. For example:

> **verb + subject**
> Sprechen + Sie Deutsch?
> *Do you speak German?*

> **verb + subject**
> Kaufte + er einen Mantel?
> *Did he buy a coat?*

With the verb *to be* and sometimes with the verb *to have*, however, the auxiliary *to do* is not needed in English. Instead, as in German, the question begins with the verb:

Ist sie wieder krank?	*Is she sick again?*
Waren sie in München?	*Were they in Munich?*
Haben Sie keinen Pass?	*Have you no passport?*

If the verb *to have* is transitive, a question can be formed either with the auxiliary verb *to do* or without it. However, the form that uses *to do* is more common in modern English:

Hast du genug Geld?	*Do you have enough money?* or *Have you enough money?*
Hatten sie kein Handy?	*Didn't they have a cell phone?* or *Had they no cell phone?*

If the verb *to have* is the auxiliary of a perfect tense, the auxiliary verb *to do* cannot be used in the formation of a question:

Hat er sein Heft gefunden?	*Has he found his notebook?*
Hatte Sonja ihre Tasche verloren?	*Had Sonja lost her purse?*

The auxiliary *to do* is used in English questions only in the present and past tenses with the exception, of course, of *to be* and *to have* as illustrated in the previous examples. The English future tense also avoids using *to do* in a question. Other auxiliaries, such as certain modal auxiliaries, also avoid it:

Wirst du auch mitkommen?	*Will you come along, too?*
Kannst du mir helfen?	*Can you help me?*

If the English modal requires the particle word *to* in order to complete its meaning, use *to do* to form a question. *To be able to* is an exception to this rule, because the verb *to be* is involved:

to be able to	*Are you able to breathe all right?*
to have to	*Does he have to shout like that?*
to need to	*Did the dogs need to be fed?*

The point being made here is that it is important to realize that you cannot translate English questions directly into German. You have to look at the structure of the English sentence and modify for the German approach to forming questions for the action of a verb: *the verb precedes the subject in a German question:*

verb + subject → eine Frage

Let's look at a few examples:

Statement: Er singt sehr gut.	*He sings very well.*
Question: Singt er sehr gut?	*Does he sing very well?*
Statement: Sie ging nach Hause.	*She went home.*
Question: Ging sie nach Hause?	*Did she go home?*

The same word order is required when a modal is used in the sentence:

Statement: Du musst so oft rauchen.	*You have to smoke so often.*
Question: Musst du so oft rauchen?	*Do you have to smoke so often?*

If the sentence is in the present perfect tense, the auxiliary verb precedes the subject.

Statement: Der Mann ist gestorben.	*The man has died.*
Question: Ist der Mann gestorben?	*Has the man died?*
Statement: Peter hat meinen Hut gehabt.	*Peter had my hat.*
Question: Hat Peter meinen Hut gehabt?	*Did Peter have my hat?*

In a future tense sentence, the auxiliary **werden** precedes the subject:

Statement: Wir werden mit ihm reisen.	*We will travel with him.*
Question: Werden wir mit ihm reisen?	*Will we travel with him?*

ÜBUNG

28·11

Rewrite each statement as a question.

1. Sein Vetter ist in der Hauptstadt gewesen.

   _____

2. Gudrun will die Wahrheit über das Unglück erfahren.

   _____

3. Die kranke Frau litt an einer Vergiftung.

   _____

4. Man muss alle Verkehrszeichen beachten.

   _____

5. Ich durfte Luise und Tanja begleiten.

   _____

6. Etwas ist in der Küche los.

   _____

7. Meine Tante freute sich auf das Wiedersehen mit ihren Verwandten.

   _____

ÜBUNG

28·12

Translate the following English questions into German.

1. Do you (**Sie**) play chess?

   _____

2. Do you (**du**) have to stay at home today?

   _____

3. Haven't you (**du**) gone to work yet?

   _____

4. Will they arrive at ten o'clock?

   _____

Interrogative words

Interrogative words are used to pose a question about a specific element in a sentence: *who, what, when, where, how,* and so on. For the most part, German and English interrogative words are used in much the same way.

Wer

The interrogative **wer** (*who*) inquires into the person or persons mentioned in a statement. But **wer** is a singular pronoun and requires a singular conjugation of the verb, even when it inquires into a plural subject. For example:

Tina wohnt jetzt in Bremen.	*Tina lives in Bremen now.*
Wer wohnt jetzt in Bremen?	*Who lives in Bremen now?*
Meine Eltern waren im Harz.	*My parents were in the Harz Mountains.*
Wer war im Harz?	*Who was in the Harz Mountains?*

If **wer** inquires into the direct object of a sentence or the object of an accusative preposition, the pronoun becomes **wen** (*whom, who*). If it inquires into an object in the dative case, the pronoun becomes **wem** (*whom, who*). And if it replaces a possessive adjective or a genitive case noun showing possession, the form **wessen** (*whose*) is used. Let's look at some example sentences.

The case of the interrogative pronoun **wer**, **wen**, **wem**, or **wessen** is determined by the case of the noun or pronoun it replaces: nominative, accusative, dative, or possessive. In the following example, the nominative subject is replaced by the nominative **wer** in a question:

Statement: Der Lehrer ist noch nicht da.	*The teacher isn't here yet.*
Question: Wer ist noch nicht da?	*Who isn't here yet?*

In the next example, the accusative noun is replaced by the accusative **wen** in a question:

Statement: Sie kennt den Lehrer.	*She knows the teacher.*
Question: Wen kennt sie?	*Whom does she know?*

If the accusative noun is introduced by an accusative preposition, that preposition will introduce **wen**:

Statement: Er wartet auf den Lehrer.	*He's waiting for the teacher.*
Question: Auf wen wartet er?	*For whom is he waiting?*

If the dative case is required to replace an indirect object or a noun introduced by a dative preposition, the interrogative **wem** will be used:

Statement: Sie gab es dem Lehrer.	*She gave it to the teacher.*
Question: Wem gab sie es?	*To whom did she give it?*
Statement: Du sprachst mit dem Lehrer.	*You spoke with the teacher.*
Question: Mit wem sprachst du?	*With whom did you speak?*

And if the noun is in the genitive case showing possession, or there is a possessive pronoun showing possession, the possessive **wessen** is required:

Statement: Der Sohn des Lehrers ist krank.	*The teacher's son is sick.*
Question: Wessen Sohn ist krank?	*Whose son is sick?*

*Rewrite the following sentences, changing the underlined word or phrase to the appropriate form: **wer**, **wen**, **wem**, or **wessen**.*

EXAMPLE:　　Er kann uns gut verstehen.
　　　　　　Wer kann uns gut verstehen?

1. Maria hatte ein Geschenk für dich.

_____

2. Peter möchte mit der neuen Studentin tanzen.

_____

3. Die Verwandten in Deutschland wollen ihr helfen.

_____

4. Ihre Kinder werden mit Liebe erzogen.

_____

5. Sie möchten mich morgen besuchen.

_____

6. Ich möchte ein neues Kleid kaufen.

_____

7. Sein Schwager ist Rechtsanwalt geworden.

_____

Was

The interrogative **was** (*what*) inquires into an object or group of objects in a sentence. It replaces the subject of the sentence or an accusative object. Its dative form is **wem**. Like **wer**, **was** is a singular pronoun.

The possessive form **wessen** is used to replace a possessive adjective or a genitive case noun showing possession.

Even if the noun or pronoun replaced by **was** is a plural, the verb in the question will have a singular conjugation:

Statement: Diese Bücher sind alt.　　*These books are old.*
Question: Was ist alt?　　*What is old?*

When replacing a direct object, the pronoun **was** is again used:

Statement: Er kauft eine neue Uhr.　　*He buys a new clock.*
Question: Was kauft er?　　*What does he buy?*

German sometimes uses an indirect object with non-human animates, a structure that would sound strange in English. To illustrate that point consider the following sentence and the question that follows:

Statement: Der Schäfer scherte den Schafen die Wolle.

The shepherd sheared the wool from the sheep.

Question: Wem scherte der Schäfer die Wolle?

From what did the shepherd shear the wool?

The possessive **wessen** replaces the genitive case noun or possessive adjective in a question.

Statement: Wir verkaufen die Wolle des Schafs.

We sell the sheep's wool.

Question: Wessen Wolle verkaufen wir?

Whose wool do we sell?

ÜBUNG
28·14

*Rewrite the following sentences as questions, changing the underlined word or phrase to the appropriate form: **was**, **wem**, or **wessen**.*

EXAMPLE: Das Buch kostet zwanzig Euro.
Was kostet zwanzig Euro?

1. Ich habe es im Schaufenster gesehen.

   _____

2. Der Gerber wird einem Tier das Fell abziehen.

   _____

3. Die Bauern ziehen Schafe auf.

   _____

4. Die Nase des Hundes war sehr kalt.

   _____

Prepositional adverbs

If an inanimate noun follows an accusative or dative preposition and you wish to replace that noun with a pronoun, a prepositional adverb is formed. In a statement, a prepositional adverb begins with **da(r)-** and ends with the preposition. In a question, it begins with **wo(r)-** and ends with the preposition. The **-r** is added before a preposition that begins with a vowel. For example:

Prepositional phrase: im Klassenzimmer   *in the classroom*
Prepositional adverb: darin, worin   *in it, in what*
Prepositional phrase: vor der Tür   *in front of the door*
Prepositional adverb: davor, wovor   *in front of it, in front of what*
Prepositional phrase: an der Wand   *at the wall*
Prepositional adverb: daran, woran   *at it, at what*

There is a tendency to use **um was** and to avoid using a prepositional adverb when saying *around what.*

Let's look at some example questions that include prepositional adverbs:

Worin sitzen sie?	*What are they sitting in?*
Worüber spricht Karl?	*What is Karl talking about?*
Worauf warte ich?	*What am I waiting for?*

ÜBUNG
28·15

Rewrite the following sentences as questions. Change the underlined word or phrase to the appropriate prepositional adverb needed for a question.

EXAMPLE: Der Zug eilt durch den Tunnel.
Wodurch eilt der Zug?

1. Herr Bauer interessiert sich für Chemie.

_____

2. Ich will nicht länger darauf warten.

_____

3. Der Lehrling hat nicht von der neuen Methode gehört.

_____

4. Die neuen Auswanderer sehnen sich danach.

_____

5. Die Kinder spielten damit.

_____

6. Ich habe meine Freunde um Hilfe gebeten.

_____

7. Der Professor kämpfte gegen falsche Meinungen.

_____

If the preposition **in**, **zu**, or **nach** is used to mean *to a place*, its interrogative form will be **wohin** (*where to, whither*). Do not form a prepositional adverb:

Wohin ging er?	*Where did he go?*
Wohin laufen sie?	*Where are they running (to)?*
Wohin reist sie?	*Where is she traveling (to)?*

If the prepositions **von** and **aus** are used to mean *from a place*, their interrogative form will be **woher** (*from where, whence*). Do not form a prepositional adverb:

Er kommt von der Arbeit.	*He's coming from work.*
Woher kommt er?	*Where is he coming from?*
Die Wanderer kamen aus dem Wald.	*The hikers came out of the woods.*
Woher kamen die Wanderer?	*Where did the hikers come from?*

Only **wer** and **was** are declined and used as pronouns. Other interrogative words are adverbial or are substitutes for modifiers. Some of the most commonly used ones are:

wann	*when*
was für	*what kind of* (plural)
was für ein	*what kind of a* (singular)
welcher	*which*
wie	*how*
wie viel(e)	*how much, many*
wo	*where (location)*

The interrogative phrase **was für (ein)** can be used with singular or plural nouns. Use **was für ein** with singular nouns and **was für** with plural nouns. For example:

Was für eine Katze hast du?	*What kind of a cat do you have?*
Was für Haustiere hast du?	*What kind of pets do you have?*

Let's look at some sentences that illustrate these interrogatives:

Statement: Der Zug kommt in zehn Minuten.	*The train comes in ten minutes.*
Question: Wann kommt der Zug?	*When does the train come?*
Statement: Karin kommt um halb elf nach Hause.	*Karin comes home at ten-thirty.*
Question: Um wie viel Uhr kommt Karin nach Hause?	*What time does Karin come home?*

Warum is used to ask a question about an entire clause that begins with *because*:

Statement: Er spricht so laut, weil er taub ist.	*He speaks so loudly because he's deaf.*
Question: Warum spricht er so laut?	*Why does he speak so loudly?*

When using **was für ein**, the case of the article **ein** is determined by the usage of the noun it modifies and not by the preposition **für** that precedes **ein**:

Statement: Sie hat einen Rennwagen.	*She has a racing car.*
Question: Was für einen Wagen hat sie?	*What kind of a car does she have?*
Ein Lehrbuch liegt auf dem Tisch.	*A textbook is lying on the table.*
Was für ein Buch liegt auf dem Tisch?	*What kind of book is lying on the table?*

Use **welcher** to ask about the distinction between two people or things:

Statement: Der neue Student ist klug.	*The new student is smart.*
Question: Welcher Student ist klug?	*Which student is smart?*

Wie is generally used to ask *how* in a question, but it also occurs in commonly used idiomatic expressions such as in the following example:

Statement: Der Junge heißt Karl.	*The boy's name is Karl.*
Question: Wie heißt der Junge?	*What is the boy's name?*

Normally, **wie viel** is used with singular nouns (*how much*) and **wie viele** with plural nouns (*how many*). (However, **wie viel** is also often used in place of **wie viele**.)

Statement: Er hat zwei Hefte.	*He has two notebooks.*
Question: Wie viele Hefte hat er?	*How many notebooks does he have?*

The interrogative **wo** inquires into location and should not be confused with **wohin**, which inquires into direction or motion:

Statement: Sie arbeiten im Garten.	*They're working in the garden.*
Question: Wo arbeiten sie?	*Where are they working?*

In addition, there is a variety of other interrogative phrases formed with **wie**. For example:

wie alt	*how old*
wie groß	*how big*
wie oft	*how often*
wie schnell	*how fast*
wie weit	*how far*
um wie viel Uhr	*at what time*

Let's look at some sentences that illustrate the use of these interrogatives:

Statement: Karin ist vier Jahre alt.	*Karin is four years old.*
Question: Wie alt ist Karin?	*How old is Karin?*
Statement: Das Zimmer hat zehn Quadratmeter.	*The room is ten meters square.*
Question: Wie groß ist das Zimmer?	*How big is the room?*
Statement: Er geht alle vier Tage in die Stadt.	*He goes to the city every four days.*
Question: Wie oft geht er in die Stadt?	*How often does he go to the city?*

In general, interrogative words are followed by the regular word order for a question:

interrogative word + verb + subject + ?
Wann + kommt + der Zug + ?
When is the train arriving?

ÜBUNG
28·16

*Rewrite each sentence as a question using the underlined word or phrase as the cue for determining which interrogative word to use: **wann**, **warum**, **was für (ein)**, **welcher**, **wie**, or **wo**.*

EXAMPLE: Sie wohnen jetzt <u>in Leipzig.</u>
            <u>Wo wohnen sie jetzt?</u>

1. Der Rechtsanwalt sprach <u>zu laut</u>.

   _____

2. Die junge Dame hat einen <u>teuren</u> Pullover gekauft.

   _____

3. Du musst einen Mantel tragen, <u>denn es ist heute sehr kalt</u>.

   _____

4. Der ältere Junge ist ziemlich dumm.

_____

5. Seine Tochter studiert an der Universität Hamburg.

_____

Rewrite each sentence as a question using the underlined word or phrase as the cue for determining which interrogative word to use: **wie alt**, **wie groß**, **wie oft**, or **wie viel**.

EXAMPLE: Sie hat zehn neue Blusen.
Wie viele neue Blusen hat sie?

1. Unser Schlafzimmer hat nur achtzehn Quadratmeter.

_____

2. Onkel Peter hat ein paar Nelken gekauft.

_____

3. Doktor Schmidt wird am elften Dezember achtzig werden.

_____

Compose questions using the words provided in each list. Add any necessary words.

EXAMPLE: kommen / er / mit / Freund / nach Hause / ?
Kommt er mit einem Freund nach Hause?

1. was / fallen / von / Dach / auf / Straße / ?

_____

2. klettern / Bergsteiger / den steilen Felsen / hinauf / ?

_____

3. mit / wer / haben / du / so lange / tanzen / ?

_____

4. wie lange / müssen / ihr / in / Hauptstadt / auf / euer / Zug / warten / ?

_____

5. können / du / mich / zu / Bahnhof / begleiten / ?

_____

6. welcher / Geschäft / haben / beste / Preise / ?

_____

7. durch / schützen / man / Pflanzen / vor / Kälte / des Winters / ?

_____

Write original sentences. Begin each one with the cue words provided.

EXAMPLE: (was)
            Was siehst du im Garten?

1. (was für ein)

_____

2. (auf wen)

_____

3. (worauf)

_____

4. (wohin)

_____

5. (wessen)

_____

_____

Compose questions using the words provided in each list. Add any necessary words. Then answer the questions appropriately.

EXAMPLE: kommen / er / mit / Amerikaner / nach Hause / ?
            Kommt er mit einem Amerikaner nach Hause?
            Nein, er kommt mit einem Ausländer nach Hause.

1. warum / spielen / du / nicht / mit / andere / Kinder / ?

   a. _____

   b. _____

2. woher / haben / er / dies / alt / Bücher / bekommen / ?

   a. _____

   b. _____

3. wie viel / Meter / Stoff / haben / Frau Benz / brauchen / ?

a. _____

b. _____

4. wie oft / sein / ihr / Ausland / reisen / ?

a. _____

b. _____

5. wohin / laufen / Fußballspieler / elf Uhr / ?

a. _____

b. _____

Compose original questions using the words in parentheses as your cues. Then answer each question.

EXAMPLE: (was)
Was haben Sie gekauft?
Ich habe einen neuen BMW gekauft.

1. (wann)

a. _____

b. _____

2. (warum)

a. _____

b. _____

3. (wie lange)

a. _____

b. _____

4. (wohin)

a. _____

b. _____

5. (wo)

a. _____

b. _____

Building more sentences ◆29◆

The main clause of a German sentence contains a subject and a verb and makes complete sense when it stands alone. Except when some element other than the subject begins a main clause, the subject precedes the verb:

Er kommt spät nach Hause.	*He comes home late.*
Tina versteht es nicht.	*Tina doesn't understand it.*
Setz dich hin! (**Du** *is understood.*)	*Sit down.*

This word order is important when using coordinating conjunctions.

Coordinating conjunctions

Coordinating conjunctions can link together words, phrases, or even complete sentences (main clauses):

word + conjunction + word
phrase + conjunction + phrase
clause + conjunction + clause

The most commonly used coordinating conjunctions are:

aber	*but*
denn	*because, for, since*
oder	*or*
sondern (*used with* **nicht** *or* **kein**)	*but (rather)*
und	*and*

When combining sentences with these conjunctions, a comma is used to mark off the two clauses. With **und** and sometimes with **aber**, however, this is optional. If the combination of two clauses with **und** is confusing, a comma can precede **und** for the sake of clarity.

Let's look at some example sentences that illustrate the use of coordinating conjunctions:

Der Mann klopfte laut an die Tür, aber niemand war zu Hause.	*The man knocked loudly on the door, but no one was home.*
Sie ging nicht zur Schule, denn sie war wieder krank.	*She didn't go to school because she was sick again.*
Du darfst hier übernachten, oder wir können ein Hotel für dich finden.	*You can stay here overnight, or we can find a hotel for you.*

Ich habe nicht nur einen Artikel, sondern ein ganzes Buch über sein Leben gelesen.	*I read not just an article, but a whole book about his life.*
Vater schläft auf dem Sofa, und Mutter arbeitet in der Küche.	*Father is sleeping on the sofa, and mother is working in the kitchen.*

sentence 1 + comma + coordinating conjunction + sentence 2
Er bleibt zu Hause + , + denn + er ist krank.
He's staying home because he's sick.

When the subject of the first clause is identical to the subject of the second clause, it is possible to omit the second subject and sometimes even the verb. For example:

Wir können bei Inge übernachten, oder ein Hotel finden.	*We can stay overnight at Inge's or find a hotel.*
Vater kann nicht schlafen und arbeitet in der Küche.	*Father can't sleep and is working in the kitchen.*

This is especially true of **sondern**:

Erik ist nicht eingeschlafen, sondern hat die ganze Nacht an Tina gedacht.	*Erik didn't fall asleep but rather thought about Tina all night.*
Ich habe nicht nur einen Artikel, sondern ein ganzes Buch über sein Leben gelesen.	*I read not just an article, but a whole book about his life.*

These five conjunctions are unique in that they require no word order change. The standard word order for a declarative, interrogative, or imperative sentence is used in both clauses that surround a coordinating conjunction.

ÜBUNG
29·1

Combine the following pairs of sentences with the appropriate conjunction. Choose the conjunction from the two provided in parentheses for each set.

EXAMPLE: (und / oder) Werner ist mein Freund. Tina ist meine Freundin.
          Werner ist mein Freund, und Tina ist meine Freundin.

1. (aber / denn) Er wollte Tennis spielen. Das Wetter war endlich gut.

   _____

2. (oder / sondern) Ich habe es nicht verloren. Ich habe es hinter dem Schrank versteckt.

   _____

3. (und / denn) Paul studiert in Berlin. Er wohnt in einem Studentenheim.

   _____

4. (aber / und) Meine Freundin hat ihre Fahrkarte verloren. Sie muss hier in Bonn bleiben.

   _____

5. (oder / aber) Sei ruhig! Geh sofort nach Hause!

   _____

6. (und / oder) Soll er einen roten Wagen kaufen? Soll er einen blauen Wagen kaufen?

   _____

7. (und / aber) Ich höre, was du sagst. Ich verstehe dich nicht.

   _____

8. (sondern / und) Angela spielt Gitarre. Ihr Bruder spielt Flöte.

   _____

ÜBUNG
29·2

Rewrite the following sentences by changing the underlined clause to an alternate clause that conforms to the meaning of the rest of the sentence.

EXAMPLE: Sie geht einkaufen, aber Peter bleibt zu Hause.
Sie geht einkaufen, aber ihre Schwester will eine Freundin besuchen.

1. Sie versuchte ihn zu warnen, aber der Junge hörte sie nicht.

   _____

2. Die Studentin konnte nicht arbeiten, denn der Lärm war zu groß.

   _____

3. Normalerweise ist der Herbst am schönsten, aber dieses Jahr ist der Winter wunderschön.

   _____

4. Karl ist nicht zum Café gegangen, sondern ist wieder zu Hause geblieben.

   _____

5. Der Schüler setzte sich auf seinen Platz und schrieb die Wörter in sein Heft.

   _____

6. Im Schaufenster stehen große Puppen, aber sie sehen alt und schmutzig aus.

   _____

7. Der Junge lernt das Gedicht nicht, sondern sieht den ganzen Abend fern.

   _____

8. Der Bauer sät das Korn, und seine Frau pflegt den Gemüsegarten.

   _____

9. Im Kühlschrank gibt es keinen Wein mehr, sondern nur ein paar Flaschen Bier.

   _____

10. Ich habe ihm mit Interesse zugehört, aber ich habe ihm kein Wort geglaubt.

   _____

ÜBUNG
29·3

Compose sentences using the words provided in each list. Add any necessary words.

EXAMPLE: morgen / kommen / er / mit / Freund / nach Hause
          Morgen kommt er mit einem Freund nach Hause.

1. tun / mir / Gefallen / und / mitkommen / !

   _____

2. Junge / müssen / gehorchen / oder / er / haben / Folgen / selbst / zu tragen

   _____

3. Kirschen / schmecken / sehr / gut / aber / wie viel / kosten / sie / ?

   _____

4. wir / machen / kein / Pause / sondern / arbeiten / bis / spät / in / Nacht

   _____

5. Mein / Vater / haben kaufen / neu / VW denn / er / haben gewinnen / 30.000 / Euro

   _____

ÜBUNG
29·4

Write an original sentence with each of the coordinating conjunctions given.

1. aber

   _____

2. denn

   _____

3. oder

   _____

4. sondern

   _____

Subordinating conjunctions

There are many subordinating conjunctions, and they all share two characteristics: (1) they introduce dependent clauses that do not make complete sense when they stand alone; and (2) the conjugated verb in such clauses is normally the last element in the clause:

main clause + subordinating conjunction + dependent clause + verb
Ich besuchte Karl, + als + ich in der Hauptstadt + war.
I visited Karl when I was in the capital.

Using subordinating conjunctions

Some of the most commonly used subordinating conjunctions are:

als	*when*	ob	*whether, if*
als ob (als wenn)	*as if*	obwohl	*although*
bevor	*before*	seit(dem)	*since*
bis	*until, by the time*	sobald	*as soon as*
da	*since*	sooft	*as often as*
damit	*so that*	soviel	*as far as*
dass	*that*	während	*while*
ehe	*before*	weil	*because*
falls	*in case*	wenn	*when(ever), if*
nachdem	*after*	wie	*as*

Let's look at a few example sentences. Take note of where the conjugated verb stands in the dependent clause:

Ich weiß, dass du lügst.	*I know that you're lying.*
Er konnte nicht einkaufen gehen, weil er pleite ist.	*He couldn't go shopping because he's broke.*
Als sie in Paris war, kaufte sie sich ein paar neue Kleider.	*When she was in Paris, she bought a couple of new dresses.*

Notice that in the first two example sentences above, the dependent clause is the second clause. In the third example, the dependent clause is the first clause. These clauses function in the same way no matter what their position in the sentence.

Er wohnte in Kiel, als er jung war.	*He lived in Kiel when he was young.*
Als er jung war, wohnte er in Kiel.	*When he was young, he lived in Kiel.*

Whatever tense the verb is in, the conjugated verb or auxiliary will be the last element of a clause introduced by a subordinating conjunction:

..., dass er krank ist.	*. . . that he's sick.*
..., dass wir nichts gehört haben.	*. . . that we didn't hear anything.*
..., dass ich gut singen kann.	*. . . that I can sing well.*

There is only one exception to that rule. When a double infinitive structure is part of the sentence introduced by a subordinating conjunction, the auxiliary verb will precede the double infinitive. This occurs, of course, with modal auxiliaries and certain other verbs such as **helfen**, **hören**, **lassen**, and **sehen** (*to help, to hear, to get* or *to have done, to see*). With modal auxiliaries, for example:

..., weil sie uns wird einladen müssen.	*. . . , because she will have to invite us.*
..., weil er mit dir hatte fahren wollen.	*. . . , because he had wanted to drive with you.*

The same kind of word order occurs with **helfen**, **hören**, **lassen**, and **sehen**. For example:

..., weil Tina mir wird kochen helfen.	*. . . , because Tina will help me cook.*
..., weil ich es habe reparieren lassen.	*. . . , because I have had it repaired.*

When as a conjunction

You need to consider the conjunction *when* carefully. Although English uses the same conjunction for three different functions, German does not. There are three distinct German words, one for each function.

When using *when* to ask a question, the German interrogative is **wann**:

Wann kommen die Gäste morgen?	*When are the guests coming tomorrow?*
Bis wann kann ich vorbeikommen?	*Until what time can I drop by?*
Seit wann wohnt Lukas in Bremen?	*How long has Lukas been living in Bremen?*

The brief response to a **wann**-question can include **wann**:

Ich weiß nicht wann.	*I don't know when.*

In general, however, responses to a **wann**-question in the present tense require **wenn**:

Wann sind die Straßen naß?	*When are the streets wet?*
Die Straßen sind naß, wenn es regnet.	*The streets are wet when it rains.*

When using *when* to mean *whenever*, the German conjunction is again **wenn**, a subordinating conjunction:

Wenn wir nach Bonn kommen, besuchen wir unsere Tante.	*When(ever) we come to Bonn, we visit our aunt.*
Wenn Sie sich erst einmal eingearbeitet haben, werden Sie unsere Ziele besser verstehen.	*When you've had a chance to get used to the job, you'll understand our goals better.*
Wenn es Sommer wird, schwimmen wir jeden Tag.	*When summer comes, we'll go swimming every day.*

When using *when* in a past tense sentence, the German conjunction is **als**, also a subordinating conjunction:

Als er ankam, sah er Maria vor dem Haus stehen.	*When he arrived, he saw Maria standing in front of the house.*
Es fing an zu regnen, als wir zum Garten gehen wollten.	*It began to rain when we wanted to go to the garden.*
Gerade als Erik hier war, wurde meine Schwester krank.	*Just when Erik was here, my sister got sick.*

Comma usage with subordinating conjunctions

When two clauses are combined by a subordinating conjunction, the two clauses are separated by a comma:

Luise versteht, dass Benno zu Hause bleiben muss.	*Luise understands that Benno has to stay home.*

The two forms of sentence formation with subordinating conjunctions are:

main clause + subordinating conjunction + clause with verb in final position
Er besuchte sie, + als + er in Berlin war.
He visited her when he was in Berlin.

subordinating conjunction + clause with verb in final position + main clause
Als + er in Berlin war, + besuchte er sie.
When he was in Berlin, he visited her.

Remember that the verb will precede the subject in the main clause if the sentence is introduced by a subordinating conjunction as illustrated in the previous example.

ÜBUNG
29·5

*Fill in each blank with the missing word: **wann**, **wenn**, or **als**.*

1. _____ legt er sich ins Bett?

2. Sie musste das Studium aufgeben, _____ ihr Vater starb.

3. _____ ich die Universität verließ, traf ich einen Freund.

4. Man geht zum Arzt, _____ man krank ist.

5. _____ hat man Husten und Schnupfen?

6. _____ er im letzten Jahr in Kiel war, begegnete er einem Schulkameraden.

7. _____ die Kinder sechs Jahre alt sind, kommen sie in die Grundschule.

ÜBUNG
29·6

Complete each sentence with any appropriate phrase.

EXAMPLE: Er starb, als _____.
           Er starb, als er im Krankenhaus war.

1. Wenn du nach Berlin reist, _____.

2. Wenn _____, dürfen Sie vorbeikommen.

3. Als die Touristen Südamerika besuchten, _____.

4. Herr Schneider trifft einen Bekannten, wenn _____.

5. Wenn du isst, _____.

6. Wenn _____, denken die Kinder an Weihnachten.

7. _____, gehst du oft ins Theater?

ÜBUNG
29·7

*Fill in each blank with an appropriate subordinating conjunction. Do not use **wann**, **wenn**, or **als**.*

1. _____ wir im Ruhrgebiet waren, besuchten wir viele Fabriken.

2. _____ Herr Bauer starb, schrieb er sein Testament.

3. _____ wir abfahren, müssen wir die Koffer packen.

4. _____ sie meine Schwester war, wollte ich ihr kein Geld leihen.

5. Wissen Sie, _____ das Rathaus weit ist?

6. Wir kommen morgen vorbei, _____ wir genug Zeit haben.

7. Fahren wir zum Bahnhof mit einem Taxi, _____ wir den Zug erreichen!

8. _____ wir wissen, ist sie wieder schwanger.

9. Sie können mit uns reiten, _____ Sie wollen.

10. Ich kann nicht warten, _____ er zurückkommt.

11. _____ er zur Party ging, kämmte er sich wieder die Haare.

12. Ich habe ihnen geholfen, _____ ich konnte.

13. _____ Lukas betrunken war, wollte sie nicht mit ihm tanzen.

14. Hast du gewusst, _____ du den letzten Bus verpasst hast?

Complete each sentence with any appropriate phrase.

EXAMPLE: Er starb, ehe _____.
Er starb, ehe er sein Testament schrieb.

1. Obwohl _____, verstand ich es nicht.

2. Während _____, haben sie oft Schach gespielt.

3. Er musste wieder zu Fuß gehen, weil _____.

4. Erik fragte uns, ob _____.

5. Sie haben nichts bezahlt, solange _____.

6. Kinder, wartet hier, bis _____!

7. Ich habe keine Ahnung, wie _____.

8. Beeilt euch, damit _____!

9. _____ er müde war, wollte er nach Hause gehen.

10. Obwohl _____, will ich nicht Skilaufen gehen.

11. Seitdem _____, ist sie nie zu Hause.

12. Nachdem er sich den Finger verletzt hatte, _____

13. _____, ob er uns versteht.

14. _____, bis du das Glas Milch ausgetrunken hast.

Interrogatives

A **ja** or **nein** question begins with the verb, which is followed by the subject:

Ist Frau Gerber zu Hause?	*Is Ms. Gerber at home?*
Ja, sie ist zu Hause.	*Yes, she's at home.*
Nein, sie ist nicht zu Hause.	*No, she's not at home.*

It is possible to use such **ja** and **nein** questions as clauses with certain pat phrases, such as **wissen Sie** or **haben Sie gehört**. When this occurs, the conjunction **ob** can be required:

Hat er genug Geld?	*Does he have enough money?*
Ich weiß nicht, ob er genug Geld hat.	*I don't know if (whether) he has enough money.*
Wohnt sie noch in Amerika?	*Does she still live in America?*
Wir haben keine Ahnung, ob sie noch in Amerika wohnt.	*We have no idea if (whether) she still lives in America.*

But when a question begins with an interrogative word, that word can be used as a subordinating conjunction with the same pat phrases and **ob** is not needed. For example:

Wer steht an der Tür?	*Who is at the door?*
Ich weiß nicht, wer an der Tür steht.	*I don't know who is at the door.*
Wem gehört dieses Buch?	*Who(m) does this book belong to?*
Weiß jemand, wem dieses Buch gehört?	*Does anyone know to whom this book belongs?*
Um wie viel Uhr ist die Vorstellung?	*What time is the show?*
Bitte sagen Sie mir, um wie viel Uhr die Vorstellung ist.	*Please tell me what time the show is.*

Since these interrogative words are now functioning as subordinating conjunctions, they have the same effect on clauses as the other subordinating conjunctions. That is, the conjugated verb or auxiliary is the last element of the clause:

interrogative conjunction + verb
Er fragt, **wer** + das gesagt **hat**.
He asks who said that.

ÜBUNG
29·9

*Change the following questions to clauses preceded by **Ich weiß nicht**. Add **ob** where necessary.*

EXAMPLE: Ist der Bahnhof weit von hier?
Ich weiß nicht, ob der Bahnhof weit von hier ist.

1. Wer schwimmt in unserem Schwimmbad?

_____

2. Hat das Mädchen das Geld verloren?

_____

3. Warum drohte er dem alten Mann?

_____

4. Kann er diese Probleme lösen?

_____

5. Wie alt war sein Urgroßvater?

_____

6. Wem ist der Sohn ähnlich?

_____

7. Wonach fragte der kranke Herr?

_____

8. Wie lange wird die Vorstellung dauern?

_____

9. Was zeigt sie ihren Gästen?

_____

10. Entwickelte der Fotograf die Aufnahmen?

_____

11. Woran denkt die alte Dame gern?

_____

12. Um wen macht er sich viele Sorgen?

_____

13. Um wie viel Uhr geht der Mann in sein Büro?

_____

14. Was wird der Fremdenführer den Touristen zeigen wollen?

_____

ÜBUNG
29·10

Compose sentences using the words provided in each list. Add any necessary words.
Compose your tenses carefully.

EXAMPLE: wann / kommen / er / mit / sein / Freund / ?
                   <u>Wann kam er mit seinem Freund?</u>

1. Tina / bleiben / in / Stadt / bis / ihr / Tante / wieder / gesund / sein

_____

2. ich / erzählen / du / sein / Geschichte / damit / du / er / besser / verstehen

_____

3. während / es / donnern / blitzen / sitzen / wir / in / klein / Paddelboot

_____

4. Frau Benz / kaufen / Bluse / obwohl / Preis / sehr / hoch / sein

_____

5. Kind / sein / so / müde / dass / es / sofort / einschlafen

_____

6. seitdem / Wetter / wieder / schlecht / werden / müssen / Kinder / in / Keller / spielen

_____

7. wenn / sie / Verwandte / besuchen / sein / sie / am glücklichsten

_____

Extended modifiers

Modifiers include those words that help to describe a noun or pronoun. Some modifiers are called adjectives. If an adjective follows a verb like **sein** (_to be_) or **werden** (_to become_), it is a predicate adjective. For example:

Der Mann ist **alt**.	_The man is **old**._
Sie wurde **krank**.	_She became **ill**._

Attributive adjectives

If the adjective stands in front of the noun, it is called an attributive adjective and in German it will have an ending, and that ending will be determined by gender, number, and case. For example:

Kennst du den **alten** Mann?	_Do you know the **old** man?_
Sie besuchte ein **krankes** Kind.	_She visited a **sick** child._

If you think about it, attributive adjectives play about the same role as certain relative clauses in which a predicate adjective is used. For example:

Kennst du den Mann, der alt ist?	_Do you know the man who is old?_
Kennst du den alten Mann?	_Do you know the old man?_
Sie besuchte ein Kind, das krank ist.	_She visited a child who was sick._
Sie besuchte ein krankes Kind.	_She visited a sick child._

The differences are the need for an ending on an attributive adjective and the need for a subject and verb in the relative clause. The use of an attributive adjective, therefore, is a bit more efficient and requires less time to say and less space to write.

Attributive adjectives can be extended somewhat by using other modifiers—adverbs—to define them. For example:

Sie hat einen ziemlich schnellen Wagen.	_She has a rather fast car._
Das ist eine sehr wichtige Tatsache.	_That's a very important fact._

The modifiers in the example sentences above were *extended* by the adverbs **ziemlich** and **sehr**. And, as you can clearly see, German and English function in the very same way when adverbs modify adjectives. By the way, that word *extended* will become important later on in this chapter.

Present participles

Present participles in German are formed quite simply. A **-d** ending is added to an infinitive. For example:

infinitive + d → present participle	
störend	*disturbing*
entsprechend	*corresponding*
anregend	*stimulating*

Notice that the absence or presence of an inseparable or separable prefix does not affect the formation of present participles. Present participles are translated into English using an *-ing* suffix.

Present participles can be used as adverbs or adjectives, and when they are used as adjectives, they function as predicate or attributive adjectives. Let's look at some examples:

Sein Verhalten war sehr störend.	*His behavior was very disturbing.*
Er machte ein störendes Geräusch.	*He made a disturbing noise.*
Sein letzter Roman war spannend.	*His last novel was thrilling.*
Das soll ein spannender Film sein.	*That's supposed to be a thrilling movie.*

Just like other modifiers, present participles can be modified by adverbs (**sehr störend**).

ÜBUNG
29·11

Form the present participle from the verb in each of the following phrases. Give the English translation of each participle.

EXAMPLE: ich laufe   laufend *running*

1. du kommst an   _____   _____

2. ich zwinge   _____   _____

3. er belastet   _____   _____

4. Sie stoßen ab   _____   _____

5. du verhältst   _____   _____

6. sie sieht an   _____   _____

7. ihr fühlt mit   _____   _____

Translate the following phrases into German. Provide the appropriate adjective ending for each present participle.

EXAMPLE: *the crying girl*   das weinende Mädchen

1. *the sleeping children*   _____

2. *the loudly barking dogs*   _____

3. *from her disappointing answer*   _____

4. *a corresponding theory*   _____

5. *next to the laughing boy*   _____

6. *in the arriving train*   _____

7. *the slowly flowing water*   _____

Past participles

Past participles are used to form the perfect tenses. But just like present participles, they can also be used as adjectives:

(auxiliary omitted) + regular or irregular past participle → adjective
(hat) gekocht	*cooked*
(hat) versprochen	*promised*
(ist) angekommen	*arrived*

Inseparable and separable prefixes affect the formation of a past participle. With inseparable prefixes, the past participle does not require an added **ge-** prefix, e.g., **besucht** (*visited*) and **vergangen** (*past*). With separable prefixes, the prefix is separated from the past participle by a **ge-** prefix (infix), placed between them, e.g., **mitgebracht** (*brought along*) and **zugenommen** (*increased*). Let's look at some example sentences that use past participles as predicate and attributive adjectives.

Er schien ganz gelassen.	*He seemed quite calm.*
Er hatte eine gelassene Reaktion.	*He had a calm reaction.*
Sie war gar nicht begeistert.	*She wasn't enthusiastic at all.*
Seine begeisterte Stimme war laut und schrill.	*His enthusiastic voice was loud and shrill.*

Translate the following phrases into German. Provide the appropriate adjective ending for each past participle.

EXAMPLE: the written word   das geschriebene Wort

1. *a broken man*   _____

2. *from the drunken man*   _____

3. *with the excited boys*   _____

4. *because of the poorly repaired motor* _____

5. *a hard-boiled egg*   _____

6. *in the recently arrived train*   _____

7. *the United States*   _____

Extended modifiers

Just as attributive adjectives can replace a relative clause that contains a predicate adjective, so, too, can participles replace relative clauses. Look at the following example with adjectives:

das Haus, das klein ist   *the house that is small*
das kleine Haus   *the small house*

Compare that with the following examples, where participles replace the verbs in the relative clauses and the phrase that was previously expressed by the relative clause now precedes the noun that is modified:

das Haus, das an der Ecke steht   *the house that stands on the corner*
→ das an der Ecke stehende Haus   *the house that stands on the corner*

das Haus, das gestern zerstört wurde *the house that was destroyed yesterday*
→ das gestern zerstörte Haus   *the house that was destroyed yesterday*

In both examples above the relative clause has been changed to an *extended modifier*, with the present or past participle acting as the modifier with the appropriate adjective ending. English does not use extended modifiers to the same degree as German, and German phrases that contain extended modifiers tend to be translated as relative clauses in English, as illustrated in the above examples.

der/die/das + participle + adjective ending
der + sitzend + -e
der vor der Tür sitzende Hund
the dog sitting in front of the door

Extended modifiers, especially those that are particularly long, tend to be used in formal writing or might be heard in a scholarly speech. When used in casual conversation, they sound cumbersome and lofty and are generally avoided.

If an active verb in a relative clause is changed into an extended modifier, a present participle is used: **der Mann, der singt = der singende Mann** (*the singing man*). If the verb is passive, a past participle is used: **das Lied, das gesungen wurde = das gesungene Lied** (*the song that was sung*). If the verb is a verb of motion or another verb that requires **sein** as its auxiliary, the tense of the participle is determined by the tense of the verb. For example:

der Zug, der gerade ankommt	*the train that is just now arriving*
der gerade ankommende Zug	*the train that is just now arriving*
der Zug, der schon angekommen ist	*the train that has already arrived*
der schon angekommene Zug	*the train that has already arrived*

If the verb is reflexive, the reflexive pronoun **sich** must be used with the participle:

der Mann, der sich schämt = der sich schämende Mann

Let's look at a sentence with an extended modifier formed from the past participle **bekannt**. Notice how it can grow with the addition of modifiers and prepositional phrases:

Er ist Politiker.	*He's a politician.*
Er ist ein bekannter Politiker.	*He's a well-known politician.*
Er ist ein sehr bekannter Politiker.	*He's a very well-known politician.*
Er ist ein in Europa sehr bekannter Politiker.	*He's a very well-known politician in Europe.*
Er ist ein bei Jugendlichen in Europa sehr bekannter Politiker.	*He's a very well-known politician among young people in Europe.*

The English translation of this final sentence could contain a relative clause:

He's a politician who is very well-known among young people in Europe.

ÜBUNG
29·14

Rewrite the following sentences by changing the verb phrase in each relative clause into an extended modifier.

EXAMPLE: Die Frau, die im Wohnzimmer sitzt, ist meine Schwester.
             Die im Wohnzimmer sitzende Frau ist meine Schwester.

1. Der Polizist, der den Rechtsanwalt anruft, ist in Not.

   _____

2. Ich hasse das Wetter, das sich so schnell verändert.

   _____

3. Sein Gewinn, der uns überrascht, erfreute seine Frau.

   _____

4. Niemand will dem Taschendieb helfen, der zum vierten Mal verhaftet worden ist.

   _____

5. Die langen Kerzen, die so trüb brennen, standen auf dem Klavier.

   _____

6. Das ist der Professor, der von seinen ehemaligen Studenten besucht wurde.

_____

7. Sie ist sehr stolz auf die Studentinnen, die konzentriert arbeiten.

_____

8. Der Kranke, der an seinen Wunden stirbt, hat keine Familie.

_____

9. Kannten Sie die Frau, die gestern Abend verstorben ist?

_____

10. Der Soldat, der sich so langsam bewegte, war verwundet.

_____

ÜBUNG

29·15

Rewrite the following sentences by adding a modifier or prepositional phrase to the extended modifier.

EXAMPLE: Er nimmt das Problem mit geöffneten Augen an.
Er nimmt das Problem mit weit geöffneten Augen an.

1. Sie bekam einen gut geschriebenen Brief.

_____

2. Er wollte die geschmückte Torte probieren.

_____

3. Das verkaufte Auto muss schon repariert werden.

_____

4. Ausgebildete Menschen werden von unserer Firma gesucht.

_____

5. Die Eltern suchten nach ihrem verschwundenen Sohn.

_____

6. Der geschiedene Mann will eine jüngere Frau heiraten.

_____

7. Das spielende Kind fing an zu lachen.

_____

8. Er findet den verlorenen Brief in einer Schublade.

_____

ÜBUNG
29·16

Combine each list of words into an extended modifier for the noun given.

EXAMPLE: schön / singen / Vogel
der schön singende Vogel

1. auf / Herd / stehen / Suppe

_____

2. von / Armee / zerstören / Dorf

_____

3. vor / Angst / zittern / Kätzchen

_____

4. laut / reden / Prediger

_____

5. vor / zwei / Jahr / bauen / Häuser

_____

6. brennen / neulich / verkaufen / Haus

_____

7. aus / zehn / Amerikaner / bestehen / Reisegruppe

_____

ÜBUNG
29·17

Write original sentences that include an extended modifier formed from the relative clause provided. **DER** *represents the definite article* **der**, **die**, *or* **das**. *The gender and case of the articles you use will change depending upon the context.*

EXAMPLE: DER das Museum besucht
Wir begegneten den das Museum besuchenden Touristen.

1. DER von dem Studenten getrunken wurde

_____

2. DER von der Köchin gebacken worden ist

_____

3. DER sich die Haare kämmt

_____

4. DER auf dem Boden eingeschlafen ist

_____

5. DER zu Hause geblieben ist

_____

Short responses

In every language there are little words that are added to sentences for emphasis or to give a particular quality to a phrase. There is only a slight difference of emphasis between the following two sentences, and it is the addition of one small adverb that causes this difference, and also adds a bit of indignation:

> I don't know.
> I certainly don't know.

German has numerous such small words, and this chapter will explain some of the important ones.

There are also in every language short, pat phrases used as a quick response to someone else's statement. They usually stand alone, because they derive their meaning from the statement to which they are responding. In English, the words *so what* and *how come* have little meaning when they stand alone, but as a response to something else, they can make quite a statement:

> —You didn't make your bed again.   —So what!
> —You're grounded for a week!   —How come?

The same thing occurs in German. And these short, pat responses are effective in sentence writing, because they make the language flow naturally and can make content more interesting. However, such phrases are often quite casual and should sometimes be avoided in formal writing.

Words for emphasis

German often adds special words to a sentence in order to emphasize a speaker's or a writer's attitude or frame of mind: impatience, enthusiasm, indignation, and so on.

Also

The word **also** (*so, well*) is usually added to a phrase to emphasize the urgency of the action of a verb or as a way of linking a phrase to a previous statement.

> Also schön!   *All right then!*
> Na also!   *You see! (I told you so!)*
> Also, kommt er jetzt oder nicht?   *Well, is he coming or not?*

Doch

Doch can be used alone as a response that says that what someone else has suggested is not true:

Du hast den Aufsatz noch nicht geschrieben!	*You haven't written the essay yet!*
Doch!	*Yes, I have!*

It is also added to a phrase to emphasize its meaning:

Los doch!	*Go ahead! Go on already!*
Das ist doch herrlich!	*That's really great!*
Das ist doch eine Lüge!	*That's such a lie!*

Gar

Gar usually means *at all* but can also be added to a phrase for emphasis:

Magst du Tee trinken?	*Do you like drinking tea?*
Gar nicht.	*Not at all.*
Hast du genug Euro?	*Do you have enough euros?*
Nein, ich habe gar keine.	*No, I have none at all.*
Tina ist wirklich hübsch.	*Tina is really pretty.*
Ja, ich hätte gar zu gern mit ihr getanzt.	*Yes, I really would have liked to dance with her.*

Kaum

The word **kaum** is an adverb and means *hardly* or *scarcely*. But it is added to other phrases to emphasize the moment when something occurs:

Sie hatte kaum Platz genommen, als sie zu weinen begann.	*She had hardly taken her seat when she began to cry.*

It is often used to modify a comparative:

Der Professor ist kaum älter als die Studenten.	*The professor is hardly older than the students.*
Das ist kaum besser!	*That's hardly better!*

It is also frequently combined with an infinitive clause introduced by **zu**:

Kaum zu glauben.	*It's hard to believe.*
Seine Handschrift ist kaum zu entziffern.	*His handwriting can hardly be made out.*

Mal

The word **mal** is a shortened version of the word **einmal** (*once*). It is often added to a phrase—particularly an imperative—for emphasis:

Komm mal her!	*Come here.*
Hört mal zu!	*Listen up!*
Hör mal damit auf!	*Stop it!*

Wie

The interrogative **wie** (*how*) is often combined with other words to form a variety of pat phrases. Many are questions that begin with *how*:

Wie oft geht ihr ins Kino?	*How often do you go to the movies?*
Wie viel kostet so ein Auto?	*How much does a car like that cost?*
Wie spät ist es?	*What time is it?*

Wie is also used in other expressions:

Wie bitte?	*What? / I beg your pardon.*
Wieso denn?	*Why?*
Und wie!	*And how!*
Wie war das?	*What did you say?*
Wie das?	*How did that happen?*

Zwar

The adverb **zwar** means *indeed* or *admittedly* and is used to stress a point in a statement or to admit to involvement in a circumstance:

Ich weiß es zwar nicht genau, aber ich nehme es als die Wahrheit an.	*I admit I'm not really sure, but I accept it as the truth.*
Onkel Karl kommt morgen, und zwar vor Mittag.	*Uncle Karl is coming tomorrow, before noon, to be precise.*
Sie ist Richterin, und zwar eine gute.	*She's a judge, and a good one at that.*

ÜBUNG
29·18

Fill in the blank of each sentence with an appropriate word from the following list: ***also,*** ***doch, gar, kaum, mal, wie,*** *or* ***zwar.***

1. _____ schnell kann das Pferd laufen?

2. Erik kennt sie _____ nicht, aber er sieht sie jeden Tag an der Ecke stehen.

3. _____ zu glauben!

4. Der hochnäsige Student ist _____ nicht so intelligent.

5. Der Dieb ist _____ auch ein Lügner!

6. _____, bis morgen. Schlaf gut!

7. „Du hast deine Handschuhe wieder verloren!" „_____ nicht!"

*Write original sentences with **also**, **doch**, **gar**, **kaum**, **mal**, **wie**, and **zwar**.*

1. also _____

2. doch _____

3. gar _____

4. mal _____

5. kaum _____

6. wie _____

7. zwar _____

Pat phrases

There are numerous short phrases that are pat responses to someone else's remarks. The following list contains some of the most frequently used ones:

Ausgezeichnet!	*Excellent!*
Das ist nicht zu glauben.	*That's unbelievable.*
Das kommt darauf an.	*That depends.*
Donnerwetter!	*For Heaven's sake!*
Du spinnst!	*You're crazy! You're nuts!*
Erstaunlich!	*Astounding!*
Großartig!	*Great!*
Keine Ahnung.	*I have no idea.*
Keine Ursache.	*Don't mention it.*
Leider nicht.	*Unfortunately, not.*
Natürlich.	*Naturally.*
Offenbar.	*Obviously. Clearly.*
Offensichtlich.	*Obviously.*
Scheinbar.	*Apparently. So it seems.*
Selbstverständlich.	*Of course.*
Super!	*Super!*
Tatsächlich?	*Really?*
Toll!	*Terrific!*
Überhaupt nicht.	*Not at all.*
Unglaublich.	*Incredible.*
Unmöglich.	*Impossible.*
Wunderbar!	*Wonderful!*

It is possible to use more than one of these expressions as a response to a particular remark. Let's look at a few example sentences that illustrate which responses are appropriate for the meaning of each sentence:

Wir gehen morgen Rad fahren.   *We're going bike riding tomorrow.*
→ Großartig!
Super!
Tatsächlich?

Herr Schneider wurde gestern verhaftet.   *Mr. Schneider was arrested yesterday.*
→ Das ist nicht zu glauben!
Donnerwetter!
Tatsächlich?

Willst du mir malen helfen?   *Do you want to help me paint?*
→ Das kommt darauf an.
Leider nicht.
Überhaupt nicht.

ÜBUNG 29·20

Fill in the blank following each sentence with an appropriate pat response.

1. Gestern abend ist mein erster Sohn geboren.

   _____

2. Ich habe eine neue Art Computer erfunden.

   _____

3. Wir haben den ganzen Tag auf der Terrasse sonnengebadet.

   _____

4. Kommt der nächste Zug um 22 Uhr?

   _____

5. Du hast 100.000 Euro gewonnen!

   _____

6. Ist Ihre Mutter wieder gesund geworden?

   _____

7. Hast du Lust, eine Fahrt nach Paris zu machen?

   _____

ÜBUNG
29·21

Write a sentence that is appropriate for the response given.

EXAMPLE: Hast du deine Handtasche gefunden?
Leider nicht.

1. _____

    Das kommt darauf an.

2. _____

    Tatsächlich?

3. _____

    Keine Ahnung.

4. _____

    Wunderbar!

5. _____

    Scheinbar.

6. _____

    Erstaunlich!

7. _____

    Toll!

Conversations

Greetings and introductions

Conversation: In der Hauptstraße (On Main Street)

Just like English speakers, Germans have a variety of ways of greeting one another. Consider the greetings used in the following dialogue.

Sabine: Hallo, Erik. **Wie geht's?**	*Hi, Erik. How are you?*
Erik: Guten Tag, Sabine. Es **geht** mir sehr gut. Danke. Und dir?	*Hello, Sabine. I'm doing very well. Thanks. And you?*
Sabine: Nicht schlecht. Wohin gehst **du**?	*Not bad. Where are you going?*
Erik: Zum Bahnhof. Ich hole meine Cousine ab.	*To the railroad station. I'm picking up my cousin.*
Sabine: Kenne ich deine Cousine? Wie heißt sie?	*Do I know your cousin? What's her name?*
Erik: Sie heißt Tina. **Du wirst** sie auf der Party kennen lernen.	*Her name is Tina. You'll meet her at the party.*
Sabine: Wie schön. Aber ich habe es eilig. **Wiedersehen!**	*How nice. But I'm in a hurry. Good-bye!*
Erik: Tschüs!	*So long!*

Du oder Sie?

Although many young Germans are quick to use **du** in their relationships, it is still common to abide by the practice of using **Sie** to show respect for someone who is older or in a position of authority. The pronoun **Sie** is almost always preferred among adults who are strangers to one another. Germans understand that many foreigners do not make this differentiation between varieties of the pronoun *you* (**du**, **ihr**, and **Sie**) in their own language and therefore do not consider it a calamity if someone makes a mistake in their choice of pronoun for *you*. If you find the practice strange or awkward, be patient, for in time it will become second nature to use **du**, **ihr**, and **Sie** correctly.

The possessive adjective form for **du**, **ihr**, or **Sie** must also be chosen using the appropriate level of formality and number (singular or plural). For example:

Du stellst deinen Freund vor.	*You introduce your friend.*
Ihr stellt eure Eltern vor.	*You introduce your parents.*
Sie stellen Ihren Bruder vor.	*You introduce your brother.*

Rewrite the dialogue **In der Hauptstraße** *as a dialogue between two people (***Frau Keller** *and* **Doktor Paulus***) who have a formal relationship and address one another with* **Sie.** *Keep all the lines of the original dialogue, making only the changes necessary to show a formal relationship.*

Frau Keller: _____

Doktor Paulus: _____

Frau Keller: _____

Doktor Paulus: _____

Frau Keller: _____

Doktor Paulus: _____

Frau Keller: _____

Doktor Paulus: _____

Based on the dialogue **In der Hauptstraße,** *supply a sentence that would be a logical response to each statement or question.*

1. Frau Keller, kennen Sie meine Cousine?

_____

2. Ich gehe zum Bahnhof.

_____

3. Sie werden meine Cousine auf der Party kennen lernen.

_____

Conversation: An der Ecke (On the corner)

Former neighbors meet on the street.

Herr Dorf: Guten Tag, Frau Schäfer. Wie geht es Ihnen?

Hello, Ms. Schäfer. How are you?

Frau Schäfer: Sehr gut. Und Ihnen?

Very well. And you?

Herr Dorf: Nicht schlecht. Wohin gehen Sie?

Not bad. Where are you going?

Frau Schäfer: Nach Hause. Wir haben jetzt eine Wohnung im Stadtzentrum.

Home. We have an apartment downtown now.

Herr Dorf: Wir wohnen noch in der Schillerstraße.

Frau Schäfer: Ach so. Was machen Sie gerade?

Herr Dorf: Ich werde **meinen** Sohn besuchen. Er wohnt hier in der Stadt.

Frau Schäfer: Grüßen Sie **Ihre** Familie von mir!

We still live on Schiller Street.

I see. What are you doing now?

I'm going to visit my son. He lives here in the city.

Say hello to your family from me.

ÜBUNG
30·3

*Based on the dialogue **An der Ecke**, supply a sentence that would be a logical response to each statement or question.*

1. Wir haben eine Wohnung im Stadtzentrum.

   _____

2. Was machen Sie gerade?

   _____

3. Mein Sohn wohnt in der Stadt.

   _____

4. Wohin gehen Sie?

   _____

ÜBUNG
30·4

*Rewrite the dialogue **An der Ecke** as a dialogue between two people (Martin and Angela) who have an informal relationship and address one another with **du**. Keep all the lines of the original dialogue, making only the changes necessary to show an informal relationship.*

Martin: _____

Angela: _____

Martin: _____

Angela: _____

Martin: _____

Angela: _____

Martin: _____

Angela: _____

ÜBUNG

30·5

In each blank provided, supply a phrase or sentence that fits logically into the three-line dialogue. For example:

Thomas: Geht es dir gut?

Erik: *Nein, es geht mir schlecht.*

Thomas: Bist du wieder krank?

1. **Sabine:** Kennst du meinen Bruder?

   Tina: Nein, ich kenne ihn noch nicht.

   Sabine: _____

2. **Erik:** Wen holst du ab?

   Karl: _____

   Erik: Ich kenne ihn nicht. Wie heißt er?

3. **Herr Keller:** Möchten Sie meinen Freund kennen lernen?

   Frau Benz: Ja, wie heißt er?

   Herr Keller: _____

4. **Maria:** Sind Sie krank, Frau Schneider?

   Frau Schneider: _____

   Maria: Es geht mir auch (*also*) gut.

5. **Thomas:** Wohin gehst du?

   Karl: _____

   Thomas: Holst du deine Tante ab?

6. **Maria:** Siezen sich Tina und Erik?

   Angela: _____

   Maria: Tina und Sabine duzen sich auch.

7. **Sabine:** Gehst du morgen zur Party?

   Martin: Ja. Aber ich habe es eilig. Tschüs!

   Sabine: _____

8. **Tina:** Wen stellt Erik vor?

   Thomas: _____

   Tina: Ich kenne ihn nicht. Wie heißt er?

9. **Frau Schneider:** Guten Tag, Doktor Paulus.

   Doktor Paulus: _____

   Frau Schneider: Ich habe es auch eilig. Auf Wiedersehen!

Conversations   523

10. **Martin:** Das ist Peter Benz.

 Sabine: _____

 Martin: Nein, er ist ein Freund von Thomas Keller.

Introducing someone

When you introduce someone or make his or her acquaintance, that person is the direct object of the verb.

Here's an important reminder: German direct objects are in the accusative case, and masculine noun phrases change their form in the accusative case. The feminine, neuter, and plural are identical in both cases.

	NOMINATIVE		ACCUSATIVE
masc.	der nette Mann	*the nice man*	den netten Mann
	ein netter Mann	*a nice man*	einen netten Mann
	dieser nette Mann	*this nice man*	diesen netten Mann
fem.	die nette Frau	*the nice woman*	die nette Frau
	eine nette Frau	*a nice woman*	eine nette Frau
	diese nette Frau	*this nice woman*	diese nette Frau
neut.	das nette Kind	*the nice child*	das nette Kind
	ein nettes Kind	*a nice child*	ein nettes Kind
	dieses nette Kind	*this nice child*	dieses nette Kind
pl.	die netten Kinder	*the nice children*	die netten Kinder
	keine netten Kinder	*no nice children*	keine netten Kinder
	diese netten Kinder	*these nice children*	diese netten Kinder

ÜBUNG
30·6

Write each word or phrase as it would appear in the given line of dialogue. Note that each completion is a direct object.

Erik kennt _____ nicht.

1. das Mädchen (*girl*) _____

2. meine Verwandten _____

3. ihr Bruder _____

4. Herr Keller _____

5. dieser Lehrer _____

Darf ich _____ vorstellen?

6. ein Freund von mir _____

7. meine Bekannte _____

8. diese Dame (*lady*) _____

9. der Ausländer _____

10. die Ausländer _____

Möchtest du _____ kennen lernen?

11. mein Sohn _____

12. unsere Tochter _____

13. Frau Dorf _____

14. diese Touristen _____

15. sein Onkel _____

Die Kinder duzen _____.

16. Erik _____

17. ihr Freund _____

18. Sabine _____

19. eine Freundin (*girlfriend*) von mir _____

20. das Mädchen _____

Thomas wird _____ abholen.

21. meine Bekannte _____

22. Doktor Paulus _____

23. der Gast (*guest*) _____

24. seine Gäste _____

25. die Ärzte _____

ÜBUNG

30·7

*Rewrite the dialogue **An der Ecke** as a dialogue between a teacher and her students.
The students address the teacher with **Sie**, and the teacher addresses the students with **ihr**.
When either Erik or Sabine speaks, they speak for both of them. Keep all the lines of the
original dialogue, making only the changes necessary to show their relationship.*

Frau Keller: _____

Erik: _____

Frau Keller: _____

Sabine: _____

Frau Keller: _____

Erik: _____

Frau Keller: _____

Sabine: _____

In the blank provided, supply a phrase or sentence that fits logically into each three-line dialogue. For example:

Thomas: Geht es dir gut?

Erik: _Nein, es geht mir schlecht._

Thomas: Bist du wieder krank?

1. Wohnen deine Eltern in der Schweiz?

   _____

   Haben sie Spanisch gelernt (_learned Spanish_)?

2. Wie alt ist sein Großvater?

   Er ist neunzig Jahre alt.

   _____

3. Was schenkst du Thomas zum Geburtstag?

   _____

   Ich habe kein Geld. Ich kaufe ihm ein Buch.

4. Ist deine Urgroßmutter sehr alt?

   _____

   Wird sie überleben?

5. Was hast du von deinem Patenonkel bekommen?

   _____

   Ist er reich (_rich_)?

6. Ich habe nur eine Schwester.

   _____

   Einundzwanzig. Genau wie du.

7. _____

   Ja, er lebt noch in Hamburg.

   Wie alt ist er?

8. Meine Tante ist fünfzig Jahre alt.

   _____

   Nein, er ist älter.

9. Mit wem wohnt Andrea? Und wo?

   _____

   München ist sehr schön.

10. _____

   Nein, sie wohnen jetzt bei unseren Eltern.

   Aber die Wohnung ist so klein.

11. Wohnt deine Tante in der Nähe?

   _____

   Sie ist also deine Nachbarin (*neighbor*)!

Verwandte (Relatives)

Let's look at sentences that describe subgroups of family members. In today's world it is common for people to have stepparents and stepchildren.

Meine Mutter ist vor drei Jahren **gestorben**.	*My mother died three years ago.*
Die zweite Frau meines Vaters ist meine **Stiefmutter**.	*My father's second wife is my stepmother.*
Ihr Sohn ist mein **Stiefbruder**.	*Her son is my stepbrother.*
Ihre Tochter ist meine **Stiefschwester**.	*Her daughter is my stepsister.*
Ich bin ihr **Stiefsohn**.	*I am her stepson.*
Meine Schwester ist ihre **Stieftochter**.	*My sister is her stepdaughter.*
Wir sind die **Stiefgeschwister**.	*We are the stepsiblings.*
Unser Vater ist **der Stiefvater** ihrer Kinder.	*Our father is the stepfather of her children.*

And when marrying, most people will inherit a group of in-laws.

Meine Frau ist die **Schwiegertochter** meiner Eltern.	*My wife is the daughter-in-law of my parents.*
Mein Mann ist der **Schwiegersohn** meiner Eltern.	*My husband is the son-in-law of my parents.*

Mein Vater ist der **Schwiegervater** meiner Frau.		*My father is my wife's father-in-law.*	
Meine Mutter ist die **Schwiegermutter** meines Mannes.		*My mother is my husband's mother-in-law.*	

The two words that describe a brother-in-law and a sister-in-law do not require the prefix **Schwieger-**.

Werner ist mein **Schwager**.	*Werner is my brother-in-law.*	
Andrea ist meine **Schwägerin**.	*Andrea is my sister-in-law.*	

At this point, you need to review the genitive case. It is used to show possession and is the equivalent of an English apostrophe + *s* or a prepositional phrase introduced by *of*.

die Frau meines Cousins   *my cousin's wife / the wife of my cousin*

The following is the genitive declension:

	NOMINATIVE		GENITIVE
masc.	der nette Mann	*the nice man*	des netten Mannes
fem.	die nette Frau	*the nice woman*	der netten Frau
neut.	das nette Kind	*the nice child*	des netten Kindes
pl.	die netten Kinder	*the nice children*	der netten Kinder

ÜBUNG
30·9

Put each group of sentences in the correct order for a conversation between two people.

1. Ist er älter als sie? / Der Mann meiner Schwester ist Lehrer. / Ja, er ist dreißig Jahre alt.

_____

_____

_____

2. Wo wohnt er denn? / Ist das das Haus deines Stiefbruders? / Nein, er wohnt nicht in der Nähe.

_____

_____

_____

3. Lebt Ihr Schwager noch? / War er sehr krank? / Nein, er ist vor einem Jahr gestorben.

_____

_____

_____

4. Der zweite Mann meiner Tante ist Professor. / Ja, in Berlin. / Wohnen sie in der Hauptstadt (*capital*)?

_____

_____

_____

5. Das ist eine große Familie. / Die Nichte meines Freundes hat sechs Geschwister. / Ja, aber sie haben eine kleine Wohnung.

_____

_____

_____

6. Es ist ein Geschenk von ihrem Sohn. / Ist das Auto deiner Schwägerin neu? / Ja, ganz (*quite*) neu.

_____

_____

_____

7. Nein, wir haben zwei alte Katzen (*cats*). / Habt ihr einen Hund?/ Meine Familie hat kein Haustier (*pet*).

_____

_____

_____

Let's review some masculine nouns that decline in a unique way. These nouns tend to be words that end in **-e**, foreign words with the accent on the final syllable, or old German words that have unique endings by tradition. For example:

nom.	der Neffe	der Tourist	der Mensch (*man, human*)
acc.	den Neffen	den Touristen	den Menschen
dat.	dem Neffen	dem Touristen	dem Menschen
gen.	des Neffen	des Touristen	des Menschen

Other words that follow this pattern are:

Löwe (*lion*)	Diplomat	Herr
Junge	Elefant	Graf (*count*)
Matrose (*sailor*)	Komponist (*composer*)	Bär (*bear*)

Using the string of words provided, form a two-line dialogue. Make the first sentence a question in the present tense with **du** as your subject. The second sentence should be either a positive or negative response (**ja** or **nein**), as indicated, to the question. For example:

kennen / die Frau / dieser Mann (nein)

Kennst du die Frau dieses Mannes? (Do you know this man's wife?)

Nein, ich kenne sie nicht. (No, I don't know her.)

1. kennen / der neue Mann / deine Nichte (nein)

   _____

   _____

2. kennen / die Freundin / der Matrose (ja)

   _____

   _____

3. kennen / der Neffe / mein Freund (ja)

   _____

   _____

4. kennen / die Gäste / unsere Großmutter (nein)

   _____

   _____

5. kennen / der Stiefsohn / der Diplomat (ja)

   _____

   _____

Now follow this example:

schenken / sie (s.) / ein Buch (nein)

Schenkst du ihr ein Buch? (Are you giving her a book?)

Nein, ich schenke ihr kein Buch. (No, I'm not giving her a book.)

6. schenken / deine Schwägerin / rote Rosen (nein)

   _____

   _____

7. schenken / er / dieser Roman (ja)

   _____

   _____

8. schenken / wir / eine Digitalkamera (nein)

_____

_____

9. schenken / der Matrose / ein neues Handy (ja)

_____

_____

10. schenken / ich / ein schicker Pulli (ja)

_____

_____

ÜBUNG

30·11

Using the noun(s) or pronoun in parentheses, ask whether the person or people named is/ are hungry. Then reply that the person is / the people are very hungry. For example:

(Stefan) Hat Stefan Hunger?
Ja, Stefan hat großen Hunger.

1. (sie [s.]) _____

_____

2. (die Kinder) _____

_____

3. (mein Sohn) _____

_____

4. (ihr) _____

_____

5. (Sie) _____

_____

6. (du) _____

_____

7. (der Reiseführer) _____

_____

8. (er) _____

_____

9. (Frau Neufeld und Sie) _____

_____

10. (Felix) _____

_____

Commands

Command forms are commonly used in conversations. Let's review how German commands function. A command is usually addressed to the second-person pronoun (*you*). Because German has three words that mean *you*, there are three forms of imperatives or commands, but all mean the same thing. In the case of the pronoun **du**, note that some verbs have an optional -**e** ending. Let's look at some examples:

INFINITIVE	DU	IHR	SIE	
kommen	Komm(e)!	Kommt!	Kommen Sie!	*come*
singen	Sing(e)!	Singt!	Singen Sie!	*sing*
bestellen	Bestell(e)!	Bestellt!	Bestellen Sie!	*order*
verkaufen	Verkauf(e)!	Verkauft!	Verkaufen Sie!	*sell*
absenden	Send(e) ab!	Sendet ab!	Senden Sie ab!	*dispatch*
aufmachen	Mach(e) auf!	Macht auf!	Machen Sie auf!	*open*

If a verb has an irregular present-tense conjugation formed by the letter -**e**- changing to -**i**- or -**ie**-, that irregularity also appears in the **du**-command and there is no optional -**e** ending.

INFINITIVE	DU	IHR	SIE	
sehen	Sieh(e)!	Seht!	Sehen Sie!	*see*
geben	Gib!	Gebt!	Geben Sie!	*give*

Note that the verb **sehen**, although irregular, has an optional -**e** in the **du**-form.

The verbs **haben, sein,** and **werden** have some unique forms.

INFINITIVE	DU	IHR	SIE	
haben	Hab(e)!	Habt!	Haben Sie!	*have*
sein	Sei!	Seid!	Seien Sie!	*be*
werden	Werde!	Werdet!	Werden Sie!	*become*

30·12

*Rewrite each statement as a command for **du**, then **ihr**, and then **Sie**. Note that the statements are provided in a variety of tenses, and no matter what the tense is, the command form remains the same. For example:*

Er lernte Deutsch.
du *Lerne Deutsch!*
ihr *Lernt Deutsch!*
Sie *Lernen Sie Deutsch!*

1. Wir finden seine Bücher.

   du _____

   ihr _____

   Sie _____

2. Ich bestellte eine Flasche Rotwein.

   du _____

   ihr _____

   Sie _____

3. Sie werden nur Milch trinken.

   du _____

   ihr _____

   Sie _____

4. Die Studenten frühstücken im Esszimmer (*dining room*).

   du _____

   ihr _____

   Sie _____

5. Stefan deckte den Tisch mit einem großen Tischtuch.

   du _____

   ihr _____

   Sie _____

6. Sie essen keinen Kuchen.

   du _____

   ihr _____

   Sie _____

7. Er grillt nicht in der Garage.

du _____

ihr _____

Sie _____

8. Mein Vater probierte die Forelle.

du _____

ihr _____

Sie _____

9. Wir werden den Vertrag mitbringen.

du _____

ihr _____

Sie _____

10. Ich machte alle Fenster zu.

du _____

ihr _____

Sie _____

ÜBUNG

30·13

Put each group of sentences in the correct order for a conversation between two people.

1. Morgen soll das Wetter besser sein. / Ja, es ist wieder sehr kalt. / Schneit es?

_____

_____

2. Ich sehe einen Fremden (*stranger*) an der Tür stehen. / Es klingelt. / Wer kommt so spät zu Besuch?

_____

_____

3. Es wird dir sicherlich gefallen. / Dieses Restaurant hat eine gute Küche. / Hoffentlich ist es nicht zu teuer.

_____

_____

_____

4. Ja, das kann der Gesundheit schaden. / Mein Mann trinkt zu viel Bier. / Aber ich bin Antialkoholikerin.

_____

_____

_____

5. Um halb zwölf. / Warum so spät? / Wann kommst du vorbei?

_____

_____

_____

Rewrite each line of dialogue with a word or phrase that can replace the underlined words. Make any necessary changes.

Zum <u>schwarzen</u> Adler

_____

Herr Benz: Ich bin sicher, dass Ihnen dieses <u>Restaurant</u> gefallen wird.

_____

Frau Neufeld: Es ist sicherlich sehr <u>elegant</u>, aber hoffentlich nicht zu teuer.

_____

Herr Benz: Ich habe <u>sehr oft</u> hier gegessen, und alles ist <u>preiswert</u>. Bitte bestellen Sie alles, was Ihnen gefällt!

_____

Frau Neufeld: Ich esse manchmal vegetarisch, aber vielleicht <u>soll</u> ich die <u>Forelle</u> probieren.

_____

Herr Benz: Bedienung! Bitte eine Flasche <u>Weißwein</u>.

_____

Frau Neufeld: Mein Mann trinkt keinen Wein. Ihm gefällt nur <u>Bier</u>.

_____

Herr Benz: Meine Frau ist Antialkoholikerin und trinkt nur <u>ein Gläschen Rotwein</u> zu Weihnachten.

_____

Frau Neufeld: Übrigens, Herr Benz, haben Sie <u>den Vertrag</u> mitgebracht?

_____

Herr Benz: Jawohl.

_____

More conversation

Conversation: **An der Bushaltestelle** (At the bus stop)

Two friends are talking about a foreigner they see standing in front of City Hall.

Tina: Wer ist der junge Mann, der vor dem Rathaus steht?

Who is the young man standing in front of City Hall?

Felix: Das ist John Weston. Er ist Amerikaner und ein **Austauschstudent** aus Kalifornien.

That is John Weston. He is an American and an exchange student from California.

Tina: Ich habe ihn gestern in der Bank **sprechen hören**. Er spricht gut aber mit einem Akzent.

I heard him speaking in the bank yesterday. He speaks well but with an accent.

Felix: Er kann auch ein bisschen Spanisch und Italienisch. Er **studiert** Medizin an der Uni.

He also knows a little Spanish and Italian. He is studying medicine at the university.

Tina: Und wer ist die junge Frau neben ihm?

And who is the young woman next to him?

Felix: Das ist seine Verlobte. Sie ist Österreicherin aus Wien.

That's his fiancée. She's an Austrian from Vienna.

Tina: Studiert sie auch?

Is she also studying? Is she a student, too?

Felix: Nein. Sie ist schon **Lehrerin** in einer **Grundschule** in einem Vorort.

No. She's already a teacher in a primary school in a suburb.

ÜBUNG
31·1

*Based upon the dialogue **An der Bushaltestelle**, supply a logical response to each statement or question.*

1. Wo steht der junge Amerikaner?

2. Er ist Amerikaner und Austauschstudent.

3. Er studiert Medizin an der Universität.

_____

4. Wer steht neben dem jungen Amerikaner?

_____

5. Seine Verlobte ist Österreicherin.

_____

Schulen

Americans tend to use the word *student* to refer to anyone involved in education. Germans make a distinction between a child who goes to school and a young adult going to college.

der Schüler, die Schülerin	*student, pupil, schoolboy/schoolgirl*
der Gymnasiast, die Gymnasiastin	*student at a preparatory high school*
der Student, die Studentin	*university student*
der Kommilitone, die Kommilitonin	*classmate, fellow student*

There is also a variety of names for educational institutions. Let's look at some sentences that illustrate these.

Gehst du gern in die Schule?	*Do you like going to school?*
Mein Sohn besucht eine Grundschule.	*My son attends a primary school.*
Meine Tochter besucht eine Hauptschule.	*My daughter attends a vocational high school.*
Unsere Kinder sind auf der Realschule.	*Our children go to a traditional high school.*
Besuchst du das Gymnasium?	*Do you attend a prep school?*

In order to attend a university, a German high school student must pass the entrance examination, called **das Abitur**.

Hast du das **Abitur** schon gemacht?	*Have you already passed the university entrance exam?*
Sie geht nächstes Jahr an die Universität.	*She is going to college next year.*
Professor Benz lehrt an einer Uni.	*Professor Benz teaches at a college.*
In Physik hat sie die beste Note bekommen.	*She got her best grade in the physics class.*
Ich bekomme dieses Jahr ein schlechtes Zeugnis.	*I am getting a bad report card this year.*

You are surely familiar with the past tense, but let's review how that tense is used differently in narratives and in conversation. When talking about the past in casual conversation, the present perfect tense is most commonly used. The simple past tense is usually used for narratives and writing. For example:

NARRATIVE	CONVERSATION
Er machte das Abitur.	Er hat das Abitur gemacht.
Sie bekam eine gute Note.	Sie hat eine gute Note bekommen.

Remember that verbs of motion and verbs that describe a change in state of being use **sein** as their auxiliary. Transitive verbs use **haben**. Let's review some regular and irregular verbs conjugated in the present perfect tense.

	besuchen (*to visit, attend*)	reisen (*to travel*)
ich	habe besucht	bin gereist
du	hast besucht	bist gereist
er	hat besucht	ist gereist

	sprechen (*to speak*)	fahren (*to drive*)
wir	haben gesprochen	sind gefahren
ihr	habt gesprochen	seid gefahren
sie (*pl.*)	haben gesprochen	sind gefahren

The verbs **haben**, **sein**, and **werden** deserve a special look.

	haben (*to have*)	sein (*to be*)	werden (*to become, get*)
ich	habe gehabt	bin gewesen	bin geworden
du	hast gehabt	bist gewesen	bist geworden
er	hat gehabt	ist gewesen	ist geworden

ÜBUNG
31·2

In the blank provided, supply a phrase or sentence that fits logically into each three-line dialogue. For example:

Thomas: Geht es dir gut?

Erik: *Nein, es geht mir schlecht.*

Thomas: Bist du wieder krank?

1. Der Professor lehrt an der Universität.

   Was lehrt er?

   _____

2. Hast du schon das Abitur gemacht?

   _____

   Was möchtest du studieren?

3. Ich bekomme dieses Semester in Physik eine schlechte Note.

   _____

   Du bist immer klüger als ich gewesen.

4. Tina steht vor dem Rathaus.

   _____

   Das ist ein Austauschstudent aus Amerika.

5. Nächstes Jahr besucht Sabine die Grundschule.

_____

Im Mai wird sie sieben Jahre alt.

6. Erik ist ein Kommilitone von mir.

_____

Nein, er möchte Lehrling (*apprentice*) in einer Fabrik (*factory*) werden.

7. Meine Tochter ist auf der Realschule.

Mein Sohn besucht das Gymnasium.

_____

8. Er kommt aus Kalifornien.

Spricht er Deutsch?

_____

9. Wer ist der Herr, der vor dem Rathaus steht?

Das ist Professor Keller.

_____

10. Felix, gehst du gern in die Schule?

Ja, aber ich bekomme schlechte Noten.

_____

Double infinitive pattern

It is important to remember that with modal auxiliaries and a few other verbs, the present perfect tense requires a *double infinitive*. Let's look at some examples.

PRESENT TENSE	PRESENT PERFECT TENSE	
ich muss lernen	ich habe **lernen müssen**	*I had to study*
du sollst arbeiten	du hast **arbeiten sollen**	*you were supposed to work*
er kann singen	er hat **singen können**	*he could sing*
wir dürfen gehen	wir haben **gehen dürfen**	*we were allowed to go*
ihr müsst helfen	ihr habt **helfen müssen**	*you had to help*
Sie wollen schlafen	Sie haben **schlafen wollen**	*you wanted to sleep*

Other verbs that follow the double infinitive pattern in the present perfect tense are **sehen**, **hören**, **helfen**, and **lassen**. Consider these example sentences.

PRESENT TENSE	PRESENT PERFECT TENSE	
ich sehe ihn schwimmen	ich habe ihn **schwimmen sehen**	*I saw him swimming*
du hörst sie singen	du hast sie **singen hören**	*you heard them singing*

| sie hilft mir arbeiten | sie hat mir **arbeiten helfen** | *she helped me work* |
| wir lassen es reparieren | wir haben es **reparieren lassen** | *we had it repaired* |

ÜBUNG
31·3

Rewrite each sentence in the present perfect tense.

1. Wir schreiben Hausaufgaben (*write/do the homework assignments*).

   _____

2. Ich lese den Artikel (*read the article*).

   _____

3. Wer unterrichtet bei dir Englisch (*teaches English to you*)?

   _____

4. Sie muss eine Berufsschule (*vocational college*) besuchen.

   _____

5. Er lässt sein Auto waschen (*has his car washed*).

   _____

6. Wie lange dauert es?

   _____

7. Ihr hört ihn Deutsch sprechen.

   _____

8. Felix bekommt eine sehr gute Note.

   _____

9. Kleine Kinder können den Kindergarten besuchen.

   _____

10. Sie hat mein Lehrbuch (*textbook*).

    _____

11. Ich belege (*take*) einen Deutschkurs (*German course*).

    _____

12. Du übersetzt einen Text.

    _____

13. Sie lernen das Lied (*song*) auswendig (*by heart*).

    _____

14. Er will seine Note verbessern (*improve*).

   _____

15. Der Schüler macht einen Fehler.

   _____

Im Klassenzimmer

Look at the following sentences, illustrating some of the things that students in a classroom might say when talking about school.

Um wie viel Uhr kommen sie zur Schule?	*What time do they come to school?*
Der Neuling aus Bonn ist sportlich.	*The new boy from Bonn is athletic.*
Die Physikaufgaben sind auf Seite elf.	*The physics assignments are on page eleven.*
Auf welcher Seite stehen die Lösungen der Übung?	*On what page are the answers to the exercise?*
Ich lese ein paar Seiten für Geschichte.	*I am reading a couple pages for history.*

Just like in any school, being on time (**pünktlich**) in a German school is essential.

Die Lehrerin ist immer **pünktlich**.	*The teacher is always punctual.*
Man muss **pünktlich** zur Schule kommen.	*You have to come to school on time.*

And just like students in any school, German students worry about being smart enough for tough subjects.

Ist Deutsch für dich leicht oder schwer?	*Is German easy or hard for you?*
Ich bin leider kein Genie.	*Unfortunately, I am not a genius.*
Mein Bruder ist in Mathe sehr klug.	*My brother is very smart in math.*

German teachers are as demanding as teachers elsewhere in the world, and they have a reputation for being strict but fair. You would probably hear statements like the following in a typical German classroom.

Nächste Stunde wiederholen wir das Gedicht noch einmal.	*We will repeat the poem one more time in the next lesson.*
Bringt eure Bücher und Hefte mit!	*Bring along your books and notebooks.*
Ruhe bitte!	*Quiet, please!*

Dedicated students take their schoolwork seriously and make every effort to keep up and to know what is required of them. The following are typical comments you might hear them make.

Was hat sie an die Tafel geschrieben?	*What did she write on the board?*
Hat er unsere Klassenarbeit korrigiert?	*Has he graded the quiz?*
Welche Fächer standen gestern auf dem Stundenplan?	*What subjects were scheduled for yesterday?*
Dieser Physikkurs ist nicht für Anfänger.	*This physics course is not for beginners.*

And a day off from schoolwork is always welcome.

Morgen haben wir keine Schule!	*We don't have school tomorrow!*

Put each group of sentences in the correct order for a conversation between two people.

1. Spielt er Fußball? / Der Neuling aus Bremen ist sportlich. / Nein, er spielt Tennis.

   _____

   _____

   _____

2. Hoffentlich bekomme ich eine gute Note. / Noch nicht. / Hat Frau Schiller das Examen korrigiert?

   _____

   _____

3. Ich kann nicht. Ich bin kein Genie. / Wir müssen achtzig Seiten lesen. / Vielleicht. Aber du musst.

   _____

   _____

4. Deutsch und Physik. / Der Physikkurs ist nicht für Anfänger. / Welche Fächer standen auf dem Stundenplan?

   _____

   _____

5. Auf Seite vierzig. / Ich verstehe kein Wort. / Auf welcher Seite steht die Hausaufgabe?

   _____

   _____

   _____

6. Ist das die neue Hausaufgabe? / Er hat etwas an die Tafel geschrieben. / Nein, das ist der Stundenplan für morgen.

   _____

   _____

   _____

7. Warum bist du so faul? / Ich habe es noch nicht gelesen. / Morgen wiederholen wir das Gedicht noch einmal.

   _____

   _____

   _____

8. Ja, aber mit einem deutschen Akzent. / Und du sprichst auch sehr gut. / Englisch ist für mich ziemlich leicht.

_____

_____

_____

9. Ich habe den Neuling schwimmen sehen. / Er ist sehr sportlich. / Er ist auch sehr klug.

_____

_____

_____

10. Wir müssen unsere Noten verbessern. / Ich werde ein schlechtes Zeugnis bekommen. / Ich auch.

_____

_____

_____

11. Nein, Physik ist zu schwer. / Haben Sie einen Physikkurs belegt? / Was für einen Kurs werden Sie belegen?

_____

_____

_____

12. Aber wir mögen diese Schule. / Ihr werdet eine andere Schule besuchen müssen. / Es tut mir leid. Wir haben keinen Platz mehr.

_____

_____

_____

13. Nein, morgen ist Sonntag. / Morgen haben wir einen Test. / Morgen haben wir keine Schule.

_____

_____

_____

14. Ja, er heißt Erik und ist sehr klug. / Er hat letzten Monat das Abitur gemacht. / Kennst du den Neuling aus München?

_____

_____

_____

15. Willst du eine schlechte Note bekommen? / Nein, Herr Braun. Ich habe sie leider vergessen. / Lars, hast du deine Bücher mitgebracht?

_____

_____

_____

Studieren and lernen

The German verb **studieren** is used specifically to describe someone taking courses at a university.

Mein Bruder **studiert** in Heidelberg.	*My brother is studying in Heidelberg.*
Haben Sie Anglistik **studiert**?	*Did you study English language and literature?*

The verb **lernen** means *to learn*, but it is also used to mean *to study* when it describes the action of sitting down with one's books and spending time studying.

Wir haben Physik **gelernt**.	*We learned physics.*
Ich kann nicht gehen. Ich muss **lernen**.	*I cannot go. I have to study.*

Now look at the following sentences that can be used with a variety of subject areas. In the example sentences that follow, you can plug in many kinds of subjects (**Chemie** *chemistry*, **Biologie** *biology*, **Erdkunde** *geography*, **Philosophie** *philosophy*, and so on).

Ich habe mich für Jura immatrikuliert.	*I enrolled in law.*
Hast du dich für Maschinenbau immatrikuliert?	*Did you enroll in mechanical engineering?*
Geschichte ist mein Lieblingsfach.	*History is my favorite subject.*
Am Montag schreiben wir einen Test in Deutsch.	*We are having a test in German on Monday.*

The following sentences are typical comments about academic work.

Seine Vorlesungen finden in diesem Hörsaal statt.	*His lectures are held in this lecture hall.*
Sie will in die Forschung gehen.	*She wants to go into research.*
Hier muss man wissenschaftlich arbeiten.	*You have to do scholarly work here.*
Der Professor hat im Labor gearbeitet.	*The professor worked in the laboratory.*
Biologie, Chemie und Physik zählen zu den Naturwissenschaften.	*Biology, chemistry, and physics belong to the natural sciences.*

And here's one last phrase, one that can be used to talk about an unsuccessful student.

Der faule Junge ist durchgefallen.	*The lazy boy failed.*

Write the word or phrase provided as it would appear in the blank in each sentence. Make any necessary changes.

Meine Lieblingsfächer sind _____.

1. Mathematik und Physik _____

2. Deutsch und Spanisch _____

3. Sport und Geschichte _____

4. Biologie und Erdkunde _____

5. Soziologie (*sociology*) und Chemie _____

_____ schreibt ihr einen Test in Latein (*Latin*).

6. am Montag _____

7. nächste Woche _____

8. im Juni (*June*) _____

9. morgen _____

10. nächsten Freitag _____

Ich habe _____ bekommen.

11. ein Stipendium (*scholarship*) _____

12. gute Noten _____

13. eine schlechte Note _____

14. ein Brief (*letter*) _____

_____ müssen wissenschaftlich arbeiten.

15. wir _____

16. man _____

17. alle (*everyone*) _____

18. du _____

19. ihr _____

Sie hat sich für _____ immatrikuliert.

20. Elektrotechnik (*electrical engineering*) _____

21. Germanistik (*German language and literature*) _____

22. Maschinenbau _____

23. Kunsterziehung (*art education*) _____

24. Jura _____

25. Geschichte _____

Shopping

Conversation: Im Einkaufszentrum (At the mall)

Mom and Dad arrive at the shopping mall and start their shopping trip.

Mutter: Endlich sind wir da! Wir **hätten** mit einem Taxi **fahren sollen**.	*We're finally here. We should have taken a taxi.*
Vater: Ja, das **Einkaufszentrum** ist weit entfernt, aber es ist gesund zu Fuß zu gehen.	*Yes, the mall is far away, but it's healthy to go on foot.*
Mutter: Wo ist meine Liste? Ich möchte Sabine eine kurze Hose und neue Strümpfe **kaufen**.	*Where is my list? I'd like to buy Sabine shorts and new stockings.*
Vater: Hans braucht nur Sportkleidung. Und neue Turnschuhe. Der Junge lebt jetzt im Turnstudio.	*Hans just needs sportswear. And new gym shoes. The boy lives at the fitness club now.*
Mutter: Guck mal! Der Anzug im Schaufenster sieht schick aus. Perfekt für dich.	*Look. The suit in the store window looks elegant. Perfect for you.*
Vater: Nein. Die braune Farbe **steht** mir nicht gut.	*No. I don't look good in brown.*
Mutter: Vielleicht der Blaue mit einem gestreiften Schlips.	*Maybe the blue one with a striped tie.*
Vater: Es ist schon elf Uhr. Ich möchte eine Tasse Kaffee und ein Sandwich.	*It's already eleven o'clock. I'd like a cup of coffee and a sandwich.*
Mutter: Es ist zu früh, und wir müssen noch viele **Einkäufe machen**.	*It's too early, and we still have a lot of shopping to do.*
Vater: Fragen wir den **Verkäufer** da, wo die Sportkleidung ist!	*Let's ask the salesman there where the sportswear is.*

ÜBUNG
31·6

*Based upon the dialogue **Im Einkaufszentrum**, supply a logical response to each statement or question.*

1. Warum hätten sie mit einem Taxi fahren sollen?

_____

2. Ich möchte Sabine eine Bluse und neue Strümpfe kaufen.

_____

3. Hans lebt jetzt im Turnstudio.

_____

4. Was sieht die Mutter im Schaufenster?

_____

5. Es ist schon elf Uhr.

_____

6. Mach schnell! Wir müssen noch viele Einkäufe machen.

_____

Einkaufen

There are numerous words that describe places where you can shop, from the tiniest corner shop to a giant mall. For example:

der Laden	_shop_
das Geschäft	_store_
das Kaufhaus	_department store_
das Einkaufszentrum	_shopping mall_

Besides stores that sell general merchandise, there are stores that sell specific kinds of goods. For example:

die Drogerie	_drugstore_
die Apotheke	_pharmacy_
die Metzgerei	_butcher shop_
die Molkerei	_dairy products store_
das Lebensmittelgeschäft	_grocery store_
die Buchhandlung	_bookstore_

Die Waren (_the goods_) sold in specialized stores are often categorized by a single word.

die Eisen**waren**	_hardware_
die Haushalts**waren**	_housewares_

And then there are businesses that sell no products at all but deal in services instead.

der Damenfriseur	_ladies' hairdresser_
der Herrenfriseur	_men's barber_

When purchasing clothing, there are some practical phrases that will come in handy.

Dieses Kleid passt mir nicht.	_This dress does not fit me._
Welche Größe brauchen Sie?	_What size do you need?_
Sagen Sie mir bitte, wo der Umkleideraum ist!	_Please tell me where the changing room is._

No matter what you buy, you always have to be concerned with how much something costs. The words **kosten** (_to cost_), **billig** (_cheap_), and **teuer** (_expensive_) will be very useful.

Wie viel **kosten** diese Handschuhe?	_How much do these gloves cost?_
Das ist **billig**.	_That is cheap._
Das ist viel zu **teuer**.	_That is far too expensive._

Some things can only be bought if they are **erhältlich** (*available/obtainable*) in a particular store or if they are **vorrätig** (*in stock*). For example:

Die Medizin ist nur auf Rezept **erhältlich**.	*The medicine is only available by prescription.*
Ist dieses Werkzeug **vorrätig**?	*Is this tool in stock?*

ÜBUNG
31·7

In the blank provided, supply a phrase or sentence that fits logically into each three-line dialogue. For example:

Thomas: Geht es dir gut?

Erik: *Nein, es geht mir schlecht.*

Thomas: Bist du wieder krank?

1. Fahren wir heute zum Einkaufszentrum!

   _____

   Ja, ich möchte einen neuen Anzug kaufen.

2. Dieses Werkzeug ist sehr preiswert. Es kostet nur dreißig Euro.

   Ist es vorrätig?

   _____

3. Ich möchte eine Tasse Kaffee.

   _____

   Wir haben genug Zeit. Es ist nur elf Uhr.

4. Passt mir dieses Kleid?

   _____

   Wo ist der Umkleideraum?

5. Wie viel kosten diese Strümpfe?

   _____

   Das ist sehr teuer. Haben Sie Billigere?

Kaufen und verkaufen (Buying and selling)

Let's look at a variety of other words and phrases shoppers commonly use.

Unsere Tochter ist **Kauf**süchtig.	*Our daughter is a shopaholic.*
Es gibt keine Ein**kauf**swagen mehr.	*There aren't any more shopping carts.*
Ich habe meine Ein**kauf**stasche mit.	*I have my shopping bag along.*
Er hat seinen Ein**kauf**szettel verloren.	*He lost his shopping list.*

The noun **der Laden** refers to a small establishment and can be translated as either *shop* or *store*.

Ein Blumen**laden** wird im Dorf eröffnet.	*A flower shop is being opened in the village.*
Der **Laden**besitzer macht eine Geschäftsreise.	*The store owner is on a business trip.*
In diesem **Laden** gibt es Lebensmittel.	*This store sells groceries.*

When shoppers complain about high prices, they openly speak their mind to friends or to a shopkeeper. For example:

Für einen Euro bekommt man heute weniger als früher.	*Today you get less for a euro than you used to.*
Das ausländische Geld hat keine **Kauf**kraft.	*Foreign money has no buying power.*

The verb **verkaufen** (*to sell*) becomes **der Verkauf** (*sale*) as a noun. Notice that the expression *for sale* in English uses a different preposition in German: **zum Verkauf**.

Er hat sein Fahrrad zum **Verkauf** angeboten.	*He put his bike up for sale.*
Endlich tätigst du einen **Verkauf**.	*You finally make a sale.*

The following phrases will come in handy for the purchaser who is looking for a bargain.

viele preiswerte Artikel	*lots of good buys*
ein Einkäufermarkt	*a buyer's market*
der Preisschlager des Monats	*the best buy of the month*
der Räumungs**verkauf**	*clearance sale*
der Schluss**verkauf**	*end-of-the season sale*
der Aus**verkauf**	*liquidation sale*
das Mindesthaltbarkeitsdatum	*sell-by date*

Die Kleidung (clothing)

After grocery shopping, shopping for clothing is probably the next most popular shopping activity. The following kinds of apparel are among the most frequently bought. For example, on a rainy day you would need:

der Regenmantel*raincoat*

For the feet, besides **Strümpfe** (*stockings*), you could buy the following items.

die Socken	*socks*
die Stiefeln	*boots*

Everyone, children and adults alike, needs undergarments. Consider these sentences.

Mein Sohn braucht eine neue Unterhose.	*My son needs new underpants.*
Zieh dir ein Unterhemd an!	*Put on an undershirt!*
Ich möchte diesen Büstenhalter **kaufen**.	*I'd like to buy this bra.*
Dieser Schlüpfer ist alt.	*These panties are old.*
die Strumpfhose	*panty hose*

And to keep your head and neck warm you need:

der Hut	hat
die Mütze	cap
der Schal	scarf

Perhaps the most common items of apparel among young and old alike are the following:

Dieses T-Shirt ist ganz modisch.	*This T-shirt is quite fashionable.*
Erik und Tina tragen teure Jeans.	*Erik and Tina wear expensive jeans.*

The verb **ziehen** (*to pull, draw*) is used with three specific prefixes (**an-**, **aus-**, and **um-**) when talking about dressing.

Ich **ziehe** meine Schuhe **an**.	*I put on my shoes.*
Die Sportler **ziehen** sich **aus**.	*The athletes undress.*
Du musst dich schnell **umziehen**.	*You have to change (your clothes) fast.*

ÜBUNG

31·8

Write the word or phrase provided as it would appear in the blank in the line of dialogue. Make any necessary changes in the rest of the line as well.

Warum hast du _____ gekauft?

1. dieser Regenmantel _____

2. eine blaue Bluse _____

3. ein roter Rock _____

4. keine Stiefeln _____

5. eine braune Strumpfhose _____

_____ zog die neue Jeans an.

6. ich _____

7. du _____

8. sie (*s.*) _____

9. wir _____

10. Sie _____

Er muss _____ ausziehen.

11. seine Jacke _____

12. sein Sakko (*sports jacket*) _____

13. sein Unterhemd _____

14. meine Handschuhe _____

15. der alte Anzug _____

Hier werden _____ eröffnet.

16. eine Apotheke _____

17. zwei Kaufhäuser _____

18. eine neue Buchhandlung _____

19. keine neuen Geschäfte _____

20. eine Metzgerei _____

Sie sollten _____ anprobieren.

21. der blaue Sakko _____

22. diese Lederjacke (*leather jacket*) _____

23. mein buntes Hemd _____

24. ein größerer Rock (*skirt*) _____

25. die billigen Handschuhe _____

_____ ziehen sich um.

26. ich _____

27. du _____

28. er _____

29. ihr _____

30. der neue Verkäufer _____

In diesem Geschäft gibt es _____.

31. nur Eisenwaren _____

32. keine Haushaltswaren _____

33. keine Lebensmittel _____

34. Kleidung für Kinder _____

35. Spielzeug (*toys*) _____

Das gestreifte Hemd steht _____ nicht.

36. ich _____

37. er _____

38. dein Vater _____

39. der Damenfriseur _____

40. der Ladenbesitzer _____

Wir bieten _____ zum Verkauf an.

41. der alte Regenmantel _____

42. die neuen Turnschuhe _____

43. dieser Badeanzug (*bathing suit*) _____

44. dieses T-Shirt _____

45. der braune Hut _____

Ich beeile mich (*hurry*) in _____ zu gehen.

46. die Molkerei _____

47. das Einkaufszentrum _____

48. das neue Kaufhaus _____

49. eine Apotheke _____

50. das Lebensmittelgeschäft _____

Subjunctive review

Let's look at a few examples of present and past subjunctive conjugations, as a review.

Regular verbs

PRESENT SUBJUNCTIVE	PAST SUBJUNCTIVE
ich mache	ich machte
du machest	du machtest
er mache	er machte
wir machen	wir machten
ihr machet	ihr machtet
sie machen	sie machten

Irregular verbs

PRESENT SUBJUNCTIVE	PAST SUBJUNCTIVE
ich sehe	ich sähe
du sehest	du sähest
er sehe	er sähe
wir sehen	wir sähen
ihr sehet	ihr sähet
sie sehen	sie sähen

There is a special phrase that can come in handy for a variety of situations. It involves the subjunctive voice of the verb **haben** and the modal auxiliary **sollen**. Look at the following examples.

Wir **hätten** mit einem Taxi fahren **sollen**.	*We should have taken a taxi.*
Ich **hätte** das nicht sagen **sollen**.	*I should not have said that.*
Du **hättest** ihr damit helfen **sollen**.	*You should have helped her with that.*

The verb **haben** is conjugated in the past subjunctive and any number of infinitives can precede **sollen** in these sentences: **hätten** + infinitive + **sollen**.

Conversation: Im Turnstudio (At the fitness club)

Two young men have just finished working out. They are discussing the shopping trip they agreed to.

Martin: Hast du noch nicht geduscht?	*Haven't you showered yet?*
Lars: Nein, ich musste Herrn Dorf helfen, ein Trainingsgerät zu reparieren.	*No, I had to help Mr. Dorf repair a piece of exercise equipment.*
Martin: Beeil dich! Wir haben Andrea und Sabine versprochen pünktlich zum **Kaufhaus** zu kommen.	*Hurry up. We promised Andrea and Sabine to get to the department store on time.*
Lars: Ich brauche nur fünf Minuten um zu duschen und noch fünf, um mich anzuziehen.	*I only need five minutes to shower and another five to dress.*
Martin: Was wollen die Mädchen **kaufen**?	*What do the girls want to buy?*
Lars: Sabine sagt, sie braucht ein neues Kleid für die Party.	*Sabine says she needs a new dress for the party.*
Martin: Ich wette, dass Andrea auch eins braucht.	*I'll bet that Andrea needs one too.*
Lars: Hast du mein Hemd gesehen? Das Blaue?	*Have you seen my shirt? The blue one?*
Martin: Mensch, es ist heute sehr heiß. **Zieh** dir ein T-Shirt **an**!	*Man, it's really hot today. Put on a T-shirt!*
Lars: Du hast Recht. Ich bin gleich wieder da.	*You're right. I'll be right back.*

ÜBUNG
31·9

Based upon the dialogue **Im Turnstudio,** *supply a logical response to each statement or question.*

1. Warum hat Lars noch nicht geduscht?

_____

2. Wir haben versprochen pünktlich zum Kaufhaus zu kommen.

_____

3. Was wollen die Mädchen kaufen?

_____

4. Andrea sagt, sie braucht eine neue Jeans.

_____

5. Hat Martin das blaue Hemd gesehen?

_____

6. Mensch, es ist sehr heiß heute.

_____

Euro und Cent

Germany no longer uses the **Mark** or **Pfennig** for its currency. Like most other members of the European Union, Germans use the **Euro** and the **Cent**. Just as with dollars and cents, one hundred **Cent** make up one **Euro**. In place of the word **Euro**, you will often see the symbol €.

Prices are given in a variety of ways.

Wie viel kostet das?	*How much does that cost?*
Das Buch kostet zehn **Euro** und achtzig **Cent**.	*The book costs ten euros and eighty cents.*
Eine Flasche Wein kostet €12,75.	*A bottle of wine costs €12,75.*
Ein Glas Limonade kostet €3,50.	*A glass of soda/pop costs €3,50.*

Note that German uses a *decimal comma* to separate euros from cents and not a *decimal point*.

ÜBUNG

31·10

Rewrite each string of words, symbols and numbers as a sentence. For example:

das Buch / kosten / €13,50

Das Buch kostet dreizehn Euro und fünfzig Cent.

1. dieser Wagen / kosten / €15 900

_____

2. ein Stück Kuchen / kosten / €1,60

_____

3. diese Handschuhe / kosten / €22,85

_____

4. ihr neues Haus / kosten / €250 000,00

_____

5. die Fliege / kosten / €8,10

_____

6. mein Pelzmantel / kosten / €925,25

_____

7. diese DVDs / kosten / €33,75

_____

8. zwei Eintrittskarten / kosten / €45,00

_____

9. ein Liter Bier / kosten / €3,50

_____

10. diese Lederstiefeln / kosten / €125,00

_____

Meter, Liter, Gramm und Pfund

Europe uses the metric system for weights and measurements. The general terms for discussing weights and measurements are as follows:

breit / die Breite	*wide/width*
lang / die Länge	*long/length*
tief / die Tiefe	*deep/depth*
schwer / leicht / das Gewicht	*heavy/light/weight*

Measurements of length and distance use the word **Meter** (*about 39.37 inches*), often together with certain prefixes.

der **Meter**	*meter*
Ich brauche etwa drei **Meter** Stoff.	*I need about three meters of fabric.*
der Milli**meter**	*millimeter*
Der Nagel ist hundert Milli**meter** lang.	*The nail is a hundred millimeters long.*
der Zenti**meter**	*centimeter*
Sie kaufte eine vierzig Zenti**meter** lange Feder.	*She bought a forty-centimeter-long feather.*

Long distances require the use of **Kilometer** (*1,000 meters*).

der **Kilometer**	*kilometer*
Wie viele **Kilometer** sind es von Hamburg nach Bremen?	*How many kilometers is it from Hamburg to Bremen?*

Square meters are called **Quadratmeter**. This term is used much the same way that *square feet* is used to describe the size of a building or a room. But remember that a **Quadratmeter** is much larger than a *square foot*: **1 Meter** = 39.37 inches, *1 foot* = 12 inches.

der **Quadratmeter**	*square meter*
Das neue Haus hat 130 **Quadratmeter**.	*The new house has 130 square meters of space.*

Liquids are measured in **Liter** (*about 33.8 fluid ounces*).

der **Liter**	*liter*
Bestell einen **Liter** Bier!	*Order a liter of beer!*

A **Gramm** is a very small unit of weight: there are approximately 453.6 *grams* in a pound. **Kilogramm**, with the prefix **Kilo-**, means *1,000 grams*. And the German word **Pfund** (*pound*) is not the same as a pound as it is understood in North America. A **Pfund** (*500 grams*) is half of a **Kilogramm**.

das **Gramm**	*gram*
Geben Sie mir hundert **Gramm** Käse!	*Give me a hundred grams of cheese.*
das **Kilogramm** / das **Kilo**	*kilogram*
Er wiegt achtundachtzig **Kilogramm**.	*He weighs eighty-eight kilograms.*
Der Hund wiegt ungefähr zehn **Kilo**.	*The dog weighs approximately ten kilograms.*
das **Pfund**	*pound (500 grams)*
Ich habe acht **Pfund** Äpfel gekauft.	*I bought eight pounds of apples.*

ÜBUNG
31.11

Rewrite each string of words and numbers as a sentence.

1. das Esszimmer / 4 Meter / breit

_____

2. dieses Brett (*board*) / 10,5 Zentimeter / lang

_____

3. der Küchentisch (*kitchen table*) / 1 Meter / hoch

_____

4. ich / kaufen / 12 Pfund / Kartoffeln

_____

5. die Katze / wiegen / 8 Kilogramm

_____

6. der Teich (*pond*) / 1 Meter / tief

_____

7. der Fluss (*river*) / 4,5 Meter / tief

_____

8. der Bleistift (*pencil*) / 125 Millimeter / lang

_____

9. der See (*lake*) / 11 Meter / tief

_____

10. die neue Wohnung (*apartment*) / haben / 95 Quadratmeter

_____

Rewrite the dialogue **Im Einkaufszentrum**, *keeping all the original sentences but making the following changes:*

The father and mother are going to a department store.

Change the son to a daughter and the daughter to a son with new names.

Change all clothing and shoes to other apparel.

Change all colors to new colors.

Change the food to new food.

Change the time of day.

Change the salesman to a saleswoman.

Im <u>Kaufhaus</u>

Mutter: _____

Vater: _____

Mutter: _____

Vater: _____

Mutter: _____

Vater: _____

Mutter: _____

Vater: _____

Mutter: _____

Vater: _____

Travel

Conversation: **Die Ferienreise (The vacation trip)**

A couple is discussing plans for a future vacation trip.

Andrea: Ich möchte so gerne nach Paris fahren. Da gibt's die besten Modehäuser.

I'd like so much to go to Paris. The best fashion houses are there.

Jörg: Wir haben vor zwei Jahren eine ganze Woche in Frankreich **verbracht**. Ich möchte lieber etwas anderes tun.

We spent a whole week in France two years ago. I'd rather do something else.

Andrea: Ja, ich weiß. Du willst fischen oder wandern gehen. Eine Großstadt ist viel interessanter.	*Yes, I know. You want to go fishing or hiking. A big city is much more interesting.*
Jörg: Wie wäre es mit Berlin oder München? Und sie sind gar nicht so weit von hier.	*How about Berlin or Munich? And they're not so far from here.*
Andrea: Nein, eine **Auslandsreise** ist ein kulturelles Erlebnis und sehr lehrreich.	*No, a foreign trip is a cultural experience and very educational.*
Jörg: Haben wir genug gespart, um eine **Amerikareise** zu machen?	*Have we saved enough to take a trip to America?*
Andrea: O, Jörg, welch eine herrliche Idee! In New York gibt es auch ausgezeichnete Modehäuser.	*Oh, Jörg, what a great idea! There are excellent fashion houses in New York, too.*
Jörg: Und Hockeyspiele in Boston, und Korbballspiele in Chicago.	*And hockey games in Boston, and basketball games in Chicago.*
Andrea: Aber nein. Die USA ist zu **weit entfernt**. Wir müssen in Europa bleiben.	*But no. The U.S.A. is too far away. We have to stay in Europe.*
Jörg: Vielleicht nicht. Nordafrika ist nur jenseits des Mittelmeers.	*Maybe not. North Africa is just on the other side of the Mediterranean.*

ÜBUNG

31·13

Based upon the dialogue **Die Ferienreise**, *supply a logical response to each statement or question.*

1. Wo gibt es die besten Modehäuser?

   _____

2. Wir haben vor zwei Jahren eine ganze Woche in Frankreich verbracht.

   _____

3. Eine Großstadt ist viel interessanter als wandern gehen.

   _____

4. Warum müssen sie in Europa bleiben?

   _____

5. Eine Auslandsreise ist ein kulturelles Erlebnis und sehr lehrreich.

   _____

6. Das ist zu weit. Wir müssen in Europa bleiben.

   _____

Comparatives and superlatives

Comparatives and superlatives are high-frequency items. Let's do a quick review of them here. They are used not only as predicate adjectives or adverbs but also as declined adjectives. First let's look at them as predicate adjectives and adverbs.

PREDICATE ADJECTIVES

Positive	Dieses Haus ist klein.	*This house is small.*
Comparative	Dieses Haus ist kleiner.	*This house is smaller.*
Superlative	Dieses Haus ist am kleinsten.	*This house is the smallest.*

ADVERBS

Positive	Sie läuft schnell.	*She runs fast.*
Comparative	Sie läuft schneller.	*She runs faster.*
Superlative	Sie läuft am schnellsten.	*She runs the fastest.*

When comparatives and superlatives are declined in the various cases, they are formed in the same way as illustrated above. But the adjective endings need to conform to the gender, number, and case of the nouns they modify.

Positive	Er liest den guten Roman.	*He reads the good novel.*
Comparative	Er liest den besseren Roman.	*He reads the better novel.*
Superlative	Er liest den besten Roman.	*He reads the best novel.*
Positive	Das kleine Kind weint.	*The little child cries.*
Comparative	Das kleinere Kind weint.	*The littler child cries.*
Superlative	Das kleinste Kind weint.	*The littlest child cries.*

Besides **gut, besser, am besten**, a few other adjectives have an irregular comparative and superlative: **bald, eher, am ehesten; groß, größer, am größten; nah, näher, am nächsten; hoch, höher, am höchsten; viel, mehr, am meisten.**

ÜBUNG

31·14

Provide the missing adjectival forms of each sentence—positive, comparative, and/or superlative.

1. Positive: Die guten Modehäuser sind in Paris.

   Comparative: _____

   Superlative: _____

2. Positive: _____

   Comparative: Ich möchte lieber nach Amerika reisen.

   Superlative: _____

3. Positive: _____

   Comparative: _____

   Superlative: Ist das Mittelmeer die größte See?

4. Positive: Es war lehrreich.

   Comparative: _____

   Superlative: _____

5. Positive: _____

   Comparative: Es ist weiter zwischen Berlin und München.

   Superlative: _____

6. Positive: _____

   Comparative: _____

   Superlative: Ist Boston am interessantesten?

7. Positive: Wir haben viel gespart.

   Comparative: _____

   Superlative: _____

8. Positive: _____

   Comparative: Sie besucht das neuere Modehaus.

   Superlative: _____

9. Positive: _____

   Comparative: _____

   Superlative: Die größten Gebäude (*buildings*) sind in dieser Straße.

10. Positive: Das Wetter im Frühling ist herrlich.

    Comparative: _____

    Superlative: _____

APPENDIX A

The principal parts
of irregular verbs

Only the second-person and third-person singular are shown in the present tense. In the past tense, the third-person singular is provided. However, because of the number of irregularities in the conjugation, the full present tense conjugation of **sein** and **tun** is shown.

INDICATIVE				SUBJUNCTIVE
INFINITIVE	PRESENT	PAST	PAST PARTICIPLE	SUBJUNCTIVE II
backen	bäckst backte	buk *or* backte	gebacken	bäckt *or* büke
befehlen	befiehlst befiehlt	befahl	befohlen	beföhle
befleißen	befleißt befleißt	befliss	beflissen	beflisse
beginnen	beginnst beginnt	begann	begonnen	begönne
beißen	beißt beißt	biss	gebissen	bisse
bergen	birgst birgt	barg	geborgen	bärge
bersten	birst birst	barst	geborsten	bärste
betrügen	betrügst betrügt	betrog	betrogen	betröge
bewegen	bewegst bewegt	bewog	bewogen	bewöge
biegen	biegst biegt	bog	gebogen	böge
bieten	bietest bietet	bot	geboten	böte
binden	bindest bindet	band	gebunden	bände
bitten	bittest bittet	bat	gebeten	bäte
blasen	bläst bläst	blies	geblasen	bliese
bleiben	bleibst bleibt	blieb	geblieben	bliebe
bleichen	bleichst bleicht	blich	geblichen	bliche

INFINITIVE	PRESENT	PAST	PAST PARTICIPLE	SUBJUNCTIVE II
braten	brätst brät	briet	gebraten	briete
brechen	brichst bricht	brach	gebrochen	bräche
brennen	brennst brennt	brannte	gebrannt	brennte
bringen	bringst bringt	brachte	gebracht	brächte
denken	denkst denkt	dachte	gedacht	dächte
dingen	dingst dingt	dingte *or* dang	gedungen *or* gedingt	dingte *or* dänge
dreschen	drischst drischt	drosch	gedroschen	drösche
dringen	dringst dringt	drang	gedrungen	dränge
dürfen	darfst darf	durfte	gedürft	dürfte
empfangen	empfängst empfängt	empfing	empfangen	empfinge
empfehlen	empfiehlst empfiehlt	empfahl	empfohlen	empföhle *or* empfähle
empfinden	empfindest empfindet	empfand	empfunden	empfände
erbleichen	erbleichst erbleicht	erbleichte *or* erblich	erbleicht *or* erblichen	erbleichte *or* erbliche
erlöschen	erlischst erlischt	erlosch	erloschen	erlösche
erschrecken	erschrickst erschrickt	erschrak	erschrocken	erschräke
erwägen	erwägst erwägt	erwog	erwogen	erwöge
essen	isst isst	aß	gegessen	äße
fahren	fährst fährt	fuhr	gefahren	führe
fallen	fällst fällt	fiel	gefallen	fiele
fangen	fängst fängt	fing	gefangen	finge
fechten	fichtst ficht	focht	gefochten	föchte
finden	findest findet	fand	gefunden	fände
flechten	flichtst flicht	flocht	geflochten	flöchte
fliegen	fliegst fliegt	flog	geflogen	flöge
fliehen	fliehst flieht	floh	geflohen	flöhe
fließen	fließt fließt	floss	geflossen	flösse

INFINITIVE	PRESENT	PAST	PAST PARTICIPLE	SUBJUNCTIVE II
fressen	frisst frisst	fraß	gefressen	fräße
frieren	frierst friert	fror	gefroren	fröre
gären	gärst gärt	gor	gegoren	göre
gebären	gebierst gebiert	gebar	geboren	gebäre
geben	gibst gibt	gab	gegeben	gäbe
gedeihen	gedeihst gedeiht	gedieh	gediehen	gediehe
gehen	gehst geht	ging	gegangen	ginge
gelten	giltst gilt	galt	gegolten	gälte *or* gölte
genesen	genest genest	genas	genesen	genäse
genießen	genießt genießt	genoss	genossen	genösse
geraten	gerätst gerät	geriet	geraten	geriete
gewinnen	gewinnst gewinnt	gewann	gewonnen	gewänne *or* gewönne
gießen	gießt gießt	goss	gegossen	gösse
gleichen	gleichst gleicht	glich	geglichen	gliche
gleiten	gleitest gleitet	glitt	geglitten	glitte
glimmen	glimmst glimmt	glomm *or* glimmte	geglommen *or* geglimmt	glömme *or* glimmte
graben	gräbst gräbt	grub	gegraben	grübe
greifen	greifst greift	griff	gegriffen	griffe
haben	hast hat	hatte	gehabt	hätte
halten	hältst hält	hielt	gehalten	hielte
hängen	hängst hängt	hing	gehangen	hinge
hauen	haust haut	hieb	gehauen	hiebe
heben	hebst hebt	hob	gehoben	höbe
heißen	heißt heißt	hieß	geheißen	hieße
helfen	hilfst hilft	half	geholfen	hülfe or hälfe
kennen	kennst kennt	kannte	gekannt	kennte

INFINITIVE	PRESENT	PAST	PAST PARTICIPLE	SUBJUNCTIVE II
klimmen	klimmst klimmt	klomm *or* klimmte	geklommen *or* geklimmt	klömme *or* klimmte
klingen	klingst klingt	klang	geklungen	klänge
kneifen	kneifst kneift	kniff	gekniffen	kniffe
kommen	kommst kommt	kam	gekommen	käme
können	kannst kann	konnte	gekonnt	könnte
kriechen	kriechst kriecht	kroch	gekrochen	kröche
laden	lädst lädt *or* ladet	lud *or* ladete	geladen *or* geladet	lüde *or* ladete
lassen	lässt lässt	ließ	gelassen	ließe
laufen	läufst läuft	lief	gelaufen	liefe
leiden	leidest leidet	litt	gelitten	litte
leihen	leihst leiht	lieh	geliehen	liehe
lesen	liest liest	las	gelesen	läse
liegen	liegst liegt	lag	gelegen	läge
lügen	lügst lügt	log	gelogen	löge
mahlen	mahlst mahlt	mahlte	gemahlen	mahlte
meiden	meidest meidet	mied	gemieden	miede
melken	melkst melkt	melkte	gemelkt *or* gemolken (*adjective*)	mölke
messen	misst misst	maß	gemessen	mässe
mögen	magst mag	mochte	gemocht	möchte
müssen	musst muss	musste	gemusst	müsste
nehmen	nimmst nimmt	nahm	genommen	nähme
nennen	nennst nennt	nannte	genannt	nennte
pfeifen	pfeifst pfeift	pfiff	gepfiffen	pfiffe
pflegen	pflegst pflegt	pflegte *or* pflog	gepflegt *or* gepflogen	pflegte *or* pflöge
preisen	preist preist	pries	gepriesen	priese
quellen	quillst quillt	quoll	gequollen	quölle

INFINITIVE	PRESENT	PAST	PAST PARTICIPLE	SUBJUNCTIVE II
raten	rätst rät	riet	geraten	riete
reiben	reibst reibt	rieb	gerieben	riebe
reißen	reißt reißt	riss	gerissen	risse
reiten	reitest reitet	ritt	geritten	ritte
rennen	rennst rennt	rannte	gerannt	rennte
riechen	riechst riecht	roch	gerochen	röche
ringen	ringst ringt	rang	gerungen	ränge
rinnen	rinnst rinnt	rann	geronnen	ränne *or* rönne
rufen	rufst ruft	rief	gerufen	riefe
salzen	salzt salzt	salzte	gesalzt or gesalzen (*figurative*)	salzte
saufen	säufst säuft	soff	gesoffen	söffe
saugen	saugst saugt	sog	gesogen	söge
schaffen	schaffst schafft	schuf	geschaffen	schüfe
schallen	schallst schallt	schallte	geschallt	schallte *or* schölle
scheiden	scheidest scheidet	schied	geschieden	schiede
scheinen	scheinst scheint	schien	geschienen	schiene
schelten	schiltst schilt	schalt	gescholten	schölte
scheren	schierst schiert	schor *or* scherte	geschoren *or* geschert	schöre *or* scherte
schieben	schiebst schiebt	schob	geschoben	schöbe
schießen	schießt schießt	schoss	geschossen	schösse
schinden	schindest schindet		geschunden	schünde
schlafen	schläfst schläft	schlief	geschlafen	schliefe
schlagen	schlägst schlägt	schlug	geschlagen	schlüge
schleichen	schleichst schleicht	schlich	geschlichen	schliche
schleifen	schleifst schleift	schliff	geschliffen	schliffe

INFINITIVE	PRESENT	PAST	PAST PARTICIPLE	SUBJUNCTIVE II
schleißen	schleißt schleißt	schliss	geschlissen	schlisse
schliefen	schliefst schlieft	schloff	geschloffen	schlöffe
schließen	schließt schließt	schloss	geschlossen	schlösse
schlingen	schlingst schlingt	schlang	geschlungen	schlänge
schmeißen	schmeißt schmeißt	schmiss	geschmissen	schmisse
schmelzen	schmilzt schmilzt	schmolz	geschmolzen	schmölze
schneiden	schneidest schneidet	schnitt	geschnitten	schnitte
schrecken	schrickst schrickt	schrak	geschrocken	schräke
schreiben	schreibst schreibt	schrieb	geschrieben	schriebe
schreien	schreist schreit	schrie	geschrieen or geschrien	schriee
schreiten	schreitest schreitet	schritt	geschritten	schritte
schweigen	schweigst schweigt	schwieg	geschwiegen	schwiege
schwellen	schwillst schwillt	schwoll	geschwollen	schwölle
schwimmen	schwimmst schwimmt	schwamm	geschwommen	schwömme or schwämme
schwinden	schwindest schwindet	schwand	geschwunden	schwände
schwingen	schwingst schwingt	schwang	geschwungen	schwänge
schwören	schwörst schwört	schwor	geschworen	schwüre or schwöre
sehen	siehst sieht	sah	gesehen	sähe
sein	bin bist ist sind seid sind	war	gewesen	wäre
senden	sendest sendet	sandte or sendete	gesandt or gesendet	sendete
sieden	siedest siedet	sott or siedete	gesotten	sötte or siedete
singen	singst singt	sang	gesungen	sänge
sinken	sinkst sinkt	sank	gesunken	sänke
sinnen	sinnst sinnt	sann	gesonnen	sänne or sönne
sitzen	sitzt sitzt	saß	gesessen	säße

INFINITIVE	PRESENT	PAST	PAST PARTICIPLE	SUBJUNCTIVE II
sollen	sollst soll	sollte	gesollt	sollte
spalten	spaltest spaltet	spaltete	gespalten *or* gespaltet	spaltete
speien	speist speit	spie	gespieen *or* gespien	spiee
spinnen	spinnst spinnt	spann	gesponnen	spönne
spleißen	spleißt spleißt	spliss	gesplissen	splisse
sprechen	sprichst spricht	sprach	gesprochen	spräche
sprießen	sprießt sprießt	spross	gesprossen	sprösse
springen	springst springt	sprang	gesprungen	spränge
stechen	stichst sticht	stach	gestochen	stäche
stecken	steckst steckt	steckte *or* stak	gesteckt	steckte *or* stäke
stehen	stehst steht	stand	gestanden	stünde *or* stände
stehlen	stiehlst stiehlt	stahl	gestohlen	stöhle or stähle
steigen	steigst steigt	stieg	gestiegen	stiege
sterben	stirbst stirbt	starb	gestorben	stürbe
stieben	stiebst stiebt	stob *or* stiebte	gestoben *or* gestiebt	stöbe *or* stiebte
stinken	stinkst stinkt	stank	gestunken	stänke
stoßen	stößt stößt	stieß	gestoßen	stieße
streichen	streichst streicht	strich	gestrichen	striche
streiten	streitest streitet	stritt	gestritten	stritte
tragen	trägst trägt	trug	getragen	trüge
treffen	triffst trifft	traf	getroffen	träfe
treiben	treibst treibt	trieb	getrieben	triebe
treten	trittst tritt	trat	getreten	träte
triefen	triefst trieft	troff	getrieft	tröffe
trinken	trinkst trinkt	trank	getrunken	tränke

	INDICATIVE			SUBJUNCTIVE
INFINITIVE	PRESENT	PAST	PAST PARTICIPLE	SUBJUNCTIVE II
tun	tue tust tut tun tut tun	tat	getan	täte
verderben	verdirbst verdirbt	verdarb	verdorben	verdürbe
verdrießen	verdrießt verdrießt	verdross	verdrossen	verdrösse
vergessen	vergisst vergisst	vergaß	vergessen	vergäße
verhehlen	verhehlst verhehlt	verhelte	verhehlt	verhelte
verlieren	verlierst verliert	verlor	verloren	verlöre
verwirren	verwirrst verwirrt	verwirrte	verwirrt *or* verworren (*adjective*)	verwirrte
wachsen	wächst wächst	wuchs	gewachsen	wüchse
wägen	wägst wägt	wog *or* wägte	gewogen	wöge *or* wägte
waschen	wäschst wäscht	wusch	gewaschen	wüsche
weichen	weichst weicht	wich	gewichen	wiche
weisen	weist weist	wies	gewiesen	wiese
wenden	wendest wendet	wandte *or* wendete	gewandt *or* gewendet	wendete
werben	wirbst wirbt	warb	geworben	würbe
werden	wirst wird	wurde	geworden	würde
werfen	wirfst wirft	warf	geworfen	würfe
wiegen	wiegst wiegt	wog	gewogen	wöge
winden	windest windet	wand	gewunden	wände
wissen	weißt weiß	wusste	gewusst	wüsste
wollen	willst will	wollte	gewollt	wollte
zeihen	zeihst zeiht	zieh	geziehen	ziehe
ziehen	ziehst zieht	zog	gezogen	zöge
zwingen	zwingst zwingt	zwang	gezwungen	zwänge

APPENDIX B

Prepositions and their required cases

Dative

aus	*out of*	**aus** der Flasche *out of the bottle*
	from	**aus** Deutschland *from Germany*
	made of	**aus** Holz *made of wood*
außer	*except for*	alle **außer** mir *everyone except for me*
	out of	**außer** Atem *out of breath*
bei	*at (someone's home)*	**bei** meinen Eltern *at my parents' house*
	near	irgendwo **bei** Hamburg *somewhere near Hamburg*
	at (a business)	**beim** Schneider *at the tailor's*
bis zu	*up to, as many as*	die Stadt hat **bis zu** 10.000 Einwohnern *the city has up to 10,000 inhabitants*
gegenüber	*opposite*	**gegenüber** der Schule *opposite the school*
	with	ihm **gegenüber** freundlich sein *be kind with someone*
mit	*with*	**mit** dem Herrn *with the gentleman*
	by (vehicle)	**mit** dem Zug *by train*

nach	*after*	**nach** der Schule *after school*
	to (a region)	**nach** Frankreich *to France*
	according to	**nach** meiner Ansicht *in my view*
seit	*since*	**seit** April *since April*
	for	**seit** Jahren *for years*
von	*from, of*	westlich **von** Berlin *west from Berlin*
	by	ein Drama **von** Goethe *a drama by Goethe*
zu	*to (someone's home)*	**zu** mir kommen *come to my house*
	with (food)	**zu** dem Käse gab es Bier *there was beer with the cheese*
	at (holiday time)	**zu** Weihnachten *at Christmas*

Accusative

bis	*till, until*	**bis** Freitag *till Friday*
	to, as far as	**bis** Bremen *to (as far as) Bremen*
durch	*through*	**durch** das Fenster *through the window*
	by	**durch** die Post *by mail*
für	*for*	ein Geschenk **für** dich *a present for you*
	as	**für** tot erklären *to declare as dead*
gegen	*against*	**gegen** mich *against me*
	toward	**gegen** Morgen *toward morning*
ohne	*without*	**ohne** seine Frau *without his wife*

um	*around*	**um** die Ecke *around the corner*
	at (time)	**um** sechs Uhr *at six o'clock*
	after, by	Stunde **um** Stunde *hour after hour*
wider	*against*	**wider** alle Vernunft *against all reason*

Dative/Accusative

an	*at*	**am** Fenster *at the window*
	on (a day)	**am** Sonntag *on Sunday*
auf	*on*	**auf** dem Boden *on the floor*
	(here's) to	**auf** Ihre Gesundheit *to your health*
hinter	*behind*	**hinter** der Tür *behind the door*
	beyond	die nächste Station **hinter** Bonn *the next station beyond Bonn*
in	*in (location)*	**in** Deutschland *in Germany*
	in (period of time)	**in** drei Tagen *in three days*
neben	*next to, beside*	**neben** dem Haus *next to the house*
über	*over, above*	**über** dem Tisch *over the table*
	about, of	**über** ihn reden *talk about him*
	over (an expanse)	**über** die Straße gehen *cross the street*
unter	*under*	**unter** einem Baum *under a tree*
	among	**unter** anderem *among other things*

vor	*before, in front of*	**vor** dem Haus *in front of the house*
	from, because of	**vor** Hunger umkommen *die from hunger*
	ago	**vor** zehn Jahren *ten years ago*
zwischen	*between*	**zwischen** seinen Eltern *between his parents*

Genitive

(an)statt	*instead of*	**statt** ihrer Schwester *instead of her sister*
angesichts	*in the face of*	**angesicht**s der Gefahr *in face of the danger*
außerhalb	*outside of*	**außerhalb** der Dienstzeit *outside of office hours*
diesseits	*this side of*	**diesseits** der Grenze *this side of the border*
jenseits	*that side of*	**jenseits** der Grenze *that side of the border*
trotz	*despite, in spite of*	**trotz** des Gewitters *in spite of the rainstorm*
unterhalb	*below*	**unterhalb** der Brücke *below the bridge*
während	*during*	**während** des Krieges *during the war*
wegen	*because of*	**wegen** des schlechten Wetters *because of the bad weather*

APPENDIX C
Summary of declensions

Declension with **der**-words

	MASCULINE	FEMININE
nom	der alte Mann	diese gute Frau
acc	den alten Mann	diese gute Frau
dat	dem alten Mann	dieser guten Frau
gen	des alten Mannes	dieser guten Frau

	NEUTER	PLURAL
nom	jenes neue Haus	die alten Leute
acc	jenes neue Haus	die alten Leute
dat	jenem neuen Haus	den alten Leuten
gen	jenes neuen Hauses	der alten Leute

Declension with **ein**-words

	MASCULINE	FEMININE
nom	ein großer Garten	meine kleine Katze
acc	einen großen Garten	meine kleine Katze
dat	einem großen Garten	meiner kleinen Katze
gen	eines großen Gartens	meiner kleinen Katze

	NEUTER	PLURAL
nom	Ihr altes Auto	keine neuen Bücher
acc	Ihr altes Auto	keine neuen Bücher
dat	Ihrem alten Auto	keine neuen Büchern
gen	Ihres alten Autos	keiner neuen Bücher

Masculine nouns requiring an -(e)n ending

nom	der Herr	dieser Löwe	kein Mensch
acc	den Herrn	diesen Löwen	keinen Menschen
dat	dem Herrn	diesem Löwen	keinem Menschen
gen	des Herrn	dieses Löwen	keines Menschen

Neuter noun **Herz** requiring an -en ending

nom	das Herz
acc	das Herz
dat	dem Herzen
gen	des Herzens

Feminine and neuter nouns ending in -a in the singular and plural

nom	die Kamera	das Drama
acc	die Kamera	das Drama
dat	der Kamera	dem Drama
gen	der Kamera	des Dramas

nom	die Kameras	die Dramen
acc	die Kameras	die Dramen
dat	den Kameras	den Dramen
gen	der Kameras	die Dramen

Unpreceded adjectives (no **ein**-word/no **der**-word)

	MASCULINE	FEMININE
nom	warmer Kaffee	kalte Milch
acc	warmen Kaffee	kalte Milch
dat	warmem Kaffee	kalter Milch
gen	warmen Kaffees	kalter Milch

	NEUTER	PLURAL
nom	frisches Brot	kleine Kinder
acc	frisches Brot	kleine Kinder
dat	frischem Brot	kleinen Kindern
gen	frischen Brotes	kleiner Kinder

Relative pronouns (**der/die/das** and **welcher**)

	MASCULINE	FEMININE	NEUTER	PLURAL
nom	der	die	das	die
acc	den	die	das	die
dat	dem	der	dem	denen
gen	dessen	deren	dessen	deren
nom	welcher	welche	welches	welche
acc	welchen	welche	welches	welche
dat	welchem	welcher	welchem	welchen
gen	dessen	deren	dessen	deren

Adjectives and participles used as nouns

	MASCULINE	FEMININE
nom	der Alte	diese Beauftragte
acc	den Alten	diese Beauftragte
dat	dem Alten	dieser Beauftragten
gen	des Alten	dieser Beauftragten

	NEUTER	PLURAL
nom	das Interessanteste	keine Angeklagten
acc	das Interessanteste	keine Angeklagten
dat	dem Interessantesten	keinen Angeklagten
gen	des Interessantesten	keiner Angeklagten

Answer key

1 Pronunciation and gender

1·1 1. g 2. o 3. f 4. n 5. e 6. m 7. l 8. d 9. k 10. j 11. c 12. i
13. b 14. h 15. a

1·2 1. der 2. die 3. die 4. der 5. die 6. der 7. der 8. die 9. die
10. der

1·3 1. das 2. die 3. die 4. der 5. das 6. das 7. die 8. die 9. die
10. der 11. der 12. das 13. die 14. der 15. der 16. die 17. die 18. die
19. die 20. die

2 Definite and indefinite articles

2·1 1. Das Kind ist da. 2. Die Blume ist da. 3. Das Haus ist da. 4. Der Garten ist da.
5. Der Wagen ist da. 6. Der Stuhl ist da. 7. Das Auto ist da. 8. Der Bruder ist da.
9. Die Schwester ist da. 10. Die Sangerin ist da. 11. Das Gymnasium ist klein.
12. Die Katze ist klein. 13. Der Sportler ist klein. 14. Das Madchen ist klein.
15. Der Boden ist klein. 16. Die Landkarte ist klein. 17. Die Universitat ist klein.
18. Der Pullover ist klein. 19. Die Schule ist klein. 20. Das Kind ist klein. 21. Das
Auto ist hier. 22. Die Gartnerin ist hier. 23. Die Frau ist hier. 24. Die Professorin
ist hier. 25. Der Junge ist hier.

2·2 1. dieser Mann 2. diese Frau 3. dieses Kind 4. diese Blume 5. dieser Garten
6. diese Gartnerin 7. diese Lehrerin 8. dieses Studium 9. dieses Bett
10. dieser Professor 11. dieser Diplomat 12. diese Bluse 13. dieser Boden
14. dieses Fenster 15. diese Schauspielerin 16. dieses Haus 17. diese Universitat
18. dieses Konigtum 19. dieser Gartner 20. dieser Lehrer 21. diese Schule
22. dieses Madchen 23. dieser Sanger 24. diese Sangerin 25. diese Landkarte

2·3 1. eine Lehrerin 2. ein Junge 3. ein Fenster 4. ein Bett 5. eine Universitat
6. eine Tante 7. ein Madchen 8. ein Arzt 9. ein Buch 10. ein Fernsehapparat
11. eine Tochter 12. ein Restaurant 13. ein Boden 14. eine Mutter 15. ein Bild

2·4 1. keine Tochter 2. kein Tisch 3. kein Fenster 4. kein Restaurant 5. kein
Gartner 6. keine Grosmutter 7. kein Arzt 8. keine Arztin 9. kein Rathaus
10. keine Butter 11. kein Junge 12. kein Schlafzimmer 13. kein Bild 14. keine
Schwester 15. keine Tante 16. kein Bruder 17. keine Zeit 18. kein
Fernsehapparat 19. keine Uhr 20. kein Fenster 21. kein Mantel 22. keine Frau
23. kein Geld 24. keine Mutter 25. keine Universitat

2·5 1. Eine Frau ist da.
Keine Frau ist da.
2. Ein Restaurant ist klein.
Kein Restaurant ist klein.

3. Eine Schule ist gros.
   Keine Schule ist gros.
4. Eine Mutter ist hier.
   Keine Mutter ist hier.
5. Ein Film ist alt.
   Kein Film ist alt.
6. Ein Bild ist klein.
   Kein Bild ist klein.
7. Eine Grosmutter ist alt.
   Keine Grosmutter ist alt.
8. Ein Tisch ist neu.
   Kein Tisch ist neu.
9. Ein Restaurant ist gros.
   Kein Restaurant ist gros.
10. Eine Landkarte ist hier.
    Keine Landkarte ist hier.
11. Eine Tante ist alt.
    Keine Tante ist alt.
12. Ein Vater ist jung.
    Kein Vater ist jung.
13. Ein Rathaus ist neu.
    Kein Rathaus ist neu.
14. Eine Tochter ist jung.
    Keine Tochter ist jung.
15. Eine Uhr ist da.
    Keine Uhr ist da.

2·6 1. Ist der Film neu? 2. Ist dieses Kind klein? 3. Ist kein Lehrer da? 4. Ist ein Restaurant da? 5. Ist die Tochter jung? 6. Ist dieser Arzt alt? 7. Ist eine Schule neu? 8. Ist kein Bild hier? 9. Ist eine Uhr da? 10. Ist die Grosmutter alt? 11. Ist dieser Professor jung? 12. Ist ein Bett hier? 13. Ist keine Butter da? 14. Ist der Boden neu? 15. Ist dieses Auto alt?

2·7 1. die eine diese keine Tochter 2. die eine diese keine Arztin 3. der ein dieser kein Bruder 4. das ein dieses kein Bild 5. die eine diese keine Uhr 6. das ein dieses kein Fenster 7. das ein dieses kein Haus 8. der ein dieser kein Wagen 9. das ein dieses kein Gymnasium 10. das ein dieses kein Rathaus 11. das ein dieses kein Schlafzimmer 12. die eine diese keine Tante 13. die eine diese keine Grosmutter 14. der ein dieser kein Mantel 15. der ein dieser kein Film 16. die eine diese keine Schauspielerin 17. der ein dieser kein Diplomat 18. das ein dieses kein Restaurant 19. die eine diese keine Schule 20. die eine diese keine Bluse 21. die eine diese keine Mutter 22. der ein dieser kein Vater 23. das ein dieses kein Buch 24. das ein dieses kein Kind 25. der ein dieser kein Garten 26. die eine diese keine Gartnerin 27. der ein dieser kein Arzt 28. das ein dieses kein Bett 29. der ein dieser kein Junge 30. das ein dieses kein Madchen

2·8 1. Dieser Wagen ist sehr alt. Welcher Wagen ist sehr alt? 2. Jene Kinder spielen Tennis. Welche Kinder spielen Tennis? 3. Sie kennt jene Frau. Sie kennt jede Frau. 4. Welchen Arzt besuchen wir? Wir besuchen diesen Arzt. 5. Thomas hat jede Zeitung. Thomas hat jene Zeitung. 6. Sie arbeiten für diesen Professor. Sie arbeiten für jenen Professor. 7. Dieses Mädchen heißt Tina. Welches Mädchen heißt Tina? 8. Herr Schneider verkauft diesen Wagen. Herr Schneider verkauft jenen Wagen. 9. Diese Lehrerin kauft das Haus. *or* Die Lehrerin kauft dieses Haus. Welche Lehrerin kauft das Haus? *or* Welches Haus kauft die Lehrerin? 10. Welche Männer helfen ihnen? Solche Männer helfen ihnen.

2·9 1. Meine Schwester wohnt in Berlin. 2. Ihre Schwester wohnt in Berlin. 3. Deine Schwester wohnt in Berlin. 4. Eure Schwester wohnt in Berlin. 5. Wessen Schwester wohnt in Berlin? 6. Sind Ihre Freunde in Heidelberg? 7. Sind ihre Freunde in Heidelberg? 8. Sind unsere Freunde in Heidelberg? 9. Wessen Freunde sind in Heidelberg? 10. Sind seine Freunde in Heidelberg? 11. Mein Bruder ist Richter. 12. Euer Bruder ist Richter. 13. Ihr Bruder ist Richter. 14. Sein Bruder ist Richter. 15. Unser Bruder ist Richter.

2·10 1. Ja, ein Lehrer wohnt in diesem Haus. Nein, kein Lehrer wohnt in diesem Haus. 2. Ja, diese Dame ist Ärztin. Nein, diese Dame ist keine Ärztin. 3. Ja, eine Katze ist unter dem Tisch. Nein, keine Katze ist unter dem Tisch.   4. Ja, ein Zug kommt. Nein, kein Zug kommt.   5. Ja, die Frau ist Richterin. Nein, die Frau ist keine Richterin.

3   Pronouns, plurals, and the verb *sein*

3·1   1. es   2. er   3. sie   4. er   5. sie   6. es   7. es   8. sie   9. er   10. es   11. er   12. Sie 13. es   14. er   15. es   16. es   17. sie   18. er   19. sie   20. es   21. er   22. er   23. sie 24. es   25. er

3·2   1. Sie sind jung.   2. Sie sind da.   3. Sie sind klein.   4. Sie sind gros.   5. Sie sind neu.   6. Sie sind hier.   7. Sie sind alt.   8. Sie sind da.   9. Sie sind jung.   10. Sie sind neu.

3·3   1. es   2. sie (*sing.*)   3. er   4. sie (*pl.*)   5. sie (*pl.*)   6. es   7. sie (*pl.*)   8. sie (*pl.*)   9. er 10. es   11. es   12. sie (*pl.*)   13. es   14. sie (*sing.*)   15. er   16. es   17. sie (*pl.*)   18. er 19. sie (*pl.*)   20. sie (*pl.*)

3·4   1. der Mantel   2. die Tochter   3. ein Auto   4. die Onkel   5. eine Kamera   6. ein Arzt   7. die Wurste   8. die Schulen   9. das Madchen   10. eine Lampe

3·5   1. Sie   2. Sie   3. du   4. ihr   5. ihr   6. du   7. Sie   8. du   9. Sie   10. Du

3·6   1. ist   2. bin   3. ihr   4. ist   5. ich   6. du   7. sind   8. sind   9. sind   10. ist   11. bist 12. seid

3·7   1. Ist das Haus gros?   2. Sind die Hauser klein?   3. Ist er jung?   4. Sind sie alt?   5. Bist du klein? 6. Sind wir Tochter?   7. Sind die Kinder hier?   8. Seid ihr Bruder?   9. Ist sie Lehrerin?   10. Sind die Stuhle alt?   11. Bin ich alt?   12. Ist dieser Mann Professor?   13. Ist sie neu?   14. Ist es gros? 15. Herr Braun! Sind Sie Arzt?

3·8   1. Er konnte ihm nicht antworten.   2. Ein Heft und Bleistifte nützen ihm.   3. Wir haben es ihm gegeben.   4. Ein kleines Segelboot hat sich ihr genähert.   5. Ich werde ihr ein paar Blumen kaufen. 6. Das wird ihnen nicht imponieren.   7. Martin schenkte es uns.   8. Der Hund ist ihr wieder entlaufen. 9. Kannst du ihnen helfen?   10. Der Professor schreibt ihm einen kurzen Brief.

4   Titles, locations, and interrogatives

4·1   1. Guten Tag. Ich heise Schafer, Martin Schafer.
Guten Tag, Herr Schafer.
2. Guten Tag. Ich heise Bauer, Boris Bauer.
Guten Tag, Herr Bauer.
3. Guten Tag. Ich heise Schneider, Angelika Schneider.
Guten Tag, Frau Schneider.
4. Guten Tag. Ich heise Schulze, Maria Schulze.
Guten Tag, Frau Schulze.
5. Guten Tag. Ich heise Neumann, Erik Neumann.
Guten Tag, Herr Neumann.
6. Guten Tag. Ich heise Kraus, Sonja Kraus.
Guten Tag, Frau Kraus.
7. Guten Tag. Ich heise Gasse, Heinrich Gasse.
Guten Tag, Herr Gasse.
8. Guten Tag. Ich heise Becker, Marianne Becker.
Guten Tag, Frau Becker.
9. Guten Tag. Ich heise Schnell, Th omas Schnell.
Guten Tag, Herr Schnell.
10. Guten Tag. Ich heise Kiefer, Gabriele Kiefer.
Guten Tag, Frau Kiefer.

4·2   1. Frau Bauer ist in Italien.
         Frau Bauer wohnt in Italien.
       2. Die Kinder sind in Russland.
         Die Kinder wohnen in Russland.
       3. Der Diplomat ist in Nordamerika.
         Der Diplomat wohnt in Nordamerika.
       4. Ein Richter ist in Rom.
         Ein Richter wohnt in Rom.
       5. Frau Professor Schneider ist in Munchen.
         Frau Professor Schneider wohnt in Munchen.
       6. Der Direktor ist in Europa.
         Der Direktor wohnt in Europa.
       7. Meine Frau ist in Frankreich.
         Meine Frau wohnt in Frankreich.
       8. Mein Mann ist in Afrika.
         Mein Mann wohnt in Afrika.
       9. Ihr Bruder ist in Warschau.
         Ihr Bruder wohnt in Warschau.
      10. Ihre Tochter sind in Spanien.
         Ihre Tochter wohnen in Spanien.

4·3   1. ist zu Hause   2. bin zu Hause   3. sind zu Hause   4. sind zu Hause   5. bist zu Hause   6. ist zu
       Hause   7. sind zu Hause   8. ist zu Hause   9. seid zu Hause   10. sind zu Hause

4·4   1. Wo ist Ihre Mutter?
         Ihre (Meine) Mutter ist im Keller.
       2. Wo ist mein Bruder?
         Mein (Ihr) Bruder ist in der Garage.
       3. Wo sind Martin und Angela?
         Martin und Angela sind in der Stadt.
       4. Wo seid ihr?
         Ihr seid (Wir sind) in der Kirche.
       5. Wo ist Th omas?
         Thomas ist im Cafe.
       6. Wo sind wir?
         Wir sind (Ihr seid) im Wohnzimmer.
       7. Wo bin ich?
         Du bist (Sie sind) im Esszimmer.
       8. Wo ist Herr Doktor Bauer?
         Herr Doktor Bauer ist im Hotel.
       9. Wo ist mein Onkel?
         Mein Onkel (Ihr Onkel) ist im Garten.

4·5   1. Wie heist der Mann?
         Der Mann heist Herr Schulze.
       2. Wie heist die Frau?
         Die Frau heist Frau Schneider.
       3. Wie heist der Mann?
         Der Mann heist Th omas.
       4. Wie heist die Frau?
         Die Frau heist Anna Schafer.
       5. Wie heist der Mann?
         Der Mann heist Martin Neufeld.
       6. Wie heist der Mann?
         Der Mann heist Erik Schmidt.
       7. Wie heist der Mann (die Frau)?
         Der Mann (Die Frau) heist Professor Benz.
       8. Wie heist die Frau?
         Die Frau heist Doktor Tina Kiefer.

9. Wie heist der Mann?
   Der Mann heist Wilhelm Kassel.
10. Wie heist die Frau?
    Die Frau heist Angela.

4·6
1. Was ist das?
   Das ist eine Kirche.
2. Was ist das?
   Das ist ein Mantel.
3. Wer ist das?
   Das ist der Polizist.
4. Wer ist das?
   Das ist die Richterin.
5. Was ist das?
   Das ist eine Bibliothek.
6. Wer ist das?
   Das ist Frau Schneider.
7. Was ist das? Was sind das?
   Das sind die Zeitungen.
8. Wer ist das?
   Das ist Herr Bauer.
9. Wer ist das? Wer sind das?
   Das sind Karl und Martin.
10. Was ist das?
    Das ist die Garage.

4·7
1. Das Konzert ist am Montag.
   Das Konzert ist im Januar.
2. Das Examen ist am Dienstag.
   Das Examen ist im Marz.
3. Die Reise ist am Mittwoch.
   Die Reise ist im Mai.
4. Die Oper ist am Donnerstag.
   Die Oper ist im Juli.
5. Ihr (Mein) Geburtstag ist am Freitag.
   Ihr (Mein) Geburtstag ist im September.

5   The verbs *haben* and *werden* and negation

5·1

1. bin
   bist
   ist
   ist
   ist
   ist
   sind
   seid
   ist
   sind
2. sind
   habe
   hast
   hat
   hat
   hat
   haben
   habt
   haben
   haben

3. werde
   wirst
   wird
   wird
   wird
   werden
   werdet
   werden
   werden
   wird

5·2   1. Wird Ihr Bruder Zahnarzt?   2. Ist sie Tanzerin?   3. Habe ich Durst?   4. Ist dieser Artikel interessant?   5. Ist es heis?   6. Wird Frau Bauer Krankschwester?   7. Haben die Kinder Hunger?   8. Wird es dunkel?   9. Haben Sie keine Fahrkarten?   10. Hat Erik Maria gern?   11. Wird mein Onkel Rechtsanwalt?   12. Ist Sonja krank?   13. Ist dieser Roman langweilig?   14. Wird es am Montag kalt?   15. Ist es kalt im Dezember?   16. Ist das Gedicht kurz?   17. Haben die Madchen Karl gern?   18. Sind wir zu Hause?   19. Heist der Herr Martin Schafer?   20. Wird Frau Keller gesund?

5·3   1. habe   2. Sind   3. ist, wird   4. hat   5. Hast   6. ist   7. bist, wirst   8. hat   9. ist, wird   10. haben   11. Haben   12. seid   13. ist, wird   14. Ist   15. Hast

5·4   1. Er hat keine Schuhe.   2. Du hast keine Zeitung.   3. Frau Bauer ist keine Krankenschwester.   4. Herr Schneider ist kein Politiker.   5. Ich habe keine Zeit.   6. Das ist kein Kleid.   7. Er ist kein Polizist.   8. Kein Tourist ist in Berlin.   9. Wir haben am Mittwoch keine Prufung.   10. Hast du kein Geld?   11. Das ist keine Bibliothek.   12. Maria ist keine Tanzerin.   13. Die Manner werden keine Politiker.   14. Er hat kein Glas Bier.   15. Das ist keine Kirche.

5·5   1. Die Touristen sind nicht in Deutschland.   2. Mein Geburtstag ist nicht im Oktober.   3. Das ist nicht Herr Dorfmann.   4. Meine Schwester wohnt nicht in der Stadt.   5. Wir haben nicht am Freitag das Examen.   6. Ist Frau Benz nicht zu Hause?   7. Es wird nicht warm.   8. Das sind nicht meine Bucher.   9. Sonja hat die Bluse nicht.   10. Das ist nicht der Lehrer.   11. Sie haben die Fahrkarten nicht.   12. Ist das nicht Herr Bauer?   13. Hast du die Zeitungen nicht?   14. Die Dame heist nicht Frau Becker.   15. Sind das nicht meine Schuhe?

5·6   1. nicht   2. nicht   3. kein   4. keine   5. nicht   6. kein   7. nicht   8. nicht   9. nicht   10. nicht   11. nicht   12. nicht   13. keine   14. nicht   15. nicht   16. nicht   17. nicht   18. nicht   19. nicht   20. kein

5·7   1. Ja, sie hat meine Bucher.
Nein, sie hat meine Bucher nicht.
2. Ja, er ist Zahnarzt.
Nein, er ist kein Zahnarzt.
3. Ja, es wird regnerisch.
Nein, es wird nicht regnerisch.
4. Ja, die Jungen werden Sportler.
Nein, die Jungen werden keine Sportler.
5. Ja, ich bin Deutscher.
Nein, ich bin kein Deutscher.
6. Ja, wir sind zu Hause.
Nein, wir sind nicht zu Hause.
7. Ja, die Tanzerin ist in Paris.
Nein, die Tanzerin ist nicht in Paris.
8. Ja, du bist krank./Ja, Sie sind krank.
Nein, du bist nicht krank./Nein, Sie sind nicht krank.
9. Ja, ich habe das Kleid.
Nein, ich habe das Kleid nicht.
10. Ja, es wird kuhl.
Nein, es wird nicht kuhl.
11. Ja, wir haben Zeit.
Nein, wir haben keine Zeit.
12. Ja, Erik wird Student.
Nein, Erik wird nicht Student.
13. Ja, der Onkel ist alt.
Nein, der Onkel ist nicht alt.
14. Ja, ihr seid in Munchen./Ja, Sie sind in Munchen./Ja, wir sind in Munchen.
Nein, ihr seid nicht in Munchen./Nein, Sie sind nicht in Munchen./Nein, wir sind nicht in Munchen.
15. Ja, ich habe Martin gern.
Nein, ich habe Martin nicht gern.

5·8   1. Sie können heute nicht lange bleiben.   2. Wohnen Sie nicht in Darmstadt?   3. Letzte Woche war sie noch nicht krank.   4. Mein Onkel singt nicht schlecht.   5. Unsere Gäste wollen heute Abend nicht tanzen gehen.   6. Warum beklagst du dich nicht?   7. Der Stuhl steht nicht zwischen dem Schrank und dem Tisch.   8. Soll die Lampe nicht über dem Tisch hängen?   9. Das alte Flugzeug fliegt nicht schnell über die Wolken.   10. Ich trage heute meinen Regenmantel nicht.   11. Der Vogel sitzt nicht auf dem hohen Dach.   12. Gudrun hat ihren kleinen Bruder nicht geschlagen.   13. Er musste mich nicht anrufen.   14. Mozart war nicht sehr musikalisch.   15. Warum hast du diesen Brief nicht zerrissen?   16. Schreiben Sie den Brief nicht an Ihre Tante?   17. Diese Studenten haben nicht fleißig gearbeitet.   18. Sie ist gestern nicht in der Nähe von Hannover gewesen.   19. Hört der Regen nicht auf?   20. Die Jungen sind nicht über die Brücke gelaufen.   21. Viele Studenten haben das Examen nicht bestanden.   22. Im Park sitzen die jungen Leute nicht auf den Bänken.   23. In der Ferne erblickte der Wanderer die Räuber nicht.   24. Wir nehmen nicht an dem Besuch der Oper teil.   25. Mein Großvater kann sich nicht an seine Jugend erinnern.

5·9   *Sample answers are provided.*   1. Wir sind nicht am Montag abgefahren, sondern am Dienstag.   2. Er will nicht das kleine Haus kaufen, sondern das große.   3. Sie fahren nicht heute ins Restaurant, sondern morgen.   4. Er nennt nicht den jungen Mann einen Dieb, sondern den alten Mann.   5. Die Studentin begegnete nicht dem Professor, sondern einem alten Freund.   6. Das alte Lehrbuch nützt nicht dem Studenten, sondern dem Professor.   7. Ich hänge das Bild nicht über das Klavier, sondern über den Spiegel.   8. Der Junge will nicht die neuen Wörter vergessen, sondern das ganze Gedicht.   9. Die Kinder bitten nicht die Mutter um Süßigkeiten, sondern die Großmutter.   10. Ich weiß nicht die Hausnummer, sondern nur die Straße.

5·10   1. In diesem Haus wohnt kein Schauspieler.   2. Hast du keine Prüfung bestanden?   3. Das Mädchen hat keine schöne Bluse verloren.   4. Keine guten Menschen helfen den Armen.   5. Der Uhrmacher zieht keine Uhr auf.   6. Im Schatten verbergen sich keine Diebe.   7. Im März können keine Obstbäume blühen.   8. Wachsen auf dieser tropischen Insel keine Tannen?   9. Dieser Fahrer hat kein Autorennen gewonnen.   10. Die Schülerin lernt keine neuen Wörter und kein Gedicht.   11. An der Straßenecke stand kein Bettler.   12. Auf dem Sportplatz rennen keine Kinder hin und her.   13. Warum reißt du kein Blatt aus dem Buch?   14. Unser Hund hat keinen Fremden gebissen.   15. Unter dem Esstisch schlafen keine Katzen.   16. Diese Sängerin hat wie keine Nachtigall gesungen.   17. Der Erfinder hat keinen neuen Motor erfunden.   18. Ich schreibe keine Ansichtskarten und keinen langen Brief.   19. Er pfeift kein Lied.   20. Sie können keine Kinder zu lernen zwingen.   21. Das Mädchen hat keinen Ball ins Wasser geworfen.   22. Keine Unfälle geschehen täglich.   23. Hast du dem Kellner kein Trinkgeld gegeben?   24. Der Verkäufer legte keine Waren auf den Tisch.   25. In dieser Straße sind keine großen Geschäfte.

5·11   1. b   2. a   3. c   4. c   5. c   6. d   7. b   8. b   9. a   10. c

6   The present tense and numbers

6·1

1. mache	gehe	frage
machst	gehst	fragst
macht	geht	fragt
2. sagen	horen	zeigen
sagt	hort	zeigen
sagen	horen	zeigen
3. lache	setze	schwimme
lacht	setzt	schwimmt
lachen	setzen	schwimmen
4. deckst	probierst	schickst
decken	probieren	schicken
deckt	probiert	schickt
5. denke	hoffe	liebe
denkst	hoffst	liebst
denkt	hofft	liebt
denken	hoffen	lieben
denkt	hofft	liebt
denken	hoffen	lieben
denken	hoffen	lieben

6·2

1. wette	meidet
wettest	meiden

wettet	meiden
wetten	4. antworte
wettet	antwortest
wetten	antwortet
wetten	antworten
2. sende	antwortet
sendest	antworten
sendet	antworten
senden	5. huste
sendet	hustest
senden	hustet
senden	husten
3. meide	hustet
meidest	husten
meidet	husten
meiden	

6·3

1.	setze	3.	tanze
	setzt		tanzt
	setzt		tanzt
	setzen		tanzt
	setzt		tanzen
	setzen		tanzen
	setzen		
2.	heise	4.	sitze
	heist		sitzt
	heist		sitzt
	heisen		sitzen
	heist		sitzt
	heisen		sitzen
	heisen		sitzen
5.	schmerze	7.	beise
	schmerzt		beist
	schmerzt		beist
	schmerzen		beisen
	schmerzt		beist
	schmerzen		beisen
	schmerzen		beisen
6.	reise	8.	niese
	reist		niest
	reist		niest
	reisen		niesen
	reist		niest
	reisen		niesen
	reisen		niesen

6·4 1. sage 2. macht 3. schmeicheln 4. horst 5. schmelzt 6. gehen 7. fragt 8. seid 9. schliest 10. wohnen 11. glaube 12. pflanzt 13. bellt 14. wandere 15. wird 16. raucht 17. wartet 18. feiert 19. badest 20. lachelt 21. hat 22. wunschst 23. findet 24. kostet 25. singe

6·5 1. Sechs plus/und eins sind sieben. 2. Funf mal drei sind funfzehn. 3. Neun minus/weniger sieben sind zwei. 4. Zwanzig plus/und drei sind dreiundzwanzig. 5. Zwolf (geteilt) durch drei sind vier. 6. Hundert minus funfzig sind funfzig. 7. Achtundachtzig plus zwei sind neunzig. 8. Zweihundert durch vierzig sind funf. 9. Neunzehn minus acht sind elf. 10. Sechzig plus zwolf sind zweiundsiebzig.

6·6 1. zweite 2. elft en 3. dritten 4. ersten 5. zwolft e 6. einunddreisigsten 7. einundzwanzigste 8. zehnte 9. sechzehnten 10. siebten

6·7 1. Schön singt Heidi. 2. Viel Geld haben Müllers. 3. Nächste Woche ist Marie in Frankfurt. 4. Weihnachten feiern wir mit den Großeltern. 5. Mein bester Freund ist Thomas.

6·8   1. Wer kommt morgen?   2. Was machen sie?   3. Wohin fahren sie?   4. Wo schwimmen sie?
5. Warum machen sie das oft?

6·9   1. Gehen wir jetzt schwimmen?   2. Singt Jakob gut?   3. Singt Paul besser?   4. Singt Emma am besten?   5. Ist Thomas oft in Leipzig?   6. Geht Mutter oft einkaufen?   7. Ziehen Müllers nach Ulm?
8. Wohnt der Bauer auf dem Land?   9. Liest der Lehrer viel?   10. Ist das Haus neu?

6·10   1. Arbeitest du/Arbeiten Sie jetzt?   2. Wo wohnen sie?   3. Was verkaufen sie hier?   4. Kaufen sie viel?
5. Singt er laut?   6. Spielen die Kinder im Park?   7. Warum lächelt sie immer?   8. Herr Braun, gehen Sie ins Kino?   9. Warum heirate ich dich nicht?   10. Beantworten wir alle Fragen?

6·11   1. Tanzt Peter gut?   2. Kommt Ulrich heute?   3. Wann kommt Ulrich?   4. Wohnen Müllers jetzt in Berlin?   5. Wo wohnen Müllers jetzt?   6. Hat er viel Geld?   7. Warum hat er viel Geld?   8. Wer ist das?/Wer ist mein Freund?   9. Kommst du bestimmt?   10. Wie heißt er?

6·12   1. frage   2. fragst   3. fragen   4. fragt   5. fragen   6. fragt   7. fragt   8. fragen   9. fragt
10. kaufst   11. kauft   12. kauft   13. kaufen   14. kaufen   15. kaufe   16. macht   17. machen
18. machst   19. macht   20. machen

6·13   1. Die Klasse beginnt.   2. Die Kinder besuchen mich.   3. Hans, was brauchst du?   4. Frau Schmidt, was brauchen Sie?   5. Der Lehrer erklärt die Aufgabe.   6. Was kaufen sie?   7. Kommt Emma?
8. Ja, Emma und Michael kommen.   9. Was fragt ihr?   10. Wo wohnen die Jungen?   11. Ich danke dir.   12. Liebst du mich?   13. Ich liebe dich nicht.   14. Ich liebe Peter.   15. Das Mädchen probiert das Sauerkraut.   16. Die Kinder spielen im Park.   17. Frau Kugel wiederholt die Aufgabe.   18. Wir weinen nicht.   19. Wir lachen.   20. Die Eltern bezahlen das.

6·14   1. beginnt   2. besuchen   3. Bezahlst   4. deckt   5. fragst   6. erzählt   7. erklärt   8. glauben
9. lebt   10. hoffen   11. lacht   12. rauche   13. weint   14. Hörst   15. machen   16. spielen
17. sucht   18. wohnen   19. Liebst   20. blühen   21. brauchen   22. zeigt   23. schaust
24. Gehorcht   25. bewegen

6·15   1. heißt   2. heiße   3. heißt   4. heißen   5. heißen   6. heißt   7. Heißen   8. heiße   9. heißt
10. heißen

6·16   1. besitzen   2. besitzt   3. heißt   4. beißt   5. Genießt   6. schließt   7. sitzt   8. tanzt
9. reist   10. setzen sich   11. putzt   12. verschmutzt   13. gießt   14. beeinflusst   15. Pflanzt

6·17   1. heißt   2. Brauchst   3. glaubst   4. Tanzt   5. beißt   6. reist   7. überraschst   8. verletzt
9. gehorchst   10. setzt   11. planzt   12. wünschst

6·18   1. heiratet   2. heiraten   3. arbeiten   4. arbeitet, beobachtet, baden   5. scheint, badet   6. bedeutet
7. beantwortet   8. Fürchtest   9. fürchtet   10. findest   11. berichtet   12. arbeitest   13. erwartest
14. redest, redest   15. betet   16. findet   17. kostet

6·19   1. feiern   2. schüttele/schüttle   3. Verbesserst   4. verbessere/verbessre   5. klingelt   6. lächele/lächle   7. erinnere/erinnre   8. ändern   9. steuere/steure   10. flüstere/flüstre

6·20   1. heißt   2. wohnst   3. kommen   4. arbeitet   5. Arbeiten   6. besucht   7. Raucht   8. Sitzt
9. Besitzen   10. Besitzt   11. Putzt   12. Benutzt   13. Kostet   14. Wanderst   15. Gehorchst
16. Findest   17. wünschst   18. Redest   19. Zeichnest   20. Reist

6·21   1. klingelt   2. liegt   3. ruft   4. geht   5. singt   6. sitzt   7. bringt   8. trinkt   9. Trinkst
10. klopft   11. steht   12. besucht   13. Besuchst   14. redet   15. hört   16. fragt   17. antwortet
18. gehen   19. wandert   20. zeichnet   21. spielen   22. kommen   23. heißt   24. beobachtet
25. grüßt   26. lachen   27. lächelt   28. kommen   29. wartet   30. findet

6·22   1. Hast   2. habe   3. hat   4. Hat   5. haben   6. habe   7. haben   8. habt   9. haben   10. haben

6·23   1. bist   2. bin   3. sind   4. bin   5. ist   6. sind   7. seid   8. sind   9. ist   10. ist

6·24   1. wird   2. werde   3. wird   4. werden   5. werdet   6. warden   7. wirst   8. werde

6·25   1. Ich bin/Wir sind zwanzig.   2. Ja, ich habe/wir haben viel Geld.   3. Ja, ich werde/wir werden oft nervös.   4. Wir sind zwölf.   5. Ja, wir haben viel Geld.   6. Ja, wir werden oft nervös.   7. Du bist zwölf.   8. Du hast/Sie haben viel Geld.   9. Ja, du wirst/Sie werden oft nervös.   10. Ja, ich habe Hunger.

6·26   1. haben   2. feiern   3. ist   4. bin   5. freue   6. lächele/lächle   7. wird   8. ist   9. sind   10. wohnen   11. sitzt   12. hat   13. sitzt   14. klingelt   15. ist   16. hat   17. arbeitet   18. haben, feiern   19. ist   20. haben   21. beginnt   22. Wartet   23. habe   24. hast

7   Direct objects and the accusative case

7·1   1. den Lehrer   2. den Roman   3. einen Artikel   4. einen Zahnarzt   5. diesen Politiker   6. diesen Mann   7. meinen Geburtstag   8. meinen Onkel   9. Ihren Wagen   10. keinen Sportler

7·2   1. den Schauspieler   2. meine Schuhe   3. Ihre Tante   4. einen Stuhl   5. das Madchen   6. ein Gymnasium   7. keine Schwester   8. dieses Wetter   9. keine Zeit   10. eine Landkarte   11. einen Mantel   12. ein Kind   13. Ihre Prufung   14. das Examen   15. meinen Garten   16. keine Universitat   17. den Boden   18. die Schule   19. meinen Pullover   20. Ihre Schwester   21. diesen Garten   22. meine Bucher   23. das Glas   24. dieses Fenster   25. eine Schauspielerin

7·3   1. keine Zeit   2. Frau Schneider   3. Radio   4. die Kinder   5. ein Kleid und einen Pullover   6. dieses Madchen   7. Maria   8. einen Wagen   9. Deutsch   10. Geld   11. keinen Mantel   12. den Roman   13. ein Problem   14. meinen Bruder   15. diese Schauspielerin

7·4   1. Kennst du mich?
Kennst du ihn?
Kennst du sie?
Kennst du uns?
2. Ja, ich habe ihn.
Ja, ich habe sie.
Ja, ich habe es.
Ja, ich habe sie.
3. Doktor Bauer hat dich gern.
Doktor Bauer hat ihn gern.
Doktor Bauer hat uns gern.
Doktor Bauer hat euch gern.
4. Meine Grosmutter liebt mich.
Meine Grosmutter liebt dich.
Meine Grosmutter liebt sie.
Meine Grosmutter liebt sie.
5. Die Manner suchen dich.
Die Manner suchen uns.
Die Manner suchen euch.
Die Manner suchen Sie.

7·5   1. Was brauchen die Frauen?   2. Wen kennt meine Schwester nicht?   3. Was liebe ich?   4. Wen suchen wir?   5. Was kauft Herr Benz?   6. Was finden Werner und Karl?   7. Was habt ihr?   8. Was braucht mein Bruder?   9. Wen sucht Martin?   10. Wen horen Sie?   11. Wen frage ich?   12. Was decken die Kinder?   13. Wen liebt Erik?   14. Was hat Sabine?   15. Was kaufen die Jungen?

7·6   1. Er   2. ihn   3. es   4. sie   5. sie   6. sie   7. sie   8. ihn   9. ihn   10. es   11. ihn   12. er   13. es   14. es   15. es

7·7   1. Was bauen die Männer?   2. Was hat Herr Schneider?   3. Wen besuchen wir? Wen besucht ihr? Wen besuchen Sie?   4. Wen kennt der Tourist?   5. Was braucht Martin?   6. Was versteht niemand?   7. Wen sehe ich? Wen siehst du? Wen sehen Sie?   8. Wen hat Karin gern?   9. Was verkauft er?   10. Wen sehen wir? Wen seht ihr? Wen sehen Sie?

7·8   1. Haben Sie ein Heft ?   2. Haben Sie die Briefe?   3. Haben Sie den Stuhl?   4. Haben Sie eine Bluse?   5. Haben Sie das Geld?   6. Ich kaufe einen Wagen.   7. Ich kaufe eine Zeitung.   8. Ich kaufe Bücher.   9. Ich kaufe eine Lampe.   10. Ich kaufe ein Handy.

7·9   1. Die Frauen sehen mich.   2. Die Frauen sehen dich.   3. Die Frauen sehen sie.   4. Die Frauen sehen es.   5. Die Frauen sehen euch.   6. Niemand versteht ihn.   7. Niemand versteht uns.   8. Niemand versteht Sie.   9. Niemand versteht sie.   10. Niemand versteht mich.

7·10   1. Die Kinder gehen durch die Straße.   2. Die Kinder gehen durch einen Tunnel.   3. Die Kinder gehen durch den Park.   4. Die Kinder gehen durch einen Garten.   5. Ich habe etwas für sie.   6. Ich habe etwas für ihn.   7. Ich habe etwas für euch.   8. Ich habe etwas für die Männer.   9. Warum ist er gegen uns?   10. Warum ist er dagegen?   11. Warum ist er dagegen?   12. Warum ist er gegen den Krieg? 13. Warum ist er gegen mich?   14. Warum ist er gegen dich?   15. Warum ist er gegen Sie?

7·11   1. Im Sommer werden wir sie besuchen.   2. Ich kenne es nicht.   3. Gudrun hat sie zu langsam beantwortet.   4. Kannst du sie lesen?   5. Wir haben ihn verpasst!   6. Wer kann es lösen?   7. Mutter hat ihn im Keller gefunden.   8. Der Blitz hat sie getötet.   9. Martin wird sie kaufen.   10. Ich liebe es.

7·12   *These are sample answers only.*   1. Ich habe den Herrn in Kanada kennen gelernt.   2. Wo hast du das Heft gefunden?   3. Er hat seine Brillen auf dem Tisch stehen gelassen.   4. Onkel Karl hat den Eimer versteckt.   5. Wirst du Karl und mich besuchen?   6. Man baut die Häuser am Rande des Waldes. 7. Tante Luise hat das Kind auf das Bett gelegt.

7·13   1. Was werde ich in Innsbruck verleben?   2. Wen kennt mein Vetter nicht?   3. Was kaufte Martin für seine Schwester?   4. Was hat sie seit ihrer Jugend getrieben?   5. Was verdient der Arbeitslose? 6. Wen treffen wir am Hauptbahnhof?   7. Wen hat meine Tante gefragt?   8. Was liebe ich am meisten? 9. Wen haben seine Eltern im Kaufhaus gesehen?   10. Wen ärgern solche Umstände?

7·14   1. es   2. ihn   3. sie   4. ihn   5. es   6. sie   7. euch   8. sie   9. ihn   10. ihn

7·15   1. er   2. sie   3. sie   4. sie   5. sie   6. es   7. sie   8. er   9. er   10. Es

7·16   1. Man erwartet von den Bürgern Respekt.   2. Oft tut man, was man nicht tun soll.   3. Die Firma soll einem mehr Lohn geben.   4. Einem soll so viel wie möglich geholfen werden.   5. Man sagt oft, dass sie miteinander nie auskommen werden.   6. Man muss ihn lange kennen, bis man ihn versteht.   7. Man stand am Fenster und klopfte.

8   Irregular verbs in the present tense

8·1   1. fahrst   2. hat   3. fallen   4. rat   5. ratet   6. backe   7. bratst   8. halt   9. lasst 10. fangen   11. waschst   12. stost   13. seid   14. wachst   15. schlafen   16. tragst   17. schlagt 18. fangt   19. fallt   20. ratst   21. schlaft   22. werdet   23. haltst   24. Wasche

8·2

1. wachse	5. brate
wachst	bratst
wachst	brat
wachsen	braten
wachst	bratet
wachsen	braten
wachst	brat
2. trage	6. stose
tragst	stost
tragt	stost
tragen	stosen
tragt	stost
tragen	stosen
tragt	stost
3. falle	7. lasse
fallst	lasst
fallt	lasst
fallen	lassen
fallt	lasst
fallen	lassen
fallt	lasst
4. schlage	8. schlafe
schlagst	schlafst
schlagt	schlaft
schlagen	schlafen
schlagt	schlaft
schlagen	schlafen
schlagt	schlafst

8·3   1. brichst   2. vergisst   3. sprecht   4. tritt   5. steche   6. messen   7. schmilzt   8. wirfst
9. erschrecken   10. gibt   11. hilft   12. sterben   13. essen   14. frisst   15. nimmt   16. triffst
17. bergen   18. gilt   19. melke   20. trittst   21. isst   22. werft   23. geben   24. stirbt   25. brechen

8·4   1. esse   5. spreche
        isst   sprichst
        isst   spricht
        essen   sprechen
        esst   sprecht
        essen   sprechen
        isst   spricht

        2. helfe   6. sterbe
        hilfst   stirbst
        hilft   stirbt
        helfen   sterben
        helft   sterbt
        helfen   sterben
        hilft   stirbt

        3. verderbe   7. gebe
        verdirbst   gibst
        verdirbt   gibt
        verderben   geben
        verderbt   gebt
        verderben   geben
        verdirbt   gibt

        4. nehme   8. treffe
        nimmst   triffst
        nimmt   trifft
        nehmen   treffen
        nehmt   trefft
        nehmen   treffen
        nimmt   trifft

8·5   1. sehe   3. empfehle
        siehst   empfiehlst
        sieht   empfiehlt
        sehen   empfehlen
        seht   empfehlt
        sehen   empfehlen
        sieht   empfiehlt

        2. stehle   4. lese
        stiehlst   liest
        stiehlt   liest
        stehlen   lesen
        stehlt   lest
        stehlen   lesen
        stiehlt   liest

8·6   1. bricht   2. fahren   3. seid   4. stiehlt   5. fallst   6. fangt   7. sehe   8. geschieht   9. nimmt
10. lassen   11. stost   12. wird   13. weis   14. hilft   15. empfehlen   16. liest   17. schlaft
18. weis   19. messt   20. lauft   21. stehlen   22. trittst   23. ratet   24. weis   25. spricht
26. rat   27. geschieht   28. lasst   29. hast   30. wissen

8·7   1. Spricht man Englisch?   2. Laufst du nach Hause?   3. Nimmt er die Fahrkarten?   4. Gebt ihr kein
Geld?   5. Fahrt er nach Hause?   6. Wer sieht die Bibliothek?   7. Essen sie kein Brot?   8. Empfehle
ich den Roman?   9. Fangst du den Ball?   10. Weis er nichts?   11. Treten Sie mir auf den Fus?
12. Hilft Thomas Sonja und Sabine?   13. Liest du die Zeitung?   14. Bricht sie sich den Arm?   15. Tragt
meine Schwester einen Pullover?

8·8   1. Der Peter schläft bis zwölf Uhr.   2. Die Eltern schlafen bis sieben Uhr.   3. Steffiund Ulla schlafen bis
zwei Uhr nachmittags.   4. Du schläfst bis zehn Uhr.   5. Luise schläft bis neun Uhr.

8·9 1. Die Liesel läuft langsam. 2. Die Kinder laufen nicht. 3. Du läufst schnell. 4. Der Lehrer läuft schneller. 5. Ihr lauft am schnellsten.

8·10 1. hat 2. empfängt 3. fährt 4. ist 5. scheint, bläst 6. wachsen, wächst 7. hält 8. verlassen 9. spielen 10. fängt 11. läuft 12. lässt 13. haben 14. brät 15. fällt 16. macht 17. waschen 18. Wäscht 19. schmeckt 20. schläft 21. lessen 22. gefällt 23. fahren

8·11 1. Ich esse Kuchen. 2. Max isst Brötchen. 3. Die Großeltern essen Schinken. 4. Der Chef isst Speck. 5. Die Familie isst Tomaten. 6. Du isst Eis. 7. Wir essen Brot. 8. Ihr esst Sauerkraut 9. Herr Schmidt, Sie essen Erdbeertorte. 10. Frau Braun isst Hähnchen.

8·12 1. Ich lese die Zeitung. 2. Er liest den Roman. 3. Wir lesen die Nachrichten. 4. Du liest den Brief. 5. Die Geschwister lesen die Postkarte. 6. Herr Wagner liest den Bericht. 7. Ihr lest die Bücher. 8. Frau Schmidt, Sie lesen das Buch. 9. Peter und ich lesen die Geschichte. 10. Fräulein Brunn und Frau Mahl, Sie lesen das Gedicht.

8·13 1. Wie lange fährst du Auto? 2. Wie lange arbeitest du hier? 3. Wie lange lernst du Deutsch? 4. Wie lange sammelst du Briefmarken? 5. Wie lange brätst du den Schinken? 6. Wie lange schläfst du am Wochenende? 7. Wie lange liest du abends? 8. Wie lange läufst du jeden Morgen? 9. Wie oft empfängst du Gäste? 10. Wie lange lächelst du schon? 11. Wie lange bäckst/backst du den Kuchen? 12. Wie lange redest du über Politik? 13. Wie lange beobachtest du die Kinder? 14. Wie lange fürchtest du dich vor dem Krieg? 15. Wie lange betest du abends?

8·14 1. Ich klingele/klingle nicht oft. 2. Ich schüttele/schüttle den Apfelbaum nicht oft. 3. Ich ändere/ändre die Haare nicht oft. 4. Ich verbessere/verbessre das Kind nicht oft. 5. Ich flüstere/flüstre nicht oft mit dem Freund. 6. Ich fahre nicht oft Auto. 7. Ich feiere/feire nicht oft Geburtstag. 8. Ich rede nicht oft mit Marie. 9. Ich bade den Hund nicht oft. 10. Ich erinnere/erinnre ihn nicht oft an den Geburtstag.

8·15 Jetzt **bin** ich schon zwei Wochen in der Schweiz. Wir woh**nen** am See. Die Berge **sind** groß und schön. Ich klett**(e)re** oft in den Bergen. Beate **hilft** mir dabei. Sie mach**t** es viel besser. Pauline klett**ert** nicht mit uns. Sie läuf**t** jeden Morgen. Dann trink**t** Pauline viel Wasser und **isst** viel Obst. Sie **gibt** mir auch Obst zum Essen. Ich nehme es natürlich gern. **Nimmst** du Obst wenn man es dir **gibt**? Später treff**en** wir uns mit Freunden. Max vergi**sst** oft zu kommen. Das **ist** schade. Luise tri**fft** uns immer. Nachmittags lesen wir oft. Pauline **liest** einen französischen Roman. Sie läch**elt** oft beim Lesen. Montags komm**t** immer eine Frau und wäsch**t** die Wäsche für uns. Sie spr**icht** nicht mit uns. Sie **ist** immer still und arbeit**et** schnell. Das s**ind** unsere Ferien. Hoffentlich **gibt** es gutes Wetter bis wir nach Hause komm**en**. Ich habe es nicht gern wenn der Wind bl**äst**. Tri**ffst** du mich im Café wenn ich wieder zu Hause bin?
Deine Emma

9 Imperatives

9·1 1. trink(e)!, trinkt!, trinken Sie! 2. stell(e) an!, stellt an!, stellen Sie an! 3. tu(e)!, tut!, tun Sie! 4. brich!, brecht!, brechen Sie! 5. empfiehl!, empfehlt!, empfehlen Sie! 6. fahr(e) ab!, fahrt ab!, fahren Sie ab! 7. sei!, seid! seien Sie! 8. nimm!, nehmt!, nehmen Sie! 9. iss!, esst!, essen Sie! 10. stiehl!, stehlt!, stehlen Sie!

9·2 *Sample answers are provided.* 1. Helft mir damit! 2. Essen Sie nicht in diesem Restaurant! 3. Schreiben Sie dem Rechtsanwalt einen Brief! 4. Besuchen Sie den neuen Patienten! 5. Sei artig! 6. Friss langsam! 7. Lade Sonja und Gudrun ein! 8. Werde gesund! 9. Antwortet schneller! 10. Steigen Sie in der Bismarckstraße aus!

9·3 *Sample answers are provided.* 1. Vorsicht! Zurückbleiben! 2. Bitte nicht anfassen! 3. Bitte von links anstellen! 4. An der nächsten Haltestelle aussteigen! 5. Während der Fahrt bitte sitzen bleiben!

9·4 1. Segeln wir in den Hafen! 2. Steigen wir am Marktplatz ein! 3. Essen wir im Schnellimbiss! 4. Lesen wir die amerikanischen Zeitungen! 5. Fahren wir nicht um die Ecke! 6. Legen wir die Kinder aufs Bett! 7. Fragen wir einen Polizisten, wo die Bank ist!

9·5 1. a. Lass sie morgen ausschlafen! b. Lass uns morgen ausschlafen! 2. a. Lass ihn den letzten Apfel essen! b. Lass uns den letzten Apfel essen! 3. a. Lass ihn nicht im kalten Fluss schwimmen! b. Lass uns nicht im kalten Fluss schwimmen!   4. a. Lasst die Mädchen mit den Kindern spielen! b. Lasst uns mit den Kindern spielen!   5. a. Lasst ihn die neue Kunsthalle besuchen! b. Lasst uns die neue Kunsthalle besuchen!   6. a. Lassen Sie sie um achtzehn Uhr anfangen! b. Lassen Sie uns um achtzehn Uhr anfangen!   7. a. Lassen Sie Herrn Bauer in die Heimat zurückkehren! b. Lassen Sie uns in die Heimat zurückkehren!

9·6   1. Trink(e)! Trinkt! Trinken Sie!   2. Kauf(e)! Kauf ! Kaufen Sie!   3. Nimm! Nehmt! Nehmen Sie!
4. Paddele! Paddelt! Paddeln Sie!   5. Schlaf(e)! Schlaft! Schlafen Sie!   6. Geh(e)! Geht! Gehen Sie!
7. Sprich! Sprecht! Sprechen Sie!   8. Hor(e)! Hort! Horen Sie!   9. Stiehl! Stehlt! Stehlen Sie!
10. Schwimm(e)! Schwimmt! Schwimmen Sie!

9·7   1. Fahr(e) ab! Fahrt ab! Fahren Sie ab!   2. Gewinn(e)! Gewinnt! Gewinnen Sie!   3. Bekomm(e)!
Bekommt! Bekommen Sie!   4. Bring(e) mit! Bringt mit! Bringen Sie mit!   5. Mach(e) zu! Macht zu!
Machen Sie zu!   6. Versuch(e)! Versucht! Versuchen Sie!   7. Erschlag(e)! Erschlagt! Erschlagen Sie!
8. Sieh an! Seht an! Sehen Sie an!   9. Hor(e) auf! Hort auf! Horen Sie auf!   10. Komm(e) an! Kommt an!
Kommen Sie an!

9·8   1. Sei gesund!   2. Stehen Sie auf!   3. Macht die Fenster auf!   4. Iss in der Kuche!   5. Besucht Onkel
Heinz!   6. Verkaufen Sie den alten Wagen.   7. Warte an der Tur!   8. Sprich nur Deutsch!
9. Kommen Sie um sieben Uhr!   10. Hilf mir damit!

10   The present perfect tense

10·1   1. Opa hat es schon gemacht.   2. Ich habe es schon gemacht.   3. Herr Lange hat es schon gemacht.
4. Wir haben es schon gemacht.   5. Jakob und Michael haben es schon gemacht.   6. Herr Müller und
Frau Müller haben es schon gemacht.   7. Emma hat es schon gemacht.

10·2   1. Ich habe Brot schon gekauft.   2. Ich habe mit Annchen schon gespielt.   3. Ich habe die Fenster schon
geöffnet.   4. Ich habe den Hund schon gebadet.   5. Ich habe den Koffer schon gepackt.   6. Ich habe
das Zimmer schon geputzt.   7. Ich habe im Garten schon gearbeitet.   8. Ich habe die Nachbarn schon
besucht.   9. Ich habe Spanisch schon gelernt.   10. Ich habe dem Vater schon geantwortet.

10·3   1. Onkel Dieter und Tante Edith haben ein neues Haus gebaut.   2. Es hat viel Geld gekostet.   3. Sie
haben Geld auf der Bank geborgt.   4. Sie haben viel im Haus gearbeitet.   5. Tante Edith hat die Fenster
oft geputzt.   6. Sie hat neue Möbel gekauft.   7. Sie hat sich einen schönen Garten gewünscht.   8. Sie
hat Blumen für den Garten gesucht.   9. Sie hat viel Geld gebraucht.   10. Sie hat das Haus den Freunden
gezeigt.   11. Das Haus hat ihr Freude gemacht.   12. Opa und Oma haben oft laut geatmet.   13. Sie
haben nicht mehr alleine gewohnt.   14. Oma hat oft geweint.   15. Sie hat nicht viel gesagt.   16. Die
Zwillinge haben Ball gespielt.   17. Sie haben oft gebadet.   18. Sie haben laut gelacht.   19. Sabine hat
mit dem neuen Freund getanzt.   20. Sie hat oft auf Post von ihm gewartet.

10·4   1. sind   2. haben   3. ist   4. hat   5. Ist   6. ist   7. hat   8. Ist   9. Ist   10. haben

10·5   1. ist   2. ist   3. hat   4. hat   5. hat   6. ist   7. hat   8. Ist   9. ist   10. ist

10·6   1. Ist   2. Ist   3. Ist   4. hat   5. sind

10·7   1. bin   2. habe   3. bin   4. habe   5. habe   6. habe   7. ist   8. ist   9. ist   10. habe
11. ist   12. bin   13. habe   14. ist   15. bin   16. bin   17. habe   18. habe   19. bin   20. bin
21. hat   22. bin   23. habe   24. bin   25. bin   26. ist   27. bin   28. habe   29. bin   30. ist

10·8   1. sind   2. haben   3. haben   4. hat   5. ist   6. sind   7. hat   8. hat   9. hat   10. habe
11. haben   12. ist   13. sind   14. haben   15. hat

10·9   1. hat gegessen   2. hat getrunken   3. hat genommen   4. hat gesessen   5. hat gelegen   6. ist
gesprungen   7. ist gekommen   8. ist gelaufen   9. ist gegangen   10. ist geschwommen   11. ist
geritten   12. hat geschrieben   13. hat gelesen   14. hat gegeben   15. hat geholfen   16. hat getroffen
17. hat gesungen   18. hat gesprochen   19. ist gestorben   20. ist gefahren   21. ist geflogen   22. ist
geworden   23. ist gewesen   24. hat gehabt   25. hat getan

10·10   1. gelernt   2. geworden   3. gesprochen   4. gefahren   5. gereist   6. gewesen   7. geritten
8. geholfen   9. unterschrieben   10. geschwiegen   11. gehabt   12. gegessen   13. getrunken
14. gezogen   15. gestorben

10·11 1. Wir haben ein gutes Frühstück gegessen. 2. Ich habe viel Kaffee getrunken. 3. Die Kinder sind in die Schule gegangen. 4. Sie sind mit dem Bus gefahren. 5. Sie haben auf dem Schulplatz gespielt. 6. Sie haben in der Klasse gelernt. 7. Ich habe die Küche geputzt. 8. Harold hat im Garten gearbeitet. 9. Er hat Tomaten gepflanzt. 10. Ich habe sie beim Gärtner gekauft. 11. Sie haben nicht viel gekostet. 12. Habt ihr dieses Jahr auch Tomaten gehabt? 13. Es ist heute Abend kalt geworden. 14. Es hat schon lange nicht gefroren. 15. Moment, hat der Nachbar gerufen?

10·12 1. Ich bin mit Michael in die Stadt gefahren. 2. Was habt ihr da gemacht? 3. Wir sind in die Geschäfte gegangen. 4. Habt ihr etwas gekauft? 5. Ja, ich habe eine neue Bluse gekauft. Sie hat nicht viel gekostet. 6. Wir haben einen Film gesehen. Ich habe ihn sehr interessant gefunden. 7. Was habt ihr dann gemacht? 8. Wir haben etwas zum Essen geholt. 9. Was hast du gegessen? 10. Ich habe ein Stück Torte gegessen und habe Kaffee getrunken. 11. Wie lange seid ihr im Restaurant geblieben? 12. Wir haben da vielleicht zwei Stunden gesessen. Wir haben viel zusammen gesprochen. Michael hat mir ein neues Foto gegeben. Ich habe es natürlich genommen. Sonst haben wir nichts getan. Wir sind ins Auto gestiegen und sind nach Hause gefahren.

10·13 1. Ich habe oft an dich gedacht. 2. Ich habe gedacht wir waren gute Freunde. 3. Du hast mir Geschenke gebracht. 4. Du hast mir Liebesbriefe gesandt. 5. Du hast mich »Liebling« genannt. 6. Jetzt hast du dich von mir gewandt. 7. Ich habe nicht gewusst was falsch war. 8. Mein Herz hat noch nie so vor Schmerz gebrannt. 9. Hast du mich nie geliebt?

10·14 1. Ich habe dich gut gekannt. 2. Wir haben alle gewusst wo du wohnst/wo du gewohnt hast. 3. Sonst hat es niemand gewusst. 4. Wir sind zu dir gekommen. 5. Zuerst haben wir einen Brief geschrieben. 6. Du hast auf der Couch gesessen. 7. Wir sind ins Haus gegangen. 8. Du hast Tee gemacht. 9. Wir haben Kuchen gegessen. 10. Das Feuer hat im Ofen gebrannt. 11. Der Hund ist im Garten herumgerannt. 12. Es hat geregnet. 13. Das Dienstmädchen hat uns einen Regenschirm gebracht. 14. Wir haben den Regenschirm genommen. 15. Wir haben »Auf Wiedersehen« gesagt.

10·15 1. abgeholt 2. angekommen 3. angezogen 4. hereingekommen 5. hereingelassen 6. mitgebracht 7. umgesehen 8. zugemacht 9. nachgedacht 10. zurückgegeben

10·16 1. Wann bist du aufgestanden? / Ich habe das immer um sieben Uhr gemacht. 2. Was ist dort niedergebrannt? / Das ist bestimmt das alte Haus gewesen. 3. Habt ihr den Müll herausgeworfen? / Das ist nie passiert. 4. Hast du das schöne Mädchen vorgestellt? / Ich habe sie nicht gekannt. 5. Wann ist der Bus angekommen? / Das ist um zwei Uhr geschehen. 6. Ist der Ball schon wieder ins Wasser hineingefallen? / Klaus hat wieder nicht aufgepasst. 7. Hat der Gärtner alle Blumen herausgerissen? / Er hat sie nicht umgepflanzt. 8. Wann seid ihr mit den Freunden zusammengekommen? / Das habe ich nicht gewusst. 9. Hast du die Äpfel mitgenommen? / Ich habe sie hier gelassen. 10. Wir haben mit dem Singen aufgehört. / Das hat sich wirklich nicht gut angehört.

10·17 1. Wir sind in die Alpen gefahren. 2. Bernd ist mitgekommen. 3. Wir haben viel Spaß gehabt./Wir hatten viel Spaß. 4. Was habt ihr alles gemacht? 5. Wir sind in den Wald hineingeritten. 6. Wir sind in den Bergen geklettert. 7. Luise ist immer schnell hinuntergeklettert. 8. Sie hat aber gut aufgepasst. 9. Sie hat sich nicht wehgetan. 10. Nachmittags sind wir viel geschwommen. 11. Die Jungen haben die Mädchen gern ins Wasser hineingeworfen. 12. Wir haben immer etwas zum Essen und Trinken mitgebracht. 13. Die Jungen haben Ball gespielt. 14. Bernd hat immer den Ball zurückgegeben. 15. Er hat das nicht gern gemacht. 16. Was habt ihr abends vorgehabt?/Was hattet ihr abends vor? 17. Wir sind in die Stadt hineingegangen. 18. Wir haben uns einen Film angeschaut. 19. Wir sind zum Essen ausgegangen. 20. Zu früh sind wir nach Hause zurückgekehrt.

10·18 1. Wir haben die Polizei angerufen. 2. Unser neues Auto ist verschwunden. 3. Wir haben nicht begriffen warum. 4. Wir haben es noch nicht lange besessen. 5. Unser Nachbar hat es uns verkauft. 6. Es hat mir sehr gut gefallen. 7. Die Polizei hat Beweis verlangt. 8. Ich habe bewiesen dass es mir gehört (hat). 9. Ich habe es genau beschrieben. 10. Ich habe genau gewusst wie das Auto ausgesehen hat.

10·19 1. 1879 ist er zur Welt gekommen. 2. Er ist in Deutschland aufgewachsen. 3. Er hat die Schule in München und in der Schweiz besucht. 4. Er hat Violine gespielt. 5. Er hat die Relativitätstheorie erfunden. 6. 1921 hat er den Nobelpreis in Physik bekommen. 7. Er hat sich mit seiner Kusine Elsa verheiratet. 8. Er hat sich entschieden nach Amerika auszuwandern. 9. Er hat Deutschland verlassen. 10. 1933 ist er nach Amerika ausgewandert. 11. Er hat an der Universität in Princeton unterrichtet. 12. Da ist er in ein einfaches Haus gezogen. 13. Er hat vieles mit seiner Frau besprochen. 14. Der

Präsident Roosevelt hat einen Brief von ihm empfangen.   15. Im Brief hat er die Entwicklung einer Atombombe in Deutschland beschrieben.   16. Er hat den Zionismus unterstützt.   17. Er hat vielen Menschen geholfen.   18. Er hat die Armen nicht vergessen.   19. In seinem Leben ist wirklich viel geschehen.   20. 1955 ist er in Princeton gestorben.

10·20 1. Was ist am Wochenende passiert?   2. Wir haben zuerst unsere Hausaufgaben korrigiert.   3. Wir haben uns dabei konzentriert und es ist schnell gegangen.   4. Dann haben wir uns amüsiert.   5. Sabine hat mit uns telefoniert.   6. Sie hat uns informiert dass sie Karten für ein Konzert hatte.   7. »Die Blonden Herren« haben schön musiziert.   8. Wir haben alle das Konzert besucht.   9. Dann sind wir in ein schönes Restaurant gefahren.   10. Wir haben Kaffee und Kuchen bestellt.   11. Heiko hat die Sachertorte probiert.   12. Die Kellnerin hat große Stücke serviert.   13. Alles hat gut geschmeckt.   14. Sie hat uns auch fotografiert.   15. Das hat alles Spaß gemacht.   16. Wir haben das Restaurant fröhlich verlassen.   17. Schreck! Das Auto hat nicht funktioniert!   18. Peter hat es aber schnell repariert.   19. Der Motor ist angesprungen.   20. Das war unser Wochenende!

11   Past perfect and future tense

11·1 1. hatten gezogen   2. war geblieben   3. hattest gesungen   4. war gereist   5. hatte zugemacht   6. war gestorben   7. waren geflogen   8. hatten gegessen   9. hattet erwartet   10. hatte gespielt   11. hatte angezogen   12. war passiert   13. hattest besucht   14. hattet gelacht   15. Hatten geschlagen   16. hattet gefallen   17. war gefallen   18. war eingeschlafen   19. waren gerannt   20. hatte gewusst   21. war gekommen   22. hattet bekommen   23. hatten zerstort   24. Hatte vergessen   25. war geschehen

11·2 1. war   2. hatte   3. waren   4. waren   5. hatte   6. hatten   7. hatte   8. war   9. hatte   10. hatte

11·3 1. Bevor wir in die Schweiz flogen, waren wir an die Nordsee gefahren.   2. Bevor wir in die Schweiz flogen, hatten wir das Reisebüro besucht.   3. Bevor wir in die Schweiz flogen, hatten wir Pläne gemacht.   4. Bevor wir in die Schweiz flogen, hatten wir die Flugkarten gekauft.   5. Bevor wir in die Schweiz flogen, hatten wir die Koffer gepackt.

11·4 1. Ich ging nach Hause, denn ich hatte den Film schon gesehen.   2. Ich ging nach Hause, denn ich hatte die Großmutter schon besucht.   3. Ich ging nach Hause, denn ich war schon in den Park gegangen.   4. Ich ging nach Hause, denn ich hatte alles eingekauft.   5. Ich ging nach Hause, denn ich hatte das Museum besichtigt.

11·5 1. Als Weihnachten kam, hatten wir schon für jeden ein Geschenk gekauft.   2. Als Weihnachten kam, hatten wir schon die Geschenke schön eingepackt.   3. Als Weihnachten kam, hatten die Eltern schon den Weihnachtsbaum geschmückt.   4. Als Weihnachten kam, hatte Hans Plätzchen gebacken.   5. Als Weihnachten kam, waren wir noch nicht in der Kirche gewesen.   6. Als Weihnachten kam, hatte der Adventskranz auf dem Tisch gelegen.   7. Als Weihnachten kam, hatten wir oft Weihnachtslieder gesungen.   8. Als Weihnachten kam, hatte Hans Tante Gretel und ihre Familie eingeladen.   9. Als Weihnachten kam, hatten die Kinder schon vier Tage Ferien gehabt.   10. Als Weihnachten kam, hatte es noch nicht geschneit.

11·6 1. Nächste Woche helfen die Jungen uns im Garten. Nächste Woche werden die Jungen uns im Garten helfen.   2. Nächste Woche erklärt die Lehrerin das Problem. Nächste Woche wird die Lehrerin das Problem erklären.   3. Nächste Woche kaufen sie ein Haus im Vorort. Nächste Woche werden sie ein Haus im Vorort kaufen.   4. Nächste Woche reiten die Reiter in den Wald. Nächste Woche werden die Reiter in den Wald reiten.   5. Nächste Woche geht er täglich spazieren. Nächste Woche wird er täglich spazieren gehen.   6. Nächstes Jahr baut die Stadt hier einen Wolkenkratzer. Nächstes Jahr wird die Stadt hier einen Wolkenkratzer bauen.   7. Nächstes Jahr schreibt der Schrift steller einen neuen Roman. Nächstes Jahr wird der Schrift steller einen neuen Roman schreiben.   8. Nächstes Jahr ziehen wir nach München. Nächstes Jahr werden wir nach München ziehen.   9. Nächstes Jahr besucht Erik ein Gymnasium. Nächstes Jahr wird Erik ein Gymnasium besuchen.   10. Nächstes Jahr wird er wieder gesund. Nächstes Jahr wird er wieder gesund werden.

11·7 1. **Past:** Tina konnte schnell tippen. **Present perfect:** Tina hat schnell tippen können. **Future:** Tina wird schnell tippen können.   2. **Past:** Wann kamst du wieder nach Hause? **Present perfect:** Wann bist du wieder nach Hause gekommen? **Future:** Wann wirst du wieder nach Hause kommen?   3. **Past:** Peter musste einen Kuchen backen. **Present perfect:** Peter hat einen Kuchen backen müssen. **Future:** Peter wird einen Kuchen backen müssen.   4. **Past:** Ich gab ihr ein paar Rosen. **Present perfect:** Ich habe ihr ein paar

Rosen gegeben. **Future:** Ich werde ihr ein paar Rosen geben.   5. **Past:** Felix wollte mit Sonja tanzen. **Present perfect:** Felix hat mit Sonja tanzen wollen. **Future:** Felix wird mit Sonja tanzen wollen.   6. **Past:** Wieder hörten wir den Mann schreien. **Present perfect:** Wieder haben wir den Mann schreien hören. **Future:** Wieder werden wir den Mann schreien hören.   7. **Past:** Der Boxer gewann den Kampf. **Present perfect:** Der Boxer hat den Kampf gewonnen. **Future:** Der Boxer wird den Kampf gewinnen.   8. **Past:** Niemand sah ihn das Buch stehlen. **Present perfect:** Niemand hat ihn das Buch stehlen sehen. **Future:** Niemand wird ihn das Buch stehlen sehen.   9. **Past:** Viele Unfälle geschahen hier. **Present perfect:** Viele Unfälle sind hier geschehen. **Future:** Viele Unfälle werden hier geschehen.   10. **Past:** Wir halfen ihr die Briefe schreiben. **Present perfect:** Wir haben ihr die Briefe schreiben helfen. **Future:** Wir werden ihr die Briefe schreiben helfen.   11. **Past:** Wir durft en nicht im Wald wandern. **Present perfect:** Wir haben nicht im Wald wander dürfen. **Future:** Wir werden nicht im Wald wandern dürfen.   12. **Past:** Man musste vorsichtig sein. **Present perfect:** Man hat vorsichtig sein müssen. **Future:** Man wird vorsichtig sein müssen.   13. **Past:** Warst du wieder in Heidelberg? **Present perfect:** Bist du wieder in Heidelberg gewesen? **Future:** Wirst du wieder in Heidelberg sein?   14. **Past:** Ich hatte leider keine Zeit. **Present perfect:** Ich habe leider keine Zeit gehabt. **Future:** Ich werde leider keine Zeit haben.   15. **Past:** Wo ließen Sie Ihre Uhr reparieren? **Present perfect:** Wo haben Sie Ihre Uhr reparieren lassen? **Future:** Wo werden Sie Ihre Uhr reparieren lassen?

11·8   1. Ich werde viel Geld haben.   2. Wir werden im See schwimmen.   3. Peter wird ein Auto kaufen.   4. Wirst du in Bonn wohnen?   5. Müllers werden ein großes Haus bauen.   6. Werdet ihr vorsichtig sein?   7. Frau Wendt, werden Sie Durst haben?   8. Die Mädchen werden Ball spielen.   9. Tante Friede wird uns besuchen.   10. In dem Kleid wirst du gut aussehen!

11·9   1. Ich werde mir ein Eis kaufen.   2. Nächstes Jahr verkaufen Müllers ihr Haus.   3. Wirst du Hunger haben?   4. Ab morgen mache ich Diät.   5. Wir besuchen morgen Onkel Alex.   6. Tante Luise wird mitkommen.   7. Alle werden ins Restaurant gehen.   8. Der Kellner wird einen guten Platz am Fenster finden.   9. Alles wird gut schmecken.   10. Nächstes Mal besuchen wir wieder das gleiche Restaurant.

11·10   1. Müllers werden an die Nordsee fahren wollen.   2. Herr Wendt wird aber in den Bergen Ferien machen wollen.   3. Das Pferd werden sie zu Hause lassen müssen.   4. Man wird Pferde nicht ins Ferienhaus mitbringen dürfen.   5. Ihren Hund werden sie mitnehmen dürfen.

11·11   1. Vater wird das Auto fahren.   2. Wir werden müde ankommen.   3. Am ersten Morgen schlafen wir lange.   4. Vater wird ein gutes Frühstück kochen.   5. Die Kinder werden Ball spielen wollen.   6. Peter und Hans werden wandern gehen.   7. Marie wird schwimmen.   8. Alle werden Hunger haben.   9. Sie werden sehr müde sein.   10. Abends spielen sie Karten./Abends werden sie Karten spielen.   11. Morgen wollen sie früh aufstehen.   12. Mutter wird ins Dorf gehen und ein gutes Bauernbrot kaufen wollen.   13. Das wird sehr gut schmecken.   14. Der Urlaub wird ihnen gut gefallen.   15. Nächstes Jahr reisen sie wieder in die Berge.

11·12   1. Sie werden wohl/sicher am Strand Ball spielen.   2. Sie werden wohl/sicher in den Wald gehen.   3. Er wird wohl/sicher Fisch essen wollen.   4. Es wird wohl/sicher gut sein./Das Wetter wird wohl/sicher gut sein.   5. Sie werden wohl/sicher lesen.   6. Sie werden wohl/sicher bis zehn schlafen.   7. Sie wird wohl/sicher Shorts tragen.   8. Sie werden wohl/sicher Milch trinken müssen.   9. Sie werden wohl/sicher Schlösser im Sand bauen.   10. Es wird wohl/sicher Fisch zum Essen geben.

11·13   1. Morgen sind Müllers und Wendts zu Hause.   2. Sie werden das Auto auspacken.   3. Sie werden die Koffer ins Haus tragen.   4. Mutter wird das Abendessen machen.   5. Alle werden viel essen wollen.   6. Es wird alles gut schmecken.   7. Sie werden Limonade trinken.   8. Marie wird ihre Freundin anrufen.   9. Peter muss morgen den Rasen mähen.   10. Herr Müller geht übermorgen zur Arbeit.   11. Die Kinder werden wohl noch keine Schule haben.   12. Sie werden zu Hause bleiben.   13. Die Mutter wird die Wäsche waschen.   14. Angela wird der Mutter helfen müssen.   15. Sie werden bestimmt über den Urlaub sprechen.

12   Separable and inseparable prefixes and imperatives

12·1   1. erfahrst   2. entlasst   3. empfangt   4. bekomme   5. empfehlt   6. verkaufen   7. besuchst   8. gefallt   9. erstaunt   10. gebrauchen   11. verstehen   12. gelingt   13. zerstoren   14. begruse   15. erschlagt   16. entlauft   17. beschreibt   18. empfinden   19. bekommt   20. gefallen   21. ertragt   22. versuche   23. gewinnst   24. enlassen   25. behaltst

12·2   1. Ich bekomme einen Brief.   2. Du bekommst einen Brief.   3. Er bekommt einen Brief.   4. Wir bekommen einen Brief.   5. Ihr bekommt einen Brief.   6. Sie bekommen einen Brief.   7. Man bbekommt einen Brief.   8. Ich empfange sie mit Blumen.   9. Du empfangst sie mit Blumen.   10. Er empfangt sie mit Blumen.   11. Wir empfangen sie mit Blumen.   12. Ihr empfangt sie mit Blumen.   13. Sie empfangen sie mit Blumen.   14. Niemand empfangt sie mit Blumen.   15. Ich entdecke eine kleine Insel.   16. Du entdeckst eine kleine Insel.   17. Er entdeckt eine kleine Insel.   18. Wir entdecken eine kleine Insel.   19. Ihr entdeckt eine kleine Insel.   20. Sie entdecken eine kleine Insel.   21. Der Professor entdeckt eine kleine Insel.   22. Ich verstehe kein Wort.   23. Du verstehst kein Wort.   24. Er versteht kein Wort.   25. Wir verstehen kein Wort.   26. Ihr versteht kein Wort.   27. Sie verstehen kein Wort.   28. Die Touristen verstehen kein Wort.   29. Ich zerreise die Zeitschrift en.   30. Du zerreist die Zeitschrift en.   31. Er zerreist die Zeitschrift en.   32. Wir zerreisen die Zeitschrift en.   33. Ihr zerreist die Zeitschrift en.   34. Sie zerreisen die Zeitschrift en.   35. Man zerreist die Zeitschrift en.

12·3   1. kommt an   2. bringen um   3. nimmt mit   4. gehen zurück   5. bereitet vor   6. ziehe um   7. fangt an   8. lauft weg   9. machen zu   10. kommen um   11. nimmt weg   12. bringe bei   13. horen auf   14. stellen vor   15. macht auf   16. lauft weg   17. bringen mit   18. setzen fort   19. bietest an   20. raumt auf

12·4   1. Ich fahre um neun Uhr ab.   2. Du fahrst um neun Uhr ab.   3. Er fahrt um neun Uhr ab.   4. Wir fahren um neun Uhr ab.   5. Ihr fahrt um neun Uhr ab.   6. Sie fahren um neun Uhr ab.   7. Man fahrt um neun Uhr ab.   8. Ich mache die Fenster und die Turen zu.   9. Du machst die Fenster und die Turen zu.   10. Er macht die Fenster und die Turen zu.   11. Wir machen die Fenster und die Turen zu.   12. Ihr macht die Fenster und die Turen zu.   13. Sie machen die Fenster und die Turen zu.   14. Niemand macht die Fenster und die Turen zu.   15. Ich bringe ihnen Deutsch bei.   16. Du bringst ihnen Deutsch bei.   17. Er bringt ihnen Deutsch bei.   18. Wir bringen ihnen Deutsch bei.   19. Ihr bringt ihnen Deutsch bei.   20. Sie bringen ihnen Deutsch bei.   21. Man bringt ihnen Deutsch bei.   22. Ich hore damit auf.   23. Du horst damit auf.   24. Er hort damit auf.   25. Wir horen damit auf.   26. Ihr hort damit auf.   27. Sie horen damit auf.   28. Martin hort damit auf.   29. Ich gebe zwanzig Euro aus.   30. Du gibst zwanzig Euro aus.   31. Er gibt zwanzig Euro aus.   32. Wir geben zwanzig Euro aus.   33. Ihr gebt zwanzig Euro aus.   34. Sie geben zwanzig Euro aus.   35. Wer gibt zwanzig Euro aus?

12·5   1. Ich komme vor Langeweile um.   2. Du kommst vor Langeweile um.   3. Er kommt vor Langeweile um.   4. Wir kommen vor Langeweile um.   5. Ihr kommt vor Langeweile um.   6. Sie kommen vor Langeweile um.   7. Man kommt vor Langeweile um.   8. Ich unterbreche die Rede.   9. Du unterbrichst die Rede.   10. Er unterbricht die Rede.   11. Wir unterbrechen die Rede.   12. Ihr unterbrecht die Rede.   13. Sie unterbrechen die Rede.   14. Niemand unterbricht die Rede.

12·6   1. Du bekommst ein paar Briefe.   2. Sie bekommt ein paar Briefe.   3. Wir bekommen ein paar Briefe.   4. Ihr bekommt ein paar Briefe.   5. Das Buch gehört einem Soldaten.   6. Sie gehören einem Soldaten.   7. Sie gehört einem Soldaten.   8. Diese Stiefel gehören einem Soldaten.   9. Ich erfahre etwas Wichtiges.   10. Du erfährst etwas Wichtiges.   11. Er erfährt etwas Wichtiges.   12. Ihr erfahrt etwas Wichtiges.   13. Empfiehlst du dieses Restaurant?   14. Empfehlt ihr dieses Restaurant?   15. Empfiehlt Herr Benz dieses Restaurant?   16. Empfiehlt sie dieses Restaurant?   17. Warum zerstören die Soldaten die alte Kirche?   18. Warum zerstört er die alte Kirche?   19. Warum zerstören die Männer die alte Kirche?   20. Warum zerstören wir die alte Kirche?

12·7   1. Du machst das Fenster zu.   2. Sie macht das Fenster zu.   3. Wir machen das Fenster zu.   4. Ihr macht das Fenster zu.   5. Sie bringen einen Freund mit.   6. Wir bringen einen Freund mit.   7. Der Arzt bringt einen Freund mit.   8. Die Ärzte bringen einen Freund mit.   9. Seine Töchter sehen sehr hübsch aus.   10. Diese junge Dame sieht sehr hübsch aus.   11. Ihr seht sehr hübsch aus.   12. Du siehst sehr hübsch aus.   13. Ich fahre morgen zurück.   14. Du fährst morgen zurück.   15. Sie fahren morgen zurück.   16. Niemand fährt morgen zurück.   17. Er läuft weg.   18. Die Katze läuft weg.   19. Der Dieb läuft weg.   20. Die Soldaten laufen weg.

12·8   *Sample answers are provided.*   1. Die Kinder stehen um sieben Uhr auf.   2. Warum machst du die Fenster auf?   3. Die Schüler hören aufmerksam zu.   4. Meine kleine Schwester schläft früh ein.   5. Die Touristen steigen am Markplatz aus.   6. Niemand macht die Tür zu.   7. Herr Schiller zieht einen neuen Anzug an.   8. Seine Freundin ruft ihn jeden Tag an.   9. Die Sportler kommen langsam und müde zurück.   10. Der Bus fährt pünktlich ab.   11. Viele Reisende steigen am Hauptbahnhof um.   12. Erik zieht sich im Umkleideraum aus.   13. Er setzt sich daneben hin.   14. Du schickst das Paket weiter.   15. Kommt deine Familie nach?

12·9

	1. beschreiben	2. anschreiben
Ich	beschreibe	schreibe an
du	beschreibst	schreibst an
er	beschreibt	schreibt an
wir	beschreiben	schreiben an
ihr	beschreibt	schreibt an
Sie	beschreiben	schreiben an
sie *pl.*	beschreiben	schreiben an
man	beschreibt	schreibt an

	3. sich ergeben	4. ausgeben
Ich	ergebe mich	gebe aus
du	ergibst dich	gibst aus
er	ergibt sich	gibt aus
wir	ergeben uns	geben aus
ihr	ergebt euch	gebt aus
Sie	ergeben sich	geben aus
sie *pl.*	ergeben sich	geben aus
man	ergibt sich	gibt aus

	5. erschlagen	6. vorschlagen
Ich	erschlage	schlage vor
du	erschlägst	schlägst vor
er	erschlägt	schlägt vor
wir	erschlagen	schlagen vor
ihr	erschlagt	schlagt vor
Sie	erschlagen	schlagen vor
sie *pl.*	erschlagen	schlagen vor
man	erschlägt	schlägt vor

12·10 *Sample answers are provided.*   1. Mein Bruder steht um sechs Uhr auf.   2. Das Rathaus befindet sich in dieser Straße.   3. Wir wachen sehr früh auf.   4. Ich empfange sie mit gelben Rosen.   5. Die Studenten erlernen zwei Sprachen.   6. Meine Tante besucht mich in der Stadt.   7. Die Mädchen ziehen sich schnell um.   8. Die Ausländer besichtigen die Altstadt.   9. Der Studienrat ruft meine Eltern an.   10. Der Lehrer benutzt die Tafel.   11. Die alten Mauern zerfallen zu Staub.   12. Die kleinen Schülerinnen erröten vor Scham.   13. Niemand lädt die neue Studentin ein.   14. Warum bricht die neue Brücke zusammen?   15. Wir kaufen beim Bäcker ein.

12·11

	1. übertreiben	2. zurückgeben
ich	übertreibe	gebe zurück
er	übertreibt	gibt wieder
wir	übertreiben	geben wieder

	3. durchdríngen	4. wíderrufen
ich	durchdringe	rufe wieder
er	durchdringt	ruft wieder
wir	durchdringen	rufen wieder

	5. vólltanken	6. únterkommen
ich	tanke voll	komme unter
er	tankt voll	kommt unter
wir	tanken voll	kommen unter

	7. wiederhólen	8. dúrchfallen
ich	wiederhole	falle durch
er	wiederholt	fällt durch
wir	wiederholen	fallen durch

12·12   1. Bringen Sie die Post rein.   2. Sortieren Sie die Briefe.   3. Tippen Sie einen Brief.   4. Bedienen Sie das Telefon.   5. Kaufen Sie Briefmarken.   6. Schalten Sie den Computer ein.   7. Bestellen Sie mehr Papier.   8. Räumen Sie den Schreibtisch auf.   9. Füllen Sie die Formulare aus.   10. Gehen Sie zur Bank.

12·13   1. Spiel in deinem Zimmer.   2. Wasch(e) dir die Hände.   3. Sitz(e) ruhig am Tisch.   4. Trink(e) die Milch.   5. Iss das Gemüse.   6. Schrei(e) nicht laut.   7. Räum(e) den Tisch ab.   8. Lies ein Buch. 9. Zieh(e) den Schlafanzug an.   10. Geh(e) ins Bett.   11. Schlaf(e) süß.   12. Steh(e) morgen früh auf. 13. Vergiss die Hausaufgaben nicht.   14. Lern(e) viel in der Schule.   15. Komm(e) nicht zu spät nach Hause.

12·14   1. Sitzt ruhig.   2. Hebt die Hand.   3. Seid still.   4. Werdet nicht laut.   5. Nehmt die Bücher. 6. Lest die Geschichte.   7. Schreibt einen Aufsatz.   8. Macht keine Fehler.   9. Sprecht nicht mit den Nachbarn.   10. Schreibt den Aufsatz noch einmal ab.   11. Seht den Film an.   12. Habt die Hausaufgaben für morgen.   13. Esst das Pausenbrot.   14. Spielt auf dem Schulplatz.   15. Geht jetzt nach Hause.

12·15   1. Gehen wir schwimmen.   2. Fahren wir in den Park.   3. Spielen wir Ball.   4. Lesen wir ein Buch. 5. Machen wir Hausaufgaben.   6. Essen wir ein Eis.   7. Trinken wir eine Limonade.   8. Bauen wir einen Turm.   9. Malen wir.   10. Besuchen wir Karl.

12·16   1. Seid still.   2. Werden Sie gesund.   3. Sei lieb.   4. Seien Sie geduldig.   5. Werde nicht krank. 6. Seien Sie nicht böse.   7. Werdet nicht nervös.   8. Seid geduldig.   9. Hab(e) Glück.   10. Werdet groß.

12·17   1. Fahren Sie, Fahr(e), Fahrt, Fahren wir   2. Helfen Sie, Hilf, Helft, Helfen wir   3. Essen Sie, Iss, Esst, Essen wir   4. Nehmen Sie, Nimm, Nehmt, Nehmen wir   5. Kommen Sie mit, Komm(e) mit, Kommt mit, Kommen wir mit   6. Schreien Sie, Schrei(e), Schreit, Schreien wir   7. Sehen Sie, Sieh, Seht, Sehen wir   8. Werden Sie, Werde, Werdet, Werden wir   9. Seien Sie, Sei, Seid, Seien wir   10. Haben Sie, Hab(e), Habt, Haben wir

12·18   1. Gehen Sie ins Café.   2. Sei still.   3. Spielt draußen.   4. Sprich leise.   5. Kauf(e) ein neues Kleid. 6. Werdet nicht krank.   7. Mäh(e) den Rasen.   8. Räumt euer Zimmer auf.   9. Wasch(e) (dir) die Hände.   10. Sitzen Sie hier.   11. Hab(e) keine Angst.   12. Seid vorsichtig.   13. Mach(e) die Tür zu. 14. Schließen Sie den Hund ein.   15. Lies die Geschichte vor.   16. Fahren Sie langsam.   17. Lauft ins Wasser.

13   Accusative prepositions and interrogatives

13·1   1. Ein Vogel fliegt durch das Fenster.   2. Ein Vogel fliegt durch die Tur.   3. Ein Vogel fliegt durch den Garten.   4. Ein Vogel fliegt durch den Wald.   5. Ich habe diese Blumen fur Ihre Mutter.   6. Ich habe diese Blumen fur Ihren Vater.   7. Ich habe diese Blumen fur meinen Onkel.   8. Ich habe diese Blumen fur meine Schwestern.   9. Ist er gegen diesen Rechtsanwalt?   10. Ist er gegen meine Idee?   11. Ist er gegen Ihre Freundin?   12. Ist er gegen meinen Bruder?   13. Kommen Sie ohne ein Geschenk? 14. Kommen Sie ohne Ihren Grosvater?   15. Kommen Sie ohne Ihren Regenschirm?   16. Kommen Sie ohne Ihre Bucher?   17. Sie sorgt sich um meinen Sohn.   18. Sie sorgt sich um dieses Problem.   19. Sie sorgt sich um meine Eltern.   20. Sie sorgt sich um den Zahnarzt.

13·2   1. Meine Familie begrust Sie.   2. Ich kenne dich nicht.   3. Die Jungen essen es.   4. Wir haben sie. 5. Die Schuler legen ihn auf den Tisch.   6. Die Touristen fotografieren uns.   7. Er liebt euch nicht. 8. Meine Eltern besuchen mich in Hamburg.   9. Wen siehst du?   10. Was schreibt der Mann?   11. Die Madchen suchen sie.   12. Niemand liest ihn.   13. Meine Mutter ruft dich an.   14. Die Frauen begrusen uns.   15. Wer bekommt es?

13·3   1. Du wohnst in Heidelberg.   2. Wir wohnen in Heidelberg.   3. Ihr wohnt in Heidelberg.   4. Sie wohnen in Heidelberg.   5. Sie wohnt in Heidelberg.   6. Erik spielt gegen mich.   7. Erik spielt gegen ihn.   8. Erik spielt gegen uns.   9. Erik spielt gegen euch.   10. Erik spielt gegen sie.   11. Meine Eltern sorgen sich um dich.   12. Meine Eltern sorgen sich um sie.   13. Meine Eltern sorgen sich um euch. 14. Meine Eltern sorgen sich um Sie.   15. Meine Eltern sorgen sich um sie.   16. Ich entdecke eine kleine Insel.   17. Er entdeckt eine kleine Insel.   18. Wir entdecken eine kleine Insel.   19. Sie entdecken eine kleine Insel.   20. Wer entdeckt eine kleine Insel?   21. Sie gehen ohne dich wandern.   22. Sie gehen ohne ihn wandern.   23. Sie gehen ohne sie wandern.   24. Sie gehen ohne uns wandern.   25. Sie gehen ohne euch wandern.

13·4   1. dadurch   2. um sie   3. fur sie   4. dafur   5. gegen sie   6. darum   7. durch ihn   8. fur uns 9. dagegen   10. ohne sie   11. wider ihn   12. um sie   13. dadurch   14. ohne ihn   15. darum

13·5   1. Sabine ist in Berlin, denn sie besucht ihren Onkel.
Sabine ist in Berlin, denn sie arbeitet in der Hauptstadt.
Sabine ist in Berlin, denn sie sucht einen Freund.
2. Er bleibt in Kanada, denn er lernt Englisch.
Er bleibt in Kanada, denn seine Eltern wohnen da.
Er bleibt in Kanada, denn seine Freundin arbeitet in Toronto.
3. Ich kaufe einen VW, denn ich brauche ein Auto.
Ich kaufe einen VW, denn ein BMW ist teuer.
Ich kaufe einen VW, denn ein VW ist billig.

13·6   1. Das ist sein Hut.   2. Das ist ihr Hut.   3. Das ist unser Hut.   4. Das ist euer Hut.   5. Das ist Ihr Hut.   6. Er sieht meinen Freund.   7. Er sieht deinen Freund.   8. Er sieht euren Freund.   9. Er sieht Ihren Freund.   10. Er sieht ihren Freund.   11. Sie kaufen dein Fahrrad.   12. Sie kaufen sein Fahrrad.   13. Sie kaufen ihr Fahrrad.   14. Sie kaufen unser Fahrrad.   15. Sie kaufen euer Fahrrad.   16. Meine Eltern wohnen in der Hauptstadt.   17. Deine Eltern wohnen in der Hauptstadt.   18. Seine Eltern wohnen in der Hauptstadt.   19. Unsere Eltern wohnen in der Hauptstadt.   20. Ihre Eltern wohnen in der Hauptstadt.

13·7   1. Wie oft fahrt sie in die Stadt?   2. Wie lange bleiben sie hier?   3. Wie viel kostet das Buch?   4. Wie spat kommt sie?   5. Wie viel Geld hat der alte Herr?

13·8   1. Gegen wen war Thomas? gegen sie   2. Ohne wen fahrt Frau Braun ab? ohne sie   3. Fur wen schreibe ich den Brief? fur ihn   4. Wodurch schwimmt der Sportler? dadurch   5. Wofur danken uns die Zwillinge? dafur   6. Wodurch laufen die Jungen? dadurch   7. Worum bittet der alte Mann? darum   8. Wogegen kenne ich ein gutes Mittel? dagegen   9. Ohne wen kommt Erik nach Hause? ohne sie   10. Wodurch schicken wir das Paket? dadurch

13·9   1. a. Eine Fledermaus ist durch das Haus geflogen.
b. Eine Fledermaus ist durch die Scheune geflogen.
c. Eine Fledermaus ist durch den großen Lesesaal geflogen.
d. Eine Fledermaus ist durch unsere Schule geflogen.
2. a. Warum ist er gegen seine Kinder?
b. Warum ist er gegen seinen Sohn?
c. Warum ist er gegen ihren älteren Bruder?
d. Warum ist er gegen seine Tante?
3. a. Der neue Manager handelte ohne jede Rücksicht auf uns.
b. Der neue Manager handelte ohne Vernunft.
c. Der neue Manager handelte ohne Überlegung.
4. a. Ich möchte bis Freitag bleiben.
b. Ich möchte bis nächsten Samstag bleiben.
c. Ich möchte bis morgen bleiben.
5. a. Welcher Weg führt den schönen Bach entlang?
b. Welcher Weg führt diesen Wald entlang?
c. Welcher Weg führt jenen Zaun entlang?
d. Welcher Weg führt keinen Fluss entlang?

13·10   1. um   2. bis   3. um   4. für   5. für   6. für   7. um   8. bis   9. um (bis)   10. um

13·11   *These are sample answers only.*   1. meine Familie   2. die Wand   3. zwanzig Uhr   4. halb elf   5. einen breiten Fluss   6. Heidelberg   7. der Stadtmauer   8. seinen Regenschirm   9. meine Enkelkinder   10. den Bach   11. meinen Pass   12. ein Gewitter   13. Hilfe   14. die neuen Schüler   15. mich

14   Regular verbs in the past tense and word order

14·1   1. spielte   2. hortest   3. sagten   4. fragten   5. reiste   6. machte   7. stelltet   8. setzten   9. diente   10. sorgte   11. holten   12. suchtest   13. kauft en   14. pflanztet   15. flusterte

14·2

1. lernte	4. lebte
lerntest	lebtest
lernte	lebte
lernten	lebten
lerntet	lebtet
lernten	lebten
lernte	lebte
2. lachelte	5. liebte
lacheltest	liebtest
lachelte	liebte
lachelten	liebten
lacheltet	liebtet
lachelten	liebten
lachelte	liebte
3. feierte	6. wohnte
feiertest	wohntest
feierte	wohnte
feierten	wohnten
feiertet	wohntet
feierten	wohnten
feiert	wohnte

14·3

1. endete	3. redete
endetest	redetes
endete	redete
endeten	redeten
endetet	redetet
endeten	redeten
endete	redete
2. furchtete	4. antwortete
furchtetest	antwortetest
furchtete	antwortete
furchteten	antworteten
furchtetet	antwortetet
furchteten	antworteten
furchtete	antwortete

14·4   1. wartete   2. besuchtest   3. erwartete   4. holten ab   5. bereitetet vor   6. fragten nach   7. verkaufte   8. horten zu   9. horte auf   10. verlangte   11. pflanzte um   12. kehrten zuruck   13. sagten   14. kauft est ein   15. ersetztet

14·5   1. Ich wohnte.   2. Er atmete.   3. Das Baby weinte.   4. Hörtest du nichts?   5. Herr Müller rauchte.   6. Wir suchten etwas.   7. Lerntet ihr viel?   8. Die Mädchen öffneten es.   9. Wartetest du?   10. Schmidts kauften es.   11. Sie arbeiteten.   12. Was sagtest du?   13. Was spieltet ihr?   14. Sie lächelte.   15. Er wohnte in Berlin.

14·6   1. machte   2. arbeitete   3. lernten   4. kochte   5. kaufte   6. schmeckte   7. ernährte   8. pflanzte, putzte   9. mähte   10. erholten, beschäftigten   11. spielten   12. übten, verbesserten   13. achtete, übten   14. kostete   15. meinten, lohnte

14·7   1. Im Sommer schwimmen die Kinder gern.   2. In Deutschland ist das Wetter oft sehr schon.   3. Gestern kauft en unsere Eltern einen neuen Wagen.   4. Heute spielen meine Tochter Schach.   5. Um sieben Uhr stehe ich auf.   6. Morgen reist meine Familie nach Paris.   7. Gestern wohnten wir noch in Munchen.   8. Im Mai feierten sie meinen Geburtstag.   9. Im Fruhling besuchte ich meine Tante in Amerika.   10. Morgen verkaufst du dein Fahrrad.

14·8   1. Ich spiele das Klavier, und Sonja singt.   2. Martin wohnt in der Hauptstadt, und ich wohne in Bremen.   3. Der Hund ist krank, und die Katze ist alt.   4. Ich lese den Roman, aber ich verstehe nichts.   5. Mein Bruder ist stark, aber er ist faul.   6. Das Wetter ist schon, aber wir bleiben zu Hause.   7. Sind sie reich, oder sind sie arm?   8. Kauft e sie ein Kleid, oder kauft e sie eine Bluse?   9. Der Mann arbeitet nicht, denn er ist mude.   10. Die Touristen verstehen nichts, denn sie sprechen kein Deutsch.

14·9   1. du einen neuen VW kauft est   2. meine Eltern viele Jahre im Ausland wohnten   3. Frau Keller deinen Bruder besuchte   4. Ihr Sohn sehr gut schwimmt   5. er sehr schlecht Klavier spielt   6. ihre Tochter da wohnt   7. ihr Mann in der Hauptstadt arbeitet   8. sie eine grose Wohnung da hat   9. Wohnungen in Berlin billig sind   10. sie gern ins Theater geht

14·10   1. c   2. b   3. a   4. c   5. d   6. c   7. a   8. d   9. a   10. a

15   Indirect objects and dative case

15·1   1. dem Rechtsanwalt   2. der Dame   3. dem Kind   4. den Leuten   5. keiner Krankenschwester   6. diesen Madchen   7. einem Schuler   8. meinen Brudern   9. unserer Freundin   10. euren Eltern

15·2   1. Ich schicke meinem Vater einen brief.   2. Ich schicke dieser Dame einen Brief.   3. Ich schicke unserem Professor einen Brief.   4. Ich schicke ihren Freunden einen Brief.   5. Ich schicke deiner Mutter einen Brief.   6. Wir schenkten unseren Tochtern einen Computer.   7. Wir schenkten seiner Tante einen Computer.   8. Wir schenkten dem Madchen einen Computer.   9. Wir schenkten dem Zahnarzt einen Computer.   10. Wir schenkten ihrem Onkel einen Computer.   11. Was geben Sie Ihrer Frau?   12. Was geben Sie seinen Kindern?   13. Was geben Sie diesen Sportlern?   14. Was geben Sie der Tanzerin?   15. Was geben Sie den Schauspielern?

15·3   1. Ich gebe es dir.   2. Ich gebe es ihm.   3. Ich gebe es ihr.   4. Ich gebe es dem Lowen.   5. Ich gebe es meinem Studenten.   6. Niemand sendet mir ein Geschenk.   7. Niemand sendet uns ein Geschenk.   8. Niemand sendet euch ein Geschenk.   9. Niemand sendet diesem Herrn ein Geschenk.   10. Niemand sendet dem Soldaten ein Geschenk.   11. Die Frau kaufte Ihnen eine Zeitschrift.   12. Die Frau kaufte ihnen eine Zeitschrift.   13. Die Frau kaufte diesem Schauspieler eine Zeitschrift.   14. Die Frau kaufte dieser Schauspielerin eine Zeitschrift.   15. Die Frau kaufte mir eine Zeitschrift.

15·4   1. dem Polizisten   2. einem Gartner   3. ihnen   4. ihr   5. uns   6. seinem Sohn   7. ihm   8. mir   9. einem Matrosen   10. dem Konzert   11. der Oper   12. ihren Vorlesungen   13. dem Stadtpark   14. der Schule   15. dir

15·5   1. von ihm   2. damit   3. bei ihr   4. ihm gegenuber   5. daraus   6. danach   7. dazu   8. zu ihnen   9. auser ihm   10. mit ihm

15·6   1. Die Jungen helfen den Frauen damit.   2. Die Jungen helfen mir damit.   3. Die Jungen helfen uns damit.   4. Die Jungen helfen ihren Freunden damit.   5. Die Jungen helfen ihnen damit.   6. Ich danke dir dafur.   7. Ich danke ihm dafur.   8. Ich danke Ihnen dafur.   9. Ich danke meiner Freundin dafur.   10. Ich danke dem Matrosen dafur.   11. Wo begegneten den Diplomaten?   12. Wo begegneten ihr?   13. Wo begegneten meinem Freund?   14. Wo begegneten ihnen?   15. Wo begegneten seiner Grosmutter?

15·7   1. c   2. a   3. a   4. a   5. d   6. d   7. c   8. d   9. d   10. a

15·8   1. seiner Freundin   2. dem Arzt   3. diesem Mädchen   4. seinen Brüdern   5. meiner Schwester   6. diesen Leuten   7. jenem Mann   8. Ihrer Tochter   9. meinen Kindern   10. dem Gast   11. jener Dame   12. seinen Lehrerinnen   13. unserem Onkel   14. den Mädchen   15. deiner Mutter

15·9   1. meinen deutschen Verwandten   2. seinem jüngeren Bruder   3. euren netten Eltern   4. seiner hübschen Schwester   5. unseren amerikanischen Gästen   6. jenen kleinen Kindern   7. diesen älteren Jungen   8. euren neuen Freunden   9. der jungen Dame   10. dem komischen Mann

15·10   1. Schenkte sie dir die Handschuhe?   2. Die Kinder bringen uns ein paar Blumen.   3. Die Touristen schickten euch Ansichtskarten.   4. Ich zeigte ihnen die alten Bilder.   5. Er gibt Ihnen die Briefe.

15·11   1. Zeigen Sie ihnen die alten Landkarten?   2. Was gibt sie ihnen?   3. Erik schenkt ihr einen Ring.   4. Seine Verwandten schickten ihm ein Geschenk.   5. Sie geben uns ein paar Euro.

15·12   1. Sie zeigten ihnen den neuen Wagen.   2. Sie zeigten ihn ihnen.   3. Gibst du ihr eine Blume?   4. Gibst du sie ihr?   5. Die Kinder bringen ihr ein Geschenk.   6. Die Kinder bringen es ihr.   7. Tina kaufte uns neue Handschuhe.   8. Tina kaufte sie uns.   9. Wir schicken ihm eine Ansichtskarte.   10. Wir schicken sie ihm.

15·13   *Sample answers are provided.*   1. Martin wohnt bei seinem alten Onkel.   2. Martin wohnt bei unseren amerikanischen Freunden.   3. Sprechen Sie mit meinen jüngeren Töchtern?   4. Sprechen Sie mit jenem alten Richter?   5. Erik wohnt gegenüber dem neuen Bahnhof.   6. Erik wohnt gegenüber unserer kleinen

Schule.   7. Niemand sieht mich außer meinem älteren Bruder.   8. Niemand sieht mich außer seiner neuen Freundin.   9. Wohin geht ihr nach dem langen Konzert?   10. Wohin geht ihr nach einer italienischen Oper?

15·14   1. Warum sprecht ihr mit uns?   2. Warum sprecht ihr mit ihm?   3. Warum sprecht ihr mit mir?   4. Warum sprecht ihr mit ihr?   5. Warum sprecht ihr mit ihnen?   6. Erik wohnt nicht weit von ihr.   7. Erik wohnt nicht weit von ihnen.   8. Erik wohnt nicht weit von dir.   9. Erik wohnt nicht weit von euch.   10. Erik wohnt nicht weit von uns.

15·15   1. Wer wohnt euch gegenüber?   2. Wer wohnt Frau Schneider gegenüber?   3. Wer wohnt gegenüber dem Bahnhof?   4. Wer wohnt gegenüber der neuen Schule?   5. Wer wohnt Ihnen gegenüber?   6. Martin und Tina sitzen der Lehrerin gegenüber.   7. Martin und Tina sitzen unseren Gästen gegenüber.   8. Martin und Tina sitzen ihnen gegenüber.   9. Martin und Tina sitzen gegenüber dem Stadtpark.   10. Martin und Tina sitzen mir gegenüber.

15·16   1. mit ihm   2. damit   3. von ihm   4. dadurch   5. danach   6. für sie   7. dafür   8. bei ihm   9. dabei   10. Daraus

15·17   1. Kannst du uns helfen?   2. Kannst du ihm helfen?   3. Kannst du diesem alten Mann helfen?   4. Kannst du meinen Eltern helfen?   5. Kannst du jedem neuen Schüler helfen?   6. Warum widerspricht er mir?   7. Warum widerspricht er jener Dame?   8. Warum widerspricht er seinem eigenen Vater?   9. Warum widerspricht er euch?   10. Warum widerspricht er ihr?   11. Sein Tanzen imponiert ihnen nicht.   12. Sein Tanzen imponiert dir nicht.   13. Sein Tanzen imponiert unseren Gästen nicht.   14. Sein Tanzen imponiert seinem jüngeren Bruder.   15. Sein Tanzen imponiert der hübschen Ärztin.

16   Irregular verbs in the past tense

16·1   1. lief   2. kamst   3. gingen   4. sprach   5. versprach   6. trank   7. ast   8. zogen   9. hies   10. sangen   11. wuschst   12. traf   13. lies   14. bekam   15. nahmen   16. riefen an   17. verstand   18. taten   19. halfst   20. schlief   21. stieg aus   22. fingen an   23. schien   24. erfandet   25. sas

16·2

1. hielt	2. fiel
hieltest	fielst
hielt	fiel
hielten	fielen
hieltet	fielt
hielten	fielen
hielten	fielen
3. schloss	5. gab aus
schlosst	gabst aus
schloss	gab aus
schlossen	gaben aus
schlosst	gabt aus
schlossen	gaben aus
schloss	gab aus
4. begriff	6. flog
begriff st	flogst
begriff	flog
begriff en	flogen
begrifft	flogt
begriff en	flogen
begriff	flog

16·3

1. hatte	3. wurde
hattest	wurdest
hatte	wurde
hatten	wurden
hattet	wurdet
hatten	wurden
hatte	wurde

            2. war
               warst
               war
               waren
               wart
               waren
               war

16·4 1. kannte   2. dachtest   3. wusste   4. brachten   5. nannten   6. rannte   7. wandten
          8. sandtet   9. branntest   10. wussten

16·5 1. kannte   3. wusste
             kanntest   wusstest
             kannte   wusste
             kannten   wussten
             kanntet   wusstet
             kannten   wussten
             kannte   wusste
          2. dachte   4. brachte
             dachtest   brachtest
             dachte   brachte
             dachten   brachten
             dachtet   brachtet
             dachten   brachten
             dachte   brachte

16·6 1. kannten   2. wusste   3. Hatten   4. war   5. wurde   6. nannte/nannten   7. dachte   8. hatte
          9. wurde   10. Warst

16·7 1. Es wurde um sieben Uhr dunkel.   2. Er kam ohne seine Frau.   3. Die Kinder hatten Durst.
          4. Was brachten Sie uns?   5. Meine Eltern fuhren zu alten Freunden.   6. Ich wusste es nicht.
          7. Sahst du die Berge?   8. Das Wetter wurde schlecht.   9. Ich sandte ihm eine Ansichtskarte.   10. Der
          Junge stand um sechs Uhr auf.   11. Kanntet ihr diesen Herrn?   12. Nannte sie ihren Namen?   13. Wo
          warst du?   14. Ich rief meine Freundin an.   15. Lasen Sie eine Zeitschrift?

16·8 1. fand   2. gewann   3. ging   4. trank   5. saß   6. sang   7. half   8. las   9. stand   10. hieß
          11. verlor   12. log   13. sprach   14. aß   15. gab   16. schrieb   17. tat   18. vergaß   19. lief
          20. kam   21. nahm   22. fand   23. blieb   24. schwamm   25. lud ein

16·9 1. ging   2. gingst   3. gingen   4. ging   5. gingt   6. gingen   7. trank   8. tranken   9. trank
          10. trankt   11. trank   12. tat   13. taten   14. taten   15. tat   16. aßest   17. aß   18. aßen
          19. aßt   20. aß

16·10 1. half   2. schliefen   3. trafen   4. nahmst   5. gab   6. ging   7. schwammen   8. warft
           9. sang   10. fandst   11. begann   12. geschah   13. fuhr   14. vergaß   15. sprach

16·11 1. Marlies und ihre Freunde fuhren nach Hamburg.   2. Ute steuerte das neue Auto.   3. Sie
           übernachteten in einer kleinen Pension.   4. Das Auto parkten sie hinter der Pension.   5. Sie standen
           früh auf.   6. Sie aßen ein gutes Frühstück.   7. Ute trank drei Tassen Kaffee.   8. Dann zogen sie sich
           die Jacken an und gingen zur U-Bahn.   9. In der Innenstadt besichtigten sie das alte Rathaus und das
           Museum.   10. Nachmittags machten sie eine Hafenrundfahrt.   11. Der Kapitän sah sehr gut aus.
           12. Viele Leute saßen im Boot.   13. Sie sahen aber alles gut.   14. Nach der Rundfahrt stiegen sie schnell
           aus.   15. Sie nahmen ein Taxi zu einem berühmten Restaurant.   16. Im Restaurant fanden sie noch
           einen freien Tisch.   17. Sie bestellten gebratenen Fisch.   18. Die Kellnerin bediente sie gut.   19. Alles
           schmeckte wunderbar.   20. Sie gaben der Kellnerin ein großes Trinkgeld.   21. Müde verließen sie das
           Restaurant.   22. Sie legten sich müde ins Bett.   23. Der Tag gefiel ihnen sehr gut.   24. Sie vergaßen
           ihn nie.

16·12 1. Das Licht brannte schon im Haus.   2. Es klopfte an der Tür.   3. Ich ging hin und machte die Tür auf.
           4. Ein fremder Mann stand da.   5. Er nannte seinen Namen.   6. Ich kannte ihn nicht.   7. Er wusste
           aber, wer ich war.   8. Ich dachte mir, »Etwas stimmt nicht!«   9. Was machten wir?   10. Wandte ich
           mich um und schloss die Tür?   11. Sandte ich den Mann weg?   12. Brachte ich ihn ins Haus?   13. Ich
           dachte nach.   14. Auf einmal erkannte ich ihn!

16·13 1. Wir fuhren zu alten Freunden.   2. Wir kannten sie schon viele Jahre.   3. Meine Frau nannte sie unsere besten Freunde.   4. Sie wussten viel über uns.   5. Manchmal dachte ich sie wussten zu viel. 6. Wir brachten frische Tomaten aus unserem Garten mit.   7. Die Fahrt dauerte lange.   8. Ihre Kinder rannten uns entgegen.   9. Alle freuten sich sehr.   10. Wir blieben den ganzen Nachmittag da.

16·14 1. hatten 2. Hattet 3. hatte 4. hatte 5. hatten 6. hatten 7. hattest

16·15 1. war 2. Warst 3. waren 4. Waren 5. war 6. waren 7. wart

16·16 1. wurden 2. wurde 3. wurden 4. wurde 5. wurdet 6. wurde 7. wurden

16·17 1. Wo war Anna? Sie war in der Schule.   2. Wurdest du oft krank? Ich wurde nie krank.   3. Hatten die Kinder Hunger? Nein, Peter hatte aber Durst.   4. Wann wurde es dunkel? Es wurde um acht dunkel. 5. Wo wart ihr? Wir waren im Auto.   6. Hattest du Durst? Ja, ich hatte Durst.   7. Hattet ihr am Wochenende Besuch? Ja, die Großeltern waren da.   8. Warst du fremd hier? Ja, ich war fremd.   9. Frau Schrank, waren Sie oft im Theater? Ich war selten im Theater.   10. Wir wurden nervös wenn er da war. Wieso denn? Er war harmlos.

16·18

	1. beschreiben/beschrieb	2. tun/tat
ich	beschrieb	tat
du	beschriebst	tatest
er	beschrieb	tat
wir	beschrieben	taten
ihr	beschriebt	tatet
Sie	beschrieben	taten
sie *pl.*	beschrieben	taten
man	beschrieb	tat

	3. fliegen/flog	4. verstehen/verstand
ich	flog	verstand
du	flogst	verstandest
er	flog	verstand
wir	flogen	verstanden
ihr	flogt	verstandet
Sie	flogen	verstanden
sie *pl.*	flogen	verstanden
man	flog	verstand

16·19 1. Du hattest ihre Tasche.   2. Sie hatte ihre Tasche.   3. Wir hatten ihre Tasche.   4. Ihr hattet ihre Tasche.   5. Wir waren in der Schweiz.   6. Sie war in der Schweiz.   7. Die Ausländer waren in der Schweiz.   8. Seine Verwandten waren in der Schweiz.   9. Wurdest du Lehrer?   10. Wurden sie Lehrer?   11. Wurden Sie Lehrer?   12. Wurde dein Sohn Lehrer?   13. Niemand hatte genug Geld. 14. Ihr wart den ganzen Tag in der Stadt.   15. Du wurdest sehr krank.

16·20 1. Martin trank keine Milch.   2. Das Kind sah sehr süß aus.   3. Lieft ihr zum Stadtpark?   4. Ich war sehr müde.   5. Er verkaufte sein Fahrrad.   6. Sabine bekam ein paar Nelken von Erik.   7. Der junge Mann stieg am Marktplatz aus.   8. Er befand sich in einer Großstadt.   9. Aßen Sie gern Rotkohl? 10. Der Ausländer sprach sehr langsam.   11. Meine Kinder lernten Deutsch.   12. Wir wohnten bei unseren Großeltern.   13. Professor Benz rief meinen Sohn an.   14. Wir blieben eine Woche in Berlin. 15. Warum schlugst du das arme Pferd?   16. Felix wusch sich die Hände.   17. Es wurde wieder kalt. 18. Gingen die Soldaten nach Hause?   19. Brauchten Sie ein Hemd?   20. Der Sportler brach sich den Finger.   21. Erik warf mir den Ball zu.   22. Ich roch die schönen Rosen.   23. Sie schloss nur ein Fenster.   24. Warum saßen deine Eltern in der Küche?   25. Mein Wörterbuch fiel in den Schmutz. 26. Hattet ihr keine Zeit?   27. Es geschah ihm nichts.   28. Stefan bat um den nächsten Tanz. 29. Viele Touristen flogen nach Europa.   30. Erik nahm das Buch unter den Arm.

17   Modal auxiliaries in the present and past tenses

17·1 1. Ich will zu Hause bleiben.   2. Du willst zu Hause bleiben.   3. Er will zu Hause bleiben.   4. Sie wollen zu Hause bleiben.   5. Sie soll ihr helfen.   6. Sie sollen ihr helfen.   7. Wir sollen ihr helfen. 8. Ihr sollt ihr helfen.   9. Du kannst den Brief nicht lesen.   10. Wer kann den Brief nicht lesen? 11. Sie konnen den Brief nicht lesen.   12. Ihr konnt den Brief nicht lesen.   13. Ich darf die Bibliothek benutzen.   14. Sie darf die Bibliothek benutzen.   15. Wir durfen die Bibliothek benutzen.   16. Die Studenten durfen die Bibliothek benutzen.   17. Du musst heute abend arbeiten.   18. Sie mussen heute abend arbeiten.   19. Ihr musst heute abend arbeiten.   20. Niemand muss heute abend arbeiten.

17·2   1. Ich mag gern Bier.   2. Du magst gern Bier.   3. Er mag gern Bier.   4. Wir mogen gern Bier.   5. Ihr mogt gern Bier.   6. Sie mogen gern Bier.   7. Sie mogen gern Bier.   8. Die Manner mogen gern Bier.   9. Ich mag junger sein.   10. Du magst junger sein.   11. Sie mag junger sein.   12. Wir mogen junger sein.   13. Ihr mogt junger sein.   14. Sie mogen junger sein.   15. Sie mogen junger sein.   16. Frau Keller mag junger sein.

17·3   1. Du solltest fleisig arbeiten.   2. Wir mussten ihnen helfen.   3. Ich wollte eine Reise durch Italien machen.   4. Der Mann mochte viel alter sein.   5. Der Auslander konnte es nicht verstehen.   6. Sie durft en nicht langer bleiben.   7. Wir sollten mehr Geld sparen.   8. Du musstest an deine Mutter schreiben.   9. Wolltet ihr bei uns ubernachten?   10. Konnten die Jungen kochen?

17·4   1. Ich mochte das Theater besuchen.   2. Mochten Sie nach Hause gehen?   3. Er mochte neue Handschuhe kaufen.   4. Frau Benz mochte den Polizisten fragen.   5. Niemand mochte die Briefe schreiben.   6. Mochtest du etwas trinken?   7. Wir mochten um neun Uhr fruhstucken.   8. Mochtet ihr mit uns fahren?   9. Sie mochte die neue Zeitung lesen.   10. Ich mochte hier aussteigen.

17·5   1. Sie lies ein neues Kleid machen.   2. Er hilft seinem Vater kochen.   3. Der Hund horte zwei Manner kommen.   4. Gingst du um elf Uhr spazieren?   5. Ich sehe sie im Garten arbeiten.   6. Die Schuler lernten lesen und schreiben.   7. Sie gehen am Montag radfahren.   8. Wir lassen das alte Fahrrad reparieren.   9. Niemand half uns die Satze ubersetzen.   10. Hort ihr ihn pfeifen?

17·6   1. Erik hort seine Freunde vor der Tur fl ustern.   2. Wir halfen Erik das Fruhstuck vorbereiten.   3. Ihr seht Thomas grose Pakete tragen.   4. Ich horte Sie Deutsch sprechen.   5. Er hilft Frau Bauer die Kuche saubermachen.

17·7   1. c   2. d   3. a   4. d   5. c   6. d   7. a   8. a   9. d   10. b

17·8   1. Ich darf zu Hause bleiben.   2. Ihr dürft in den Park gehen.   3. (Die) Kinder dürfen nicht rauchen.   4. Ich kann Auto fahren.   5. Wir können Deutsch lernen.   6. Die Kellnerin kann viel erzählen.   7. Die Freunde können die Speisekarte lesen.   8. Ihr könnt den heißen Kaffee trinken.   9. Du darfst ins Kino gehen.   10. Wir dürfen den Film sehen.   11. Frau Kranz darf den Kuchen nicht essen.   12. Die Ferien dürfen jetzt beginnen.   13. Herr Bohl, können Sie das Auto kaufen?   14. Kannst du tanzen?   15. Die Sekretärin kann den Brief schreiben.

17·9   1. Ich muss Deutsch lernen.   2. Wir müssen so leise sprechen.   3. Die Kinder müssen so schnell laufen.   4. Der Vater muss so spät arbeiten.   5. Ihr müsst/Wir müssen zu den Nachbarn gehen.   6. Ich muss in Berlin wohnen.   7. Wir müssen unsere Autos verkaufen.   8. Ja, du musst/Sie müssen zu den Nachbarn gehen.

17·10   1. möchten   2. möchte, möchte   3. sollen   4. soll, soll   5. möchten, Möchtest, möchte   6. möchtest   7. möchtet

17·11   1. Magst   2. mag   3. mag   4. mögen   5. mögt   6. mögen   7. mögen

17·12   1. willst   2. will   3. Will   4. wollt   5. wollen   6. wollen

17·13   1. Ich esse nicht viel, weil ich abnehmen möchte.   2. Er treibt Sport, da er fit sein will.   3. Sie ziehen an den Bodensee, weil sie da immer schwimmen können.   4. Lotte muss viel lernen, wenn sie die Prüfung bestehen will.   5. Wir verkaufen unser Haus, damit wir viel Geld haben können.   6. Die Kinder wissen nicht, warum sie still sein sollen.   7. Es muss still sein, damit das Kind schlafen kann.   8. Die Mädchen verstehen nicht, warum sie nicht ins Kino gehen dürfen.   9. Anton lernt viel, weil er nicht dumm bleiben will.   10. Wir besuchen Tante Margarete, da wir mit ihr sprechen möchten.

17·14   1. Herr Volker, möchten Sie mehr Kaffee?   2. Leo, kannst du Deutsch?   3. Ich muss.   4. Wir wollen es.   5. Was will er hier?   6. Ich will es.   7. Müsst ihr?   8. Er kann nicht.   9. Du darfst.   10. Möchten Sie es?

17·15   1. Wir bekommen Besuch.   2. Alte Freunde wollen uns besuchen.   3. Sie sollen heute Nachmittag ankommen.   4. Ich hoffe dass sie ein paar Tage bleiben wollen.   5. Wir haben immer viel Spaß wenn sie hier sind.   6. Es gibt viel zu tun.   7. Das Haus muss sauber sein.   8. Mutter muss das Essen vorbereiten.   9. Vater will noch im Garten arbeiten.   10. Er und Peter wollen den Rasen mähen.   11. Peter soll auch die Blumen gießen.   12. Mutter sagt dass ich frische Blumen ins Haus bringen soll.

13. Ich mag die gelben Tulpen.   14. Ich möchte einen großen Strauß auf den Tisch stellen.
15. Mutter will noch schnell einen Kuchen backen.   16. Er darf nicht zu lange im Ofen bleiben.
17. Ich kann ihn schon riechen.   18. Endlich ist alles fertig.   19. Wir müssen noch etwas warten bis
der Besuch kommt.   20. Peter steht am Fenster und wartet.   21. Jetzt kann er das Auto sehen.
22. Wir wollen sie alle begrüßen.   23. Die Gäste sollen sich setzen.   24. Sie möchten aber in den
Garten gehen.   25. Wir wollen da essen.   26. Das Wetter soll schön sein.   27. Frau Marx möchte
etwas trinken.   28. Herr Marx will viel erzählen.   29. Wir müssen viel lachen.   30. Die Kinder
dürfen lange aufbleiben.

17·16   1. Sie kann Deutsch und Italienisch sprechen.   2. Sie will Deutsch und Italienisch sprechen.   3. Ich
muss den ganzen Tag zu Hause bleiben.   4. Ich soll den ganzen Tag zu Hause bleiben.   5. Meine
Schwester darf nicht mitkommen.   6. Meine Schwester will nicht mitkommen.   7. Kannst du ihm einen
Brief schreiben?   8. Musst du ihm einen Brief schreiben?   9. Was mag sie zu ihrem Essen essen?
10. Was will sie zu ihrem Essen essen?

17·17   1. **Present:** er will **Past:** er wollte **Present perfect:** er hat gewollt   2. **Present:** wir müssen **Past:** wir
mussten **Present perfect:** wir haben gemusst   3. **Present:** ihr sollt **Past:** ihr solltet **Present perfect:** ihr
habt gesollt   4. **Present:** er kann **Past:** sie konnten **Present perfect:** ich habe gekonnt   5. **Present:** sie
mag **Past:** du mochtest **Present perfect:** wir haben gemocht   6. **Present:** er darf **Past:** ich durfte **Present
perfect:** du hast gedurft

18   *Wissen* and *kennen*

18·1   1. Weißt   2. weiß   3. Weiß   4. wissen   5. wisst   6. wissen   7. wissen   8. wissen

18·2   1. kennen   2. weiß   3. Kennst   4. weiß   5. weiß   6. Wissen/Weiß   7. kennst   8. wissen
9. Wisst   10. kennt

18·3   1. Paul, was weißt du?   2. Ich weiß nichts.   3. Herr Brach kennt Köln gut.   4. Sie kennt das Mädchen.
5. Fräulein Schmalz, kennen Sie Hamburg?   6. Lotte und Beate, wisst ihr wie viel das kostet?   7. Wir
wissen das nicht.   8. Ich kenne Frau Broch.   9. Mädels/Mädchen, wisst ihr wo das Buch ist?   10. Wir
kennen die Gegend gut.

18·4   1. Sag(e) es auf Deutsch! Sagt es auf Deutsch! Sagen Sie es auf Deutsch!   2. Empfiehl ein Restaurant!
Empfehlt ein Restaurant! Empfehlen Sie ein Restaurant!   3. Bleib(e) in der Hauptstadt! Bleibt in der
Hauptstadt! Bleiben Sie in der Hauptstadt!   4. Probier(e) den Kuchen! Probiert den Kuchen! Probieren Sie
den Kuchen!   5. Probier(e) den Mantel an! Probiert den Mantel an! Probieren Sie den Mantel an!
6. Fahr(e) nach Hause! Fahrt nach Hause! Fahren Sie nach Hause!   7. Jag(e) den Hund weg! Jagt den
Hund weg! Jagen Sie den Hund weg!   8. Sing(e) lauter! Singt lauter! Singen Sie lauter!   9. Zerreiß(e) den
Brief! Zerreißt den Brief! Zerreißen Sie den Brief!   10. Sei artig! Seid artig! Seien Sie artig!

19   The accusative-dative prepositions

19·1   1. das Haus   2. die Tur   3. die Baume   4. die Garage   5. den Laden   6. diesem Madchen
7. unseren Eltern   8. seiner Freundin   9. einem Schulkameraden   10. dem Fernsehapparat   11. den
Keller   12. die Kirche   13. das Restaurant   14. die Garage   15. diesen Laden   16. unserem Bett
17. dem Sofa   18. einer Decke   19. diesen Kissen   20. dem Boden   21. das Klavier   22. den Tisch
23. den Schrank   24. die Stuhle   25. das Sofa

19·2   1. auf dem Sofa   2. in der Schule   3. am Theater   4. im Wasser   5. vor der Tur   6. am Fluss
7. aufs Bett   8. ins Rathaus   9. am Bahnhof   10. auf den Stuhlen

19·3   1. Er geht zwei Schritte vor ihm.   2. Der Hund erkennt die Frau daran.   3. Hier sind wir endlich wieder
unter ihnen.   4. Warum stehst du davor?   5. Die Kinder fürchten sich davor.   6. Sie irren sich in
ihnen.   7. Jemand steht dahinter.   8. Man soll sich davor schützen.   9. Die Jungen warten neben ihr.
10. Er schläft dazwischen.   11. Worunter spielen die Kinder?   12. Auf wen ist der Mann sehr
eifersüchtig?   13. Wovor steigen die Touristen aus?   14. Worüber hängt ein großes Bild?   15. Worin
verbirgt sich die Katze?

19·4   1. Jetzt fahren wir in die Berge.   2. Jetzt fahren wir in einen langen Tunnel.   3. Jetzt fahren wir in die neue Garage.   4. Sie hängt einen Spiegel über den Esstisch.   5. Sie hängt einen Spiegel über mein Bett. 6. Sie hängt einen Spiegel über den Bücherschrank.   7. Was stecktest du in deine Tasche?   8. Was stecktest du in ihre Handschuhe?   9. Was stecktest du in deinen Mund?   10. Der Bus fährt bis vor den neuen Bahnhof.   11. Der Bus fährt bis vor das neue Einkaufszentrum.   12. Der Bus fährt bis vor unsere Schule.   13. Herr Keller stellte den Korb hinter die Tür.   14. Herr Keller stellte den Korb hinter den alten Esstisch.   15. Herr Keller stellte den Korb hinter den großen Bücherschrank.

19·5   *Sample answers are provided.*   1. Warum laufen die Jungen an das Tor?   2. Erik legt das Buch auf seinen Schreibtisch.   3. Mein Vater fährt den Wagen hinter die Mauer.   4. Ich stellte die Bücher in den Bücherschrank.   5. Die neue Studentin setzt sich neben ihren neuen Professor.   6. Tina hängt einen Spiegel über das Klavier.   7. Der Hund kriecht unter den langen Esstisch.   8. Eine Straßenbahn fährt bis vor das Einkaufszentrum.   9. Sie stellt eine Stehlampe zwischen das Sofa und den Fernsehapparat. 10. Der Junge steckte einen Bleistift in seine Tasche.

19·6   1. Worin schläft eine Katze? Wo schläft eine Katze?   2. Vor wem steht der Junge?   3. Zwischen wem will das Kind sitzen?   4. Worunter kriecht eine Maus? Wohin kriecht eine Maus?   5. Worin stellt sie die Milch? Wohin stellt sie die Milch?   6. Worüber hängt ein Poster? Wo hängt ein Poster?   7. An wen schreibt sie einen Brief?   8. Woran steht sein Moped? Wo steht sein Moped?   9. Sie fahren ihre Fahrräder (bicycles) hinter das Haus. Wohinter fahren sie ihre Fahrräder? Wohin fahren sie ihre Fahrräder? 10. Worin essen alle? Wo essen alle?

19·7   1. b   2. c   3. d   4. b   5. a   6. c   7. b   8. b   9. d   10. a   11. c   12. b   13. d   14. b 15. a

20   Genitive case, the comparative, and the superlative

20·1   1. der Tasse   2. dieses Glases   3. meiner Eltern   4. seiner Tochter   5. einer Prufung   6. Ihres Bleistifts   7. des Geldes   8. ihrer Gesundheit   9. unseres Gartens   10. des Flugzeugs   11. Dieses Zuges   12. der Blume   13. dieser Nacht   14. deines Geburtstags   15. unserer Freundinnen 16. des Hundes   17. ihrer Katze   18. des Jahres   19. dieser Pferde   20. eines Apfels   21. Keines Dichters   22. der Gaste   23. des Studenten   24. eines Lowen   25. des Schiffes

20·2   1. seiner Schwester   2. der Lehrer   3. dieses Herrn   4. meiner Tochter   5. unseres Gastes   6. des Chefs   7. ihres Freundes   8. dieses Problems   9. deiner Tante   10. Ihrer Freundin

20·3   1. Wegen des Regens bleiben alle zu Hause.   2. Wegen des Gewitters bleiben alle zu Hause.   3. Wegen seiner Erkaltung bleiben alle zu Hause.   4. Wegen des Wetters bleiben alle zu Hause.   5. Wegen der Prufungen bleiben alle zu Hause.   6. Wir waren wahrend meines Geburtstags in Kanada.   7. Wir waren wahrend des Krieges in Kanada.   8. Wir waren wahrend des Angriffs in Kanada.   9. Wir waren wahrend der Konferenz in Kanada.   10. Wir waren wahrend der Verhandlungen in Kanada.   11. Anstatt meines Onkels musste ich ihr helfen.   12. Anstatt der Jungen musste ich ihr helfen.   13. Anstatt eines Matrosen musste ich ihr helfen.   14. Anstatt der Familie musste ich ihr helfen.   15. Anstatt unserer Eltern musste ich ihr helfen.   16. Trotz unserer Freundschaft wollte sie nicht Tennis spielen.   17. Trotz des Wetters wollte sie nicht Tennis spielen.   18. Trotz des Sonnenscheins wollte sie nicht Tennis spielen. 19. Trotz meines Alters wollte sie nicht Tennis spielen.   20. Trotz meiner Bitte wollte sie nicht Tennis spielen. 21. Wir wohnten diesseits des Flusses.   22. Wir wohnten diesseits der Grenze.   23. Wir wohnten diesseits der Brucke.   24. Wir wohnten diesseits der Berge.   25. Wir wohnten diesseits der Alpen.

20·4   1. Er will den Wagen eines Freundes kaufen.   2. Er will das Fahrrad dieser Kinder kaufen.   3. Er will den Hut eines Generals kaufen.   4. Er will die Bücher jener Lehrerin kaufen.   5. Er will den Regenschirm meines Onkels kaufen.   6. Er will die Blumen dieses Mädchens kaufen.   7. Er will die Katze dieser Mädchen kaufen.   8. Er will den Ring seiner Freundin kaufen.   9. Er will die Schuhe eines Tänzers kaufen.   10. Er will den Spiegel ihres Großvaters kaufen.

20·5   1. alten   2. jüngeren   3. neuen   4. deutschen   5. großen   6. älteren   7. jungen 8. amerikanischen   9. russischen   10. ersten

20·6   1. Wo ist das Spielzeug der jüngeren Kinder?   2. Wo sind die Bücher des neuen Schülers?   3. Wo ist das Hotel meiner ausländischen Gäste?   4. Wo ist das Rathaus dieses kleinen Dorfes?   5. Wo sind die

Schuhe der hübschen Tänzerin?   6. Die Schwestern meiner neuen Frau fahren nach Frankreich.   7. Der Chef Ihres jüngeren Bruders fährt nach Brüssel.   8. Die Wirtin deiner kranken Mutter fährt nach München.   9. Der Sohn der jungen Ärztin fährt nach Heidelberg.   10. Der Freund des hübschen Mädchens fährt nach Österreich.   11. Sehen Sie den Freund meines älteren Bruders?   12. Sehen Sie das Haus des reichen Richters?   13. Sehen Sie die Tante ihrer ausländischen Verwandten?   14. Sehen Sie das Fahrrad unserer jüngeren Tochter?   15. Sehen Sie die Kleider dieser hübschen Tänzerinnen?

20·7 *Sample answers are provided.*   1. des letzten Krieges   2. der verdorbenen Milch   3. ihrer langen Krankheit   4. einer zweiten E-Mail   5. meines hohen Fiebers   6. des heißen Sommers   7. des schrecklichen Gewitters   8. meines jüngeren Cousins   9. unserer nächsten Europareise   10. der langen Parade   11. seiner weißen Haare   12. eines silbernen Rings   13. eines unerwarteten Schneesturms   14. der letzten Hitzewelle   15. des kalten Wetters

20·8   1. schneller   2. langsamer   3. gruner   4. weiser   5. dicker   6. neuer   7. langer   8. schwerer   9. leichter   10. kurzer   11. naher   12. heller   13. alter   14. fleisiger   15. Breiter

20·9   1. Seine Tochter war junger als seine Schwester.
Tante Angela war am jungsten.
2. Die Kinder laufen langsamer als Thomas.
Mein Sohn lauft am langsamsten.
3. Das Gymnasium ist groser als die Grundschule.
Die Universitat ist am grosten.
4. Erik spricht besser als seine Kusine.
Der Professor spricht am besten.
5. Der Doppendecker fliegt hoher als der Zeppelin.
Diese Flugzeuge fliegen am hochsten.
6. Unsere Gaste kamen spater als ich.
Du kamst am spatesten.
7. Diese Geschichte war langweiliger als ihr Roman.
Sein Gedicht war am langweiligsten.
8. Diese Strasen sind breiter als unsere Strase.
Die Autobahn ist am breitesten.
9. Diese Prufung ist schwerer als die Hausaufgabe.
Das Examen ist am schwersten.
10. Frau Bauer kam fruher als ihr Mann.
Ihr kamt am fruhesten.

21   The future perfect, negation, and imperatives

21·1   1. werden, sein
2. werden, haben
3. wird, haben
4. werden, haben
5. werden, sein
6. wird, haben
7. wird, haben
8. werden, haben
9. wirst, haben
10. wird, haben

21·2   1. Sie wird das Gymnasium beendet haben.
2. Sie wird die Universität besucht haben.
3. Sie wird einen Beruf gelernt haben.
4. Sie wird ein Auto gekauft haben.
5. Sie wird eine Ferienreise in die Alpen gemacht haben.
6. Sie wird in die eigene Wohnung gezogen sein.
7. Sie wird wenig Geld gehabt haben.
8. Sie wird die Bekanntschaft eines jungen Mannes gemacht haben.
9. Sie wird sich verliebt haben.
10. Sie wird geheiratet haben.

21·3
1. Sie werden in die Berge gefahren sein.
2. Sie werden gut angekommen sein.
3. Sie werden im See geschwommen sein/haben.
4. Sie werden ins Dorf gegangen sein.
5. Sie werden Souvenirs gekauft haben.
6. Sie werden in einem guten Restaurant gegessen haben.
7. Sie werden eine Spazierfahrt gemacht haben.
8. Sie werden einen Film gesehen haben.
9. Sie werden sich geküsst haben.
10. Sie werden viel miteinander gesprochen haben.

21·4
1. Die Eltern werden sich bei den Gästen bedankt haben.
2. Die Eltern werden sich von den Gästen verabschiedet haben.
3. Vater wird die Hochzeitsrechnung bezahlt haben.
4. Vater wird zur Arbeit gegangen sein.
5. Mutter wird sich ausgeruht haben.
6. Mutter wird im Garten gearbeitet haben.
7. Die Großeltern werden nach Hause gefahren sein.
8. Die Geschwister werden den Kuchenrest aufgegessen haben.
9. Tante Erika wird mit Mutter telefoniert haben.
10. Alle werden uns vermisst haben.

21·5
1. Wir werden sechs Stunden lang gefahren sein.   2. Die Touristen werden wohl nach Polen gereist sein.
3. Die Jungen werden Fusball gespielt haben.   4. Die Wanderer werden Durst gehabt haben.   5. Der
Schuler wird ein Wurstchen gekauft haben.   6. Du wirst den ganzen Kuchen gegessen haben.   7. Karl
wird wohl einen Beruf gelernt haben.   8. Die Party wird allen gefallen haben.   9. Wir werden mehr als
neun Stunden geschlafen haben.   10. Die Reisenden werden zu spat angekommen sein.

21·6
1. Mein Onkel bezahlte die Rechnung.
   Mein Onkel hat die Rechnung bezahlt.
   Mein Onkel hatte die Rechnung bezahlt.
   Mein Onkel wird die Rechnung bezahlen.
   Mein Onkel wird die Rechnung bezahlt haben.
2. Die Madchen schwammen im Fluss.
   Die Madchen sind im Fluss geschwommen.
   Die Madchen waren im Fluss geschwommen.
   Die Madchen werden im Fluss schwimmen.
   Die Madchen werden im Fluss geschwommen sein.
3. Wir sprachen oft mit unseren Nachbarn.
   Wir haben oft mit unseren Nachbarn gesprochen.
   Wir hatten oft mit unseren Nachbarn gesprochen.
   Wir werden oft mit unseren Nachbarn sprechen.
   Wir werden oft mit unseren Nachbarn gesprochen haben.
4. Meine Verwandten reisten nach Amerika.
   Meine Verwandten sind nach Amerika gereist.
   Meine Verwandten waren nach Amerika gereist.
   Meine Verwandten werden nach Amerika reisen.
   Meine Verwandten werden nach Amerika gereist sein.
5. Ich arbeitete fur Herrn Dorf.
   Ich habe fur Herrn Dorf gearbeitet.
   Ich hatte fur Herrn Dorf gearbeitet.
   Ich werde fur Herrn Dorf arbeiten.
   Ich werde fur Herrn Dorf gearbeitet haben.
6. Mein Sohn besuchte die Universitat.
   Mein Sohn hat die Universitat besucht.
   Mein Sohn hatte die Universitat besucht.
   Mein Sohn wird die Universitat besuchen.
   Mein Sohn wird die Universitat besucht haben.

7. Sie zog sich eine schone Bluse an.

Sie hat sich eine schone Bluse angezogen.

Sie hatte sich eine schone Bluse angezogen.

Sie wird sich eine schone Bluse anziehen.

Sie wird sich eine schone Bluse angezogen haben.

8. Viele Jugendliche wanderten im Wald.

Viele Jugendliche sind im Wald gewandert.

Viele Jugendliche waren im Wald gewandert.

Viele Jugendliche werden im Wald wandern.

Viele Jugendliche werden im Wald gewandert sein.

9. Er machte alle Fenster auf.

Er hat alle Fenster aufgemacht.

Er hatte alle Fenster aufgemacht.

Er wird alle Fenster aufmachen.

Er wird alle Fenster aufgemacht haben.

10. Die Gaste asen mehr als dreimal mexikanisch.

Die Gaste haben mehr als dreimal mexikanisch gegessen.

Die Gaste hatten mehr als dreimal mexikanisch gegessen.

Die Gaste werden mehr als dreimal mexikanisch essen.

Die Gaste werden mehr als dreimal mexikanisch gegessen haben.

21·7 1. Sie können heute nicht lange bleiben. 2. Wohnen Sie nicht in Darmstadt? 3. Letzte Woche war sie noch nicht krank. 4. Mein Onkel singt nicht schlecht. 5. Unsere Gäste wollen heute Abend nicht tanzen gehen. 6. Warum beklagst du dich nicht? 7. Der Stuhl steht nicht zwischen dem Schrank und dem Tisch. 8. Soll die Lampe nicht über dem Tisch hängen? 9. Das alte Flugzeug fliegt nicht schnell über die Wolken. 10. Ich trage heute meinen Regenmantel nicht. 11. Der Vogel sitzt nicht auf dem hohen Dach. 12. Gudrun hat ihren kleinen Bruder nicht geschlagen. 13. Er musste mich nicht anrufen. 14. Mozart war nicht sehr musikalisch. 15. Warum hast du diesen Brief nicht zerrissen? 16. Schreiben Sie den Brief nicht an Ihre Tante? 17. Diese Studenten haben nicht fleißig gearbeitet. 18. Sie ist gestern nicht in der Nähe von Hannover gewesen. 19. Hört der Regen nicht auf? 20. Die Jungen sind nicht über die Brücke gelaufen. 21. Viele Studenten haben das Examen nicht bestanden. 22. Im Park sitzen die jungen Leute nicht auf den Bänken. 23. In der Ferne erblickte der Wanderer die Räuber nicht. 24. Wir nehmen nicht an dem Besuch der Oper teil. 25. Mein Großvater kann sich nicht an seine Jugend erinnern.

21·8 *Sample answers are provided.* 1. Wir sind nicht am Montag abgefahren, sondern am Dienstag. 2. Er will nicht das kleine Haus kaufen, sondern das große. 3. Sie fahren nicht heute ins Restaurant, sondern morgen. 4. Er nennt nicht den jungen Mann einen Dieb, sondern den alten Mann. 5. Die Studentin begegnete nicht dem Professor, sondern einem alten Freund. 6. Das alte Lehrbuch nützt nicht dem Studenten, sondern dem Professor. 7. Ich hänge das Bild nicht über das Klavier, sondern über den Spiegel. 8. Der Junge will nicht die neuen Wörter vergessen, sondern das ganze Gedicht. 9. Die Kinder bitten nicht die Mutter um Süßigkeiten, sondern die Großmutter. 10. Ich weiß nicht die Hausnummer, sondern nur die Straße.

21·9 1. In diesem Haus wohnt kein Schauspieler. 2. Hast du keine Prüfung bestanden? 3. Das Mädchen hat keine schöne Bluse verloren. 4. Keine guten Menschen helfen den Armen. 5. Der Uhrmacher zieht keine Uhr auf. 6. Im Schatten verbergen sich keine Diebe. 7. Im März können keine Obstbäume blühen. 8. Wachsen auf dieser tropischen Insel keine Tannen? 9. Dieser Fahrer hat kein Autorennen gewonnen. 10. Die Schülerin lernt keine neuen Wörter und kein Gedicht. 11. An der Straßenecke stand kein Bettler. 12. Auf dem Sportplatz rennen keine Kinder hin und her. 13. Warum reißt du kein Blatt aus dem Buch? 14. Unser Hund hat keinen Fremden gebissen. 15. Unter dem Esstisch schlafen keine Katzen. 16. Diese Sängerin hat wie keine Nachtigall gesungen. 17. Der Erfinder hat keinen neuen Motor erfunden. 18. Ich schreibe keine Ansichtskarten und keinen langen Brief. 19. Er pfeift kein Lied. 20. Sie können keine Kinder zu lernen zwingen. 21. Das Mädchen hat keinen Ball ins Wasser geworfen. 22. Keine Unfälle geschehen täglich. 23. Hast du dem Kellner kein Trinkgeld gegeben? 24. Der Verkäufer legte keine Waren auf den Tisch. 25. In dieser Straße sind keine großen Geschäfte.

21·10 1. b 2. a 3. c 4. c 5. c 6. d 7. b 8. b 9. a 10. c

22 Relative pronouns

22·1   1. das   2. mit denen   3. dessen Buch   4. denen   5. den   6. in der   7. nach dem   8. deren Eltern   9. von denen   10. dessen Bucher   11. dem   12. in das   13. deren Vater   14. die   15. durch den

22·2   1. das ein Dusenjager ist   2. auf dem ein kleiner Vogel sitzt   3. das niemand reparieren konnte   4. in das die Fluggaste einsteigen   5. die Amerikanerin ist   6. deren Kinder eine Schule in der Stadt besuchen   7. mit der viele Manner tanzen wollen   8. auf die ich gestern gewartet habe   9. die alles verloren haben   10. deren Tochter ihnen nicht helfen konnen   11. fur die wir einmal gearbeitet haben   12. die alle Nachbarn lieben   13. das viel zu gros ist   14. auf dem der Hund auch schlaft   15. Das sein Grosvater vierzig Jahre vorher gekauft hatte

22·3   1. welches ein Dusenjager ist   2. welches der Tourist fotografiert hat   3. von welchem alle reden   4. uber welche er einen Artikel geschrieben hat   5. mit welchen die groseren Jungen gern spielen   6. deren Bruder das Geld gestohlen hat   7. durch welche ich die Nachricht bekommen habe   8. Welcher keinen Fuhrerschein hat   9. welchen Frau Keller gern hat   10. mit welchem diese Fusganger sprechen wollen   11. welchem der Polizist einen Strafzettel gab   12. welche Thomas ihr geschenkt hat   13. fur welche sie ihm danken will   14. von welchen ihre Schwester nicht sprechen will   15. welche leider schon welken

22·4   1. Wem der Roman nicht gefiel, der soll ihn nicht lesen.   2. Wem man traut, der ist ein treuer Freund.   3. Wer nicht fur uns ist, der ist gegen uns.   4. Wen wir einladen, dem geben wir den teuersten Sekt.   5. Wessen Wein ich trinke, dem bleibe ich treu.   6. Wen der Freund liebt, den hasst der Feind.   7. Wen man nicht kennt, dem bleibt man fern.   8. Wen ich gesehen habe, den werde ich nie vergessen.   9. Mit wem der Politiker spricht, der wird der neue Kandidat.   10. Wessen Freundschaft ich habe, dem bleibe ich ein guter Freund.

22·5   1. Der Mann sagte alles, was voller Unsinn war.   2. Das ist das Schrecklichste, was ich gesehen habe.   3. Es gibt vieles, was sehr gefahrlich ist.   4. Sie hat das Teuerste, was nicht immer das Beste ist.   5. Singe etwas, was wir noch nicht gehort haben!   6. Thomas hat ein Auto gestohlen, wovon seine Eltern nichts gewusst haben.   7. Unsere Tante muss heute abreisen, was wir sehr bedauern.   8. Sie hat nichts verstanden, was ich gesagt habe.   9. Wir vergessen alles, was der Politiker versprochen hat.   10. Unsere Nachbarn machen Krach, was uns stort.

22·6   1. Das ist die Lehrerin, die mir helfen wird.   2. Das Land, das ich liebe, ist meine Heimat.   3. Es war einmal eine Königin, die eine hübsche Tochter hatte.   4. Wo ist der Hund, der so laut bellt?   5. Seht ihr die Vögel, die so schön singen?   6. Sie haben die Weingläser verloren, die sehr teuer waren.   7. Warum kaufst du das Pferd, das alt und krank ist?   8. Wir besuchten unsere Verwandten, die in Leipzig wohnten.   9. Erik hat einen Fernsehapparat, der einen großen Bildschirm hat.   10. Ihr Sohn, der neun Jahre alt wird, hat morgen Geburtstag.

22·7   1. Sie findet das Kleid, das sie gestern gekauft hat. Sie findet die Briefmarken, die sie gestern gekauft hat. Sie findet den Hut, den sie gestern gekauft hat.   2. Kennen Sie den Ausländer, der in Darmstadt wohnt? Kennen Sie die Studenten, die in Darmstadt wohnen? Kennen Sie die Studentin, die in Darmstadt wohnt?   3. Ich begegnete einer Dame, deren Vater gestorben ist. Ich begegnete den Brüdern, deren Vater gestorben ist. Ich begegnete einem Kind, dessen Vater gestorben ist.   4. Das sind die Leute, von denen ich das Geschenk bekommen habe. Das ist der Richter, von dem ich das Geschenk bekommen habe. Das sind unsere Gäste, von denen ich das Geschenk bekommen habe.   5. Die Männer, für die wir gearbeitet haben, sind nach Bonn gezogen. Der Engländer, für den wir gearbeitet haben, ist nach Bonn gezogen. Das Mädchen, für das wir gearbeitet haben, ist nach Bonn gezogen.

22·8   1. Ich habe den Roman, den Karl übersetzen will.   2. Ich habe den Roman, von dem viele Leute begeistert sind.   3. Ich habe den Roman, dessen Schrift steller Hesse war.   4. Sabine spielte mit den Kindern, über die der Reporter geschrieben hat.   5. Sabine spielte mit den Kindern, deren Eltern krank waren.   6. Sabine spielte mit den Kindern, nach denen der Lehrer fragte.   7. Die Witwe, deren Mann vor zwei Monaten gestorben ist, wohnt jetzt in Bayern.   8. Die Witwe, der niemand helfen wollte, wohnt jetzt in Bayern.   9. Die Witwe, für die ihre Kinder nicht sorgen können, wohnt jetzt in Bayern.   10. Sie erzählte von einem König, der vier starke Söhne hatte.   11. Sie erzählte von einem König, den das Volk sehr liebte.   12. Sie erzählte von einem König, dessen Tochter goldene Haare hatte.   13. Stefan fotografiert die

Soldaten, die der Bürgermeister des Dorfes hasst.   14. Stefan fotografiert die Soldaten, von denen niemand sprechen will.   15. Stefan fotografiert die Soldaten, die tapfer im Kampf waren.

22·9   1. Sie findet das Kleid, welches sie gestern gekauft hat. Sie findet die Briefmarken, welche sie gestern gekauft hat. Sie findet den Hut, welchen sie gestern gekauft hat.   2. Kennen Sie den Ausländer, welcher in Darmstadt wohnt? Kennen Sie die Studenten, welche in Darmstadt wohnen? Kennen Sie die Studentin, welche in Darmstadt wohnt?   3. Ich begegnete einer Dame, deren Vater gestorben ist. Ich begegnete den Brüdern, deren Vater gestorben ist. Ich begegnete einem Kind, dessen Vater gestorben ist.   4. Das sind die Leute, von welchen ich das Geschenk bekommen habe. Das ist der Richter, von welchem ich das Geschenk bekommen habe. Das sind unsere Gäste, von welchen ich das Geschenk bekommen habe.   5. Die Männer, für welche wir gearbeitet haben, sind nach Bonn gezogen. Der Engländer, für welchen wir gearbeitet haben, ist nach Bonn gezogen. Das Mädchen, für welches wir gearbeitet haben, ist nach Bonn gezogen.

22·10   *Sample answers are provided.*   1. Er besuchte seinen Onkel, der ein Haus in Hamburg hat.   2. Der Kaufmann, dem ich im Restaurant begegnete, reist sehr weit.   3. Erik verkaufte die Bücher, die er nicht mehr braucht.   4. Kennen Sie die Amerikanerin, deren Bruder Diplomat ist?   5. Die Künstlerin, von der ich dir erzählte, ist gestorben.   6. Heidelberg ist eine Stadt, die für ihre Schönheit berühmt ist.   7. Die Herren, mit denen wir sprechen, sind Ausländer.   8. Die Leute, deren Kinder so jung sind, sind umgezogen.   9. Frau Benz ist jetzt eine Witwe, deren Mann sehr lange krank war. 10. Der Aufsatz, welchen Sabine schreibt, ist schwer.   11. Die Polizei fand die Wanderer, welche in den Bergen verloren waren.   12. Der Wagen, welchen Frau Keller kauft, ist ein BMW.   13. Wir wohnen in einem Land, welches viele Touristen besuchen.   14. Viele helfen dem Jungen, dessen Eltern arm sind.   15. Ist das das Pferd, welches Herr Kamps verkaufen will?   16. Ich sehe das Fenster, welches Thomas zerbrochen hat.   17. Mein Nachbar, mit welchem ich oft Karten spiele, ist krank geworden. 18. Er sitzt auf einem Stuhl, welcher hundert Jahre alt ist.   19. Wir begegneten der Richterin, deren Bruder Taschendieb ist.

22·11   1. a. Er findet einen Handschuh, der seinem Freund gehört.
     b. Er findet eine Mappe, die seinem Freund gehört.
     c. Er findet die Anzüge, die seinem Freund gehören.
 2. a. Ich sprach mit einer Freundin, die Liese neulich kennen gelernt hat.
     b. Ich sprach mit dem Mädchen, das Liese neulich kennen gelernt hat.
     c. Ich sprach mit den Ausländern, die Liese neulich kennen gelernt hat.
 3. a. Klaus kennt den Herrn, von dem die anderen gesprochen haben.
     b. Klaus kennt die Leute, von denen die anderen gesprochen haben.
     c. Klaus kennt das Kind, von dem die anderen gesprochen haben.
 4. a. Sie besuchte ihre Verwandten, deren Nachbar aus England kommt.
     b. Sie besuchte den Professor, dessen Nachbar aus England kommt.
     c. Sie besuchte die Krankenschwester, deren Nachbar aus England kommt.

22·12   1. Der Tourist, mit welchem er gesprochen hat, war Ausländer.   2. Der Schriftsteller, dessen Romane viel bewundert werden, ist jetzt achtzig Jahre alt.   3. Sie haben Beethoven ein Denkmal gesetzt, welches ein junger Bildhauer geschaffen hat.   4. Sie kauft neue Gläser, aus welchen man nur Wein trinken wird. 5. Der Zug, welcher langsam fährt, ist kein Eilzug.

22·13   1. der   2. die   3. was   4. Wer   5. den   6. das   7. dem   8. dem   9. dessen   10. den

22·14   *These are sample answers only.*   1. ... die so hell leuchten.   2. ... was mir sehr gefiel.   3. ... er einen Artikel geschrieben hat.   4. ... der ihm gar nicht passt.   5. ... ich mich nicht interessiere.

23   Modifiers, adverbs, reflexive pronouns, and conjunctions

23·1   1. einem, alten   2. diese, hubsche   3. solche, interessanten   4. deine, erste   5. unsere, besten   6. jedem, guten   7. seine, neue   8. einer, kleinen   9. jenem, grosen   10. ein, solches   11. solche, lauten   12. welchen, jungen   13. keinem, kleinen   14. Ihr, schoner   15. einer, langen

23·2   1. solche netten Kinder
     solche netten Kinder

solchen netten Kindern
solcher netten Kinder
2. wenige deutsche Manner
wenige deutsche Manner
wenigen deutschen Mannern
weniger deutscher Manner
3. jeder alte Herr
jeden alten Herrn
jedem alten Herrn
jedes alten Herrn
4. ein solches Flugzeug
ein solches Flugzeug
einem solchen Flugzeug
eines solchen Flugzeugs
5. deine beste Prufung
deine beste Prufung
deiner besten Prufung
deiner besten Prufung
6. gutes Wetter
gutes Wetter
gutem Wetter
guten Wetters

23·3 1. Die Kinder waren ganz mude. 2. Die Kinder waren sehr mude. 3. Die Kinder waren ziemlich mude. 4. Die Kinder waren gar nicht mude. 5. Die Kinder waren total mude. 6. Sein Gedicht ist ziemlich gut. 7. Sein Gedicht ist uberhaupt nicht gut. 8. Sein Gedicht ist ganz gut. 9. Sein Gedicht ist sehr gut. 10. Sein Gedicht ist gar nicht gut.

23·4 1. Martin kaufte etwas fur sich. 2. Ihr habt nur an euch gedacht. 3. Wir helfen uns, so oft wir konnen. 4. Ich verberge das Geschenk hinter mir. 5. Er setzte sich auf den kleinen Stuhl. 6. Wer wollte sich ein Wurstchen bestellen? 7. Sie konnte sich nicht helfen. 8. Waschst du dich im Badezimmer? 9. Ich frage mich, warum er weint. 10. Warum widersprecht ihr euch? 11. Mutter wird sich ein paar Nelken kaufen. 12. Sie finden gar keine Platze fur sich. 13. Karl hat sich an die grose Prufung erinnert. 14. Wo kann er sich waschen? 15. Wir argern uns nicht daruber.

23·5 1. Ich möchte mich vorstellen. 2. Wir haben uns wieder geärgert. 3. Du musst dich vor einer Erkältung schützen. 4. Habt ihr euch angekleidet? 5. Wie können sie sich ändern? 6. Meine Mutter fragt sich, was geschehen ist. 7. Frau Schneider hat sich auf einen Stuhl gesetzt. 8. Du hast dich schon überzeugt. 9. Der wahnsinnige Mann hat sich getötet. 10. Ich wasche mich.

23·6 1. Die Mutter putzt sich die Zähne. 2. Gudrun hilft sich, so gut sie kann. 3. Martin und Erich wollen sich ein Spiel kaufen. 4. Warum musst du dir widersprechen? 5. Ich kämme mir die Haare. 6. Darf ich mir ein Stück Kuchen nehmen? 7. Meine Schwester hat sich ein interessantes Buch gefunden. 8. Er kaufte sich eine Armbanduhr. 9. Das wird sie sich nie verzeihen. 10. Habt ihr euch die Mäntel ausgezogen?

23·7 1. Was hat sich bewegt? 2. Ich kann mir nicht helfen. 3. Haben Sie sich nicht widersprochen? 4. Wir haben uns vorgestellt. 5. Wer hat sich gewaschen? 6. Sie hat sich an die Italienreise erinnert. 7. Man soll sich nicht ärgern. 8. Herr Finkler hat sich einen neuen Wagen gekauft. 9. Sie haben sich ein paar Pralinen genommen. 10. Du musst dich ändern.

23·8 1. a. Ich denke nur an mich.
b. Du denkst nur an dich.
c. Die Kinder denken nur an sich.
d. Sie denken nur an sich.
2. a. Ich kaufte mir neue Handschuhe.
b. Er kaufte sich neue Handschuhe.
c. Wir kauften uns neue Handschuhe.
d. Du kauftest dir neue Handschuhe.

3. a. Der alte Mann braucht Hustentropfen für sich.
   b. Sie braucht Hustentropfen für sich.
   c. Ihr braucht Hustentropfen für euch.
   d. Erich braucht Hustentropfen für sich.

23·9 *These are sample answers only.* 1. Wir werden dem neuen Angestellten diese Arbeit zutrauen. 2. Braucht ihr das Geld für euren Onkel? 3. Ich kann meinen Chef nicht davon überzeugen. 4. Sie dürfen das Kind auf diese Bank setzen. 5. Marianne stellte die Stehlampe neben ihren Vater. 6. Meine Eltern haben einem Freund einen bunten Teppich gekauft. 7. Er fragt Gudrun, ob das eine Dummheit ist. 8. Du sollst deine Eltern sofort vorstellen. 9. Karl hat seiner Freundin einen guten Platz gesucht. 10. Ich ziehe dem Kind das Hemd an.

23·10 1. mich 2. dich 3. sich 4. sich 5. euch 6. sich 7. sich 8. mir 9. dich 10. mir

23·11 1. Wir wussten nicht, warum sie nach Hause gegangen ist. 2. Wir wussten nicht, was er im Einkaufszentrum gekauft hat. 3. Wir wussten nicht, mit wem Sabine Tennis gespielt hat. 4. Wir wussten nicht, wie lange sie im Ausland bleiben mussten. 5. Wir wussten nicht, fur wen Erik die Blumen gekauft hat. 6. Jemand fragte, wann der Bus abgefahren ist. 7. Jemand fragte, wessen Mercedes der Mann gestohlen hat. 8. Jemand fragte, wohin die Jungen gelaufen sind. 9. Jemand fragte, wofur sich der Wissenschaft ler interessiert. 10. Jemand fragte, warum du dir immer widersprichst. 11. Konnen Sie mir sagen, um wie viel Uhr der Zug kommt? 12. Konnen Sie mir sagen, wem ich damit helfen soll? 13. Konnen Sie mir sagen, was geschehen ist? 14. Konnen Sie mir sagen, wie viel diese Hemden kosten? 15. Konnen Sie mir sagen, wonach der Polizist gefragt hat?

23·12 *Sample answers are provided.* 1. Ich habe ein neues Fahrrad, aber Felix hat ein altes Fahrrad. 2. Meine Cousine wohnt in Bayern, aber ihre Eltern wohnen in Kiel. 3. Peter mag kaltes Wetter, denn er geht oft Ski laufen. 4. Wir werden bis morgen warten, denn es regnet. 5. Sollen wir ins Theater gehen, oder sollen wir zu Hause bleiben? 6. Du kannst dich im Keller waschen, oder du kannst dich im Badezimmer waschen. 7. Ich höre nicht gern Radio, sondern ich sehe lieber fern. 8. Er möchte keinen Kuchen essen, sondern ich möchte ein bisschen Eis essen. 9. Tina deckt den Tisch, und Erik macht die Küche sauber. 10. Im Juni fliegen wir nach New York, und im Juli sind wir wieder in Deutschland.

23·13 *Sample answers are provided.* 1. ich in einem Dorf wohnte 2. der Mann betrunken war 3. ich etwas bestelle 4. wir starke Männer sind 5. ich das Museum besuchte 6. Professor Benz frei ist 7. alle Schüler die Prüfung bestanden haben 8. er in London wohnt 9. die Wellen zu hoch sind 10. Seine Frau einkaufen geh

24 Double infinitive structures

24·1 1. Du hast deine Pflicht tun sollen. 2. Der Mann hat nicht schwimmen konnen. 3. Man hat sehr vorsichtig sein mussen. 4. Haben sie mit der Katze spielen durfen? 5. Niemand hat mit mir tanzen wollen. 6. Haben Sie die Berge sehen konnen? 7. Er hatte ins Ausland reisen wollen. 8. Was hatte er tun sollen? 9. Die Jungen hatten fur Sie arbeiten konnen. 10. Ihr hattet den Hund waschen mussen. 11. Hier hatte man nicht rauchen durfen. 12. Erik wird ins Restaurant gehen wollen. 13. Wirst du ihm helfen konnen? 14. Ich werde in die Stadt fahren sollen. 15. Wir werden ihn vom Flughafen abholen mussen.

24·2 1. Er hat das neue Auto waschen lassen.
   Er wird das neue Auto waschen lassen.
2. Er hat seine Eltern im Keller flustern horen.
   Er wird seine Eltern im Keller flustern horen.
3. Wir haben den Dusenjager uber dem Wald fliegen sehen.
   Wir werden den Dusenjager uber dem Wald fliegen sehen.
4. Herr Dorf hat einen neuen Anzug machen lassen.
   Herr Dorf wird einen neuen Anzug machen lassen.
5. Der Junge hat mir das alte Radio reparieren helfen.
   Der Junge wird mir das alte Radio reparieren helfen.

24·3
1. Sie kann seine Rede nicht verstehen.
   Sie konnte seine Rede nicht verstehen.
   Sie hat seine Rede nicht verstehen konnen.
   Sie wird seine Rede nicht verstehen konnen.
2. Wir horen den Mann Gitarre spielen.
   Wir horten den Mann Gitarre spielen.
   Wir haben den Mann Gitarre spielen horen.
   Wir werden den Mann Gitarre spielen horen.
3. Du musst ins Ausland reisen.
   Du musstest ins Ausland reisen.
   Du hast ins Ausland reisen mussen.
   Du wirst ins Ausland reisen mussen.
4. Wer sieht die Madchen im Fluss schwimmen?
   Wer sah die Madchen im Fluss schwimmen?
   Wer hat die Madchen im Fluss schwimmen sehen?
   Wer wird die Madchen im Fluss schwimmen sehen?
5. Der kranke Mann darf nicht nach Hause gehen.
   Der kranke Mann durfte nicht nach Hause gehen.
   Der kranke Mann hat nicht nach Hause gehen durfen.
   Der kranke Mann wird nicht nach Hause gehen durfen.
6. Ich soll eine neue Schule besuchen.
   Ich sollte eine neue Schule besuchen.
   Ich habe eine neue Schule besuchen sollen.
   Ich werde eine neue Schule besuchen sollen.
7. Viele Leute konnen schwimmen.
   Viele Leute konnten schwimmen.
   Viele Leute haben schwimmen konnen.
   Viele Leute werden schwimmen konnen.
8. Er will die Suppe probieren.
   Er wollte die Suppe probieren.
   Er hat die Suppe probieren wollen.
   Er wird die Suppe probieren wollen.
9. Der Wissenschaft ler lasst die Soft ware installieren.
   Der Wissenschaft ler lies die Soft ware installieren.
   Der Wissenschaft ler hat die Soft ware installieren lassen.
   Der Wissenschaft ler wird die Soft ware installieren lassen.
10. Die Soldaten helfen ihnen die Tulpen pflanzen.
    Die Soldaten halfen ihnen die Tulpen pflanzen.
    Die Soldaten haben ihnen die Tulpen pflanzen helfen.
    Die Soldaten werden ihnen die Tulpen pflanzen helfen.

24·4
1. c   2. a   3. b   4. d   5. c   6. a   7. c   8. b   9. a   10. c   11. a   12. d   13. b   14. c
15. c   16. a   17. b   18. d   19. d   20. a

24·5
1. eine Sprache zu lernen   2. ihr sechs Euro zu geben   3. ihm ein Glas Wasser zu bringen   4. an der
Ecke zu warten   5. mehr Zeit zu haben   6. nach meiner Tochter zu fragen   7. in einer Fabrik zu
arbeiten   8. ihn nicht zu sehen   9. schlechter zu werden   10. heute in der Hauptstadt zu sein

24·6
1. eine Schule in Bremen zu besuchen   2. die Fahrkarten zu vergessen   3. um acht Uhr anzukommen
4. sich umzuziehen   5. bald zuruckzukehren   6. es zu empfehlen   7. einen Freund mitzubringen
8. einen alten Koff er zu verkaufen   9. die Gaste vorzustellen   10. in der Schillerstrase auszusteigen

24·7
1. zum Einkaufszentrum gefahren zu sein   2. ihnen danken zu sollen   3. sehr kalt geworden zu sein
4. die Polizei angerufen zu haben   5. nicht schneller laufen zu konnen   6. eine Tasse Tee bestellt zu
haben   7. in die Schweiz reisen zu mussen   8. einen Regenschirm mitgenommen zu haben
9. langsam hereingekommen zu sein   10. nicht alleine fahren zu durfen

24·8
1. den kranken Mann zu verstehen   2. in dem dunklen Wohnzimmer zu lesen   3. so schnell wie ein
Pferd zu rennen   4. in einer kleinen Wohnung zu wohnen   5. ohne einen Computer zu arbeiten

6. einen neuen Ausweis zu bekommen   7. elf Kinder zu erziehen   8. einige Pakete nach Afghanistan zu schicken   9. die schweren Koffer zum Bahnhof zu tragen   10. Politiker zu sein

24·9 1. im Garten zu arbeiten   2. den wichtigen Brief zu schreiben   3. die Suppe vorzubereiten   4. Den armen Mann aufzuheben   5. noch eine Flasche Wein zu bestellen   6. den unartigen Jungen zu strafen   7. eine Fahrkarte gekauft zu haben   8. von uns Abschied zu nehmen   9. zu weinen   10. deine Kleider auszuwahlen   11. beim Militar zu dienen   12. in der Fabrik zu arbeiten   13. mehr Geld verdienen zu konnen   14. einen guten Job zu suchen   15. Goethes Leben zu untersuchen

24·10 1. Es wird unmöglich sein, eine Amerikareise zu machen.   2. Es wird unmöglich sein, genug Geld zu verdienen.   3. Es wird unmöglich sein, heute Abend spazieren zu gehen.   4. Es wird unmöglich sein, mit euch zu frühstücken.   5. Es wird unmöglich sein, die ganze Stadt zu besichtigen.   6. Es ist notwendig, einen anderen Brief zu schreiben.   7. Es ist notwendig, zwei fremde Sprachen zu erlernen.   8. Es ist notwendig, die Kinder richtig zu erziehen.   9. Es ist notwendig, die Stadt besser zu verwalten.   10. Es ist notwendig, das lange Gedicht jeden Tag zu wiederholen.   11. Es ist sehr gesund, täglich joggen zu gehen.   12. Es ist sehr gesund, früh aufzustehen.   13. Es ist sehr gesund, die Ruhe zu behalten.   14. Es ist sehr gesund, ohne Salz und Fett zu kochen.   15. Es ist sehr gesund, das Rauchen aufzugeben.

24·11 1. Es war Schade, das Spiel verloren zu haben.   2. Es war Schade, den Mann entlassen zu haben.   3. Es war Schade, nach Schweden ziehen zu müssen.   4. Es war Schade, zu viel Geld ausgegeben zu haben.   5. Es war Schade, vergebens so weit gefahren zu sein.   6. Es war eine gute Idee, an eine Universität zu gehen.   7. Es war eine gute Idee, einen guten Job zu finden.   8. Es war eine gute Idee, gesund und froh zu bleiben.   9. Es war eine gute Idee, zwei musikalische Instrumente spielen zu können.   10. Es war eine gute Idee, ein neues Kleid machen zu lassen.

24·12 1. Ich vergesse, von meiner Europareise zu erzählen.   2. Wir haben versucht, mit dem Bürgermeister zu sprechen.   3. Meine Eltern hoffen, jeden Abend spazieren gehen zu können.   4. Du musst aufhören, mit den kleinen Welpen zu spielen.   5. Sie fangen an, früh am Morgen zu arbeiten.   6. Ich hoffe, in den Ferien länger schlafen zu können.   7. Niemand versucht, dem entlaufenden Taschendieb zu folgen.   8. Sabine will nicht aufhören, mit ihrem Freund zu tanzen.   9. Die Großeltern wünschen sehr, ihre Kinder und Enkel in Bremen zu besuchen.   10. Tina hat vergessen, ein Geschenk mitzubringen.

24·13 *Sample answers are provided.*   1. Fleißig zu arbeiten ist notwendig. Immer pünktlich anzukommen ist notwendig.   2. In Heidelberg zu studieren war nicht leicht. Die großen Koffer zu tragen war nicht leicht.   3. Erik hat mir versprochen eine Ansichtskarte zu schicken. Erik hat mir versprochen Onkel Heinz in München zu besuchen.   4. Kleine Sabine träumt davon Schauspielerin zu werden. Kleine Sabine träumt davon einmal ins Ausland fahren zu können.   5. Freuen Sie sich darauf wieder nach Kanada zu reisen? Freuen Sie sich darauf einen Job in Basel zu finden?

24·14 *Sample answers are provided.*   1. Er sieht den ganzen Abend fern, anstatt ins Bett zu gehen.   2. Er sieht den ganzen Abend fern, anstatt einen Brief an Oma zu schreiben.   3. Er sieht den ganzen Abend fern, anstatt ins Lokal zu gehen.   4. Er sieht den ganzen Abend fern, anstatt den neuen Roman zu lesen.   5. Er sieht den ganzen Abend fern, anstatt die Küche sauber zu machen.   6. Die Touristen sind nach Hause gefahren, ohne Abschied von uns zu nehmen.   7. Die Touristen sind nach Hause gefahren, ohne ihre Pässe mitzunehmen.   8. Die Touristen sind nach Hause gefahren, ohne die Fahrkarten zu kaufen.   9. Die Touristen sind nach Hause gefahren, ohne den alten Dom besichtigt zu haben.   10. Die Touristen sind nach Hause gefahren, ohne Frau Kamps kennengelernt zu haben.   11. Tina und Felix müssen viel arbeiten, um mehr Geld zu verdienen.   12. Tina und Felix müssen viel arbeiten, um ein Haus in Oldenburg zu kaufen.   13. Tina und Felix müssen viel arbeiten, um eine Garage bauen lassen zu können.   14. Tina und Felix müssen viel arbeiten, um für meine lange Krankheit zu bezahlen.   15. Tina und Felix müssen viel arbeiten, um den Sommer in Italien zu verbringen.   16. Stefan wird nicht vergessen, seinen Cousin vom Bahnhof abzuholen.   17. Stefan wird nicht vergessen, einkaufen zu gehen.   18. Stefan wird nicht vergessen, Brot und Milch zu kaufen.   19. Stefan wird nicht vergessen, den Fernsehapparat reparieren zu lassen.   20. Stefan wird nicht vergessen, drei Glas Bier zu bestellen.   21. Meine Mutter träumt davon Schriftstellerin zu werden.   22. Meine Mutter träumt davon einmal nach Afrika zu reisen.   23. Meine Mutter träumt davon wieder ganz gesund zu sein.   24. Meine Mutter träumt davon ihren ältesten Sohn wieder umarmen zu können.   25. Meine Mutter träumt davon eine moderne Küche zu haben.

25 The passive voice

25·1
1. Die Maus wurde von der Eule gefressen.
Die Maus ist von der Eule gefressen worden.
Die Maus wird von der Eule gefressen werden.
2. Der Kranke wird von der Arztin geheilt.
Der Kranke ist von der Arztin geheilt worden.
Der Kranke wird von der Arztin geheilt werden.
3. Der Artikel wird von ihm gelesen.
Der Artikel wurde von ihm gelesen.
Der Artikel wird von ihm gelesen werden.
4. Die Briefe werden von mir geschrieben.
Die Briefe wurden von mir geschrieben.
Die Briefe sind von mir geschrieben worden.
5. Die Schuler werden vom Lehrer unterrichtet.
Die Schuler sind vom Lehrer unterrichtet worden.
Die Schuler werden vom Lehrer unterrichtet werden.
6. Die Anzuge werden vom Schneider genaht.
Die Anzuge wurden vom Schneider genaht.
Die Anzuge sind vom Schneider genaht worden.
7. Das Brot wurde von Herrn Benz gekauft.
Das Brot ist von Herrn Benz gekauft worden.
Das Brot wird von Herrn Benz gekauft werden.
8. Eine Tasse Kaffee wird von der Kellnerin gebracht.
Eine Tasse Kaffee wurde von der Kellnerin gebracht.
Eine Tasse Kaffee wird von der Kellnerin gebracht werden.

25·2
1. Das Dorf ist vom Feind zerstort worden. 2. Der Bauernhof wird von einem Waldbrand bedroht.
3. Der alte Hund wurde durch einen Schuss getotet. 4. Viele Schweine werden vom Bauer aufgezogen werden. 5. Die Aufsatze sind vom Lehrer verbessert worden.

25·3
1. Dem Professor wurde von seinem Gedicht imponiert. 2. Der alten Frau ist von mir geholfen worden.
3. Dem Konig ist von dir gut gedient worden. 4. Das Lied wird von allen gesungen werden. 5. Uns wird vom Dieb mit einer Pistole gedroht. 6. Der Mann ist von mir in Berlin gesehen worden. 7. Mir wurde vom Soldaten fur das Geschenk gedankt. 8. Das Eis wird von den Kindern gegessen werden.
9. Der Gesundheit wird durch das Rauchen geschadet. 10. Ihm ist von einem guten Freund geraten worden.

25·4
1. Ein Haus muss hier gebaut werden. 2. Ein Haus kann hier gebaut werden. 3. Ein Haus soll hier gebaut werden. 4. Ihm wollte damit geholfen werden. 5. Ihm sollte damit geholfen werden. 6. Ihm konnte damit geholfen werden. 7. Das Problem kann auch von ihr verstanden werden. 8. Das Problem muss auch von ihr verstanden werden. 9. Das Auto wird nicht repariert werden konnen. 10. Das Auto wird nicht repariert werden mussen.

25·5
1. Das lies sich nicht leicht andern.
Das hat sich nicht leicht andern lassen.
Das wird sich nicht leicht andern lassen.
2. Das Geld kann nicht gefunden werden.
Das Geld hat nicht gefunden werden konnen.
Das Geld wird nicht gefunden werden konnen.
3. Diese Probleme lassen sich schnell losen.
Diese Probleme liesen sich schnell losen.
Diese Probleme haben sich schnell losen lassen.
4. Ihnen wird dafur gedankt.
Ihnen wurde dafur gedankt.
Ihnen wird dafur gedankt werden.
5. Der Hund war gewaschen.
Der Hund ist gewaschen gewesen.
Der Hund wird gewaschen sein.

25·6　　1. Der Brief ist von der Mutter geschrieben worden.　　2. Der Brief war von der Mutter geschrieben worden. 3. Der Brief wird von der Mutter geschrieben werden.　　4. Der Brief wird von der Mutter geschrieben worden sein.　　5. Der Brief wurde von der Mutter geschrieben.

25·7　　1. Das gute Restaurant wird von den Freunden besucht.　　2. Der gebratene Fisch wird von dem jungen Mann bestellt.　　3. Die Sachertorte wird von dem Mädchen gegessen.　　4. Das Essen wird von dem Kellner zum Tisch gebracht.　　5. Die Rechnung wird von dem Paar bezahlt.

25·8　　1. Deutsch wurde durch viel Mühe gelernt.　　2. Das Kind wurde durch laute Musik geweckt. 3. Die Kirche wurde durch den Sturm zerstört.　　4. Ich wurde durch Medizin geheilt.　　5. Die Ratte wurde durch Gift getötet.

25·9　　1. wird, gespült　　2. werden, gemacht　　3. wird, gewaschen　　4. werden, gegossen　　5. wird, besucht

25·10　　1. Es wird abends musiziert.　　2. Es wurde dem Lehrer nicht geantwortet.　　3. Es wird dem Kind nichts geglaubt.　　4. Es wurde viel am Wochenende gegessen.　　5. Es wurde viel in den Ferien gewandert.

25·11　　1. Die Getränke sind gekühlt.　　2. Die Würstchen sind gebraten.　　3. Der Kuchen ist serviert. 4. Die Küche ist aufgeräumt.　　5. Die Wohnung ist geschmückt.　　6. Die Haare sind gekämmt.　　7. Das Gesicht ist gewaschen.　　8. Die Zähne sind geputzt.　　9. Der Bart ist rasiert.　　10. Die Krawatte ist gebunden.

25·12　　1. Das Buch war gelesen.　　2. Der Aufsatz war geschrieben.　　3. Die Tasche war gepackt.　　4. Das Frühstück war gegessen.　　5. Die Zähne waren geputzt.　　6. Der Mantel war angezogen.　　7. Die Tasche war genommen.　　8. Die Tür war geschlossen.

25·13　　1. Wie schreibt man das Wort?　　2. Das Lied singt man laut.　　3. Den Kuchen isst man mit der kleinen Gabel.　　4. Man kocht die Suppe langsam.　　5. Man bezahlte viel Geld für diese Bilder.　　6. Man bringt das Kind ins Bett.　　7. Man machte die Tür zu.　　8. Man macht das Licht aus.

25·14　　1. Es wird ruhig gesessen.　　2. Es wird die Hand gehoben.　　3. Es wird ins Heft geschrieben. 4. Es wird nicht mit den Nachbarn gesprochen.　　5. Es wird gut aufgepasst.

25·15　　1. Ja, er ist billig herzustellen.　　2. Ja, sie ist leicht leise zu öffnen.　　3. Ja, sie ist leicht zu lernen. 4. Ja, es ist schwer zu verkaufen.　　5. Ja, es ist gut zu verstehen

25·16　　1. Der Stuhl lässt sich reparieren.　　2. Der Patient lässt sich retten.　　3. Lässt sich das Lied leicht singen? 4. Lässt sich die Straße gleich finden?　　5. Das lässt sich mit Schwierigkeit machen.　　6. Das ließ sich schnell erklären.　　7. Die Frage ließ sich schwer beantworten.　　8. Das Geld ließ sich schnell ausgeben. 9. Das Mädchen lässt sich sehen.　　10. Das Geld lässt sich leicht verlieren.

25·17　　1. Viel Spätzle werden von den Leuten im Süden gegessen.　　2. Die linke Hand wird nicht in den Schoß gelegt.　　3. Getränke werden ohne Eis getrunken.　　4. Die Hauptmahlzeit wird meistens mittags gegessen.　　5. Frische Brötchen werden oft zum Frühstück von den Leuten gegessen.　　6. Viel Kartoffelsalat und Würstchen werden abends gegessen.　　7. Ein Pausenbrot wird von den Kindern in die Schule mitgebracht.　　8. Kaffee und Kuchen werden Sonntagnachmittags serviert.　　9. Besuch wird oft zum Kaffee eingeladen.　　10. Obstkuchen wird oft mit Schlagsahne gegessen.　　11. Kakao wird von den Kindern getrunken.　　12. Blumen werden vom Besuch gebracht.

25·18　　1. Die Arbeit im Haus wurde von Frauen gemacht.　　2. Die Kinder wurden von der Frau versorgt. 3. Das Geld wurde von dem Mann ins Haus gebracht.　　4. Ein Beruf wurde von jungen Männern gelernt. 5. Die Arbeit im Haus wurde von jungen Mädchen gelernt.　　6. Das Brot wurde zu Hause gebacken. 7. Kuchen wurde selten gegessen.　　8. Viele Briefe wurden von Leuten geschrieben.　　9. Die Wäsche wurde von der Waschfrau mit der Hand gewaschen.　　10. Es wurde viel mit dem Rad gefahren oder zu Fuß gegangen.

25·19　　1. active　　2. passive voice with sein　　3. passive　　4. substitute for passive　　5. substitute for passive 6. passive　　7. passive　　8. passive　　9. passive　　10. active　　11. substitute for passive

12. substitute for passive   13. passive   14. passive   15. substitute for passive   16. passive
17. substitute for passive   18. passive   19. active   20. passive

25·20   1. **Past:** Der Anzug wurde von dem Schneider genäht. **Present perfect:** Der Anzug ist von dem Schneider genäht worden. **Future:** Der Anzug wird von dem Schneider genäht werden.   2. **Present:** Von wem wird das Haus gebaut? **Present perfect:** Von wem ist das Haus gebaut worden? **Future:** Von wem wird das Haus gebaut werden?   3. **Present:** Die Schüler werden von dem Lehrer unterrichtet. **Past:** Die Schüler wurden von dem Lehrer unterrichtet. **Future:** Die Schüler werden von dem Lehrer unterrichtet werden.
4. **Present:** Die neue Übung wird von ihr gelesen. **Past:** Die neue Übung wurde von ihr gelesen. **Present perfect:** Die neue Übung ist von ihr gelesen worden.   5. **Past:** Ein Glas Wein wurde von dem Kellner gebracht. **Present perfect:** Ein Glas Wein ist von dem Kellner gebracht worden. **Future:** Ein Glas Wein wird von dem Kellner gebracht werden.   6. **Present:** Kleider und Blusen werden von ihr verkauft. **Present perfect:** Kleider und Blusen sind von ihr verkauft worden. **Future:** Kleider und Blusen werden von ihr verkauft werden.   7. **Present:** Die alte Kirche wird von den Touristen besucht. **Past:** Die alte Kirche wurde von den Touristen besucht. **Future:** Die alte Kirche wird von den Touristen besucht werden.
8. **Present:** Die Wörter werden von der Schülerin gelernt. **Past:** Die Wörter wurden von der Schülerin gelernt. **Present perfect:** Die Wörter sind von der Schülerin gelernt worden.   9. **Past:** Die Fenster wurden von meiner Tante aufgemacht. **Present perfect:** Die Fenster sind von meiner Tante aufgemacht worden. **Future:** Die Fenster werden von meiner Tante aufgemacht werden.   10. **Present:** Wer wird von ihnen verhaftet? **Present perfect:** Wer ist von ihnen verhaftet worden? **Future:** Wer wird von ihnen verhaftet werden?

25·21   1. Neue Schuhe wurden von dem Studenten gebraucht.   2. Ein belegtes Brot wurde von der Malerin gegessen.   3. Die Pferde wurden von diesen Männern dressiert.   4. Diese Gedichte sind von einer neuen Dichterin geschrieben worden.   5. Die Lehrbücher werden von den Kindern gelesen werden.
6. Die Ausländer sind von meinen Eltern eingeladen worden.   7. Eine neue Werkstatt wird von ihnen gebaut werden.   8. Die Arbeit wurde von den Arbeitern beendet.   9. Ein Kuchen wird von meiner Großmutter gebacken.   10. Die Kinder sind von Herrn Keller gerufen worden.   11. Die Tiere werden von dem Fleischer geschlachtet werden.   12. Die Schweine werden von dem Bauern aufgezogen.   13. Drei Flaschen Wein sind von dem Gast bestellt worden.   14. Viele Sprachen werden von einem Gelehrten erlernt.   15. Der alte Wagen wird von den Mechanikern repariert werden.   16. Das Baby wurde von meiner Frau gefüttert.   17. Ein Hammer und eine Säge sind von dem Tischler benutzt worden.   18. Einige Angestellte werden von Frau Schäfer entlassen.   19. Das große Zimmer wird von den Studentinnen gemietet werden.   20. Die Fahrkarten sind von Felix wieder vergessen worden.

25·22   1. von einem Wolf   2. durch ein Gewitter   3. durch einen Waldbrand   4. durch einen Virus
5. Von einem Fremden

25·23   1. **Past:** Ihr wurde von niemandem geglaubt. **Present perfect:** Ihr ist von niemandem geglaubt worden. **Future:** Ihr wird von niemandem geglaubt werden.   2. **Present:** Dem Herrn wird für seine Hilfe von uns gedankt. **Present perfect:** Dem Herrn ist für seine Hilfe von uns gedankt worden. **Future:** Dem Herrn wird für seine Hilfe von uns gedankt werden.   3. **Present:** Den Schülern wird von dem Lehrer gratuliert. **Past:** Den Schülern wurde von dem Lehrer gratuliert. **Future:** Den Schülern wird von dem Lehrer gratuliert werden.   4. **Present:** Der Gesundheit wird durch Rauchen geschadet. **Past:** Der Gesundheit wurde durch Rauchen geschadet. **Present perfect:** Der Gesundheit ist durch Rauchen geschadet worden.   5. **Past:** Den Touristen wurde von dem Dieb gedroht. **Present perfect:** Den Touristen ist von dem Dieb gedroht worden. **Future:** Den Touristen wird von dem Dieb gedroht werden.   6. **Present:** Dem Professor wird nicht von den Studenten widersprochen. **Present perfect:** Dem Professor ist nicht von den Studenten widersprochen worden. **Future:** Dem Professor wird nicht von den Studenten widersprochen werden.   7. **Present:** Der alten Dame wird von ihm geschmeichelt. **Past:** Der alten Dame wurde von ihm geschmeichelt. **Future:** Der alten Dame wird von ihm geschmeichelt werden.   8. **Present:** Uns wird immer von ihnen vertraut. **Past:** Uns wurde immer von ihnen vertraut. **Present perfect:** Uns ist immer von ihnen vertraut worden.
9. **Past:** Den verlorenen Kindern wurde von dem Polizisten geholfen. **Present perfect:** Den verlorenen Kindern ist von dem Polizisten geholfen worden. **Future:** Den verlorenen Kindern wird von dem Polizisten geholfen werden.   10. **Past:** Dem König wurde von einem jungen Mädchen gedient. **Present perfect:** Dem König ist von einem jungen Mädchen gedient worden. **Future:** Dem König wird von einem jungen Mädchen gedient werden.

25·24 1. Mir wurden Blumen von ihr gebracht. Blumen wurden mir von ihr gebracht. 2. Der Amerikanerin ist ein Teller Suppe von Thomas bestellt worden. Ein Teller Suppe ist der Amerikanerin von Thomas bestellt worden. 3. Das Museum wird von den Touristen fotografiert werden. 4. Der armen Frau wird Geld von Vielen geschickt. Geld wird der armen Frau von Vielen geschickt. 5. Ihr wurde eine kleine Überraschung von mir gegeben. Eine kleine Überraschung wurde ihr von mir gegeben. 6. Ihnen sind die Bücher von der Lehrerin ausgeteilt worden. Die Bücher sind ihnen von der Lehrerin ausgeteilt worden. 7. Uns wird ein Fernsehapparat von unserem Sohn geschenkt werden. Ein Fernsehapparat wird uns von unserem Sohn geschenkt werden. 8. Ihm werden viele E-Mails von seiner Cousine gesandt. Viele E-Mails werden ihm von seiner Cousine gesandt. 9. Seiner Tochter wird ein Wagen von ihm gekauft werden. Ein Wagen wird seiner Tochter von ihm gekauft werden. 10. Uns wurden die Gemälde von der Malerin gezeigt. Die Gemälde wurden uns von der Malerin gezeigt.

25·25 1. b 2. a 3. a 4. a 5. a 6. d 7. b 8. d 9. d 10. b 11. a 12. d 13. d 14. c
15. a

26 The subjunctive

26·1

1. müsse	trage	versuche
müssest	tragest	versuchest
müsse	trage	versuche
müssen	tragen	versuchen
müsset	traget	versuchet
müssen	tragen	versuchen
2. sehe an	laufe	interessiere
sehest an	laufest	interessierest
sehe an	laufe	interessiere
sehen an	laufen	interessieren
sehet an	laufet	interessieret
sehen an	laufen	interessieren
3. wisse	wolle	gebe aus
wissest	wollest	gebest aus
wisse	wolle	gebe aus
wissen	wollen	geben aus
wisset	wollet	gebet aus
wissen	wollen	geben aus

26·2

1. schliefe	äße	wollte
schliefest	äßest	wolltest
schliefe	äße	wollte
schliefen	äßen	wollten
schliefet	äßet	wolltet
schliefen	äßen	wollten
2. lüde ein	tränke	ginge mit
lüdest ein	tränkest	gingest mit
lüde ein	tränke	ginge mit
lüden ein	tränken	gingen mit
lüdet ein	tränket	ginget mit
lüden ein	tränken	gingen mit
3. dürfte	verstünde/verstände	riefe an
dürftest	verstündest/verständest	riefest an
dürfte	verstünde/verstände	riefe an
dürften	verstünden/verständen	riefen an
dürftet	verstündet/verständet	riefet an
dürften	verstünden/verständen	riefen an

26·3

1. nennte	erkennte	wäre
nenntest	erkenntest	wärest
nennte	erkennte	wäre
nennten	erkennten	wären

nenntet	erkenntet	wäret
nennten	erkennten	wären
2. hatte	brachte	wurde
hattest	brachtest	wurdest
hatte	brachte	wurde
hatten	brachten	wurden
hattet	brachtet	wurdet
hatten	brachten	wurden

26·4 1. Der Reporter berichtete, dass der Kanzler bald gesund werde.   2. Der Reporter berichtete, dass niemand die Rede verstehe.   3. Der Reporter berichtete, dass die Touristen nach Italien reisten.   4. Der Reporter berichtete, dass die alte Frau gestorben sei.   5. Der Reporter berichtete, dass Herr Dorf in Polen wohnen werde.   6. Sie haben ihn gefragt, ob seine Frau wieder in der Schweiz sei.   7. Sie haben ihn gefragt, ob die Kinder Fusball spielen konnten.   8. Sie haben ihn gefragt, ob er genug Geld habe.   9. Sie haben ihn gefragt, ob sie wussten, wo sie ist.   10. Sie haben ihn gefragt, ob der Junge bestraft warden musse.

26·5 1. Der Richter hat gesagt, dass der Junge mit dem Hund gespielt habe.   2. Der Richter hat gesagt, dass wir die Uhr verloren hatten.   3. Der Richter hat gesagt, dass sie mit dem Bus gefahren seien.   4. Der Richter hat gesagt, dass Erik das Auto gestohlen habe.   5. Der Richter hat gesagt, dass der Dieb zwei Stunden im Keller gewesen sei.   6. Sonja berichtete, dass sie eine neue Speise gekocht hatten.   7. Sonja berichtete, dass Karl zu spat gekommen sei.   8. Sonja berichtete, dass ihre Tochter gut getanzt habe.   9. Sonja berichtete, dass mein Vater ihr zehn Euro gegeben habe.   10. Sonja berichtete, dass Martin oft an uns gedacht habe.

26·6 1. Wenn ich in meiner Heimat ware!   2. Wenn er mehr Mut hatte!   3. Wenn wir mehr Gluck gehabt hatten!   4. Wenn er nicht in die Stadt gefahren ware!   5. Wenn du besser gearbeitet hattest!

26·7 1. er verletzt ware   2. er uns hasste   3. wir taub waren   4. sie sehr krank gewesen ware   5. sie ihm uberhaupt nicht glauben konnte   6. sie ein Ungeheuer gesehen hatte   7. sie ihn liebte   8. sie den Mann nie kennen gelernt hatte   9. ich ihr Diener ware   10. sie perfekt Deutsch sprechen konnte

26·8 1. Wenn Tina im Lotto gewanne, wurde sie sich einen Pelzmantel kaufen.   2. Wenn der Mann lange schliefe, konnte er nicht arbeiten.   3. Wenn sie das verlorene Geld gefunden hatte, hatte sie es dem Polizisten geben mussen.   4. Wenn das Wetter schlecht gewesen ware, ware ich nicht auf das Land gefahren.   5. Wenn der Student nicht aufmerksam gewesen ware, hatte er einen grosen Fehler gemacht.   6. Wenn es nicht so weit ware, wurde ich dorthin zu Fus gehen.   7. Wenn das Madchen ein Gymnasium besucht hatte, hatte sie an einer Universitat studieren konnen.   8. Wenn die Frau besser arbeitete, wurde sie mehr verdienen.   9. Wenn sie uns angerufen hatte, hatte ich sie vom Bahnhof abgeholt.   10. Wenn du wieder gesund warest, musstest du wieder einen Job finden.

26·9 1. Er sagt, er finde mich sehr schön.
2. Er sagt, ich habe schöne Augen.
3. Er sagt, er sei so gern mit mir zusammen.
4. Er sagt, er kaufe mir ein schönes Geschenk.
5. Er sagt, er wolle mit mir ins Theater gehen.
6. Er sagt, er gehe im Sommer gern mit mir spazieren.
7. Er sagt, mein Gang sei so anmutig.
8. Er sagt, er singe gern mit mir.
9. Er sagt, er denke oft an mich.
10. Er sagt, es sei recht langweilig ohne mich.

26·10 1. Sie sagte, sie habe zehn Pfund abgenommen.
2. Sie sagte, ihre Frisur sei sehr modern gewesen.
3. Sie sagte, sie habe viermal in der Woche Gymnastik gemacht.
4. Sie sagte, sie habe jede Woche eine neue Speise gekocht.
5. Sie sagte, sie habe immer den besten Kuchen gebacken.
6. Sie sagte, ihr Wohnzimmer habe einen neuen Teppich gehabt.
7. Sie sagte, Anton, ihr Sohn, habe immer gute Noten bekommen.

8. Sie sagte, Gabriela, ihre Tochter, sei die schönste in der Klasse gewesen.
9. Sie sagte, ihr Mann habe die zweite Lohnerhöhung bekommen.
10. Sie sagte, ihr Vater habe ihr oft Geld gegeben.

26·11
1. Sie wollte wissen, wie sie heiße.
2. Sie wollte wissen, wie sie aussehe.
3. Sie wollte wissen, ob sie intelligent sei.
4. Sie wollte wissen, wo sie wohne.
5. Sie wollte wissen, wer ihre Eltern seien.
6. Sie wollte wissen, was für eine Arbeit der Vater habe.
7. Sie wollte wissen, ob die Familie Geld habe.
8. Sie wollte wissen, was sie in ihrer Freizeit mache.
9. Sie wollte wissen, ob sie gutes Deutsch spreche.
10. Sie wollte wissen, ob sie gut kochen könne.

26·12
1. Er sagte, ich solle jeden Tag üben.
2. Er sagte, ich solle gerade sitzen.
3. Er sagte, ich solle nicht auf die Finger schauen.
4. Er sagte, ich solle am Ende des Stückes leiser spielen.
5. Er sagte, ich solle ein neues Musikheft kaufen.

26·13
1. Thank goodness! (Thanks be to God!)   2. Your will be done!   3. God protect you!   4. Your kingdom come!   5. Long live freedom!

26·14
1. Sie schreibt, sie habe im Flugzeug geschlafen.
2. Sie schreibt, Frankfurt sei eine schöne Stadt.
3. Sie schreibt, sie habe die Altstadt besichtigt.
4. Sie schreibt, sie habe das Goethehaus interessant gefunden.
5. Sie schreibt, sie sei nach München gefahren.
6. Sie schreibt, sie sei einen ganzen Nachmittag im Englischen Garten gewesen.
7. Sie schreibt, sie sei zweimal in den Alpen geklettert.
8. Sie schreibt, sie habe viele Souvenirs gekauft.
9. Sie schreibt, sie habe oft Wiener Schnitzel gegessen.
10. Sie schreibt, sie habe Luthers Wartburg in Thüringen interessant gefunden.
11. Sie schreibt, sie habe genug Geld mitgebracht.
12. Sie schreibt, sie habe auch eine Schifffahrt auf dem Rhein gemacht.
13. Sie schreibt, Andreas habe auch viel Spaß.
14. Sie schreibt, er habe ein schönes Mädchen kennen gelernt.
15. Sie schreibt, sie wohne in Bonn.

26·15
1. ginge   2. gingen   3. gingen   4. gingest   5. ginget   6. ginge   7. ginge   8. gingen

26·16
1. Wir kauften es gern.
2. Wir hätten aber kein Geld.
3. Mutter müsste es uns geben.
4. Gäbe sie es gern?
5. Das wüsste ich nicht.
6. Die Kinder sagten immer, Vater verdiene viel.
7. Brächtet ihr das Geld dann?
8. Wir dächten nicht daran.
9. Kennte er die neuen Nachbarn?
10. Wär(e)st du am Wochenende hier?
11. Ich sollte jetzt gehen.
12. Kämest du morgen wieder?
13. Wenn du es wolltest.
14. Wir gingen jetzt nach Hause.
15. Schrieb(e)t ihr uns einen Brief?
16. Arbeitetest du lange?
17. Nein, ich wäre zu müde.

18. Nännte sie das Kind Rumpelstilzchen?
19. Das wollte ich nicht.
20. Er hätte es aber gern.

26·17 1. Dürfte ich ein Stück Schokolade essen?
2. Könntest du das Licht ausmachen?
3. Dürfte ich fernsehen?
4. Könnte der Vater ein Buch lesen?
5. Dürfte Paul mit mir spielen?

26·18 1. Inge hätte gern eine neue Puppe.
2. Die Zwillinge hätten gern einen elektrischen Zug.
3. Der Vater hätte gern einen neuen Pullover.
4. Ich hätte gern einen Fußball.
5. Peter und ich hätten gern viel Schokolade.

26·19 1. Ich hätte gern ein Stück Torte.
2. Marie hätte gern eine Limo.
3. Hans und Lars hätten gern eine Pizza.
4. Frank, was hättest du gern?
5. Beate und ich hätten gern ein Erdbeereis.

26·20 1. Er wäre heute nicht gekommen.
2. Sie hätte wieder nichts mitgenommen.
3. Das wäre nett gewesen.
4. Wir hätten viel Geld gehabt.
5. Die Kinder hätten viel gelernt.
6. Er wäre schnell nach Hause gegangen.
7. Hätte sie die Stadt gekannt?
8. Ich hätte nichts davon gewusst.
9. Wir hätten die Oma oft besucht.
10. Er hätte die Reise gemacht.
11. Axel hätte einen neuen Anzug gekauft.
12. Peter hätte nie seine Hausaufgaben gemacht.
13. Er hätte das langweilig gefunden.
14. Das hätte den Lehrer geärgert.
15. Peter hätte aber lieber gespielt.

26·21 1. Emma hätte mehr Geld mitnehmen müssen.
2. Sie hätte alles sehen wollen.
3. Andreas hätte mehr Zeit in Deutschland haben wollen.
4. Sie hätten länger in Deutschland bleiben sollen.
5. Sie hätten dann mehr sehen können.
6. Ich hätte auch mitfahren wollen.
7. Ich hätte nicht immer zu Hause bleiben müssen.
8. Die Reise hätte länger sein sollen.
9. Sie hätten nicht so früh zurückkommen müssen.
10. Hättest du auch eine Reise machen wollen?

26·22 1. würde
2. würde
3. würdest
4. würden
5. würden
6. würdet
7. würden

26·23 A.
1. hättet
2. nähmet

3. lerntet
4. ausginge
5. besuchtet
6. umtauschte
7. reserviert
8. sprächet
9. nähme
10. wäre

B.

1. Es wäre schön, wenn ihr mehr Zeit hättet.
2. Es wäre besser, wenn ihr nur zwei Koffer nehmen würdet.
3. Es wäre besser, wenn ihr mehr Deutsch lernen würdet.
4. Es wäre besser, wenn Emma nicht allein ausgehen würde.
5. Es wäre schön, wenn ihr meinen Freund in Duisburg besuchen würdet.
6. Es wäre besser, wenn Andreas das Geld hier umtauschen würde.
7. Es wäre besser, wenn ihr ein Hotelzimmer reservieren würdet.
8. Es wäre besser, wenn ihr nur Deutsch sprechen würdet.
9. Es wäre besser, wenn Andreas die Koffer nehmen würde.
10. Es wäre sicherer, wenn Emma nie allein wäre.

26·24
1. Ich würde nur einen Koffer packen.
2. Ich würde auf die Insel Sylt fahren.
3. Ich würde mir neue Kleider kaufen.
4. Ich würde mit dem Taxi zum Flugplatz fahren.
5. Ich würde oft Schwarzwälder Torte essen.
6. Ich würde nach Thüringen reisen.
7. Der Vater würde mir bestimmt mehr Geld schicken.
8. Meine Freundin und ich würden jeden Tag spazieren gehen.
9. Meine Reise würde nicht so viel kosten.
10. Ich würde in einer Jugendherberge übernachten.

26·25
1. Wenn Klaus Hunger hat, isst er sein Pausenbrot.
2. Wenn ich Geld habe, fahre ich nach Freudenstadt.
3. Wenn die Sonne scheint, gehen die Kinder schwimmen.
4. Wenn es regnet, gehen sie nach Hause.
5. Wenn sie müde sind, gehen sie ins Bett.

26·26
1. Wenn sie nur nicht so lange am Telefon sprechen würde.
2. Wenn sie nur mehr zu Hause helfen würde.
3. Wenn sie nur bessere Noten bekommen würde.
4. Wenn sie nur nicht so oft in die Disko gehen würde.
5. Wenn sie nur nicht so viel Geld ausgeben würde.
6. Wenn sie nur bessere Freunde hätte.
7. Wenn sie nur nicht so lange schlafen würde.
8. Wenn sie sich nur nicht mit der Schwester streiten würde.
9. Wenn sie nur die Kleider aufhängen würde.
10. Wenn sie nur die Oma besuchen würde.

26·27
1. Wenn ich Geld hätte, würde ich mir etwas schönes kaufen.
2. Wenn ich Lust hätte, würde ich ins Kino gehen.
3. Wenn ich ein gutes Buch hätte, würde ich lesen.
4. Wenn das Wetter schön wäre, würden meine Freunde und ich einen Ausflug machen.
5. Wenn es warm wäre, würden wir schwimmen gehen.

26·28
1. Wenn ich klug gewesen wäre, hätte ich weniger Geld gespart.
2. Wenn ich klug gewesen wäre, hätte ich mehr Reisen gemacht.
3. Wenn ich klug gewesen wäre, hätte ich weniger Kinder gehabt.
4. Wenn ich klug gewesen wäre, hätte ich einen reicheren Mann geheiratet.

5. Wenn ich klug gewesen wäre, hätte ich mich nicht so viel mit meiner Schwester gestritten.

6. Wenn ich klug gewesen wäre, hätte ich mehr Sport gemacht.

7. Wenn ich klug gewesen wäre, hätte ich mir schönere Sachen gekauft.

8. Wenn ich klug gewesen wäre, hätte ich auf dem Land gewohnt.

9. Wenn ich klug gewesen wäre, hätte ich Auto fahren gelernt.

10. Wenn ich klug gewesen wäre, hätte ich mir ein Dienstmädchen genommen.

26·29 1. Wenn Emma nicht nach Deutschland fahren könnte, würde sie weinen.

2. Wenn Emma nicht nach Deutschland fahren könnte, würde sie böse sein.

3. Wenn Emma nicht nach Deutschland fahren könnte, würde sie nach Chicago fahren.

4. Wenn Emma nicht nach Deutschland fahren könnte, würde sie in ihrem Zimmer sitzen.

5. Wenn Emma nicht nach Deutschland fahren könnte, würde sie ihre Freundin anrufen.

26·30 1. Wenn Müllers eine Million Euro hätten, würden sie ein neues Haus bauen.

2. Wenn Müllers eine Million Euro hätten, würden sie nach Australien fliegen.

3. Wenn Müllers eine Million Euro hätten, würden sie ein Haus an der Nordsee kaufen.

4. Wenn Müllers eine Million Euro hätten, würden sie zwei neue Mercedes kaufen.

5. Wenn Müllers eine Million Euro hätten, würden sie keine Geldsorgen haben.

27 More on the subjunctive mood

27·1 1. Der Reporter berichtete, dass die Kanzlerin eine Reise nach Russland mache.   2. Der Reporter berichtete, dass die Touristen in der Hauptstadt gewesen seien.   3. Der Reporter berichtete, dass der Dieb gestern Abend verhaftet worden sei.   4. Der Reporter berichtete, dass die deutsche Wirtschaft immer stärker werde.   5. Die Dame hat gefragt, ob er das Problem verstanden habe.   6. Die Dame hat gefragt, ob Ihr Sohn auch spielen wolle.   7. Die Dame hat gefragt, ob die Gäste noch im Wohnzimmer seien.   8. Die Dame hat gefragt, ob du so laut singen müssest.   9. Jemand fragte, wo Frau Keller jetzt arbeite.   10. Jemand fragte, warum Felix so viele Schulden habe.   11. Jemand fragte, wohin dein Bruder fahre.   12. Jemand fragte, wie viel Geld der reiche Herr ausgebe.   13. Sie sagte, dass Lars wieder sehr krank geworden sei.   14. Sie sagte, dass die laute Musik sie störe.   15. Sie sagte, dass ihr Mann seinen Pass vergessen werde.   16. Sie sagte, dass das Unwetter bald aufhören solle.   17. Der Reiseführer hat uns erzählt, dass die alte Burg vor hundert Jahren zerstört worden sei.   18. Der Reiseführer hat uns erzählt, dass der letzte König in der Burg gewohnt habe.   19. Der Reiseführer hat uns erzählt, dass ein neues Theater neben dem Rathaus gebaut werde.   20. Der Reiseführer hat uns erzählt, dass man im Garten spazieren könne.

27·2 1. Frau Schneider teilte mit, dass mein Bruder vor einem Jahr in Afrika gewesen sei.   2. Frau Schneider teilte mit, dass der neue Professor aus Amerika gekommen sei.   3. Frau Schneider teilte mit, dass der Gast noch nicht gefrühstückt habe.   4. Frau Schneider teilte mit, dass die Ausländer zu lange im Museum geblieben seien.   5. Frau Schneider teilte mit, dass das Mädchen zu wenig Geld gehabt habe.   6. Der Richter hat geschrieben, dass niemand dieses Gebiet habe betreten dürfen.   7. Der Richter hat geschrieben, dass der Fluss viel Land überschwemmt habe.   8. Der Richter hat geschrieben, dass meine Frau sich nicht an die Seeluft gewöhnt habe.   9. Der Richter hat geschrieben, dass der Verbrecher seine Rechte verloren habe.   10. Der Richter hat geschrieben, dass es nichts Schöneres als den Anblick der Berge gäbe.

27·3

subjunctive I	subjunctive II	subjunctive I	subjunctive II
1. schlafen		2. reisen	
ich schlafe	schliefe	reise	reiste
du schlafest	schliefest	reisest	reistest
er schlafe	schliefe	reise	reiste
wir schlafen	schliefen	reisen	reisten
ihr schlafet	schliefet	reiset	reistet
sie schlafen	schliefen	reisen	reisten

3. austrinken

ich trinke	aus tränke	
du trinkest	aus tränkest	
er trinke	aus tränke	
wir trinken	aus tränken	
ihr trinket	aus tränket	
sie trinken	aus tränken	

4. vergessen

aus vergesse	vergässe
aus vergessest	vergässest
aus vergesse	vergässe
aus vergessen	vergässen
aus vergesset	vergässet
aus vergessen	vergässen

5. wissen

ich wisse	wüsste
du wissest	wüsstest
er wisse	wüsste
wir wissen	wüssten
ihr wisset	wüsstet
sie wissen	wüssten

6. aufmachen

mache auf	machte auf
machest auf	machtest auf
mache auf	machte auf
machen auf	machten auf
machet auf	machtet auf
machen auf	machten auf

7. denken

ich denke	dächte
du denkest	dächtest
er denke	dächte
wir denken	dächten
ihr denket	dächtet
sie denken	dächten

8. abfahren

fahre ab	führe ab
fahrest ab	führest ab
fahre ab	führe ab
fahren ab	führen ab
fahret ab	führet ab
fahren ab	führen ab

9. erwarten

ich erwarte	erwartete
du erwartest	erwartetest
er erwarte	erwartete
wir erwarten	erwarteten
ihr erwartet	erwartetet
sie erwarten	erwarteten

10. dürfen

dürfe	dürfte
dürfest	dürftest
dürfe	dürfte
dürfen	dürften
dürfet	dürftet
dürfen	dürften

27·4 1. Der Arzt fragte, ob sie ein Rezept dafür hätten. 2. Der Arzt fragte, ob ich einen Preis gewonnen hätte. 3. Der Arzt fragte, ob wir unsere Verwandten besuchen würden. 4. Der Arzt fragte, ob die Sportler schon auf dem Sportplatz seien. 5. Der Arzt fragte, ob ich nur Deutsch spräche. 6. Herr Benz antwortete, dass die Männer Überstunden machten. 7. Herr Benz antwortete, dass diese Bücher ihm gehörten. 8. Herr Benz antwortete, dass die älteren Schüler im Wald wanderten. 9. Herr Benz antwortete, dass Sonne und Meer jeden Menschen gesund machten. 10. Herr Benz antwortete, dass wir um vier Uhr abreisen würden.

27·5 1. Der neue Student hat gefragt, woher wir darüber wüssten. 2. Der neue Student hat gefragt, warum sie die Vorträge nicht besucht hätte. 3. Der neue Student hat gefragt, was man mit 200. Euro kaufen könnte. 4. Der neue Student hat gefragt, wie lange das Theaterstück gedauert hätte. 5. Der neue Student hat gefragt, wem du diesen alten Laptop schenken wolltest. 6. Doktor Frank erzählte, dass seine Geschichte total richtig gewesen wäre. 7. Doktor Frank erzählte, dass die Studentin aus Frankreich leider durchgefallen wäre. 8. Doktor Frank erzählte, dass viele Einwohner des Dorfes dadurch krank warden würden. 9. Doktor Frank erzählte, dass er dem Diplomaten aus Asien nicht geglaubt hätte. 10. Doktor Frank erzählte, dass sein Sohn mit dem Präsidenten ins Gespräch gekommen wäre.

27·6 *Sample answers are provided.* 1. Wenn der Neue nur ein bisschen schneller arbeiten könnte! 2. Wenn ich nur reich wäre! 3. Wenn mein Sohn einen guten Job hätte! 4. Wenn wir unsere Eltern besuchen könnten! 5. Wenn Sabine mich liebte!

27·7 1. Wenn Martin Deutsch spräche, könnte er mit seinem Urgroßvater sprechen. 2. Wenn sie damals gesund gewesen wären, hätte sie den Arzt nicht gebraucht. 3. Wenn Lars es gewusst hätte, hätte er nicht gefragt. 4. Wenn wir im Lotto gewönnen, würden wir ein neues Haus in der Stadt kaufen. 5. Wenn er ihr helfen könnte, würde sie sehr dankbar sein. 6. Wenn du Flügel hättest, könntest du wie ein Vogel fliegen. 7. Wenn Erik den Bürgermeister getroffen hätte, hätte er mit ihm darüber gesprochen. 8. Wenn sie mehr arbeiteten, würden sie mehr Geld verdienen. 9. Wenn das Wetter schlecht gewesen wäre, wäre ich nicht aufs Land gefahren.   10. Wenn die Studentin aufmerksam wäre, würde sie keine Fehler machen.

27·8   1. Der Gast machte ein Gesicht, als ob die Suppe nicht gut schmeckte.   2. Der Gast machte ein Gesicht, als ob er sehr traurig wäre.   3. Der Gast machte ein Gesicht, als ob er sie falsch verstünde.   4. Der Gast machte ein Gesicht, als ob der Gastgeber unhöflich gewesen wäre.   5. Der Gast machte ein Gesicht, als ob das Essen zu scharf wäre.   6. Mein Bruder führt ein Leben, als wenn er reich geworden wäre.   7. Mein Bruder führt ein Leben, als wenn unser Vater Millionär wäre.   8. Mein Bruder führt ein Leben, als wenn man von Wein und Bier leben könnte.   9. Mein Bruder führt ein Leben, als wenn seine Gesundheit nie ein Ende haben könnte.   10. Mein Bruder führt ein Leben, als wenn er keine Freunde mehr hätte.

27·9   1. helfe, hälfe   2. bleibe, bliebe   3. besuche, besuchte   4. bringe mit, brächte mit   5. sei gekommen, wäre gekommen   6. werde sprechen, würde sprechen   7. müsse lachen, müsste lachen   8. esse, äße   9. nenne, nennte   10. werde gefunden werden, würde gefunden warden

27·10   *Sample answers are provided.*   1. a. Der Reporter berichtete, dass die junge Schauspielerin ihn geküsst habe. b. dass jemand seine Brieftasche gestohlen habe. c. dass der alte König nicht mehr regieren könne. d. dass die Kanzlerin in Berlin bleiben werde.   2. a. Professor Benz fragte, ob der Student einen Aufsatz schreibe. b. ob sein Kollege eine neue Stellung gefunden habe. c. ob sein Sohn sich gut benehme. d. ob das Feuer die Bibliothek zerstört habe.   3. a. Sie teilte mit, dass der Dieb bestraft werde. b. dass die Armee das kleine Dorf verteidigen müsse. c. dass die Gemeinde eine neue Kirche nicht bauen könne. d. dass die Zeugen nichts gesehen hätten.   4. a. Frau Kamps erzählte, dass seine Geschichte ihr kaum imponiere. b. dass der Millionär sehr wenig Geld ausgeben wolle. c. dass sie seine Fehler verbessert habe. d. dass der Feind nicht angreifen könne.

27·11   *Sample answers are provided.*   1. a. Meine Schwester tut so, als ob sie sehr intelligent wäre. b. als ob das Wetter schön wäre. c. als ob sie helfen wollte.   2. a. Der alte Mann lacht, als ob er nicht krank wäre. b. als ob seine Frau nicht gestorben wäre. c. als ob er den Witz verstünde.   3. a. Die Kinder singen, als ob sie schöne Stimmen hätten. b. als ob sie die Worte wirklich verstünden. c. als ob das Volkslied eine Oper wäre.   4. a. Meine Mutter weinte, als ob ich gestorben wäre. b. als ob wir arm geworden wären. c. als ob es eine Tragödie wäre.   5. a. als ob er das Gedicht auswendig gelernt hätte. b. als ob seine Frau wieder krank wäre. c. als ob sein Sohn an der Universität Hamburg studierte.

27·12   1. a. Wenn ihr nur bei mir wäret! b. Wäret ihr nur bei mir!   2. a. Wenn das Kind nur fleißig wäre! b. Wäre das Kind nur fleißig!   3. a. Wenn der arme Mann doch nicht so unglücklich wäre! b. Wäre der arme Mann doch nicht so unglücklich!   4. a. Wenn ich ihnen nur helfen könnte! b. Könnte ich ihnen nur helfen!   5. a. Wenn du mehr Glück gehabt hättest! b. Hättest du mehr Glück gehabt!

27·13   *Sample answers are provided.*   1. Wenn der Wagen nicht kaputt wäre, würden wir in die Stadt fahren.   2. Wenn es nicht regnete, könnten die Jungen im Garten spielen.   3. Wenn ich den Zug verpasste, würde ich in Hamburg übernachten.   4. Wenn ihr Kind wieder gesund wäre, würde sie aufhören zu weinen.   5. Wenn Erik reicher wäre, würde er einen Rennwagen kaufen.   6. Wenn Onkel Hans das Klavier spielen könnte, könnten die Mädchen tanzen.   7. Wenn Frau Benz ihn kennte, würde sie ihn einladen.   8. Wenn sie auf dem Balkon stünden, könnten sie das ganze Dorf sehen.

27·14   *Sample answers are provided.*   1. Wenn wir in Süddeutschland gewesen wären, wären wir nach München gefahren.   2. Wenn der Kerl hilfsbereit gewesen wäre, hätte er länger bleiben können.   3. Wenn es das Medikament genommen hätte, wäre das Kind schneller gesund geworden.   4. Wenn sie besser Deutsch hätte sprechen können, hätte ich ihre Rede verstanden.   5. Wenn Sonja nicht krank gewesen wäre, wäre sie zum Faschingsfest gegangen.   6. Wenn das Wetter besser geworden wäre, wären wir noch einen Tag in den Bergen geblieben.   7. Wenn ich einen neuen Laptop gekauft hätte, hätte ich den Aufsatz schneller schreiben können.   8. Wenn das Baby hätte schlafen können, hätte es nicht andauernd geweint.

27·15   *Sample answers are provided.*   1. Wenn Sabine nach Hause käme, würde ihre Mutter sehr glücklich sein.   2. Wenn der Bus pünktlich gekommen wäre, wären wir nicht so böse gewesen.   3. Wenn wir

Thomas damit geholfen hätten, wäre er noch unser Freund gewesen.   4. Wenn ich das gewusst hätte, hätte ich nicht danach gefragt.   5. Wenn der Schüler aufmerksam wäre, würde er keine Fehler machen.   6. Wenn sie wieder gesund wäre, würde Vater wieder froh sein.   7. Wenn sie mehr Geld hätte, würde sie immer noch Probleme haben.   8. Wenn Tina in die Stadt gefahren wäre, hätte ich mit den Kindern zu Hause bleiben müssen.   9. Wenn ihr Mann noch zu Hause gewesen wäre, wäre Frau Keller zum Park gegangen.   10. Wenn es nicht so kalt wäre, dann würden wir schwimmen gehen.

28   Building sentences

28·1   1. a. Martin sprach kein Englisch. b. Martin hat kein Englisch gesprochen. c. Martin wird kein Englisch sprechen.   2. a. Ich kann es machen. b. Ich konnte es machen. c. Ich habe es machen können.   3. a. Eine Schlange frisst den Frosch. b. Eine Schlange frass den Frosch. c. Eine Schlange wird den Frosch fressen.   4. a. Über dem Wald fliegen viele Vögel. b. Über dem Wald sind viele Vögel geflogen. c. Über dem Wald werden viele Vögel fliegen.

28·2   1. Das ist nicht das beste Buch.   2. Sie ist nicht am Nachmittag angekommen.   3. Ihr Mann ist nicht bei einem Unglück umgekommen.   4. Er hat nicht helfen wollen.   5. Frau Schneider hat sich nicht wohl gefühlt.   6. Die Studenten sitzen nicht im Lesesaal.   7. Seine Frau hat ihn nicht betrogen.

28·3   1. Meine Großmutter trinkt keinen Kaffee.   2. Boris hat keine interessanten Bücher gefunden.   3. Ich habe keine Tante in London.   4. Der Dieb hat kein Wort gesagt.   5. In diesem Wald gibt es keine Bären.   6. Ich werde das unter keinen Umständen tun.   7. Ich habe heute Abend keine Zeit.

28·4   1. Ihr Sohn hat nicht mitgehen wollen.   2. Die Leute gehen nicht in seinen Laden.   3. Ich klebte die Marke nicht auf den Brief.   4. Der Bodensee ist nicht der größte See.   5. Kein Mann spricht mit ihm.   6. Die Lehrerin brauchte keinen Kugelschreiber.   7. Der betrunkene Mann fährt nicht schnell.

28·5   1. Niemand will Schlittschuh laufen.   2. Der Polizist wird niemanden verhaften.   3. Manfred geht niemals in die Stadt.   4. Meine Verwandten waren nie in Berlin.   5. Sonja wird niemanden in Hamburg besuchen.   6. Er will nichts zu essen haben.   7. Sonja hat nichts gekauft.

28·6   1. Leider ist sie wieder krank geworden.   2. Den ganzen Tag blieb Martin zu Hause.   3. Meine Freizeit verbringe ich in der Bibliothek.   4. Als ich um die Ecke kam, begegnete ich meinen Nachbarn.   5. Im Herbst möchte ich nach Italien reisen.   6. Wenn sie in London ist, geht sie oft ins Theater.   7. Letzten Sommer wohnte meine Tante bei ihrem Sohn.

28·7   1. Den Wecker hat er reparieren lassen.   2. Das wissen sie nicht.   3. Schach spielen die Jungen.   4. Das muss man nicht.   5. Einen Mantel kaufte die Frau im Kaufhaus.

28·8   *Sample answers are provided.*   1. a. Oft isst meine Familie italienisch. b. Am Wochenende isst meine Familie italienisch. c. Wenn Onkel Otto uns besucht, isst meine Familie italienisch.   2. a. Gestern spielte Sonja Tennis. b. Nach der Schule spielte Sonja Tennis. c. Nachdem sie von der Schule kam, spielte Sonja Tennis.   3. a. Jetzt wird seine Freundin einen neuen Wagen kaufen. b. Im Februar wird seine Freundin einen neuen Wagen kaufen. c. Bevor sie abfährt, wird seine Freundin einen neuen Wagen kaufen.   4. a. Damals komponierte Beethoven diese Sinfonie. b. Vor zwei Jahren komponierte Beethoven diese Sinfonie. c. Als er noch in Bonn war, komponierte Beethoven diese Sinfonie.

28·9   1. In einer Woche werden wir wieder in Wien sein.   2. Meine Mutter musste um sechs Uhr aufstehen und in die Stadt fahren.   3. Als ich in der Hauptstadt war, ging ich oft ins Museum.

28·10   *Sample answers are provided.*   1. Jemand steht an der Tür und klopft.   2. Vor einer Woche kaufte mein Vater einen gebrauchten Wagen.   3. Um zehn Uhr begann die Vorstellung.

28·11   1. Ist sein Vetter in der Hauptstadt gewesen?   2. Will Gudrun die Wahrheit über das Unglück erfahren? 3. Litt die kranke Frau an einer Vergiftung?   4. Muss man alle Verkehrszeichen beachten?   5. Durfte ich Luise und Tanja begleiten?   6. Ist etwas in der Küche los?   7. Freute sich meine Tante auf das Wiedersehen mit ihren Verwandten?

28·12   1. Spielen Sie Schach?   2. Musst du heute zu Hause bleiben?   3. Bist du noch nicht zur Arbeit gegangen? 4. Werden sie um zehn Uhr ankommen?

28·13   1. Für wen hatte Maria ein Geschenk?   2. Mit wem möchte Peter tanzen?   3. Wem wollen die Verwandten in Deutschland helfen?   4. Wessen Kinder werden mit Liebe erzogen?   5. Wen möchten sie morgen besuchen?   6. Wer möchte ein neues Kleid kaufen?   7. Wessen Schwager ist Rechtsanwalt geworden?

28·14   1. Was habe ich im Schaufenster gesehen?   2. Wem wird der Gerber das Fell abziehen?   3. Was ziehen die Bauern auf?   4. Wessen Nase war sehr kalt?

28·15   1. Wofür interessiert sich Herr Bauer?   2. Worauf will ich nicht länger warten?   3. Wovon hat der Lehrling nicht gehört?   4. Wonach sehnen sich die neuen Auswanderer?   5. Womit spielten die Kinder? 6. Worum habe ich meine Freunde gebeten?   7. Wogegen kämpfte der Professor?

28·16   1. Wie sprach der Rechtsanwalt?   2. Was für einen Pullover hat die junge Dame gekauft?   3. Warum muss ich einen Mantel tragen?   4. Welcher Junge ist ziemlich dumm?   5. Wo studiert seine Tochter?

28·17   1. Wie groß ist unser Schlafzimmer?   2. Wie viele Nelken hat Onkel Peter gekauft?   3. Wie alt wird Doktor Schmidt am elften Dezember werden?

28·18   *Sample answers are provided.*   1. Was fiel von dem Dach auf die Straße?   2. Klettert der Bergsteiger den steilen Felsen hinauf?   3. Mit wem hast du so lange getanzt?   4. Wie lange müsst ihr in der Hauptstadt auf euren Zug warten?   5. Kannst du mich zum Bahnhof begleiten?   6. Welches Geschäft hat die besten Preise?   7. Wodurch schützt man die Pflanzen vor der Kälte des Winters?

28·19   *Sample answers are provided.*   1. Was für ein Geschenk haben Sie gekauft?   2. Auf wen wartet ihr so lange?   3. Worauf freuen sich die Schüler?   4. Wohin reisen deine Eltern im Sommer?   5. Wessen Mantel hat der Dieb gestohlen?

28·20   *Sample answers are provided.*   1. a. Warum spielst du nicht mit den anderen Kindern? b. Ich spiele nicht mit den anderen Kindern, weil sie zu jung sind.   2. a. Woher hat er diese alten Bücher bekommen? b. Er hat diese alten Bücher von einem Freund bekommen.   3. a. Wie viel Meter Stoff hat Frau Benz gebraucht? b. Frau Benz hat vier Meter Stoff gebraucht.   4. a. Wie oft seid ihr ins Ausland gereist? b. Wir sind nur einmal ins Ausland gereist.   5. a. Wohin laufen die Fußballspieler um elf Uhr? b. Um elf Uhr laufen die Fußballspieler nach Hause.

28·21   *Sample answers are provided.*   1. a. Wann musst du aufstehen? b. Ich muss morgen früh aufstehen.   2. a. Warum bleibt ihr zu Hause? b. Wir bleiben zu Hause, weil wir kein Geld haben.   3. a. Wie lange dauert der Film? b. Der Film dauert zwei Stunden.   4. a. Wohin wollen sie heute gehen? b. Sie wollen heute ins Kino gehen.   5. a. Wo wohnt Dr. Schäfer? b. Dr. Schäfer wohnt in der Schillerstraße.

29   Building more sentences

29·1   1. Er wollte Tennis spielen, denn das Wetter war endlich gut.   2. Ich habe es nicht verloren, sondern hinter dem Schrank versteckt.   3. Paul studiert in Berlin und wohnt in einem Studentenheim. 4. Meine Freundin hat ihre Fahrkarte verloren und muss in Bonn bleiben.   5. Soll er einen roten Wagen kaufen, oder soll er einen blauen Wagen kaufen?   6. Ich höre, was du sagst, aber ich verstehe dich nicht. 7. Angela spielt Gitarre, und ihr Bruder spielt Flöte.

29·2   *Sample answers are provided.*   1. Sie versuchte ihn zu warnen, aber seine Brieftasche fiel doch ins Wasser. 2. Die Studentin konnte nicht arbeiten, denn sie hörte die laute Musik. 3. Normalerweise ist der Herbst am schönsten, aber letztes Jahr war der Frühling schön. 4. Karl ist nicht zum Café gegangen, sondern hat eine alte Freundin besucht. 5. Der Schüler setzte sich auf seinen Platz und nahm seinen Bleistift in die Hand. 6. Im Schaufenster stehen große Puppen, aber niemand kauft sie. 7. Peter schreibt den Aufsatz nicht, sondern sieht den ganzen Abend fern. 8. Herr Benz pflegt den Blumengarten, und seine Frau pflegt den Gemüsegarten. 9. Ich habe kein Sprudelwasser gekauft, sondern nur ein paar Flaschen Bier. 10. Ich habe sein letztes Buch gelesen, aber ich habe ihm kein Wort geglaubt.

29·3   *Sample answers are provided.*   1. Tun Sie mir den Gefallen und kommen Sie mit! 2. Der Junge muss gehorchen, oder er hat die Folgen selbst zu tragen. 3. Die Kirschen schmecken sehr gut, aber wie viel kosten sie? 4. Wir machen keine Pause, sondern arbeiten bis spät in die Nacht. 5. Mein Vater hat einen neuen VW gekauft, denn er hat 30.000 Euro gewonnen.

29·4   *Sample answers are provided.*   1. Ich habe kein Geld, aber ich will eines Tages eine Europareise machen. 2. Die Bauern hoffen auf Regen, denn der Sommer ist wieder trocken. 3. Hast du genug Geld, oder bist du wieder pleite? 4. Sie reisen nicht nach Kanada, sondern nach Amerika.

29·5   1. Wann legt er sich ins Bett? 2. Sie musste das Studium aufgeben, als ihr Vater starb. 3. Als ich die Universität verließ, traf ich einen Freund. 4. Man geht zum Arzt, wenn man krank ist. 5. Wann hat man Husten und Schnupfen? 6. Als er im letzten Jahr in Kiel war, begegnete er einem Schulkameraden. 7. Wenn die Kinder sechs Jahre alt sind, kommen sie in die Grundschule.

29·6   *Sample answers are provided.*   1. Wenn du nach Berlin reist, sollst du deinen Personalausweis bei dir haben. 2. Wenn Sie in Düsseldorf sind, dürfen Sie vorbeikommen. 3. Als die Touristen Südamerika besuchten, lernten sie ein paar spanische Wörter. 4. Herr Schneider trifft einen Bekannten, wenn er im Stadtpark sitzt. 5. Wenn du isst, sollst du nicht sprechen. 6. Wenn es anfängt zu schneien, denken die Kinder an Weihnachten. 7. Wenn du London besuchst, gehst du oft ins Theater?

29·7   *Sample answers are provided.*   1. Während wir im Ruhrgebiet waren, besuchten wir viele Fabriken. 2. Bevor Herr Bauer starb, schrieb er sein Testament. 3. Bevor wir abfahren, müssen wir die Koffer packen. 4. Obwohl sie meine Schwester war, wollte ich ihr kein Geld leihen. 5. Wissen Sie, ob das Rathaus weit ist? 6. Wir kommen morgen vorbei, falls wir genug Zeit haben. 7. Fahren wir zum Bahnhof mit einem Taxi, damit wir den Zug erreichen! 8. Soviel wir wissen, ist sie wieder schwanger. 9. Sie können mit uns reiten, sooft Sie wollen. 10. Ich kann nicht warten, bis er zurückkommt. 11. Ehe er zur Party ging, kämmte er sich wieder die Haare. 12. Ich habe ihnen geholfen, soviel ich konnte. 13. Da Lukas betrunken war, wollte sie nicht mit ihm tanzen. 14. Hast du gewusst, dass du den letzten Bus verpasst hast?

29·8   *Sample answers are provided.*   1. Obwohl ich gut zuhörte, verstand ich es nicht. 2. Während sie im Lager wohnten, haben sie oft Schach gespielt. 3. Er musste wieder zu Fuß gehen, weil er eine Panne hatte. 4. Erik fragte uns, ob wir ins Theater gehen wollen. 5. Sie haben nichts bezahlt, solange sie kein heißes Wasser hatten. 6. Kinder, wartet hier, bis die Ampel grün ist! 7. Ich habe keine Ahnung, wie die Dame aussieht. 8. Beeilt euch, damit wir den Bus nicht verpassen! 9. Da er müde war, wollte er nach Hause gehen. 10. Obwohl es kalt und sonnig ist, will ich nicht Skilaufen gehen. 11. Seitdem sie ihren Führerschein bekam, ist sie nie zu Hause. 12. Nachdem er sich den Finger verletzt hatte, fing er an zu heulen. 13. Wir wissen nicht, ob er uns versteht. 14. Du musst am Tisch bleiben, bis du das Glas Milch ausgetrunken hast.

29·9   1. Ich weiß nicht, wer in unserem Schwimmbad schwimmt. 2. Ich weiß nicht, ob das Mädchen das Geld verloren hat. 3. Ich weiß nicht, warum er dem alten Mann drohte. 4. Ich weiß nicht, ob er diese Probleme lösen kann. 5. Ich weiß nicht, wie alt sein Urgroßvater war. 6. Ich weiß nicht, wem der Sohn ähnlich ist. 7. Ich weiß nicht, wonach der kranke Herr fragte. 8. Ich weiß nicht, wie lange die Vorstellung dauern wird. 9. Ich weiß nicht, was sie ihren Gästen zeigt. 10. Ich weiß nicht, ob der Fotograf die Aufnahmen entwickelte. 11. Ich weiß nicht, woran die alte Dame gern denkt. 12. Ich weiß nicht, um wen er sich viele Sorgen macht. 13. Ich weiß nicht, um wie viel Uhr der Mann in sein Büro geht. 14. Ich weiß nicht, was der Fremdenführer den Touristen wird zeigen wollen.

29·10 *Sample answers are provided.* 1. Tina blieb in der Stadt, bis ihre Tante wieder gesund war. 2. Ich erzähle dir seine Geschichte, damit du ihn besser verstehst. 3. Während es donnerte und blitzte, saßen wir im kleinen Paddelboot. 4. Frau Benz kaufte die Bluse, obwohl der Preis sehr hoch war. 5. Das Kind war so müde, dass es sofort einschlief. 6. Seitdem das Wetter wieder schlecht wurde, mussten die Kinder im Keller spielen. 7. Wenn sie ihre Verwandten besuchen, sind sie am glücklichsten.

29·11 1. ankommend, arriving 2. zwingend, forcing 3. belastend, burdening 4. abstoßend, repellent 5. verhaltend, restraining 6. ansehend, looking at 7. mitfühlend, being sympathetic

29·12 1. die schlafenden Kinder 2. die laut bellenden Hunde 3. von ihrer enttäuschenden Antwort 4. eine entsprechende Theorie 5. neben dem lachenden Jungen 6. im ankommenden Zug 7. das langsam fließende Wasser

29·13 1. ein gebrochener Mann 2. von dem betrunkenen Mann 3. mit den aufgeregten Jungen 4. wegen des schlecht reparierten Motors 5. ein (hart) gekochtes Ei 6. im neulich angekommenen Zug 7. Die Vereinigten Staaten

29·14 1. Der den Rechtsanwalt anrufende Polizist ist in Not. 2. Ich hasse das sich so schnell verändernde Wetter. 3. Sein uns überraschender Gewinn erfreute seine Frau. 4. Niemand will dem zum vierten Mal verhafteten Taschendieb helfen. 5. Die langen so trüb brennenden Kerzen standen auf dem Klavier. 6. Das ist der von seinen ehemaligen Studenten besuchte Professor. 7. Sie ist sehr stolz auf die konzentriert arbeitenden Studentinnen. 8. Der an seinen Wunden sterbende Kranke hat keine Familie. 9. Kannten Sie die gestern Abend verstorbene Frau? 10. Der sich so langsam bewegende Soldat war verwundet.

29·15 *Sample answers are provided.* 1. Sie bekam einen von ihrem Freund gut geschriebenen Brief. 2. Er wollte die mit Zuckerblumen geschmückte Torte probieren. 3. Das vorgestern verkaufte Auto muss schon repariert werden. 4. Gut ausgebildete Menschen werden von unserer Firma gesucht. 5. Die Eltern suchten nach ihrem vor einer Stunde verschwundenen Sohn. 6. Der von seiner zweiten Frau geschiedene Mann will eine jüngere Frau heiraten. 7. Das mit dem Hund spielende Kind fing an zu lachen. 8. Er findet den vor einem Jahr verlorenen Brief in einer Schublade.

29·16 1. die auf dem Herd stehende Suppe 2. das von der Armee zerstörte Dorf 3. das vor Angst zitternde Kätzchen 4. der laut redende Prediger 5. die vor zwei Jahren gebauten Häuser 6. das brennende und neulich verkaufte Haus 7. die aus zehn Amerikanern bestehende Reisegruppe

29·17 *Sample answers are provided.* 1. Das von dem Studenten getrunkene Bier war gar nicht kalt. 2. Ich kann die von der Köchin gebackene Torte riechen. 3. Das sich die Haare kämmende Mädchen ist meine Freundin. 4. Sie betrachtet die auf dem Boden eingeschlafenen Kinder. 5. Sie haben den zu Hause gebliebenen Kindern geholfen.

29·18 *Sample answers are provided.* 1. Wie schnell kann das Pferd laufen? 2. Erik kennt sie gar nicht, aber er sieht sie jeden Tag an der Ecke stehen. 3. Kaum zu glauben! 4. Der hochnäsige Student ist gar nicht so intelligent. 5. Der Dieb ist doch auch ein Lügner! 6. Also, bis morgen. Schlaf gut! 7. „Du hast deine Handschuhe wieder verloren!" „Gar nicht!"

29·19 *Sample answers are provided.* 1. Also, gehen wir schon! 2. Das ist doch nicht wahr! 3. Ich verstehe gar nicht, warum du lügst. 4. Sei mal ruhig! 5. Seine Worte sind kaum zu verstehen. 6. Wie kommt so etwas? 7. Ich komme morgen zu euch, und zwar um elf Uhr.

29·20 *Sample sentences are provided.* 1. Ausgezeichnet! 2. Erstaunlich! 3. Offenbar. 4. Keine Ahnung. 5. Großartig! 6. Leider nicht. 7. Selbstverständlich.

29·21 *Sample answers are provided.* 1. Kannst du mir fünfzig Euro leihen? 2. Alle zwei Minuten startet ein Flugzeug von diesem Flughafen. 3. Ist Andrea achtzehn oder neunzehn Jahre alt? 4. Unsere Mannschaft hat den Pokal gewonnen. 5. Sie ist eine sehr gute Tänzerin. 6. Nach zwei Jahren haben sie das Problem endlich gelöst. 7. Ich möchte dir ein paar neue CDs kaufen.

30 Conversation

30·1 In der Hauptstraße
Frau Keller: Hallo, Doktor Paulus. Wie geht es Ihnen?
Doktor Paulus: Guten Tag, Frau Keller. Es geht mir sehr gut. Danke. Und Ihnen?
Frau Keller: Nicht schlecht. Wohin gehen Sie?
Doktor Paulus: Zum Bahnhof. Ich hole meine Cousine ab.
Frau Keller: Kenne ich Ihre Cousine? Wie heißt sie?
Doktor Paulus: Sie heißt Tina. Sie werden sie auf der Party kennen lernen.
Frau Keller: Wie schön. Aber ich habe es eilig. Wiedersehen!
Doktor Paulus: Auf Wiedersehen!

30·2 *Sample answers are provided.*   1. Nein, ich kenne sie nicht.   2. Holen Sie Ihre Cousine ab?   3. Wie schön!

30·3 *Sample answers are provided.*   1. Ich wohne noch in der Hauptstraße.   2. Ich werde meinen Sohn besuchen.   3. Grüßen Sie Ihren Sohn von mir.   4. Ich gehe nach Hause.

30·4 An der Ecke
Martin: Guten Tag, Angela. Wie geht es dir?
Angela: Sehr gut. Und dir?
Martin: Nicht schlecht. Wohin gehst du?
Angela: Nach Hause. Wir haben jetzt eine Wohnung im Stadtzentrum.
Martin: Wir wohnen noch in der Schillerstraße.
Angela: Ach so. Was machst du gerade?
Martin: Ich werde meinen Sohn besuchen. Er wohnt hier in der Stadt.
Angela: Grüße deine Familie von mir!

30·5 *Sample answers are provided.*   1. Sabine: Ich werde ihn dir vorstellen.   2. Karl: Ich hole meinen Bruder ab.   3. Herr Keller: Er heißt Martin Bauer.   4. Frau Schneider: Nein, es geht mir gut.   5. Karl: Ich gehe zum Bahnhof.   6. Angela: Nein, sie duzen sich.   7. Sabine: Auf Wiedersehen!   8. Thomas: Er stellt einen Freund vor.   9. Doktor Paulus: Guten Tag, Frau Schneider. Ich habe es heute leider eilig.   10. Sabine: Ist er ein Freund von dir?

30·6 1. das Mädchen   2. meine Verwandten   3. ihren Bruder   4. Herrn Keller   5. diesen Lehrer   6. Einen Freund von mir   7. meine Bekannte   8. diese Dame   9. den Ausländer   10. die Ausländer   11. meinen Sohn   12. unsere Tochter   13. Frau Dorf   14. diese Touristen   15. seinen Onkel   16. Erik   17. ihren Freund   18. Sabine   19. eine Freundin von mir   20. das Mädchen   21. meine Bekannte   22. Doktor Paulus   23. den Gast   24. seine Gäste   25. die Ärzte

30·7 An der Ecke
Frau Keller: Guten Tag, Erik. Guten Tag, Sabine. Wie geht es euch?
Erik: Sehr gut. Und Ihnen?
Frau Keller: Nicht schlecht. Wohin geht ihr?
Sabine: Nach Hause. Wir haben jetzt eine Wohnung im Stadtzentrum.
Frau Keller: Wir wohnen noch in der Schillerstraße.
Erik: Ach so. Was machen Sie jetzt?
Frau Keller: Ich werde meinen Sohn besuchen. Er wohnt hier in der Stadt.
Sabine: Grüßen Sie Ihre Familie von uns.

30·8 *Sample answers are provided.*   1. Nein, sie wohnen in Spanien.   2. Und lebt seine Großmutter noch?   3. Ich habe ihm ein Handy gekauft.   4. Ja, sehr alt und sehr krank.   5. Ich habe ein Auto von ihm bekommen.   6. Wie alt ist sie?   7. Lebt Ihr Urgroßvater noch?   8. Ist Ihr Onkel jünger als sie?   9. Sie wohnt mit ihrem Mann in München.   10. Wohnen deine Geschwister in der Stadt?   11. Ja, im Haus gegenüber von hier.

30·9 1. Der Mann meiner Schwester ist Lehrer.
Ist er älter als sie?
Ja, er ist dreißig Jahre alt.

2. Ist das das Haus deines Stiefbruders?
   Nein, er wohnt nicht in der Nähe.
   Wo wohnt er denn?
3. Lebt Ihr Schwager noch?
   Nein, er ist vor einem Jahr gestorben.
   War er sehr krank?
4. Der zweite Mann meiner Tante ist Professor.
   Wohnen sie in der Hauptstadt?
   Ja, in Berlin.
5. Die Nichte meines Freundes hat sechs Geschwister.
   Das ist eine große Familie.
   Ja, aber sie haben eine kleine Wohnung.
6. Ist das Auto deiner Schwägerin neu?
   Ja, ganz neu.
   Es ist ein Geschenk von ihrem Sohn.
7. Habt ihr einen Hund?
   Nein, wir haben zwei alte Katzen.
   Meine Familie hat kein Haustier.

30·10 1. Kennst du den neuen Mann deiner Nichte? Nein, ich kenne ihn nicht.   2. Kennst du die Freundin des Matrosen? Ja, ich kenne sie.   3. Kennst du den Neffen meines Freundes? Ja, ich kenne ihn.   4. Kennst du die Gäste unserer Großmutter? Nein, ich kenne sie nicht.   5. Kennst du den Stiefsohn des Diplomaten? Ja, ich kenne ihn.   6. Schenkst du deiner Schwägerin rote Rosen? Nein, ich schenke ihr keine roten Rosen. 7. Schenkst du ihm diesen Roman? Ja, ich schenke ihm diesen Roman.   8. Schenkst du uns eine Digitalkamera? Nein, ich schenke euch keine Digitalkamera.   9. Schenkst du dem Matrosen ein neues Handy? Ja, ich schenke dem Matrosen ein neues Handy.   10. Schenkst du mir einen schicken Pulli? Ja, ich schenke dir einen schicken Pulli.

30·11 1. Hat sie Hunger? Ja, sie hat großen Hunger.   2. Haben die Kinder Hunger? Ja die Kinder haben großen Hunger.   3. Hat mein Sohn Hunger? Ja, mein/Ihr/dein Sohn hat großen Hunger.   4. Habt ihr Hunger? Ja, ihr habt / wir haben großen Hunger.   5. Haben Sie Hunger? Ja, ich habe / Sie haben / wir haben großen Hunger.   6. Hast du Hunger? Ja, du hast / ich habe großen Hunger.   7. Hat der Reiseführer Hunger? Ja, der Reiseführer hat großen Hunger.   8. Hat er Hunger? Ja, er hat großen Hunger.   9. Haben Frau Neufeld und Sie Hunger? Ja, Frau Neufeld und Sie haben / wir haben großen Hunger.   10. Hat Felix Hunger? Ja, Felix hat großen Hunger.

30·12 *Sample answers are provided.*
1. Finde seine Bücher!
   Findet seine Bücher!
   Finden Sie seine Bücher!
2. Bestell(e) eine Flasche Rotwein!
   Bestellt eine Flasche Rotwein!
   Bestellen Sie eine Flasche Rotwein!
3. Trink(e) nur Milch!
   Trinkt nur Milch!
   Trinken Sie nur Milch!
4. Frühstück(e) im Esszimmer!
   Frühstückt im Esszimmer!
   Frühstücken Sie im Esszimmer!
5. Deck(e) den Tisch mit einem großen Tischtuch!
   Deckt den Tisch mit einem großen Tischtuch!
   Decken Sie den Tisch mit einem großen Tischtuch!
6. Iss keinen Kuchen!
   Esst keinen Kuchen!
   Essen Sie keinen Kuchen!

7. Grill(e) nicht in der Garage!
   Grillt nicht in der Garage!
   Grillen Sie nicht in der Garage!
8. Probier(e) die Forelle!
   Probiert die Forelle!
   Probieren Sie die Forelle!
9. Bring(e) den Vertrag mit!
   Bringt den Vertrag mit!
   Bringen Sie den Vertrag mit!
10. Mach(e) alle Fenster zu!
    Macht alle Fenster zu!
    Machen Sie alle Fenster zu!

30·13 *Sample answers are provided.*
1. Schneit es?
   Ja, es ist wieder sehr kalt.
   Morgen soll das Wetter besser sein.
2. Es klingelt.
   Wer kommt so spät zu Besuch?
   Ich sehe einen Fremden an der Tür stehen.
3. Dieses Restaurant hat eine gute Küche.
   Hoffentlich ist es nicht zu teuer.
   Es wird dir sicherlich gefallen.
4. Mein Mann trinkt zu viel Bier.
   Ja, das kann der Gesundheit schaden.
   Aber ich bin Antialkoholikerin.
5. Wann kommst du vorbei?
   Um halb zwölf.
   Warum so spät?

30·14 *Sample answers are provided.*
Zum weißen Adler
Herr Benz: Ich bin sicher, dass Ihnen dieses Café gefallen wird.
Frau Neufeld: Es ist sicherlich sehr schön, aber hoffentlich nicht zu teuer.
Herr Benz: Ich habe schon zweimal hier gegessen, und alles ist billig. Bitte bestellen Sie alles, was Ihnen gefällt!
Frau Neufeld: Ich esse manchmal vegetarisch, aber vielleicht will ich die Würstchen probieren.
Herr Benz: Bedienung! Bitte eine Flasche Rotwein.
Frau Neufeld: Mein Mann trinkt keinen Wein. Ihm gefällt nur Kaffee.
Herr Benz: Meine Frau ist Antialkoholikerin und trinkt nur Mineralwasser.
Frau Neufeld: Übrigens, Herr Benz, haben Sie meine Bücher mitgebracht?
Herr Benz: Jawohl.

31 More conversation

31·1 *Sample answers are provided.*   1. Er steht vor dem Rathaus.   2. Kann er Deutsch?   3. Was für ein Arzt möchte er werden?   4. Neben ihm steht seine Verlobte.   5. Sie ist Lehrerin in einer Schule in einem Vorort.

31·2 *Sample answers are provided.*   1. Er lehrt Physik und Chemie.   2. Ja, vor drei Monaten.   3. Ich bekomme eine gute Note in Physik.   4. Wer ist der junge Mann neben ihr?   5. Wie alt ist Sabine jetzt?   6. Will er an einer Universität studieren?   7. Wird er das Abitur machen?   8. Ja, sehr gut aber mit einem Akzent.   9. Lehrt er an der Universität?   10. Du solltest besser aufpassen.

31·3   1. Wir haben Hausaufgaben geschrieben.   2. Ich habe den Artikel gelesen.   3. Wer hat bei dir Englisch unterrichtet?   4. Sie hat eine Berufsschule besuchen müssen.   5. Er hat sein Auto waschen lassen. 6. Wie lange hat es gedauert?   7. Ihr habt ihn Deutsch sprechen hören.   8. Felix hat eine sehr gute Note bekommen.   9. Kleine Kinder haben den Kindergarten besuchen können.   10. Sie hat mein Lehrbuch gehabt.   11. Ich habe einen Deutschkurs belegt.   12. Du hast einen Text übersetzt.   13. Sie haben das Lied auswendig gelernt.   14. Er hat seine Note verbessern wollen.   15. Der Schüler hat einen Fehler gemacht.

31·4   1. Der Neuling aus Bremen ist sportlich.
Spielt er Fußball?
Nein, er spielt Tennis.
2. Hat Frau Schiller das Examen korrigiert?
Noch nicht.
Hoffentlich bekomme ich eine gute Note.
3. Wir müssen achtzig Seiten lesen.
Ich kann nicht. Ich bin kein Genie.
Vielleicht. Aber du musst.
4. Welche Fächer standen auf dem Stundenplan?
Deutsch und Physik.
Der Physikkurs ist nicht für Anfänger.
5. Auf welcher Seite steht die Hausaufgabe?
Auf Seite vierzig.
Ich verstehe kein Wort.
6. Er hat etwas an die Tafel geschrieben.
Ist das die neue Hausaufgabe?
Nein, das ist der Stundenplan für morgen.
7. Morgen wiederholen wir das Gedicht noch einmal.
Ich habe es noch nicht gelesen.
Warum bist du so faul?
8. Englisch ist für mich ziemlich leicht.
Und du sprichst auch sehr gut.
Ja, aber mit einem deutschen Akzent.
9. Ich habe den Neuling schwimmen sehen.
Er ist sehr sportlich.
Er ist auch sehr klug.
10. Ich werde ein schlechtes Zeugnis bekommen.
Ich auch.
Wir müssen unsere Noten verbessern.
11. Haben Sie einen Physikkurs belegt?
Nein, Physik ist zu schwer.
Was für einen Kurs werden Sie belegen?
12. Ihr werdet eine andere Schule besuchen müssen.
Aber wir mögen diese Schule.
Es tut mir leid. Wir haben keinen Platz mehr.
13. Morgen haben wir einen Test.
Nein, morgen ist Sonntag.
Morgen haben wir keine Schule.
14. Kennst du den Neuling aus München?
Ja, er heißt Erik und ist sehr klug.
Er hat letzten Monat das Abitur gemacht.
15. Lars, hast du deine Bücher mitgebracht?
Nein, Herr Braun. Ich habe sie leider vergessen.
Willst du eine schlechte Note bekommen?

31·5   1. Mathematik und Physik   2. Deutsch und Spanisch   3. Sport und Geschichte   4. Biologie und Erdkunde   5. Soziologie und Chemie   6. Am Montag   7. Nächste Woche   8. Im Juni   9. Morgen   10. Nächsten Freitag   11. ein Stipendium   12. gute Noten   13. eine schlechte Note   14. einen Brief   15. Wir müssen   16. Man muss   17. Alle müssen   18. Du musst   19. Ihr müsst   20. Elektrotechnik   21. Germanistik   22. Maschinenbau   23. Kunsterziehung   24. Jura   25. Geschichte

31·6   *Sample answers are provided.*   1. Weil das Einkaufszentrum weit entfernt ist.   2. Hans braucht nur Sportkleidung.   3. Er ist sehr sportlich.   4. Sie sieht einen schicken Anzug.   5. Es ist zu früh zu essen.   6. Fragen wir den Verkäufer da, wo die Sportkleidung ist.

31·7   *Sample answers are provided.*   1. Warum? Willst du Einkäufe machen?   2. Nein, aber es ist in unserem anderen Geschäft erhältlich.   3. Es ist zu früh, und wir haben noch so viel zu tun.   4. Nein, du brauchst eine kleinere Größe.   5. Sie sind ziemlich teuer. Zwölf Euro.

31·8   1. diesen Regenmantel   2. eine blaue Bluse   3. einen roten Rock   4. keine Stiefeln   5. eine braune Strumpfhose   6. Ich zog   7. Du zogst   8. Sie zog   9. Wir zogen   10. Sie zogen   11. seine Jacke   12. seinen Sakko   13. sein Unterhemd   14. meine Handschuhe   15. den alten Anzug   16. wird eine Apotheke   17. werden zwei Kaufhäuser   18. wird eine neue Buchhandlung   19. werden keine neuen Geschäfte   20. wird eine Metzgerei   21. den blauen Sakko   22. diese Lederjacke   23. mein buntes Hemd   24. einen größeren Rock   25. die billigen Handschuhe   26. Ich ziehe mich   27. Du ziehst dich   28. Er zieht sich   29. Ihr zieht euch   30. Der neue Verkäufer zieht sich   31. nur Eisenwaren   32. keine Haushaltswaren   33. keine Lebensmittel   34. Kleidung für Kinder   35. Spielzeug   36. mir   37. ihm   38. deinem Vater   39. dem Damenfriseur   40. dem Ladenbesitzer   41. den alten Regenmantel   42. die neuen Turnschuhe   43. diesen Badeanzug   44. dieses T-Shirt   45. den braunen Hut   46. in die Molkerei   47. ins Einkaufszentrum   48. ins neue Kaufhaus   49. in die 50. ins Lebensmittelgeschäft

31·9   *Sample answers are provided.*   1. Er musste Herrn Dorf helfen.   2. Kein Problem. Es ist nur vierzehn Uhr.   3. Sie brauchen neue Kleider.   4. Die besten Jeans kosten mehr als sechzig Euro.   5. Er weiß nicht, wo das Hemd ist.   6. Du hast Recht. Ich werde mir ein T-Shirt anziehen.

31·10   1. Dieser Wagen kostet fünfzehntausendneunhundert Euro.   2. Ein Stück Kuchen kostet einen Euro und sechzig Cent.   3. Diese Handschuhe kosten zweiundzwanzig Euro und fünfundachtzig Cent.   4. Ihr neues Haus kostet zweihundertfünfzigtausend Euro.   5. Die Fliege kostet acht Euro und zehn Cent.   6. Mein Pelzmantel kostet neunhundertfünfundzwanzig Euro und fünfundzwanzig Cent.   7. Diese DVDs kosten dreiunddreißig Euro und fünfundsiebzig Cent.   8. Zwei Eintrittskarten kosten fünfundvierzig Euro.   9. Ein Liter Bier kostet drei Euro und fünfzig Cent.   10. Diese Lederstiefeln kosten hundertfünfundzwanzig Euro.

31·11   1. Das Esszimmer ist vier Meter breit.   2. Dieses Brett ist zehn Komma fünf Zentimeter / zehn und halb Zentimeter lang.   3. Der Küchentisch ist einen Meter hoch.   4. Ich kaufe zwölf Pfund Kartoffeln.   5. Die Katze wiegt acht Kilogramm.   6. Der Teich ist ein Meter tief.   7. Der Fluss ist vier Komma fünf Meter / vier und halb Meter tief.   8. Der Bleistift ist hundertfünfundzwanzig Millimeter lang.   9. Der See ist elf Meter tief.   10. Die neue Wohnung hat fünfundneunzig Quadratmeter.

31·12   *Sample answers are provided.*
Im Kaufhaus
Mutter: Endlich sind wir da! Wir hätten mit einem Taxi fahren sollen.
Vater: Ja, das Kaufhaus ist weit entfernt, aber es ist gesund zu Fuß zu gehen.
Mutter: Wo ist meine Liste? Ich möchte Andreas einen Anzug und einen neuen Schlips kaufen.
Vater: Tanja braucht nur ein schönes Kleid. Und neue Strümpfe. Das Mädchen lebt jetzt im Tanzlokal.
Mutter: Guck mal! Der Sakko im Schaufenster sieht schick aus. Perfekt für dich.
Vater: Nein. Die schwarze Farbe steht mir nicht gut.
Mutter: Vielleicht der Graue mit einem blauen Hemd.
Vater: Es ist schon zwölf Uhr. Ich möchte ein Glas Bier und ein Würstchen.
Mutter: Es ist zu spät, und wir müssen noch viele Einkäufe machen.
Vater: Fragen wir die Verkäuferin da, wo die Lederjacken sind!

31·13 *Sample answers are provided.* 1. Die besten Modehäuser sind in Paris. 2. Vielleicht sollen wir dieses Jahr eine Amerikareise machen. 3. Wie wäre es mit Wien oder Zürich? 4. Die USA sind zu weit entfernt. 5. Aber wir haben nicht genug gespart, um eine Auslandsreise zu machen. 6. Aber Nordafrika ist nur jenseits des Mittelmeers.

31·14 1. Positive: Die guten Modehäuser sind in Paris.
Comparative: Die besseren Modehäuser sind in Paris.
Superlative: Die besten Modehäuser sind in Paris.
2. Positive: Ich möchte gern nach Amerika reisen.
Comparative: Ich möchte lieber nach Amerika reisen.
Superlative: Ich möchte am liebsten nach Amerika reisen.